T0283922

Advance Prais
Japan's Holoc.....

"Rigg's thorough exploration of Japanese atrocities in China and during the Pacific War drives home the totality and scale of the utter depravity of the Japanese government and its armed forces. He makes it clear that this trait was ingrained in the very culture of the Imperial Army and pervasive in every locale and against everyone it encountered, civilian or military. One cannot fully understand the conflict without comprehending this aspect of the Japanese approach to war."
— Colonel Jon T. Hoffman USMC (Retired), author of *Chesty: The Story of Lieutenant General Lewis B. Puller, USMC* and *Once a Legend: Red Mike Edson of the Marine Raiders*

"Once again Bryan Rigg has shown himself to be a distinguished military historian, writing with passion, power, and flair about Japanese actions in Asia and the Pacific during World War II. His grasp of the battles and atrocities are deep, his passion for the codes of war fierce as only one schooled in those codes and respectful of them as essential to the morality of war can be. His portrayal of the battles and mass-murder actions are vivid and his grasp of their geopolitical implications insightful. I learned a lot, and I thought ever more deeply about the ethics of war."
— Michael Berenbaum, author of *The World Must Know: The History of the Holocaust as Told in the United States Holocaust Memorial Museum* and distinguished professor of Jewish Studies at American Jewish University

"Exploding onto the historical scene with *Hitler's Jewish Soldiers* Bryan Rigg exposed a long-held secret. In this book, he exposes an international tragedy of epic proportions, and exposes the shameful, willful and determined ignorance of the history he has chronicled by the nation responsible for it. An instant classic."
— Colin D. Heaton, author of *Above the Pacific: Three Medal of Honor Fighter Aces of World War II Speak*

"Most discussions of the Holocaust of World War II center around the atrocities perpetrated by Nazi Germany. Much less studied or even acknowledged is the Holocaust perpetrated by Imperial Japan. Historian Bryan Rigg has documented in his exhaustive research possibly the definitive work on the subject. The reader will learn about the sick culture of Japan in the first part of the twentieth century that gave rise to a warrior society that decreed Emperor Hirohito an infallible god, and the Japanese race as the superior militaristic race destined to rule the world. Rigg documents the wanton killings of civilians, the widespread rape committed by the Japanese troops and the sickening treatment of POWs in violation of the Hague Convention to which Japan was a signatory. In addition, the Japanese military was instructed to die rather than surrender or else lose their honor. Even more sobering is the failure of Japan, unlike Germany, to this day to acknowledge the horrors that they committed from the 1920s through the end of the war. *Japan's Holocaust* is must reading for any student of World War II."

— Captain (USN) Lee R. Mandel (Retired), author of *A Pacifist at Iwo Jima: Rabbi Roland Gittelsohn from Pulpit to the U.S. Marine Corps' Bloodiest Battle*

"*Japan's Holocaust* is a very important and groundbreaking work. Rigg has done tremendous research once again."

— Richard Frank, author of *Downfall: The End of the Imperial Japanese Empire* and *Tower of Skulls: A History of the Asia-Pacific War: July 1937–May 1942*

"Bryan Rigg's *Japan's Holocaust* is an important book, and it deserves a wide readership."

— Sir Andrew Roberts, author of *Churchill: Walking with Destiny* and *The Storm of War: A New History of the Second World War*

JAPAN'S HOLOCAUST

HISTORY OF IMPERIAL JAPAN'S MASS MURDER AND RAPE DURING WORLD WAR II

BRYAN MARK RIGG

A KNOX PRESS BOOK
An Imprint of Permuted Press
ISBN: 978-1-63758-688-4
ISBN (eBook): 978-1-63758-689-1

Japan's Holocaust:
History of Imperial Japan's Mass Murder and Rape During World War II
© 2024 by Bryan Mark Rigg
All Rights Reserved

Cover art by Cody Corcoran

Permuted Press, LLC
New York • Nashville
permutedpress.com

Published in the United States of America
2 3 4 5 6 7 8 9 10

This book is dedicated to my beloved children, Ian, Justin, and Sophia. May they each contribute to the fortification of the United States as a thriving democracy. May they answer the call, whenever it arises, to confront the malevolent forces that frequently emerge across the globe, whether through military service, political engagement, or education. In short, may they each play their part in vanquishing such evils as we saw in World War II and as we will, unfortunately, see again and again, in the future. Moreover, I would like to thank my dear wife, Dr. Emelie Karlsson, for her words of encouragement and support during this project.

Furthermore, this book is dedicated to the countless Asian and Pacific victims who suffered unimaginable horrors at the hands of the Japanese between 1927 and 1945. May their memories be honored, their stories heard, and their suffering *never forgotten*.

The only thing necessary for the triumph of evil is for good men to do nothing.
Edmund Burke, Anglo-Irish statesman and philosopher (1729–1797)

Generally speaking, the errors in religion are dangerous.
David Hume, Scottish Enlightenment philosopher (1711–1776)

TABLE OF CONTENTS

FOREWORD

by Andrew Roberts

ALTHOUGH MOST EDUCATED PEOPLE KNOW about the Nuremberg Trials of the senior Nazis after World War II, relatively few are at all cognizant of the International Military Tribunal of Japanese war criminals at Tokyo, which concluded in 1948. In all, some 920 Japanese war criminals were executed, 475 received life sentences, and 2,944 prison sentences of varying lengths.

Yet as this well-researched and searing book proves beyond doubt, tens of thousands—perhaps more—Japanese war criminals escaped punishment altogether. This book expertly examines the religious, psychological, societal, political, and other factors that turned the Japanese armed forces of 1927 to 1945 into such an astoundingly vicious killing (and raping) machine. Dr. Bryan Rigg writes of "a dark web of complicity, where the monarchy, government, military, and religions of Japan all played their part in reinforcing totalitarianism, fanaticism, and the perpetration of mass murder."

Dr. Rigg analyzes unflinchingly all the myriad ways that Imperial Japan abused the countries that fell under the yoke of its so-called "Greater East Asia Co-Prosperity Sphere," the title intended to hide the reality of life (and death) of an empire that at one point stretched over no less than one-seventh of the planet.

Dr. Rigg lays bare the truth behind the monstrous culture behind Bushido, *Banzai* attacks (which accounted for 200,000 out of Japan's 1.4 million soldiers killed), *Samurai* "honour," *seppuku* (mass suicide), *jikyusen* (attritional strategy), *Kamikaze*, and so on. He shows how, far from being an ancient and noble calling, *Bushido* was in fact little more than a necro-sadistic death cult steeped in the blood of innocents, with no uplifting features. Small wonder, therefore, that it appealed—and indeed still appeals today—to Fascists, nihilists, and totalitarians.

The author is rigorous in his examination of each of these phenomena (and more), which dealt such untold misery to so many millions of people across so much of the globe. (When the war ended, there were 5.2 million Japanese soldiers stationed in China alone.) Nor did the death cult succeed even according to its own lights, because Japan lost the war. "Cultural norms, religious creeds, and moral codes break down under extreme physical and mental stress," the author points out. All too often, it came down to Japanese officers killing their own men to prevent surrenders, once it became clear that fighting spirit alone was not enough to bring victory.

Imperial Japan's armies had been defeated in Burma, the Pacific, and elsewhere before the atomic bombs were dropped on Hiroshima and Nagasaki, yet as Dr. Rigg proves beyond doubt, it was essential to drop them because they saved hundreds of thousands of American and Japanese lives in averting the final *Götterdämmerung* that would have resulted from an invasion of the Japanese home islands. If anyone still believes that Japan was on the point of surrender after Hiroshima, and that it did not require the second bomb to be dropped for it to change its mind, they should read the contemporary evidence presented here.

There are few people who are better qualified than Dr. Rigg to write this important work. A BA in history from Yale University, PhD in history from Cambridge University, with six books on various aspects on World War II to his name, as well as a veritable blizzard of published articles and reviews, he is a meticulous researcher steeped in the all-important historical context. He has walked a number of the key battlefields that he discusses, and his expertise in Judeo-Christian morality makes him particularly adept at spotting how the warped and twisted view of religion espoused by the Tokyo regime of 1927–45 underpinned much of the abhorrent behaviour that he describes, behaviour that was mirrored virtually wherever the Japanese Army (and Navy) went throughout Asia and the Pacific.

There are very few equivalents for Imperial Japan of the kind of comprehensive work that Sir Martin Gilbert, Raul Hilberg, and many others have done for the Nazi Holocaust, but Dr. Rigg's book is an attempt to rectify that, especially in its coverage of Japan's use of biological warfare, chemical weapons, the torture and execution of prisoners of war, forced labor, and sexual slavery. Dr Rigg is particularly good on a very little-known aspect of the war, namely Japan's massive pushing of opium and heroin onto the Chinese, an operation that he estimates was some two hundred times the size of the largest of today's Mexican and Colombian cartels.

Sexual abuse has been a feature of warfare for centuries. It tends to happen when soldiers are badly led, both by their officers and their non-commissioned officers. Yet as Dr. Rigg shows in example after example—including the mass-rapes of Nanking, Hong Kong, Singapore, Guam, and Manila—Japanese officers and non-commissioned officers actively encouraged the practice, as a way of "rewarding" their soldiers and hoping to imbue them with a macho fighting spirit. Because foreign women were considered sub-human in Fascist ideology, it did not matter what happened to them.

Bushido's combination of racial and sexual supremacy meant that unnumbered South Korean "comfort women" were used as sex slaves by the Japanese Army. Even Lt. Col. Tadamichi Kuribayashi—who seemed to be presented as an attractive figure in Clint Eastwood's movies about Iwo Jima—had been chief of staff in Hong King when tens of thousands of women were raped. Shockingly, there are only two occurrences of rape being punished by the Japanese army during the war, otherwise orders given by generals on the subject were strictly Potemkin ones intended for public relations, and they had no expectation or interest in their being obeyed.

The fact that there was no Japanese officers' plot against the leadership once the war was obviously being lost—as there was against Adolf Hitler in July 1944—says a good deal about their fanaticism. Imperial Japan's disgusting ill-treatment of prisoners of war (POWs) also derived from Japanese officers' contempt for a foe who surrenders rather than fighting to the last man, as happened on Okinawa, Iwo Jima, and elsewhere. The Japanese Army was fortunate indeed that the Allies adhered to a different code when it finally surrendered in August 1945.

Although modern Japan has officially apologized on many occasions for what happened during the Second World War, there is a sense that what happened has gone far beyond what any apology can achieve. The first such statements were made in 1957 when then Prime Minister Kishi Nobusuke told the people of Burma, "We view with deep regret the vexation we caused to the people of Burma in the war just passed. In a desire to atone, if only partially, for the pain suffered, Japan is prepared to meet fully and with goodwill its obligations for war reparations. The Japan of today is not the Japan of the past, but, as its Constitution indicates, is a peace-loving nation."

That is true: like modern Germany, today's Japan is an impressively peace-loving, democratic nation, partly because of the whirlwind that it sowed and subsequently reaped during the Second World War. Modern critics of the Allied policy of unconditional surrender for Germany and Japan ought to consider this more than they do.

Although there were other apologies made by senior Japanese statesmen in the 1960s, 1970s, and 1980s, the most important are considered to be the Murayama Statement issued on the fiftieth anniversary of the end of the war, the Koizumi Statement on the sixtieth anniversary, and Shinzo Abe's on the seventieth. Yet the reparations that Japan has paid over the years—such as $550 million to the Philippines in 1956 and $39 million to South Vietnam in 1959—have tended to be too little, too late.

Similarly, reparations for POWs and "comfort women" were minimal and had to be squeezed out of a reluctant Tokyo that all too often seemed to be playing for time while its former victims were succumbing to the Grim Reaper. Furthermore, the practice of Japanese premiers between 1975 and 2006 making pilgrimages to the Yasukuni Shrine in Tokyo—where fourteen Class A war criminals' "souls" were enshrined—understandably drew (ultimately unfounded) fears from Japan's neighbours about the resurgence of Japanese militarism.

There are also serious questions to be asked—and Dr. Rigg certainly does not shy away from asking them—about the way that Japanese history from 1927 to 1945 is taught in Japanese schools today. When I visited Japan half a decade ago, it was very noticeable how Japanese museums were still massively downplaying the scale of the atrocities, and instead attempting to claim victimhood status because of the fact that Japan is the only nation to have suffered a nuclear attack.

The personal responsibility of the god-king Emperor Hirohito for wartime atrocities is repeated regularly in these pages, and rightly so. With his profound understanding of Japanese culture, Bryan Rigg unfailingly places Hirohito in the celestial dock for the events of his reign, even though political considerations meant that that was impossible to do in the actual dock of the International Military Tribunal in the late 1940s. After reading the author's unsparing analysis, it is hard to escape the conclusion that Hirohito ought to have been hanged alongside his more junior co-conspirators, such as General Hideki Tojo, Koki Hirota, and General Kenji Doihara. This is an important book, and it deserves a wide readership.

Andrew Roberts
The House of Lords, London, August 2023

INTRODUCTION

"Goodness without knowledge is weak…yet knowledge without
goodness is dangerous, and that both united form the noblest
character, and lay the surest foundation of usefulness to mankind."

—**John Phillips**, Founder of Phillips Exeter Academy 1791[1]

WHILE SOME INDIVIDUALS MAY TAKE umbrage with this study's use of the term
"Holocaust" in relation to Japan's mass murder during the Asian and Pacific
Wars (1927–1945), it is important to note that this study draws upon various
reputable sources that have employed this title. Renowned journalist Iris Chang,
in her book *The Rape of Nanking*, referred to the massacre in Nanking as the
"Forgotten Holocaust" of World War II.[2] The *Merriam-Webster* dictionary
defines holocaust as "mass slaughter," which accurately characterizes the actions
perpetrated by Japan during this period. *The Memorial Hall of the Victims in
Nanjing Massacre by Japanese Invaders* in Nanking, China, refers to this event
as "a Human Holocaust,"[3] and journalist and historian Arnold C. Brackman,
in his work *The Other Nuremberg: The Untold Story of the Tokyo War Crimes
Trials*, labels Japan's actions on the Asian mainland as a "Holocaust in China."[4]
Furthermore, lesser-known works on these events, such as Armando A. Ang's
Brutal Holocaust: Japan's World War II Atrocities and Their Aftermath and Koken
Tsuchiya's *The Asian Holocaust 1931-1945: Hidden Holocaust of World War II by
the Japanese Army* obviously also incorporate the term Holocaust in their titles.[5]
Even the U.S. Congress' Committee on Ways and Means declared in 1945 that
Japan's actions in China was a "Holocaust."[6]

So, the term "Holocaust" accurately captures the nature of what Japan did
during the Asian and Pacific Wars and can be used for what both Japan and
Germany did during their Fascist reigns. However, it is worth noting that some
Jewish scholars dislike this term being used for what the Nazis did during the
Third Reich because the Jews were not a sacrificial burnt offering, which is its

original meaning, although it universally is understood today as meaning the mass murder under Hitler. Many Jewish scholars, particularly in Israel, prefer the term *Shoah*, which means "catastrophe" in Hebrew and specifically refers to the Nazi extermination of the Jews. Even with these opinions out there, I, as a Holocaust historian, think such a term is appropriate for Germany's extermination policies during the Second World War. In addition, I also believe the events described here that Japan did during the Asian and Pacific Wars also indeed make up its *Holocaust*, which denotes a distinct and terrible slaughter perpetrated by the Japanese against millions of innocent people during their Imperial, expansionist rule from 1927 to 1945.

In summary, the term "Holocaust" is not limited to one specific version of history when its true definition and historiography are examined. As already explained, it can be applied to both the atrocities committed by Nazi Germany and the heinous actions of Imperial Japan during their respective reprehensible regimes. In short, by considering the broader historical context, it becomes apparent that the term "Holocaust" can encompass and accurately describe the immense suffering and mass killings perpetrated by both nations.

Now that I have defined in general terms what I believe to be Japan's Holocaust and that the term is appropriate for this time period and nation, one might find it interesting how I came to research this disturbing subject matter. During my extensive research on the Pacific War, which led to the publication of my book *Flamethrower: Iwo Jima Medal of Honor Recipient and U.S. Marine Woody Williams and His Controversial Award, Japan's Holocaust and the Pacific War*, conducted between 2015 and 2020, I was continuously horrified by the behavior of the Japanese during their conquests throughout Asia and the Pacific from 1927 to 1945. As I delved into various archives in Guam, the United States, China, Germany, and Japan, I encountered a disturbing pattern of criminal behavior that, if possible, surpassed the horrors documented in the archives related to Nazi Germany. Historians Haruko Taya Cook and Theodore Cook vividly captured the nature of the Japanese society under Hirohito's rule, describing it as deeply racist, paternalistic, and aggressive. These deeply ingrained convictions and cultural beliefs "left Japanese soldiers and civilians capable in wartime of committing shocking and widespread war crimes… without a prevailing feeling that *these were morally reprehensible* [author's italics]."[7] This analysis by the Cooks, and verified by my study, presents a stark contrast to the situation with the Germans under Hitler, as many of them were aware of the moral reprehensibility of their actions. However, what troubled me deeply was the realization that this awareness was not as prevalent among the Japanese as the Cooks above noted.

To provide a comprehensive understanding of the comparisons drawn between the totalitarian pasts of Germany and Japan with respects to their citizenry and genocide just mentioned, a deeper analysis is warranted. In contrast to the Japanese, who displayed a disturbing lack of remorse and an apparent enjoyment in their acts of murder and rape, there were cases among the Germans who showcased varying responses to the atrocities committed during World War II. Christopher Browning's book, *Ordinary Men*, provides compelling examples of individuals who actively avoided participation in the killings when given a choice.[8] Furthermore, some German soldiers and *SS* personnel who did the killing experienced profound psychological distress, leading to drug addiction, alcoholism, and even suicide as a means to cope with the weight of their actions. Adolf Hitler, recognizing the potential social unrest that would arise if death camps like Auschwitz were located within Germany's borders, deliberately situated them hundreds of miles away in foreign lands. Within these camps, the Nazis often assigned inmates, such as the *Sonderkommandos*, the gruesome task of herding prisoners into gas chambers and operating the crematoriums. The decision stemmed from the difficulty faced by certain frontline soldiers, as observed in the *Einsatzgruppen* (killing squads), who found it challenging to personally carry out the up-close and personal killings. *The Japanese, on the other hand, did not have these problems.* When given the opportunity, the vast majority participated in murder and rape and seemed to enjoy it, and rarely felt remorse for doing so. Historian John W. Dower astutely highlights this phenomenon, writing,

> Such [barbaric] acts [by the Japanese] commonly reflect oppressive social
> and racial hierarchies, as well as pathological transfers of oppression that,
> in the cauldron of war, all too often culminated in indiscriminate killing,
> wanton murder, rape, and *the utter obliteration of any sort of empathy
> whatsoever* [author's italics].[9]

Consequently, the magnitude of these atrocities and the apparent lack of remorse from their perpetrators compelled me to write this book and better understand why they did so. By delving into the depths of their actions, motivations, and the historical context, my aim is to gain a deeper understanding of why such horrors unfolded during this dark period in history.

Upon learning these unsettling facts, my disgust only deepened when I discovered that to this day, Japan ignores the victims of its mass murders and sexual crimes, failing to acknowledge their suffering. The absence of monuments or museums within the country to commemorate these atrocities from its fascistic rule is in stark contrast to Germany, which has taken significant steps since 1945 to confront its dark past, acknowledging the horrors it committed during the Nazi regime.

Historians Haruko Taya and Theodore F. Cook write:

> There is no national museum or archive [in Japan] to which children can go to find out about the war, or where students can freely examine wartime documents; no neutral national setting where one could study wartime art, explore major photo collections, or examine artifacts of daily life. Although there are certainly displays in local museums devoted to those years, there is no concerted national effort to preserve, accumulate, and reconstruct the war from an historical perspective. Indeed, the only significant large collection of war memorabilia is held in the memorial hall at Yasukuni Shrine, which itself served as the focal point of the cult of the war dead in prewar and wartime Japan. Without a neutral public space for public investigation of, or reflection on, the war experience, scholars of today—and more importantly, those who wish to study the war years in the future—must depend on what little private documentation reaches the public.[10]

The glaring contradiction between a nation that prides itself on honor, respect, and manners and its dishonorable approach to commemorating the victims of the Asian and Pacific Wars and documenting its past leaves me deeply perplexed. The answers I uncovered as to why this is the case were disheartening and fell far short of expectations. This was yet another reason why I wanted to write this book.

The pivotal moment that propelled me to study this subject more closely occurred in 2015 when I embarked on researching General Tadamichi Kuribayashi, the commanding officer of Iwo Jima. Renowned as one of the most formidable Imperial Japanese Army (IJA) leaders encountered by the Allied forces during World War II, Kuribayashi's reputation intrigued me.[11] However, along the way, I uncovered troubling facts about this warrior that made me struggle with a different battle—the pursuit of evidence against interest. The prevailing image of Kuribayashi, both in Japan and portrayed in Clint Eastwood's films *Flags of Our Fathers* and *Letters from Iwo Jima*, had been distorted. While he undoubtedly displayed bravery and operational acumen, a darker truth emerged. Kuribayashi, in addition to his military prowess, was also a monster who ordered his men to slaughter innocent POWs and civilians and allowed his soldiers to violate tens of thousands of women under his control. Furthermore, he actively encouraged his men to choose death over surrender. These failings of Kuribayashi have rarely, if ever, been explored.

In the end, through my extensive research, I discovered that no historian has yet attempted to do a comprehensive overview of Japan's Holocaust comparable to the renowned works of Raul Hilberg and Martin Gilbert on Hitler's Holocaust. This book also tries to accomplish this lofty goal. It has been a struggle to gather the truth and publish this book, but I firmly believe that it has faithfully portrayed the Japanese men, encompassing both military personnel and political leaders, as well as the untold stories of their victims who suffered under their rule.

This book has been crafted with deep introspection, profound sorrow, and countless nights of restless contemplation. Nonetheless, it is both with great honor, but also with much sadness, that I present this book. I sincerely hope that you will recognize the importance of confronting uncomfortable truths rather than embracing beautiful lies if we are to glean valuable lessons from history and strive towards the creation of a more just society. It is crucial to acknowledge that grappling with the harsh realities of the past is a necessary step towards growth and progress. We must not shy away from the difficult truths that challenge our preconceptions and force us to confront the darker aspects of human history. By doing so, we can uncover a clearer understanding of the world we inhabit today and the steps needed to forge a better future. Furthermore, it is imperative that we transcend any attempts to suppress or censor the truth, which notable Japanese politicians and book translators tried to do to me. In the words of Thomas Jefferson, one of the founding fathers of the United States, "There is not a truth existing which I fear...or would wish unknown to the whole world."[12] These words resonate strongly, emphasizing the importance of *embracing the truth in its entirety*, irrespective of its discomfort or potential consequences.

This book presents a dual narrative that aims to provide a comprehensive account of both General Kuribayashi's crimes and Japan's broader atrocities, encompassing its society, military, and religious institutions throughout its Imperial history. By delving into various themes and events, it endeavors to offer readers a profound understanding of the significant occurrences within Japan's Holocaust, shedding light on the intricacies of how and why they unfolded.

Upon engaging with the difficult contents of this book, it is my sincere aspiration that readers will gain new perspectives and profound insights into Imperial Japan, its culture of denial, and the magnitude of its war crimes across Asia and the Pacific. By delving into the depths of this harrowing history, I aim to unravel the reasons behind Japan's mass murders and shed light on the forces that propelled such atrocities. As the adage goes, "those who forget the past are condemned to repeat it." It is in this spirit that I present this historical account, with the hope that it will serve as a vital reminder to humanity, and particularly to Japan, of the critical importance of remembering this dark chapter in history. By confronting the truth and acknowledging the depths of these atrocities, we aspire to foster collective growth, understanding, and a resolute commitment to ensuring that such horrors are never repeated.

Bryan Mark Rigg, Ph.D.
Dallas, Texas, December 2022

PREAMBLE

"A Lesson From the Holocaust:
Never Stop Telling the Terrible Stories."
—Chicago Tribune[13]

Author Bryan Rigg outside the Nanking Massacre Memorial Museum at Nanking, China. This 36-foot statue of a mother holding her murdered child by Japanese soldiers greets visitors at the entrance gate. 11 May 2019. *Author's Collection*

As my 18-year-old daughter Sophia and I stepped into a grand museum in Nanking, the former capital of the Chinese Empire, a profound sense of gravity enveloped us. Crossing a glass walkway suspended above an ancient footpath, we peered down through the transparent floor, the dimly lit room below casting an eerie glow on the scene. To our right, a somber black wall displayed a series of photographs, meticulously illuminated, unveiling the unfathomable atrocities committed by the Japanese against Chinese citizens in December 1937. The images captured the grotesque reality of that dark period: Dead babies, severed heads, and piles of corpses strewn along the banks of the Yangtze River. Executed prisoners of war also stared back at us, their haunting faces frozen in time. Each photograph, a testament to the brutality and mercilessness of the perpetrators, was captured by their very hands with their own personal cameras, leaving no room for denial or escape from the truth.[14] The photo collage documented an orgy of slaughter that defied comprehension.

As we continued along the pathway, a rectangular centerpiece stood before us, enclosed by low walls. Many, on gazing over the lips of the precipice, shook their heads. Some put their hands together and offered prayers to the heavens. Others whispered to companions, "Bastards," "I hate the Japanese," "How can Japan deny this?" or "America should've dropped more bombs on the assholes." A mother pointed to one of the pictures depicting a Japanese soldier callously executing a defenseless Chinese citizen, and imparted a painful lesson to her young child, ensuring that the memory of these atrocities would not fade. "Remember," she said, "this is how the Japanese behave. Never forget that the Japanese are always like this." The air trembled with anger and horror, as tears welled in many eyes.

Amidst the predominantly *Han* Chinese crowd, my daughter Sophia stood tall at 5'11", her flowing blonde hair and piercing blue eyes marking her as distinct. A hushed silence enveloped the room from most of those there, broken only by the shuffling footsteps or an angry curse against the Japanese of those departing from the centerpiece. Sophia approached the low wall, her gaze drifting towards the deep pit below, and then she turned to me, her eyes widened with a profound sadness that echoed within my own heart as I too looked down below on what lay beneath us. The words of Dante came to my mind: "In truth I found myself upon the brink of an abyss, the melancholy valley containing thundering, unending wailings."[15]

Before us lay a haunting sight—a sprawling mass grave, an unsettling testament to Japan's human cruelty. Countless skulls bore the marks of brutality, some crushed under the weight of a heavy object, while others bore the unmistakable scars of bullet wounds. Other skulls had been removed from their bodies, settling several feet away from their shoulders. Shocked, we gazed upon the gruesome aftermath of a merciless crime. Unbeknownst to us, this crime scene was not even close to being the museum's biggest. With heavy hearts, we continued to walk on a massive unplanned cemetery where everyone had met an untimely and murderous end. The Japanese had "stained the world with blood"[16] and jars of human remains mixed with the earth that had absorbed their flesh lined the exhibit. As we moved forward, the weight of history pressed upon us, as the very earth beneath our feet cried out for remembrance.

Nanking Memorial second hall's mass grave of butchered Chinese by the Japanese, December 1937. Notice the bullet hole in the skull that is staring out at us from the middle of the pile. 11 May 2019. *Author's Collection*

My daughter and I found ourselves standing in the heart of one of the most harrowing crime scenes in human history. Sophia, with her fluency in Chinese, had accompanied me to aid in our research efforts. It was a solemn day as we ventured into *The Memorial Hall of the Victims in Nanjing Massacre by Japanese Invaders* in Nanking, China. Having visited notable Holocaust sites such as the Holocaust Museum in Washington D.C., Yad Vashem in Jerusalem, Israel, the poignant and extensive Holocaust Memorial in Berlin, Germany, and the haunting grounds of the Nazi death camp Auschwitz near Krakow, Poland, I believed I had witnessed the depths of human suffering. Little did I know that the experience awaiting me within this vast complex, dedicated to commemorating the Rape of Nanking, would leave an indelible mark on my soul. Unlike the European sites, which showcased evidence of mass murder, Auschwitz being the most dramatic with large rooms full of shoes, piles of shaven female hair, and suitcases of the deceased, the Memorial Hall in Nanking presented a unique and haunting spectacle. Within its walls, we encountered the sober presence of hundreds of skeletons, their empty black eye sockets seemingly staring at us as if pleading for us to not forget them. The complex itself stood upon a site known as the "Mass Grave of 10,000," a chilling reminder of the immense loss of life that occurred there. Throughout the museum, the remains of these victims were on display, a poignant testimony to the atrocities committed.

Each step took immersed us further into a tragic realm, where the fragmented whispers of shattered bones conveyed tales of anguish and despair. The weight of their existence resonated deeply within me, urging me to bear witness to their suffering and to ensure that their stories would never fade into oblivion. The sheer size of the extermination reminded me of Dante's phrase: "I should never have believed that death could have unmade so many souls."[17]

CHAPTER 1

JAPAN'S EMPEROR CULT, INTOLERANT RELIGIONS, HIROHITO, FASCISTIC IDEOLOGY, AND RACIST BELIEFS

"Moral imagination requires us to take responsibility for past
wrongdoings and, at the same time, stimulates us to project
our thoughts toward a more human future through the creative
examination of our past...investigating the war crimes and atrocities
committed by the Japanese is, therefore, to master the past."

—Japanese historian Yuki Tanaka, *Hidden Horrors:*
Japanese War Crimes in World War II[18]

DURING HIROHITO'S RULE FROM 1925 to 1945,[19] Japan produced horrors on the scale of Hitler's evils. Hirohito's and Hitler's rule shock most, particularly those who have only experienced the democracies of present-day Japan and Germany. The WWII behavior of both countries was deplorable.[20] Japan's legacy from 1927 to 1945 was marred by atrocities, war crimes and "suicidal disgrace."[21] Japan at that time was ruled by an absolute ruler in Hirohito, just like Russia was by Stalin and Germany by Hitler. However, Hirohito had a long tradition of dictatorships on which he based his rule that was more supreme than in Russia and Germany. To understand this, one must have a basic understanding of Japanese history leading up to Hirohito.

The homogeneous island nation of Japan had lived in self-imposed isolation as a feudal state ruled by *shoguns* (hereditary commanders-in-chief) from the *samurai* warrior class for two and a half centuries before Commodore Matthew Perry and the U.S. Navy's "Black Ships" forced it to open itself to world trade in 1854, thereby shattering "the 'closed door' policy of the Tokugawa government."[22] The arrival of Perry and the subsequent opening of Japan to the world triggered social upheaval within the nation. The emperor had long been a cultural and religious figure, apart from and nominally superior to the warrior class, but his power was not absolute or universal at this time.[23] For centuries, the *shoguns* had held power until the advent of Western influence. Although some Japanese leaders had heard of the American and French Revolutions and the expansion of colonial empires, they took little notice of global events and remained largely isolationists.

The Opium Wars of the 1840s and 1850s, along with the subsequent granting of extensive privileges to European powers in China, sent shockwaves through Japan's elite circles. "[T]o see China humiliated, to see its major ports occupied and administered by barbarians from the West made it obvious… that a great shadow had begun to fall over East Asia, one that Japan could not escape."[24] Japan became hyper-focused on ensuring Western powers would not do to it what they had to China.[25] One crucial measure taken by Japan to combat Western influence and colonial expansion was to unify the nation under the emperor (*tenno*). By consolidating power under a centralized authority, Japan aimed to fortify itself and counter the encroachments of external forces.

In 1868, the Meiji Restoration marked Japan's return to imperial rule and during this era, a constitution was written for the nation. Emperor Mōsuhito, who would come to be known as Meiji after his reign as emperor, ascended the throne in 1868. Unlike the U.S. Constitution, which was developed through a process involving widespread public discourse, Japan's constitution was drafted by a group of elites in secret and then presented to the people as a gift from the emperor.[26] One of the primary purposes of the Meiji's constitution was to impress the West, which Japan aspired to join and prove it had modern institutions. It wanted respect from powerful countries, equal treatment, and protection from Western imperialism. Yet, Japan's constitution was not meant to make her institutions viable or ensure genuine rights for its citizens. While the constitution did include a provision guaranteeing religious freedom, a provision of interest in the West, it is important to note that in practice, regulations, law, and social pressure suppressed non-Japanese faiths.[27] State Shintō observances, complete with priests, spirits, gods, shrines, and myths, could not be questioned and were civic requirements, especially since they embraced certain aspects of revering the emperor.

There were elections in which a small percentage of men could vote, but the military was not accountable to elected officials, answering only to the emperor. Although male suffrage increased before WWII, the military remained in many areas beyond the voters' control of their elected officials. In fact, the army often manipulated elections and influenced the passage of laws. Yes, the Japanese legislative assembly, known as the Diet, could indirectly exercise control over the military through budgetary measures, but when it came to matters of strategy, training, and military actions, the military enjoyed full autonomy from political leaders. Japan did adopt certain institutions from the West, altered of course to suit Japan's culture, but the country's elite chose not to adopt liberal institutions fully. Japan strove to secure independence from other nations to avoid the risk of becoming one of Europe's dominions. Taking inspiration from Europe and the United States, Japan embarked on building its empire by seizing Okinawa and other Ryukyu islands from China in 1871.[28] These acts were seen as necessary in creating a buffer zone for Japan against the Western incursions in Asia.

In the 1870s, Japan needed a new focus to inculcate patriotism and transfer loyalties previously centered on family, region, or one's local lord to that of a national level like Europe was doing.[29] To achieve this, glorification and deification of the emperor was the chosen path. The constitution had declared Japan had been "ruled over and governed by a line of emperors unbroken for ages eternal" and the emperor "symbolized the unity of the...people (*ue no zettai*)," but now Japan needed and got the educational system to reinforce these concepts.[30] The nation encountered challenges during this transition from a feudal state to a progressive society under one leader, the emperor. It was plagued by civil wars pitting the modern military against conventional-minded *samurai* who wished to keep Japan "traditional," meaning that Japan would remain a fragmented state with different fiefdoms. Thousands died as Japan was dragged "kicking and screaming" into the modern age.[31] Most elites believed that the only way to successfully enter the modern age was to unite the nation under the emperor, which they slowly but surely accomplished using civil war, religion, and education to accomplish this goal. To ensure the Shintō and Zen-Buddhist creeds of emperor worship took hold, between 1870 and 1884, 10,000 evangelists were "employed in a massive campaign to promulgate" this renewed focus on the emperor and sacred country in a large-scale proselytizing operation.[32] Everything in society took on a religious-tent-revival-like atmosphere. For instance, schools taught the "imperial throne was as ancient as the very origins of heaven and earth...The state supported financially this intensely nationalistic cult...[which produced] the blind loyalty and devotion Japan's leaders required."[33]

Concurrently, the country underwent rapid industrialization and urbanization during which time it created a large, modern, conscript military. Unsurprisingly, the military was accountable only to the emperor, considered a direct descendent of the sun goddess, *Amaterasu Omikami*, one of the most powerful Shintō gods. This was why their servicemen were called *Soldiers of the Sun*. The creeds and traditions surrounding the sun goddess stemmed from a pre-Bronze age culture that supported the belief they were the special objects of the divine—our solar system's star, *the Sun*. The belief that the Sun was the sole progenitor of the Japanese shows their heliocentric conviction that everything in life was arranged with them in mind. Consequently, the Sun became the emblem of their national and military flags, further serving to unite the nation as one people under one god, the emperor. It was the Japanese version of *E Pluribus Unum*.

Japan's pathetic solipsism that they were the direct descendants of the gods and ruled by one of them fostered an extreme egotism that helped create an unforgiving citizenry willing to commit some of the most grotesque atrocities any modern power has ever performed precisely because they believed they had divine permission to do so. Their delusions justified their goal "to acquire and wield power over others." To them everybody non-Japanese were the gods' unfavored children. During the late 19th century and 20th century, Japan was the only modern nation still ruled by a god who espoused totalitarian convictions supported by a state requiring all to worship him.[34] These forms of "arrogance and servility, both of which flow directly from the power of the passions," were evident throughout Japanese culture and defined its beliefs.[35]

So, by the late 19th century, Japan was fully instilled with an "emperor-centered ideology." The IJA used this ideology to "validate [its actions in the emperor's name and] [it] as a special institution in the Japanese polity" to unite its men for whatever campaign or political endeavor it focused on.[36] Such a focus by the IJA allowed Hirohito, and his predecessors, to maintain more control over the military, and by extension, over their subjects than the Nazi or Fascist dictators of Germany and Italy. Yes, there were some commanders who ignored Hirohito's ideas and orders when given without much publicity, but when Hirohito was clear and direct, especially in a public format, his subordinates followed him without deviation. The heavy focus on the emperor was fully supported by Shintō- and *Bushido*/Zen-Buddhist-doctrines. And these doctrines made the Japanese feel superior and justified in murdering anyone not Japanese for the slightest of reasons.[37] No one was permitted to question the Imperial institution, even foreigners, that permitted anything in the emperor's name. Unlike in Germany, which had known enough of democracy and enlightened ideas for many to recognize the evil in Nazi rule, few in Japan dared to ever question the emperor—he was always good, right, and unerring. This was reinforced by government documents since some of them ensured the emperor was untouchable, especially since the Meiji Constitution had declared him "sacred and inviolable" and "free from all worldly responsibilities."[38]

> To anyone reading the Japanese [press] of the period, it could easily have appeared that the whole of Japanese life centered on the slightest whim of the emperor. Dire punishments threatened anyone who dared to suggest that everyone and everything in the Imperial realm was not subject to his divine judgment.[39]

In Shintō belief, the emperor held a divine role as an intermediary between the people and the gods, providing the link they needed mentally to uphold the illusion they were a heavenly guided people. Starting from 1890 on, after Japan had already experienced 20 years of religious indoctrination, an Imperial rescript (*tokuhō*), similar to a Catholic *Encyclical*, mandated that school children memorize and recite an oath to "offer yourselves courageously to the State" and "thus guard and maintain the prosperity of Our Imperial Throne coequal with heaven and earth" as well as affirm the emperor's teachings, decisions, and decrees *as infallible.*[40] Shintō priests developed rites to pay homage to the rescript and the imperial photograph. "Every aspect of life took on a military coloring. Boys went off to school in [army] uniforms...Instructors often drilled the children indoctrinating them with military values. Every day, boys would face a picture of the emperor and be asked 'What is your dearest ambition?'" and in unison, they would answer, "To die for the Emperor! (*chūkun aikoku*)." Seeing his school catch fire, one boy rushed in to save the emperor's photo trying to prevent the flames from destroying god's image but died in the blaze. Instead of viewing this as a tragedy, it was hailed as a "happy manifestation" "of love for the emperor." "These pathetic martyrdoms swelled the hearts of the people rather than depressed them." Children were taught "myths" as truth that the emperor discussed decisions with the Shintō gods, "in pitch-black darkness," and after receiving wisdom from on high, would declare it to the nation. Japanese faith had become "nothing now but credulity and prejudices" and "absurd mysteries," creating unquestioned obedience to the emperor, who was recast as a military figure who was owed incontestable loyalty.[41] Admiral Kanji Katō, occupying "all the major educational and 'command' posts in the prewar" navy, wrote in 1933:

> Whence comes the strength of our army, that during the three thousand years since the founding of our country has protected us and has not yielded an inch of land to the enemy? 'For generations, the emperor has led our Imperial Forces.'...It is the pride of the Imperial Forces to submit to...the emperor...around whom everything centers...The soldier dies for the emperor...When he is about to die, the last words that break forth from his lips are '*Tennō Heika, Banzai!*' (Our emperor, lives 10,000 years). We die gladly. We are happy to float in his spiritual grace...Under the [emperor's] supreme command there is no limit to our power.[42]

The military focused on the emperor as the "foundation of our national strength" to explain Japan's "invincibility, equaled by no country in the world."[43] Unquestioning allegiance to the emperor instilled during military training permeated into civilian life when soldiers left active duty. It was a vicious circle, teaching xenophobic "virtues" as being the highest forms of behavior to unify the country using Shintō beliefs as a foundation.[44] Although many would also have called themselves Zen Buddhists, to be Japanese was by default to also be Shintōist.[45] "State Shintō, the government's artificial construct, was purposely designed as a cult of national morality and patriotism, to which followers of all religions [Buddhists, Taoists, Christians, and Confucianists] must subscribe."[46] This amalgamation of Japanese-religious beliefs created a Fascist and imperialistic nation.

By WWII, no Japanese dared question the emperor, especially since for 70 years leading up to 1941, the nation had been totally indoctrinated with this religion of emperor worship.[47] Hirohito, following in the footsteps of his father and grandfather, enjoyed maintaining his people "in a condition of political tutelage and immaturity."[48] The government's propaganda machinery relied heavily on elite religious teachings, creating an exaggerated metaphysical and epistemological solipsism making Japanese feel they were the best of humanity led by the best the gods could create, the emperor. As Japan modernized, these beliefs manifested themselves into aggressive militarism and territorial expansion. Having one dominant sect did not contribute to a culture of moral restraint and thus, Japan's society embraced violence as justifiable means to achieve its theological mandate to rule the world.[49] Thus, the political beliefs of Japan were not liberated from religion, but rather, were theocratic and not subordinate to a secular state like in the U.S.[50]

One would think Buddhism would have prevented Japan from becoming Fascist, but that was not so. Zen Buddhism also took on Shintō-like characteristics and willingly made itself subservient to the emperor, nation, and military. Although today, most Buddhists would identify themselves as pacifists, under Fascist Japan, their beliefs inverted.[51] For Zen Buddhists, "warfare and killing were described as manifestations of Buddhist compassion." Historian and Buddhist priest Brian Victoria continued: "The 'selflessness' of Zen meant absolute and unquestioning submission to the emperor's will and dictates. And the purpose of religion was to preserve the state and punish any country or person who dared interfere with its right of self-aggrandizement."[52] As Japan descended further into Fascism, it had its two major religions of Buddhism and Shintōism in its back pocket. Buddhism "was indeed one, if not the only, organization capable of offering effective resistance to state policy," but instead, it offered its unquestioning loyalty.[53] Zen Buddhism became Fascist claiming it was the best Buddhism:

> Buddhism in India collapsed due to…Indian culture, Buddhism in China collapsed because it ran directly contrary to the history of nature of the Chinese state, and was therefore only able to produce a few mountain

temples. On the other hand, thanks to the rich cultivation Japanese Buddhism received on Japanese soil, it gradually developed into…[what] Buddhist teaching was aiming toward.[54]

Many Japanese believed Japan was "the only Buddhist country" in existence because Buddhism "didn't simply spread to Japan but was actually created there."[55] So, not surprisingly, Japanese troops often disparaged foreign religions, viewing their adherents as heathens, including members of non-Japanese denominations of Buddhism.[56] And spreading Japanese Buddhism by the sword, killing "unruly heathens" (*jama gedō*), was supported by Zen Buddhists: "discharging one's duty to the state on the battlefield is a religious act."[57] "Buddhism doesn't merely approve of wars that are in accord with its values; it vigorously supports such wars to the point of being a war enthusiast."[58] And concerning the emperor, Zen Buddhist leaders believed he was the long-term "protector" of their religion and a "Gold Wheel-Turning King" (*konrin jōō*), "one of the four manifestations of the ideal Buddhist monarch or *cakravartin-raja*." They believed he was a "*Tathagata* [fully enlightened being] of the secular world."[59] And since Japanese religion, a synthesis of Shintō and Buddhist ideologies, was martial to its core (*Bushido*—"the Way of the Warrior"),[60] it was just a matter of time before Japan's indoctrinated legions swarmed out beyond the nation's borders to enact *their* "God-given right" to rule everyone, especially since that had been preached to them for decades. As one can see, "Japanese racism" was extremely dangerous "for being firmly rooted in religion."[61]

So, not surprisingly, Hirohito was an absolute and religious ruler when he seized the throne by the very fact of how the whole of Japan had been indoctrinated to view the cult of the emperor. Hirohito was Emperor Meiji's first grandson, born on 29 April 1901.[62] At eleven, he became the crown prince and received the ranks of army second lieutenant and navy ensign.[63] In 1926, he officially became the emperor (to become known after his death as the *Shōwa* Emperor, or the "Enlightened" Emperor), although for a year, he had already been acting as such for his insane father. Again, it must be emphasized, the Japanese believed he *was a god in human form* (*arahitogami*) and the nation's "high Shintō Priest."[64] And as head of the armed forces, he was "a real war leader," "exercising his constitutional prerogatives of supreme command" (*daigensui*), doing so with impunity.[65]

However, Hirohito's slight physique and bookish demeaner did not embrace the title just given him as being a "war leader." He did not look like a prototypical bloodthirsty dictator embodied by the Axis powers although he would become one in deeds. His build was slight, weighing 150 pounds, and he was short, standing at 5'5". His voice was squeaky, and he behaved in a docile and wispy manner. His gait was somewhat awkward, as if he was extremely flat-footed, walking not heel to toe, but placing his entire foot down with each step as if his ankles were incapable of bending. This made him pick up his knees in an artificial manner, giving him a cartoonish appearance that he was unsure of himself. In addition to these unwarlike mannerisms, he also wore simple, metal round-rimmed eyeglasses that gave him a nerd-like quality, not the hawk-eyed, single eyeglass *pince nez* that many German generals wore giving them a martial appearance, for example. It is intriguing to ponder why, if he was really a god, did he have poor eyesight? Nevertheless, Japanese were not allowed to question any physical shortcomings that Hirohito might have had. Close associates described him as a passive, sensitive man who sometimes did not take his emperor duties seriously, especially since he enjoyed studying marine biology and fungi, and not Sun Tzu or Musashi, for instance. Such subjects were unusual for a brutal dictator's curriculum.

Emperor Hirohito in a military dress uniform. Although he never trained as a soldier or officer, he was the highest military authority in the land during the war. He liked playing soldier. *National Archives, College Park*

Nonetheless, as a ruler, Hirohito was all powerful and he, "as a source of law, transcended the constitution, whose purpose was not to place limits on his powers, but the...opposite—to protect him and provide a mechanism enabling him to exercise authority unimpeded by limits."[66] Hirohito, being an intelligent man, knew he reigned with unquestioned authority, and he took pleasure in it. So, in contrast to his passive demeanor, Hirohito often met with his commanders to dictate strategy and enjoyed playing soldier. He freely, and carelessly, ordered "his men to commit acts in violation of laws and customs of war."[67] Few WWII leaders wielded such extensive control over the halls of power as Hirohito did.[68] Contrary to his outwardly passive and meek personality, he was indeed land-driven, empire-hungry, and indifferent to the suffering of conquered peoples and his own citizens. From 1927 until mid-1942, Hirohito's Japan conquered areas throughout Asia and the Pacific and Indian Oceans in its "reckless expansionist policy," deploying millions of troops and investing billions of yen in the enterprise.[69] He seized more land, conquered more countries, and killed more people than Hitler. Similar to the Nazi dictator, Hirohito rarely allowed his forces to retreat. It became a hallmark for soldiers to fight relentlessly in place until they died. Hirohito's armed forces accomplished some amazing feats, but the military was marred by rape, atrocities, suicidal *Banzais* and dramatic defeats. Hirohito ruled a Japan with an "army run amok, led by fanatics whose blind devotion to the emperor encouraged barbaric behavior."[70] This "barbaric behavior" was defined by excessive rape, murder, torture, and looting.

In many respects, Japanese Imperial society, Shintōism, and Zen Buddhism were obviously highly unstable, and certainly self-destructive. Japan's history, myths, and religion contained notable gaps and, it must be noted, plenty of plagiarisms, which caused some of that instability. For example, it borrowed many of its beliefs from China and India, specifically Buddhism, Taoism, and Confucianism, and adapted the conviction in the emperor's Divine Origin from the political theories of China's Chou kings (1100 to 300 B.C.E.). Furthermore, it took its "system of...writing using Chinese-derived characters" or ideographs (*kanji*) and drew much of its legal theory from China, and its ethnic origins were largely Mongolian, Chinese, and Korean.[71] China and Korea were Japan's forebears genetically, culturally, spiritually, and linguistically.[72] Japan's society was showing its schizophrenia in that it taught its people to hate these Asian civilizations that had actually given birth to many of its cultural mores, creating self-loathing that was deep-seated and often subconscious. Like many cultures with fanatical and fascistic beliefs about a nation's origins being "pure," the Japanese exaggerated their beginnings and destiny. The more extreme Japan became in its mission to rule *everyone and everywhere* because they were superior, the more extraordinary, fanciful, mythical, and fallacious its claims became about its origins, emperor, people, and role in the world.[73]

Despite the inherent logical inconsistencies of their pursuits, the Japanese nonetheless strove to elucidate and ultimately create that new world order where they controlled everything. Instead of relying on argument, education, and intelligence to convince the world of their superiority, the Japanese resorted to brute force. As a result, the Japanese soldiers the Allies and Chinese fought were some of the most ruthless any modern nation has produced. Allied troops who fought the IJA troops were up against experienced, well-trained, well-equipped, fanatical, and brainwashed adversaries. Japanese military men were committed fighters, willing to endure tremendous hardship and sacrifice their lives for their emperor. These superhuman deeds were fueled, in part, by their unwavering belief in Hirohito, who gave them "fantasies of a strong father" and myths about their origins and greatness "in a more abstract and irrational way" than Hitler did for Germans.[74]

With this background, one starts to understand how and why the Japanese committed atrocities. The political, religious, and ideological convictions most Japanese shared in their group-think and rule-oriented society made them into some of the most intolerant, chauvinistic, nationalistic, and sadistic people any modern nation has ever produced. It is no wonder it required the collective strength of the Allies, combined with superior weaponry and scientific advancements, to utterly defeat this nation. There was no reforming Imperial Japan or modifying its society. It would have to be demolished, the power of its emperor-god crushed and his divinity debunked. The world would have to experience much death and destruction before realizing the ultimate demise of Imperial Japan.

CHAPTER 2

JAPAN'S RACIAL TENSIONS WITH NAZI GERMANY AND BLENDING FASCIST IDEOLOGIES

"The factor most responsible for the miseries
of mankind is man himself."
—**Mikiso Hane**, *Modern Japan*[75]

JAPAN'S ADHERENCE TO A DOCTRINE of racial superiority presented a unique predicament—it found itself in competition with its allies for the claim of genetic, eugenic, and cultural greatness. The Germans propagated the notion of Aryan superiority, placing the Japanese in an inferior position within this hierarchy. Yet Japan itself also espoused a master-race theory that positioned the Germans in a lower position—thus, there couldn't be two chosen people: The *Yamato* race was distinct from the *Aryan* race. These conflicting race theories proved irreconcilable, or as a Japanese journalist noted, were "like trying to mix oil and water."[76]

The Germans appeared to be the first to take proactive measures to address this issue between their nation and Japan. In order to navigate the challenge posed by having such an Asian ally, the Nazis devised a plan. Justifying the alliance with the Japanese, who fit into the Nazi category of "Asiatic barbarians" and whom Hitler had disparaged in *Mein Kampf*, required a creative rationalization (Japanese translations edited these sections out of the *Führer*'s work).[77] Hitler's armament minister, Albert Speer, referred to Germany's alliance with Japan "from the racist point of view a dubious affair."[78] Party members disapproved of associating with "barbarian midgets," and the Japanese did not appreciate being labelled inferior "non-Aryans." Given the importance of the 1936 Anti-Comintern Pact, aimed at creating a unified front for Japan and Germany to confront the spread of Communism, Hitler needed to ease the racial tension both internally and externally. Consequently, Hitler officially designated the Japanese as "honorary Aryans," because they possessed Germanic qualities, calling them the "Prussians of the East." However, in private, he harbored concerns about the Japanese as a potential threat to the white race and confided to his pilot, Hans Baur, that these "yellow men" would "be a problem…after we won the war."[79]

Hitler's racist mindset towards the Japanese was demeaning, but it also was parasitical. *SS* Lieutenant General (*Obergruppenführer*) Karl Wolff, a close associate of the head of the *SS*, *Reichsführer* Heinrich Himmler, described *der Führer's* convictions:

> Hitler was impressed with the speed by which Japan had industrialized in less than a century. He was also surprised at how quickly they created an empire after the Great War, and then expanded into China. He had met with the Japanese ambassador, [Baron Hiroshi] Oshima. I was there with them a couple of times… Later, after the Japanese attacked the Americans, Hitler said, "Looks like they joined the fight. They do have this idea of racial superiority, so we can let them believe that as long as they keep the Americans busy over there. Let them have their empire and the colonies of the Europeans. We will have Europe and Africa. But we know, and I think deep inside even the Japanese knows, the Aryan is superior. That was why they abandoned the Middle Ages and westernized their culture, politics, industry, and military and not the other way around. I'll bet that they probably use forks now instead of chop sticks."[80]

Hitler's remarks here, made in the aftermath of the Pearl Harbor attack, revealed his perspective on Japan as the superior Asian race, albeit still inferior to the Germans. Surprisingly, he entertained the idea of allowing Japan to exercise dominion over China and the European Asian colonies on the condition that they relinquished control over Africa and Europe to him. Thus, he did not care what Japan would do with China, and other Asian nations, and viewed them as inferior by the fact of approving what Japan was doing there at that time, endorsing its mass murder, colonization, and economic exploitation. Nonetheless, in arrogant fashion, he believed Japan really felt the Aryans were superior to themselves and strove to become like them, something Hitler knew could never happen. The Japanese could not grow blonde hair, change their brown eyes to blue, or increase their average height and modify their skeletons, especially their skulls, enough to be like what Hitler felt were ideal Aryans (Hitler faced a similar predicament, to some degree, since he was average height at 5'8" and had dark hair, but that is another matter altogether). The fact Hitler felt Japan wanted to "Aryanize" their population, proven, according to him, by how they had copied everything in their nation after the European model, gave Hitler proof that, indeed, the Aryans were the best of humankind.

Interestingly, regardless of Hitler's analysis of the Japanese, the Japanese continued to call Germans *gaijin*, meaning barbarians, even as they were undeniably copying Germany's roadmaps for nation formation and empire expansion. The mental and verbal gymnastics both nations performed to ally themselves with people they ridiculed were trumped by the satisfaction they felt of being allied in the 1930s and early 1940s with countries that were powerful and dominant in the regions they controlled. Its military triumphs and First-World nation status allowed Japan to save face being dependent, to some degree, on western nations like Germany. Similarly, Germany sought to justify its alliance with "inferior" nations composed of *Untermenschen* like Japan since they fought a common enemy and embraced similar political ideologies. Nonetheless, the racial tensions would never really go away. For instance, when the Tripartite Pact was signed on 27 September 1940, Hitler subtly took a dig at the Japanese in the preamble that the "strongest" race (i.e. Aryans) would ultimately prevail in the ongoing global conflict. In response, Prime Minister Fumimaro Konoe, Foreign Minister Yōsuke Matsuoka, and War Minister Hideki Tōjō skirted the issue Hitler had raised saying if Japan should fail in "her 'grand mission of spreading the Imperial Way,'" then she did not deserve to exist.[81] In the end, these racist regimes demonized those not allied with them as inferior and viewed the other Axis nations as racially acceptable, at least in official documents intended for public consumption. They both were racially acceptable if both kept their empire building within their respected hemispheres and their racial propaganda benign regarding each other.

During this period, an interesting development with these Axis nations' racism unfolded as the Nazis dragged the Japanese into their world of antisemitism. Nazi naval attaché in Tokyo, Captain Paul Wenneker, reported to the Ministry for the Armed Forces in Berlin on 13 May 1935 that the "Jewish Question" had found "a lot of interest" among many Japanese naval officers. Wenneker identified IJN Captain Koreshige Inuzuka as the person responsible for spreading this information through the ranks of the Japanese military. Inuzuka was a believer in the racist, fabricated Tsarist anti-Semitic document called the *Protocols of the Elders of Zion*. This unscientific and bogus document supposedly "proved" the inherent danger of Jews because they desired to rule the world, and already did through "international finance and banking controls." Inuzuka confided in Wenneker that, based on their study of WWI, numerous naval officers believed the Jews had plunged the world into a global conflict from 1914 to 1918 to benefit financially from the arms race. Consequently, these "elements" should be closely watched and controlled.[82]

In November 1936, following the Anti-Comintern Pact with Italy and Germany, the Japanese government interjected numerous anti-Semitic arguments into "mainstream public discussion—where defamation of the Jews was already widespread."[83] From 1936 onwards, the Japanese civil servants responsible for propaganda "shamelessly manipulated the popular image of the Jews, not so much to persecute them as to strengthen domestic ideological conformity."[84] Whereas the Nazis wanted to kill all the Jews, Captain Inuzuka, an ardent anti-Semite, eventually devised the *Fugu* Plan, which aimed to exploit the Jews' perceived malevolence and economic influence for Japan's global dominance (this partly explains why Japan allowed Jews to move to Japanese-controlled Shanghai). Maybe these racist regimes could not agree on who was the best of humanity, the Aryans or the *Yamato* race, but at least they could agree the Jews were dangerous and warranted persecution. But while Nazi Germany felt the threat of the Jews with their ability to "control money" among other deficiencies had signed their death warrants for Auschwitz, under the leadership of such types as Captain Inuzuka, the Japanese felt that if the Jews could control the world economically and the Japanese could control them, that would ensure Japan could rule the world with the most efficient measures of domination. So, the help rendered to Jewish refugees, especially in Shanghai, by Chiune Sugihara, Japan's vice-consul for the Empire in Kaunas, Lithuania, must be looked at with a skeptical eye.[85]

And interestingly, as Germany distanced itself from China in 1938, many Germans succumbed to Japanese propaganda that portrayed Japan as a worthy ally, while deeming the Chinese, due to their laziness, lack of organization, and their physical weaknesses, as sub-humans unworthy of German alliance. That partially explains why the Germans pulled away from the Chinese and embraced the Japanese, since Japan appeared to be proving their superiority through their conquests, positioning itself as the lessor of racial Asian inferiorities. Indeed, General Georg Wetzell, the leader of the German military delegation to China from 1930 to 1934, and his successor, Lieutenant General Alexander von Falkenhausen, who held that position from 1935 to 1938, both grew increasingly frustrated with Chiang Kai-Shek, noting his soldiers were inferior to the Japanese, especially since they rarely went on the offensive. Moreover, they also held a general view that the Chinese people were primitive.[86] One of Falkenhausen's staff members, Major Robert Borchardt, gave further analysis on Wetzell's and Falkenhausen's opinions, saying, "The Japanese were right about the Chinese. Although there're many good Chinese I've worked with, they're, in general, indeed inferior racially to the Japanese and unworthy of a nation because they cannot organize themselves."[87] As one can see, both Japan and Germany rubbed off on one another, imparting to each other their views of their enemies of Jews and Chinese, forcing one another, in some forms, to embrace their own prejudices. When illogical and intolerant beliefs gain the support of powerful nations, they can influence policies and global perspectives. Japan and Germany at this time gave each other more reasons to hate others rather than try and understand them.

CHAPTER 3

JAPAN'S MARTIAL CULTURE

"Every morning be sure...to think of yourself as dead."
—18th Century *Samurai* Death Code[88]

IN THEIR PURSUIT OF GLOBAL domination and the cultivation of a "super race," the Japanese military employed abusive practices to enforce their objectives, subjecting their men to draconian punishments and brainwashing conditioning. Leaders beat their subordinates, and they in turn harmed those under them, perpetuating a cycle of harm within the ranks. They were not allowed to question, criticize, or strike back against superiors.[89] Fighter ace IJN Sub-Lieutenant Saburō Sakai wrote, "We were automatons who obeyed without thinking."[90] The practice of "harsh discipline" was referred to as *tekken seisai* (iron fist) and *ai-no-muchi* (whip of love).[91] Navy sailor Naoji Kōzu wrote about his superiors: "They beat us up regularly...In the navy, they put almost superstitious faith in the belief that brutality and physical punishment made better sailors."[92] This bully-like behavior took the form of blood, broken bones, and incredible humiliation for subordinates and had been part of the military for generations, creating a community of men who *always obeyed their orders.* Dating back to the army regulations of 1912, an Imperial rescript from the emperor obligated servicemen to exhibit absolute, unthinking obedience to orders. So, because officers had a direct connection to the emperor, their orders came with divine authority making them infallible. Unlike their counterparts in the U.S military, the Japanese had no concept of unlawful orders, as their unwavering adherence to obedience was deeply ingrained.[93]

From a young age, these men had been socialized with the belief that subordination to the group was of the utmost importance. As a result, when the group, particularly their superiors, engaged in criminal activities, the vast majority of them unquestioningly followed suit. They adhered to the Japanese proverb: "The nail that sticks up gets pounded down," which epitomized the pressure to conform within their community. Consequently, they found themselves bound by a sense of duty to align with the group's norms, seldom deviating from them, even when the group was involved in heinous acts against humanity. That mindset, coupled with the harsh and rigorous training they endured, instilled in these men a strong group bond that worked against individual conscience as the western world would understand it.[94]

The IJA also taught its soldiers the belief that death should never be avoided in war. It propagated the idea that to truly live, one must always be willing to die for the emperor and nation. If death came, it should be welcomed. Fighter ace Sakai claimed they lived by *Hagakure* (a popular *Bushido* text); to "live in such a way…[to] always be prepared to die."[95] More was "expected of the Japanese soldier than any soldier" of WWII.[96] As history would prove, the average fighting man was extremely brave, embraced an extreme form of loyalty and honor to comrades and country to overcome the fear of death, and continuously did his best to fulfill his orders to kill the enemy. As historian Richard Frank noted, their collective "valor [was] on a scale never surpassed,"[97] and this was a direct result of their rigorous training and conditioning.

This "valor" exhibited by Japan's military men was a product of a system built on militarism, racism, and unquestioning obedience enforced through strict press censorship, religious indoctrination, and intimidation.[98] While this system's instruction molded young men into efficient killing machines, it also led to the development of bizarre behaviors within its ranks. A striking example of this happened when an IJA officer, upon making a mere slip of the tongue while reading an emperor rescript to his troops, felt compelled afterwards to commit suicide by falling on his sword. Instead of condemning such a display as a tragic consequence of blind loyalty, people actually praised him for his actions.[99] Despite being taught that they were exceptional, the Japanese military superiors treated their subordinates as inferior beings. They demanded perfection in everything the men did, fostering a zero-defect mentality that was impossible to achieve, thus causing many to live in fear. And when one lives in fear, he does not create healthy environments for himself and others. It was evident that the military hierarchy in Japan at this time created a distorted sense of values and detrimental effects on the well-being of their troops up and down the entire chains of command.

Furthermore, as often is the case with cultures that try to make their citizenry more than they can become, Japan resorted to extreme measures to create an enemy and demonize him to keep control over its citizens while attempting to also instill in its people a sense of superiority. Ironically, in their pursuit of making the Japanese population feel superior to others, the military instructors employed training and education methods that subjected recruits to corporal punishment and verbal abuse, as mentioned earlier. It is important to highlight the contradiction here: While Japan propagated the notion that foreigners were inferior, they often did so by using pedagogic techniques that treated the very individuals receiving these lessons as inferior themselves. This self-defeating education was constantly cancelling itself out. Nevertheless, using the military apparatus, Japan made every effort to demonize the enemy and fuel hatred towards anyone, real and perceived, who was an enemy of the state.

As a result, Japanese Fascism within the military preached everything Japanese was superior and anything non-Japanese barbaric. The term *"gaijin"* (foreigners), often used with disdain, were viewed as non-human, and such terms were often used in military literature. For decades, Japanese military men had been indoctrinated with "evidence" that their enemies, such as Caucasians and Chinese, "were inferior, even subhuman creatures for whom no respect was possible."[100] IJA regular Shintarō Uno, who beheaded prisoners, wrote of the Japanese perspective: "[W]e never really considered the Chinese humans. When you're winning, the losers look…miserable. We concluded that the Yamato race was superior."[101] George Orwell wrote that for centuries, the Japanese preached, especially for their soldiers, "a racial theory…more extreme" than the Nazis, claiming "their own race to be divine and all others hereditarily inferior."[102] James Young, a former Japanese prisoner, supported Orwell's conclusions in an insightful 1940 book *Our Enemy*, writing about the Nanking massacre: "[The Japanese soldiers] duplicat[ed] all Nazi brutalities, exceed[ed] them, and add[ed] a whole satanic range of their own peculiar cruelties."[103] When the breakdown of their ritualistic environment occurred as Japanese soldiers invaded other countries, the "collapse of the subliminal restraints against aggressive impulses [happened] with catastrophic consequences. Frustration…pent up by the regimented rituals of social interaction within Japan exploded with…savagery against enemies abroad."[104]

The army created certain rites for recruits that created that "savagery against enemies abroad." In 1941, when Officer Candidate Shōzō Tominaga assumed command of a platoon in China within the 232nd Regiment of the 39th IJA Division from Hiroshima, he noticed the men "had evil eyes. They weren't human eyes, but the eyes of leopards or tigers… The longer the men had been at the front, the more evil their eyes appeared."[105] Upon joining this unit, fresh conscripts were compelled to bayonet Chinese POWs. These unfortunate victims were bound to stakes with a circle drawn around their hearts. The soldiers' superiors instructed them to avoid puncturing the prisoners' hearts, but to inflict injuries in other areas, prolonging their suffering and agony. Any Japanese who hesitated was "kicked, beaten, and prodded by their officers."

That was for enlisted men. For officers to "qualify" as platoon leaders, they had to cut off prisoners' heads. Second Lieutenant Tanaka provided a demonstration to the men on the proper technique of beheading. These gruesome executions took place in the presence of the regimental commander, Colonel Toraichi Ōsawa, who watched approvingly, having issued the original order for these executions. When Candidate Officer Tominaga's turn arrived, he took up his sword and slashed down on his victim's neck with such force that his "head flew away and the body tumbled down, spouting blood."[106] Another comrade's attempt at beheading was less successful, botching his stroke since the blade hit the skull and not the flesh of the neck. Suffering a horrible injury but still alive, the prisoner sprung up and ran around with a bleeding head. In response, the 22 officer candidates present at this "ceremony" descended upon the prisoner and hacked him to death with their swords. "Everyone got covered with blood as we butchered him," Tominaga noted clinically.[107] According to Tominaga, they "became…demon[s] within three months."[108] "Men were able to fight courageously only when their human characteristics were suppressed. So, we believed. It was a natural extension of our training back in Japan. This was the emperor's army."[109] Even years after these events, Tominaga could still write: "At that moment [after cutting off a head of a Chinese man], I felt something change inside me. I don't know how to put it, but I gained strength somewhere in my gut."[110] This collective slaughter gave them community, identity, and their first taste of blood, and this rite of passage made them into ruthless, uncaring killers. Disturbingly, there were instances after the Japanese murdered Chinese POWs when they would even eat the deceased's flesh, muscle, and livers.[111]

IJA soldiers were also indoctrinated with the belief that if they ever found themselves about to be defeated, they were to kill themselves instead of surrendering.[112] The IJA soldier's manual implicitly stated: "Bear in mind the fact that to be captured means not only disgracing the Army but your parents and family will never be able to hold up their heads again. Always save the last round for yourself."[113] Prime Minister and General Hideki Tōjō signed off on the Field Service Code in 1941 that contained this injunction, "Do not be taken prisoner alive."[114] Officers had the responsibility to ensure that they and their men upheld this standard with the 1908 army criminal code containing the following mandate: "A commander who allows his unit to surrender to the enemy without fighting to the last man or who concedes a strategic area to the enemy *shall be punishable by death* [author's italics]."[115]

Since Japan's military treated surrender as a crime, it led to a disturbing practice of encouraging captured servicemen to take their own lives. Many military personnel complied with this expectation.[116] By way of illustration, after the Shanghai Incident of 1932, Captain Noboru Kuga was repatriated to Japan through a prisoner exchange. He committed suicide soon thereafter. His *seppuku* (ritualistic suicide by disembowelment, also known as *hara-kiri*) was praised by War Minister General Sadao Araki, and his "spirit" was enshrined at the Yasukuni shrine in Tokyo, perpetuating this weird martial tradition.[117] For example, during the battle of Nomonhan in August of 1939 with the Soviets, Lieutenant Colonel Eiichi Ioki performed a heroic defensive action that disrupted Russian General Georgy Zhukov's timetable. When his "last capacity for defense evaporated," Ioki removed his survivors without orders to a more advantageous position. This retreat disgraced Ioki, and he was forced to commit suicide by his superiors.[118] Before committing *seppuku*, these men who had "retreated" or had become POWs were already considered socially dead. "They could not return to their families," and even if they had done so, their families would have rejected them.[119] If a Japanese soldier was unable to fight, wounded, or threatened with capture, his fellow soldiers often killed him instead of leaving him to be taken prisoner. Frequently, wounded soldiers were booby-trapped by their comrades to eliminate advancing enemy forces, reflecting a willingness to assassinate enemy combatants while ensuring the eradication of their own injured comrades.

Japanese bayonet prisoners at the Rape of Nanking. December 1937. *Nanking Massacre Memorial*

So, with these disturbing facts in mind, it becomes evident that enemy POWs were held in utter contempt by Japan's military, and it degraded, beat, and killed them. One harrowing example occurred after American prisoners surrendered to the Japanese at Wake Island. After several days once leaving the island on the ship *Nitta Maru* for a prison camp, Japanese naval personnel took some of the POWs from the ship's hold and brought them top deck. The navy lieutenant in charge, Toshio Saitō, announced that because the Marines had inflicted so much death on the Japanese, they were to be executed. Before their sentence was carried out, he coldly stated, "Since you have committed a crime, it will do no good to the world to let you live. I hope you will find happiness in the next world. When you are born again, I hope you will become peace-loving citizens."[120] In fulfilling Saito's execution order, Chief Petty Officer Yasuo Kohara said that an order from "his Commanding officer...was an order from his emperor and must be obeyed."[121] The Japanese beheaded and then mutilated the headless Americans before callously dumping them overboard. The perpetrators of this atrocity received the wedding rings, watches, and other personal effects of the men they had just murdered.[122] The Japanese would go on to murder thousands of innocent Allied POWs, particularly following the fall of the Philippines in 1942, including the infamous Bataan Death March. Downed airmen were often executed shortly after being taken prisoner, and in some cases, the POWs were brutally dismembered and eaten as meals. Shockingly, approximately 37% of all Western Allied POWs died while in Japanese hands.[123] Although this horrific treatment and high mortality rate shock the modern-day reader, one will find it disturbing that these rates were much lower than the death rates for other non-White POWs in Japanese custody. This is shown dramatically by the fact that out of the hundreds of thousands of Chinese POWs seized from 1931 until 1945, only 56 were found alive in camps at the war's end, indicating an alarmingly almost 100% kill rate![124]

So, Japan had an insatiable appetite for slaughtering defenseless POWs. Their methods of execution often reached unimaginable levels of cruelty and creativity. One such instance occurred near Menado, Indonesia, where Japanese guards tied Dutch prisoners together near crocodiles, and then left them there to be devoured alive. Laughing and joking with each other, the Japanese guards watched the reptiles tear the terrified, screaming victims into pieces.[125] In another sickening display of their barbarity, the Japanese placed Allied soldiers inside three-foot-long bamboo pig baskets while out in the ocean near Java, Indonesia, before casting them into shark-infested waters. Those who were not immediately devoured by the sharks faced a gruesome fate as their cages sank below the surface, leading to their drowning.[126] These acts were nothing short of sadistic entertainment for the Japanese personnel involved, who callously laughed as the POWs suffered agonizing deaths.

Japan's brutality extended beyond the slaughter of innocent prisoners of war, as they also perpetrated massacres against defenseless populations in conquered regions, resulting in millions of deaths. As a nation, the Japanese accepted killing the "other," and thought of world conquest as a given, thus removing any obstacles to committing atrocities. The Japanese treated conquered peoples as disposable resources, to be exploited for their benefit, without regard for their well-being. The entirety of Japan's culture was conditioned towards preparing its citizens for mass murder. While Germany primarily targeted the Jews as being the worst of humanity, Japan's ideology went further, deeming anything non-Japanese as unworthy of life. This ideology manifested in widespread acts of homicide wherever Japan gained control. Other Asians were considered inferior to the Japanese, and treated with disdain, persecution, and frequent murder. In general, the minds of the Japanese were "stuffed with martial dreams of grandeur [and a] political philosophy [that was] a pungent admixture of National Socialism, Fascism and medieval superstition."[127] Upon conquering a territory, the Japanese expected absolute obedience and reverence from the inhabitants, driven by their "martial dreams." However, they failed to realize that "to force men to say they believe what they do not, is vain, absurd, and without honor."[128] Most Japanese did not care that such measures were immoral, so they embraced a movement that imposed their will on nations they ruled because they thought they were the best race. Any form of resistance was met with death. This should not be surprising since for decades cadets were taught, "above all, the ethics of the warrior, the cult of *bushido*,"[129] which preached a fanatical dedication to fulfilling orders and destroying the enemy. By the time of WWII, these warrior codes had morphed into dangerous religious death cults, further fueling the fanaticism and dedication to fulfilling orders while annihilating the enemy.

These death cults resulted, in part, because the Japanese had preached for decades their "Aryan-like" myth that they, the *Yamato* race (the Sun clan), were the sun goddess' children and better than everyone else and destined to rule over these so-called sub-humans. Such beliefs inundated every facet of society and found fervent support among Japanese leaders and scholars. Examining the following men and leaders will shed light on how these beliefs were taught and embraced.

Widely read pseudo-scientist Colonel Kingorō Hashimoto wrote, "there's no nation that can compare with our national blood solidarity which makes possible a unification like ours with the emperor in the center."[130] Hashimoto also believed Japan's sphere of influence should include the following sub-human nations to be ruled by Emperor Hirohito: "Manchuria, China, the Soviet Far East, Malaya, Netherlands, India, British East India, Afghanistan, Australia, New Zealand, Hawaii, the Philippines and the islands of the Pacific and Indian oceans."[131] Similar to the Nazis' "Aryan"-myth teachings, many Japanese leaders and self-proclaimed "scholars" propagated the notion that the Japanese had once ruled the entire world in the not-so-distant past and that Japan's quest for world domination was to return her to her rightful place she had achieved during this ancient order.[132] Professor and IJA veteran Chikao Fujisawa from Nihon University, author of the bestselling book *Zen and Shintō: A History of Japanese Philosophy*, wrote,

> Excavations of ancient relics carried out in various regions of the world testify to the authenticity of the descriptions of the Japanese annals. They brought to light the wonderful fact that in the prehistoric age, mankind formed a single worldwide family system with the Japanese emperor at its head. Japan was highly respected as the land of parents, while all other lands were called the lands of children, or the branch lands. Eminent scholars are unanimous in concluding that the cradle of mankind was neither the Pamir plateau nor the banks of the Tigris-Euphrates, but the middle mountainous region of the Japanese mainland.[133]

Fujisawa skillfully cloaked his teachings in pseudo-science, artfully presenting the Japanese with a grandiose notion of their inherent superiority over other nations. This belief system aimed to justify their dominion over others, effectively reducing them to a state of servitude. However, similar to the Nazis' Aryan domination myths, neither the Germans nor the Japanese could provide "logical" explanations as to why these superior ancient races, supposedly more advanced in every way, had lost their power and dominance in the past. In some Nazi circles, they attributed the decline of the Aryans to intermarriage with Jewish communities, but the Japanese had stayed homogenous, so they could not blame their historical setbacks to genetic influences as Hitler did with the Jews. In the end, Fujisawa's preachings and "academic" claims, that humankind's origins came from Japan and that the original metaphorical Adam and Eve had not been in the Tigris-Euphrates region (or Africa), but rather near Mt. Fuji, shifted the focus of his listeners about human origins away from science and into legend. His diatribe here illustrated Imperial Japan was doing all it could to create a xenophobic, power-hungry, racist population that could justify violating human rights and international law in the quest of returning Japan to its rightful place as the master of all humankind. In other words, the

Japanese had historical justification to rape and dominate the entire world because archeological evidence, historical analysis and Japanese annals proved it!

The Japanese preached their master-race theories for three generations, successfully brainwashing millions by the time the Second World War erupted on the world's stage. The state-controlled Shintō religion played a significant role in inundating society with the belief in the "superiority of the Japanese as a race [*Nihonjin*], their divine mission in the world, and their supreme devotion to the emperor…Japan was pictured as an invincible nation."[134] Prominent figures like IJN officer and influential politician Chikuhei Nakajima boldly asserted in 1940 that it was their duty to exert control over others because they "were pure-blooded [and] had descended from the gods. The Greater East Asia War was thus no ordinary conflict but rather a divine mission."[135] Leaders such as War Minister General Sadao Araki (1931–34) devoted themselves to "the spiritual side of warfare," firmly believing their divine mission to rule made them superior and assured victory.[136] Lieutenant Colonel Gorō Sugimoto, a Buddhist philosopher, penned the bestselling book *Great Duty* (*Taigi*) that recruits, officers, and school children admired.[137] In this influential work, he wrote what many believed, intertwining Shintō, Buddhist, and Fascist convictions into one ideology:

> The Emperor is identical to the…[Sun] Goddess *Amaterasu*. He is the… only God of the universe…[T]he many components [of a country] including such things as its laws and constitution, its religion, ethics, learning, and art, are expedient means by which to promote unity with the Emperor…Stop such foolishness as respecting Confucius, revering Christ, or believing in [Buddha]! Believe in the Emperor, the embodiment of Supreme Truth, the one God of the universe!… Imperial subjects…should not seek their own personal salvation. Rather their goal should be the expansion of Imperial power…The Imperial way is…the fundamental principle for the guidance of the world…The Emperor's way is what has been taught by all the saints…The wars of the Empire are…holy…They are the [Buddhist] practice (*gyō*) of great compassion (*daijihshin*). Therefore the Imperial military must consist of holy officers and…soldiers…Warriors who sacrifice their lives for the Emperor will not die. They will live forever. Truly, they should be called gods and Buddhas for whom there is no life or death.[138]

Sugimoto preached a xenophobic, radical, religiously racist, Japanese-centric ideology that found resonance among IJA personnel in particular and *Nippon*'s society in general. Sugimoto believed by surrendering oneself completely to the emperor, a soldier could secure salvation, eternal life, and *even deification*, particularly if he died for the Empire's preservation. However, as is often the case with radical religious explanations, Sugimoto's ideology revealed inherent contradictions. Unknowingly, he somewhat cancelled out his dogma when he first wrote people should only believe in the emperor, not Buddha, but then later pronounced they should aspire to become gods and Buddhas! Wait, what should one do? He then declared Hirohito as the one true "God of the universe," being equal to the sun goddess although, since Shintō ideology claims *Amaterasu* gave birth to Hirohito's line, the Imperial household occupied an inferior position. Nonetheless, apparently Sugimoto was convincing with his illogical arguments, as is often the case with charismatic men. Comparable examples can be found in Hitler's *Mein Kampf* and his speeches, where pseudo-religious allusions and illogical concepts are present (such as Hitler's claim that Jesus was "Aryan" and a fighter against Jews, who wanted the *Volk* to rule all mankind).[139] The world during this era was rife with fanatical visions of what a future humanity should look like and what gods or beliefs a society should embrace. Sugimoto devoted his life to military campaigns, joining the IJA in 1921. When the Second Sino-Japanese war broke out, he died in battle on 14 September 1937 in Shanxi Province. In his unwavering conviction, he met his fate as a self-proclaimed god and Buddha, gazing toward the Imperial throne as he took his last breath.[140]

The hyperbolic language espousing the destiny of omnipresent rule as embraced by Hashimoto, Fujisawa, Nakajima, Araki and Sugimoto, buoyed the Japanese national self-concept. However, there existed a yawning gap between their religious pretensions, historical claims, and self-proclaimed elite warrior status on the one hand, and the stark reality that they possessed only a fraction of the resources available to their enemies on the other.[141] As a tiny minority in the world of nations with an island land poor in raw materials that had just gone through an industrial revolution, they lagged economically behind other "inferior" nations. Many Japanese felt frustrated by their manifest inability to solve their political problems and to control Asia. They were reliant on more powerful Allied countries who could abruptly cut off commodities, especially oil, without notice, severely crippling their economy and military. This raised troubling questions about the nation and its religion. Was there not something dramatically wrong with Japan that claimed its values, people, gods, and society were the best humanity had to offer, yet the world around them was disproving these assertions with the U.S., Britain, and Germany being far superior powers in empire building? Japan's sense of inadequacy was further compounded by the undeniable superiority of Western technology, especially with military hardware and machines. They must have wondered, if they were indeed the chosen people of the gods, then why were they so much smaller physically and technologically weaker than other ethnicities, especially Caucasians. Japan had a social structure that had a "tendency to exclude and denigrate others," which is usually a sign of deep-rooted insecurities.[142]

Furthermore, Japanese culture, to some extent, paradoxically, held a fascination with "White people" and desired to emulate them.[143] Even if there were individuals among the body politic who did not necessarily feel physically inferior due to their height and pigmentation, the pervasive depiction of Japanese as "little yellow men" and "monkeys" by the Western world only deepened their sense of inferiority. They hungered to be like the Europeans and Americans who appeared more physically formidable, held greater political power, and possessed superior military capabilities. However, the Japanese also despised them for their dominance in Asia and their ridicule of Asian races.[144] The disconnect between their cult-like indoctrination and their personal views kept the Japanese world in a perpetual belligerence that would later erupt into a global conflict of an unprecedented scale.

During the course of this global conflict, Japan's religious institutions, educational system, military services, and news agencies embraced and propagated Fascist ideologies that led it to becoming a leader among the Axis nations in its thirst for international power and disregard for human rights. Everything Japan did was dramatically reflected in its barbaric rule. Educators have often wondered how one teaches a subject matter so well it becomes internalized and shapes action. Japan was excellent in this pedagogic technique, but it was not to create enlightened people; it used educational techniques for sinister goals, creating mass murdering, intolerant, and racist soldiers, diplomats, and rulers, and did so by giving them intellectual license and psychological conditioning to commit crimes wherever they pleased, with grotesque regularity. The prevailing culture in Japan during this period reminds one of Martin Luther King Jr.'s famous quote: "Nothing in all the world is more dangerous than sincere ignorance and conscientious stupidity." The Japanese were in general ignorant to think they were the best the human race had to offer and everyone else inferior. When they started to rape and slaughter everywhere they went, they demonstrated their overt stupidity, foolishly believing that such abhorrent behavior would be tolerated, accepted, or even lauded by the rest of the world.

Although Japan did not set out to commit ethnic cleansing, even though its teachings often espoused it, its military servicemen almost always treated the non-Japanese in conquered lands with the same brutality the Nazis treated

Jews, Gypsies (Roma and Sinti), Communists, and male homosexuals. The Japanese killed their victims up close and inefficiently, yet with *gusto*. It took them *longer* to accomplish their killing by gang-raping women, lopping off heads, bayonetting POWs, starving citizens, deploying biological and chemical weapons against Nationalist Chinese, and burying people alive than by using Nazi-like extermination camps, but they would never be deterred from doing so. Unlike the Germans who occluded their crimes, only allowing a "select" few to participate in the extermination, the Japanese military personnel did not try to separate the people killed from those allowed to live. They did not bury them in mass graves or cremate them as the Germans did when trying to hide their atrocities, but instead, they just left the slaughtered to rot in the sun or threw them in a river or ocean. Japanese troops committed extermination from the front lines to the rear echelons. International news outlets reported the atrocities, turning public opinion against Japan.[145] Despite the widespread knowledge of these crimes, neither Hirohito nor his subordinates stopped this slaughter. Historian Edward J. Drea wrote: "War crimes may afflict all armies, but the scope of Japan's atrocities was so excessive and the punishments so disproportionate that no appeal to moral equivalency can excuse their barbarity."[146]

In conclusion, Japanese soldiers were dehumanized by their own chains of command and indoctrinated to have no feelings for those they conquered. The common soldier was trained to unquestioningly obey every order and to rape and slaughter wherever he went. When faced with defeat, he was taught to kill himself. Japan's modern military was indeed strange, based on primitive, feudalistic, Fascistic, and intolerant religious convictions. As historians Meirion and Susie Harries wrote: "The Imperial Army was suffused with a spirit of feudal origins. In many ways *the soldiers of the sun were in the twentieth century, but not of it* [author's italics]."[147]

CHAPTER 4

JAPANESE XENOPHOBIC AND IMPERIALISTIC GOALS IN PRACTICE

"Justice is only superficial courtesy among nations and
the ultimate resort is military power alone."

—Japanese Minister **Kentarō Kaneko**, Privy Council, 1930

"How courteous is the Japanese; He always says, 'Excuse it, please.'
He climbs into his neighbor's garden, and smiles, and says, 'I beg your
pardon'; He bows and grins a friendly grin, and calls his hungry family
in; He grins, and bows a friendly bow; So sorry, this my garden now."

—**Ogden Nash**, an American poet commenting on
Japan's brutal takeover of Manchuria in 1931[148]

YEARS PRIOR TO THE PEARL Harbor attack in 1941, Japan had already embarked
on a path of aggression starting with the First Sino-Japanese War (1894–1895).
Eager to utilize the modernized military into which much effort and treasure
had been expended, Japan crushed China in this war and acquired Taiwan/
Formosa, the adjoining Pescadores and Manchuria's Liaodong Peninsula.[149]
During this time, IJA soldiers unleashed terror upon the populations under
their control, committing horrifying acts of violence, such as bayoneting
children through their anuses and then holding them up in the air "for fun."[150]
One of the most egregious instances of Japan's brutality occurred during the
sacking of Port Arthur in Manchuria under the command of General Yamaji
Motoharu. His troops slaughtered between 2,000 and 3,000 men, women,
and children, although some accounts suggest the number could be as high
as 60,000. Additionally, Motoharu's soldiers perpetrated thousands of rapes,

reflecting a *modus operandi* Japan embraced when taking a city.[151] Shockingly, even elementary school teachers in Takamatsu, Kagawa Prefecture, compiled a war report celebrating Japan's slaughter and success against China, which they proudly displayed on the bulletin board for all to see:

> September 22, 1894. Battle Report. Japanese troops defeat Chinese at P'yongyang and win a great victory. Chinese corpses were piled up as high as a mountain, Oh, what a grand triumph. Chinka, Chinka, Chinka, Chinka, so stupid and they stinka.[152]

In Taiwan, Japanese soldiers showed themselves to be "arbitrary, arrogant and cruel," massacring thousands of civilians.[153] Their ruthless tactics included publicly beheading those who dared to resist their authority.[154] Moreover, the imposition of the Japanese language became compulsory in schools, while the publication of Chinese newspapers was strictly prohibited. Whenever feasible, the Japanese sought to supplant the foreign cultures they governed with their own language and customs, erasing the cultural heritage of the local populace. These actions underscored the oppressive and assimilationist policies employed by the Japanese during their occupation of Taiwan.[155]

Through an alliance with Great Britain during this period, Japan obtained a modern fleet which included European warships that the British taught the Japanese to operate. With its military of "leather-skinned dwarves" as the Russians called them, Japan shocked the world in the Russo-Japanese War (1904–1905) with a naval victory at Tsushima (the strait between Japan and Korea) in May 1905. This conflict marked a significant milestone as it was the first major battle at sea with steam-powered vessels.[156] Additionally, with the aid of Krupp siege guns, the Japanese military successfully defeated Russia at its Port Arthur base on the Manchurian Coast. It was the first modern victory of an Asian country over a Western power, boosting the confidence of Japanese militarists.[157]

This victory gave the Japanese a free hand to rule without restraint in parts of Manchuria and in Korea. However, the manner in which Japan consolidated its power in these regions came at a great cost, especially for Koreans who resisted their new rulers and faced brutal reprisals. Thousands lost their lives, with the death toll reaching at least 18,000 until Korea was formally annexed by Japan in 1910.[158] According to historian Saburō Ienaga, this annexation "started Japan on the road to empire and aggression" in a more accelerated manner than before.[159] The subjugation of Korea involved forceful measures, such as replacing the Korean language with Japanese in schools, mandatory attendance of Shintō services, and the violent punishment of those who struggled to adopt the Japanese language and culture or resisted Shintō worship. Christians who clung to their faith also faced persecution. Moreover, the Japanese imposed a systematic erasure of Korean identity by pressuring Koreans to adopt Japanese names and suppressing any expression of desire for independence.[160] Impoverished Korean women were compelled into Japanese brothels, while Imperial soldiers brutally quashed revolts and demonstrations through tactics like arrests, beatings, and killings to uphold their control. These oppressive actions solidified Japan's dominion over Korea and showcased the uncompromising nature of its imperialistic and totalitarian regime, which brooked no disobedience.[161]

Japan also exploited Korean men for its military goals, adding yet another dark chapter to its rule of this country. Official Japanese military post-war rolls indicate that around 150,000 Korean soldiers lost their lives from the Asian and Pacific Wars. However, it is crucial to recognize that most of these Koreans were forcibly coerced into fighting for Japan against their will.[162] The Japanese authorities compulsorily conscripted a staggering total of 370,000 Koreans into service.[163] Furthermore, the toll extended beyond the battlefield. Approximately, 64,000 Korean workers perished in Japan during the war, with 30,000 of them dying in the atomic blast at Hiroshima alone.[164] Additionally, between 670,000 and 1,000,000 Koreans were forcefully shipped to Japan to labor in "coal mines, on construction sites, and at other difficult tasks throughout the country."[165] During this period, the hundreds of thousands of Japanese occupying and governing Korea rarely complained about the miserable mistreatment of civilians. Likewise, when Koreans were deployed to Japan or served in combat units, their miserable plight went largely unacknowledged. Head of the War Ministry, Lieutenant General Seishirō Itagaki, even expressed that one goal Japan had in Korea was to "stamp out the respect and admiration of the Korean people for Britain and America and establish a strong faith in Japanese victory."[166] Paradoxically, Japan's actions in Korea only served to "stamp out" any remaining respect for the Japanese and their culture. As a Japanese Cabinet resolution had read as early as 1903: "It is inevitable that we should keep Korea under our thumb by force whatever happens," and for the ensuing four decades, Japan demonstrated its commitment to this declaration through the practice of cultural and physical genocide.[167] All these activities just mentioned could be summed up as being part of the Rape of Korea.

Driven by a relentless desire for expansion, Japan's ambitions extended beyond its control over Korea. The outbreak of WWI (1914–1918) presented Japan with more opportunities to expand its empire. Through its alliance with Britain, Japan capitalized on the situation and seized Germany's eastern territories, including islands in the Carolines, Marshalls, and northern Marianas, along with concessions in northern China. Of particular significance was Japan's acquisition of the Shantung Peninsula, which it regarded as a stepping stone toward establishing China as its second colony, following Korea. This aggressive pursuit of territorial dominance was driven by Japan's aspiration to establish itself as a major global power, capable of becoming one of the world's select few "governing nations."[168]

By the 1920s, Japan had emerged as the sole Asian state with a "modern army, navy and air force—in fact among the best in the world."[169] This military prowess was underscored by Japan's construction in 1922 of the first aircraft carrier any nation had ever built, the *Hōshō*, and its unwavering focus on developing a navy that could rival that of the mighty British Empire. These triumphs on the expansionist front, coupled with Japan's rapid military buildup, caused concern among notable figures such as the future chairman of the Joint Chiefs-of-Staff, Fleet Admiral William D. Leahy, as well as many in the U.S. Marine Corps. As a lieutenant commander and the navigator on the armored cruiser USS *California*, Leahy visited Japan in 1910. Ever since Japan had won its war against Russia in 1905, Leahy had been monitoring its society and military, viewing it as a future enemy. His interactions with numerous IJN officers, including the victor of Tsushima, Admiral Heihachirō Tōgō himself, left a lasting impression. Reflecting on his time in country, Leahy observed that Japan was ruled "by a people with a high order of military talent and an intense nationalism, it will be a menace to our institutions."[170] These experiences and insights shaped Leahy's strategic thinking and approach in the 1930s and 1940s as he grappled with the evolving challenges posed by Japan. He drew upon his firsthand exposure to Japan's military capabilities and nationalist fervor to inform his assessments and guide his strategic handling of Japan during this crucial period in history.[171]

Long before World War II, other officers besides Leahy also viewed Japan as America's nemesis and actively worked to ensure the Marine Corps' war doctrine acknowledged this nation as a serious threat. After WWI, the brilliant and prophetic USMC Major Earl H. Ellis thought about what country in the Pacific could challenge America. He saw what was going on in Japan and cautioned his superiors of the danger of a future war with the Empire of the Sun. To support his warning, he researched and compiled a divinatory study between 1920 and 1921 entitled *Advanced Base Operations in Micronesia*. With his superiors' support, Ellis dedicated years to analyzing Japan, the Pacific, Asia, and the intricacies of amphibious warfare to prepare for the possibility of future hostilities. His comprehensive study convinced some officers higher up, like

USMC Commandant John Archer Lejeune, to recognize the significance of amphibious warfare for future military operations in the Pacific against Japan. His study provided "the framework for the American strategy for a Pacific war, adopted by the Joint Board of the Army and Navy in 1924 as the 'Orange Plan.'" Tragically, he mysteriously died in 1923 while on Japanese-held Palau. Many speculate that the Japanese sent an assassin for this Marine Corps' Messiah, viewing him as a threat due to his profound understanding of the future challenges Japan posed and his insights into what America's defensive preparation should focus on.[172]

Leahy's and Ellis' concerns about Japan were well-founded, particularly as its society turned more radical throughout the early 1900s. Following the onset of political violence in 1905, an even stronger wave of Fascist ideology emerged within the country.[173] Notably, a die-hard Shintō ideologist held a close relationship with the empress and imparted his teachings to Hirohito, who served as the acting regent for his mentally unstable father.[174] These influential lectures significantly shaped Hirohito's thoughts and were subsequently published as imperial edicts upon his coronation in 1926. As a consequence, these edicts played a significant role in shaping Japan's political climate, especially by emphasizing the importance of military might.[175]

In 1927, Japan deployed additional troops throughout Shantung Province in northern China, a region it had dominated since taking it from the Germans after WWI. In the following years, from 1928 to 1929, Japan dispatched more troops to Tsingtao, a port city in Shantung Province, and subsequently to Tsinan. During the occupation of Tsinan, approximately 17,000 soldiers seized and controlled the city, perpetrating acts of rape and murder without restraint.[176] To the far north, Japan's entire behavior in Manchuria was characterized by violence and clandestine activities. It orchestrated the assassination of Manchuria's warlord, Chang Tso-lin, on 4 June 1928, in the "vain hope" that the regional government would not pledge allegiance to Chiang Kai-Shek's Nationalist government.[177] The next year, Hirohito "condoned the army's cover-up of this [assassination], thereby encouraging further acts of military defiance."[178]

With the Mukden Incident on 18 September 1931, Japan fabricated an attack on the South Manchuria Railway, blowing it up themselves, and then used this ruse to invade Manchuria. This act was akin to how Hitler invaded Poland eight years later.[179] According to historian Saburō Ienaga, "The bombing [of the railroad station] was a planned criminal act by the Kwantung Army."[180] This fabricated attack devised by numerous officers not only violated the nonaggression treaties and the Nine-Power Treaty Japan had previously signed, but it also was a direct violation of domestic law. According to the

IJA criminal code (Article 35), initiating "hostilities with a foreign country without provocation" was punishable "by death." Article 37 further stated that when a commander, "except in an extreme emergency, moves troops beyond his area of jurisdiction, [he] shall be punished by death or imprisonment of not less than seven years."[181] However, the Kwantung Army commander, General Baron Shigeru Honjō, along with his staff members, like Colonel Kenji Doihara and Colonel Seishirō Itagaki, who concocted this attack, were never prosecuted or reprimanded under the law. Instead, they continued to receive promotions and gain authority. The military failed to uphold its moral and ethical codes, allowing its leaders to act recklessly in China. Even Hirohito himself eventually approved of his soldiers' Manchurian invasion, thereby absolving men like Honjō, Doihara, and Itagaki from the "crime of insubordination."[182] Hirohito, like many senior army leaders in Tokyo, "approved of the troop movements in Manchuria after the fact because they were sympathetic before the fact."[183]

In taking Manchuria, Japan ultimately sanctioned this operation because it wanted this buffer state between it and the Soviet Union, which Japan felt it would have to fight.[184] The government declared in 1932: "Manchuria and Mongolia are the Empire's first line of defense against Russia and China; no external interference will be tolerated."[185] In 1932, Japan renamed Manchuria as *Manchukuo*, using it as its *Lebensraum*, and sent over a million colonists there in the coming years.[186]

Besides Manchuria's strategic value as a buffer zone against Russia, Japan's perceived necessity for Manchuria was driven by other factors as well, including the region's abundant mineral resources and its flourishing illegal drug trade. Beginning in 1927, Japan initiated a significant migration effort, sending 1.5 million settlers to Manchuria by 1945. Astonishingly, very few, if any, of these citizens or military personnel voiced complaints about the Rape of Manchuria, characterized by widespread murder, sexual assaults, and property confiscation.[187] Historians Meirion and Susie Harries described Japan's behavior in northern China as reaching "genocidal proportions."[188]

The eruption of hostilities in 1932 around Shanghai's international settlement can be largely attributed to massive Chinese protests of Japan's illegal invasion of Manchuria. Japan swiftly deployed its troops, leading to multiple clashes with Chinese forces, resulting in thousands of casualties on each side. Shockingly, Japan resorted to aerial bombardments of the city with the expressed intent of killing non-combatants, killing an estimated 2,000 to 6,000 innocent civilians. Emperor Hirohito issued an Imperial rescript praising his Kwantung Army commanders and soldiers "for having fought courageously in 'self-defense' against Chinese 'bandits.'"[189] As a reward, he then granted 3,000 awards and promotions upon military personnel and civil servants involved in the exploitation of Manchuria and the military actions around Shanghai.[190] The ruthless manner in which Japan took over and then ruled Manchuria, coupled with its conduct at Shanghai, elicited widespread condemnation from the international community. U.S. President Herbert Hoover strongly criticized Japan's actions as "immoral" and "outrageous."[191] Thousands of foreigners witnessed how Japan conducted war, observing how they murdered civilians in Shanghai by shooting them or bombing them without restraint. The disturbing scenes deeply disgusted the American people, prompting them to exert pressure on Secretary of State Henry Stimson to impose sanctions on Japan. This marked a defining moment that set the tone for America's approach towards Japan throughout the rest of the 1930s.[192]

Recognizing the tide of world public opinion was turning against Japan, Japan's delegation head to the League of Nations, Yōsuke Matsuoka, justified Japan's position to a joint session of the member states on 24 February 1933. Displaying an arrogant demeanor, he audaciously claimed all government factions in China were legal fictions, and consequently, Japan had a duty and right to reorganize China, citing it as a "bandit-ridden hopelessly disorganized country."[193] He blatantly lied to *everyone*, asserting Japan "had always upheld the principles of international law." Moreover, Matsuoka sought to instill fear by warning that if the League did not support Japan's actions in northern China, a potential alliance between Red China and the Soviet Union would follow, posing a worldwide threat to other governments by strengthening Communism's control across the globe. Pleading with the representatives, he stated, "Gentlemen, our desire is to help China as far as it is within our power. This is the duty we must assume...I beg you to deal with us on our terms and give us your confidence. To deny us this appeal will be a mistake."[194] He then concluded his address by requesting the nations to officially recognize *Manchukuo*. However, Matsuoka's efforts proved to be a resounding failure as the attending nations' representatives uniformly rejected his requests, refusing to be swayed by his arguments.

In response to the Western world's negative feedback and the imposition of sanctions for its actions in Manchuria, Japan made the decision to withdraw from the League of Nations in March 1933. This decision came after the League adopted a resolution, with a vote of forty-two to one (with Japan being the sole dissenter), adopting "a resolution disapproving of Japan's control of Manchuria."[195] In typical fashion, if Japan did not get its way using diplomacy, they ignored international law and public opinion and refused to deal with the problem. This behavior caused primarily the United States and Great Britain to place embargoes on Japan of increasing severity from 1933 until 1941. In some respects, these policies prompted Japan to attack the U.S. at Pearl Harbor in an effort to forcefully secure natural resources since other powers were slowly but surely choking her off from the world's supply of iron and oil.

In supporting actions like the invasion of Manchuria and further retarding international relations, War Minister General Sadao Araki (1931–34) "extended his professional support to colonels who were most passionately committed to the ideas of *total war* [author's italics]," namely, colonels Hideki Tōjō, Yoshijirō Umezu, and Tomoyuki Yamashita, some of the future major war criminals.[196] Unfortunately, having such figures in positions of power was contrary to Japan's interests if they sought to establish positive relationships with other nations. As historian Ienaga astutely observed, "The military comprehension of world power relationships suffered from a subjective astigmatism."[197] This observation highlights the military's distorted perspective, which hindered its comprehension of the complex interplay of power among nations.

The world's disapproval, as expressed by the League of Nations, proved insufficiently forceful enough to deter Japan from its aggression. Historian Barbara Tuchman noted that the League's lack of courage to slap crippling sanctions on Japan and to provide more aide to China "brewed the acid appeasement that gutted the League, encouraged further aggression and opened the decade of descent to war."[198] Japan's subsequent military campaigns in 1933 vividly exemplified the accuracy of Tuchman's observations. These campaigns involved the conquest of Jehol Province and "crossed over into Hopei, where [Japanese troops] established a demilitarized zone 30 to 40 miles wide between Peiping and Tientsin into which Chinese troops could not enter without Japanese consent."[199] Despite Japan's blatant acts of aggression and violation of international law, both the League and the Western powers failed to take decisive action against the nation (obviously the sanctions had not been powerful enough to deter Japan's actions in the short term). U.S. military advisor in China, Colonel Joseph "Vinegar Joe" Stilwell, perceptively remarked, "Paradoxically, each successful encroachment will be accepted more and more as inevitable and the foreign powers will be less and less inclined to call a halt."[200] This observation underscored the dangerous precedent of appeasement set by the lack of consequences for Japan's transgressions, leading to a diminishing resolve among foreign powers to confront its actions. In other words, sanctions rarely, if ever, deter military action of totalitarian regimes.

Not content with these conquests throughout Manchuria from 1931 to 1933, in July 1937 Japan launched a full-scale war against China, ultimately taking over the equivalent to half of the U.S. in landmass over the next year.[201]

This conflict was ignited by the Marco Polo Bridge incident near Beijing on 7 July when Japanese and Chinese troops clashed. Japan used this event to commence war primarily against Chiang Kai-Shek's Nationalist forces (*Kuomintang*) with Hirohito's explicit blessing ordering his men to "chastise Chink forces."[202] The chief of staff of the Kwantung Army, Major General Hideki Tōjō, had previously communicated to Army Vice Minister Major General Yoshijiro Umezu and vice chief of the General Staff, Lieutenant General Kiyoshi Imai, that the sooner Japan destroyed Chiang Kai-Shek's forces, the sooner Japan could protect its back and focus on destroying the Soviet Union.[203] At that time, the Nationalist forces constituted Japan's primary adversary on China's mainland (trained and supplied by Germany from 1934 to 1938, and then the Soviet Union for a limited amount of time, and then the U.S. thereafter, especially from 1940 to 1945).[204]

Concurrently, China was undergoing a major civil war with Chiang Kai-Shek's armies battling Mao Zedong's Communist forces to the north. Complicating matters further, both factions also were fighting numerous warlords (*tuchuns*) scattered across the country.[205] Essentially, it was a civil war within a civil war. China was a chaotic land unable to expel the Japanese invaders largely due to the nation's inability to unite under a single leader.

Japan saw China's instability as a threat to its own security vis-à-vis Communist Russia and the Allied powers, while also recognizing an opportunity to exploit China's internal turmoil to seize more territory and access valuable resources. In 1939, Prime Minister Kiichirō Hiranuma addressed the Diet, expressing his hope for Chinese corporation, which effectively meant becoming subservient to Japan as its slaves. He unequivocally stated, "As for those who fail to understand we have no other alternative but to exterminate them."[206] Japan regarded Chinese resistance as absurd and dishonorable, deeming those who resisted its rule worthy of deserving the harshest of punishments "for their refusal to acknowledge the superiority and leadership of the Japanese race and to co-operate with them."[207]

Japan conducted this war with China with such "ruthlessness and brutality," it shocked the "great powers" of the day.[208] The Japanese atrocities at the Rape of Nanking in 1937, where German military officers were stationed, "horrified" the *Wehrmacht* advisors.[209] Even Germany's Supreme Army Command in 1938, after observing Japan's combat, wrote that the IJA's bravery, loyalty to the fatherland, and lack of fear for death baffled it, and could not be "measured with European sensibilities."[210] That Japanese soldiers made the Nazi army stand back in awe for its brutality makes one take note of IJA extremism born from "a fanatical nation at war."[211] *SS* Lt. General (*Obergruppenführer*) Karl Wolff, following a dinner with the Japanese ambassador, remarked, "If these reports are accurate [of how the Japanese raped and slaughtered everywhere], I can see why the Japanese would think they're the superior race. I cannot imagine our soldiers sleeping well after displaying such ruthless efficiency. I don't know whether to admire or fear them."[212] Following the successful campaigns of 1937 and 1938, these newly occupied regions of China became home to over 500,000 Japanese colonists in addition to millions of IJA troops.[213] The scale of Japan's territorial expansion and occupation was remarkable, with far-reaching consequences for the affected areas, and now millions more Chinese were subjected to constant rape, murder, and exploitation.

The large emigration of Japanese citizens to mainland Asia demonstrated widespread support of Japanese for Japan's campaigns in China and the colonization of foreign lands. Citizens felt a sense of national destiny, believing it was their duty to spread their culture and beliefs worldwide. Such convictions were ingrained in the educational system. To illustrate how people had been conditioned for this exploitation, the following story is telling. When a boy cried about dissecting a frog during school, his teacher reprimanded him with a blow, accompanied by a question, "Why are you crying about one lousy frog? When you grow up you'll have to kill a hundred, two hundred Chinks."[214] As we know, when we teach children certain values when they are young, they often do not depart from them when they are older, and the behavior of the Japanese in China seemed to prove they were good students in the Japanese school system illustrated by this disturbing example. The seeds of inculcation of such values gave rise to a harvest of sorrow throughout Asia as these boys, now grown, became soldiers ruling over unprotected populations or colonists replacing the indigenous people. They indeed often treated foreigners as if they were dissecting frogs, echoing the callousness witnessed in their earlier classroom experiences.

On 27 September 1940, Japan forged a stronger alliance with Nazi Germany and Fascist Italy through the Tripartite Pact.[215] Hirohito wrote that these countries benefited Japan because they "share the same intentions as ourselves."[216] Exploiting the vulnerable state of Vichy France, Hirohito's Japan wrested control of Indochina from 1940 to 1941, edging closer to the coveted Dutch East Indies' oil reserves.[217] On 7 December 1941, emboldened by his conquests, Hirohito escalated his aggression to new heights, by going to war against Great Britain, the Netherlands, the United States, Australia, and New Zealand. The destruction of America's Pacific battleships at Pearl Harbor left Japan with a significant advantage, enabling them to pursue the conquest of other Southeast Asian and Pacific islands. In the following months, America received only bad news as Japan's military enjoyed one success after another. Not only was America's Pacific Fleet licking its wounds, but the British navy also suffered a grievous loss when Japanese planes sank the battleship HMS *Prince of Wales* and battlecruiser HMS *Repulse* off Singapore's coast on 10 December taking 840 sailors to the ocean's bottom. Churchill, now feeling what Roosevelt had a few days before, aptly captured the gravity of the situation:

> In all the war, I never received a more direct shock [with the sinkings of the *Prince of Wales* and *Repulse*]…As I turned over and twisted in bed the full horror of the news sank in…There were no British or American ships in the Indian Ocean or the Pacific except the American survivors of Pearl Harbor, who were hastening back to California. Across the vast expanse of waters, Japan was supreme, and we everywhere were weak and naked.[218]

While there were months of tremendous Filipino and U.S. heroism in defense of the Philippines, as well as notable successes achieved by the Flying Tigers (American fighter pilots provided to China), these were rare "success" stories in the war's early months. America found itself unprepared for the conflict that was thrust upon her on both sides of the world, and at first, "the chances for an Allied victory" seemed remote.[219] During the first six months following the surprise attack on the U.S., Japan secured a series of victories over unprepared British, Dutch, Australian, and American forces. This relentless onslaught granted Japan control over an enormous area, including the Philippines, Guam, Burma, Malaysia, Singapore, Hong Kong, and the Dutch East Indies (Indonesia). Japanese triumphs extended further into parts of Thailand, New Guinea, and numerous Pacific islands. With each invasion and occupation of these objectives, which were ripe for exploitation, Japan showed her true *casus belli*. Hirohito himself helped play a role in planning these aggressive actions, getting "caught up in the fever of territorial expansion and war."[220] Japan dealt harshly with anybody who tried to resist its expansion. In the occupied areas, grim reminders of *Nippon*'s brutality became all too common. Decapitated heads of those who dared to challenge Japan's invasion were often put on gruesome display. Severed skulls adorned telephone poles, lined fences, and were placed along roads, serving as a macabre warning to all who defied Japanese rule.[221]

Japanese soldiers hung up the heads they had cut off of "bandits" in Kharbine,
Manchuria, 19 November 1937. *National Archives, College Park*

Just weeks after the devastating attack on Pearl Harbor, Japanese forces were
knocking on Australia's doors and launching bombing raids on its northern
city of Darwin. The defense of Australia was severely handicapped by the fact
that the majority of its troops were engaged in combat against Field Marshal
Erwin Rommel's *Afrika Korps* in North Africa. "In the early days of the War,
the Japanese were an invincible force in the Pacific, moving swiftly and easily
from victory to victory—and island to island."²²² Hirohito played a pivotal role
as one of the driving forces for Japan's aggression, and his empire "dwarfed
Hitler's" in size. "The Rising Sun was blinding" and anyone who consulted
an atlas in 1942 would have to conclude the Allies were losing on all fronts

and that the Japanese reigned supreme in Asia.[223] It "appeared that [Japanese] policies were also being blessed by the Shintō gods" with their conquests.[224] The extent of Japan's territorial gains was staggering, encompassing an area equivalent to one-seventh of the Earth's circumference, three times larger than the combined landmass of the U.S. and Europe. In developing their vision of the "Co-Prosperity Sphere," Japan's self-proclaimed "super race" exerted dominion over 500 million people.[225] Even Lieutenant General Kuribayashi's grandson Yoshitaka Shindo, a politician in Japan's Liberal Democratic Party (a right-wing, nationalistic, conservative party actually), observed:

> Just like America seized lands from the Indians and Mexicans or ruling people like in Guam and the Philippines, we were building a nation. It was our Manifest Destiny. It was our time to spread our borders. To prevent colonization of ourselves could only be done, we felt, by spreading our physical influence throughout Asia. Although the Japan of that time did this with the wrong means by killing people and without the freedom of speech and democracy. I...tell you this to help you understand why the Japanese felt the way they did back then.[226]

Japan's Pacific War brought about the demise of "White" colonial rule in Asia, masquerading under the guise of Pan-Asianism. However, in reality, Japan emerged as the supreme ruler of the territories it occupied.[227] As historian Saburō Ienaga accurately pointed out, "To call Japan's disgraceful and bloody rampage [throughout Asia and the Pacific] a crusade for liberation [for Asians] is to stand truth and history on their heads."[228] By 1942, the western Pacific had "become a Japanese lake," where their authority was enforced with draconian measures.[229] The impact of Japan's conquests was far-reaching, as they extended their control over vast expanses of land and subjected the occupied populations to oppressive rule. In the aftermath of the Pearl Harbor attack, Prime Minister and General Tōjō (appointed by Hirohito)[230] could confidently reaffirm his declaration to citizens given on 8 December 1941:

> The key to victory lies in a "faith in victory." For 2600 years since it was founded, our Empire has never known a defeat. This record alone is enough to produce a conviction in our ability to crush any enemy no matter how strong. Let us pledge ourselves that we will never stain our glorious history, but will go forward...[231]

Tōjō remained undeterred by the fact that to "crush" America required more aircraft carriers and field armies than he and his Axis allies had altogether. His best hope was to "deter or convince" the U.S. to cease further fighting in Asia and the Pacific, while anticipating a triumph of the Nazi regime over Britain and the U.S.S.R. Such an outcome would isolate America and consume its attention with self-preservation. In a twist of logic, once Tōjō, Hirohito, and others initiated the war with the U.S. and Great Britain, an "irrational belief in victory…became the strategy."[232] Issues about securing victory were removed from most civilians' consciousness and they felt pride at Japan's success.[233] The German naval attaché in Tokyo, Rear Admiral Paul Wenneker, recounted how his contact Captain Masao Nakamura depicted the war with the U.S. as ushering the empire into its greatest epoch and that both nations should collaborate towards achieving victory.[234] Prior to this attack, Tōjō had solemnly declared in the presence of Hirohito that their new plans for a southward and southeastward strike had placed the empire "at the threshold of glory or oblivion." [235] At the present moment, Japan reveled in glory, yet they had not adequately prepared for how to prevent oblivion.

Japan's Prime Minister General Hideki Tōjō (1941–1944). He sent armies overseas knowing full well they were murdering and raping everywhere they went. He did not care. In 1948, the International Tribunal in Tokyo found him guilty of war crimes and he was executed by hanging. *National Archives, College Park*

The audacious surprise attack on Pearl Harbor was executed without a realistic follow-up plan for bringing the war to a conclusive end.[236] In some respects, it was conducted in response to the Nazis' remarkable successes throughout Europe. As Hitler's invasion of Russia and his ongoing conflict against Britain appeared to yield significant dividends for the Third Reich, the Japanese felt compelled to act quickly in Asia to secure their share of the spoils before others claimed them, since it appeared *der Führer* was about to defeat Stalin and Churchill.[237] The constant portrayal of Hitler's triumphs in newsreels showing throughout Japan "reinforce[d] this sense of urgency."[238] British ambassador to Japan Sir Robert Craigie, who detested the militaristic Japanese and felt nauseated by having to maintain a veneer of being polite with "the little blighters," wrote, "How, they urged, could Japan expect Hitler to divide the spoils with them unless she had been actively associated in the spoliation."[239] Foreign Minister Yōsuke Matsuoka echoed Craigie's observation, claiming, "When Germany wipes out the Soviet Union, we can't simply share in the spoils of victory unless we've done something…We must either shed our blood or embark on diplomacy. And it's better to shed blood."[240]

Japanese war hawks also wanted more dividends on the investment of the 400,000 men it had sacrificed in China, an adventure "proven to be a disaster," and secure their Asian gains by knocking the Americans back into the Western Hemisphere. Compounding this objective was the U.S.-enforced oil embargo in July/August 1941, which could have crippled the Empire's economy. This provided a further impetus for Japan to attack America, and the Netherlands, with the goal of seizing the oil-rich Dutch East Indies. U.S. Secretary of State Cordell Hull at the same time told the Japanese, whom he despised for their false pretenses of politeness, smiles, bowing, and "hissing," that if they wanted peace, they "would have to abandon the Tripartite Pact" and withdraw their troops from several areas in China. Hirohito's government found these demands unacceptable. Furthermore, the restrictions on the sale of petroleum and scrap iron to Japan further aggravated the situation. Admiral Isoroku Yamamoto felt the only way to secure a victory over the U.S. was to deliver a crippling, preemptive blow that would destroy most of its navy. These combined factors prompted the Japanese to stealthily move a formidable armada from Tokyo to Hawaii and smash the U.S. fleet at Pearl Harbor on a Sunday morning when America's guard was down.[241]

According to military philosopher Carl von Clausewitz, the Japanese failed to grasp the fundamental principle that "an enemy who violates a frontier will be made to pay a penalty in blood."[242] They were already paying a high price in China fighting along a 2,800-mile front against three million Chinese troops.[243]

However, they dramatically increased that debt by violating the Allies' frontiers. Similar to Hitler's costly dual campaigns against Russia and England, Japan left its rear vulnerable while it opened a gigantic front to the east against one of the most powerful countries in the world. While Japan launched its attacks against Western powers, Chinese Nationalists diligently had completed training of "another million of [its] soldiers to replenish the 'wall of steel and flesh'" which had been "checking and throwing back Japan's repeated attacks."[244] If Japan could not defeat a rag-tag group of Chinese soldiers with inferior weaponry and limited supplies, how was it going to tackle the first-world nations of the U.S., Great Britain and her Commonwealth territories?[245] Moreover, if they waged a war against China "without just cause or cogent reason," why in the world open another front with the Allies without a clear and definitive end goal?[246] Their fanaticism had blinded them to the realities of *Realpolitik*.

After declaring war with the United States in December 1941, and achieving overwhelming success against this superpower and others like Great Britain, the Japanese highlighted their unique superior racial status as being the Yamato *Übermenschen*, destined to deliver Japan ultimate victory. After destroying several naval ships at Pearl Harbor and taking over vast tracts of territory across Asia and the Pacific throughout 1941 and 1942, the Japanese succumbed to *shoribyo*, or "victory disease." This affliction fostered the dangerous belief "that Japan was invincible and could afford to treat its enemies with contempt."[247] They truly felt that they were on the cusp of fulfilling their racial destiny of ruling the world. These victories provided the proverbial "pouring gasoline on the fire" for them when embracing the false belief that they were indeed the master race. Their ideological and racial nonsense was disseminated through newspapers, schools, radio, and films using such slogans as: "100 million advancing like a ball of flame," or "Think as one, act as one," or "Extravagance is the enemy."[248] The most potent slogan, embodying this superior race theory, was one espousing the tenents of *Hakko Ichiu* ("eight corners of the world under one roof"), meaning Japan should control the entire globe.[249] Such notions, embraced by the majority of the population, illustrated the Japanese wanted all to adhere to their beliefs regarding Hirohito and the *Yamato* race. Ironically, these viewpoints made the Japanese "at home and on the front lines" capable of enduring "privations and hardships that the enemy could never withstand— they would work harder and face death with samurai-like indifference."[250] But in the end, despite their unwavering determination, their ambitions proved insufficient to take on the whole world although it still motivated the small nation of Japan to try and do so.

But in late 1941 and throughout 1942, the Japanese felt confident in their future prospects. After the Pearl Harbor attack, Hirohito issued the declaration of war as an Imperial rescript. It placed blame on the U.S. and England for causing war by supporting China and undermining Japan's efforts to establish an Asian Co-Prosperity Sphere. Essentially, Japan contended that the war started because the Allies had disturbed "the peace in East Asia." "Our Empire, for its existence and self-defense, has no other recourse but to appeal to arms and to crush every obstacle in its path."[251] Soon overwhelming military successes greeted Japan, further reinforcing its citizens' belief that they were the gods' chosen people. On the day of the attack, Hirohito donned his naval uniform and was in a "splendid mood," gloating over the victories. Hirohito lavished praise upon frontline units and sent rescripts to commanders "which carried far more honor and prestige than did presidential citations for American commanders."[252] By 12 December, Hirohito expressed gratitude to "the gods" for Japan's victories and "asked for their protection" as he led the "nation in this time of…national emergency."[253] However, as usual, there was no justification provided for Japan's violation of international law, as their attack violated the principles outlined in the Hague Convention. The convention stipulated that "the contracting parties accept that hostilities should not be opened unless there has been an explicit prior announcement in the form of a reasoned declaration of war or a final ultimatum which includes conditions."[254] Japan ignored these international legal mandates in conducting its war efforts, launching massive surprise attacks throughout the Pacific and Asia at the time of Pearl Harbor. And with each victory achieved through these unlawful acts, Japan propagated the notion that its triumphs would herald a new world order characterized by peace and prosperity.

However, instead of peace and prosperity, its conquests brought forth a harrowing reality of hardship, disease, starvation, slavery, and mass slaughter. The acts of rape, brutality, and torture were not only prevalent but actively encouraged and publicized,[255] common occurrences when a Japanese army was in control. In short, as historians Meirion and Susie Harries wrote, "The atrocities committed by the Imperial Japanese [military] are impossible to catalog. The number and the hideous variety of the crimes defy even the most twisted imaginations: murder on a scale amounting to genocide; rapes beyond counting; vivisection; cannibalism; torture…"[256] In the upcoming chapters, I will endeavor to "catalog" and shed light on some of these atrocities. To the best of my knowledge, this book represents the first comprehensive attempt to compile and chronicle many of these appalling events in history, providing a thorough account of these crimes against humanity.[257]

CHAPTER 5

THE RAPE OF NANKING

"Those who can make you believe absurdities
can make you commit atrocities."

—Voltaire[258]

THE BRUTAL NATURE OF JAPAN'S conquests of cities in WWII is starkly illustrated by the horrific events that make up the atrocity known as the Rape of Nanking. Taking place from July 1937 to March 1938, the Japanese forces unleashed a wave of unspeakable violence, spanning from Shanghai to Nanking. The scale of the crimes committed is unfathomable, with a minimum of 300,000 Chinese civilians brutally slaughtered and over 80,000 women subjected to rape.[259] These acts of savagery were carried out by the Shanghai Expeditionary Army, later renamed the Central China Expeditionary Force, consisting of approximately 200,000 soldiers. The campaign in this region lasted for five to six months, during which an average of 50,000 innocent lives were claimed each month. This reign of terror culminated with the sacking of Nanking. All told, from Shanghai to Nanking and the surrounding regions, Japan laid waste to 4,000 square miles of China or the size of Connecticut during this operation.[260]

As the National forces withdrew to the interior of China towards Nanking, the horizon following them was dotted with plumes of fire rising to the heavens from burning villages and towns. These grim scenes marked the relentless advance of the attacking Japanese army. Throughout the next weeks, Japanese troops plundered, raped, and slaughtered as they marched to Chiang Kai-Shek's capital. "A progression of smoke pillars visually charted the approach of the Japanese spearheads as soldiers engaged in a frenzy of arson" and destruction, ensuring they left no potential threat in their rear. Picking off straggling Chinese forces and the wounded, they left behind along their "advancing columns" a "thick wake of murdered prisoners and violated women."[261] At one rape victim's crime scene a few months after the actual campaign to conquer Nanking, but in the same region, IJA soldier Kōsuke Gomi witnessed a soldier assault a woman during a rest break. To accomplish his vile deed quickly, he mounted the defenseless female in full uniform with his web belt and ammunition. As he pumped away, she screamed in pain and terror. No one came to her aid or thought twice about stopping a fellow soldier from doing what he was doing. As historian Ienaga aptly wrote, "Rape was an accepted prerogative of the Imperial Army."[262] In another horrendous scene during this war in China, described by Taijirō Tamura, as a regiment of marching soldiers neared a position, onlookers saw "patches of white mixed in with the marching column." Closer inspection revealed that the patches of white were naked Chinese women, forced to march with the grunts. An NCO callously shouted, "If you want to get your hands on these Chink broads, you better keep up with the march. Right? Keep your eyes on those Chink bitches and keep going."[263] Later on, after the troops got their hands on the ladies and violated them, they often killed them because, as one soldier chillingly revealed, "They say the raped women must *always be killed* [author's italics]."[264] Sadly, the retreating Chinese forces could do little to protect their citizens they had to leave behind as they retreated west.

Upon reaching their capital, the surviving remnants of the National forces found themselves engulfed in chaos and disarray. This dire situation was exacerbated by the abandonment of Nanking by the Chinese commander, General Shengzhi Tang, who deserted the city and the majority of his troops at a critical moment when strong leadership was needed. Chiang Kai-Shek had indeed ordered him to leave, something he and his wife themselves had also already done. One could argue Tang's disgraceful behavior mirrored that of Chiang Kai-Shek's. The absence of leadership on many levels plunged the remaining Chinese forces into a state of panic and terror, especially when the Japanese launched mustard gas attacks on their static positions. Without effective leadership, the Chinese soldiers displayed little initiative and caused much "military confusion."[265] Colonel Stilwell, an astute observer of these events being in country himself, bluntly criticized Chiang Kai-Shek, referring to him as "an ignorant, illiterate peasant son-of-a-bitch" and that "the Chinese soldiers [are] excellent material, wasted and betrayed by stupid leadership."[266] In this state of disarray, the Chinese defenders in Nanking were quickly overwhelmed and defeated by the advancing Japanese forces.

The photograph claims it is of Chunking, China, showing civilians killed when a Japanese bomb hit their shelter. Since many of the women are nude and on stairs way above ground, it is felt this is of Nanking and shows evidence of rape and murder. December 1937. *National Archives, College Park*

Japanese bombing of South Station in Shanghai on 28 August 1937. H. S. "Newsreel" Wong took this photograph of the baby. His mother lay dead nearby. The baby was one of the only survivors of the attack on the station. *National Archives, College Park*

A Japanese sailor stands proudly with the head of a Chinese man
he has just cut off. *National Archives, College Park*

The escalation of slaughter occurred primarily after the disintegration of the Nanking Garrison Force, consisting of around 150,000 soldiers who had been defending the city's "fortress." By mid-December, relentless attacks from the better-equipped Japanese forces had shattered their resistance. Approximately 90,000 Chinese soldiers had laid down their arms, 10,000 had died in battle defending Nanking, and another 47,000 had fled west.[267] Chiang Kai-Shek's army, originally with a total of 750,000 men, had fought bravely in and around Shanghai for months, inflicting significant casualties on the 250,000 IJA personnel in protracted urban warfare, by far the largest city battle of World War II prior to Stalingrad.[268] However, when Kai-Shek's forces retreated to Nanking in November, they were exhausted, and their leaders had not adequately prepared the capital for a defensive stand. Despite outnumbering the Japanese divisions confronting them at Shanghai, the National forces suffered losses six times larger (250,000) than those suffered by the IJA (40,000) by the time they commenced their retreat.[269] Almost all the Chinese causalities were killed-in-action (KIAs) including many women and children "who had fought on the front lines" whereas the Japanese only suffered 9,115 dead and 31,257 wounded.[270] In foreshadowing what was to come throughout the campaign to Nanking and within the city itself, during this conflict just at Shanghai alone, Chinese-held postwar trials documented 30,000 cases of atrocities against civilians.[271] Obviously, tens of thousands more were soon to come in the near future.

During this battle for Nanking, American military personnel were present. Japanese planes sank the U.S. gunboat USS *Panay* on the Yangtze River near Nanking, killing three sailors and injuring 48 others. In addition, the Japanese aircraft attacked three Standard Oil tankers, which may have resulted in the murder of numerous Nanking evacuees. Despite these grave incidents, isolationist sentiments prevailed in America, urging the country to refrain from taking action. In the aftermath of the devastating carnage of World War I, most Americans desired to avoid any further entanglements, putting pressure on government officials to avoid conflict in Asia. It worked, and the officials complied. Tokyo did issue an apology, claiming ignorance about the *Panay's* American identity, while Japanese politicians at home jeered at what they perceived as American weakness. Admiral Yamamoto, in a display of contrition, "tearfully" presented himself at the U.S. Embassy, offering an apology and a "cash indemnity of $2.2 million [$45,961,667 in 2023]." However, he faced threats of assassination for his conciliatory actions from militant diehards, suggesting that he was an exception to the prevailing sentiment in Japan. Most Japanese people welcomed the attack on the Americans, with certain military leaders, contrary to their government's stance, having planned the attack with the intention of drawing America into the war to remove the "White man's" presence from Asia. However, their efforts failed to achieve the desired outcome.[272] Colonel Stilwell strongly denounced the Japanese "bastards" who were fully aware of their actions. He harbored intense hatred toward them for their brutal treatment of China, and the world at large for that matter, describing them as "arrogant, cynical, truculent, ruthless, brutal, stupid, treacherous, lying, unscrupulous, unmoral, unbalanced and hysterical."[273] Later 25th USMC commandant, Robert E. Cushman Jr., who was a lieutenant in

Shanghai during these events, supported Stilwell's assessment, proclaiming, "[The Japanese] knocked off *Panay* and in effect, told us to go to hell."[274]

Simultaneously to the assault on the *Panay*, Japanese pilots and shore batteries also targeted several British gunboats, namely HMS *Ladybird*, HMS *Bee*, HMS *Cricket*, and HMS *Scarab*. The attack resulted in the death of one sailor and caused injuries to the commander and several sailors on the *Ladybird*, yet England, like the U.S., refrained from responding with violence.[275] One of the main officers ordering the artillery fire from the land on these vessels was pseudo-scientist Colonel Kingorō Hashimoto who knew the ships' identities and was well aware that Japan was engaging in acts of killing innocent and non-combatant people and destroying international "property" that violated international law.[276]

Not to be outdone by ground troops and air forces, the Japanese Navy under Fleet Commander Vice Admiral Kiyoshi Hasegawa dispatched its gunboats (17 ships in the 11th Battle Fleet) on the Yangtze River hugging Nanking to its north to prevent any Chinese citizens or troops from fleeing northwest. According to Japanese scholar Yutaka Yoshida, the IJN attacked small boats and even people floating on house doors fleeing the city, "either strafing them with machinegun fire or taking pot shots at them with small arms. Rather than a battle this was more like a game of butchery."[277] The IJN did not take prisoners, but the IJA took tens of thousands immediately following the Chinese defeat, and thereafter, resorted to "a game of butchery" like their sailor comrades. Military correspondent Yukio Omata provided testimony to the POW executions:

> Those in the first row were beheaded, those in the second row were forced to dump the severed bodies into the river before they themselves were beheaded. The killing went on non-stop, from morning until night, but they were only able to kill 2,000 persons in this way. The next day, tired of killing in this fashion, they set up machineguns. Two of them raked a cross-fire at the lined-up prisoners. Rat-atat-tat. Triggers were pulled. The prisoners fled into the water, but no one was able to make it to the other shore.[278]

Executed Chinese Nationalist POW troops by IJA soldiers at Nanking, December 1937. These men were murdered in a clear violation of the Hague Convention of 1907, which Japan had signed. *Second Historical Archives, Nanking, China*

Chinese cadavers killed by IJA personnel piled on the shore of the Yangtze River, Nanking (Murase Moriyasu's photo). December 1937. *Second Historical Archives, Nanking, China*

Bodies of the victims of Nanking on a riverbank, December 1937 (Murase
Moriyasu's photo). *Second Historical Archives, Nanking, China*

Out of the 300,000 murdered during the campaign from Shanghai to
Nanking in the winter of 1937–38, 80,000 to 90,000 were Chinese POWs—
"it was a slaughter, a massacre."[279] Although the one treaty the Japanese had
signed and ratified, the Hague Convention of 1907, forbade the killing of
enemy soldiers, "who having laid down [their] arms, or having no longer means
of defense, have surrendered at discretion,"[280] the Japanese ignored this accord
and killed without remorse. The entire acts of Japan and its army at Nanking
also violated the Kellogg-Briand Pact from 1928 which Japan had signed which
forbade nations from committing crimes against peace and using war to resolve
international disputes.

The IJA commander at Nanking, General Iwane Matsui defied the
prototypical image of a bloodthirsty field commander. Standing at a modest
5'0" even, the rather short and tubercular reservist flag officer was a devout
Buddhist who harbored reservations about Japan's actions in China.[281] Born
on 27 July 1878, Matsui entered the military in 1896. He fought as a platoon
leader in the Russo-Japanese War and steadily climbed the ranks. During his
career, his fascination with China led him to become one of the army's foremost
experts on the country. In 1935, he retired from active duty, but then was

subsequently summoned back to service in August 1937 to participate in the Battle of Shanghai, where he assumed command of the Shanghai Expeditionary Force.[282] Before departing for China, he had a private audience with Hirohito at the Imperial Palace, during which the emperor charged him with the following mandate: "Break the Chinese government's will to resist by capturing Nanking."[283] Matsui promised his leader to do so. However, in fulfilling his promise, Matsui's forces endured significant losses. On the war path to Nanking, his troops suffered 110,000 casualties before they would even reach the walls surrounding the Chinese capital.[284]

Knowing his troops were tired, hungry, and "eager for revenge,"[285] Matsui did "issue orders before the capture of the city, enjoining propriety of conduct upon his troops, and later issued further orders to the same purport."[286] Yet, like with most moral codes like the laws they indeed had inside Japan like outlawing murder and rape, the Japanese as a collective group ignored all humane behavior while engaged in war outside their country, and as one could also say, outside the reach of their domestic law. Although he issued orders to the contrary, General Matsui's actions of doing "nothing effective"[287] to curtail the atrocities evidenced he "lacked any idea that the killing of POWs was a violation of international law and a grave crime against humanity"[288] that would elicit widespread condemnation and future war crime trials.

Despite having issued orders for his troops to exercise restraint, General Matsui witnessed his soldiers committing acts that he had secretly envisioned for years. In a top-secret memorandum for the Army in 1923, Matsui outlined some of this vision, writing: "We must substitute economic conquest for military invasion, financial influence for military control..."[289] He was aware of the potential consequences when a conquered nation is subjected to economic exploitation, often resulting in immense suffering and loss of life throughout history. Furthermore, considering Matsui's army was already living off the land they currently occupied, it was impractical for them to accommodate the nearly 100,000 prisoners they had just captured. The options available to them were either to confine the prisoners in concentration camps and allow them to starve to death, as Hitler would do with Soviet POWs in 1941, or to release them, knowing that they would potentially resume fighting against the Japanese forces in the future.[290] Both choices presented significant challenges and moral dilemmas.

Matsui made the fateful decision to execute the POWs, viewing it as a quick and convenient resolution to his logistical problems, enabling him to implement "military control." Although being fully aware that such actions were in violation of international law, Matsui showed a blatant disregard for these legal constraints. While the killing of defenseless POWs took place under Matsui's 10th Army, rapes were rampant throughout the occupied territories.[291] Women, desperate and defenseless, beseeched their captives for mercy, as a "starving man" would "for food and drink,"[292] but that mercy rarely came. The chilling recollection of IJA soldier Shirō Azuma, who was involved in these horrific acts, provides a grim and heartbreaking testimony:

> At first we used some kinky words like *Bikankan*. *Bi* means "[hip or pelvis, but in this case it really means Pussy]," *Kankan* means "look." *Bikankan* means, "Let's see a woman open up her legs." Chinese women didn't wear underpants. Instead, they wore trousers tied with a string. There was no belt. As we pulled the string, the buttocks were exposed. We "*Bikankan*." We looked. After a while we would say something like, "It's my day to take a bath," and we took turns raping them. It would be all right if we only raped them. I shouldn't say all right. But we always stabbed and killed them. *Because dead bodies don't talk.*[293]

Renowned Yale University historian Jonathan Spence accurately described the events in Nanking as a "period of terror and destruction" that ranks "among the worst in…modern warfare…[It was] a storm of violence and cruelty that has few parallels."[294] Today, in the Chinese consciousness, it is as significant for them as Auschwitz is for Jews and "still stands as the icon of Imperial Army bestiality."[295] The 200-mile stretch between Shanghai and Nanking during the autumn and winter of 1937 was a flotsam of rape and dead bodies, a literal "carnival of death."[296] The town of Soochow, situated along this path, witnessed horrifying executions and senseless killings, mirroring the devastation that befell countless other towns in the region. The streets were plagued by wild dogs that feasted upon the lifeless bodies, an eerie testament to the depths of the atrocities committed.[297] Tragically, even those desperate souls attempting to escape the marauding Japanese forces on foot found no respite. Japanese pilots mercilessly strafed groups of terror-stricken citizens along the crowded roads heading west, leaving them with no escape from the relentless violence that pursued them.[298]

Similar atrocities unfolded in cities surrounding Nanking, including Mufushan, Wuhu, Nit'ang, Wuxi, and Suzhou. Unlike in Nanking, these cities lacked the presence of International Safety Zones that could offer protection against the brutal actions of the IJA soldiers. In contrast, Nanking being the Chinese Nationalists' capital and housing diplomatic offices and embassies, benefited from the establishment of an International Safety Zone, providing a haven for tens of thousands of its citizens.[299] Meanwhile, as other combat operations raged across China, such as in Pingting, T'ai-yüan, K'ai-feng, Jilin

City, and Hangchow, the Japanese troops unleashed a wave of murder and rape in those areas as well, with the citizens there having no area or people to turn to for help.[300] The extent of these crimes becomes evident when considering just one "small" Japanese operation that recorded 20,000 rapes against Russian women alone in the northern regions, accompanied by thousands of fatalities.[301] This pattern of abhorrent behavior, not only confined to China, but also extending to Pacific Island nations, highlights that "these murders followed such a similar pattern over such a wide range of territory and covered such a long period of time, and so many were committed after protests had been registered by neutral nations that…only positive orders from above [like Tōjō, Hirohito, and Matsui] made them possible."[302]

A Japanese soldier beheads a Chinese citizen at Nanking, December 1937. Note that several of the IJA soldiers are taking pictures with their cameras. Taking photos of crimes was common for the Imperial Japanese Army. *Second Historical Archives, Nanking, China*

A Japanese officer at Nanking proudly displays the head he has just cut off of a Chinese citizen. Notice how he is smiling holding the severed head and his bloody sword. *Second Historical Archives, Nanking, China* and *The Alliance for Preserving the Truth of Sino-Japanese War*

Sent to conquer Nanking without adequate supplies, the Japanese troops were forced to forage for their own sustenance. However, in their actions, they needlessly destroyed thousands of homesteads, leaving a trail of devastation in their wake.[303] The hapless victims dubbed the IJA *Huang-chün*, an "army of locusts."[304] In a chilling depiction of the IJA's campaign tactics, a regimental commander unabashedly informed Hirohito's brother, Captain Prince Mikasa Takahito, that its policy was "to burn every enemy house along the way as we advance. You can tell at a glance where our forward units are."[305] During such campaigns, the Japanese army unashamedly claimed it conducted them according to its "extermination policy." This ruthless strategy entailed burning everything to the ground and cold-bloodedly slaughtering all civilians in its way.[306] Even in the face of such uncaring and immoral behavior, Takahito expressed his grievances to Hirohito, pleading for intervention to halt the atrocities. Regrettably, the emperor remained passive, failing to take *any action* to curb the acts being committed by his military forces.[307]

Japan employed this Nanking campaign in a deliberate manner to instill fear and submission among the civilian population. Horrifically, massacres were conducted openly, serving as a gruesome spectacle meant to entertain soldiers and encourage others to similar conduct, often accompanied by a disturbing air of merriment. Sub-Lieutenants Tsuyoshi Noda and Toshiaki Mukai shamelessly engaged in a macabre competition, publicly reported in newspapers such as the *Nichinichi Shinbun*, to tally the civilian heads they had cut off.[308] They were photographed, smiling, and holding their swords proudly. The Japanese everywhere in China acted "beyond the bounds of permitted aspirations."[309] Historian Werner Gruhl observed that the fact that such reports were disseminated in newspapers without repercussions "indicates a level of public and government acceptance of these acts."[310] *Manchester Guardian* journalist Harold John Timperley succinctly encapsulated the magnitude of these atrocities:

> Should anyone believe that the Japanese army is in this country to make life better…for the Chinese, then let him travel over the area between Shanghai and Nanking…and witness the unbelievable…destruction. This area, six months ago, was the most densely populated portion of the earth…and…prosperous section of China. Today the traveler will see only cities bombed and pillaged; towns and villages reduced to shambles; farms desolated…The livestock has been either killed or stolen, and every sort of destruction that a brutal army…can inflict has been done… Countless numbers have been killed; others have been maimed for life; yet others are huddled in refugee camps; or hiding in mountain caves, afraid to return to their desolate farms, their empty shops and ruined businesses. Those who would dare return are not permitted to do so by the war-mad Japanese army. It is shameful…that the Japanese who control communication lines, are proclaiming to the world that they are inviting Chinese back to their ancestral homes to live in peace and plenty.[311]

The audacity that Japan thought it could commit such atrocities without incurring the world's disdain revealed it had a disturbing arrogance and a belief that it played by a different set of rules than the rest of humanity. The martial culture practiced in China, where most of the Japanese troops of WWII were conditioned to be "warriors," transformed them into hardened individuals who were uncaring, unsympathetic, and indifferent. This lack of empathy coupled with their warrior conditioning created a perilous combination, making them formidable yet dangerous adversaries.

In addition to its strategic significance in expanding Japan's territory and resources, the capture of Nanking held immense political and psychological value for the IJA due to its status as Chiang Kai-Shek's capital. This conquest was not only a military victory, but also a win politically and psychologically, showing the world Japan waged a "war of annihilation."[312] The Japanese High

Command believed that if Nanking fell, then the "Chinese house of cards would collapse and the immediate goal—an autonomous region in North China dominated by Japan—would be achieved."[313] This strategy bears some resemblance to Hitler's later perspective on the battle for Stalingrad, although his ambitions were ultimately unsuccessful. It is crucial to note that such a victory did not secure peace or bring a conclusion to hostilities. Instead, it proved to be a pyrrhic victory in some respects, somewhat like when Napoleon sacked Moscow in 1812 without achieving a cessation of hostilities. Historian Edwin P. Hoyt points out that Japan's capture of Nanking "had solved no problems; the Chinese government simply moved farther west, and the Japanese had a much larger area to police and control."[314]

Emperor Hirohito, in recognition of the destruction and atrocities committed in Nanking, dishonorably bestowed decorations and awards upon his generals.[315] On 14 December, he conferred an Imperial message extending congratulations to his chiefs of staff on Nanking's conquest.[316] In February 1938, the emperor issued an official rescript commending General Matsui praising him for his "great military accomplishments" at Nanking.[317] Lieutenant General Asaka eventually received the Order of the Golden Eagle in April 1940 in part for his duties during the Rape of Nanking.[318] Historian Herbert P. Bix observes that when Hirohito awarded men responsible for one of the most horrendous WWII atrocities, he indirectly condoned "the criminality of his troops."[319] Such actions cast a dark shadow on the emperor's legacy and his role in enabling the horrific crimes committed during the Rape of Nanking.

It is worth noting that within all ranks, Zen Buddhist monks and priests encouraged and fought with IJA troops. As the Japanese forces advanced and conquered territories, these monks exported their version of Buddhism while seeking to undermine and eradicate Chinese Buddhism wherever possible. For instance, IJA Buddhist monks invaded the Nanking temple estates and preached their theological beliefs, extolling Japan's holy war and denouncing Chinese Buddhism as inferior and heretical. Consequently, Nanking not only underwent the brutal slaughter of its citizens, but also the displacement and erasure of its cultural heritage.[320]

All these wicked acts just described were not only carried out under the authority of Japanese commanders but were actively encouraged by them. Among those responsible were, as already mentioned, General Matsui (Commander 10th Army), Lieutenant General Hisao Tani (6th Division Commander), Lieutenant General Kesago Nakajima (16th Division Commander) and Lieutenant General Prince Yasuhiko Asaka (Hirohito's 50-year-old granduncle and ultranationalist on the Supreme War Council).[321] Once the battle commenced, Lieutenant

General Nakajima went so far as to lend his own sword to aid a subordinate in fulfilling these criminal orders. He recounted in his diary: "Takayama Kenshi visited me at noon today [13 December]. There happened to be seven captives, so I asked him to try to behead them with *my sword*. I did not expect him to do such a good job—he cut off two heads."[322] Nakajima further confided in his diary that the IJA's policy was to "Accept no prisoners!" He noted his entire staff got on board without protest and laid out a plan of how to "dispose of a batch of 7,000 or 8,000 prisoners, until 'someone suggested this plan: Divide them up into groups of 100 to 200, and then lure them to some suitable spot for finishing off.'"[323] Nakajima and his men committed murder with enthusiasm and efficiency, often laughing as they executed their murderous tasks. Alongside these atrocities, the IJA soldiers continued to rape women everywhere. It became their obsession.

General Iwane Matsui's victory march through Nanking on 17 December 1937. Although Matsui knew his men were raping women and killing thousands of POWs and citizens, he did nothing to stop their barbarity. *Nanking Massacre Memorial, Nanking, China*

At the Nanking War Trials in 1947, the military judges brought skulls of victims from Nanking to bear witness to the proceedings against Lieutenant General Hisao Tani (6th Division commander at Nanking). *Nanking Massacre Memorial, Nanking, China*

General Iwane Matsui stands trial at the Tokyo War Trials in 1948. He was found guilty and executed by hanging. His soul has been enshrined at the Yasukuni Shintō Shrine, Tokyo, Japan, by the Japanese for future generations to honor. *Nanking Massacre Memorial, Nanking, China*

"Chinese witnesses saw Japanese rape girls under ten years of age...and then slash them in half by sword. In some cases, the Japanese sliced open the vaginas of preteen girls...to ravish them more effectively."[324] Heartbreakingly, numerous girls lost their lives as a result of the internal bleeding caused by the cruelty they endured.[325] Australian journalist Harold John Timperley fittingly described the Japanese soldiers involved in these acts as being "lust-mad."[326] Disturbingly, there were instances where soldiers would enter villages, round up the men, escort them outside town and place them under armed guard. Then, IJA soldiers would take turns returning to the village to subject the women to unspeakable acts of gang rape. At one village, Chinese men sat on the roadside "trembling" as they heard the screams from their mothers, wives, daughters and sisters but unable to protect them.[327] Nearby in Nanking, two husbands who courageously ran back to save their wives were tragically shot dead.[328] Countless women were taken to IJA camps, never to be heard of again, their fate forever shrouded in sorrow and uncertainty.[329] When the IJA was in control of a city, women's screams echoed throughout the streets not only during the nights, but also during the days.[330] Lower-level command, obviously having been given permission from higher command, brazenly instructed their troops they "could kill and rape as many of 'the Chinese enemy' as we pleased."[331] One sergeant went so far as to encourage a subordinate to kill civilians, telling him that "Killing a Chinese is just like killing a dog! You'll feel nothing! Try it and you'll see!"[332] The soldier acted upon this encouragement and shot an elderly woman, causing her brains to splatter against a nearby wall. To the soldier's delight, his comrades cheered and applauded his deed, goading him to commit similar acts on others. Emboldened, he killed "Chinese of all ages, even children."[333] And after he raped girls, he would kill them too. He performed his horrific deeds with a disturbing enthusiasm.[334]

The intricate coordination and network that evolved within such platoons, companies, battalions, and regiments during this period lay bare a diabolical structure that aimed at ripping apart everything that holds a decent society together. Instead of winning Chinese hearts and minds in creating their Greater East Asia Co-Prosperity Sphere, the Japanese instead spawned guerilla networks costing more casualties for themselves. This in turn fostered a generational hatred that would take decades or longer to repair. The consequences were far-reaching, leading to the breakdown of infrastructure, the devastation of farms that could have helped them by eating the livestock, and a military environment ill-equipped for training and maintenance of weapons required for future battles.[335] "These activities are not the normal manifestations of a nation of the 20th century imbued with altruistic and humanitarian ideals of helpfulness toward a weaker neighboring people. They are the actions of a nation still steeped in the traditions and barbaric conceptions of a nationalistic aggrandizement."[336]

Japanese "went beyond rape," delving into the most monstrous depths of inhumanness. They cruelly sliced off women's breasts and cut open pregnant women's bellies and decapitated the infants in front of their bleeding mothers. And they took a perverse pleasure in taking the time and effort to bury people alive. To give concrete examples of how their brutal deeds played out, the following examples give vivid mental scenes for the reader. In the midst of raping a woman, this soldier's act was interrupted by the cries of her five-month-old baby nearby. The man stopped, went to the child, callously smothered it, and then returned to the woman and resumed raping her. In another heart-wrenching incident, after killing a nursing mother, soldiers failed to kill her small baby boy. He mustered the strength to crawl to his nude mother's breast to suck what milk remained inside and was later found "glued to his mother's corpse by frozen cubes of milk, tears and snot." The depravity continued unabated, with soldiers castrating prisoners before using them for bayonet practice or subjecting them to agonizing deaths by dousing them with gasoline and setting them ablaze. The savagery did not spare small children, as they too fell victim to the soldiers' violence. Soldiers "impaled babies on bayonets and threw some into pots of boiling water." Other soldiers took a baby from its mother, placed it on the ground, and hammered a nail through its forehead. The soldiers reveled in their sadistic acts, hanging people by their tongues on iron hooks or burying them to their midsections and releasing ravenous dogs upon them. Even the most vulnerable were not spared, as one 80-year-old woman died when a soldier skewered "her vulva with his bayonet." Other elderly women were "lucky" and just got raped. Even some Nazis in the International Safety Zone like John Rabe *pleaded with Hitler* to help stop these atrocities, calling the IJA "bestial machinery."[337] He also wrote the Japanese Embassy, along with others, for help detailing IJA crimes. Yet, their appeals fell on deaf ears, and the Embassy did nothing.[338] The city streets became haunting galleries of death with dead women laying in the streets, nude, with their legs spread and their orifices pierced with rods and tree branches. One witness reported to Rabe, "You can't breathe for sheer revulsion when you keep finding bodies of women with bamboo poles thrust through their vaginas. Even old women over 70 are constantly being raped."[339]

Corpses of raped, killed, and desecrated women by Japanese soldiers in the streets of Nanking in December 1937. Notice that the Japanese IJA personnel took the time after they killed these women to shove sticks into their vaginas. *Universal History Archive/Universal Images Group and Getty Images*

Other times, Japanese men stuck sticks of dynamite into women's vaginas and blew them to pieces. Japanese "hunted" citizens "like rabbits."[340] Soldier Hakudo Nagatomi wrote:

> I beheaded people, starved them to death, burned them, and buried them alive, over two hundred in all. It is terrible that I could turn into an animal and do these things. There are really no words to explain what I was doing. I was truly a devil.[341]

Another soldier, Shintarō Uno, described cutting off heads as a sexual experience and felt "refreshed" after the killings, having first dragged the prisoner from the stockade, forced him to dig his grave, and then pushed him into a kneeling position by the hole to be his final resting place. Uno gripped his sword and swung down, hard, to sling the head from the body. By his own admission, he beheaded at least 40 innocent Chinese.[342]

German military advisor Major Robert Borchardt, who was attached to the armor units of the Chinese forces at Nanking and assisted them in escaping capture, provided this revealing commentary about Hirohito's legions:

> The Japanese are undoubtedly better equipped and organized compared to the Chinese, and without us Germans, Chiang Kai-Shek could never have put effective units in the field against Japan. However, despite this advantage, I consider the Japanese military to be second rate. They're second rate for not only their inability to think critically during battle and adapt to new situations, but also, they're second rate for their lack of morals. After what I've seen the Japanese do to helpless Chinese civilians and the wanton rape and executions of non-combatants, they're a disgrace to humanity. Knowing that I helped…Chinese units fight effectively against them and kill many of them gives me much satisfaction. Although we're allied with them, we should try to distance ourselves from the Japanese. The people of China need protection from Japan because Japan will destroy this nation if left to its own devices.[343]

Borchardt's superior and head of the Nazi military attaché in China, General Alexander von Falkenhausen, also witnessed the Japanese barbarity and was sickened by it. He described the IJA as a "brutal military mob" and that "the Japanese soldiers raged like savages." Drawing from accounts of Borchardt and others, as well as his own experience, Falkenhausen reported the situation to Hitler's foreign minister, Joachim von Ribbentrop, urging them to do something about the atrocities.[344] Not surprisingly, the Nazi leadership did nothing.

The scale of the killings and rapes in Nanking would have been more widespread if it had not been for the efforts of the expatriate community, led by of all people a Nazi Party member named John Rabe, who chaired the "International Committee for the Nanking Safety Zone." Alongside individuals such as Americans Professor Miner Bates, Rev. Charles Riggs, Rev. John Magee, and Professor Minnie Vautrin, they, along with others, helped Rabe set up a precinct to protect civilians. Through their diplomatic skills and international pressure, they managed to keep the Japanese forces at bay, resulting in the saving of approximately 200,000 lives. However, beyond the safety zone, most Chinese suffered horribly.[345] In one unsettling example alone, roughly 60 miles away from Nanking, Japanese forces rounded up some 57,000 civilian refugees, only to rape, starve, and execute many of them.[346] These actions feature the brutal reality experienced by many innocent individuals in dozens of other locations outside the protective confines of the Nanking Safety Zone during these Japanese operations.

Babies slaughtered by Japanese soldiers at Nanking, December 1937. Japanese soldiers seemed to have no moral compass when it came to killing innocent children. *Second Historical Archives, Nanking, China* and *The Alliance for Preserving the Truth of Sino-Japanese War*

In addition to the immense toll on human life at Nanking, the Japanese invaders laid waste to the natural and urban resources in the area as well. The unyielding rampage resulted in the demolition of hundreds of buildings, with approximately 80% of commercial and industrial structures being reduced to ruins. Furthermore, they coldly slaughtered and plundered thousands of farm animals, while also wreaking havoc on farming equipment and implements, either through destruction or confiscation. Grain stores were set on fire, and vast stretches of crop land were left devastated. If the Japanese could not steal it, they smashed it. The consequences of this destruction were dire for the citizens of Nanking. In the following year, many survivors would endure untold suffering due to the scarcity of food and shelter.[347] Hundreds of thousands of Nanking refugees, and as many as 20 million people throughout China affected by the Japanese military campaigns of 1937–1938, were forced to abandon their homes in search of safer regions to live. Untold thousands died while desperately seeking survival away from the marauding Japanese forces.[348] The scale of the displacement and the human toll inflicted during this period remain immeasurable and largely unresearched.

On 17 December, General Matsui and his staff, accompanied by Vice Admiral Kiyoshi Hasegawa, the highest-ranking naval officer in the region, staged a triumphal procession through the streets of Nanking. Mounted on horseback, Matsui led his officers and a contingent of chosen troops, parading before an assembled mass of 20,000 soldiers, gathered along Nanking's main thoroughfare. The spectacle served as a symbol, boldly proclaiming the establishment of a new order over the former capital of Chiang Kai-Shek.[349] On this day, he declared,

> Now the flag of the Rising Sun is floating over Nanking, and the Imperial Way is shining forth in the area south of the Yangtze. The dawn of the renaissance is about to take place. On this occasion, it is my earnest hope that the four hundred million people of China will reconsider.[350]

Interestingly, General Matsui demonstrated an ability to organize a grand victory parade on short notice, yet he seemed unable to exert control over his men to halt their rampant acts of rape and murder. In his speech, he conveyed his desire for the Chinese people to submit to Japanese rule, suggesting they become slaves to their conquerors. Despite years of resistance against Japanese dominance, Matsui, in a haughty manner and in the flush of victory, made it clear that the fate of Nanking would befall other Chinese cities unless they acquiesced to Japanese authority. There was no other way to interpret his speech. Loosely translated, his speech said, "Either submit to our rule or we will rape, murder and conquer your other cities." Historian Robert J. C. Butow commented on Matsui's address, noting "this was a favorite Japanese theme of those years. Regardless of the injustice done them, the Chinese were supposed to 'reconsider' once they had been beaten nearly to death."[351] Fortunately, Chiang Kai-Shek's China rejected Matsui's advice, a decision that would have far-reaching implications for subsequent conflicts. In later battles between the Soviet Union and Japan in 1938 (Lake Khasan) and 1939 (Nomonhan), [352] and Russia's fight against Germany from 1941–1945, as well as the United States' campaign across the Pacific from 1942–1945 fighting Japanese island strongholds, China's resistance tied down millions of Japanese troops. This, in turn, helped Stalin and Roosevelt to fight Hirohito's and Hitler's forces more effectively. Had China surrendered, Japan could have used more forces on challenging Russian and American military personnel, potentially altering the course of the global conflict that engulfed much of the world by 1941. Fortunately for the Allies, millions of Nationalist soldiers continued fighting after Nanking in protracted warfare to tie down millions of Japanese troops. Luckily for the Allies in particular and the Chinese in general, the Rape of Nanking did not force the collapse of the Nationalist government, although it indeed suffered heavy losses and had to surrender large tracts of its land to the enemy.

Undoubtedly, the Rape of Nanking has garnered significant attention through numerous books and remains one of the most notorious atrocities of the Asian War in particular and the Second World War in general. However, it is still a topic that requires further examination and research. Regrettably, much of the existing research has struggled to gain widespread visibility within Japan, the very place where it is of utmost importance to be thoroughly studied and understood.

These Japanese troops during the Rape of Nanking who perpetrated the violent crimes against humanity were incredibly resourceful and energetic. Having endured grueling combat operations in Shanghai, one of the most brutal WWII urban warfare battles, they then marched almost 200 miles to Nanking without proper supplies, engaging in protracted attacks along the way. In addition to them having to find their food, keeping weapons clean, maintaining equipment and vehicles, conducting patrols and assaults, establishing bivouacs, and ensuring field sanitation, they also found time to rape and slaughter the local populations all the way to the capital. And they continued perpetrating these atrocities while conducting siege operations to that city. Once they conquered Nanking, their criminal, inhumane activities increased tenfold when they no longer had to fight.

Matsui's assertions during the Tokyo War Crimes Tribunal that he did not know about the Nanking crimes and that he had issued orders for his men not to commit these felonies was a weak defense based on outlandish lies. Before executing him, the Tribunal concluded that Matsui knew his officers and he "had the power, as he had the duty, to control his troops and to protect the unfortunate citizens of Nanking. He must be held criminally responsible for his failure to discharge this duty."[353] Throughout the Asian and Pacific Wars, when orders or tacit approval were given to rape and murder, Japanese soldiers did so with zest, but when ordered to not rape and murder, they still did so with zest.

For Germany, most often there existed a clear distinction between the units responsible for carrying out Holocaust crimes and those engaged in combat operations. For instance, the *SS-Einsatzgruppen* killing squads had a different mission and were smaller in scale compared to the regular army units involved in battle. While some military outfits did indeed assist in the systematic killing process of the Jews, most *Wehrmacht* units focused on prosecuting the war.

In juxtaposition, the primary focus of the *SS* was on the targeted killing of innocent civilians. In contrast to the German military and extermination units, Japan combined both combat and genocidal activities within its Imperial forces. Japanese soldiers and sailors played dual roles as both agents of civilian killings and active combatants. When examining the evolution of the *SS-Einsatzgruppen*, it becomes evident that extensive conditioning was necessary to prepare its members for the task of mass murder. *SS* Lieutenant General (*Obergruppenführer*) Karl Wolff said,

> The *SS* field commanders, who had their orders, needed men to carry out the killings. They couldn't just go to their men and say, 'here we have some Jews who must be killed,' and expect the men to just follow those orders to kill civilians. They were often told 'we have some partisans who killed Germans' and that would often ease the minds of the men who would then shoot these people. The result of these operations upon the soldiers forced Himmler to tell Heydrich to take charge and find another way.[354]

However, the average Japanese soldier did not require the same kind of conditioning to conduct mass murder as the *SS* troops serving Hitler did, as Wolff's testimony helps to illustrate. The cultural evolution of Japan at that time seemed to have already produced individuals who were capable of committing *SS-Einsatzgruppen*-like activities without having the need for fabricated justifications for doing so or having to be dissuaded from thinking such acts were immoral. This was seen with how many German commanders viewed the *SS* with disdain, an organization they felt was foreign and illegal, something you *never* see from Japanese commanders about their own outfits.

For example, the atrocities against Jews during the Polish campaign in 1939 were so shocking that even members of the German armed forces protested. *Wehrmacht* General Johannes Blaskowitz voiced his concerns to Hitler that "this state of affairs undermines order and discipline…It is necessary to forbid summary executions forthwith. The German army is not here to give its support to a band of assassins."[355] He further warned that the *SS* atrocities would have a devastating impact on the German people because "unlimited brutalization and moral depravity [would spread]…like an epidemic through the most valuable German human material. If the high officials of the SS continue to call for violence and brutality, brutal men will soon reign supreme." Hitler ignored Blaskowitz's complaints. Even figures like the notorious "Nazi general," Walter von Reichenau, did not approve of the actions carried out by the *SS*. However, Hitler remained indifferent to these misgivings, declaring one cannot "wage war with Salvation Army methods."[356] Although the Holocaust continued to march on, leaders like Blaskowitz and Reichenau noted that this was improper behavior and should cease. In Japan, one *never has documented* a general or admiral writing to his superiors, or Hirohito himself, to stop the mass murder and rape inflicted upon enemy societies.

The fact that *no Japanese commander* in the Shanghai Expeditionary Force or Central China Expeditionary Force recognized how damaging Japanese soldiers' behavior was to creating a lasting peace or how counterproductive it was to have one's troops spend so much time slaughtering civilians and raping women (and young boys) instead of fighting a war baffles the mind.[357] It indicates that Japan had created a culture that embraced satanic impulses that most civilized societies would universally reject in their legal and social codes. This demonstrates that Japan believed what it was doing overseas was acceptable.

The Japanese would never embrace the wise words of the Jewish sage Hillel the Elder, who said, "What is hateful to you, do not do to others."[358] Japan would not have tolerated foreign powers invading its nation to rape and slaughter its citizens, nor would it have tolerated that within its own society. This is proven by Hirohito's wise decision to surrender to the Americans at the war's end, rather than to the Russians. Had he allowed the Soviets to occupy his country, Hirohito knew they would rape and slaughter his people, just like they were doing to his citizens in Manchuria and how they were also treating the Germans in the areas they currently occupied. This extreme double standard showcased Hirohito's desire for his people to be spared from the very atrocities his soldiers had perpetrated during the Rape of Asia. This same double standard was apparent when Hirohito's government cited the Hague Convention with the Allies to secure humane treatment for their POWs in 1945, despite their refusal to follow the Hague mandates throughout the war themselves.[359] The Japanese were the very definition of hypocrites.

Returning to the leaders during the Rape of Nanking, one must repeat yet again that rarely does one find anyone, especially lower-level officers or NCOs, questioning the mistreatment meted out to the Chinese civilians and POWs. *This study has not uncovered a single line- or field-grade officer protesting these acts.* It appears that the soldiers, without exception, embraced the open display of brute force against unarmed civilians and prisoners. Unfortunately, the Rape of Nanking's atrocities offer numerous examples of what Japanese soldiers and leaders engaged in during their campaigns. It was not a one-off situation. It was indeed their *modus operandi.*

CHAPTER 6

THE RAPE OF SINGAPORE AND MALAYA

"The Western mind cannot grasp the realities of this awful crime [of Japanese atrocities]. One must grope into the shadows of history to find a parallel [like when] Genghis Khan [and his]... Mongol Horde [blazed] a trail of utter destruction [across Asia]."

—**U.S. General Headquarters**, SW Pacific Area, Military Intelligence Sec., General Staff[360]

ON 8 DECEMBER 1941, JAPAN launched its invasion of Malaya, with the ultimate objective of capturing Singapore. Among the key masterminds of this invasion was Lieutenant Colonel Masanobu Tsuji, head of operations and planning for the 25th Army and called the "God of strategy" due to his organizational brilliance. For at least six months before the attack, Tsuji meticulously studied maps and military units in order to seize this landmass which he believed was the gateway to India, Australia, and Indonesia. The 25th Army and Tsuji were both under the command of Lieutenant General Tomoyuki Yamashita, a tall and homely man who later got the nickname from his victims of "Old Potato Face" due to his large, spherical skull.[361] Before the battle, Yamashita "immediately enjoined his soldiers: 'no looting, no rape, no arson.'" [362] Fully aware of the behavior exhibited by his troops in China, he sought to avoid such misconduct in the presence of Western powers. However, and not surprisingly, he would soon be sorely disappointed with the widespread disobedience to this order, as his troopers engaged in acts of murder, rape, and arson wherever they went. The reports of Japanese savagery, many based on factual accounts from China and Hong Kong, had instilled fear in some Allied servicemen who, upon encountering the assaulting Japanese forces near Kota Bharu on 8 December, chose a hasty retreat towards Singapore.[363] Yamashita's apprehensions regarding his soldiers' conduct during the invasion of this region were justified as the following events will prove in droves.

Lieutenant Colonel Masanobu Tsuji perpetrated crimes during the Rape of Malaya and the Rape of Singapore. He was also one of the major masterminds of the Bataan Death March as well. *Second Historical Archives, Nanking, China*

Lieutenant General Tomoyuki Yamashita was in overall command during the Rape of Malaya, the Rape of Singapore, the Rape of Manchuria, the Rape of the Philippines and the Rape of Manila. He was found guilty of war crimes after the war and executed for crimes against humanity and peace. *Second Historical Archives, Nanking, China*

As the Japanese forces advanced along the Malayan peninsula, they unleashed a wave of brutality, targeting both civilians and Allied POWs. In Penang, on 17 December, Chinese citizens were mercilessly killed, and numerous women were subjected to rape. Surprisingly, Yamashita did have a few Japanese soldiers "tried and executed."[364] However, these isolated instances of justice failed to curtail the widespread atrocities unfolding throughout Malaya. Even when Lieutenant General Yamashita was made aware of Tsuji's involvement in numerous crimes, he chose not to take any action against his operations officer. This demonstrated a clear lack of resolve on Yamashita's part to hold offenders accountable, thereby neglecting his duty to uphold both legal and moral standards. Regrettably, history would reveal that Yamashita's limited use of his legal and moral compass in punishing offenders, especially those high up in his chain of command, fell far short of what was necessary.[365]

While Yamashita deliberated on taking action against Tsuji, he tragically allowed him and others to continue their spree of atrocities. On 7 January 1942, following the Allied defeat at Slim River, the Japanese executed dozens of British-Indian prisoners.[366] The news of Japan's appalling treatment of prisoners had spread, prompting a heart-wrenching scene at Bakri on 19 January. A group of wounded Australians, unable to retreat due to their injuries, made a solemn request to their healthier comrades that they end their suffering before the Japanese reached them. Their wishes were honored, and they were compassionately dispatched "with pistol shots to the heart."[367] Then, on 22 January 1942, in the vicinity of Parit Sulong, the true extent of the IJA's brutality was once again revealed. Approximately 150 wounded Australian and Indian troops were subjected to a massacre. The Japanese soldiers callously shot many at close range, beheaded others in an execution-style manner with their swords, and even resorted to dousing some victims in gasoline and setting them afire.[368]

Atrocities were happening out at sea too. On 27 January, a distressing incident unfolded as Japanese destroyers and a minesweeper targeted and sank the British destroyer HMS *Thanet*. Among the survivors of this attack were 31 British sailors, who found themselves taken aboard the destroyer *Shirayuki* skippered by Lieutenant Commander Rokurou Sugawara. Sadly, the fate that awaited these prisoners of war was grim. It is believed that they most likely were beheaded and/or bayoneted, or a combination of both, before being callously thrown into the depths of the sea. Tragically, their voices were forever silenced, as they "were never heard from again."[369]

On January 26–27, a sickening incident occurred when the Japanese forces captured an Australian ambulance convoy around northwestern Johore. In a display of utter cruelty, IJA soldiers extracted the defenseless wounded and medical personnel from the vehicles, soaked them with petrol, and set them on fire. Those who refused to sit still *as they were burning alive*, making a desperate bid to escape the agonizing flames, were shot and bayoneted. Nearby, yet another ambulance convoy met a similar fate at Kotonga. Although they, like their comrades near Johore, had Red Cross symbols prominently displayed on their uniforms and vehicles and were clearly non-combatants, they were tied together and executed with gunshots to their heads.[370]

On 31 January, the Japanese landed and swiftly captured the Malayan island, Amboina. Over 220 Australian troops were taken captive, their lives hanging by a thread. In the coming weeks, however, their fate took a harrowing turn. Under Rear Admiral Koichiro Hatakeyama's orders, guards of these men executed the Allied POWs. The command cascaded down the chain of command, reaching Sub-Lieutenant Kakagawa, who meticulously organized his men for the murderous task at hand. Over the course of several days, he had his men bayonet and behead all prisoners.[371]

In the aftermath of the invasion of Singapore, some Japanese took three Chinese girls into plain view of battle, lashed them to poles, and then bayoneted them to death, their lives snuffed out in a wave of brutality. Their crime was the suspicion that they had been signaling Japanese hideouts to the British.[372] Simultaneously, on this very same day, another group of Japanese troops infiltrated Alexandra Hospital and slayed over 300 doctors, nurses, and patients, including one unfortunate soul being actively operated on, along with his surgeon and anesthesiologist.[373] The sacred grounds of healing were stained with the blood of innocent lives. As night fell on 13 February, the desperate exodus of frightened citizens seeking refuge reached a crescendo. Hundreds of small craft, crammed with thousands of fleeing citizens from all walks of life, embarked on a perilous journey to escape the horrors of Singapore, with the hope of reaching Australia. However, soon thereafter, Japanese planes and naval vessels had a heyday attacking these defenseless crafts, "leaving a four-hundred-square-mile area speckled with debris, bodies, oil, and desperate survivors of all races, ages, and backgrounds." Amidst the chaos, one Japanese ship took aboard 21 Australian nurse survivors who had miraculously survived the ordeal. Tragically, their hopes for survival were shattered as they were machinegunned and thrown into the ocean. Remarkably, Vivian Bullwinkel emerged as the sole survivor of this atrocity, and after the war, she would testify at a war trial to help shed light on these crimes that befell her comrades.[374]

On the fateful day of 15 February 1942, a little over two months after the relentless onslaught began, the British forces found themselves in a dire predicament. Despite outnumbering the opposing Japanese by a significant margin, with 80,000 troops compared to the enemy's 30,000, they were cut off from vital supplies. Succumbing to the overwhelming circumstances, the British made the difficult decision to surrender. At the helm of this ill-fated campaign was Lieutenant General Arthur Percival, whose leadership had been marred by a series of poor decisions and operational missteps. The loss of the island under his command became a stain on his legacy, as he faced the ignominy of defeat. Prime Minister Winston Churchill called it the "worst disaster" in British military history.[375]

After Japan defeated Britain and its Commonwealth troops, mainly from India and Australia, Lieutenant Colonel Tsuji unleashed his fury on POWs and the population. Lieutenant General Yamashita, who had earned the moniker "The Tiger of Malaya," ordered a "systematic combing of Singapore for hostile Chinese and then enacted *Ganja Shogun* ('severe [or harsh] disposal')."[376] His troops would not disappoint him, and they never questioned the contradiction between this directive and his earlier call for moral conduct. In one of many rounds of butchery, the Japanese murdered 6,000 Chinese, often tying their hands behind their backs before throwing them off ships into the ocean while several miles away from shore. The ensuing days witnessed the haunting sight of lifeless, bloated bodies washing ashore on nearby beaches. The Japanese forces also engaged in acts of grotesque symbolism, such as isolated instances of crucifixion, a grim mockery of Christianity.[377] One such instance occurred at Sandakan, Borneo, where an Allied prisoner from Singapore underwent an unimaginable ordeal. After being led to a large cross, a Japanese officer had his men affixed the Australian POW on the cross, hammering nails through his hands and feet. The prisoner screamed and tried to yank one of his hands away. Amidst his agonized screams, a rag was shoved into his mouth by an irritated Japanese officer, because, *for some reason, he would not remain quiet!* While this ill-fated prisoner was writhing in pain, bleeding from his hands and feet, the officer took a long nail, his hammer, and with a mighty blow, drove the nail through the man's forehead, securing it firmly to the cross. As if that were not enough, the officer disemboweled the unfortunate prisoner and placed fragments of his organs over the beams of the cross, nailing them in place. The cross, with the tormented prisoner attached, was then transported to Sandakan POW camp, where fellow inmates were forced to bear witness to this gruesome spectacle. After he rotted on the cross for days, the Japanese put it to flame, reducing the cross and corpse to ashes.[378]

Although precise statistics are difficult to obtain, it is estimated that during the Sook Ching massacres in February and March 1942, approximately 40,000 to 50,000 individuals, primarily Chinese (with 600,000 residing in Singapore and two million in Malaya at that time), were executed. These criminal acts left a horrifying trail, with streets adorned by rows of severed heads impaled on the end of wooden poles. These massacres represented only a portion of the atrocities inflicted by the Japanese during their rule of Singapore and the surrounding region. Over the course of Japan's occupation, at least 100,000 would be killed by the Japanese, and tens of thousands of women fell victim to rape and sexual abuse.[379] The secret police of the Japanese forces, the *Kempei Tai*, operated extensively throughout the region, relentlessly pursuing Chinese individuals suspected of harboring Communist sentiments or holding anti-Japanese views. In one particularly heinous incident in Penang, two women faced brutal repercussions at the hands of the *Kempei Tai* when they refused to provide, or could not provide, the information sought. Stripped naked, the Japanese tied them to motorcycles and dragged them around the prison yard, subjecting them to unimaginable humiliation, physical torment, and lasting scarring since large sections of skin were removed from their bodies during this ordeal.[380]

The initial wave of mass murder in Singapore and its surrounding regions was meticulously planned by Tsuji, leaving little room for Yamashita to plead ignorance of his subordinate's orders given its extensive scale. Tsuji, in defense of his actions, asserted that he was merely following orders. For example, just three days after Singapore's fall on 18 February 1942, Yamashita had issued an order that, in part, ordered his men to "select and remove hostile Chinese,"[381] with *remove* indicating the extermination of those Chinese with "anti-Japanese sentiments."[382] `Months before the invasion, Tsuji had already compiled a pamphlet that he had distributed amongst his subordinates, containing a comprehensive list of anti-Japanese Chinese residing in Malaya and in Singapore. Exploiting the British defeat in his sector of operations, Tsuji orchestrated a massive Gestapo-like operation, mobilizing his legions to round up thousands of Chinese thought to be hostile to Japan, particularly targeting Communists, and slaughtered them all.[383] Tsuji had further articulated his contemptuous views in his lengthy report on the strategy to conquer Malaya and Singapore, asserting that "Overseas Chinese" stood apart from the "Asian Brotherhood" and were therefore deemed fair game for extermination.[384]

Similar to the early days of the Nazi Holocaust in Poland, Tsuji adopted a strategy reminiscent of Hitler's treatment of the Jews in Poland in 1939, targeting the educated and the intelligentsia. This included rounding up civil servants, teachers, and lawyers, trucking them to secluded beaches and then mowing them down with machinegun fire.[385] As part of their oppressive measures, the Japanese authorities in Malaya took control of the educational system, shutting down schools and repurposing many of them as military barracks. All-girls schools were particularly affected, being transformed into establishments such as restaurants and "whorehouses" catering to servicemen. The dire economic circumstances imposed upon the population "forced many female students and widows to work" in the newly made Japanese brothels, further exacerbating the plight of the affected individuals.[386]

After gloating about his triumph over the British and supporting his troops' actions against the local population, Lieutenant General Yamashita arrogantly announced: "The Japanese were descended from gods, while Darwin had demonstrated that European ancestors were monkeys. In this war between gods and monkeys, the gods must prevail."[387] Yamashita's hubris fueled the actions of his subordinate, Tsuji, and others in conducting their torture and executions of the "monkeys." Both Lieutenant General Takuma Nishimura (the Imperial Guard Division's commander) and Major General Saburō Kawamura (9th Infantry Brigade's commander), were both implicated in massacres. Nishimura, whose men, with assistance from Tsuji, oversaw the Parit Sulong and Sook Ching massacres, was sentenced to life in prison after his initial trial by the Allies in 1947. Kawamura, whose troops collaborated with the *Kempei Tai*, helped slaughter thousands of Chinese in and around Singapore, and subsequently was executed after standing trial under British jurisdiction that same year.[388] In a separate trial conducted by the Australian War Crimes Tribunal a few years later, Nishimura was found guilty of crimes against humanity and hanged in 1951.[389] The revelations about Japan's conduct during the war in Singapore led Prime Minister Churchill to say, "They have proved themselves formidable, deadly and—I am sorry to say—*barbarous antagonists* [author's italics]."[390]

After successfully orchestrating the Malaya and Singapore crimes against humanity, Tsuji was recalled to Tokyo and hailed as a hero by the populace. He was celebrated as one of the key commanders responsible for the victory at Singapore over the "White man" and "British devils." In April, he was transferred to the Philippines to assist Lieutenant General Masaharu Homma with his disappointingly slow progress against the resilient American forces at Bataan. Here, the "monkeys" proved to be a formidable challenge for the supposed Japanese "gods," and thus, they needed Tsuji's help.[391] In this arena, Tsuji continued his criminal behavior and masterminded one of the cruelest treatments of POWs during the Pacific War after the Philippines fell to Japan, the Bataan Death March.

Before we turn to the Bataan Death March, it is crucial to examine the atrocities committed during the Rape of Singapore and Malaya. Many have argued that Japanese soldiers behaved poorly when they were frustrated by their inability to conquer China, like with the Rape of Nanking in 1937. Yes, the Japanese conquered the Nationalist capital, but it did not move them closer to winning the war. Some theorists propose that the pent-up rage and frustration in their failure to secure victory over all of China at Nanking unleashed uncontrollable outbursts of violence from the Japanese conquerors. Conversely, others argue that in the face of defeat and with nothing else to lose, Japanese soldiers unleashed their rage and dark desires upon helpless populations, seen so dramatically with the Rape of Manila in 1945 soon to be covered in a later chapter. However, even when the Japanese had massive success and clear-cut victories, such as in the Malaya peninsula campaign and the conquest of Singapore, their behavior mirrored the atrocities witnessed in Nanking and Manila, despite emerging as the victors. This suggests that the Japanese never required any specific justification to engage in acts of barbarity; they simply needed a foreign society upon which to enact their evil deeds. In a rare display of honesty for an IJA officer, Lieutenant Colonel Iwaichi Fujiwara wrote the following reflection after the war:

> There was no room for the Japanese Army to counterargue the charge of the inhumane murders in which countless Chinese were executed indiscriminately on the beaches, in rubber plantations and in the jungles without investigations or trials [during the Malaya and Singapore campaigns]. There was no justification for the massacres even if some Chinese had fought us as volunteers and collaborated with anti-Japanese elements.[392]

In light of Fujiwara's declaration that he knew that what he and his fellow soldiers had done was wrong, it obviously came too late to save millions of lives. Fujiwara's statement gives evidence the Japanese should have known what they were doing was illegal and immoral, but when IJA and IJN personnel were in positions of power, they acted with reckless abandon, disregarding the principles of humanity. During the "Double Tenth" Trial in Singapore, Lieutenant Colonel Colin Sleeman, in his opening speech for the prosecution on 18 March 1946, expressed his deep perplexity at Japanese behavior during WWII:

> It is with no little diffidence and misgiving that I approach my description of the facts and events in this case. To give an accurate description of the misdeeds of these men it will be necessary for me to describe actions which plumb the very depths of human depravity and degradation. The keynote of the whole of this case can be epitomized by two words— unspeakable horror. Horror, stark and naked, permeates every corner and

angle of the case from beginning to end, devoid of relief or palliation...
I have searched diligently, amongst a vast mass of evidence to discover
some redeeming feature, some mitigating factor in the conduct of these
men which would elevate the story from the level of pure horror and
bestiality, and ennoble it, at least, upon the plane of tragedy. I confess
that I have failed.[393]

The atrocities that transpired in Singapore and Malaya, as in China, bear a
haunting resemblance, reflecting a pattern that persisted throughout Japanese
conquests in Asia and the Pacific. Lieutenant Colonel Sleeman's description
of the Japanese in Singapore and Malaya could easily be applied to describing
their deeds in Nanking. The evidence collected against Japanese commanders
accurately portrays a gruesome narrative of rape, torture, murder, and executions,
reaching the "very depths of human depravity and degradation."[394] Sleeman's
characterization of these Japanese crimes as "unspeakable horror" resonates with
anyone attempting to comprehend how such acts could be carried out on such
a massive scale, devoid of moral reflection or hesitation. It is indeed difficult
to find "some mitigating factor in the conduct of [the Japanese] which would
elevate the story from the level of pure horror and bestiality, and ennoble it, at
least, upon the plane of tragedy."[395]

CHAPTER 7

THE BATAAN DEATH MARCH

"In conducting war all of the ferocity of
humanity is brought to the surface."
—**Arthur MacArthur Jr.**, Congressional Testimony, 8 April 1902[396]

AFTER JAPAN ATTACKED PEARL HARBOR, it invaded the Philippines in Luzon on 10 December 1941. Despite having ample warning of Japan's aggression at Pearl Harbor, General Douglas MacArthur was ill-prepared for the invasion. Once the Japanese landed in Luzon, MacArthur initiated a strategic retreat, relocating his troops southward to Bataan and Corregidor. Eventually, on 2 January 1942, Manila fell to the Japanese after the Allies were forced to abandon the city.[397] Although American troops with Filipino soldiers fought valiantly throughout the campaign, they eventually had to face the harsh reality that reinforcements were unlikely to arrive, and, as a result, the American and Filipino forces surrendered to the Japanese by 9 April (Bataan) and 6 May (Corregidor) 1942. Nearly 100,000 Allied troops gave themselves up to the forces under Lieutenant General Homma.[398] Considering the brutality exhibited by the Japanese towards prisoners during the campaign, it was surprising that he Allied troops chose to surrender *en masse*.

For example, Marines and Army soldiers were horrified to discover murdered comrades with their severed penises in their mouths to greet the Americans.[399] One unlucky soul who had the barbaric ritual of having his severed member stuffed in his mouth actually was not dead, only unconscious, when the Japanese took down his pants, sawed off his penis and testicles with a knife, and stuffed them in his mouth. When he came to, spewing out his own organs, with blood and sperm running down his face, he begged for his countrymen to kill him.[400] Even with such atrocities being known, the Americans, after a valiant fight, felt

103

they only had one option left, knowing they had no support coming to them, and that was surrender.

Clearly concerned about the well-being of his men upon laying down their arms, Major General Edward P. King, the Luzon Force commander, engaged in discussions with Colonel Motoo Nakayama, senior operations air officer of the 14th Army. However, King's requests concerning the treatment of wounded soldiers were repeatedly denied by Nakayama, leaving him exasperated, especially with Nakayama's evasive mannerisms. Seeking reassurance, King directly asked for Nakayama's assurance that his men would "be treated as prisoners of war under international law."[401] In response, Nakayama answered, "We are not barbarians."[402]

Contrary to their deceptive declarations of treating foreign citizens and prisoners of war with dignity and respect, Japanese leaders consistently failed to uphold these principles. Tragically, soon after this surrender, around 400 Filipino officers and NCOs of the 91st Division of the Philippine Army were separated from a larger group of POWs, lined up, and slaughtered. At one end, Japanese officers drew their swords and started decapitating these defenseless prisoners, while at the other end, soldiers commenced with bayonetting them.[403] The Japanese indeed were "not barbarians." They were worse than that.

The surviving American and Filipino servicemen on Bataan, comprising approximately 80,000, faced a harrowing ordeal. Despite their sickness and wounds, they were forced to march over 60 miles to Camp O'Donnell in the north. Deprived of food and water, they endured unimaginable hardships, including physical abuse, torture, and often death at the hands of their captors. The scorching temperatures, exceeding 100° Fahrenheit, exacerbated their suffering, leading to the tragic loss of many lives due to heat stroke and dehydration.[404]

It is challenging to ascertain the precise figures, but it is estimated that between 500 to 1,000 Americans and 5,000 to 10,000 Filipinos fell victim to the ruthless acts of the Japanese and their Korean guards during the horrific Bataan Death March, which took place from 9 April to 17–18 April 1942.[405] These atrocities occurred under the command of Lieutenant Colonel Tsuji, who "believed it was morally just and politically expedient to kill [POWs]. Japan was fighting a racial war in the Philippines, he insisted, and the white colonialists should be killed. The Filipinos who fought alongside [the Americans] had betrayed the Asian cause…and should be eliminated as well."[406] Tsuji encouraged, urged, "and in some cases, ordered the killing of American and Filipino POWs and civilians."[407] One notable instance of his involvement happened when he oversaw the Pantingan River massacre, where another 400 Filipino officers and NCOs were murdered.

The accounts of atrocities committed during this dreadful march are legion. On a certain day of this march, a guard demanded a POW's wedding band. Despite the prisoner's attempts, the ring wouldn't budge. In a shocking act of cruelty, the guard ran out of patience and cut off the prisoner's hand with a machete and then mutilated the severed hand to get the ring. Bleeding profusely, the prisoner was pitilessly forced to continue marching. In a state of shock, he managed to take a mere 50 steps before collapsing. Without mercy, the guards then promptly ran him through with bayonets.

Trucks passing by marching POWs contained sword-wielding Japanese soldiers brandishing swords. They would yell "duck" and then strike at the column, decapitating any Americans who failed to stoop quickly enough.[408] The Japanese "took sport swinging their rifle butts, bayonets, rods of bamboo, and even looted golf clubs at walking prisoners,"[409] often laughing as they committed these acts. Sentries compelled Filipinos to bury an American POW alive. A fellow American and witness, horrified, "saw a hand feebly, hopelessly, claw in the air above the grave."[410] POWs who dared to ask for water were shot, and those too sick or exhausted to continue the march, as well as those who stumbled along the way, were run over by trucks with Japanese soldiers laughing at the victims. Anyone who fell and could no longer rise again was immediately dispatched to "the undiscovered country," usually with a bayonet through the temple.[411] The column moved forward, leaving behind roads littered with decapitated bodies, rotting corpses, and bayoneted prisoners.[412]

The Japanese mindset supported and welcomed Tsuji's leadership. IJA soldier Hino Ashihei aptly captured this sentiment when he observed: "As I watch large numbers of the surrendered soldiers, I feel like I am watching filthy water running from the sewage of a nation which derives from impure origins and has lost its pride of race."[413] *The Japan Times and Advertiser*, in an analysis published on 24 April 1942, echoed this perspective, stating:

> They [the Allies] surrender after sacrificing all the lives they can, except their own, for a cause which they know well is futile; they surrender merely to save their own skins…They have shown themselves to be utterly selfish throughout all the campaigns, and they cannot be treated as ordinary prisoners of war. They have broken the commandments of God, and their defeat is their punishment. To show them mercy is to prolong the war. Their motto has been "Absolute unscrupulousness." They have not cared what means they employed in their operations. An eye for an eye, a tooth for a tooth. The Japanese Forces are crusaders in a holy war. Hesitation is uncalled for, and the wrongdoers must be wiped out.[414]

Unlike Nazi Germany, where the press concealed the crimes by its military and *SS*, the Japanese employed the largest English-language daily newspaper to openly declare their intention to exterminate the Allied troops captured after the conquest of the Philippines. They ridiculed the American and Filipino soldiers' willingness to surrender, portraying such acts as pathetic and deserving of mistreatment and death. It is unclear which of God's commandments the authors had in mind when referencing them, but if they were referring to Japan's deity, Hirohito, or specific Shintō gods, like the war-gods *Hachiman Daimyōjin* and *Takemikazuchi-no-kami*, then they might have claimed that these Allied troops violated the divine commandment of never surrendering. In their conclusion, the authors advocated for the complete eradication of these prisoners, using phraseology derived from Judo-Christian principles, namely, "an eye for an eye, and a tooth for a tooth" (Exodus 21:23–25).[415] While this ancient Jewish legal code calls for reciprocal justice, it is important to note that the Allies did not have a comparable legal code or societal conditioning that justified killing prisoners of war. Only the Japanese adhered to such codes, and the writers here projected these norms onto a situation that did not exist, as the Allies generally treated POWs humanely according to the Hague and the Geneva Conventions. Ultimately, this article aimed to condition Japan's reading public to perceive the extermination of POWs as justifiable and to endorse the actions of Tsuji and his sycophants. It twisted historical facts and projected a distorted narrative to legitimize the inhumane treatment of prisoners, thus manipulating public opinion to support these reprehensible acts.

As news of this atrocity leaked out throughout the world, many in America voiced their protest against Japan's ill treatment of POWs. In response to the Allied claims of Japanese atrocities, the spokesperson for Tokyo radio made the following statement:

> If American and British leaders are so ready to raise a hue and cry over the 'maltreatment' of their War Prisoners, why don't they teach their men to stand up and fight to the finish? The way the Americans threw up their hands at Corregidor and the way the British gave up Singapore—on the heels of loud mouthed assertions that they would fight to the finish—surely shows that the men must have carried on their backs a pretty wide streak of yellow.[416]

Interestingly, Tokyo radio did not deny the claims of atrocities. Instead, the show's producers seized the opportunity to ridicule the Allies for their loses and what the Japanese perceived as a lack of courage based on their own standards. When the Japanese held positions of power, they manipulated the laws of war to suit their agenda and dismissed any objections raised by the Allies regarding their disregard for established laws. Consequently, their crimes against humanity persisted for many more months.

Once the survivors of this death march reached their POW camps, their plight did not improve significantly. Sadly, thousands of them succumbed to the dire conditions characterized by a severe lack of medical care, inadequate provisions of food and water, and an overall absence of basic human compassion. In the following weeks alone, another 20,000 souls perished, and over the course of the next few years, tens of thousands more would meet their untimely demise due to blatant neglect and mistreatment.[417] It is estimated that a staggering 36,000 individuals lost their lives solely due to tropical diseases and malnutrition, underscoring the profound toll of suffering inflicted upon them.[418]

The Bataan Death March, although dreadful, was sadly not unique. Throughout the war, the Japanese employed a brutal tactic of forcing POWs to undertake grueling forced marches, often with the deliberate aim of causing numerous deaths along the way. In May 1945, a similar tragedy like Bataan unfolded when the Japanese forced 536 Allied POWs to embark on a treacherous 140-mile trek from Sandakan to Ranau in Borneo, Indonesia. Shockingly, by the time the survivors reached their destination after a month of unimaginable hardship, only 183 of them remained alive. This group of POWs was under the authority of Captain Takuo Takakuwa and Lieutenant Genzo Watanabe, both of whom disposed of wounded and sick POWs with murderous intent. Once they arrived in Ranau, the situation did not improve as the prisoners continued to die at an alarming rate. Of the 2,396 POWs who endured the multiple death marches from Sandakan to Ranua, a mere six men managed to survive until the end of the war, highlighting the extent of the tragedy that transpired.[419]

After the war, Lieutenant General Homma faced trial for his involvement in war crimes and was ultimately sentenced to death in 1946. Reflecting on Homma's actions, General of the Army Douglas MacArthur offered his perspective:

> If this defendant does not deserve his judicial fate, none in jurisdictional history ever did. There can be no greater, more heinous or more dangerous crime than the mass destruction, under guise of military authority or military necessity, of helpless men incapable of further contribution to a war effort. A failure of law process to punish such acts of criminal enormity would threaten the very fabric of world society.[420]

Homma's actions were emblematic of the widespread disregard for international conventions exhibited by many Japanese commanders upon capturing prisoners of war. They demonstrated a blatant disregard for the provisions set forth in the Hague Convention of 1907 and the Geneva Convention of 1929. Even Prime Minister Tōjō was aware of the atrocities committed during the Bataan Death March but failed to take any action to prevent or address them.[421] As for Tsuji, he managed to evade accountability in 1945 and lived a comfortable life in Japan for 16 years. However, sensing the possibility of arrest, he disappeared in Laos during the 1960s, never having to face justice in a courtroom. According to historians Meirion and Susie Harries, he was "an exceptionally intelligent staff officer with a flair for operational planning—talent vitiated by megalomaniac ambition, violent prejudices, and ruthless disregard for human life."[422]

Many have been taught the metaphorical tale that has elements of truth in it that when a wolf in a pack shows any weakness, the others who are stronger often gang up on the weaker one and kill it. Similarly, the Japanese viewed a person who had the ability to continue fighting but chose to surrender as the epitome of weakness. Chapter 3 highlights how Japanese soldiers were trained never to surrender, often resorting to self-inflicted death rather than facing capture. Those who hesitated or showed signs of surrender were met with disdain and frequently killed by their own comrades. So, when it came to an enemy surrendering, the Japanese took their disdain and hatred to an even higher level with this despised person, who had just *neutered himself totally* in the eyes of Japanese when he laid down his arms expecting to be treated humanely. In the Japanese mindset, such a human being was one of the lowest forms of humanity. When Allied military personnel in the Philippines surrendered to Homma's forces in 1942, they unknowingly consigned themselves to a cruel fate. By now, it was to be expected that Japanese education and training would dictate what had happened. The Bataan Death March was not a random anomaly, like one sees with the Mỹ Lai massacre of 1968 by American military personnel against innocent Vietnamese civilians, but the executions and atrocities of the Bataan Death March accurately reflected Japan and its men. Based on their training, culture, religion, and mindsets, the Bataan Death March was a normal Japanese POW operation. And its scale and barbarity might have made it the most well-known and maybe even extreme, if that was possible, since Homma and his men felt they had lost face compared to their counterparts in Malaya, Singapore, Hong Kong, Burma, and Indonesia since it took them almost half a year to defeat the brave Filipino and American soldiers.[423]

CHAPTER 8

THE RAPE OF GUAM

"History is dangerous because the truth can be uncomfortable.
War probably brings out this reality more than any other human
activity, and World War II is replete with uncomfortable truths."

—Alexandra Richie[424]

THE UNITED STATES ACQUIRED GUAM as a result of the Spanish American War
in 1898. Located in the North Pacific within Micronesia, Guam is the largest
and most populous island in the Marianas. Its strategic location along the route
from North America to the Asian continent, the Philippines, and Japan made
it a valuable acquisition.[425] Guam boasts stunning natural beauty, characterized
by clear skis, flourishing coconut groves, dense jungle growth in its interior,
and aqua ocean waters lapping sandy white beaches that encircle the island.
Guam and its sister island to the north called Saipan "were big, rugged islands,
dominated by steep peaks, yawning gorges, undulating tablelands," fields of
sugarcane, and thick vegetation.[426]

Guam played a significant role as a coaling and supply station for ships
traversing the Pacific Ocean, serving as a vital stopover for various vessels.
Additionally, it became a prominent destination for air travel, accommodating
iconic planes like the Pan American Airways clippers.

The island was home to approximately 22,000 indigenous Chamorro
farmers and fishermen, whose lives revolved around the core values of family,
church, and village community. The future first chairman of the joint chiefs-of-
staff, Fleet Admiral William D. Leahy, depicted the pre-war Chamorro people
as follows: "They have little and want nothing. Living in little grass huts one
story above the pigs and chickens; wearing what clothes they can find, or none
at all, and subsisting on whatever fruit happens to grow near, they appear to

be happy and contented beyond the usual lot of humans."[427] The majority of Chamorros were Catholic, with a Protestant minority, and the population as a whole was characterized by their simplicity and amiable nature. Although not U.S. citizens during WWII, they enjoyed many of the rights and privileges afforded to citizens. They spoke English fluently, were permitted to travel to the U.S. mainland, and possessed official U.S. identity documents.

A number of Chamorro actively served in the military, and unfortunately, 12 of them lost their lives on ships during the devastating attack on Pearl Harbor.[428] Prior to World War II, Gaum maintained a modest U.S. government presence, comprising 153 Marines, 271 sailors, 5 nurses, 134 civilian construction workers, 247 insular Guard members (Chamorros under Marine NCOs), and a few civilian administrators. The governor was a U.S. Navy captain and the island, in effect, was under martial law.[429] The military garrison on Guam possessed a decommissioned oil storage ship, a lightly armed mine sweeper, and two patrol boats, which constituted the extent of its naval assets.[430]

In Asia, the attack on Hawaii happened on 8 December 1941 since Pearl Harbor lies over the International Date Line. On this day, Chamorros were celebrating the Feast of the Immaculate Conception as Japanese planes attacked.[431] Panic gripped the parishioners, who cried out, "*Asaina Yu'os! Santa Maria!*" ("Lord God! Holy Mary!"). The capital Agaña (Hagåtña) was engulfed in flames as bombs relentlessly fell from the sky, compelling frightened people to flee towards the inland hills. Illegally, Japanese fighter planes targeted civilians, firing upon the fleeing crowds, and causing numerous casualties. The blaring of car horns filled the air. Two days later, 6,000 Japanese sloshed ashore and overwhelmed Guam's small and lightly armed American garrison.[432] The U.S. detachment valiantly attempted to defend its territory, but in the end, it was "manifestly hopeless."[433] The most powerful weapon the U.S. had, the minesweeper USS *Penguin*, engaged enemy planes with antiaircraft fire. However, in the face of certain loss, the ship was intentionally scuttled to prevent capture. When it went down, the only guns on the island larger than .30 caliber went to the ocean's bottom. On 10 December, the garrison's commander, USN Captain George J. McMillin, made the difficult decision to surrender. The Japanese commander, Major General Tomitarō Horii, a seasoned veteran of the Sino-Japanese War, then commenced with the occupation.[434] Atrocities began to unfold immediately after the Japanese landed. Rosa Baza, who fled alongside others near Tumon, witnessed several dead Americans and Chamorros near a location known as Cinema, which had come under attack by the Japanese. In her testimony, she recounted: "We continued on, passing more dead people. We saw a jitney carrying dead women who had been bayonetted…Several other dead people were near the river, including a pregnant woman whose baby died with her."[435]

In an attempt to mask his true motives, Horii, shortly after seizing control of the island, issued a proclamation that purported to "welcome" the 22,000 Chamorros into "The Greater East Asia Co-Prosperity Sphere" (*Dai Tō Kyōei Ken*). This sphere aimed to eliminate the influence of the "White Man" in Asia and establish a Pan-Asian domain. In his proclamation, Horii stated:

> It is for the purpose of restoring liberty and rescuing the whole Asiatic people and creating the permanent peace in Asia. Thus our intention is to establish the New Order in the World…You all good citizens need not worry anything under the regulations of our…authorities and my [authority] enjoy your daily life as we guarantee your lives and never distress nor plunder your property [sic].[436]

Sadly, but not surprisingly, these assurances quickly proved to be hollow promises.

The occupation of Guam was carried out by Kwantung Army troops, who had previously occupied different posts in Manchuria. Shortly after the island's conquest, these troops forcibly loaded American POWs into cargo areas of the ship *Argentina Maru* and transported them to the Zentsuji camp on the Japanese island of Shikoku.[437] Many died *en route* to Japan in such "hell ships" in which prisoners were packed together for weeks in hulls without nourishment. Many starved to death. The lack of basic provisions caused some others to lose their sanity. For instance, a doctor with a stash of morphine committed suicide. Others, "crazed by thirst, went berserk; they slashed at the throats and wrists of companions to suck blood." Some licked and slurped up sewage from "open drains."[438] Those who died were unceremoniously dumped overboard by their Japanese guards. Upon their arrival at Zentsuji, the survivors were dispersed to various camps, where they were subjected to slave labor. Unfortunately, over the course of the following years, many would die due to the cruel conditions they endured, including "starvation, disease, and beheadings."[439]

With the beginning of the occupation, the Japanese embarked on a campaign of oppression and brutality. They confiscated farms and subjected the local population to a reign of terror, characterized by arbitrary arrests, brutal beatings, interrogations, sexual assault, and torture. The Japanese forced civilians into labor, compelling them to cultivate crops, construct fortifications, lay mines, dig caves, and provide women for their gratification. Anyone who dared to resist or refuse their demands was met with immediate and merciless execution.[440]

Under the Japanese occupation, Guam underwent a forced cultural transformation. The occupiers rebranded the island as *Omiyajima*, meaning

Great Shrine Island, and renamed the capital city of Agaña to *Akashi* (Bright Stone), in homage to the rising sun. The Japanese did not stop with these landmarks, and eventually gave Japanese names to all other towns and regions throughout the island. The Japanese authorities also imposed their language and customs upon the local population, forcing school children to participate in rigorous Japanese language and cultural education. Speaking and writing English were strictly forbidden and carried severe consequences for those caught doing either one. Every morning, before commencing their assigned jobs or forced labor, adults were required to form orderly lines, face the sun, and perform deep bows, symbolizing their reverence for Emperor Hirohito. The Japanese occupiers envisioned their rule lasting for an unprecedented ten thousand years. They would be off by a little more than 9,996 years.[441]

After firmly securing the island militarily, thousands of Japanese troops took control of government buildings and private residences. The garrison size would eventually swell to 14,000 troops by 1944. Tragically, this occupation brought about immense suffering for the local population. Over 2,000 residents were forcibly evicted from their homes, some of whom were confined to substandard and squalid living conditions. Disturbing reports consistently emerged about rape, adding to the harrowing experiences endured by the Chamorro people.[442] The IJA and IJN servicemen looted countless homes, stealing everything from the inhabitants, "even our beds and our clothes."[443] Since Japan had controlled Saipan since the end of WWI, they had previously indoctrinated the Chamorros there in Japanese language and culture. They deployed dozens of people from Saipan as interpreters and overseers of forced-labor details, some of whom relished in their newfound power and treated their brother Chamorros on Guam with disrespect and violence. Their behavior mirrored that of the *Kapos* in Nazi concentration camps, as they assumed roles of authority over compulsory labor and carried out administrative tasks.[444] One particularly notorious case involved not a person from Saipan, but a local citizen of Guam, Samuel T. Shinohara. He was a Japanese immigrant who had settled on Guam in 1905 as a teenager, and later married a local woman and had two children. He knew the people, language, and customs, but when the Japanese came, he took over a governor-like role under the Imperial occupation, moved into a nice home taken from others, and helped the Japanese administer the island. He even assaulted Captain McMillin and aggressively provided the Japanese, under false pretenses, island women to rape. In the aftermath of the war, on 27 August 1945, a commission under the United States Pacific Fleet found Shinohara guilty of treason and crimes against humanity. He was condemned "to death, to be executed by hanging…by the neck until he is dead."[445] Besides using the local Japanese already on the island like Shinohara, Japan actively imported other Japanese families to colonize Guam, further solidifying their control over the island and its population.[446]

Upon thorough examination of numerous war crime affidavits on Guam and in collaboration with park ranger Kina Doreen Lewis, this study unequivocally concludes that a significant number of Chamorro women and young girls fell victim to rape by Japanese soldiers, who engaged in what was commonly referred to as "girl hunting." Accounts reveal that such incidents were distressingly prevalent during the Japanese occupation, with witnesses attesting that when the soldiers were drunk, which was quite often, "they went out raping."[447] Remarkably, many archival reports document instances of violence and abuse without explicitly using the term "rape," although the nature of these accounts makes it abundantly clear that sexual assault was the horrifying reality experienced by these women. Given the overwhelming numerical advantage of the Japanese garrison, with a male-to-female ratio of 2:1, it is highly likely that the majority of women on Guam endured unimaginable suffering throughout the nearly three years of Japanese rule, with little chance of escaping unscathed. Maria Ninete Baza, a courageous survivor of rape on Guam, bravely shared her harrowing experience, reporting:

> Whatever they told us to do, we would bear with it and we did it, everything...And if he said to stay here and this is what you're to do; then we'd stay there and that was what we did...We were grouped; I was in the second group. They said that the second group was the clean group; you already showered and change. Those were the women that they took after the Japanese got drunk [to abuse and rape].[448]

"Rape is an immeasurably traumatic experience for the females involved; it leaves lifelong emotional scars. Given the shame-inducing nature of this crime, victims naturally wish to keep it secret," especially for such a community like Guam where Catholic values shaped the societal fabric.[449] One sees this culture of shame and silence also in China, since "most families [were] unwilling to admit that their women had been abused by Japanese soldiers."[450] "Comfort Women" were also brought to Guam to join the already-abused native girls. Authorities callously established a brothel where Japanese, Korean, and Chamorro women were subjected to repeated acts of rape, sometimes over a dozen times a day.[451] The Japanese also conducted medical experiments on civilians, further demonstrating their complete disregard for human dignity and rights.[452] The systematic efforts undertaken by Japan to demoralize and debase the Chamorro people represent a calculated strategy to crush their spirit and eradicate their cultural identity.

Despite the strict prohibition on owning radios, a courageous group of Chamorros clandestinely possessed them and managed to pick up news from a station broadcasting from San Francisco's Fairmont Hotel. Regardless of the occupiers' efforts to block outside news from reaching the native population, the people received word American forces were defeating the Japanese everywhere.[453] Even though the occupiers made numerous and desperate attempts to block any external information from reaching the people, the truth eventually seeped through. Within a remarkably short span of six months, Guam's resilient citizens became aware that America's offensive operations were steadily pushing back against the Japanese forces, turning the tide of the war. However, maintaining this lifeline of communication with the outside world came at great risk, as discovery of radios by the Japanese occupiers meant certain death for the individuals involved. Nevertheless, their unwavering determination to stay connected to the news of American triumphs served as a beacon of hope and inspiration in the face of adversity.[454]

Meanwhile, the occupying forces were determined to bolster agriculture production to support a massive garrison of 30,000 troops. This led to an intensified imposition of forced labor, and the islanders' meager rations were further diminished as their food was seized. Women were coerced into tending crops, while men were required to perform grueling tasks such as constructing tank traps and fortifications, and transporting food and ammunition. Failure to meet the oppressors' demands resulted in brutal beatings and, in some cases, executions. Many Chamorro families "were all crying because they were very, very skinny and sick" from starvation. The repercussions of these harsh conditions left many Chamorro families emaciated and suffering from illness, prompting desperate cries for help. By the time of Operation *Stevedore*, the recapture of Guam, was underway, the Japanese had committed many massacres, claiming the lives of a few thousand. During forced marches to concentration camps that commenced in earnest on 10 July, atrocities continued to increase. Some unfortunate individuals were beaten to death or subjected to lynching, while others were deliberately herded with their carabaos through minefields to kill them.[455] "It was a pitiful sight when they went flying in the air, because of the bomb explosions."[456] The Japanese forcibly relocated 80% of the population to seven camps, where they endured conditions of utter deprivation. "[T]here was very little food or medicine, no potable water, no sanitary facilities, and…only makeshift or temporary shelter from the torrential rains."[457] Many Chamorros understood that the purpose behind confining them to these camps was to "kill us all."[458] At the Alaguag camp, Alberto Babauta Acfalle described the conditions as such:

Some just died in the camp because of infection and the severity of their sickness, of fever from lack of water, from lack of food, and other forms of sickness. Some had tuberculosis because there was no more food... Some were beaten by the Japanese, not because they could not do their work, but because of the sufferings they had to endure and the lack of strength to endure them. When a person couldn't do anything anymore, he gave up his body and let God take him...We gave God an abundance of gratitude from us who are now still alive and we pray and have compassion and grief for our peers who have gone from this life, who died in Alaguag. At that time, you could not do anything. Sometimes you just got hit on the back, on your head, and you would get knocked, and you couldn't do anything about it, you could not do something in return to try and defend yourself. The life of a person, an individual at that time was taken very lightly by the Japanese. But for us Chamorros, it was very hard because we never knew what war was really like.[459]

The Japanese administration of these camps mirrored the oppressive practices employed by the Nazis at the infamous concentration camps like Dachau and Sachsenhausen during the 1930s. The camps on Guam served as tools of population control and manipulation, where every detainee was treated like a criminal. As the conditions within these camps deteriorated, the guards and commanders exhibited a callous indifference toward the suffering and death, particularly among the frail and old Chamorro population. This uncharacteristic brutality from the Japanese shocked the inherently peaceful Chamorro people, leaving them in a state of disbelief and despair. This sense of despair plagued individuals like Alberto Babauta Acfalle, and they felt utterly powerless and unable to retaliate against their mistreatment. Even 40 years after the events took place, Acfalle still struggled to comprehend the Japanese disregard for human life and their inhumane treatment of the detainees, which, he acknowledged, was something that he and his fellow captives had great difficulty understanding. They simply could not fathom "what [Japanese] war was really like." Thousands like Acfalle endured unimaginable suffering within these camps, and sadly, hundreds of them succumbed to their ordeal.

Outside the camps, the Japanese committed a constant stream of atrocities. For example, some Chamorros were ordered to dig graves before being beheaded. Edward L.G. Aguon watched soldiers tie four people to a cotton tree, then the "Nips" slapped and beat them, tormenting them like a cat toying with a mouse. The executioners proceeded to bayonet them even after "it was obvious [they] were...dead." "The most painful thing I remember...[was] to see the looks on their faces when the final stab of the bayonet pierced their flesh; to hear their cries, as their last breath left their bodies." As the tide of war turned against the Japanese, the frequency of executions escalated, particularly after the American capture of Saipan. Even innocent teenagers who were simply seeking food in the jungle were tied to trees and decapitated.[460] The Japanese executed one man when they found out his son was a U.S. sailor.[461] Just a week before American forces stormed the beaches of Guam to retake the island, the Japanese rounded up families of U.S. servicemen and others deemed "rebellious" in Libugon, and mercilessly slaughtered them in a cave at Tinta.[462] In the final days of Japanese rule on Guam, public executions became "frighteningly common."[463] As Francisco Chargulaf reported: "There were lots of people [who] got killed in Fouha and Tinta. They were the only ones who dug their own graves. It was like a foxhole, long and big and they were killed there. The Japanese were going crazy because the Americans were very near."[464]

Photo of Chamorro skulls. The Japanese executed these victims by decapitation during the occupation. *Guam Public Library System*

This photo shows Japanese atrocities with them beheading three men on Guam. This happened shortly after they took over the island in December 1941. Maria Ninete Baza may have described this execution when she testified: "While [I was in Tai], there were about... three men to be killed. They were made to dig their own graves. They were sentenced to die because they were suspected as spies. They were from Piti." *National Archives, College Park*

The Japanese also had imported Korean forced laborers to toil alongside the enslaved Chamorro. Those who failed to meet the harsh demands were whipped, beaten, or slaughtered. Sadly, many, especially native children, died from malnutrition, further adding to the toll of lives lost. The population decreased by 10% during the occupation, claiming 2,000 lives.[465] Japanese authorities bragged about their reign of terror, arrogantly proclaiming that if Americans were to return to Guam, they would encounter an island strewn with rotting corpses full of "flies."[466] In the years they controlled Guam, they marched toward this goal proving "Japanese civilization had come to Guam."[467]

While the war spiraled into defeat for the Japanese near their front lines as American planes bombed and strafed them, their terrible behavior reached even greater depths. "As the Marianas-based Japanese prepared to defend the islands to the death, Chamorro lives became expendable. Atrocities increased in both frequency and ferocity."[468] This was especially the case for those Japanese who had been stationed in China who had "slaughtered Chinese peasants."[469] Once the Chamorro population was placed in the concentration camps, hundreds died of disease and malnutrition, "in conditions of indescribable squalor," especially the infants.[470] Despite their dire circumstances, the native people clung to hope, and anxiously awaited the Americans' return, fantasizing about how the "Yanks" would kill every one of the "yellow devils."[471] In their toil during details, once out of earshot of the Japanese, they would often find solace in singing the song: "Uncle Sam, Please Come Back to Guam."[472] The prayers of the Chamorro were eventually answered on 21 July 1944, when the American forces successfully landed and then slowly but surely liberated Guam in a grueling battle that persisted until 10 August. The recapture of Guam brought an end to one of the worst atrocities committed against American nationals by a foreign power on American soil. After Admiral Chester Nimitz assumed his post on Guam, he received a heartfelt letter from Chamorro elders, expressing their profound gratitude:

> Dear Sir:
>
> [On] behalf of the people of Guam, we take this opportunity to express to you and our common nation our heartfelt thanks for the recapture of Guam by the…forces under your command. The recapture of Guam was opportune. Had it been delayed longer the native inhabitants would have barely withstood the ill-treatments and atrocities received from the Japanese. What kept us up throughout the thirty-two months of Japanese oppression was our determined reliance upon our mother country's power, sense of justice, and national brotherhood. We rejoice the recapture of Guam and are extremely grateful for the timely relief we are now getting. In closing we request…our note of appreciation be transmitted to the Honorable President, and to the people of the United States of America.[473]

Obviously, the elders' expression of gratitude was far from being hyperbolic. The end of Japanese rule on Guam brought to light the extent of their brutality and their complete disregard for any accountability for their actions in the post-war era. However, the arrival of American forces marked a turning point for Guam. The island's inhabitants now had access to the abundant resources that America offered, and they found themselves under a rule of law that upheld justice and human rights. This transformation was evident as Guam's citizens were soon donning GI-issued boots and clothes and receiving plenty of food.[474] Their heartfelt thanks conveyed to the U.S. Armed Forces and FDR for restoring peace were more than mere words. They were a token of appreciation that would forever be cherished. Supposedly even as of the time of this writing, Guam boasts the highest percentage of individuals serving in the U.S. Armed Forces compared to any other territory or state.[475] Services of thanksgiving, which had been prohibited during the occupation, reverberated through the island, with many offering prayers of gratitude to God for their newfound freedom.

CHAPTER 9

THE RAPE OF THE PHILIPPINES AND MANILA

"Japan's atrocities...are the worst of any nation during [WWII].
They are the worst not only for their scope, but also because this...
violence was [inflicted] by what many considered a cultured nation.
They are the worst because Japan was too wise to have conducted
such slaughter, but not wise enough to follow its conscience."

—Japanese Fighter Ace **Saburō Sakai**[476]

IN THE AFTERMATH OF THE Pearl Harbor attack, the Japanese swiftly launched their invasion of the Philippines. By the summer of 1942, the Philippine islands had fallen into Japanese hands. As was becoming horrifyingly common in lands where Japan set up its rule, rapes, executions, and oppression followed military conquest. Numerous accounts from the occupation of the Philippines by the Japanese shed light on the atrocities committed by the Japanese soldiers and sailors, offering chilling examples of their viciousness.

In one harrowing incident in Canangay, a young woman seeking refuge in the grass was discovered by a patrol of Japanese soldiers. Instead of extending compassion, "for fun," they tore off her clothes and raped her. To further inflict suffering, the patrol's commander took out his saber and "cut off her breasts and cut open her womb...At first the girl screamed but finally lay silent and still... the Japanese then set fire to the shelter [they had drug her to in order to perform this torture]."[477] The girl was so right to try and hide from Japanese soldiers.

Similar acts of sadistic brutality unfolded in Manila, where a group of Japanese on patrol became unsatisfied with a person's houseboy and resorted to a gruesome display of violence. While the victim was still alive, they tied him to a pillar, cut off his genitals, and shoved "his severed penis into his mouth."[478]

It goes without saying, these grotesque acts demonstrated the depths of their depravity and were quite commonplace.

Japanese soldiers about to bayonet children in the Philippines, 1945. *National Archives, College Park*

The wave of violence extended to all provinces, with countless innocent lives being mercilessly snuffed out. In one such incident in Lanao Province in 1942, a barrio was brutally attacked by 100 soldiers, resulting in a staggering loss of life.[479] A year later, in Iloilo Province, 24 men and three women were bound together and beheaded. To compound the horror, before their executions, the soldiers callously took a three-month-old baby and threw it in the air, impaling it on a bayonet in front of the group. This act was accompanied by a chorus of laugher emanating from all Japanese involved.[480]

Once again, mocking the Christian faith, the Japanese military personnel took pleasure in conducting crucifixions. The chilling fate of Lucas Doctolero in Iloilo Province on 18 September 1943 epitomized this sadistic cruelty. Witnessing the gruesome demise of his fellow citizen, Aurelio Artacho, who was hacked in the neck with a sword, thrown into a house, and set on fire, Doctolero himself now knew he faced a nightmarish ordeal. Pinned down on pieces of wood, he pleaded for mercy as a soldier approached him with a hammer and three six-inch nails. With precision and a steady hand, the soldier nailed Dotolero's wrists into a cruciform position, and then, holding Doctolero's head steady, he commenced to hammer his last six-inch piece of metal "through the base of [the victim's] skull."[481] These acts of unspeakable horror not only inflicted physical pain but also fueled a deep-seated hatred among the Filipino people towards their Japanese oppressors, and the spirit of defiance spread throughout the nation. By the time the American forces arrived in late 1944 to initiate the liberation of the nation from Japanese occupation, a formidable force of 270,000 guerrilla fighters had emerged, united in their struggle against the despicable *Nipponese*.[482]

As World War II dragged on and the U.S. reclaimed island after island in the Pacific, Japanese brutality seemed to know no bounds. With the grim reality of their impending defeat dawning upon Hirohito's legions, their acts of violence grew even more savage, as evidenced by the atrocities committed in Guam and other occupied territories. In these areas, innocent civilians were ruthlessly slain, women were subjected to unspeakable acts of rape, and even American troops, both living and deceased, fell victim to unimaginable mutilation. Technician 5th Grade Burdett Andrews, in a haunting discovery, encountered a fellow serviceman who had been gruesomely severed and dismembered. Despite tireless efforts, Andrews and his comrades were unable to recover the scattered remains, ultimately laying to rest only a torso cruelly sliced in half.[483]

In the grim month of November 1944, Japanese troops moved into Cebu Province, rounded up 1,000 innocent men, women, and children, and cut them down. So even before the Rape of Manila, the Japanese commander in the Philippines, General Yamashita, and his troops were drunk on violence. *Shockingly, no one in the chain of command complained about the atrocities Imperial troops were committing during the Rape of the Philippines.*[484]

In a chilling display of the disregard for justice and due process, Colonel Hideo Nishiharu, the head of Yamashita's 14th Army's Judge Advocate Section, delivered a grave report to the general on 14 December 1944. Startlingly, the report indicated that 600 suspected guerrillas were in custody. Without conducting a review of the evidence or granting them a fair trial, Yamashita callously authorized their execution. Immediately thereafter, IJA troops slaughtered the unfortunate souls.[485] In the same fateful month, the horrors continued unabated, with an additional 2,000 labelled as "guerillas [i.e. bandits]" falling victim to this merciless cycle. These unsuspecting souls were also denied their right to a fair trial and only discovered their grim fate when they were led to a vast cemetery, where their lives were abruptly and brutally extinguished.[486]

During this fateful month of December 1944, under command of General Yamashita, 1,650 American prisoners boarded the ill-fated vessel known as the *Oryoku Maru*, destined for Japan. Unfortunately, the *Oryoku Maru* would fall victim to an Allied attack, further exacerbating the plight of the already suffering prisoners. The captain of the *Oryoku Maru* decided to transfer the prisoners to other ships in the fleet due to the damage his ship had sustained. Throughout the stressful transfers to other ships, the prisoners endured mistreatment and cruelty at the hands of their captors. They were beaten, clubbed, and many would die during the transfers or soon thereafter from their wounds. Those who survived were sometimes starved and killed in the new ships that held them prisoner. Weeks later, when the surviving POWs arrived in Japan, the shocking truth became apparent—their numbers had dwindled to a mere 450.[487] The majority of their comrades had met a grisly fate, ruthlessly murdered at sea.

This study has already given instances of the killing of POWs and civilians under the command of General Yamashita, which commenced when he assumed control of the IJA 14th Army in the Philippines in September 1944, overseeing approximately 200,000 men in Luzon. However, one of the most appalling atrocities occurred after the Allies landed in Luzon on 9 January 1945. In a brutal act of reprisal for guerrilla activities, Yamashita's forces slaughtered 25,000 men, women, and children.[488] Such atrocities were regrettably commonplace for Yamashita's subordinates. The Allied prosecution struggled after the war to organize all the atrocities among Yamashita's command, writing:

> The Commission established hundreds of incidents which included the withholding of medical attention from, and starvation of, prisoners of war and civilian internees, pillage, the burning and destruction of homes and public buildings without military necessity, torture by burning and otherwise, individual and mass execution without trial, rape, and murder, all committed by members of the Japanese forces under the command of [Yamashita]. *These offences were widespread as regards to both space and time*.[489] [author's italics]

Hence, it becomes evident that the Rape of Manila was not an isolated event under Yamashita's leadership during the Rape of the Philippines. Instead, it served as a culmination of the escalating and intensified misconducted exhibited by his troops as they came to terms with their imminent defeat and impending demise.

By 1945, Japan's utter contempt for the welfare of conquered civilians in its Greater East Asia Co-Prosperity Sphere was glaringly evident, with few places exemplifying this brutality more horrifically than Manila. These depths of this persecution were reached in March, coinciding with the fall of Iwo Jima to the U.S. Marines, when the U.S. Army initiated its mission to liberate the city. The people of Manila had already endured months of suffering, with a staggering death toll of 500 individuals per day from starvation since December 1944.[490] Little did they know that their plight was about to worsen even further.

In anticipation of the impending takeover of their operational area, numerous Japanese personnel chose to pitilessly murder their POWs under their custody rather than allow them to be liberated by the advancing American forces. One disturbing account recounts a sickening incident at Puerto Princesa prison on Palawan Island on 14 December 1944, where approximately 150 U.S. soldiers, sailors, and Marine POWs, survivors of Bataan and Corregidor, were herded into an air raid shelter. Soon thereafter, these prisoners were drenched in gasoline and set ablaze, burning them alive.[491] The guards conducting this slaughter were heard laughing as the agonized prisoners cried out for help as the flames consumed them. The few who managed to escape from the burning tomb were "bayoneted, shot, clubbed or stabbed" to death, with only six men surviving the ordeal to testify later to the unspeakable atrocity.[492]

Following the liberation of the Palawan Island by American forces and discovering the crime scene, the U.S. government expressed its strong condemnation of the heinous acts committed there by the Japanese military. Through the Swiss legation, a message was conveyed to the Japanese foreign minister, Shigenori Tōgō, on 19 May 1945, denouncing "such barbaric behavior on the part of the Japanese armed forces [which] is an offence to all civilized people. The Japanese government cannot escape punishment for this crime."[493] In response to the communication, Tōgō promised an "*immediate investigation*" would be conducted. However, in reality, nothing was done. It became evident that the Japanese authorities had no genuine intention to address the issue, particularly given their official policy of executing POWs to prevent their rescue by friendly forces.[494] The vice minister of war, General Hajime Sugiyama, had already issued an order instructing Imperial forces to slaughter prisoners rather than allowing them to be recaptured by Allied troops.[495]

So, war crimes, especially against POWs, were rampant under Yamashita's authority even prior to the battle for Manila. It was not surprising considering that this was the *modus operandi* adopted by Japanese commanders. A stark example of this occurred over a year earlier when IJN Captain Shigematsu Sakaibara, the Wake Island commander, machinegunned 98 American POWs, including many Chamorros, on one of the island's beaches. Sakaibara acted out of fear that an imminent amphibious assault by the U.S. forces would result in the prisoners falling back into enemy hands.[496] These senseless acts constituted war crimes, and Sakaibara would face justice for his actions, being executed in Guam on 19 June 1947.[497]

In the lead-up to the battle with the Americans in Manila, Rear Admiral Sanji Iwabuchi, along with Japanese sailors and soldiers under his command, disregarded Lieutenant General Yamashita's orders to withdraw and instead turned Manila into a battleground. While Japanese commanders often carried out atrocities against civilians without justification, Iwabuchi's stubborn decision to fight in Manila may have been motivated by his desire to compensate for previous failures. For instance, having experienced defeat with the loss of his battleship *Kirishima* during the battle for Guadalcanal on 15 November 1942 and the ground war at Munda Point with his combat troops on New Georgia in the Solomon Islands from 22 July to 5 August 1943, Iwabuchi possibly sought redemption for his past missteps or sought to create a dramatic spectacle before his intended suicide. Regardless of his motives, he would ultimately live up to expectations of how Japanese commanders behaved in the face of defeat with tragic consequences.[498]

Despite being under Yamashita's command, Rear Admiral Iwabuchi took his orders from his naval superior, not his legal superior, Vice Admiral Denshichi Okochi, commander of the Southwestern Area Fleet based in the Philippines. Okochi explicitly instructed Iwabuchi to hold Manila.[499] Although Okochi had transferred command of naval personnel in Manila to Yamashita on 5 January 1945, he disregarded this arrangement and ensured Yamashita's order for Iwabuchi to evacuate Manila was countermanded.[500] As Yamashita's units moved out, Iwabuchi's troops, consisting of 12,500 sailors and 4,500 soldiers, remained in and around Manila with the intention of devastating the city.[501] Under Iwabuchi's authority, instructions were issued for the Navy Defense Force in Manila that claimed throughout December 1944 to February 1945 that,

> When killing Filipinos, assemble them together in one place, as far as possible, thereby saving ammunition and labor. The disposal of dead bodies will be troublesome, so either collect them in houses scheduled to be burned or throw them into the river.[502]

Iwabuchi's sailors and soldiers energetically carried out his orders. Subjected to incessant pounding by U.S. forces and facing certain death or capture, the beleaguered Japanese, predominantly naval personnel, vented their anger and frustration on civilians, perpetrating what would be known as the Manila Massacre, or what I refer to as the Rape of Manila.[503]

One witness, San Juan, horrifyingly observed a group of children and infants subjected to savage attacks by Japanese soldiers. Some troopers forcibly snatched babies from their mothers' arms and then held them in the air while soldiers nearby impaled them with bayonets. In a morbid display, other babies were heartlessly thrown into the air and caught on "the point of the bayonet," while the soldiers reveled in sadistic laughter.[504] In another case, as a Japanese soldier "caught" a baby with his bayonet, the baby did not immediately die, and as the Japanese laughed and enjoyed their play, the suffering infant "dangled moving his hands," crying as he attempted to escape from the cold, metallic blade.[505] The Japanese took sick pleasure carrying out these terrible acts in front of the anguished parents to see their reactions as their babies were killed.[506] In another horrific incident, one pregnant woman, who happened to be San Juan's wife, was bayoneted through her belly, instantly snuffing out the life of her unborn child. With her dying breath, she gazed up at the soldiers and cried out in agony, "Oh, how painful!" before succumbing to her own fate.[507] A nearby husband, who dared to raise his voice against such brutality, had his tongue gruesomely cut out.[508] One expectant mother had to endure the unspeakable agony of having her belly sliced open, only to witness her newborn baby roll on the floor, still connected by the umbilical cord. A soldier, devoid of any humanity, cut off the infant's head before the aghast eyes of the grief-stricken mother.[509]

The Japanese soldiers and sailors displayed a shocking degree of sexual sadism, engaging in unspeakable acts of cruelty and perversion.[510] They burned men's testicles while the person screamed or inserted matchsticks into the penises of others. They put out their cigarettes in women's vaginas and rammed large sticks into women after having burned off their pubic hair. In one case, the Japanese took pleasure in hanging one Chinese prisoner upside down and then inserting a wire deep into his body by way of his anus. After painful minutes of torture, the prisoner died, most likely from internal bleeding.[511] When raping a young teenage girl, a Japanese sailor found he could not penetrate her because her vagina was too small. He took out his knife, cut her open, and then "finally succeeded" in entering her and ejaculating. In this case, he did not kill her, and as blood was running down her legs, he said with glee, "You will have Japanese baby, not American baby."[512]

In a heartbreaking scene, as the Americans advanced, they discovered a young woman who had been subjected to a brutal rape. Even though her whole lower jaw had been shattered by a butt of a rifle, thus causing her severe problems and pain in breathing, she still miraculously clung to life. The American GIs did their best to render aid to her to get her immediately to a doctor. In close proximity to this crime scene, another woman, also a rape victim, lay in bed in severe shock because the Japanese "had hacked her feet off," leaving her in a state of unimaginable agony and despair.[513] Sadly, the suffering inflicted upon these women was not confined to the initial acts of violence. Many endured repeated acts of rape, sometimes enduring the horrors more than two dozen times in a single day. And quite often, the aftermath of such brutal violations took a further toll on these survivors as they suffered from venereal diseases and internal trauma, a constant reminder of the despicable acts committed against them.[514]

In further exploring the butchering going on in Manila, a later war trial revealed the following testimony from a witness: "Hospital patients were strapped to their beds and set afire; babies' eyeballs were gouged out and smeared on walls like jelly...others were ordered to dig their own graves and then shot down."[515] Army private Cam Dowell was left stunned by the heart-wrenching sight encountered in the main bank downtown. As he descended into the vaults below, he was confronted with a horrifying scene that would forever haunt his memory. The once secure confines of the bank now housed a macabre collection of decaying corpses. These innocent civilians, victims of the Japanese, had been ruthlessly raped and murdered, their lifeless bodies callously arranged in the vaults with the explicit intent to shock and horrify the approaching American forces.[516] The Japanese succeeded in their goal.

In yet another disgusting display of depravity, deeply disturbing scenes unfolded. After 20 sailors raped a 12-year-old girl, a few of them sliced off her breasts. One sailor picked up her severed organ, placed it on his chest and wiggled his shoulders, laughing while doing so.[517] Another girl, while fighting to prevent her rape, had her head cut off by a sailor. He then mounted her headless body, sexually assaulting her remains.[518] Others tried to perform necrophilia with another murdered woman but were unable to do so due to rigor mortis that prevented them from spreading her legs.[519] Many civilians, including dozens of women who had endured the trauma of rape but been spared death, were locked into the walls of Fort Santiago. As the imminent fall of Manila loomed, the Japanese forces sealed off the entrances to this fort, poured gasoline over the structure, and set it afire, burning hundreds to death, their desperate cries drowned in the engulfing flames.[520] One soldier, burdened by the weight of his own atrocities, etched his guilty reflections in the pages of his diary, writing:

> Every day is spent in hunting guerrillas and natives. I have already killed well over 100. The innocence I possessed at the time of leaving the homeland has long since disappeared. Now I am a hardened sinner and my

sword is always stained with blood. Although it is for my country's sake, it is sheer brutality. May God forgive me. May my mother forgive me.[521]

Undoubtedly, the God this man worshiped and the mother who raised him did not give him the moral fortitude required to refuse to obey unlawful orders to slaughter defenseless Filipino citizens. This soldier's self-reflection that he was indeed a sinner and committing "sheer brutality" on people indicates he had enough morality to know what he was doing was wrong. However, he lacked the integrity and inner strength to halt his compliance with these orders. His justification that his actions were carried out in service of his country revealed his deficiency in logical reasoning. It is perplexing how he could believe that the indiscriminate killing of innocent people, particularly in a losing effort against the Americans, could possibly benefit Japan. Despite his awareness of the criminal nature of his actions, he persisted in carrying them out, driven by a combination of efficiency in executing evil deeds and twisted moral rationalizations.

During the destruction of the city by IJA and IJN units, at least 100,000 *Manileños* lost their lives.[522] The destruction wrought upon the city was immense, with over 70% of its utilities and factories razed, 80% of the southern residential district reduced to ruins, and the entire business district decimated beyond recognition. Hospitals, tragically, were not spared, as many were deliberately set ablaze, often with the patients inside. The entire city's sanitation system, an essential lifeline, was obliterated, plunging Manila into chaos, filth, and disease. Renowned historian James M. Scott, in his book *Rampage*, aptly described Manila as being engulfed by a "tsunami of barbarity," ranking the war crimes committed there as among "one of the worst human catastrophes" of World War II.[523] As the war crimes trial of General Yamashita concluded, his troops' "acts constitute a deliberate, planned enterprise."[524] General of the Army MacArthur received a report about this slaughter, which declared the responsibility of the Manila crimes "rests with the Japanese High Command and the government of Japan, represented by the Emperor, while the people of Japan itself cannot ultimately escape the awful weight of moral participation and moral guilt."[525] Journalist Henry Keys of the *London Daily Express* drew a chilling parallel, asserting, "At last the Japanese have matched the Rape of Nanking."[526] "Trapped in the doomed city, knowing that they had only a few days at best to live, the Japanese went berserk, unloosed their pent-up fears and passions in one last orgy of abandon."[527]

In his cold-hearted diary entry, Japanese Warrant Officer Yamaguchi documented his criminal chain of command: "We are ordered to kill all the males we find. Mopping up the bandits from now on will be a sight indeed…

Our aim is to kill or wound all the men...Women who attempt to escape are to be killed. All in all, *our aim is extermination* [author's italics]."[528] The Japanese acts during the Rape of Manila were indeed wholesale extermination, leaving no room for mercy or escape. Rear Admiral Iwabuchi, before taking his own life, transmitted a radio message to his superior, Vice Admiral Okochi, the following:

> I am overwhelmed with shame for the many casualties among my subordinates and for being unable to discharge my duty because of my incompetence...Now, with what strength remains, we will daringly engage the enemy. '*Banzai* to the Emperor!' We are determined to fight to the last man.[529]

A few days later, Iwabuchi killed himself feeling "shame," not for atrocities, but because of his men dying while slaughtering civilians and his inability to conduct land warfare properly. How erudite and "moral," one might add. Iwabuchi's admissions here serve as a stark reminder of the distorted values and warped sense of honor that many Japanese leaders embraced during this tumultuous period of the war.

While Iwabuchi and his officers escaped taking responsibility for their crimes by committing *seppuku* on 26 February, General Yamashita, the overall commander, was eventually apprehended, imprisoned, and brought to trial. Following months of rigorous hearings and depositions, he was ultimately found guilty and executed in 1946 for his involvement in these atrocities. It is important to note that Yamashita's troops behaved no better in the Philippines than they had during their conquest of Malaya and Singapore in 1942.[530] The horrors his troops unleashed on the people of Manila in particular, and the Filipinos throughout the Philippines in general, was actually their *modus operandi* throughout the entire war.

The Japanese military instilled terror and occupied the Philippines for a traumatic period of three years until General of the Army MacArthur led the successful campaign to liberate the country. Although the exact number of casualties during this dark chapter is challenging to ascertain, it is estimated that between 900,000 and 1,000,000 Filipinos lost their lives as a result of various factors, including widespread starvation, cold-blooded executions and guerilla warfare, and the perpetration of hundreds of thousands of rapes.[531]

It is both sobering and poignant to acknowledge that General Yamashita was compelled to face the testimonies of his victims during his court proceedings. One could even say it is gratifying to know that he was indeed required to do so. The stories shared by survivors revealed the depths of the atrocities committed by his troops. One particularly sad story came from a Chinese mother who recounted the traumatic loss of her three-year-old son, torn from her arms and mercilessly bayoneted by an IJA soldier. Overwhelmed by grief and rage after finishing her testimony, she leaped over the witness stand and rushed the general, clawing at his face as he sat, sphinxlike, in the dock. The guards pulled her away and ushered her from the courtroom with her crying and cursing on the way out, leaving all there stunned into silence at the dramatic illustration of just how devasting Yamashita's army had been on the population.[532] Seventeen-year-old Julieta Milanes also confronted Yamashita, recounting the brutal murder of her parents by his troops. Her anguished words reverberated through the courtroom as she condemned the general, screaming, "If I could only get near you. You don't have shame. You ought to be hung. You ought to be cut to pieces. You can still laugh?" Maybe Yamashita was laughing or maybe he was just puzzled by the whole ordeal—Japanese generals in particular, and Japanese men in general, usually did not have women speak to them in such a manner, especially when they were girls.[533] Another victim who took the stand against Yamashita was 11-year-old Rosalinda Andoy. She described how soldiers had not only murdered her parents but also subjected her to 38 brutal bayonet wounds, leaving her for dead. When asked to reveal her injuries to the court, she lifted her little pink frock and showed her skinny body, covered in grotesque, red, and swollen scar tissue, everywhere, a testament to the unimaginable suffering she endured. The sight was so distressing that even the seasoned Allied generals on the bench, hardened combat veterans themselves, broke down and cried.[534]

In the end, the prosecution at Yamashita's trial concluded he:

> ...knew or must have known of, and permitted, the widespread crimes committed in the Philippines by troops under his command (which included murder, plunder, devastation, rape, lack of provision for prisoners of war and shooting of guerrillas without trial), and/or that he did not take the steps required of him by international law to find out the state of discipline maintained by his men and the conditions of prevailing in the prisoner-of-war and civilian internee camps under his command.[535]

Yamashita claimed ignorance of his troops' behavior (*any of it in its entirety*). He even had his defense present his case before the United States Supreme Court, filing "a petition for writs of *habeas corpus* and prohibition." However, this defense tactic proved unsuccessful.[536] Chief Justice Harlan F. Stone, after examining the evidence and consulting with others on the Supreme Court, firmly said: "A commanding general must be held responsible for the conduct of his troops."537 One aspect of Yamashita's defense was that there was no written order under his name explicitly commanding his troops to commit the atrocities they always had carried out—rape and murder. This defense, however, was weak. Even Hitler had not issued a written order to exterminate the Jews. Immoral commanders rarely give such instructions in writing; they usually rely on oral directives.538 During Yamashita's trial, it was learned that his subordinate, Colonel Fujishige Masatoski, had ordered his officers and NCOs to kill anyone suspected of "opposing" the emperor, "even women and children."539 Under his command, hundreds died. Masatoski's commander, Lieutenant General Isamu Yokoyama (sentenced to death at the Tokyo Tribunal for conducting medical experiments and vivisections on POWs), in typical Japanese euphemistic fashion, suggested that the colonel "might have" come under Yamashita's command and received his orders from the general.540 No, Masatoski was under Yamashita's command and would have only enacted such widespread operations after receiving Yamashita's approval. As one witness, who had intimate contact with Yamashita, testified, right after he arrived at his Philippines command, General Yamashita "issued a general order" to his chain-of-command "to wipe out the whole Philippines, if possible...since everyone in the Islands were either guerrillas or active supporters of the guerrillas; wherever the population gave signs of favoring the Americans the whole population of that area should be exterminated."541 As history has shown, Yamashita's troops dutifully fulfilled his orders.

Considering the actions of Yamashita's troops throughout the war, it is difficult to view him as anything other than either grossly ignorant or a pathetic liar. During his assignment as commander of the First Area Army in Manchuria from July 1942 until September 1944, overseeing a force of 700,000 soldiers, it is implausible that he remained unaware of the atrocities committed against "bandits," the horrible medical experiments conducted by Unit 731 (which will be discussed shortly), Japan's oppressive economic policies, and the IJA's involvement in the drug trade (which will also be addressed shortly).

Yamashita's role as the commanding general in several of the most horrific crimes of the Asian War/Pacific War cannot be overlooked. The Rape of Singapore and Malaya, the Rape of Manchuria, the Rape of the Philippines, and the Rape of Manila fill his resume and stain his record. To fully comprehend the magnitude of death resulting from Yamashita's actions (excluding combat-related casualties), let us examine the data. Rough estimates suggest that under Yamashita's command, at least 350,000 to 450,000 died at the hands of his troops. To put this into perspective, Yamashita's atrocities surpassed the combined death toll of two Nazi death camps, Sobibór and Majdanek (circa 230,000), and approach the total deaths in Chelmno (circa 330,000).

CHAPTER 10

SIAM-BURMA RAILWAY OR "RAILROAD OF DEATH"[542]

"Hell is empty. All the Devils are here."
—**William Shakespeare**, *The Tempest*[543]

THE JAPANESE FORCED LABOR PROJECT aimed at constructing a railway between Burma and Siam (Thailand) extended across a distance of 258 miles. Military headquarters in Tokyo had strategic objectives for this project, desiring a rail link to connect the armies in India and Thailand and improve logistics support for food, supplies, and munitions. The railway connected the Thai city of Ban Pong with the Burmese city of Thanbyuzayat. The project commenced in late 1942 and came to a halt in early 1944. It involved more than 400,000 civilian laborers, including Malayan, Tamil, Javanese, Burmese, Chinese, Thai, and other Southeast Asians workers, as well as over 61,000 Allied POWs. Among the POWs, half were British, a quarter were Australian, and the remainder consisted of Dutch and about 700 Americans. Tragically, the conditions the laborers endured, including the lack of medical care, inadequate food, beatings, executions, overwork, and the exposure to harsh environments, resulted in the deaths of possibly over 330,000 indigenous workers and over 15,000 Allied POWs. These figures indicate an appalling loss of life, averaging around 1,337 fatalities for every mile of rail laid and approximately 24,642 deaths per month.[544] The Japanese had not been hyperbolic when they warned arriving prisoners: "This railway will go through even if your bodies are to be used as sleepers [railroad ties or crossties]."[545] This kill-quota per month rivalled the Nazi death camp Auschwitz. Prime Minister Tōjō was aware of these atrocities but took no action to improve the conditions under which the slave laborers toiled.[546]

This construction project stands as a remarkable feat, both in terms of its sheer size and the speed at which it was accomplished. Structural engineer Bashar Altabba aptly describes its engineering significance, writing:

> What makes this an engineering feat is the totality of it, the accumulation of factors. The total length of miles, the total number of bridges—over 600, including six to eight long-span bridges—the total number of people who were involved...the very short time in which they managed to accomplish it, and the extreme condition they accomplished it under. They had very little transportation to get stuff to and from the workers, they had almost no medication, they couldn't get food let alone materials, they had no tools to work with except for basic things like spades and hammers, and they worked in extremely difficult conditions—in the jungle with its heat and humidity. All of that makes this railway an extraordinary accomplishment.[547]

The men involved in this project, often sick and surviving on meager rations, performed truly remarkable feats. They managed to build this extensive railway "through the densest jungle in the world apart from the Amazon Basin."[548] If their achievement was solely attributed to enduring starvation and exposure to tropical weather, it would be exceptional in itself. However, they also faced constant harassment, abuse, and executions while working exhausting shifts of 18 to 20 hours per day. Furthermore, these diverse groups, comprising individuals who spoke ten different languages, had limited knowledge of civil engineering. Yet, they found a way to collaborate, utilizing inadequate tools, materials, and machinery to accomplish this extraordinary engineering project. The resilience and resourcefulness displayed by the POWs and "coolies" or civilian laborers (rōmusha) defy the limits of imagination.

Despite enduring a grueling schedule and facing harsh conditions, the POWs faced additional burdens. Alongside their arduous labor, they were tasked with the somber responsibility of conducting burial details for their fallen comrades. Additionally, they had to scavenge for food to supplement the meager rations provided by their Japanese captors. In their desperate pursuit of nourishment, they resorted to consuming insects, frogs, snakes, snails, rats, and anything else they could catch. Unfortunately, even these desperate measures proved insufficient. Sadly, within a mere 10 weeks of their arrival, approximately 1,700 men, out of nearly 9,000 in the "F Force" POW group from Singapore, succumbed to the dire circumstances they faced.[549]

According to British doctor Robert Hardie, the conditions endured by the POW-laborers were equally dire for Japan's "brother Asians" involved in the project. In his own words, he penned the following:

> The conditions in the coolie camps down river are terrible. They are kept from Japanese and British camps. They have no latrines. Special British prisoner parties at Kinsalyok bury 20 coolies a day. These coolies have been brought from Malaya under false pretenses—'easy work, good pay, good houses!' Some have even brought wives and children. Now they find themselves dumped in these charnel houses, driven and brutally knocked about by the Jap and Korean guards, unable to buy extra food, bewildered, sick, frightened. Yet many of them have shown extraordinary kindness to sick British prisoners passing down the river, giving them sugar and helping them into the railway trucks at Tarsao.[550]

For all of Japan's rhetoric of liberating the Asians from their European masters, it becomes evident once again that they were not "liberating" the locals from their previous rulers, but rather replacing European rule with their own, and in doing so, they exhibited even greater malevolence. While Europe had not always treated the regions now under Japanese control favorably, the indigenous populations soon realized that they longed for their former colonial masters, as Japan demonstrated a complete disregard for the well-being of those under its control.

The Japanese dispatched a force of 12,000 soldiers, including 800 Korean forced laborers, to provide engineering expertise and carry out guard duties for the project. Following the war, 111 Japanese and Koreans were convicted for atrocities committed against those forced to work on the railway, with 32 of them receiving a death sentence.[551] Prime Minister Tōjō, in violation of international law, supported the utilization of POWs for the construction of the railway. This evidence, among others, contributed to his death sentence at the Tokyo War Crimes Tribunal.[552] Vice Minister of War, Lieutenant General Heitarō Kimura, was executed by hanging for his role in ordering "the employment of…prisoners on the construction of the Burma-Siam Railway."[553] Like many Japanese commanders, he did indeed issue orders for his men to "refrain from ill-treating prisoners," something his soldiers disregarded just like all other Japanese soldiers in the field did when given "moral" directives.[554] One of the men, Sergeant Seiichi Okada, earned his nickname "Doctor Death" due to his sadistic conduct as a medical orderly, helping hundreds of prisoners die in the area of Hintok-Konyu. He served 10 years in a Singapore prison.[555] To describe some of the horrible "medical treatment," out of 1,200 coolies treated at the Kanburi Hospital, only 10 survived the war.[556] Another soldier, Arai Koei, a Korean known as "Boy Bastard," was sentenced to the gallows to hang for his treatment of prisoners on the Burma section of the railway.[557] It was tragic that millions of Koreans suffered under Japan's oppressive rule as forced laborers and "Comfort Women." However, there were others who succumbed to the culture of oppression and willingly emulated their Japanese masters, exemplifying the age-old adage of "abuse begets abuse." As Korean guard, I Gil (Yoshikichi Kasayama), stated,

> My duty was to guard prisoners and assist in the operation of the camps where they were held, not to fight battles...Above us [Korean guards] were a Japanese lance corporal, a sergeant, and an officer, usually a first or second lieutenant. We simply followed their orders, which were absolute.[558]

I Gil even visited "Comfort Women," some of whom were fellow Koreans enslaved by the Japanese.[559] His behavior underscores the extent to which he had been brainwashed to obey the Japanese, who dehumanized him and his fellow guards, perpetuating a constant state of oppression in their home country. He was found guilty of war crimes and, after serving his jail time, spent his remaining days in Japan rather than returning to his home country of Korea that he had betrayed on many levels.[560]

It is essential to acknowledge that Korea had been under Japanese colonial rule for over three decades since 1905, resulting in widespread indoctrination to perceive Japan as superior and as Korea's master. Despite Koreans being categorized as Japanese citizens, they were never treated as such, neither in legal nor in social terms. As an illustration, after the massive earthquake that struck Japan on 1 September 1923, thousands of Japanese vigilantes, with the support of local police and military personnel, launched a pogrom against Koreans based on unfounded rumors of arson, looting, and well poisoning. In the Kantō region and other areas, more than 6,000 Koreans were mercilessly hunted down, raped, and slaughtered.[561] Few perpetrators, if any, faced any consequences, exemplifying the lack of humanity and justice within Japanese society at this time. Koreans, whether in Japan and Korea, were simply treated as second-class citizens. Slave laborer Ahn Juretsu described the situation by stating, "Korea was a colony. No human rights at all. We were just the same as slaves."[562] Many Koreans were conscripted into the IJA, most against their will, and experienced horrendous treatment while wearing the Japanese uniform, resulting in tens of thousands of fatalities during training or at their duty stations.[563] But some rose to high-ranking positions within the military, such as Lieutenant General Hong

Sa-ick (Shiyoku Kō), the commandant of Manila's notorious POW camp, who was executed as a war criminal in Manila in 1946. Future Korean President Park Chung-hee also graduated from the Japanese Military Academy and fought for Japan in Manchuria. Additionally, there were some brainwashed Korean youths who became *Kamikaze* pilots. Due to Japan's prolonged control over Korea, it is important to acknowledge that not all Koreans in the IJA were second-class citizens or victims, although they were generally treated as inferior.[564] It is astonishing that some Koreans became perpetrators of Japanese war crimes, but historical evidence shows that oppressed individuals sometimes turn on their own, and Koreans were not absolved from this cruel truism.

Returning to the discussion of the crimes committed on the Railroad of Death, Major Hikosaku Kudo of the 19th Ambulance Corps took sadistic pleasure in inflicting punishment on coolies for minor offenses. His methods involved stripping them naked, immobilizing their arms and legs to prevent them from standing, and leaving them exposed to the scorching sun for three consecutive days. On other occasions, he would subject a victim to hold a heavy log or stone above his head until exhaustion forced him to collapse. When a prisoner would do so, Kudo would beat him and force him to repeat the agonizing process for hours. Not only did Kudo subject male prisoners to such tortuous treatment, but he also targeted women and children in the coolie camp. He subjected them to prolonged exposure under the blazing sun for hours, often engaging in acts of rape during these horrific episodes. Furthermore, during his alcohol-fueled parties, Kudo would compel Tamil women to dance naked before him and his comrades. Upon the conclusion of their performances, these innocent women would be gang-raped. One brave woman who resisted such abuse met a gruesome fate, while her husband descended into madness from observing the unspeakable horrors inflicted upon his beloved wife.[565]

The military project to build the railroad from Burma to Thailand caused unbelievable suffering upon hundreds of thousands of innocent people. The utilization of Allied POWs in this military endeavor violated the Geneva Convention, and the ill treatment of these POWs constituted a violation of both the Geneva and Hague Conventions. The mass murder of civilians was indeed a crime against humanity, and a clear violation of the Kellogg-Briand Pact of 1928. Japan found unique ways throughout its empire to rape, persecute, and abuse those under its yoke of oppression. Unlike the Nazi death camps like Auschwitz or Majdanek, which were situated far from Hitler's homeland, away from his troops, and in secluded areas, Japan operated openly and incorporated its entire military apparatus into its acts of brutality. Whether engaged in combat or assigned other tasks, Imperial troops seemingly always found opportunities to commit rape and murder against those under their control. The Railroad of Death represented a moving horror characterized by rape, torture, humiliation, death marches, sickness, and slaughter. It stands as Japan's largest project involving prisoners of war and forced laborers, and thus, its deadliest.[566] Regrettably, this event was not the only instance of a Railroad of Death, as Japan also constructed the Sumatra Railway between Pekanbaru to Muarakalaban from 1944 to 1945, spanning 153 miles. More than 700 Allied POWs and around 20,000 Indonesian forced laborers perished during the construction of this project. As one sees, atrocities almost always followed everything Japan did during World War II.

CHAPTER 11

LIEUTENANT GENERAL TADAMICHI KURIBAYASHI

"The weak-willed man makes mistakes. Willpower is the essence of manhood. A man's strength is determined by the strength of his will."

—**Lieutenant General Tadamichi Kuribayashi**[567]

KURIBAYASHI, THE COMMANDING OFFICER OF Iwo Jima, was an innovative leader with a unique background. He was born into a *samurai* family on 7 July 1891 in Nagano Prefecture and displayed exceptional abilities early on. After attending the IJA Academy, he ranked second in his class, an impressive achievement. He was also taller than the average Japanese man of his generation, standing 5'9" and weighing 200 pounds. Later, what really set Kuribayashi apart from most IJA generals was his time spent in North America.

In 1928, when he was a captain, the IJA honored Kuribayashi with an educational tour in America. It was a rare privilege for an officer, and he embarked on a three-year journey across the United States.[568] During this time, he studied at Harvard University, similar to Admiral Isoroku Yamamoto, although Yamamoto never finished his studies there whereas Kuribayashi did. At Harvard, he immersed himself in his courses in English, American history, and U.S. current affairs.[569] Even though he attended this Ivy League University, it seems he did not apply himself because he finished at the bottom of his English class, earning a D+ (it's possible his duties gathering intelligence hurt his studies).[570] Additionally, he attended the U.S. Army War College, enjoyed the works of Shakespeare and Carl Sandburg's *Lincoln*, watched tackle football games, and engaged with numerous Americans. He also acquired a Chevrolet K automobile and learned how to drive under the guidance of an American officer, embarking thereafter on a remarkable 1,000-mile cross-country trip. These experiences left a lasting impression on Kuribayashi of the strength of American citizens and their nation, writing: "The United States is the last country in the world Japan should fight. Its industrial potential is huge and fabulous, and the people are energetic and versatile. One must never underestimate the American fighting ability."[571]

Furthermore, he underwent training with the U.S. Army at Fort Bliss, Texas, where he gained firsthand knowledge of the caliber of the American fighting man. The base commander, Brigadier General George Van Horn Moseley, forged a friendly bond with Kuribayashi and gifted him a signed photograph along with an inscription with these heartfelt words: "I shall never forget our happy association together in America. Best wishes to you and Japan."[572] Promoted to major in August 1931, Kuribayashi continued his North America journey as a military attaché in Canada at the Japanese legation, where he served for an additional two and a half years until December 1933.[573]

In addition to his military career and extensive travels, Kuribayashi held a deep love for his wife and family, cherishing their bond immensely. However, it is regrettable to note that he engaged in relationships with "Comfort Women" while stationed in China.[574] Despite this flaw, when he was away from home, he dedicated himself to writing heartfelt letters and even illustrated his experiences for his beloved son and daughters. Within the family circle, he displayed a gentle and caring nature towards his women, while his interactions with his son were marked by strictness. As a boy, his son would grow into an adult who would carry on the *samurai* tradition of his ancestors of the esteemed Matsushiro clan. Kuribayashi embodied the values of a traditional Japanese man, instilling in his sons the ways of the warrior and nurturing his daughters to become supportive wives and mothers, upholding their crucial roles in society.[575]

Many have an imperfect understanding of the *samurai* culture (literal meaning of *samurai* 侍 is "those who serve").[576] These men were poets, leaders, politicians, warriors, fathers, and husbands. While different sects existed, the essence of *samurai* life can be described as spartan. Kuribayashi's grandson, Yoshitaka Shindo, sheds light on this way of life:

> To be *Samurai*, one must be strong and learn how to fight. Yet, to be *Samurai*, one must demonstrate strength for the sake of others, and at the same time, one must be kind to the people who should be protected. Happiness of others must coincide with the happiness of oneself. One must hold the right convictions and the right beliefs so in the view of others, his actions would not bring shame on himself or those he serves or commands.[577]

Guided by these principles, Kuribayashi fulfilled his responsibilities as an officer, steadily advancing through the ranks.

Upon returning to Japan from Canada in 1933, Kuribayashi's career took various turns within the military. Initially, he served in the Main Ordnance, Military Service Department of the War Ministry. Then, in August 1936, he assumed command of the 7th Calvary Regiment, leading a contingent of 500 men until August 1937.[578] At the end of his command of the regiment, he obtained the rank of colonel and thereafter became the divisional chief of the "Remount Administrative Section, Military Service Bureau of the War Ministry," which brought him in touch with IJA supply and mobilization capabilities.[579] His specialty within this ministry was horses. He was tasked with increasing the number, size, and strength of horses and became the chief organizer for horse husbandry. Despite Japan having 1.5 million horses in 1937, he embarked on efforts to expand this population. He acquired 7,500 stallions for breeding purposes and coordinated the transfer of thousands of horses to China to support the over one million troops engaged there. For example, when Hirohito ordered the takeover of Chinese cities at Beijing and Tientsin in July 1937, he deployed 209,000 troops with 54,000 horses. During this period, horses played a crucial role in the transportation of supplies and artillery pieces for the military. It was a critical job for militaries during operations (Hitler sent 625,000 horses in support of his 3.5 million soldiers when they invaded Russia on 21 June 1941 for example). Although no detailed numbers were given, during Kuribayashi's tenure at this post until March 1940, he met with success—he produced stronger and more horses.[580] Many of these horses were utilized by General Matsui during his invasion of northern China, including the infamous takeover of Nanking in 1937, an event that held such widespread news attention Kuribayashi could not have been unaware of it.[581] In fact, during his subsequent command in Hong Kong, it was observed that numerous officers under Kuribayashi's command rode "exceptionally fine horses, proof of the reports that for the last fifty years the Japanese have been buying up the finest Arab stallions and breeding the showiest possible mounts for their high officers."[582] He even dabbled in propaganda efforts for his units. For instance, in 1940, his department contributed to the production of the film *Praying at Dawn*, which showcased the vital role of war horses within the Imperial Japanese Army and glorified their achievements in China.[583] Overall, Kuribayashi's involvement in horse procurement and management showcased his organizational skills and ability to contribute to the military's operational needs during this time.

With his firsthand knowledge of America's capabilities and industrial might, Kuribayashi expressed his concerns to his superiors before 1941 about making the U.S. a major enemy. He warned them that in the event of war, the U.S. peacetime industry could transform overnight to produce vast quantities of munitions that could overpower anything Japan could muster. Despite Kuribayashi's efforts to convey to his superiors the danger an enemy like America posed, "they didn't get it," and ignored his warnings.[584]

Soon after his tenure in the "Remount Administrative Section," he assumed the role of the chief of staff[585] for General Takashi Sakai's 23rd Army stationed in China. It was during this time that they conducted war games and, under secret orders, meticulously planned the invasion of Hong Kong to coincide with the Pearl Harbor attack. As part of the preparations for this assault, Kuribayashi contributed to the strategic plans that gave special attention to attacking pillboxes (knowledge he would use later during the Battle of Iwo Jima).[586]

He also had the responsibility of disseminating the instructions from an Imperial conference held in Tokyo on 5 November 1941. These instructions implored the forces under his and Sakai's command to "behave themselves." Since "the eyes of the world would be watching," the Japanese government wanted its troops invading southern China to not repeat "the excesses committed by the Japanese soldiers on the Chinese mainland."[587] Of course, Kuribayashi understood what his government was asking him to command his troops to do—they were not to practice the Nanking-like crimes they had been committing on the northern Chinese.[588] Indeed, Kuribayashi's subordinate, 38th Division commander, Major General Sano, duly conveyed the order to his regiments "to treat any British and other Allied prisoners they might take in Hong Kong with humanity and justice," especially the Indian auxiliaries, whom the Japanese believed had been coerced into fighting for their colonial masters.[589] However, despite these efforts, Sakai, Kuribayashi, and Sano would ultimately fail miserably in ensuring that their troops would comply with this directive in such a way that they would obey it. As historian Philip Snow astutely observed: "It was one thing to urge moderation on the relatively educated officer caste; quite another to implant it in the line troops, who were for the most part ignorant, xenophobic and brutalized by a training intended to turn them into mindless fighting machines."[590]

One could argue that changing the behavior of these men, who had grown accustomed to raping and killing during their campaigns, would have been challenging if for no other reason than that they had no theoretical, moral, nor ethical codes that forbade such actions. As Snow further pointed out, "so the... rank and file troops [under Sakai, Kuribayashi, and Sano]...had learned in the course of [the Second Sino-Japanese War] to perceive the Chinese masses as less than human. And it would seem that in the heat of triumph the habits of a decade were hard to break."[591] The Japanese were quite honest with how they viewed "inferior" people. For example, the Japanese journalist Shigeharu Matsumoto, working for *Domei News Agency* in Shanghai, interviewed a Kwantung staff officer, Colonel Ryūkichi Tanaka, who admitted: "To be perfectly frank, the ways you [Matsumoto] and I look at the Chinese are fundamentally different. You seem to think of them as human, but I see them as pigs."[592] The tragic events of soldiers slaughtering non-Japanese in Hong Kong solely based on their nationality unfortunately confirmed the observations made by Snow and Matsumoto in spades and substantiated that the moral orders Sakai, Kuribayashi, and Sano issued were never honored.

Just one hour after the assault on Pearl Harbor, the 23rd Army launched its attack on the British Crown Colony of Hong Kong, located on the southern coast of China. The operation was codenamed *Hara-Saku*, meaning "Haller Work," striking the colony from the rear with the hope of driving the 12,000 British, Canadian, Indian, and Chinese troops toward the sea.[593] Despite Churchill's public encouragement for the garrison to never surrender, he knew that no immediate relief could be provided by his command there and that they would soon run out of suuplies forcing them to surrender. The Allied troops were in a perilous position, reliant on a potential attack from a Nationalist army to the north for their salvation. The hope was that the Chinese forces, led by General Yu Hanmou, commander of Seventh War Zone (12th Army Group) under Chiang Kai-Shek, would be able to launch a counterattack and strike the rear of the IJA 23rd Army.[594] However, Hanmou required until January to properly organize his forces for an effective assault in support of the besieged defenders of Hong Kong. It was unclear whether the British could hold out the one month needed for the Chinese Nationalists to come to their aid.[595]

The 23rd Army consisted of three divisions: the 18th, 38th and 104th, totaling 48,000 men. Kuribayashi issued orders and coordinated units as Sakai's chief of staff when launching the attack on 8 December, initially deploying 15,000 men across the border. He took charge of the "Hong Kong capture operation," playing a prominent role with the 38th Division as it advanced into the peninsula.[596] As the Japanese troops flooded into the Kowloon peninsula, Chinese families took desperate measures to hide their daughters in basement hovels, in attics, or in closets. Many locked their whole family in their cramped homes. "Women skulked out of sight of the troops and wore dingy black as a form of protective coloring. To reduce their attraction still further, they hunched their backs, daubed their faces with mud, and wore sanitary pads irrespective of the time of the month."[597] The city, with an estimated one million refugees fleeing the conflicts unleashed by Japan in China and Manchuria, was well aware of the horrors that awaited it. In an attempt to reassure the population, General Sakai ordered his staff to post a "reassurance proclamation" throughout the Kowloon peninsula, declaring: "We protect Chinese property. The war in Hong Kong is a war against the Whites."[598] However, as the actions of his troops would soon reveal, these words rang hollow.

Later, Kuribayashi helped conduct the amphibious assault on Hong Kong Island on 18 December, following the successful push of Allied troops into a full retreat from the mainland to the isle. The British forces had initially believed they could hold out on the island for months, but as events would soon reveal, their hopes were unfounded. Preparing for the attack on Hong Kong Island, Kuribayashi issued orders to various units, coordinating their assaults to hit the beaches on Hong Kong Island.

Ramped boats were assembled along the shores of the mainland, as Kuribayashi oversaw the order to carry at least 10,000 men in an amphibious invasion against the isle traversing a mile of ocean of Victoria Harbor. In total, they had three 47-feet-long *Daihatsu* ramped landing craft capable of carrying 70 men, 18 35-feet-long *Shohatsu* landing craft that could ferry 35 men, and 200 13.6-feet-long collapsible boats that could transport 20 men each. The goal was to ensure the success of these assaults, unlike previous failed attempts on 15–16 December when the Japanese landing parties were caught by searchlights and repelled by Commonwealth troops during a night crossing. Despite these initial failures, the landing for 18 December was hastily thrown together and lacked sufficient planning. The Japanese admitted later it was a "boar-like blind rush" (*chototsu-mōshin*) "without adequate intelligence about the British or cooperation with Japanese artillery." Nevertheless, the landing proceeded, and the battle-hungry Japanese troops crossed the channel in two waves, totaling 7,500 men. They made landfall at the districts of North Point and Shaukeiwan.

Kuribayashi quickly learned the challenges posed by the British pillboxes and their crossfire, causing confusion and casualties. However, the IJA eventually overcame these obstacles. As they penetrated the island, they faced fierce resistance at the Stanley fortifications. Kuribayashi felt impressed by how difficult it was to locate weak spots and prevent crossfire from these fortified positions. The British especially utilized crossfire near the narrow entrance of Stanley Village, employing a two-pounder anti-tank gun, machinegun positions, and a searchlight beam. They managed to destroy three Japanese Type-94 tankettes and cut down several soldiers. Kuribayashi later drew from this experience to design his Iwo Jima defense.[599]

During this engagement, Kuribayashi's unorthodox and rebellious nature became evident as he defended Colonel Teihichi Doi's aggressive disobedience to orders at the battle's beginning. He also visited wounded men in field hospitals, an unheard-of act for a senior IJA commander.[600] Within a week after landing on the island, the Japanese had deployed at least 20,000 soldiers to conquer the British colony.[601] Since the Commonwealth units, as well as a few Nationalist Chinese naval outfits, had not trained long with one another, and had not prepared the island for defense, the Japanese units successfully overran them.

On 25 December, which became known as Black Christmas for the Allied troops, Hong Kong fell into Japanese hands.[602] As the British raised the white flag over Victoria Barracks, the victorious Japanese soldiers marched in, shouting, "*Banzai! Banzai!*" Kuribayashi had played a significant role in delivering a devastating "blow to the British in Asia [and helped]…deprive Chiang Kai-shek's [China] of a window to the world."[603]

The British forces suffered 3,445 casualties, while the Japanese reported 2,118.[604] Since Hong Kong had become a "symbol of British determination to restrain Japan, and a more subtle symbol for British support of Chinese resistance," this victory became highly significant both psychologically and militarily for Japan.[605] The conquering of Hong Kong also severed the vital supply route of 100,000 tons of goods that Chiang Kai-Shek had been receiving through this port, a large percentage of what he received from the outside world.[606]

The battle lasted much longer and resulted in higher casualties than the Japanese had initially anticipated. The pre-battle planning, primarily led by Kuribayashi under Sakai's command, "was inadequate at best."[607] The Japanese achieved victory primarily due to their overwhelming numerical superiority over the British forces.

Kuribayashi remained with the 23rd Army for eighteen months after the defeat of Hong Kong, carrying out occupational duties. His exceptional leadership skills led to his promotion to lieutenant general in 1943. In June of that year, he left China and returned to Japan, where he was assigned to the prestigious position of commanding the Emperor's Tokyo Division (Imperial Guards).[608] However, he eventually lost this post, possibly due to an incident where one of his cadets set fire to "one of the barracks, so he 'was fired.'"[609]

Even with this professional setback, in April 1944, he was appointed to defend Iwo. By May, the army officially selected him as the island's commander. On 27 May, he had a private meeting with Emperor Hirohito, an uncommon "honor for a commoner."[610] Kuribayashi returned home from this sacred encounter filled with excitement, as it was one of the most remarkable events in his life.[611] During their conversation, Emperor Hirohito emphasized the importance of preventing the Americans from invading Japan's main islands. He told Kuribayashi, "Only you among all generals is qualified and capable of holding this post. The entire army and nation will depend on you."[612] The significance of Kuribayashi's mission was further underscored by a meeting with Prime Minister Tōjō, who admonished him to perform well and either secure a victory or lead his garrison to fight to the last man in their defense.[613] Over a week later, on 8 June 1944, Kuribayashi officially assumed command of Iwo.[614]

Before praying to his ancestors and "begging for their blessing and guidance on his mission," Kuribayashi expressed his unwavering determination to fight to the end in a letter to his brother. He stated, "I will fight as a son of Kuribayashi, the *Samurai*, and will behave in such a manner as to deserve the name of Kuribayashi. May my ancestors guide me."[615] These were not mere words for Kuribayashi. In the Shintō religion, everyone was taught from birth to respect and revere the *kami*, the spirits of the household clan and the imperial ancestors. It was believed that these spirits intimately influenced one's life and neglecting them would bring about misfortune for the warrior. Kuribayashi also wrote to his wife before the Battle of Iwo Jima, expressing his belief that his soul would join other warriors at the Yasukuni shrine and live on with other warriors after his impending death.[616] This belief in the continuity of the soul and the connection to ancestral spirits was deeply ingrained in Japanese culture and religious traditions. Kuribayashi's grandson, Yoshitaka Shindo, delved into these beliefs and their significance, stating:

> What makes Japan dear to the heart? It is the knowledge that the energy, the work, the fruits of the labor of past generations live in the soil, the rocks and the buildings of the land. The cause was indeed to die for the emperor, but the Emperor was symbolic of those things dear to the Japanese since He and His royal line have been around for 2,600 years. The gods we worship are symbolic of larger feelings about nature...our world and...culture. To be Japanese is to focus on the...nation, past and present, as a nation full of loved ones and those loved ones include *kami*, gods, spirits—one might say sacred energy or inner voice. Worshiping our ancestors' souls and dying for them and the emperor make a Japanese Japanese. Not to focus on these spirits and the emperor would be shame on oneself and family.[617]

This religious fervor fortified Kuribayashi's resolve. One of his guiding forces to defend Iwo was his conviction he was protecting his divine country, one that admonished all to "Honor the Gods and serve loyally their descendants [the emperors]," creating a martial religion for "a race of warriors."[618]

Over the course of several months, Kuribayashi transformed Iwo Jima into one of the most impressive fortifications any Axis commander built, showcasing his remarkable military skills. With an unwavering resolve, Kuribayashi assembled a garrison of 22,000 men who would fight to the death, including himself. Their objective was to inflict significant losses on the American forces. They would accomplish this goal in an impressive manner, inflicting 7,000 deaths and 19,000 casualties on the Americans. This would prove to be the most formidable resistance any Japanese commander offered against the Americans during the Pacific War. Kuribayashi was nothing if not an organized and intelligent fanatic. He hoped to make the Americans give up their desire to conquer Japan by looking at how zealously his men would defend sovereign territory. Kuribayashi's main strategic goal was to inflict massive casualties against the Americans, and in this regard, he would prove quite effective. But even though his battle plan was sound, his ultimate "object was mad."[619] It was sound in that he was prepared to inflict maximum damage on the enemy, but mad in that by doing so, there was no hope America would settle for less than total victory and unconditional surrender. He forced the Americans to rethink their strategy, but not necessarily in the manner he had hoped. Instead of causing the U.S. to shrink from war, it motivated America to intensify its bombing of Japan and drop the atomic bombs on two of its major cities to prevent further battles like Iwo Jima. Neither Kuribayashi, Tōjō, nor Hirohito understood that the excessive cost of victory through conventional means at Iwo Jima would make the deployment of super-weapons against Japan an inevitable reality.[620] Their failure to anticipate the consequences of their actions played a significant role in shaping the subsequent events of the war. Kuribayashi would die on Iwo Jima, and America would continue its aggressive march toward Japan thereafter.

CHAPTER 12

THE RAPE OF ASIA AND HONG KONG UNDER KURIBAYASHI

"Do not stand idly by while your neighbor's blood is being shed."
—**Talmud** [Jewish Oral Bible][621]

MANY JAPANESE SOLDIERS WHOM THE Allies battled against during WWII were veterans of Japan's brutal, criminal warfare. Among them was Iwo Jima garrison's commander, Lieutenant General Tadamichi Kuribayashi. Had he survived the war, he would likely have faced charges for crimes against humanity and peace.[622] Here are only a few of his misdeeds catalogued below.

In April 1939, Kuribayashi toured Manchuria and China as divisional chief of the "Remount Administrative Section, Military Service Bureau of the War Ministry," where he gathered data on the logistics needs of the IJA.[623] During his time there, he must have witnessed the Manchurian operation was "a mad carnival of debauchery carried out by gangs of ignorant bullies."[624] Enemy combatants there were labelled "bandits" and universally "exterminat[ed]" when taken prisoner.[625] Sometimes the "bandits'" villages also were "liquidated" as evidenced by the Pingdingshan (P'ingtingshan) Incident in September 1932 when Japanese troops executed 3,000 citizens, because everyone was assumed to have supported the "guerillas."[626] Similar massacres had occurred just a month before in three towns near Fushun, were 2,700 civilians were slaughtered for allegedly aiding insurgents. The commander of Kwantung Army, General Baron Shigeru Honjō, justified these killings of innocent women and children as part of a plan to "exterminate bandits."[627] Upon his return to Japan, Honjō was hailed as a war hero and subsequently appointed as Hirohito's *aide-de-camp*.

146

It is highly likely that Kuribayashi was aware of these activities taking place under the leadership of Japanese commanders before his visit to Manchuria.

Prisoners were also cruelly labelled as "bandits" and subjected to horrific human experiments by Unit 731, a biological and chemical warfare laboratory based in Manchuria. These inhumane trials ultimately led to the prisoners' deaths. Given Kuribayashi's expertise in logistics for operations in China, he could not have been unaware of the existence of this killing center.[628]

The atrocities committed by Unit 731 were also well-known among many Manchurians, who hated the Japanese for these heinous acts. The Japanese themselves were aware of this animosity, and Kuribayashi was most assuredly briefed on this fact. To prove this point, multimillionaire and businessman Kinmochi Okura expressed his observations after visiting Manchuria at this time, stating: "Under the present circumstances, if a war breaks out between Japan and Russia, *all Manchurians* will rise in revolt against the Japanese [author's italics]."[629] This sentiment reflects again the profound anger and hostility that many Manchurians felt towards their Japanese oppressors, and Kuribayashi was indeed one of them.

From September 1941 until June 1943, Kuribayashi served as the 23rd Army's chief of staff during the battle and occupation of Hong Kong, where numerous atrocities took place. Tragically, throughout the course of the short campaign, Kuribayashi's troops slaughtered defenseless POWs. For example, on 11 December 1941, after seizing ten "unresisting" British Royal Army Medical Corps officers and privates, as well as eight wounded Canadians, the Japanese stabbed them with bayonets and cut off their heads "amid shouts of laughter."[630] Furthermore, a day before the British surrendered on 25 December, a certain Japanese flag officer known as General Spinach due to his weird mustache gathered 150 civilians and forced a group of Commonwealth prisoners to stand in front of them, their hands tied behind their backs. In a horrifying display, the prisoners were executed in full view of the civilians. Shockingly, none of the Japanese present saw anything wrong with the actions. Later, a Chinese coolie who recognized his master among this civilian group approached them with his hands above his head, only to be impaled with a bayonet by a soldier.[631] Other coolies were subjected to further cruelty, being used as test cases for some soldiers to practice their ju-jitsu moves on. After several of them were no longer able to fight or stand due to their broken bones, the soldiers would then cut off their heads using swords.[632] In Happy Valley, numerous civilians were tied up outside their homes on their fences and either bayoneted to death or decapitated. The streets were strewn with the bodies of innocent victims, and to further compound the horror, IJA truck drivers took sadistic pleasure in running over these corpses, deliberately veering out of their lanes for that purpose.[633] It is deeply distressing to note that there are no documented records suggesting that Kuribayashi made any efforts to stop these abhorrent acts committed against prisoners of war and innocent civilians.

During the conflict and in the aftermath of the city's conquest, the Japanese perpetrated widespread rape: "Over 10,000 Chinese [and foreign] women, from the early teens to the sixties, are reckoned to have been raped or gang-raped by the Japanese...during the sack of Hong Kong."[634] However, this number was a dramatic "underestimation" according to the head of the Hong Kong Sanatorium and Hospital, Dr. Shu-Fan Li, an eyewitness to these crimes who rendered medical care to victims.[635] Dr. Li believed that tripling the estimated figure would not be an exaggeration. Among the targeted victims, Catholic nuns were especially sought out by Japanese soldiers since they believed them to be virgins.[636] One tall, stately 6'0" Australian nurse was raped repeatedly, but after the war, she defiantly reported: "It didn't hurt that much since all the little buggers had small pricks."[637] Was this nurse telling the truth or devising a story of defiance to help cope with her trauma? Either way, she was a victim of horrific behavior. Her flippant comments about Japanese manhood belie the fact many rape victims, even probably she herself, suffered psychological wounds. Some who survived these deplorable acts "walked and talked like zombies" afterwards, having suffered severe trauma.[638] Others throughout China "ended their own lives" while others "went insane."[639] Dr. Li wrote, "I...treated...women with their teeth bashed in, their noses broken, their bodies showing bayonet prods; wives so heavy with child that the assault had brought on miscarriage; and young...girls whose minds had been affected by the pain and horror of multiple rapes."[640] These fates were the reality for many rape victims who were fortunate enough to survive physically. The trauma inflicted upon these women was unimaginable, leaving deep scars that would last a lifetime.

Later, in a horrifying incident at St. Stephen's College, seven nurses were "dragged, crying and writhing," to a room full of already butchered men. Once there, IJA soldiers held them down on top of a pile of dead, ripped off their clothing, and gang-raped them. After several finished raping a nurse, others would bayonet her to death. Blood-curdling screams echoed throughout the halls as the men either thrusted their penises or their blades into the women. They would place the next victim on the burial mound next to her freshly killed colleague and then one soldier after another would violate her until someone made the decision she was no longer useful and would dispatch her to the "undiscovered country."[641] The room became a grotesque tableau of horror, with fresh victims continually joining their deceased colleagues on the burial mound. The gutters of St. Stephen's College, once a place of learning and hope, now "ran with blood."[642] One "Jap" later remarked these victims "cried like a lot of pigs," displaying a complete lack of empathy or regard for their humanity.[643] This chilling statement serves as only one example out of thousands of the magnitude of the dehumanization and cruelty inflicted upon these innocent women.

In an alarming act of cruelty, a British lieutenant, held as a prisoner of war, pleaded with a Japanese officer to allow him to see his wife, who was among the nurses at St. Stephen's College. The officer took the unsuspecting prisoner outside the building to a stack of lifeless bodies. There, the lieutenant witnessed the brutal violation of his wife, her nude body covered in bruises, wounds, and blood. Overwhelmed by shock and anger, he attempted to attack his captors, but was quickly overpowered and thrown back into the storeroom with the other incarcerated POWs. Devastated, he succumbed to a state of incoherent babbling, descending into a catatonic state of shock as he rocked back and forth.[644] The surviving, semi-functional POWs were then ordered by their captors to gather the bodies of their fallen comrades and nurses, numbering over a hundred, and pile them outside in the courtyard. Then, they were forced to set fire to this macabre pyre. As the bodies burned, guards laughed nearby.[645]

Canadian Army chaplain James Barrett, who witnessed the aftermath of this massacre, described the dreadful scene of this crime:

> The next day I made a tour of the [St. Stephen's College] hospital. It was in a dreadful state. I found the two men who had been taken out of our room. Their bodies were badly mutilated, their ears, tongues, noses and eyes had been cut away from their faces. About 70 or more wounded men had been killed by bayonets…In the bushes…we found the bodies of the…dead nurses, one of whom had her head practically severed from her body.[646]

The lack of compassion displayed by the Japanese soldiers towards the hospital patients and those who cared for them reveals a twisted and tyrannical mindset. It is deeply troubling that Kuribayashi, as the commander, *never once* raised his voice in opposition to these heinous acts. This failure reflects his defective leadership that was psychopathic at its core. Decadently, one might add, he protested the ill treatment meted out to Colonel Doi for his disobeying orders by being too aggressive in his combat tactics, but he did not protest his men cutting off the heads of raped nurses or the slicing off of body parts of hospital patients.[647] Such crimes were unfortunately common throughout the campaign and its aftermath, further highlighting the depths of depravity reached by the Japanese forces.

As a further example of these crimes, after hostilities ceased in one area now controlled by the Japanese, a British businessman was having dinner with his wife and teenage daughter when IJA troops barged into his home, tied him to a chair, and then raped his wife in front of him and their child.[648] Upon this unsuspecting population, Japan had unleashed a generation of psychopaths, manifesting mental disorders, and abnormal and violent social behavior. Such were the men under Kuribayashi's command. Such was Kuribayashi who never protested these crimes.

The actions of Kuribayashi's troops in Hong Kong were nothing short of despicable. And in addition to his troops raping women in the city by the thousands, they also pitilessly murdered countless civilians, resulting in at least 4,000 killed during the battle and 50,000 during the occupation.[649] As a British eyewitness noted, the attack on Hong Kong was accompanied with a strong "taste of Nanking."[650] On 12 December, the first night spent on Hong Kong Island by the Allied troops, was an indescribable nightmare for them as they heard the echoes of screams from the mainland, serving as a chilling reminder of the rampant rape and murder being carried out by the Japanese soldiers.[651] As Kuribayashi was deployed in this sector, it is inconceivable that he could have been oblivious to these criminal acts. Yet, once again, he failed to take any action or intervene to prevent these atrocities.

During his address to the House of Commons, British Foreign Secretary Anthony Eden candidly exposed the disturbing violence committed by the Japanese forces in Hong Kong. He described Japan's adherence to *Bushido* as "nauseating hypocrisy" in light of their destruction in property and lives at Hong Kong. He then noted the IJA had "perpetrated against their helpless military prisoners and civil population…the same kind of barbarities which aroused the horror of the civilized world at the time of the Nanking massacre of 1937…It is known that women both Asiatic and European were raped and murdered."[652] He concluded that the barbaric "little men" had executed defenseless POWs in cold blood.[653] The Japanese executed most of the wounded and POWs they found, numbering in the hundreds, outright crimes against the principle of *hors de combat*.[654] As mentioned before, others were mutilated: "Soldiers cut out one man's tongue and chopped off another man's ears."[655] While the screams of these victims rang out in the Red Cross Hospital, IJA soldiers gouged out others' eyes and sliced off limbs and noses. Almost 100 defenseless Commonwealth soldiers were slaughtered at this hospital, many dying by blade thrusts while laying sick in their beds.[656]

During the occupation of Hong Kong, the Japanese raped, killed, and resettled tens of thousands of natives that devastated the local population. This once vibrant city saw its population dwindled from 1.6 million in 1941 to just 600,000 in 1945 due to a combination of forced evacuations, resettlement, murder, disease and starvation.[657] In the immediate aftermath of the IJA's takeover of Hong Kong, the 23rd Army "chopped off a few hundred heads a day for some time."[658] "Guidelines adopted by the 23rd Army" and sanctioned by Kuribayashi called for the "immediate suppression of hostile influences"; namely, all Communist or Nationalist elements were to be "imprisoned or liquidated."[659] The consequences were grim, and by New Year's Day, a former playing field in Hong Kong was "piled high with the corpses of Chinese who had been bayoneted or shot."[660] The actions of the *Kempei Tai* in Kowloon at King's Park were relentless, using citizens "for shooting and bayonet practice and even beheading some."[661] By the end of January 1942, corpses littered Hong Kong's coastline.[662] Unlike in Nanking, there was no International Safety Zone to offer protection to the citizens of Hong Kong, as Japan's belligerence had severed any hope of honoring such agreements since it was at war with the world by now.

The 23rd Army proved to be a disastrous city administrator, leaving Hong Kong in a state of chaos and despair. "The colony lay prostrate in the absence of any firm order. The streets were a mess of corpses and shell-holes and severed lines, and the harbor was clogged with the sunken hulls of two hundred vessels."[663] The once thriving colony now lay prostrate, ravaged by the absence of any semblance of order or stability.

Several months later, on 25 September 1942, a catastrophic event unfolded involving 1,816 British POWs under the control of Kuribayashi. They were forced to board the *Lisbon Maru* bound for Japan, a ship woefully inadequate for the number of prisoners it held. Originally designed to accommodate only 28 passengers, the ship became a nightmarish multi-level cattle hold with no proper sanitation facilities, insufficient food, and limited water for the inmates. Those confined in the lower decks were subjected to the constant filth of their fellow prisoners, enduring showers of diarrhea, urine, and defecation of the men above them. Those who died due to disease or sickness were unceremoniously thrown overboard. The grim conditions aboard made it a true "hell-ship." On 1 October 1942, the American submarine USS *Grouper*, unaware of the "cargo" aboard the *Lisbon Maru*, torpedoed it. The Japanese crew battened down the hatches on the rooms where the POWs were confined and then abandoned ship, hoping it would be the final mass grave for these Allied soldiers. Meanwhile, safely in their lifeboats, the Japanese sailors made their way to nearby ships in this fleet. Some of the Allied prisoners eventually managed to break free from the ship and ascend to the top decks, only to be met with machinegun fire from Japanese sailors on other neighboring ships. As the *Lisbon Maru* took on water, one compartment remained sealed, and the haunting sound of the doomed men singing in beautiful harmony "It's a Long Way to Tipperary" was the last thing the survivors heard from their doomed comrades. Eventually, the Japanese sailors ceased their gunfire as the torpedoed ship disappeared beneath the waves. On 5 October, the Allied survivors, now aboard other ships in the fleet, arrived at Shanghai. They were mustered, and a roll call was conducted, revealing the devastating news that 840 of their comrades had lost their lives during this treacherous journey.[664] This criminal act, and many others, serves as a testament to Kuribayashi's uncaring attitude toward POWs.

Kuribayashi never protested such crimes that are now known as crimes against humanity. As an obsessive man of detail and micromanager of troops, Kuribayashi had to not only have known of these crimes, but also had to have supported and/or ordered them.[665] He was not one to shy away from challenging commanders when he thought them wrong.[666] Kuribayashi was stationed during part of the battle at Kowloon where "the murder of civilians, looting, plunder, serious abuse, and sexual violence" became routine.[667] The IJA "systematically looted the city because it stored useful resources such as food, motor vehicles, medical and scientific equipment, but it was in a rather 'orderly manner' because it was organized by the 23rd Army."[668] Kuribayashi's commanding officer, 23rd Army commander Lieutenant General Takashi Sakai, was later executed at the Chinese war crime trials in Nanking in 1946 for his actions during the Rape of Hong Kong.[669] The Tribunal wrote: "All the evidence goes to show that [Sakai] knew of the atrocities committed by his subordinates [like Kuribayashi] and deliberately let loose savagery upon civilians and prisoners of war."[670] The sentence further read:

> The defendant, Takashi Sakai, having been found guilty of participating in the war of aggression and having been found guilty of inciting or permitting his subordinates [Kuribayashi was his highest-ranking subordinate] to murder prisoners-of-war, wounded soldiers and non-combatants; to rape, plunder, deport civilians; to indulge in cruel punishment and torture; and to cause destruction of property, is hereby sentenced to DEATH.[671]

For one disturbing example out of hundreds that illustrate the grotesque nature of Sakai's command, he allowed two subordinates to rape two women, mutilate their bodies and then feed their butchered body parts to dogs in a

Jeffrey Dahmer-like manner.[672] Just like Lieutenant General Yamashita and his right-hand man, 25th Army's chief of operations Lieutenant Colonel Tsuji, committed thousands of war crimes in Malaya and Singapore as a team, General Sakai and his right-hand man, 23rd Army's chief of staff Lieutenant General Kuribayashi, performed Nanking-like rape, looting, and murder while conquering Hong Kong and its surrounding region.

Lieutenant General Takashi Sakai and Lieutenant General Tadamichi Kuribayashi lead their victorious troops of the 23rd Army through the streets of Hong Kong on 28 December 1941 (Kuribayashi occupies the central position in this image, positioned directly behind Sakai, who was leading the procession). All during this time, their troops murdered and raped innocent civilians throughout the city. *National Archives, College Park*

After leading a triumphant march through Victoria's center on 28 December, Sakai and Kuribayashi gave their victorious troops a "three-day 'holiday'" in which they engaged in rampant acts of rape, pillage, and plunder throughout the city.[673] Sakai's history of such behavior dated back to his time in China, most notably the butchering of people at the Jinan battle in May 1928, where he slaughtered thousands of innocent civilians. His men had been conditioned to carry out such actions, and this behavior was *normal Japanese behavior*.[674] Out of 123 who stood trial at Hong Kong, 21 were executed, many junior in rank and responsibility to Kuribayashi *and under his command*.[675]

Had Kuribayashi survived the war, he probably would have been right next to them during their trials. Historian Dennis Showalter remarked, "Kuribayashi's poor leadership and support of the crimes in his region of operations in China would've definitely put him in the cross hairs of the war trials after the war."[676] Historian Philip Snow highlights the failure of Kuribayashi's leadership, writing: "Few officers [at Hong Kong] seem to have made any notable effort to hold the men back, and one or two were even prodding them to commit their excesses."[677] Additionally, men under Kuribayashi, like commanding officers Ryossaburo Tanaka of the 299th Regiment and Takeo Ito of the 298th Infantry Unit of the 38th Division, slaughtered defenseless POWs and were convicted of war crimes after the war.[678] Tanaka issued orders to kill all "prisoners of war."[679] Kuribayashi was above Tanaka, and orders usually did not get issued to the chain of command without a superior's sign-off.

Under Kuribayashi's command, the POW camps in Hong Kong and its region experienced numerous avoidable deaths, which were largely attributed to the actions of his subordinates. Colonel Isao Tokunaga, who served as the commandant of all camps, carried out policies and actions under Kuribayashi's orders that led to unnecessary loss of life.[680] In fact, Takunaga's medical doctor in charge of the POWs' physical welfare, Captain Shunkichi Saito, caused much death through his gross medical negligence.[681] Despite Kuribayashi visiting these camps, the prevailing pattern of senseless death persisted.[682] This suggests once again a failure of leadership and morality on Kuribayashi's part to address and rectify the dire conditions and mistreatment of these POWs, which violated numerous international laws.

According to Hong Kong's war crimes judge and prosecutor Major Murray Ormsby, the burden of proof to convict someone of war crimes was to prove their subordinates acted against the laws of war and committed atrocities, which Kuribayashi's subordinates did on a massive scale.[683] USMC Colonel Mant Hawkins, advisor to the commander of Centcom 2005–07 and director of Global Combatting Terrorism Network Special Operations Command 2007–08, stated, "As the chief of staff of the 23rd Army, Kuribayashi knew about everything Sakai and their men did. That no action was taken to curtail the atrocities is a testament to Kuribayashi's fascist mindset and brutal uncaring."[684] Presiding judge and Major General Russel Reynolds, in rendering a judgement about General Yamashita at his trial for the Rape of Manila, could have been writing about Kuribayashi when he proclaimed:

> Where murder and rape and vicious, revengeful actions are widespread offenses, and there is no effective attempt by a commander to discover

and control the criminal acts, such a commander may be held responsible, even criminally liable, for the lawless acts of his troops.[685]

General Yamashita's chief of staff, Lieutenant General Akira Mutō, was sentenced to death for his involvement in the Rape of Manila. Had Kuribayashi survived the war, he likely would have faced a similar fate as Sakai's chief of staff for failing to protect POWs and civilians during the Rape of Hong Kong. As General of the Army MacArthur said, "a soldier's duty included the protection of the weak and unarmed," a duty Kuribayashi shirked.[686] When discussing this with a retired Marine Corps lieutenant colonel and Japanese language expert, and cousin by marriage to Kuribayashi, he suggests that as chief of staff, Kuribayashi was limited in being able to change anything while at his Hong Kong command. According to this expert, if he had tried to stop the crimes he would have been killed.[687] The Tokyo War Crimes Tribunal disagreed with this assessment, writing that a chief of staff "was in a position to influence policy."[688] The Tribunal rejected the defense of ignorance, stating about Mutō, but it might as well have been for Kuribayashi:

> During his tenure of office a campaign of massacres, torture and other atrocities was waged by the Japanese troops on the civilian population, and prisoners of war and civilian internees were starved, tortured and murdered. Mutō shares responsibility for these gross breaches of the Laws of War. We reject his defense that he knew nothing of these occurrences. It is wholly incredible.[689]

As chief of staff, Kuribayashi had not only had a military duty, but also a legal obligation to put an end to the murders, rapes, and pillaging taking place. General of the Army MacArthur's assessment of Yamashita's leadership failures during the Manila incident resonates when describing Kuribayashi's actions, as they were "a blot upon the military profession [and] a stain upon civilization."[690]

After Hong Kong's fall, Kuribayashi continued his activities as chief of staff for the 23rd Army, which held control over Guangdong Province, the southernmost of the mainland provinces which channels most of South China's trade. It has one of the longest coastlines of any province and encompasses the cities of Hong Kong, Shenzhen, and Guangzhou (also known as Canton) where numerous crimes transpired of "Comfort Women," rape, murder, human medical experiments, and pillage, all under Kuribayashi's command. Unit 8604, akin to the notorious Unit 731, conducted horrible medical experiments on civilians in Canton, and this operation received the support of Kuribayashi's command.[691] Since Kuribayashi's 23rd Army controlled Guangdong Province for "security maintenance…maintenance of facilities such as airfields and economic measures (finance, currency, distribution of goods, [and total] control," he had to have known of these atrocities.[692] The 23rd Army served as the main hub for the IJA's "military training…and logistics base" in Guangdong that committed these crimes above.[693] Historian Robert Burrell writes: "Kuribayashi provided prominent leadership in…these horrific arenas where Japanese brutality was the norm."[694]

A massacre of civilians in Canton in 1938 by the Japanese military. The men who committed these atrocities were under General Kuribayashi's command. *Three Lions and Getty Images*

It does appear that under Kuribayashi's and Sakai's leadership, the 23rd Army did hold meetings to address the "rape epidemic" during the occupation. Months into the occupation, they did arrest some soldiers newly guilty of such crimes, though there was little effort to punish those who had already committed such transgressions. To mitigate future instances of rapes, the 23rd Army resorted to establishing brothels and actively looked for "non-family women to staff them. Posters appeared on the streets advertising for 'comfort women,' some hundreds of whom were recruited…[from] Guangdong Province."[695] Kuribayashi helped establish these prostitution houses, not because of his concern for the "Chinese victims of rape by [his] soldiers but because of [his] fear of creating antagonism among the Chinese civilians."[696] Sakai and Kuribayashi enlisted the assistance of their chief medical officer, Colonel T. Eguchi, who consulted with the head of the Hong Kong Sanatorium and Hospital, Dr. Shu-Fan Li, to gather 500 women (prostitutes) in one place for the creation of a large brothel so they could curb the raping epidemic.[697] Also, localizing the women being "used" allowed the medical personnel to better manage and reduce the spread of venereal diseases, something authorities worried about because such diseases "undermine the strength of their men (and hence their fighting ability)."[698] Since they needed more than these hundreds of local women to "service" the men, Kuribayashi and his staff imported an additional 1,700 Japanese prostitutes from Canton, treating them as mere "military supplies."[699] It is worth noting that Kuribayashi had already trucked in numerous Chinese and Russian women near the battle's end on 24 December—that these truckloads of women were sent there before the battle was even finished illustrates the meticulous planning involved in ensuring a steady supply of women to rape.[700] While senior officers visited "Comfort Women" alongside their men, it is interesting that Kuribayashi brought in Japanese prostitutes. These women, probably *geishas*, "were in a different position from the comfort women" in that they mainly serviced "high-ranking officers" and were given better food and accommodations.[701] Kuribayashi was not only taking care of his flag- and field-grade officers, but he was probably also taking care of his own personal needs. He and his command helped organize and take part in what would become "the largest and most elaborate system of trafficking in women in the history of mankind and one of the most brutal."[702]

After nine months since the fall of Hong Kong, a tragic consequence was observed in the city, and it was a definite certainty that similar occurrences took place in various regions. Dr. Li provided testimony about a significant increase in the number of newborns in Hong Kong, which he referred to as a massive "baby crop." He explained this tragedy thusly: "The loss of virginity, which is sacred in the eyes of the Chinese, the inflicting of venereal diseases upon innocent girls, and the army of enemy babies they carried in their bodies and finally bore—this was a mass crime which cannot be paid for by reparations."[703]

Kuribayashi and Sakai also implemented a deliberate strategy from the moment the "White" troops surrendered, to inflict the "maximum humiliation on the 10,000-odd British and Canadian soldiers who had fallen into Japanese hands."[704] They were beaten, forced to bow to Chinese citizens, required to collect trash in the streets, and garrisoned in some of the worst parts of the city. "[E]very opportunity was taken to drive home the message that the ethnic tables had been turned."[705] They were put under Colonel Tokunaga, nicknamed "the pig" by the inmates, who was "gross, cruel and sadistic" and subjected his prisoners to starvation diets and soon, all were wracked by "wound sepsis, dysentery and diphtheria...[and] deficiency diseases such as pellagra and beriberi."[706] All this occurred while Kuribayashi continued to labor away at Sakai's staff duties growing a nice, fat belly.[707]

Under the leadership of Sakai and Kuribayashi, a series of measures were implemented to assert Japanese dominance and control over the city. One significant aspect was the imposition of Japanese as the colony's official language, accompanied by the renaming of various areas using Japanese names. They also enforced the observance of religious festivals dedicated to honoring Hirohito and the Imperial forces. The "local citizens were expected to play a full part in them" or they would be punished.[708] As the Hong Kong landscape was Nipponized, a massive monument called *The Tower of Triumph* was constructed on a "spur of Mount Cameron overlooking the Wanchai District" designed to honor those who died fighting to conquer Hong Kong and glorify "Japanese power." As a symbol of their power, Sakai's and Kuribayashi's engineers embedded a *samurai* sword in the foundation, which was solemnized "by a bevy of Shintō priests dressed in white." Chinese leaders were forced to attend the ceremony, donate money, and display "their conversion to Japanese values."[709]

Like with most Japanese occupational duties, Sakai's and Kuribayashi's men continued to kill citizens for the slightest of offenses.[710] The actions in Hong Kong were part of a broader pattern seen throughout the Japanese Empire, where cultures and traditions of the conquered territories were systematically eradicated in an attempt to assimilate them into Japanese culture. Similar practices took place in other regions under Japanese control, such as Taiwan, Korea, Manchuria, and Guam. While the period following the battle witnessed widespread chaos and crimes in Hong Kong, by the summer of 1942, some semblance of order had been restored and efforts were made to rebuild the city as a functioning metropolis. However, the crimes perpetrated by the 23rd Army, led by Kuribayashi and Sakai, left an indelible stain on their legacies, forever associating them with the atrocities committed during their command.[711]

Similar to General Yamashita's defense of pleading *total* ignorance of his troops' crimes in the Philippines after the war, Lieutenant General Sakai also denied any knowledge of the atrocities committed by his troops, stating he was "not guilty to the charges concerning atrocities on the grounds that he was not responsible for the acts of his subordinates as he had *no knowledge of them* [author's italics]."[712] The ability for the Japanese to tell tall tales and think others could believe them with the evidence before them baffles the imagination. Either Sakai was one of the most vacuous commanding generals of the war bordering on being a total moron oblivious to everything around him or he was an out-and-out fraudster. The war crime trials recognized the implausibility of Sakai's claims that he was an idiot and ignoramus concerning his troops, and found him guilty of:

> ...inciting or permitting his subordinates to murder prisoners of war, wounded soldiers, nurses and doctors of the Red Cross and other non-combatants, and to commit acts of rape, plunder, deportation, torture and destruction of property, he had violated the Hague Convention concerning Laws and Customs of War on Land and the Geneva Convention of 1929. These offences are war crimes and crimes against humanity.[713]

The Tribunal wrote further that Sakai's claims of ignorance were utterly bogus since:

> ...a field Commander must hold himself responsible for the discipline of his subordinates [like Kuribayashi] as an accepted principle. It is inconceivable that he should not have been aware of the acts of atrocities committed by his subordinates...All the evidence goes to show that the defendant knew of the atrocities committed by his subordinates and deliberately let loose savagery upon civilians and prisoners of war.[714]

While with the 23rd Army, Kuribayashi also forced 1,600 conscripts from Korea to take care of horses in Guangdong, and while in command of Iwo Jima, he used the same number of Korean enslaved laborers (*senjin* or *chōkō*) to build defenses. During both duties, he knew full well most of these Koreans were there against their will.[715] So whether it was raping Chinese women, killing POWs, pillaging Chinese cities' resources, slaughtering civilians, dealing in human trafficking, or enslaving Korean men, the list of misdeeds Kuribayashi was *directly* responsible for was legion. He was intimately aware of the crimes committed by his country because he actively participated in them.

When Kuribayashi's grandson, Liberal Democratic Party (LDP) politician Yoshitaka Shindo, was asked about his grandfather's actions, he said,

> I must be honest. I don't know about what my grandfather did in Hong Kong. I only really learned about my grandfather and what he did at Iwo Jima when Clint Eastwood made his film...There were difficult things during the war. If you find things based on historical fact, then write them.[716]

Such honesty and integrity among Japanese politicians, especially those who are members of the LDP and of the revisionist group *Nippon Kaigi* (Japan Conference), are rare. For a man who uses his grandfather to further his political career, placing images of his grandfather in uniform on political posters next to pictures of himself, one might find it strange Shindo has not done more research or exercised more caution in using pictures of a man who led an army of rapists, murderers, and war criminals.

After examining the Rape of Nanking, the Rape of Singapore and Malaya, the Rape of Guam, and the Rape of Manila, one sees that the Rape of Hong Kong was not unique, but just another common way Japan practiced conquest in the lands it conquered. After watching Clint Eastwood's films about Kuribayashi, it could be hoped that one would have found Kuribayashi's behavior to have been different than what it was when he and his legions seized Hong Kong, but alas, while Kuribayashi was strong in thinking out of the box when it came to military matters, he was weak when it came to stopping mass murder and rape. Sadly, he encouraged mass murder and rape because that apparently was viewed universally as a good way to take over an enemy's territory and Kuribayashi embraced this *modus operandi* with enthusiasm.

CHAPTER 13

"COMFORT WOMEN": JAPANESE SEX-SLAVE CULTURE

"We are all born mad. Some remain so."
—**Samuel Beckett**, *Waiting for Godot*[717]

DURING THE ASIAN AND PACIFIC Wars, the Japanese military and government established numerous rape-centers throughout their empire, providing military personnel with easy access to sexual services. Japan's WWII sex slaves or "Comfort Women [*ianfu*]," as they were euphemistically called, have rarely been acknowledged by Japan's government. Using the term "Comfort Women," a term embraced by the perpetrators themselves, denies the victims an accurate description of what happened to them; namely, they were violated emotionally and physically, oftentimes murdered in the process. Therefore, when one studies this dark chapter of Japanese history, one needs to exercise caution when using the term "Comfort Woman," since such a term, still often used by the Japanese themselves, continues to perpetuate the oppression and marginalization of these women who were victimized by the Japanese who oppressed them.

During World War II, it is estimated by historians that a minimum of 200,000 women were systematically abused—it would not be an exaggeration to double this number. These women were tragically taken to stations in war zones, and many lost their lives when their brothels were attacked or overrun during combat. The age of these victims is particularly distressing, as the average age of these enslaved women was only 15 years old. Knowing this fact, one could easily argue the Japanese were not only rapists, but also pedophiles. Soldiers often raped girls between the ages of 10 and 15, many of whom died due to internal hemorrhage.[718] In some of their rape brothels, the Japanese imposed

161

daily quotas on women/girls: "[T]wenty enlisted men in the morning, two NCOs in the afternoon, and the senior officers at night."[719] In other brothels, some women were forced to endure the horrifying ordeal of servicing between 40 and 70 soldiers per day.[720] Jeanne Ruff-O'Hearne, a Dutch "Comfort Woman," voiced what Japanese did to her, echoing what happened to thousands: "During that time the Japanese had abused me and humiliated me. They had ruined my young life. They had stripped me of everything, my self-esteem, my dignity, my freedom, my possessions, my family."[721] Since the majority of Japanese troops were guilty of raping women when deployed overseas, as acknowledged by the head of the War Ministry (1938–1939), Lieutenant General Seishirō Itagaki, one cannot help but wonder about the relationships these soldiers had with their own daughters, sisters, aunts, or mothers.[722] How in the world did the grandmothers, aunts, sisters, and mothers of these men interact with them during their formative years to create a collective group who willingly, and frequently, enjoyed violating women wherever they were stationed. *Disturbingly, no documents have been found that proves that anyone, from private to general, ever protested against the rape of foreign women and the institution of setting up "Comfort Women" stations for soldiers to "enjoy."*

Japan treated "Comfort Women" like cattle, utterly dehumanizing them as clearly illustrated with Lieutenant General Kuribayashi "shipping in" almost 2,000 and "recruiting" thousands more from the local population to "service" him and his 23rd Army. Unfortunately, Kuribayashi's actions were not an isolated case, as every Japanese commander made it a priority to organize "Comfort Women" centers for their men when operating in foreign lands. Often, these commanders enticed local women under false pretenses to "labor" at these rape houses, exploiting their vulnerability. In other instances, they resorted to outright coercion, threatening murder if the women refused to comply. It is essential to highlight that the mindset of viewing women as mere objects for rape and abuse, particularly when in positions of power, reveals a deeply grotesque mindset most Japanese males were raised with during Imperial Japan.

Through history, the horrifying realities of rape and pillaging have been sadly intertwined with warfare, especially Asian warfare such as the actions of Genghis Khan and his warriors prove. However, in the modern era, especially in Western nations during the 20th century, women's rights were gaining momentum, which curtailed and even outlawed abuse against women. Enlightened societies began recognizing that women, as fellow human beings and "people makers," deserved honor, protection, suffrage, and the opportunity to participate in the workforce. Slowly but surely sexual abuse and rape were defined and outlawed. In most enlightened nations, military codes of honor and law prevented men from wholesale rape when garrisoned or deployed. Even in the Nazi military, although German soldiers did have problems with rape, especially in Russia, it was neither nearly as widespread nor as widely accepted as it was among Japanese soldiers and *it was illegal*. Unlike with Japan, German legal authorities actively prosecuted thousands of soldiers for rape, making it a punishable offense under their penal code. In contrast, the Imperial Japanese military lacked such codes that explicitly forbade violence against women, or if they did exist, they were not consistently or often followed. In fact, the military establishment often encouraged and supported the mass rape and abuse of women, a deeply disturbing contradiction given that society relies on the military to uphold order and justice. While isolated cases of rape by American occupational forces in Germany and Japan did occur during and after the war, those responsible were held accountable and punished. This was an amazing testament to the principles by which governments and militaries should operate. Unfortunately, the same level of accountability and justice was not seen within the Imperial Japanese military's handling of such crimes.[723]

Japanese leaders, both political and military, displayed mindsets akin to that of Jeffrey Epstein in their lust for abusing women, especially when it came to "Comfort Women." The depths of their depravity sometimes culminated in acts reminiscent of those committed by Jeffrey Dahmer, with the "happy ending" leading to the brutal slaughter of their victims through overt killings or the consequences of severe physical trauma. As a result, Japanese men *en masse* inflicted profound psychological devastation upon an entire generation of women throughout Asia and the Pacific, robbing them of their dignity, their potential for healthy relationships, and their ability to lead balanced and fulfilling lives. While it is true that individuals who have experienced abuse can overcome their trauma and build confident, healthy lives, the heinous sexual abuse, venereal diseases, physical violence, and psychological torment inflicted upon hundreds of thousands of women by the Japanese military made their path to recovery far more challenging than that of the average person. That Japan devastated millions of families and prevented the healthy evolution of millions of other families by violating almost a quarter of a million women during their occupational history is one of the biggest crimes against humanity the Japanese instigated. According to some research, only 10% of the estimated 200,000 "Comfort Women" survived their harrowing ordeals. Many perished due to internal bleeding, within combat zones, or as a result of diseases, while others were ruthlessly murdered by their perpetrators once they were deemed no longer useful.[724] Japan had raised a generation of sexual deviants who were unworthy of being called honorable men.

CHAPTER 14

UNIT 731/JAPAN'S HUMAN MEDICAL EXPERIMENTATION CENTER AND DEATH CAMP

"There is no weapon against cruelty, against
warped minds and warped souls."

—**Pacita Pestaño-Jacinto**, Diary Entry, 6 January 1945
(Witness to Japanese barbarity in Manila)[725]

UNIT 731 WAS A COVERT research facility of the Imperial Japanese Army dedicated to conducting biological and chemical warfare experiments. Its operations involved the brutal murder of tens of thousands of individuals, primarily Chinese civilians, and Allied POWs, through lethal medical experiments and procedures. The headquarters of this complex was located in the Pingfan district of Harbin, the largest city in Japan's puppet state of Manchuria, also known as *Manchukuo*. It was established shortly after Japan took over Manchuria in 1931 and did not stop operations until 1945.[726] Initially, Unit 731 was known as the Water Supply and Prophylaxis Administration or Ishii Detachment after its commander. In 1941, the commander-in-chief of the Kwantung Army, General Yoshijirō Umezu, gave it its numerical designation, which it has since become known by historically.[727]

The facility's head was Lieutenant General Shirō Ishii, a medical officer in the Kwantung Army. Born on 25 June 1892 into a wealthy landowning family in Chiyoda, he developed an early interest in science and medicine, leading him to pursue university studies in 1916.[728] During his college years, he gained notoriety for his rigorous academic pursuits during the day, followed by late-night visits to bars and prostitutes, showing a disturbing preference for underage girls between 15 and 16. Even with these late-night escapades, this pedophile

164

graduated as a doctor from Kyoto Imperial University in 1921, entering the army as a surgeon that same year. He was a fervent nationalist and became passionate about chemical and biological warfare after studying its effects on the battlefields of World War I. He was a brilliant doctor, inventing one of the military's first water-filtered machines, which he shamelessly demonstrated by urinating in it and then drinking the filtered fluid in front of others, *even including Emperor Hirohito*. His audacious presentations impressed Navy and Army leaders, who purchased thousands of these machines, making Ishii a wealthy man and enhancing his reputation within the ranks.[729] In 1928, he self-funded an extensive tour to 20 European nations, the United States, Canada, and others, where he studied their advancements in chemical warfare. His experiences abroad strengthened his conviction to establish a specialized branch of the military dedicated solely to chemical and bacteriological warfare.[730] Interestingly, Japan knew it was going to take on populations larger than its own, notably in its enemies of the U.S.S.R. and China, and a decisive difference maker for it, according to historian Richard Frank, would be its ability to fight its larger enemies with more deadlier, and easily mass-produced, weapons of chemical and biological agents.[731]

After Japan's complete occupation of Manchuria in 1931, Ishii immersed himself in the development of vaccines. He made trips to Manchuria in 1931 and 1932, eventually establishing a laboratory in Harbin that would evolve into the massive organization known as Unit 731 by 1941. The army provided its full support for this endeavor, with the official sign-off given by War Minister General Sadao Araki. From the outset, Ishii conducted experiments using prisoners or local civilians, all of whom were provided by the Kwantung Army. Tragically, the vast majority of these subjects were killed in the process. To conceal the evidence of these heinous acts, the bodies of the murdered prisoners were incinerated in an electrical furnace on Unit 731's premises.[732]

Lieutenant General Shirō Ishii was head of Unit 731 during most of its existence. He was responsible for most of Japan's biological warfare developments and deployment during the war. His organization killed thousands in grisly human experiments. *National Military Archives, Japan*

By 1936, Ishii had assembled a workforce of 1,000 personnel at his extensive base, along with satellite complexes, all dedicated to the development of biological weapons.[733] On 1 August 1936, he was officially appointed as the commanding officer of the unit.[734] The scale of Unit 731 continued to grow, with 3,000 personnel by 1940 and probably reaching up to 5,000 people under Ishii's authority when considering the five satellite bases connected to Unit 731.[735] Ishii's units were established "in accordance with secret edicts of the Emperor Hirohito, the General-Staff and War Ministry of Japan."[736] Hirohito's fascination with science took a sinister turn when he approved of the use of biological warfare and supported the human experimental activities carried out by Unit 731.[737] While some argue that the emperor may not have fully understood what the unit's activities were when he approved it, his senior commanders disagreed. During his trial under the Soviets, General Otozō Yamada, the last Kwantung commander from 1944 to 1945, claimed that Unit 731 in Harbin and Pingfan, along with its sister Unit 100 in Mokoton, were actually established "by *secret order* of the Emperor [author's italics]."[738] Major General Kiyoshi Kawashima, who served in the Army Medical Services, corroborated Yamada's claims, confirming that Unit 731 was set up under "secret instructions from Emperor Hirohito."[739] Hence, Hirohito did put his science background to evil use during his rule and knew about Unit 731 *because he actually approved of it from the outset.* Unlike Hitler, who never put his name to any written order concerning the extermination of the Jews, although he made public speeches to that effect, Hirohito's seal can be found on numerous documents concerning Unit 731.[740] He regularly read about the unit's research and accomplishments and approved everything that took place within it.[741]

With ample backing and support, Ishii's units' coffers overflowed, allowing him to construct a luxurious and sprawling complex resembling a college campus. The elaborate facility boasted state-of-the-art heating, lavatories, prison blocks, laboratories, dormitories, restaurants, athletic fields, and even a grand Shintō shrine.[742] Filled with pride for his newly created village, Ishii honored one of his wartime heroes, the victorious admiral from the Russo-Japanese war from 1904–1905, Admiral Tōgō, by naming Unit 731 "Tōgō Village."[743] Owing to his relentless use of human subjects in cruel experiments, Ishii established a research center that aimed to "master the twin fields of biological warfare—offence and defense."[744] Not even the Nazis came close to touching the research Ishii performed in this particular area of military science.

During Ishii's tenure at Unit 731, a staggering number of lives were lost due to his horrific medical experiments. Estimates range from at least 3,000 to possibly 10,000 people subjected to these inhumane trials. Furthermore, the development and deployment of the biological weapons created at the unit caused a catastrophic death toll, primarily among the Chinese population, amounting to approximately 580,000 victims.[745] However, some scholars, like Peter Li and James Yin, assert that this figure could be much higher, with estimates ranging from 750,000 to 2 million deaths attributed to the deadly biological weapons.[746]

One of the deadliest weapons developed under Ishii's command was a virulent strand of bubonic plague. Obedient to Hirohito's orders, Unit 731 personnel released fleas and rats infected with the "Black Death" into native populations.[747] Here was an example of how this played out. Chinese witness Wang Peigen vividly recounted the horrifying attack on her village, Gongshan, when an airplane dropped the bubonic weapons, releasing a "kind of smoke from its butt."[748] The aftermath was tragic, and a few weeks later, people started dying of the Black Death in excruciating agony:

The screams sundered the night from behind shattered windows and some of the most delirious victims ran or crawled down the narrow alleys to gulp putrefied water from open sewers in vain attempts to vanquish the septic fire that was consuming them. They died excruciating deaths. You buried the dead knowing that the next day you would be buried.[749]

Out of a village of 1,200 people, 392 perished due to the horrific plague. The Japanese army then entered the village to collect data for Ishii, and then they callously burned the plague-ridden homes, further adding to the misery and destruction caused by their actions.[750]

Ishii's twisted idea of using fleas as carriers of infection proved to be horrifyingly efficient, something that made him very proud. Unlike the ineffective method of spraying the disease on victims, using fleas to transmit the pestilence through their bites was highly successful. To breed these disease-carrying fleas, Unit 731 maintained tens of thousands of rats in their laboratories, breeding a staggering number of fleas—billions upon billions, with a rate of 100 million every few days.[751] Under Emperor Hirohito's orders, other units in China were also involved in deploying poison gas against civilians, with many of these agents tested and produced at Ishii's facility.[752] Detailed records show the extent of these horrific attacks: nine times in 1937, 185 in 1938, 465 in 1939, 259 in 1940, and 48 in 1941. The use of poison gas continued throughout 1942 to 1945, although specific numbers for these later years were not available.[753] In one instance, Emperor Hirohito sanctioned a particularly devastating attack in March 1939 when the 11th IJA Army, under the command of Lieutenant General Yasuji Okamura, employed 15,000 canisters of gas "in the largest chemical attack of the war" against Chinese forces.[754] It is crucial to note that these chemical agents had been perfected in laboratories using human subjects. Many "young boys, mothers and children, even pregnant women," were lured into Unit 731's compound under the guise of being offered employment, food, or medical care. The mentally handicapped were also gathered and "used" there. Once a person entered the nightmarish confines of Unit 731, there was no escape, as they never left there alive.[755]

Unit 516, in collaboration with Unit 731, was also focused on perfecting poison gas, with a particular emphasis on hydrogen cyanide. In one haunting experiment, they placed a mother and her young child inside a gas chamber, observing with callous amusement as the mother valiantly tried to shield her baby from the poisonous fumes. "She died lying on top of her child," both innocent victims of this evil act.[756] Amidst these macabre medical experiments, there was one IJA doctor, Dr. Ken Yuasa, who after the war could honestly claim that he was willing to do anything his country asked of him, even if it meant participating in these evil experiments. Shockingly, he believed he was acting morally by implementing Ishii's orders to commit crimes against humanity.[757] Despite having signed the Versailles Peace Treaty, which explicitly banned the use of poison gas under Article 171, Japan shamelessly ignored its commitments when confronting what it considered "a technologically inferior enemy," just like it had disregarded the Hague Convention concerning the treatment of prisoners.[758] As their *modus operandi* proved to be time and time again, the pursuit of victory led the Japanese military to commit unspeakable atrocities in flagrant violation of international agreements and basic human decency.

Due to the high numbers of soldiers throughout Asia and the Pacific raping women, violating "Comfort Women," and going to prostitutes without practicing any sexual protection, the ranks were riddled with venereal diseases. Unit 731 studied numerous sexually transmitted diseases, with a particular focus on syphilis. Tragically, hundreds of female *marutas* (i.e. logs, derisive term the Japanese gave inmates) died during these inhumane experiments. In one particularly diabolical experiment, the researchers deliberately infected a pregnant woman with syphilis, and when her baby was born, both were dissected. They were not killed beforehand and died during the vivisections.[759]

As mentioned earlier, Lieutenant General Ishii's underlings heartlessly referred to these human guinea pigs at Unit 731 as *marutas*, and during experiments, the staff members would callously inquire of one another, "How many logs fell today?" This derogatory term originated from the false narrative spread by Japanese officials to the local population, claiming that this complex was a lumber station.[760] One of the Unit 731's stenographers and clerks, Uezono Naoji, described the *marutas* as mere "lumps of meat on a chopping block," illustrating the dehumanizing perspective of the researchers.[761] The inmates endured horrific abuse, being repeatedly infected with diseases such as bubonic plague, typhoid, and gonorrhea. Guards and even some doctors would engage in reprehensible acts, raping both female and, shockingly, male inmates before and sometimes after infecting them with diseases. A disturbing incident exemplifying this utter lack of empathy within the walls of Unit 731 was when two researchers, having some leisure time, used their authority to unlock prison cells in order to rape some women. The first researcher opened a cell with a healthy woman, went in, and violated her. The second researcher went to the next cell, went in and was about to assault the woman until he discovered she was missing some fingers due to a frostbite experiment and suffering other egregious wounds, and that her vagina was swollen with syphilis. He turned away and left her alone. At least the Japanese have their standards when it comes to rape![762]

Likely thousands of men, women, and children were subjected to excruciating vivisections without any anesthesia at Unit 731. They were strapped down to surgical beds and cut open, screaming their lungs out while the doctors conducted their research. Some prisoners had their limbs cut off just solely for the purpose of studying blood loss to develop methods to aid wounded soldiers in the field. Most humans experimented on were sourced from the Kwantung Army's stockades, particularly during the commands of General Yoshijirō Umezu (1939–1944) and General Otozō Yamada (1944–1945).[763] Unit 731, along with its sister Unit 100, which focused both on animals and people,[764] conducted nightmarish experiments on thousands of human guinea pigs. Regrettably, the use of prisoners for medical experiments was disturbingly common, not only within Unit 731 but also in numerous other locations outside and inside Japan. Even after the war, it was discovered that nine hospitals around Tokyo had conducted such trials on POWs. For example, away from the Japanese island of Honshu where Tokyo was, the Japanese Military Western Army on the island of Kyūshū conducted "appalling experiments to which they [had subjected POWs to]…vivisection and the substitution of sea-water for their blood."[765]

As one has just seen, although Unit 731's scale and barbarity were horrifying, it was not an isolated case. The knowledge of these abominable activities extended to the highest levels of leadership, with Emperor Hirohito, as mentioned before, being well aware of the atrocities. Other senior leaders, such as Prime Minister and General Tōjō, actually watched films prepared by Unit 731, which were so ghastly that even Tōjō eventually refused to watch them because they disturbed him! However, despite his discomfort, he did not take any action to halt these atrocious experiments.[766]

At a minimum, using Unit 731 research, the IJA conducted 12 large-scale field operations deploying biological weapons against 11 Chinese cities. One of the most devastating attacks happened at Changde in 1941, where around 10,000 Chinese civilians died. However, the indiscriminate nature of these biological agents also led to approximately 1,700 IJA soldiers losing their lives from this attack since they were ill-prepared for how to deal with the spread of biological agents. So, as one can see, Ishii's forces proved adept in making lethal biological agents, but were unsuccessful in how to properly control who the agents would kill and in what geographical region they could be contained.[767] The same number of Japanese soldiers also died and countless suffered when Ishii unleashed his biological agents against the Chinese after the Doolittle Raid in April 1942.[768] Historian Daniel Barenblatt calls this "biological friendly fire."[769] Although both campaigns seemingly killed more

Chinese than Japanese soldiers, Ishii's uncontrollable waging of biological warfare showed how unrealistic it was to think such warfare could be controlled once unleashing a disease. Some evidence suggests that since so many IJA troops died and thousands more became sick during these operations, Ishii "suffered a serious reverse in his fortunes." This probably is why he left that command soon thereafter.[770] Even after he left, his minions continued their work and operations. After his apparent dismissal, Ishii took up activities in Nanking and continued overseeing biological warfare attacks against the Chinese with Unit Ei 1644.[771]

In their ruthless quest to spread the "Black Death" amongst the Chinese population, the Japanese authorities devised various diabolical methods. For instance, thousands of fleas were intentionally infected with the disease and then enclosed in clay bombs, which were dropped over cities. At a low altitude, a small explosive charge would break open the shells above the targeted area, releasing the fleas into an unsuspecting population. At other times, the infected fleas were simply dropped in bundles of paper. Ishii's obsession with causing "massive outbreaks of epidemics" by deploying the agents from attacking bombers using clay bombs was his idea alone, a method he took great pride in inventing.[772] Additionally, the Japanese employed similar tactics with other biological warfare agents, such as typhoid and paratyphoid germs. They would release these agents into Chinese wells, marshes, and neighborhoods, rapidly spreading the deadly diseases into unsuspecting populations. In a shocking display of cruelty, they even placed these biological diseased agents into food and candy, distributing them out to civilians as "snacks."[773]

The horrors committed at Unit 731 extended to a whole range of medical experiments that continues to defy the imagination. In some experiments, researchers burned people with flamethrowers or exploded grenades at various distances from inmates tied to wooden stakes to observe the effects of the fire and bomb blasts.[774] Personnel would tie down prisoners with protective metal shielding on their bodies except for their limbs and buttocks and shower them with shrapnel from explosive charges laced with gas gangrene germs. Then, for the next week, the effects were studied until the prisoners "died in great torment."[775] They experimented on people with poison gas to see the effects it had on them, attacking victims often with mustard gas, causing them to cough up their lungs and die. They transfused different blood types into people to see the adverse side effects on the subjects. To study embolisms, they injected air into *marutas'* veins. Shockingly, and illogically, some experiments seemed totally devoid of any military application, such as documenting the time it took for three-day-old babies to freeze to death when left exposed to the elements.[776] For frostbite research, they placed prisoners out in the Manchurian cold, enduring temperatures as low as 40 to 50 degrees below zero Fahrenheit, leading to their deaths from freezing. In other instances, only specific body parts of a prisoner were exposed until the appendage froze, allowing for later amputation due to necrosis, which prolonged the *marutas'* lives for further experimentation.[777]

It is difficult to comprehend what unfolded within the confines of Unit 731. Again, as mentioned in passing already, one must never forget that thousands were killed at the Unit 731 compound "in grisly experiments involving tolerance for freezing temperatures, poison gas, starvation, X-rays, boiling water, and pressure so extreme that their eyes came out of their sockets."[778] Exploring the last cruel experiment mentioned here, many in the pressure chambers lost their eyes when their membranes ruptured, leading to fatal bleeding as their blood was forced out through their pores in the skin due to the extreme suction within the chamber.[779] As historian Sheldon Harris aptly wrote, "Some of the tests conducted by 'scientists' and 'medical doctors' defy imagination today."[780]

As mentioned, while Unit 731's main operations were centered at Pingfan and Harbin, numerous satellite stations were scattered throughout Manchuria, China, and Japan, each conducting their own ominous experiments. Among these sites, the city of Mukden, located south of Harbin, became a grim laboratory where thousands of Allied prisoners were subjected to inhumane studies and medical trails. Not surprisingly, most of these prisoners lost their lives due to the appalling experiments conducted on them.[781]

In its heyday, Unit 731 possessed the capacity to manufacture "bacteria to kill the world's population several times over."[782] In theory, although its entire arsenal of weapons was never fully unleashed on Japan's enemies, Unit 731 "had the power to rival the Manhattan Project, America's program to build the atomic bomb."[783] In their misguided pursuit of what they believed to be the ultimate weapon of war, Unit 731's personnel "tampered with, and destroyed, the lives of [thousands of] others in their efforts to produce what they thought, erroneously, would be the ultimate weapon of war."[784]

When the war finally ended, before all the staff left Harbin, they committed one more overt act of war although Hirohito had commanded them to lay down their arms. They deliberately released thousands of infected rats into the neighboring region of Pingfan, killing thousands of innocent citizens. The devastating impact continued throughout the rest of 1945 and persisted into 1946, 1947, and 1948, with a staggering 30,000 people dying in 1947 alone. This appalling act reflects the disturbing mentality of Japan's so-called medical "researchers."[785]

Only in 2018 did the Japanese National Archives finally release the names of 3,607 scientists, doctors, and military personnel who had worked at Unit 731. The eerie similarities between Dachau's and Auschwitz's medical doctors and "treatments" are legion, and the sheer depravity of the people involved at Unit 731 is mind-numbing. Medicine under the Japanese while stationed in China turned into a horror-house of activity and they inverted everything a doctor promises to do when reciting the Hippocratic Oath. Japanese medicine was organized to harm and slaughter. Also under Ishii's leadership, Japan established itself as a world leader in microbiology, making significant advancements in various fields. During the war, Japan even outpaced the U.S. in the mass-producing of penicillin and likely led the world also in "research on vitamins, especially the 'B' complex, and nutrition." These advancements were in part due to their inhumane experimentation on human subjects. It is a tragic paradox that such scientific progress came at the terrible cost of countless innocent lives and unspeakable suffering.[786]

After the war, Ishii managed to evade capture by going into hiding. His subordinates attempted to mislead the Allied investigators, claiming that he was either still in Manchuria or dead, even staging a mock funeral.[787] However, the Allies were skeptical of these accounts and eventually located him. Disappointedly though, despite the gravity of his crimes against humanity, Ishii never stood trial due to striking a deal with the Americans to disclose his research in exchange for immunity. In 1947, General of the Army Douglas MacArthur wrote Washington, D.C., that, "…additional data…[coming] from Ishii probably can be obtained by informing the Japanese involved that information will be retained in intelligence channels and will not be employed as 'War Crimes' evidence."[788] In supporting even more damning evidence against MacArthur for not bringing Ishii to justice in order to get what he thought were valuable weapons, he gave direct orders to his staff to "keep quiet about [Ishii's] human experiments."[789] Obviously, Ishii committed grave crimes against humanity, a new crime enacted at the Nuremberg and Tokyo Trials, but Ishii got a hall pass from MacArthur personally and did not suffer any legal or professional repercussions.[790] On 2 February 1950, the Soviet ambassador in Washington demanded additional war crime trials for many Japanese leaders, particularly Ishii and Hirohito, for their crimes against humanity, especially in the realm of biological warfare. However, the United States disregarded the Soviets' request, counterarguing that until they accounted for all the missing Japanese POWs in Russian camps, they need not lecture America about morality and future war crime trails.[791] This response underscored the complexities and political motivations surrounding the pursuit of justice for war crimes committed during World War II.

It is evident that both the Soviet Union and America had moral failures in their policies, especially when dealing with war criminals like Ishii. The fact that Ishii's case was ignored by American authorities at the highest levels, "obscured by a fog of Cold War bitterness and laid to rest because it suited the Allies to do so, is one of the scandals of the Second World War. The interests of justice were not served."[792] Simply, MacArthur and others wanted more weapons in their arsenal in which to fight the Communists in some possible World War III, and consequently, they let a mass-murdering thug get away with despicable crimes. MacArthur was not alone in showing an Allied commander could compromise his morals when making decisions for the nation. For instance, President Roosevelt, and other Allied leaders, chose to ally themselves with Stalin and the U.S.S.R. even though the Soviet dictator and his legions had killed at least 9 million people before Hitler ever invaded Russia, documented well in Timothy Snyder's book *Bloodlands*.[793] Although we knew something about the atrocities, we decided not to condemn him and his regime since we felt Hitler was the greater evil, and thus, needed him to fight the Nazis. We indeed, in some respects, allied ourselves with Beelzebub to cast out Satan from this world. So, MacArthur's working with an evil man like Ishii was not an isolated event although his decision to do so was wrong.

Supposedly for the rest of his life, Ishii spent time in the U.S. helping America with its biological warfare program and practicing medicine in Japan when back in his homeland. Displaying his lack of shame and regret, he gave a talk to a group of Unit 731 alumni in 1958 at a secret meeting in Japan that was "rich in xenophobia and elitism," talking about how noble their work and accomplishments had been.[794] Shortly before his death from throat cancer, he converted to Catholicism and took the name of Joseph in 1959. According to his family, only when he converted to Christianity did he feel "relieved" from what he had done in life. Perhaps his shame and sense of guilt led him to a religion that preached forgiveness and reward in Heaven if he confessed his sins, receiving, in his mind at least, the redemption he desperately needed. In the end, it is quite telling that he was drawn to such a religion knowing death was approaching him.[795] And although the government knew about his crimes, he and his wife enjoyed a government pension throughout their lives after WWII.[796] This lack of accountability is a troubling example, but sadly a common one, of how Japanese officials have often responded when confronted with their WWII crimes.

In 1997, a Chinese lobbyist named Wang Xuan filed a lawsuit in Tokyo's District Court demanding compensation and recognition for victims of Ishii's diabolical Unit 731. She was the team leader, and a niece of one of the 180 plaintiffs who were filling complaints on behalf of themselves as victims of, and on behalf of 2,100 people killed due to, Japan's germ warfare.[797] On 30 August 2002, the court ruled "that Japan would neither formally apologize nor give any compensation to the plaintiffs."[798] Ironically, the court acknowledged the occurrence of germ warfare and its deadly consequences, but it refused to offer any apology or compensation to the plaintiffs.[799] Under Xuan, the plaintiffs appealed the Tokyo District Court's decision and it was then, not surprisingly, rejected by the Tokyo High Court in 2005. Ms. Xuan declared, "It's not a right verdict. It's not a verdict of justice."[800] The court's decision was met with criticism from former Unit 731 member, Yoshio Shinozuka, who had given testimony against his former superiors and admitted to the crimes he and his colleagues had committed. He went on the record about the court, saying: "It's not a verdict you could reach if you were human. The judge was just making excuses for the Japanese government."[801] This is one example, out of millions, of how most Japanese officials, leaders, and educators behave when confronted with their WWII crimes. They simply continue to fail to take responsibility for the atrocities Japan committed during World War II, and the history of Unit 731 stands as one of the nation's dramatic examples of how its citizens fail repeatedly to address the sins of the past and seek justice for the victims after the crimes that harmed them become known.

CHAPTER 15

JAPAN AS A DRUG-DEALING NATION

"Of all tyrannies a tyranny sincerely exercised for the *good of its victims* may be the most oppressive [author's italics]."

—**C. S. Lewis** (1970)

GENERAL KENJI DOIHARA'S MONSTROUS CRIMES against humanity, including his involvement in the sale of opium and heroin throughout China, led to his execution in 1948 after standing trial during the Tokyo War Crimes Tribunal. Despite being a charming, intelligent, and sophisticated man, he was, without a doubt, also an evil psychopath. In the dark annals of drug lords, Doihara stands as one of the most cunning masterminds the world has ever known.

The scale of devastation caused by Doihara's drug operations is unparalleled. The number of people he got addicted, the massive profits he earned in millions of yen, the millions he was indirectly responsible for killing, and the havoc he wrought on countless families would make the major drug dealers of South and Central America and Mexico look like amateurs. Even major drug organizations, like the notorious Mexican cartel *Mara Salvatrucha*, or more popularly known as MS-13, with around 50,000 members worldwide with around 10,000 inside the U.S., pale in comparison to the vast network Doihara commanded. Doihara's operation benefited from the fact that he had the whole network of the Japanese army, millions of armed men throughout China, and an entire nation supporting his activities. This is why in today's money, his operation earned a staggering 200 times more than the amount MS-13 makes today on an annual basis, when adjusted for inflation.

Although from humble origins, Doihara's criminal mindset and ambition became apparent early in life. He displayed exceptional academic prowess, graduating in the top echelon of the Imperial Japanese Army Academy in 1904 and from the Army Staff College in 1912. As a low-ranking officer, he realized that his modest background might hinder his rise through the ranks without a powerful sponsor. In a regrettable and reprehensible act, Doihara made a grave decision to exploit his sister. After careful planning, he pimped out his 15-year-old sister to a nobleman. This transaction proved successful and in exchange for these sexual services, the nobleman got him a higher military rank and a duty station in Beijing as the *aide-de-camp* to the military attaché, Lieutenant Colonel Hideki Tōjō. This career move propelled his trajectory, but it came at the expense of his sister's dignity and reputation, as she was subjected to harmful rumors and disparaging labels such as being the family's "slut."

As Japan expanded its presence in northern China in 1927 and 1928, Doihara was attached to the IJA 1st Division, participating in operations to fight "bandits." Recognizing the strategic importance of understanding the local language and culture, he displayed remarkable intelligence by hiring tutors and immersing himself in extensive reading. Through diligent efforts, he achieved fluency in Mandarin and other Chinese dialects. In fact, it was noted that he could speak Chinese like a native and blend into the local culture.[802] His mastery of the Chinese language proved invaluable in his future endeavors, eventually helping him to secure a high-level position in the IJA Intelligence Service in 1928.

During this time, Doihara was instrumental in orchestrating the assassination of Chang Tso-lin, the warlord of Manchuria, in 1928. This calculated move aimed to further Japan's interests in seizing control of Manchuria in its entirety, but the plan did not succeed. However, soon thereafter, he would get another opportunity to help Japan in this quest with the Mukden Incident of 1931 that allowed Japan to seize control of northern China. It is important to note that one year before this pivotal incident, Doihara also commanded the 30th Infantry Regiment, a unit marred by actions of rape and murder wherever it was stationed. These events occurring under Doihara's leadership up until 1931 already underscore the destructive impact of his goals and the consequences of Japan's policies of unleashing military commanders in China like Doihara who had unchecked power.

During the beginning of the 1930s, he became part of a secret society called the "Eleven Reliable" which further solidified his connection with influential figures like Colonel Tōjō and Colonel Seishirō Itagaki, both wielding significant power within the army. Their support played a crucial role in elevating Doihara to the position of the head of the Houten Special Agency, the military intelligence service of the entire Kwantung Army, in 1931. After the successful seizure of Manchuria in that same year, Colonel Doihara played a key role in organizing and commanding a force comprising 150,000 soldiers, 18,000 military police, and 4,000 members of the *Kempei Tai*. With this formidable military apparatus at his disposal, he imposed a reign of terror on the 30 million inhabitants of *Manchukuo*. Under his command, the region experienced the horrors of slave labor, forced prostitution, and the distribution of drugs, leaving the population in a state of absolute fear and distress. As part of the army's establishment of a drug empire, the Japanese authorities in Tokyo dispatched its high-level politician and bureaucrat, Naoki Hoshino (a later convicted war criminal at the Tokyo Tribunal), to Manchuria to oversee the opium monopoly, ensuring that the financial gains from these illicit activities were funneled back to Japan.[803] This ruthless exploitation of *Manchukuo*'s resources and people was a testament to the dark and oppressive side of Japan's imperial ambitions during that era.

Throughout 1932 and 1933, Doihara held a combat post as the commanding officer of the 9th Infantry Brigade, operating under the 5th Infantry Division in northern China. In February and March 1933, he led his troops successfully during the Battle of Rehe (Jehol Province) as part of Operation *Nekka* against Nationalist troops. This victory was of significant importance to the Japanese as it secured their control over a critical source of income from the opium trade in the region.

In 1934, Doihara returned to his covert activities, resuming his role as the head of the Houten Special Agency. From 1936 until 1937, he held positions in Japan until the Marco Polo Bridge Incident in July 1937, when he assumed command of the 14th Division and returned to the battlefields in China. Leading his division through various operations, he notably played a crucial role at the Battle of Lanfeng in May 1938. However, his leadership came under scrutiny in June 1940 during the events around Honan, particularly when Chiang Kai-Shek's flooding strategy of the region resulted in significant losses for his troops. Subsequently, Doihara resumed his intelligence activities as part of the Army General Staff, heading the Doihara Special Agency. Soon thereafter, he was promoted yet again and appointed commanding officer of the Japanese 5th Army in Manchuria. His rise to power continued at an accelerated pace, and from 1940 until 1941, he became the member of the Supreme War Council, focusing on exploiting and raping all of China under Japan's control.[804] Because of his perceived role in the Tripartite Pact with Germany in 1940, Adolf Hitler even awarded him with the Grand Cross of the German Eagle in 1941.[805] From 1941 to 1943, he held administrative positions in Japan until he became the governor of Johor State in Malaya in 1944. By the war's end in 1945, he had assumed command of the IJA 7th Army based in Singapore.

Throughout his tenure in China, Doihara did more than anyone else in facilitating drug addiction among the Chinese population and establishing a bureaucracy that controlled the sale and distribution of illicit drugs, not only in Asia, but globally. While Japan was a major player in the arena, it's worth noting that Mao's Communist movement was also partly "sustained by the sale of opium."[806] Nonetheless, Doihara's involvement in perpetuating drug addiction and exploiting vulnerable populations remains a dark chapter in Japan's history since this nation was the major player of drug trafficking in the world. Before we conclude this chapter, it is important to explore Doihara and his history further to better understand his personality and how he accomplished his sordid and massive misdeeds.

While stationed in Beijing from 1935 to 1937, Marine Lieutenant Colonel Graves Erskine had several meetings with Lieutenant General Kenji Doihara referred to as the "Lawrence of Manchuria" due to his instrumental role in organizing the invasion of Manchuria. However, this nickname and comparison was a misnomer, as Lawrence of Arabia fought to liberate people, not oppress them. Doihara, along with others like Colonel Seishirō Itagaki, played a significant role in concocting this invasion, something they ultimately were doing by obeying illegal orders from the Kwantung Army commander, General Baron Shigeru Honjō.[807] Doihara liked bragging that it was he who had conquered Manchuria, and his reputation spread far and wide, leading Erskine to believe Doihara was solely responsible for the successful operation. One day, Erskine questioned Doihara, "Just what are you doing over here [in China]?" Doihara answered, "I think old lady China sick old lady. I speak in parable about China. She do not need Uncle Sam, but what she need is Doctor Japan." Unfortunately, this "doctor" was not there to heal and help, but rather to exploit and oppress, finding ways to keep the "old lady" so sick that she would be a slave and unable to offer resistance.[808] This conversation reveals Doihara's sinister intentions to subjugate China, using his power and military strategy to dominate and control the Chinese population, rather than providing any genuine assistance or support.

Ironically, an opium addict himself, Doihara, as proven above, masterminded the Chinese drug trade, which kept some parts of "old lady" China sick on opium. In 1937, the League of Nations pointed out that 90% of all "illicit drugs in the world," primarily heroin, cocaine and opium, were of Japanese origin, largely due to Doihara's activities.[809] This drug trafficking extended "into America and Europe to pay for the weapons of war" Japan needed.[810] Stuart J. Fuller, the American representative to the Opium Advisory Committee at the League of Nations, had warned a year prior, "Let us face facts. Where Japanese influence advances in the Far East, what goes with it? Drug traffic."[811] His observation highlighted the connection between Japan's growing influence in the region and the proliferation of drug trafficking, fueling the illicit trade that funded their military endeavors.

And Doihara found clever ways to amass the millions of yen of profit for Japan using illicit drugs. For instance, to propagate drug addiction, Doihara cunningly dispatched agents on "humanitarian" missions to establish health centers in various Japanese-occupied regions of China. Under the guise of medical assistance, his personnel deceitfully administered medicines laced with opium to unsuspecting patients, thus rapidly creating millions of Chinese addicts.[812] Exploiting their addiction, Doihara ran brothels with women who were already hooked on drugs, manipulating them to spread heroin and opium to their customers.[813] He incentivized these women with more drugs if they could ensnare their patrons into addiction as well.

Additionally, Doihara collaborated with the Japanese tobacco industry, particularly Mitsui of Mitsui *Zaibatsu* (conglomerates), to produce "special" cigarettes laced with opium or heroin, selling these brands to native Chinese, further proliferating drug use. To extend his malevolent reach, Doihara employed about 80,000 Chinese villains to spread drug addiction.[814] Furthermore, Japanese personnel frequently paid Chinese laborers in opium, thereby perpetuating drug dependency across China's society.[815]

The entire chain of command reaped significant benefits from this malevolent enterprise.[816] At its zenith, the Japanese drug trade generated a staggering $300 million annually in 1939 (equivalent to $6.5 billion in 2023 currency).[817] By comparison, the current MS-13 network's earnings amount to approximately $30 million per year.[818] With its vast empire, including around 500 million people under its control in 1942, Japan had a vast population, primarily in China, to spread its drug culture throughout.[819] During its peak, Japanese narcotic production imported a mind-boggling 30 tons "of high-grade Iranian opium for processing in one year alone."[820] The motive behind inducing drug addiction was twofold: It provided immense profits and granted the Japanese authorities control over the affected population, undermining the Chinese "people's will to fight."[821] Prior to the Japanese occupation, Chiang Kai-Shek had made commendable efforts to eradicate drug use, having studied the devastating impact of the Opium Wars of the 1840s and 1850s, and witnessed the opium addictions that had plagued his countrymen throughout the 1920s and 1930s.[822] Tragically, Doihara undid all these efforts, leaving behind a trail of destruction and addiction in China.

Once Japan assumed control, the drug culture spread like wildfire. After Mukden was taken over by the Japanese in 1931, a tragic scene throughout the city was often witnessed of trash dumps becoming "littered with the corpses of addicts, gray-faced from the morphine, and usually naked, their clothes having been stripped from them by other addicts."[823] In contrast, before the Rape of Nanking, the city had virtually no drug issues under the Nationalist Chinese rule. However, just one year after the fall of this city, the number of addicts skyrocketed to 50,000, paying the IJA a total of $3 million per month (equivalent to $62.9 million in 2023 currency). After seizing Beijing in 1937, Japanese authorities went on to license 600 opium dens by 1940.[824] A similar pattern emerged in numerous cities throughout China, with the other two big centers being Hankow with 460 dens and Canton with 852.[825] Hong Kong, following its fall, succumbed to the drug culture, initially spreading throughout this city starting in the brothels amongst the prostitutes.[826] Shockingly, in Manchuria alone, out of a population of 30 million, a staggering *10 million individuals became opium addicts.*[827] Knowing these numbers above, Prime Minister Konoe was laughing all the way to the bank with the profits the drug trade in China brought Hirohito's regime.[828]

Before the hanging of the "Lawrence of Manchuria" at the Sugamo Prison in Tokyo, a significant part of his indictment stated:

> [Doihara] pursued a systematic policy of weakening the native inhabitants' will to resist…by directly and indirectly encouraging the increased production and importation of opium and other narcotics and by promoting the sale and consumption of such drugs among such people.[829]

Interestingly, he maintained complete silence during his trial, well aware that his horrible crimes spoke volumes on their own. Similar to General Yamashita, he attempted to appeal his case to the U.S. Supreme Court, but, like Yamashita, his request was denied.[830]

Accurately quantifying the devastating impact of Doihara's actions is challenging, as it involves not only calculating the lives lost but also accounting for the immeasurable toll on individuals' well-being, lost livelihoods, and shattered families. While obtaining precise statistics is difficult, it is evident that Doihara's criminal behavior and Japan's drug trade had far-reaching consequences. Drawing a parallel to some of the drug issues in present-day America might help shed light on the gravity of Japan's actions and Doihara's involvement.

Present-day pharmaceutical companies in the U.S. are undeniably driven by profits, largely due to the nation's excessive reliance on drugs, not necessarily because these drugs are the best for our overall health. Their soaring revenues are a testament to the addictive nature of these substances, and they capitalize on our vulnerabilities. It's alarming to note that even though the U.S. population represents 5% of the global population (circa 336 million in 2023), Americans consume an astounding 80% of the world's opioids.[831] Such an overreliance raises questions about the underlying factors contributing to this dependence. Are we that pain-filled and depressed compared to the rest of the world that warrants such a high consumption of these drugs? And with such drugs killing or negatively affecting so many, one would think Americans would reduce the production of these drugs and limit how doctors can prescribe them. Since 1999, 400,000 Americans have tragically lost their lives to opioid use. Our government fined Purdue Pharmaceuticals, owned by the evil Sackler family, $8 billion in 2020 for promoting the use of and selling opioids to the public "without legitimate medical purpose."[832] The National Center for Health Statistics reported overdose deaths in America alone rose from 50,963 in 2019 to 69,710 in 2020.[833] These are deaths that have occurred in a land where heroin and opium use is *illegal,* and "official" opioid use done only under a physician's care. Our entire law enforcement structure and legal system is designed to prevent illicit drug use and to punish those who sell such illegal drugs on the black market or sell legal opioids to people in unhealthy doses or for the wrong reasons, like the Sackler family has done. Just imagine what these numbers would be if the government actually was sponsoring the use of heroin and opium in order to destroy a society and gain profits.

Giving these startling statistics and that Japan was sponsoring drug use throughout China as early as 1931, it becomes evident that Doihara's sinister enterprises likely resulted in the loss of several million lives due to direct drug use, and indirectly, the destruction of tens of millions of lives. Such was the nation of Japan during Hirohito's regime that it could support a drug lord like Doihara, letting him and the army wreck the lives of millions through drug addiction. The nation's complicity in supporting such a destructive operation is deeply troubling and speaks volumes about the moral bankruptcy of the regime during this time.

CHAPTER 16

OTHER JAPANESE ATROCITIES AND COUNTING THE VICTIMS

"I observed with assumed innocence that no man
was safe from trouble in this world."

—**Joseph Conrad**, *Heart of Darkness*[834]

BESIDES NANKING, SINGAPORE, MALAYA, GUAM, Manila, and Hong Kong, numerous other cities and regions bore witness to the horrific atrocities committed by the Japanese throughout the Asian and Pacific Wars. The scale of Japan's campaigns extended far beyond these well-known names already explored, and hundreds of places experienced the brutal wrath of its military forces. The campaigns Japan waged throughout China and elsewhere were "undertaken in order to 'punish the [Chinese and foreign] people…for their refusal to acknowledge the superiority and leadership of the Japanese race and to co-operate with them.'"[835] As was often the case with Japan, its martial behavior "was an uneasy blend of ancient thought and modern methods."[836] Lord Russell of Liverpool, chief legal advisor for the British during the post-WWII war trials, eloquently captured the relentless brutality of Japan's actions when writing: "Month after month, and year after year, throughout the whole duration of the Sino-Japanese war the Japanese armies continued to fight like barbarians, and brought death and destruction to innocent people and defenseless villages wherever they went."[837] The following examples below give more evidence to what already has been given to support Lord Russell's conclusion here.

As the war raged around Shanghai in 1937, the situation in northern China was equally dire. By the end of July, Beijing had fallen, and on 24 September, Baoding (Paoting) collapsed to the IJA as other forces readied themselves to move on to Nanking. The aftermath of Baoding's capture was a devastating display of brutality, as 30,000 troops "burst out in a week's rampage of murder, rape and pillage." As they would later burn down a third of Nanking's city, they also burned Baoding's main buildings and deliberately destroyed all the schoolbooks they could find in a week-long bonfire. In addition to this, they set fire to Hopei Medical College's library and laboratory equipment, reducing them to ashes. "A decade's records of crop statistics at the Agriculture Institute, the basis of its program for improved farming methods, were also deliberately destroyed." The Japanese killed at least 25,800 civilians and soldiers in their merciless actions. Japan's relentless onslaught extended beyond military victories; it was a war on an entire society.[838] Unfortunately, almost everywhere Japan attacked in the late 1930s, it met with success. American military advisor Colonel Stilwell had to deal with the successful IJA officers, found them insufferable, and noted how "Beijing under the control of the 'arrogant little bastards' was hard to bear.'"[839]

One day, in the desolate northern region of China, a heart-wrenching incident unfolded when a group of IJA soldiers inexplicably attacked a defenseless man. Brutally wielding rocks, they savagely beat his head, causing his skull to split open, and blood spewed forth, drenching his lifeless form as he collapsed in a tangled mess. Although dead, the soldiers showed no mercy, and continued to kick him and "throw more stones" at his corpse. Shockingly, the soldiers' officers stood nearby, indifferent to the senseless murder unfolding before their eyes. As the troops moved away from the lifeless man, a "weeping woman," likely his wife, clung to the mangled remains that once had been her husband. *No one lifted a finger* to prevent this crime or offered comfort to the grieving woman.[840]

During that harrowing time, there was another deeply distressing incident that unfolded. Inside a home, soldiers found an old lady and a young woman cradling an infant in her arms. Their feet were already bound, likely indicating they had been subjected to unspeakable violence by other soldiers who possibly wanted to return to them and continue their crimes against these innocent victims. Without a shred of mercy, the soldiers forcibly dragged these defenseless women from their home. In a horrifying display of cruelty, one soldier ruthlessly bayoneted the old lady, while another heartlessly shot the young woman in the head. Tragically, the baby was now left all alone, lying on the ground, kicking its legs and arms in a feeble attempt to find comfort. Filled with confusion and uncertainty, one soldier turned to his squad leader for guidance. He asked, "The baby is still alive. What shall I do?" The man in charge responded with chilling coldness: "Kill it!" Without a moment's hesitation, his subordinate carried out the appalling order immediately.[841]

In the summer of 1938, the Japanese attacked cities along the Yangtze River, west of Nanking. Their assault began with the swift capture of Anqing, and on 29 June, they overpowered Madang after dousing it with poisonous gas, securing yet another victory. Their march of aggression continued as they seized control of Hukou and then set their sights on the river port city of Jiujiang. Here, too, they likely employed poison gas, resulting in its rapid fall to the invading forces. Thereafter, the IJA troops fell upon the citizens with utter abandon, raping and slaughtering the inhabitants, producing "a miniature…Nanking massacre."[842] After their trail of destruction, the Japanese moved on under Hirohito's direct order and eventually conquered Wuhan in October 1938, perpetrating their common crimes when they seized a city.[843] Throughout this campaign, Japan's use of poison gas reached a shocking tally of 375 separate occasions, leaving in its wake a trail of devastation and suffering.[844]

In another disturbing account of the war, Japanese troops found themselves dangerously close to a minefield. In a grotesque display of callousness, they resorted to forcing Chinese peasants to walk 50 meters ahead of them, essentially using them as human shields to trigger the deadly detonators. If any of the innocent civilians refused to march through the perilous minefields, they were shot.[845]

In a daring and desperate move, Chiang Kai-Shek, after consulting with his German advisors, decided to take drastic action to halt the relentless onrush of Japanese forces across his region of rule. On the fateful night of 20 June 1938, Chiang ordered the strategic breach of the dikes holding back the Yellow River near Chengchow. Swollen with the winter snow melt from the Mongolian mountains, the powerful and fast-moving river burst forth with immense force, following its old route of flow in a southeastward direction. The consequences of this decision were profound and devastating. Within a matter of days, vast areas of eastern China were submerged by the raging floodwaters. Sadly, the innocent civilians in the path of this raging wall of water had no warning of what their leaders had decided. Millions were displaced by the catastrophic flood, and the toll of human suffering was unimaginable. It is estimated that at least a million people lost their lives either by drowning or due to the ensuing sickness and starvation.[846] Despite the immense human cost, this desperate measure did succeed in preventing the Japanese from conquering even more of China. Moreover, it inflicted significant losses upon Japanese units, including the drowning of the majority of the IJA 14th Division under General Doihara's command with most of his soldiers succumbing to the raging waters.[847] Since Chiang had limited resources at his disposal to push back Japanese forces, he resorted to utilizing the natural defenses his country could offer to stave off

Hirohito's advancing armies. It was a time of immense sacrifice and strategic maneuvering in the face of overwhelming odds.

On 20 March 1939, Japan's 11th Army, led by Lieutenant General Yasuji Okamura, launched a ferocious attack on Nanchang, a city located south of Nanking and the capital of Jiangxi Province. The Japanese forces unleashed the most massive artillery barrage of the entire war on this city, coupled with devastating air strikes. Although targeting military positions, they also focused on civilian sectors. In addition to these conventional weapons, they hit the city and Chinese troops with poison gas. Within a week, on 27 March, the Japanese forces managed to breach the city's defenses, ushering in a nightmarish reign of terror. As soon as they seized control of the metropolis, they commenced with raping and killing citizens and "expelling hundreds of thousands of refugees in their path."[848] During these crimes being perpetuated against these innocent civilians, Lieutenant General Okamura failed to intervene, doing nothing to stop these atrocities.

Throughout 1941 and 1942, Officer Candidate Shōzō Tominaga, who later attained the rank of captain, was attached to the 232nd Regiment in the 39th Division. Disturbingly, he openly discussed how he and his men routinely massacred civilians as a matter of course in Henan Province, Suizhou prefecture-level city (Hubei province), and Changsa (capital of Hunan Province). During the winter months, they destroyed whole villages and whenever they found anyone in the open, they "captured and killed them. Spies! This was war."[849] Tominaga himself confessed to ordering the shooting of POWs and the destruction of hundreds of homes, stating that these actions were carried out under "direct orders."[850] Even more troubling is the fact that he further admitted: "Most of us thought then that murdering, raping, and setting fire to villages were unavoidable acts in war, nothing particularly wrong."[851] Tominaga eventually stood trial in a Chinese war crimes trial, where he surprisingly admitted to his crimes and displayed signs of genuine remorse, a rare occurrence among Japanese officers. In an unprecedented twist, he was released in 1957, a decision influenced by his decade-long period of "self-examination" and the humane treatment he received from his Chinese captors.[852]

During the full-scale invasion of Burma in February 1942, before taking Sittang Bridge, the 33rd Divisional commander, Lieutenant General Seizo Sakurai, ordered his troops to refrain "from engaging in rape, pillage, and arson" just like Lieutenant General Sakai had commanded before invading Hong Kong and General Yamashita did before assaulting Malaya. However, despite this directive, Sakurai's men still committed crimes of killing defenseless wounded enemy soldiers and newly seized POWs.[853] The British troops who faced the

Japanese assault conducted one of the longest retreats in British history, and the civilians attempting to also escape the Japanese suffered horrifically. Tragically, at least 50,000 refugees died trying to flee the Imperial troops.[854] After securing the land, numerous reprisals were carried out against the civilian population in Burma who were suspected "to have given assistance" to British soldiers and Burmese guerrillas."[855] One such example occurred on 7 July 1945, when the 3rd Battalion of the 215th Regiment, accompanied by secret police personnel from the *Kempei Tai* under orders from Major General Seiei Yamamoto, chief of staff of the 33rd Army, rounded up and executed at least 600 civilians from the town of Kalagon, accusing them of helping British commandos. During these executions, the Japanese soldiers also subjected many women and children to rape and abuse. On 11 July, they pillaged the village and then burned it to the ground. From the survivors, they picked out ten young women to rape and abuse. The women were subsequently taken away by the Japanese troops, and they were never heard from again.[856]

After the Doolittle raid in April 1942, the Japanese launched an offensive around Chekiang and Kiangsu Provinces, prompted by the American pilots' plans to use airfields in those areas (due to fuel shortages all the planes either crash-landed in fields or the men bailed out of them). Hirohito himself signed the order to destroy and occupy this region, deploying 100,000 soldiers under General Shunroku Hata, primarily from the 13th Army.[857] The devastating offensive covered towns and cities like Chü Hsien, Chuchow, Yüshan, Ihwang, Kinhwa, Nancheng, Peipo, and Futsing, encompassing a total area of 20,000 square miles. In Chuchow alone, the Japanese mercilessly murdered 10,246 people, "destroyed 62,146 homes, stole 7,620 head of cattle and burned 30% of the crops."[858] IJA forces machinegunned large groups of captured men and raped and skewered women with their penises and bayonets. They also ruthlessly ended the lives of innocent children through the use of bullets, bayonets, and clubs, and even sometimes resorted to the horrifying act of throwing some of them into wells, subjecting them to a tragic fate of drowning and contaminating the water sources of several villages. The use of biological agents, including cholera, typhoid, and dysentery pathogens from Unit 731, resulted in the destruction of entire towns and villages. By the end of the campaign, tens of thousands of women had been raped, and "at least 250,000 Chinese civilians lay dead."[859] Chiang Kai-Shek cabled FDR: "The Japanese troops slaughtered every man, woman, and child in those areas—let me repeat—*these Japanese troops slaughtered every man, woman, and child in those areas* [author's italics]."[860] Japanese forces proved to be excellent butchers of innocent civilians. General Hata was later found guilty of war crimes and sentenced to life in prison. The

Rape of Chekiang marked one of Lieutenant General Ishii's largest operations involving chemical and biological agents in combat. During this campaign, he left Unit 731 and returned to Japan to lecture and conduct more research, eventually returning to China and operating his duties and research in Nanking. Thereafter, he turned over the helm of his medical center to his colleague, Major General Masaji Kitano, a man who continued the evil research from 1942 until 1944.[861]

Japan's odious crimes extended even to the high seas, where every Japanese organization seemed to relish in committing atrocities. Despite Japan having signed and ratified Article 22 of the London Navy Treaty of 1930, which guaranteed the right of crew members and civilians of sunken ships by submarines to use their lifeboats and be granted safe passage to land, they shamelessly, not surprisingly, disregarded their obligations. Although the Treaty expired in 1936, Article 22 remained binding by virtue of Article 23, which dictated the expected moral conduct by submarine crews. However, as was often the case with the Japanese, they flagrantly violated moral codes they had once agreed to abide by. For example, the First Submarine Force commander at Truk, Rear Admiral Takero Kouda issued a chilling order on 20 March 1943: "Carry out the complete destruction of the crews of enemy's ships; if possible seize part of the crew and endeavor to secure information about the enemy [before killing them]."[862] Between 13 December 1943 and 29 November 1944, IJN submarines sank eight Allied vessels in the Indian Ocean and one American ship in the Pacific Ocean. Appallingly, in every case of Allied vessels being sunk by Japanese submarines, the IJN sub-commanders selected a few for interrogation, usually the commanders, and then instructed their sailors to machinegun and cannon-blast the remaining survivors in their rafts and lifeboats. At other times, Allied crews were taken aboard and bayoneted to death. Hundreds of Allied sailors died in such unimaginably brutal ways.[863]

In September 1944, General Tanaka in Timor, Indonesia, issued a cold-blooded order that led to the execution of several civilians from Loeang and Sermata for supposedly orchestrating the assassination of two members of the secret police, the *Kempei Tai*. At least 96 innocent islanders were arbitrarily selected and pitilessly slaughtered. A lieutenant who bore witness to this gruesome act recounted the horror: "The natives were killed by bayoneting, three at a time, by 21 Japanese soldiers. After the execution, I organized a brothel in which I forced native girls to act as prostitutes *as a punishment for the deeds of their fathers* [author's italics]."[864] The sheer cruelty of such actions is unbelievable. Imagine the anguish these women faced, who after witnessing their fathers being cut down in cold blood, were then subjected to the additional indignity of being raped by their fathers' murderers. Regrettably, such appalling behavior was all too common among the "Knights of Bushido."[865]

Throughout Japanese-conquered lands, there were numerous cases of cannibalism of their enemies, even frying up entrails, penises, and testicles. It was done by "choice and not of necessity." Bestial acts were the sons of Japan's *modus operandi* driven by brutality and cruelty.[866] While stationed in Burma in 1944, Lieutenant Colonel Tsuji, the butcher of Singapore and at the Bataan Death March, exhibited a particularly sadistic nature in these matters. He ordered the execution of an American prisoner, FirstLieutenant Benjamin Parker, gruesomely beheading him with a dull sword. It took three hacks to sever the skull from the body. Afterwards, Tsuji ordered meat from Parker's thigh to be cooked and served to his officers, claiming it would grant them special strength by consuming their enemies' flesh.[867] Tsuji even bragged to his troops and fellow officers that he derived vigor from a secret medicine he imbibed that derived from the livers of prisoners boiled in a soup.[868] Many soldiers seemed to relish in their demonic exploits: "No law could curb their reckless debauches, no ray of wisdom penetrate their blindness."[869] When they did not have Allied prisoners to eat, they resorted to eating their own. In a rare case when a soldier surrendered, he told his Australian interrogator he did so because he had been ordered to the cookhouse without his cooking pail to be sacrificed for his unit. He didn't like that order and bolted for the enemy's lines—so, indeed sometimes, a soldier was capable of disobeying an immoral order when self-interest was at hand.[870] Japan had produced a nation of Hannibal Lecters from the movie *Silence of the Lambs* (1991).[871] Joseph Conrad's *Heart of Darkness* could have described them:

> They were conquerors, and for that you want only brute force—nothing to boast of, when you have it, since your strength is just an accident arising from the weakness of others. They grabbed what they could get for the sake of what was to be got. It was just robbery with violence, aggravated murder on a great scale, and men going at it blind—as is very proper for those who tackle a darkness. The conquest of the earth, which mostly means the taking it away from those who have a different complexion or slightly flatter noses than ourselves, is not a pretty thing when you look into it too much.[872]

In taking over nations, the Japanese often encountered what they thought were "weaker" communities. Vast tracts of China were rural and any armed resistance there depended on the U.S. and Soviet Union providing it supplies. Citizens of the Philippines and Guam had neither the training, weapons, nor infrastructure to repel the Japanese. Yes, the Filipinos did have several thousand of their men trained as soldiers, but once American forces were kicked out of the Philippines, the Filipinos had neither the industrial foundation nor the leadership to conduct major actions against the Japanese. Many occupied islands had communities of unsophisticated tribesmen like in Papua New Guinea. The Japanese easily used brute force, conducting their "robbery with violence." As shown before, initiations into the IJA fraternity often involved officers beheading and the enlisted men bayoneting prisoners. The military turned men into "murdering demons."[873] It is difficult to fathom the "darkness" Japan had to overcome to do what it did. One man could have stopped this: Hirohito. Instead, he, "being knowledgeable about political and military affairs...participated in the making of national policy and issued the orders of the imperial headquarters to field commanders and admirals. He played an active role in shaping the barbaric Japanese war strategy."[874]

According to extensive research, Japan committed the horrifying mass murder of at least 30 million from 1927 through 1945,[875] giving it eighteen years to exterminate "inferior peoples." The National Museum of the Pacific War reports that the Japanese slaughtered 22,617,242.[876] The *Encyclopedia of Genocide* notes that a minimum of 15 million Chinese died from "bombing, starvation, and disease that resulted from the Japanese terror campaign."[877] "China paid the highest price of any of the Allied nations in the war with Japan."[878] "Asia under the Japanese was a charnel house of atrocities,"[879] and Japan treated subjected people with "beastialization."[880] Historian Martin Morgan even suggests that the death toll may exceed 40 million, considering whole cities vanished under Japanese control and mass graves are continually discovered.[881] Those Chinese suffering under IJA rule said the Japanese had a motto: *sanko seisaku* meaning, "kill all, burn all, destroy all."[882]

Here is a rough breakdown of those killed, mostly civilians, POWs, and even their own people, by the Japanese during the Asian and Pacific Wars (1927–1945):

China: 20 million (minimum and conservative)
Indonesian: 4 million
Vietnam: 2 million
Bengal Famine: 1.5 million[883]
Philippines: 1 million
Korea: 500,000
Burma/Siam Railroad: 345,000
Malaya/Singapore: 200,000
India: 180,000

Okinawa: 150,000
Saipan: 16,751
Tinian: 4,000
Guam: 2,000
Total: 29,897,751

"The suffering inflicted upon the victims of Japanese imperialism remains incalculable," but it is larger than what most have estimated.[884] England's chief advisor during the postwar trials, Lord Russell of Liverpool, remarked, "The full extent of [Japanese] crimes will never be accurately known, but in China they will never be forgotten."[885] It is difficult to find an "obvious explanation" for Japan's slaughter of millions. The Japanese targeted Chinese for mass murder "regardless of sex or age" and simply marked them "out as victims" to be dispensed without any justification except that they were poor, defenseless, and non-Japanese.[886] Japan disputes the numbers. However, Japan knows how many it lost in the war (3 million),[887] but does not *care to know* the numbers other nations give of those who died under its rule.[888] While there may be challenges with documenting the extent of the barbarism, the summary assessments made by nations after WWII cannot be denied—Japan was responsible for the murder of millions.

CHAPTER 17

PROBLEMS JAPAN HAS DOCUMENTING AND ATONING FOR ITS PAST

"Though he should conquer a thousand men in the battlefield a thousand times, yet he, indeed, who would conquer himself is the noblest victor."

—**The Buddha**[889]

WHEREAS THE NAZIS METICULOUSLY RECORDED how they "processed death," the Japanese, on the other hand, sloppily maintained records of their atrocities. "One argument could be that they were so disinterested in the actions their soldiers committed, and with documenting the murder of civilians to be totally unimportant they just ignored the process."[890]

The infrastructure of the societies Germany destroyed had government records on civilians. The Chinese system of documenting people was primitive, making it arduous to verify the exact number of civilians living in an area before and after the war. Although there are holes in authenticating the extent of Nazi destruction, there are historians who tenaciously ferret out the truth. However, in Japan, the government and much of its academic community have shown an aversion to facing their past, and there are few willing to document it.[891] Historians Meirion and Susie Harries explain: "The exhaustive and cathartic examination of the Holocaust by Germans...has no Japanese equivalent. *There has been no easy explanation of Japanese atrocities* [author's italics]."[892] They go on to explain Japan's avoidance culture has actively prevented the Japanese from coming to terms "with their own past." It has similarly prevented the rest of the world from coming to terms with the past as well. Although not a perfect analogy, their behavior is akin to a violent crime scene when a man brutally beats and rapes a woman, only then to act as if he has done nothing wrong when she is standing there with a broken nose, bloody face, and a violated body.[893] The need for open examination and acknowledgment of historical crimes is crucial for genuine reconciliation and understanding, something the majority of Japanese seem oblivious to apprehending.

This was seen recently when I submitted my manuscript *Flamethrower* to numerous translators from Japan only to be refused service. The issues I had raised in that book about Japan caused many to respond with: "Very problematic and difficult. Very sad. I regret that I am unable to help you." When I inquired about the reasons behind their refusal, none of them were willing to explain them. However, the truth emerging from these exchanges show that Japanese society, in some respects, is in a conspiracy to prevent the truth from coming out in their history books.

Japanese officials and many historians have "systematically kept all mention of their atrocities out of the nation's history textbooks." Journalist Katsuichi Honda wrote, "Unlike the Germans and Italians, the Japanese have not made their own full accounting of their prewar actions."[894] Historian Saburō Ienaga emphasized the gravity of this issue by asserting that falsifying textbooks "prohibits the completion of the people's development as human beings."[895] Historian John W. Dower echoes Ienaga's sentiments that what Japan's Department of Education does creates "nationalistic mythmaking."[896] Unlike Germany, which has taken significant steps to atone for its crimes by paying reparations and facing its dark past, Japan has neither atoned for its crimes by paying sufficient reparations nor, at the very least, even *admitted* its atrocities.[897]

In 1994, justice minister and former Army chief of staff Shigeto Nagano controversially declared the Rape of Nanking to be a fabrication, and he even attempted to justify Japan's actions during WWII as "'liberating' Asian countries from Western colonial powers."[898] This statement would be akin to a German politician denying the existence of Auschwitz and claiming Hitler was "liberating" Russia from Communism. Tokyo's *Yushukan* War Museum mentions nothing of the atrocities, and only writes that General Matsui in 1937–38 warned his men not to commit unlawful acts. It further claims he destroyed the Chinese at Nanking and then notes: "The Chinese soldiers disguised in civilian clothes were severely prosecuted."[899] They were not "prosecuted," they were slaughtered! As the 32nd Army's operations officer on Okinawa, Colonel Hiromichi Yahara, wrote in his memoir: "Without solid facts there can be no truth."[900] However, in his entire account, Yahara shamefully avoids addressing the over 100,000 civilians who died under his command, sometimes at the hands of his own soldiers, to "prevent" them from falling into Allied hands or being subjected to battlefield realities. He revealingly admitted: "We had to close our eyes to their plight."[901] Moreover, Yahara refused to discuss the policies of commanding his soldiers to kill themselves rather than surrendering to Americans, although he knew they would have been treated fairly, as he had firsthand experience with American culture during his time spent in the United States.[902]

To hammer home this point, it is important to highlight the perspective presented by Japan's A-Bomb Peace Museum in Hiroshima. While the museum emphasizes the horrors of the aerial bombardment that destroyed Hiroshima, it notably omits any mention of Japan's own bombings of numerous Chinese cities, which resulted in an estimated 350,00 civilian deaths.[903] There is no mention of the fact that the IJA used factories and assembling plants in Hiroshima prefecture to manufacture poison gas it deployed against civilians. Additionally, the museum fails to note that the city garrisoned 43,000 servicemen. It is essential to recognize that while the Japanese suffered the agony at Hiroshima and in other cities like the Tokyo Fire Bombing of March 1945, these events only happened after they inflicted great suffering on the Chinese, having killed tens of thousands in bombing and incendiary aerial raids. This was especially seen during Japan's campaigns in 1932 and from 1937 to 1940 when they terror-bombed Chapei, Tientsin, Shanghai, Nanking, Lanchow, Guangzhou, and Chongqing (Chungking), just to name a few. For instance, at Chongqing alone, Japan conducted 200 air raids from 1937 to 1940, killing 12,000 and wounding tens of thousands more, mostly non-combatants. Unlike American bombing raids, which aimed to cripple the enemy's war industry and ultimately end the war, Japan deliberately targeted civilians in their bombing campaigns and used them in such a way that prolonged the war.[904]

Luckily for these Chinese victims, Japanese planes and bombs were far inferior to America's. Had they had atomic bombs and better planes, they would have used them. Prime Minister Tōjō had already "planned to wage nuclear war if his nuclear scientists had prevailed."[905] The League of Nations Chinese delegation, represented by Wellington Koo, wrote the *Société des Nations'* general secretary in 1937 documenting Japan's terror-bombing operations against civilians which violated international law. Koo pleaded with the *Société des Nations* to use its resources to condemn and put an end to such illegal and inhuman war practices.[906] While U.S. bombing raids against Japan killed thousands of civilians, the strategy was always to cripple the war industry and end the war: *It was never designed to kill civilians* unlike Japan's goal. By 1945, after learning about the atrocities of these Axis regimes, most Americans believed Nazi Germany and Imperial Japan "deserved every bomb that fell on their countries," yet they still would have opposed any action solely to kill elderly men, women, and children—aka non-combatants.[907]

The blatant omission of Japan's violations of other nations and illegal acts from Japanese museums reveals the hypocrisy of those running these institutions. Commenting on Japan's falsifications, historian Yuki Tanaka writes that this dishonorable behavior "naturally hinders full recognition of responsibility for Japan's abhorrent military acts and the losses its Asian neighbors suffered as a result of war and colonialism."[908] In fact, this lack of historical accuracy extends to Japan's educational system, where important events such as the Battle of Pearl Harbor are either misrepresented or entirely ignored. A Marine Corps acquaintance who married a woman from Kuribayashi's family had to take her to Pearl Harbor to teach her how war with Japan and the U.S. started, highlighting the prevailing ignorance among many Japanese citizens regarding their country's war responsibility.[909] Historian Yuki Tanaka writes that Japan's fabrication of its history resulted in "the majority of Japanese…remain[ing] ignorant not only of Japan's war responsibility but also of the history of the Asia-Pacific War in general."[910] In the context of Holocaust survivor Primo Levi's statement, "Those who deny Auschwitz would be ready to remake it,"[911] it is pertinent to apply this principle to Japanese leaders who deny the atrocities committed under Hirohito's regime. Such denial raises concerns about the potential for similar acts to be repeated if history is not fully acknowledged and learned from. As former prime minister of Singapore Lee Kuan Yew aptly expressed, "Asian nations can never trust a Japan that cannot acknowledge its own misdeeds."[912]

This is particularly evident with politicians in Japan's current ruling party, the Liberal Democratic Party, which is really ultra-conservative. The late former Prime Minister Shinzo Abe, a colleague and friend of Shindo (General Kuribayashi's grandson), has tried to whitewash Japan's history and even attempted to retract apologies to other nations for Japan's actions, including the tragic "Comfort Women" issue and the mass slaughter of millions during the war. Shockingly, he denies that "Comfort Women" even existed, despite overwhelming evidence to the contrary. He is viewed by many as a right-wing nationalist, a revisionist historian, and a "Japanese Holocaust denier."[913] He appears to be a new nationalist who wants to produce "an evangelical edition of history with the inconvenient facts omitted."[914] Knowing his grandfather, Economic Minister Nobusuke Kishi, who was classified as a Class-A war criminal for his involvement in the brutal rule of Manchuria, perhaps Abe's behavior is not entirely surprising. Abe has never condemned his grandfather's actions, who believed in the *Yamato* race theory (describing the Chinese as dogs), supported the opium trade, conducted sexual abuse against women, and facilitated the death of hundreds of thousands of Manchurians.[915] He actually has given words of deep respect about his grandfather. That Japan's head of state could embrace such a man as being honorable shows how far his nation needs to go before it can be taken seriously amongst enlightened and democratic nations. To be taken seriously in the international community, Japan must demonstrate a commitment to truth, accountability, and reconciliation, acknowledging past wrongs and actively working towards a future built on peace and cooperation with its neighbors, something Abe (the longest serving prime minister Japan had since WWII) and other politicians have failed to do.

After my meeting with the "Honorable" LDP politician Shindo, I collaborated with my interpreter, Ms. Uo of Simul, to translate and transcribe our interview and the information Shindo provided. Thereafter, I sent the document to him and his government contact in the Ministry of Foreign Affairs, Iba Takamasa, and waited patiently for six months for a reply. Eventually, I received a response, but to my dismay, I found that Shindo had made corrections to only half of the notes I gave him and then insisted I take the other half out entirely. It was clear that he did not want to be quoted saying what he had said during our interview. I surmise that upon reviewing his translated and transcribed remarks, his advisors, Shindo, and his team deemed them too controversial for his conservative support base. Moreover, it is possible that he faced pressure from some of his colleagues to distance himself from an American *gaijin* who was reigniting the contentious discussion about Japan's wartime past. This interview, coupled with the criminal information about his grandfather, could potentially be politically devastating for Shindo, especially since he has used the image of General Kuribayashi in political posters defending Japanese islands from China, Korea, and Russia, or in efforts to reclaim islands these three nations seized after WWII. The revelation of his family's dark history may undermine his credibility and image among his constituents and the broader public.

In 1951, historians Philip A. Crowl and Jeter A. Isely astutely warned about the danger posed by Shindo, stating, "[Kuribayashi] was a man to be feared alive, but is probably even more dangerous to America dead, since he is capable of becoming a hero of a resurgent nationalism in Japan."[916] Their prophetic words proved to be alarmingly accurate when, in 2018, Shindo's unguarded comments spoken truthfully for this research apparently jeopardize his position within his own party. And his party has proven that it has difficulty apologizing properly to the world for Japan's crimes against humanity and for *its Holocaust*. Moreover, Shindo's party's reluctance to apologize sincerely for Japan's past actions has contributed to the creation of a misguided nationalism, precisely as Crowl and Isely had forewarned. In 2019, Shindo's frustration with the attention drawn to our research led to an unfortunate incident where he made a veiled threat to the Iwo Jima American Association (IJAA), suggesting that he might shut down Iwo Jima to Americans if they did not address my book and my role on the board![917] His attempt to use airport maintenance as leverage was not only childish, but also indicative of the lengths some might go to suppress inconvenient truths that challenge the prevailing narrative.

I should not be surprised by Shindo's behavior since as a member of the revisionist lobby *Nippon Kaigi*, he aims to erase Japan's crimes from history books, promote nationalistic education, support official visits to the Yasukuni Shrine, and promote a nationalist interpretation of Shintō for citizens. This lobby group wants the nation to reinstate a standing army. One of its influential leaders, Hideaki Kase, until his death in 2022, even wanted Japan to return to a monarchy and Imperial state.[918] The lobby group stands for xenophobic, misogynistic, anti-modern, anti-liberal, and anti-democratic principles. One could call it a fascist organization, which *National Review* journalist Josh Gelernter indeed does.[919] It supports the myth that Imperial Japan tried to "liberate" East Asia from Western colonial powers, that the Tokyo war trials were illegitimate (a clear violation of San Francisco Peace Treaty's Article 11) and that the IJA massacre at Nanking in 1937 was fabricated. Moreover, it fights against feminism, LGBT rights, and the 1999 Gender Equality Law.[920] *Nippon Kaigi* would make Tōjō, Hirohito, Matsui, Tsuji, and Kuribayashi proud. Shindo would be wise to listen to historian Liu Yizheng when he writes: "Historical records can be used to contribute to national prosperity and world peace or to spell disaster by covering up or even glorifying the evil."[921] It looks like Shindo, unfortunately, is doing the latter. He might be wise to harken to the admonition by chief of counsel of the International Military Tribunal for the Far East, Joseph B. Keenan: "If there is no justification for punishment of individuals who have already brought civilization to the brink of disaster, then justice itself is a mockery."[922]

Politician Yoshitaka Shindo uses images of Kuribayashi in campaign posters saying he defends Japan like his grandfather. Knowing his grandfather committed crimes during WWII, one would think Shindo would be wise not to do this. *Author's Collection*

Ironically, revisionists like Shindo and Abe, who align themselves with revisionist organizations denying WWII atrocities, perform a "pivotal role in publicizing" Japan's mass murder during the Pacific and Asian Wars "beyond national boundaries."[923] Their intense resistance to acknowledging Japan's crime and the historical massacres like Nanking only serves to make these events headline news. According to historian Takashi Yoshida, "[these atrocities] might have remained a domestic issue rather than becoming an international symbol of Japan's wartime aggression" had Japanese leaders just been honest about their past.[924] Contrary to Shindo's and Abe's beliefs that their behavior will make these "issues" go away, it has the opposite effect. According to historian Zhang Sheng and vice president of *The Society for Research on the History of the Nanjing*

Massacre by Japanese Invaders, people like Shindo and Abe have "distorted East Asia's history and played havoc with its present."[925] These Japanese leaders might take their education and cue from German chancellor Willy Brandt when he knelt down before the Warsaw Ghetto monument in 1970 in an overt act of asking for forgiveness and in acknowledging the horrible history Germany had conducted there. How many Japanese prime ministers have done a similar symbolic gesture in Nanking at its memorial? The answer is simple: None!

If Japan and its leaders persist in refusing to acknowledge their country's dark past and continue supporting jingoistic organizations like *Nippon Kaigi*, they dishonor not only the victims of 20th-century Japanese atrocities, but also the millions of others who fought for freedom against totalitarian regimes like Hirohito's Japan. Moreover, they dishonor the deaths of their own countrymen who, although they died under an evil regime, at least could have taken hope that their deaths indirectly helped create a better government for future generations. Although Japan's present government is undoubtedly better than its Imperial predecessor, it still falls short in fully recognizing the extent of its country's criminal history, much like Turkey's denial of its Armenian genocide. As long as this denial persists, leaders like Shindo will dishonor the positive attributes of his grandfather's leadership seen on Iwo Jima and will implicitly condone his despicable behavior seen during the battle for Hong Kong. Shindo, Abe, and others pervert what the *Nippon Times* asked its readers to embrace in 1945:

> If we use this pain and this humiliation [of our defeat and surrendering] as a spur to self-reflection and reform, and if we make this self-reflection and reform the motive force for a great constructive effort, there is nothing to stop us from building, out of the ashes of our defeat, a magnificent new Japan free from the dross of the old which is now gone, a new Japan which will vindicate our pride by winning the respect of the world.[926]

However, it seems that Abe and Shindo are not getting the "respect of the world," but instead distrust for what historian Michael Weiner calls their "mytho-history."[927] Nevertheless, it is hoped, however unlikely, that this book might help the Japanese people to accept their ancestors' wrongs so they will never be repeated.

There are indeed some Japanese who are honest about their country's past atrocities, including historians Saburō Ienaga, Keiichi Tsuneishi, Yoshiaki Yoshimi, Hirofumi Hayashi, Yutaka Yoshida, and Yuki Tanaka to name some, but they represent only a minority among Japan's political and academic leaders. While there are a few courageous souls in government, they are few and far between. For example, Japanese consul-general in Houston, Texas, Tetsuro

Amano, said in January 2018 that Japan should never forget the victims of Hirohito's Japan and that apologies and tangible economic activity should support this remembrance.[928] Likewise, in 2000, a brave Japanese journalist and women's rights activist, Yayori Matsui, organized a women's war crimes tribunal in Tokyo which sought to procure some form of justice for Japan's sex slavery campaign during WWII. Although it brought a lot of victim testimony to light and found Hirohito guilty of these crimes, it did not procure reparations from the government or changes in the textbooks for children.[929] Regrettably, when the government was invited to participate, it declined to send representatives, and Prime Minister Abe, not surprisingly, suppressed information about it in the press.[930] This is not surprising, given Japan's history of downplaying and whitewashing its wartime actions.

Since 1945, there have been some attempts at reparations from Japan; however, these efforts pale in comparison to Germany's approach. Astonishingly, despite Japan slaughtering three times as many as the Nazis did (Hitler murdered 11.7 million),[931] Japan has paid a meager amount, barely reaching over 1% of what Germany has contributed ($1 billion compared to *Deutschland's $90 billion*).[932] This significant disparity in reparations has led many to claim that the "Japanese are both morally and monetarily deficient by comparison."[933] The lack of substantial reparations is not the only issue; many Japanese have little knowledge about or remorse for their country's past atrocities. With the official stonewalling and avoidance of facing their history, it is highly improbable that there will be significant progress in educating the Japanese people about their nation's dark past and fostering a sense of genuine remorse.[934]

Although more died during the Rape of Nanking and the rampage Japan conducted in China after Doolittle's raid than the Japanese who died from the atomic bombs, some Japanese persist in maintaining an illusion of victimhood, pointing to the nuclear bombings as evidence of their suffering while conveniently ignoring their role in initiating the Asian and Pacific Wars.[935] Regrettably, this distorted perspective has led to demands from certain Japanese quarters for apologies from America regarding the use of nuclear weapons. Yet, these same individuals only offer half-hearted apologies, if any, to the countless victims who suffered due to Japan's brutal wartime actions.

Often when apologies are offered by the Japanese, they are insincere and dishonest since they are not backed with reparations or explorations of these crimes in state-sponsored textbooks.[936] And when apologies are asked for or a request to recognize the victims is made, the Japanese often respond in childish and disgraceful ways. A glaring example of this is the response by the Japanese in 2018 to the memorial in San Francisco dedicated to remembering the sex slaves (i.e. "Comfort Women") abused by the Japanese military called the *Column of Strength*. Instead of acknowledging the historical truth and expressing remorse, the mayor of Japanese sister city Osaka to San Francisco, Hirofumi Yoshimura, cut ties with the city and called the memorial "Japan-bashing." This reaction reflects a prevalent pattern of denial and deflection among Japan's political leaders. Notably, the previous mayor Tōru Hashimoto first denied the existence of "Comfort Women" in 2013 and then revised his statement saying they existed but were necessary so soldiers could "rest."[937] Even the senior fellow at their National Institute for Defense Studies, Colonel Yukio Yasunaga, claimed in 2018 that "Comfort Women" followed the Japanese armies in China "and were paid for their services. All the talk today about them is political."[938] Yasunaga's sentiments are unfortunately all too common, exemplified by the examples of political leaders mentioned here. These individuals dismiss the plight of the victims of Imperial Japan with political talking points and hyperbolic denials.

When the World Heritage Foundation UNESCO included the Rape of Nanking documents as part of humanity's heritage, Japan responded by halting its funding for the organization in 2016, an amount totaling $40 million. This decision significantly hindered UNESCO, as Japan had been one of its major contributors.[939] And in the tradition of hindering historical research and justice, unlike Germany, which actively investigated and collaborated with foreign nations to prosecute its war criminals, Japan did not undertake a similar comprehensive effort to bring its own perpetrators to justice.

Whereas Germany condemns Hitler, Japan has never held Emperor Hirohito accountable for his role in leading the country into fascism, mass murder, and a disastrous war. Instead, Japan allowed him to hold his throne until 7 January 1989 when he, a fallen god and war criminal, died of colon cancer. For many years, he lived a life of leisure, often playing "rounds of golf in the postwar era, blithely oblivious to his sordid wartime past."[940] "He lacked all consciousness of personal responsibility for what Japan had done abroad and never once admitted guilt for the war of aggression" that was sanctioned by him.[941] The lack of accountability is a significant injustice, as the authority to act as Japan did derived from him as the emperor.[942] Some argue that he should have faced charges for war crimes and that the judges at the Tokyo Tribunal should have executed him.[943]

In the 44 years after WWII, during which Hirohito's rule continued albeit without the power he had before and during the war, he *never* publicly discussed the conflict or his role in it (his diary remains unreleased).[944] Although he was revered by the wartime generation, Hirohito, the ex-god, never took responsibility for Japan's atrocious crimes during the war. "Despite the fact that the war was fought under his command," he refused to accept "responsibility for the...acts which occurred during it" in his *holy name*.[945] Even today, many in Japan refuse to denounce Hirohito and his actions. When asked to denounce Hirohito in 2018, Japanese deputy consul general for Houston Ryuji Iwasaki, presenting a sphinxlike expression, declined to do so, perhaps fearing the consequences of expressing such a conviction by his own government.[946] Iwasaki maybe had legitimate fear for admitting such a conviction if he had it. For instance, in 1990, when the mayor of Nagasaki, Hitoshi Motoshima, claimed Hirohito was to blame for the war, a right-wing nationalist shot him. He fortunately survived the attack.

After World War II, General of the Army MacArthur made the strategic decision to retain Emperor Hirohito as a symbolic figurehead of Japan in order to secure the peace, promote liberalization, and democratize the country. The Allies controlled the war trials, and the responsibility of not holding Hirohito accountable lay in MacArthur's hands.[947] MacArthur's military secretary, Brigadier General Bonner F. Fellers, explained the reasoning behind sparing Hirohito's life, describing the emperor as the "incarnation of national spirit, incapable of wrong or misdeeds [and thus,] to try him as a war criminal would not only be blasphemous but a denial of spiritual freedom."[948] General Curtis LeMay explained MacArthur's position, saying the Allies left Hirohito alone "because of his anti-communist posture and willingness to work with the U.S. during the Cold War [which President] Truman saw as valuable...Personally, I would've strung the bastard up by his balls."[949] In the end, MacArthur and his advisors were worried that trying "Hirohito as a war criminal would cause Japan's government to collapse and might result in an uprising requiring a larger expeditionary force and prolonging the occupation."[950]

Unsurprisingly, Japan's WWII commemorative ceremonies remain silent about Emperor Hirohito's or the nation's crimes. Every 15 August, on Japan's anniversary of surrender, the country recalls "the war" "with a government-sponsored 'Day Commemorating the End of the War.'" Though not a national holiday, Tokyo's *Nihon Budôkan* hall, "normally the site of concerts, professional wrestling matches and martial-arts events," is used, where national leaders and honored guests participate in ceremonies to "Mourn the War Dead."[951] In a sea of Japanese flags and chrysanthemum banners, leaders such as the prime minister, government and local officials, as well as family members of famous military dead are among the VIP guests. The emperor reads a statement covered by the press, followed by a moment of silence. "No apologies or regrets are offered to the millions...who survived the depredations of the Japanese, and no one seems to consider anything to be amiss in that."[952] Although apologies are demanded of the Japanese, they rarely comply. The "disingenuous" Hirohito, when he participated in these events, "lacked all consciousness of personal responsibility for what Japan had done…and never once admitted guilt for the war of aggression that…cost so many lives."[953]

However, it is ironic and pathetic that Japan, despite its own reluctance to apologize for its wartime actions, demands apologies from others. For instance, in May 2016, when U.S. President Obama visited Hiroshima, Terumi Tanaka, secretary general of Japan's Confederation of A-Bomb and H-Bomb Sufferers, urged Obama to apologize to the "victims," claiming the weapon "inhumane and against international law."[954] Tanaka attempted to convince the world to view the Japanese as victims instead of as the aggressors whose actions had caused the use of the bombs in the first place.[955] Historian John W. Dower writes, "a collective sense of Japanese victimization in that terrible war generally prevails over recollection of how grievously Imperial Japan victimized others."[956] On the other side of the equation, some veterans' groups advised President Obama not to visit Hiroshima, fearing that it might be interpreted as an "implicit apology" disrespecting the sacrifices of U.S. veterans. Retired Rear Admiral Lloyd "Joe" Vasey, a WWII submarine officer, wrote:

> Any presidential action or policy that even appears as an implicit apology for the use of the atomic bomb would be a gross insult to us and our valiant comrades who fought and sacrificed…to win the war and bring us a peace that liberated Asia.[957]

President Obama made clear there would be no apology but that his visit would serve as an opportunity to reflect on the bombs' destructiveness and recommit to preventing nuclear war.[958] President Obama's visit was followed by one of Japan's Prime Minister Abe to Pearl Harbor, offering condolences to the Americans who lost their lives there, but not addressing Japan's own wartime atrocities or violations of international law. Although WWII events "seem far behind us, in many ways they continue to structure mentalities in the contemporary world."[959]

One of the most glaring examples of justice denied and historical understanding disregarded is what happened with the butcher of Singapore and organizer of the Bataan Death March, Lieutenant Colonel Masanobu Tsuji. After the war, he evaded capture and went into hiding as a Buddhist monk in Bangkok. He then spent two years in China, accomplishing little. Through one of his old army contacts, he returned to Japan in 1948 and was shockingly put on the payroll of the United States as a CIA covert agent. Like with General Ishii, General of the Army MacArthur allowed his intelligence chief, General

Charles Willoughby, to allow Tsuji to go un-prosecuted because of his planning abilities and his anti-Communist "bona fides," making him "one thus worth protecting."[960] Tsuji capitalized on his notoriety and started writing books, the first entitled *Underground Escape*, chronicling how he avoided Allied capture after the end of WWII. Published in 1950, it quickly became a run-away bestseller. In 1952, he released his second work, *Japan's Greatest Victory, Britain's Worst Defeat*, boasting how he had masterminded the victory of Malaya and Singapore. It also became a bestseller and he rose to even more prominence. With his newfound fame, Tsuji easily won election to the Diet in 1952, the lower house of Japan's parliament, advocating for Japan to re-militarize and to fight against Communism. In 1959, he won election to the upper house of Japan's parliament in a landslide victory. However, his political ambitions faced a major setback when a military enemy from his time in the Philippines, who had knowledge of his crimes in Singapore and Bataan, exposed him by writing a scathing article in 1959 which crippled Tsuji's political aspirations, and he left parliament in 1961. Instead of the government seizing Tsuji and putting him on trial immediately after the revelations in 1959 of his crimes, he continued to live as a free man from 1959 until 1961.

In stark contrast, Germany has taken responsibility for its wartime atrocities and has conducted several trials against its own war criminals over the years, demonstrating a commitment to justice and historical accountability. Deplorably, Japan *has failed to follow suit.*[961] Although the treaty with the U.S. after WWII may have restricted Japan from holding its own trials, it could have at least extradited Tsuji to the authorities in Singapore, the Philippines, or the United States to stand trial. However, instead of facing the consequences of his actions, Tsuji, soon after leaving parliament, disappeared, donning the robes of a Buddhist monk, seamlessly "blending" into the society in the country of Laos. After seven years of being a "missing person," the Japanese government conveniently declared him dead.[962] This lack of accountability is deeply troubling and raises questions about Japan's commitment to justice. Adding to the distressing situation, in 2008, the city of Kaga in Ishikawa prefecture, Tsuji's birthplace, erected a large monument with a bronze life-size sculpture of him on a pedestal. Japan honors its war criminals and forgets its victims. This monument is one action out of thousands that serve as painful reminders of Japan's failure to fully reckon with its dark history, embracing their fascist past as something to honor and not condemn.

Japan's persistent culture of denial continues to plague the nation to this day, especially since this culture was established right at the start of the post-war political environment. Despite being confronted with extensive evidence of his own wrongdoings and the atrocities committed by the military and government, one of Tōjō's statements was nothing short of audacious when he claimed:

> Since the end of the war, I have read about the inhumane acts committed by the Japanese Army and Navy. These were certainly not the intention of those in authority, namely the General Staff, or the War or Navy Departments or myself. We did not even suspect that such things had happened. The Emperor especially, because of his benevolence, would have had a contrary feeling. Such acts are not permissible in Japan, the character of the Japanese people is such that they believe that neither Heaven nor Earth would permit such things. It will be too bad if people in the world believe that these inhumane acts are the result of Japanese character.[963]

Tōjō's attempt to portray Japan as a nation that would never permit such acts seen from 1927 to 1945 is not only disgraceful but also lacks moral integrity. In exploring Japanese culture, one could analyze their concepts of "what is perceived" *tatemae* (建前) and "what is actual" *honne* (ほね) in interpreting Tōjō's words. Tōjō's words were clearly meant to create a perception that Japan was innocent of such crimes, absolving Emperor Hirohito, government and military leaders, and ordinary citizens of any responsibility for the heinous acts committed by commanders and soldiers in the field. However, as history has proven, no one believes his words, as they fail to convince anyone of Japan's innocence outside Japan. Tōjō wanted the Japanese to feel the crimes their nation committed were not their fault and that they were honorable. However, this perception was not the case. Tōjō's statement does indeed prove he had to acknowledge Japan's crimes, but in doing so, he further deflects the blame for those crimes from being assigned to *anybody*. It sought to protect him and his cohorts from being held accountable for their misdeeds committed during the Asian and Pacific Wars.

In claiming the entire military and government structure had nothing to do with the crimes when all the evidence showed they knew about everything that was happening illustrates Tōjō's unbelievable arrogance. As a former head of the army and government, his audacity to make such claims, which by and large have not been rejected by present-day Japanese, reveals why it remains challenging for modern-day Japanese to confront their past honestly and seek redemption for their actions. Unfortunately, there are many Tōjō-like-minded people in Japan presently, and thus, their culture is grossly lacking when it comes to honoring the truth. They would do themselves a great favor if they focused more on *honne* (ほね) "what is actual" than *tatemae* (建前) "what they wish to be perceived," because their perception of the facts is downright dishonorable.[964]

One event after the war's end that starkly illustrates the dishonorable nature of Japanese leaders happened when they suddenly took a profound "interest in the niceties of the Hague Convention," pointing out how Japanese POWs should be treated humanely.[965] Now, the Japanese were willing to invoke laws they knew the Allies would follow and had pledged to uphold, something the Japanese never had done although their signatures were on the same document. The hypocrisy goes beyond mere two-faced behavior and highlights a deep-seated flaw in Japanese culture at the time. They manipulated international laws to their advantage, receiving humane treatment for their prisoners while showing no regard for the same laws when they were the aggressors.

And concerning post-war apologies and reparations, Korea has borne the brunt of Japan's lackluster compensation, especially for the tens of thousands of "Comfort Women" who came from there and suffered immensely during the war. Even more shocking is Japan's denial of benefits to 370,000 Korean veterans, embracing their still racist mandate "that they were not Japanese."[966] The same fate befalls Korean victims of the atomic bombs, leaving them in "legal and medical limbo."[967] All these policies conducted by Japan post-1945 prove this nation is still racist and continues to struggle with its criminal past.

Japan's inability to deal with their crimes has become a tradition, dating back to the International Tribunal on War Crimes in Tokyo from 1946 to 1948. Prime Minister and General Tōjō set the tone for this at his trial when he had the hubris to testify that his actions as a general and politician were without blemish, declaring, "I feel that I did no wrong. I feel I did what was right and true."[968] The Tribunal disagreed with Tōjō and sentenced him to death, writing, "He bears major responsibility for Japan's criminal attacks on her neighbors. In this trial he defended all these attacks with hardihood, alleging that they were legitimate measures of self-defense. We have dealt with that plea. It is wholly unfounded."[969] Brazenly, Tōjō wrote right before he was hanged, "But internationally, I declare myself innocent."[970] For a man who commanded the Japanese Secret Police (*Kempei Tai*) in 1935 for the Kwantung Army in Manchuria; who was the Kwangtung Army's chief of staff from 1937 to 1938; who had personally conducted military operations in 1937 Chahar Province during the Second Sino-Japanese War;[971] who was vice minister of war from 1938 to 1940;[972] and who was prime minister from 1940 until 1944, he had to have known about the Rape of Asia and the Rape of the Pacific in all its forms. He either was a pathological liar or an idiot, or both. The day his guilty verdict was issued, he wrote the following poem: "Gazing upward, I hear reverently the voice of the Buddha, calling me from the pure and boundless sky."[973] Several weeks later, before stepping onto the trapdoor on the gallows, he yelled out "*Tenno Haikai! Banzai* [Long Live the Emperor]."[974] No self-reflection. No apologies. No regrets. Fanatic ignorance must surely be the ultimate bliss.

If one considers all the evidence of denial and deception, one realizes how defiant the Japanese still are to this day when it comes to embracing facts from the war, still following Tōjō's disgraceful example. They behave as if no one sees the tens of millions of murdered bodies and treat everyone who confronts them with historical facts about Japan's atrocities as if they are blind and racist towards Japan. Until Japan changes its educational system and its moral and ethical character, it should face consequences for its actions. Perhaps during the next Olympics, they should not be invited, and restrictions on Japanese products should be enforced, preventing them from entering free markets, especially those from companies that supported Japan during the war. Moreover, several times a year, first-world nations that suffered under the Japanese during the Asian and Pacific Wars, like the United States, Britain, France, the Philippines, and China, etc. should issue statements on key anniversaries, like the end of WWII or the Rape of Nanking, to confront Japan's leadership with these uncomfortable truths until the nation finds the moral strength to own up to its crimes and establish a museum in Tokyo's center honoring the victims. Only then can Japan begin to truly heal and move forward with integrity.

CHAPTER 18

MASS MURDER AND COMPULSORY SUICIDE OF JAPANESE CIVILIANS *BY THE JAPANESE*

"In war, truth is the first casualty."

—**Aeschylus**, 5th century B.C.E. Greek tragedian[975]

ONE ASPECT OF JAPAN'S HOLOCAUST that should be focused on is how the Imperial Japanese leaders convinced their civilians to kill themselves instead of surrendering to American forces. Many of those who refused to commit suicide were killed by their own soldiers, since those soldiers were ordered to do so. To explore this history, the battles of Saipan, Tinian, and Okinawa will be reviewed.

SAIPAN

In June and July 1944, American forces fought the Japanese on Saipan and conquered the island. At the battle's end, U.S. Marines and Army soldiers cornered what was left of the Japanese garrison to the island's north. Civilians moved with retreating troops stopping at the shore with no place to escape.

Many Marines did what they could to help civilians left behind. Even after experiencing enemy cruelty and fanaticism, American servicemen displayed kindness. As soon as the Marines ascertained what was occurring at Marpi Point, when civilians started killing themselves, they brought up interpreters on megaphones and loudspeakers, telling them they would not hurt them.[976] Scout planes dropped fliers notifying civilians of U.S. servicemen's good intentions.

Seabees had to bulldoze the hundreds of dead Japanese soldiers into a mass grave from the *Banzai* attack on Saipan from 7 July 1945. *National Archives, College Park*

Marine Jim Reed witnessed a father throw his children, wife, and then himself off a cliff. After observing such scenes, Reed wanted to help. When he encountered some children and women, he gathered them up before they jumped. In other island battles, the natives melted into the hills beforehand or sailed to nearby islands and returned after fighting stopped, but there were still over 20,000 in the Japanese-controlled area on northern Saipan.[977]

The civilians had a difficult time avoiding the conflict and behaved in bizarre ways when facing defeat. During the campaign's final days, Marines witnessed hundreds of civilians kill themselves to avoid falling into American hands. One of Japan's commanders on Saipan, Lieutenant General Yoshitsugu Saitō, had ordered civilians to commit suicide in the event of defeat.[978] For years, Japan fed its citizens the propaganda describing Americans wanting to cut the testicles off of Japanese and as "sadistic, redheaded, hairy monsters who committed unspeakable atrocities before putting all *Nipponese*, including women and infants, to the sword."[979] One document claimed Americans were "barbarous and execute all prisoners" and kill some "by cutting them up and crushing them with steam rollers."[980] Japanese "were taught to despise Marines, who purportedly had to murder their own parents to qualify for enlistment."[981] Many Japanese believed these lies.[982] A few civilians did take up arms against the Marines, though not many.[983] Believing the propaganda, many civilians trapped at Marpi Point killed themselves. Mothers threw their infants off cliffs and then jumped. A group of a hundred of all ages passed grenades out to one another, pushed the pins, and blew themselves up. Women, men, boys, and girls slit each other's wrists and bled out. Others took cyanide.[984] Young children hugged the necks of soldiers as they waded out to sea to collectively drown together.[985] The 4th Marine Division (MarDiv) reported: "Enemy soldiers, and civilians killed their families and themselves rather than surrender."[986]

A patrol boat's commander said as he motored along the coast by Marpi cliff by the ocean, his craft's progress "was slow and tedious because of the hundreds of corpses floating in the water." One of the dead was a nude woman who had killed herself while giving birth: "The baby's head had entered the world but that was all of him."[987] Piles of bodies floated in the surf and along the rock jetties, most of them dead, but many not. Sickening, gut-wrenching moans echoed throughout the canyon walls from those still alive, suffering from compound fractures, lacerations, and internal bleeding.[988]

As civilians stood at Marpi Point debating whether to jump, a Japanese sniper shot those reluctant to commit suicide. While two parents agonized over whether they should throw themselves and their small children over the cliff, the sniper killed the parents. This revealed his position to Marines nearby who zeroed in on him. Realizing his position had been given up, he defiantly walked out of his cave and "crumpled under a hundred American bullets."[989] In another cave, IJA soldiers hid with women and children. When some infants started crying, threatening to reveal their hideout, a sergeant said, "Kill them yourself or I'll order my men to do it." With that order, "several mothers killed their own children."[990] A 4th MarDiv observed that the Japanese "reputation for butchery did stand up. This was…illustrated in the days at Marpi Point where great numbers of civilians were slaughtered by maddened soldiers."[991]

Marine Gunnery Sergeant Keith A. Renstrom witnessed a family of seven near the lip of a cliff struggling with whether to jump or not. A father, a mother clutching her young infant, a young boy and girl of about five years of age, and two elder siblings, both in their young teens and dressed in exquisite kimonos. The family stood together; their forms pronounced at the cliff's edge with the seamless backdrop of the ocean behind them. With their hair whipping around their faces wildly, they stared at the position of Renstrom and his Marines. Suddenly, with a flash of movement, the father snatched the tiny infant bundle from his wife's protective arms and hurled the baby into the air over the jagged rock face. Renstrom watched the child roll down the face of the cliff until it stopped near the bottom, where it got hung on the sharp coral edges by its blanket. The baby dangled, moving its tiny arms and legs, and the men glared in horror as the waves relentlessly pummeled its little body against the jagged wall. Its life ebbed away on each crest of a whitecap. The Marines returned their attention back to the remaining family members to see the two eldest children solemnly bow to each other, turn, and throw themselves off the ledge. The father then grabbed the young son and attempted to throw him over the ledge, but the little boy fought his father with fierce determination. The father was able to disengage with the boy and then heaved him over the cliff. Then the father did the same with his little girl, throwing her mercilessly to her death too. He then turned to his wife. High on the cliff with the shattered bodies of their children below, they began to argue. Running out of patience with her as she hesitated in the face of her own death, he leapt forward and shoved her over the jagged ledge to join her dead children. Examining the scene of his family below him, he turned to Renstrom and his Marines and yelled "*Banzai! Banzai!*" and then jumped. As the men watched his descent, they saw that instead of falling directly onto the rocks below, in a dark twist of comedic fate, he was instead caught and spared his intended show of Japanese stoicism, landing in an embarrassment of failure cradled by the crest of an untimely large wave, having only injured himself. Obviously in extreme agony, but still alive, the current carried him further away out to sea. After a short internal debate, Renstrom raised his tommy gun and fired three shots, all of them missing his intended target. A Marine nearby said, "Gunny, let me take care of this." He raised his M1 rifle and shot the father in the head. As the blood rushed out of the father's skull, his body slowly disappeared into the sea. This was to become Renstrom's biggest regret that followed him throughout his life, in that he had not recognized what these people were about to do in order to stop the pointless slaughtering of themselves.[992]

Government-controlled news reports in Japan glorified this suicidal fanaticism. One newspaper extolled Saipan mothers who killed their children and themselves as *the flowers of womanhood*.[993] Historian Edward J. Drea wrote:

> This was obviously crude propaganda, but to its underlying purpose was chilling to convince…[homeland] civilians that they too were expected to fight to the bitter end to protect the homeland. The army had imposed its standard of no surrender onto the civilian population to legitimize the notion of death before dishonor and collective suicide for all Japanese.[994]

This "carnival of death" and "frenzied extinction" at Marpi Point shocked "battle-hardened Marines."[995]

V Amphibious Corps, responsible for the entire campaign for Saipan, reported after the conflict that 27,000 Japanese and Korean citizens were living on the island at the time when the Marines had landed. After the conflict, only 9,091 Japanese and 1,158 Koreans were found. This leaves 16,751 who killed themselves, were murdered by other Japanese, or were caught in the battle's maelstrom (62%).[996] Historians Haruko and Theodore Cook wrote, "Japanese women, children and other noncombatants were driven into the northern corner of the island, where most committed mass suicide."[997] The commandant of Hong Kong POW camps Colonel Isao Tokunaga under General Kuribayashi explained after the war:

> According to a Japanese, not only military personnel but women and children will think it better to die than to become a POW. This principle was strongly taught [to] women and children and in this war, in the Pacific area, many women and children died rather than be POWs.[998]

Unfortunately, Tokunaga knew his fellow countrymen well. Often Japanese citizens were to be exploited for military goals. The 4th MarDiv reported numerous Japanese soldiers had used civilians as human shields, resulting in innocent women and children dying.[999] The report noticed a "peculiar trait" when the soldiers knew civilians were surrendering. They set up snipers to hit the roads coming and going to the evacuation points, putting their own citizens in harm's way, and killing any Americans who helped civilians.[1000]

Due to suicide, disregard for the safety of their own citizens, dehydration, diseases, malnutrition, and combat, 16,000 Japanese and Korean citizens died on Saipan (most of the 16,000 were Japanese).[1001] The 4th MarDiv concluded, "No quarter can be given to the Jap soldier. He will employ every trick or ruse possible that will profitably yield several American lives for the sacrifice of his own."[1002]

Japanese behavior perplexed Americans. One Marine labelled it: "These Nips Are Nuts." Another Marine wrote the "Japs" were "plain crazy, sick in the head, that's all."[1003] Marines, witnessing this fanaticism, started calling one another "Asiatic" if one acted oddly, meaning they were behaving like the wacky "Nips."[1004] Japan had created a collective death cult: "Suicide became ritualized, and formally institutionalized, in the army's ethos as a laudable goal and a testament to the unique Japanese spirit."[1005]

There were cases where some of Saipan's citizens started to realize Americans would not hurt but help them. Reed showed he had water and chocolate for them, sharing them with the children. Before he knew it, he had a crowd around him. They gathered the kids and adults in a truck and drove them away from Marpi Point to where Marines took care of the civilians.[1006]

As they drove between the suicide cliffs and the beachhead, rogue Japanese units fired at them. Marines did their best to protect themselves, counterattack, and kill these IJA soldiers. Reed remembered one girl of about four years old who was terrified at first. Slowly, through his acts of kindness, she started to trust him until he was teaching her how to play "patty-cake" and giving her candy. When it came time for him to save more civilians, she jumped into his arms, and refused to let go. He freed himself from her embrace and tearfully said goodbye. She stood waving as he drove away. He told his buddy, "I wish I could take her home with me."[1007]

Gunny Renstrom also took care of a little girl. Most likely an orphan like the child Reed showed kindness to, she stood wet and shivering in the rain. Looking at the Marines, she saw something in Renstrom. She walked to him and nestled next to his leg under his poncho. Soon thereafter, he took off his poncho, wrapped her in it, and laid her gently in the cranny of a large rock. Renstrom gave his canteen to her, and she had to hold the bottle with both of her teeny hands. Water flowed over her mouth dribbling down both sides of her face as she gulped as fast as she could. After she finished, she handed the canteen back to the Gunny and smiled, her white teeth gleaming in the dull light of day. Renstrom also fed her some of his food. "She ate two full rations," and Renstrom was shocked such a "little thing" could eat so much. After, she curled back into her poncho-bed and drifted off to sleep as evening approached. Marines nearby shook their heads and laughed as they watched their fearless leader turn "into putty" as he doted on this child. Gunnys were to be feared and they never showed weakness in front of their men, but these Marine-laws had disappeared when this innocent, frightened girl entered Renstrom's life.[1008]

As the day turned to dusk, the salty, filthy, heavily armed Renstrom stood watch over the girl. Throughout the night, he would bend down and tuck the poncho around her slender torso and skinny legs. A few times, he patted her head and brushed her coal-black hair away from her face. As he cared for her, a Japanese patrol hit his outfit. His men returned fire, killing the enemy right and left. Renstrom grabbed his tommy gun but did not fire it for fear of hitting his men. It was fierce hand-to-hand combat and he sat there with the weapon at the ready, right by the girl, watching the shadows of fighting around him. After the engagement ended, he noticed his small friend "never even woke up. She slept through the whole engagement."[1009]

The next morning, Renstrom estimated there were around 15–20 dead Japanese around their position. A few of his men, finding some of the Japanese still alive, shot these enemy soldiers in their heads and "put them out of their misery." Single shots from rifles echoed across the landscape. When "the beautiful girl" awoke, she smiled, stood up, and then grabbed Renstrom's hand. He walked some distance away from his platoon, heading toward other Marines who were gathering civilians to take them to the camps. The girl looked at Renstrom with adoring eyes as they meandered around dead enemy bodies, hand-in-hand.

On reaching the gathering point, he pointed to the men who would care for her. Perceiving the Gunny was saying goodbye, her tiny hand squeezed his in a death grip. Since Renstrom outranked most there, he made sure those collecting civilians would protect "his little girl" because he did not want to chance her going back to some crazed Japanese adult who would launch her and himself off a cliff. Prying her wee fingers away from his palm with his free hand, he hugged her and sent her on her way. When the girl left him to join a group of other children under Marine sentries, she waved to him walking backwards with tears dripping from her eyes. This hardened Gunny and grizzled warrior raised his hand and waved back at her, then wiped the tears away from his own eyes, his other hand holding his tommy gun pointing at the ground. For this devout Mormon, the carnage of war and destruction of Saipan's society were events his conservative, religious upbringing in Utah had not prepared him for. He sat there and cried for several minutes while the girl disappeared in the distance, skipping along with the other children into her unknown future. After a few minutes, Renstrom checked the grenades hanging on his webbing, his ammunition, and his machinegun and then returned to his men. He immediately started to bark orders and made sure his Leathernecks were sharp and ready for their next patrol. The men moved quickly under his instructions: The Gunny had returned.[1010]

And to explore another fact which proved that Japan in general did not care for either the civilians on Saipan or its troops fighting there, they had planned to do a chemical warfare attack on the island to kill everyone on it when faced with losing it.[1011] General Ishii masterminded this attack and dispatched an elite team of 20 special biological warfare experts from his alma mater of Kyoto Imperial University to unleash a massive attack of plague on the island that would have killed friend and foe alike (even the men he had sent there). This was a unique *Kamikaze* mission. Luckily for the surviving civilians and the Americans on the island, U.S. submarines sank the ship while *en route* to the island.[1012]

The actions of Saipan's civilians were a harbinger of things to come as the U.S. inched its way toward the empire's heart.[1013] Journalist Robert Sherrod stated the Japanese behavior on Saipan was "intended to make the U.S. think it would be that way all across Japan." Events on Saipan did register in U.S. leaders' minds.[1014] Pacific Fleet commander, Admiral Chester Nimitz, and chief of naval operations (i.e. head of the Navy), Admiral Ernest King, agreed that the "riot of self-destruction and the suicidal banzai charges of the Japanese soldiers [on Saipan] were a miniature preview of what an invasion of the Japanese home islands would be like."[1015] They were convinced even more so after Saipan that they must find another way to get Japan to surrender other than a full-scale invasion of that country.

As American forces neared Japan, the enemy had much larger armies and civilian populations to bring to the war zone willing to fight to the death. Typical was Lieutenant General Saitō at Saipan who ordered his charges to swear allegiance to the ethical tenet *Senjinkum* (Battle Ethics): "We must utilize this opportunity to exalt true Japanese manhood...I will never suffer the disgrace of being taken alive."[1016] When asked about the civilians, Saitō responded with, "There is no longer any distinction between civilians and troops. It would be better for them to join in the attack with bamboo spears than be captured."[1017] The actions at Marpi Point illustrate the results of such orders on civilians and IJA personnel conditioned to follow his thoughts about how the battle should unfold. As the fighting on Saipan dwindled down by 6 July, Vice Admiral Chūichi Nagumo, who had led the Pearl Harbor raid and was stuck on this island, committed *hari-kari*, shooting out his brains.[1018]

By 9 July 1944, the Marines under Lieutenant General Holland McTyeire "Howlin' Mad" Smith declared Saipan secure. Sporadic fighting continued, but the Americans had won the island. America suffered 17,537 casualties taking Saipan, with 3,426 killed.[1019] On 10 July, Lieutenant General Saitō declared "*Tenno Haikai! Banzai!*" and then disemboweled himself with his sword. As Saitō lay over his bleeding belly with his sword shoved into his guts, his orderly shot him in the head to finish him off.[1020]

After securing the island, the Marines cared for civilians. In contrast to how the Japanese treated conquered peoples, the U.S. collected non-combatants and provided them "food, water, first aid and transportation" to internment camps where shelter was given.[1021] When the Americans discovered at the enemy camp that the Japanese did not care for orphaned babies, allowing 21 to die, they intervened. Interestingly, Chamorros had been caring for these orphans for days without incident, but the children were neglected when turned over to their own countrymen. One woman was witnessed taking an orphan to the edge of the camp where she deposited the child "over the fence and wandered away." Shocked and disgusted, the Marines set up an orphanage and cared for the children themselves.[1022] The Americans set up three different groups; they established one camp with 9,091 Japanese, one with 1,158 Koreans, and another with 2,258 Chamorros and 782 Carolinians for a total of 13,289. All were cared for equally, both enemy and friend.[1023] The Chamorros stated to U.S. authorities that they were glad the "Americans were there and that they hoped the Japanese would never return to govern them."[1024]

TINIAN

On 24 July 1944, the U.S. Marines invaded Tinian. It was quickly defeated. At the battle's end, just like as on Saipan, many of the 13,000 Japanese civilians and 2,700 Korean laborers committed suicide or were murdered by their own soldiers. Like at Saipan's Marpi Point, 2,500 adults threw small children and themselves off Marpo Point at the southeastern coast of Tinian.[1025] The 23rd Marine Corps Regiment issued the following report on 3 August:

> Several freak incidents occurred during the day: (1) Jap children thrown [by their parents] over cliff into ocean; (2) [Japanese] military grouped civilians in numbers of 15 to 20 and attached explosive charges to them, blowing them to bits; (3) Both military and civilians lined up on the cliff and hurled themselves into the ocean; (4) Many civilians pushed over cliff by [Japanese] soldiers.[1026]

Between the mass suicides, murders by their own military personnel and deaths due to getting caught in the crossfire, it was estimated that a total of 4,000 citizens out of an original 13,000 died in this battle (31%).[1027]

As on Saipan, the Tinian commanders, IJN Captain Goichi Oya and IJA Colonel Kiyochi Ogata, committed suicide. Imperial servicemen, often after helping citizens take their own lives, killed themselves by either jumping off cliffs or shooting themselves.[1028] The battle officially came to an end on 1 August 1944.

OKINAWA

The last major battle of the Pacific War started on 1 April 1945 and ended on 22 June 1945. At least a third of the 300,000 Okinawan civilians died during this battle alone.[1029] The following scene was typical: While hiding in a cave with soldiers away from the Americans, a frightened child screamed out in fear while being held by its mother. A soldier near her grabbed the child from her and "strangled the child to death in front of everyone."[1030] This was just one example of many of how IJA soldiers treated children within their units while on Okinawa, the largest Japanese civilian population the Americans would encounter to date.

After the battle, countless civilians "perished from wounds and malnutrition."[1031] How many committed suicides, were killed by their own soldiers, or got caught in the battle thereafter remains unknown, but they were the "real victims."[1032] Most of the killing of the civilians was done due to Imperial Japanese Army procedures. As historian Edward J. Drea wrote:

> During the battle, soldiers murdered civilians who got in their way. They confiscated food from starving women and children. They executed islanders speaking in the local dialect as spies. On smaller outlying islands, fanatical junior officers imposed draconian measures, executing scores of Okinawans as alleged spies or for disobeying army orders. The most notorious crime occurred on Tokashiki, where an army captain [Yoshitsugu Akamatsu]…executed dozens of villagers and coerced more than 300 survivors into committing collective suicide [*shūdan jiketsu*].[1033]

The last event Drea described done by Akamatsu happened all throughout the island. Those Okinawan men/boys who were not forced to kill themselves were "impressed into service and thrown into battle with little training or equipment," with 24,000 of them dying.[1034] The Japanese command sent many conscripts out with bamboo spears to attack heavily armed American troops and Marines. The result was predictable. During one such engagement, a unit of these conscripts "were all destroyed *in one day* [author's italics]."[1035] Describing these young people of Okinawa, former Naval Intelligence officer and Japanese expert Frank B. Gibney wrote:

> The flower of the island's youth—teenage girl nurses' aides as well as *beoitai* boy soldiers—were sacrificed to the directives of the Japanese army command. In many cases they were forced to hurl themselves from the low southern cliffs [just like at Saipan and Tinian] into the sea, so they too, could "die for the Emperor."[1036]

Operations officer of the 32nd Army on Okinawa, Colonel Hiromichi Yahara, rightly wrote: "Fear had robbed them of their faculties," a fear, that actually was instilled in them by commanders like Yahara.[1037] The entire chain of command on Okinawa appears to have never questioned this *modus operandi* of convincing civilians, or forcing them, to kill themselves in defeat as something immoral.

The 32nd Army commander, General Mitsuru Ushijima (who had participated in the Rape of Nanking), committed suicide at the battle's end along with seven of his officers, including his second in command, General Isamu Chō (another man, like Ushijima, who committed crimes at Nanking).[1038] Before committing their last act together, Chō joked: "Excellency, you will go to paradise. I to hell."[1039] Before Chō committed *seppuku*, he wrote the surviving troops: "Do not suffer the shame of being taken prisoner. You will live for eternity."[1040] Right before he sliced open his belly and had his officer and master swordsman Captain Sagaguchi behead him, Ushijima, in one of the greatest understatements of the war, declared: "The Okinawans must resent me."[1041] Like Kuribayashi experienced on Iwo Jima, right before Ushijima and Chō committed their *seppukus*, they received a request to surrender from the American commander on Okinawa, General Simon Bolivar Buckner Jr. which they laughed off declaring *samurai* did not do such childish things.[1042] At the battle's end, thousands of soldiers and sailors took their lives "rather than face capture. Soldiers [and sailors] would either die fighting in *Gyokusai* suicide charges against American tanks or simply [push] a grenade pin and blow themselves up."[1043] Hundreds of tiny *Banzais* or *jiketsus* happened as the battle died down, often including Okinawan citizens in the carnage. Their deaths were irrational. Even the 32nd Army's operations officer, Colonel Yahara, who ordered these deaths, admitted after the war these "suicide tactics that were resorted to in our grand actions" were, in the end, "*absurd* [author's italics]."[1044] Many of the 107,539 Japanese combatants and militiamen under Yahara's authority died in these *absurd* ways.[1045]

Just like with Saipan, General Ishii's Unit 731 and its subsidiary in Beijing, Unit 1855, made plans to hit Okinawa with massive amounts of bacterial warfare. They wanted to send a strong message to the Americans of the cost Japan was willing to pay if they neared the home islands any further. Luckily for the Americans on the island and the surviving civilians, the "attack never came together in time for execution."[1046]

CONCLUSION

Having close to 50% of one's civilians die during battles like Saipan, Tinian, and Okinawa displays that millions of Japanese civilians would have died in Japan had the United States and Russia been forced to invade the nation's four main islands. As former WWII Naval Intelligence officer and Japanese expert, Frank B. Gibney, said: "Our experience with the die-hard resistance on Okinawa [of the soldiers and civilians] seemed to presage an even bloodier struggle for the Japanese homeland."[1047]

Throughout the summer of 1945, over 3,000 ships were being readied for this invasion while millions of Allied troops trained for it. Our leaders felt the Japanese were really going to continue fighting until the bitter end.[1048] Had Hirohito not been brought to his knees to surrender in August 1945 after the atomic bombs were dropped, millions of his subjects would have either killed themselves, been slaughtered by their own troops after the invasion started, died in senseless attacks against well-trained and supplied Allied troops, or starved to death due to the supply chain being horribly disrupted. Hirohito was nowhere near surrendering before the bombs were dropped. Historian Richard Frank said, "In face of [the] evidence, it is fantasy, not history, to believe that the end of the war was at hand before the use of the atomic bomb."[1049] The Japanese were willing to kill themselves or support a military that would do the killing of their civilians, which showed that Japan's behavior was beyond irrational and was so extreme that it would "eat its own."

For instance, in invading Japan, the Allies would have encountered more *Kamikaze* planes than any U.S. military force to date, as many as 10,000. Father of the *Kamikazes*, Vice Admiral Takijiro Ōnishi, believed if the nation was willing "to sacrifice *twenty million Japanese* lives in a special attack [*Kamikaze*] effort, victory will be ours! [author's italics]."[1050] One Japanese Zen Buddhist priest, Dr. Reihō Masunaga, wrote of these *Kamikazes*: "The source of the spirit of the Special Attack Forces lies in the denial of the individual self and the rebirth of the soul, which takes upon itself the burden of history. From ancient times Zen has described this conversion of mind as the achievement of complete enlightenment."[1051] So *Kamikaze* pilots were enlightened Buddhas who would gain reincarnation at the moment they rammed their planes into U.S. Navy ships. Japanese religion had truly embraced extreme militarism and radical, self-destructive principles. Despite being aware Japan would lose the war, Zen master Sōgaku Daiun Harada wrote in late 1944 that it "is necessary for all one hundred million subjects [of the emperor] to be prepared to die with honor…If you see the enemy you must kill him; you must destroy the false and establish the true—these are the cardinal points of Zen."[1052] With defeat and destruction of their nation a certainty, Japanese leaders encouraged their citizens to sacrifice themselves for their country and Hirohito in literally suicidal activities. Prime Minister Kantarō Suzuki said in June 1945:

> If our hundred million people fight with the resolve to sacrifice their lives,
> I believe it is not at all impossible to attain the great goal of preserving
> the essence of Japan…None of our fighting men can understand how it
> is that Germany, with such a large army left, was not able to hold out
> until the end. In quantities of arms and supplies, we may not compare

favorably with the enemy, but our determination as we stand on the firing line is peculiar to us alone. With this formidable strength we must fight to the end, the entire population uniting as one body.[1053]

The frightening fact emerging from this monologue was that the Japanese citizenry were willing to follow such mandates. Most were conditioned to fight to the bitter end, probably the only people in the world who would do so under such circumstances. Suzuki brought out an interesting point about how his citizens viewed the Nazis. If the average Japanese did not understand how passionate Nazis could lay down their arms in the face of defeat, that indeed shines a light on how fanatical the Japanese were. That fanaticism would have carried them into the next phase of war if not for Hirohito surrendering to avoid annihilation. Suzuki's interpretation of German acquiescence was that although most German cities had been bombed flat, Germany had been split in two and largely occupied, and the *Luftwaffe* had been neutered, Suzuki and many of his cohorts expected the Nazis to continue fighting. Nobody will ever know how much longer the Germans could have fought had their charismatic leader not committed suicide, but without a functioning army, there was little left with which to fight—a fact that Suzuki clearly overlooked. By his calculus, whereas the Germans no longer had the stomach to do so, Suzuki would have expected every Japanese citizen to fight until his own house was conquered and his own family was dispatched to the afterlife. It was indeed, as historian Richard Frank wrote, "a recipe for extinction."[1054] Japan's leadership continued with their final plans "for the suicidal defense of the Homeland—Operation Decision (*Ketsu-Go*)."[1055] As historian Saburō Ienaga wrote, echoing Frank, "Japan's leaders showed a supreme indifference to the suffering and despair of the populace to the very end. That callous determination was unshaken by two atomic bombings. The 'national polity' took precedence over the people."[1056]

During the planning for this last-ditch operation, Japan mobilized all its citizens. Out of a population of 71 million, they had six million servicemen and an additional 18 million citizen soldiers (men between the ages of 15–60 and women between ages 17–40). Children were even trained "to carry backpacks of explosives and to throw themselves under the treads of tanks [as] 'Sherman carpets.'" The government renamed schools "National Schools" and assigned teachers "the crucial task" of educating the "children of the Emperor" to sacrifice themselves for Japan. Children 12 years and older were trained to fight the invasion, and even married women exercised with bamboo spears to combat invaders.[1057] Right before this invasion, had it taken place, a senior army officer in Osaka had laid out plans to slaughter all "the infirm old people, the very young and the sick" because the nationwide food shortage could not sustain them and military operations.[1058] "We cannot allow Japan to perish because of them."[1059]

For these reasons, land war on Japan's mainland would have seen not only some of the bloodiest battles of WWII, but also some of the bloodiest in history. Conservative estimates of Japanese deaths for the total invasion numbered upwards of 10 million. Japanese leadership "willfully consigned" their countrymen to death. "It was, [no doubt], a recipe for extinction."[1060] This self-imposed Japanese Holocaust against the Japanese was truly insane. And we know they would have done so on the homeland by witnessing their behavior on Saipan, Tinian, and Okinawa. We did not have to guess what Japanese citizens would do once an invasion happened because we already knew what they would do. *They would have continued to conduct mass murder against themselves.* By way of illustration, Dr. Michihiko Hachiya, a doctor in a Hiroshima hospital taking care of the atomic blast victims, recorded how people there responded to Hirohito's announcement to lay down arms and stop the war on 15 August 1945. In short, even they wanted to fight on.

> By degrees people began to whisper and then to talk in low voices until, out of the blue sky, someone shouted:
>
> "How can we lose the war!"
>
> Following this outburst, expressions of anger were unleashed.
>
> "Only a coward would back out now!"
>
> "There is a limit to deceiving us!"
>
> "I would rather die than be defeated!"
>
> "What have we been suffering for?"
>
> "Those who died can't go to heaven in peace now!"
>
> The hospital suddenly turned into an uproar, and there was nothing one could do. Many who had been strong advocates of peace and others who had lost their taste for war following the [atomic bomb] were now shouting for the war to continue… The one word—surrender—had produced a greater shock than the bombing of our city.[1061]

Takaaki Aikawa, former president of Christian university Kanto Gakuin in Yokohama, stated people knew about the Bataan Death March and that their leaders under Hirohito "did not make only American captives participate in such a march. They made our whole civilian population take part in it! We marched day after day, not knowing our destination nor the time of the end."[1062] Had Hirohito not ended the conflict, the Japanese, even those suffering from radiation poisoning and blistered over their entire bodies, would have continued marching to their deaths, fighting the Americans as best they could.

CHAPTER 19

BANZAIS, SEPPUKU, JIKETSU, AND *KAMIKAZES*

"Duty is weightier than a mountain, while
death is lighter than a feather."[1063]

—One creed of Imperial Japanese soldiers

ALTHOUGH THE JAPANESE MILITARY EXHIBITED skill, determination, and boldness of leadership, they glorified death, preferring *Banzais* to less glorious but more effective methods. One historian estimates that out of the 1,140,000 Japanese army dead, 200,000 of them died in inefficient charges. The highest value to which a Japanese subject could aspire was "death in the nation's [and emperor's] service, followed by apotheosis as a national deity."[1064] It has been said that "[r]eligion's surest foundation is the contempt for life."[1065] Japanese disregard for life gave them *Kamikazes* and glorified the desire of millions *to die in battle.* If they could not die in battle, they were encouraged to take their own lives by *seppuku* and *jiketsu* (literally self-determination, but in this context, suicide other than disembowelment). For example, "a tiny fraction" of the 8,212 Japanese wounded during the Luzon battle in 1945 survived the war. Before leaving them in field hospitals, their comrades murdered them or encouraged them to commit suicide. When the Allies found them, many "had killed themselves with grenades; some had been beheaded by their officers and others had been shot."[1066] One commander ordered: "Concerning those wounded: Men who are slightly wounded will participate in this battle. When men wounded are not able to participate in battle their leaders will see to it they end their lives." At one Luzon hospital, Americans found 1,810 dead who either committed *seppuku* or *jiketsu* or were killed by comrades.[1067] An IJA doctor volunteered to shoot patients in "sacred murder" so they would not become prisoners, and often medics and doctors injected morphine, cyanide, opium,

222

and corrosive sublimate (mercury chloride) into injured men's veins. One soldier even killed his brother who could no longer fight.[1068] On average, the Japanese had a fatality rate of 98% in combat zones, which has never been surpassed in modern warfare.[1069] According to Yale University scholar Paul Kennedy, "While other armies merely talked of fighting to the last man, Japanese soldiers took the phrase literally, and did so."[1070]

In this chapter, the battles of Saipan, Tinian, Guam, and Iwo Jima give examples of these Japanese military policies that encouraged its men to die in the face of defeat instead of surrendering. Most modern nations encourage their military units to fight until they cannot any longer, but once they can no longer offer resistance, they are allowed to raise the white flag and spare their men death. This was not the case with Japan. Its military embraced a dark dimension that once a man put on the uniform, he must win or die. There was no grace or mercy for those who would spare their men and themselves useless deaths when defeat was inevitable. Japan's society embraced a weird, suicidal mass murder of their men when suffering defeat in battles and war.

SAIPAN

Marching toward Japan's mainland across the Pacific, the U.S. decided Saipan must be taken first in the Marianas in the summer of 1944. Over 60,000 Marines and soldiers from the V Amphibious Corps under Vice Admiral Kelly Turner and Lieutenant General Smith (2nd and 4th MarDivs and the Army 27th Infantry Division) fought 30,000 Japanese there. Smith's trusted chief of staff for the landing force, Brigadier General Graves B. Erskine, planned the invasion. The commanders felt they would defeat the enemy quickly since they thought only 12,000 to 15,000 Japanese defended the island.[1071]

Due to the real numbers, it took the Americans longer to defeat the Japanese on Saipan than thought. However, by the end of the first week of July, the Marines and U.S. Army had cornered the Japanese to the island's north. On 6 July, Lieutenant General Saitō ordered a *gyokusai* ("honorable death/defeat"): "Whether we attack or…stay where we are, there is only death. However, in death there is life. I will advance with you to deliver another blow to the American devils and leave my bones on Saipan as a fortress of the Pacific."[1072] He was correct they were all going to perish. However, even in defeat, he characterized it as a victory, claiming that by fighting on the gods' side, they would gain eternal life. Japanese troops tenaciously brawled with U.S. forces hoping to win the spiritual battle, because in the physical world, they were losing everywhere. After weeks of fighting, U.S. forces had corralled them to the isle's far north. The enemy was now crowded around hundred-foot cliffs that

BRYAN MARK RIGG

plummeted from a plateau surrounding Mount Marpi. It was an onerous place for the Japanese to offer effective defense. However, they actually wanted to go on the offense. Although all was lost for the Japanese, instead of surrendering, they would launch an attack.

In a last-ditch effort to kill Marines, many Japanese died in *Banzais*, the last of which happened on 7 July when over 3,000 (some reports claim 4,300 if one includes the second wave) charged south screaming out of Paradise Valley, shattering two Army battalions along the west coast.[1073] Japanese medics killed soldiers too sick to participate.[1074] One soldier who joined this charge wrote a diary entry after bowing north to the emperor: "I, with my scarified body, will become the whitecaps of the Pacific and will stay on this island until the friendly forces come to reclaim the soil of the Emperor."[1075] He joined the ranks, shouted *"Banzai"* and rushed toward the Americans. The men looked like "spiritless sheep being led to the slaughter" with their officers taking on the roles of being "guides to the Gates of Hell."[1076] The mass coming down the hills at the Americans resembled a "stampede staged in the old Wild West movies."[1077] Within the "second wave," even wounded men hobbling or on crutches came at the Americans. Eventually, after running over the Americans' initial lines, Marine and Army gunfire mowed them down. They had done their best to obey the emperor to fight until the last, but their tactics proved ineffective against the well-armed, trained, and disciplined Marines and soldiers. "The carnage [was] beyond belief. Burial parties needed days to deal with the great number of dead."[1078] These suicidal attacks were ordered by Lieutenant General Saitō, in control of operations, and the island commander Major General Iketa.[1079]

After this *Banzai*, the island fell to the Americans. All those Japanese who charged in the *Banzai* could have surrendered, but their command refused them that option. On 10 July, Saipan's 43rd Division commanding officer, Lieutenant General Saitō, committed *seppuku*.[1080] The majority of his troops either died in battle or killed themselves along with civilians, especially at Marpi Point. Most taken prisoner were Korean laborers or men too sick or wounded to take their own lives, numbering around 1,500 out of the original 30,000!

TINIAN

On 24 July 1944, two weeks after Saipan fell, the invasion began of Tinian only a few miles to the south of Saipan, code name Jig-Day. After a diversionary landing on the southwest coast off Tinian Town, an amphibious force of 39,000 Marines of the 2nd and 4th MarDivs invaded Tinian on the northwest coast, three and a half miles from Saipan. Over 9,000 Japanese defended the island. In a brilliant landing, the Marines achieved "complete tactical surprise" from staging areas at Saipan's most southern end, arriving on two tiny beaches at the northern tip that the Japanese had deemed impossible for landings. Following Brigadier General Erskine's instructions, the Marines placed their artillery south of Saipan's Aslito airfield and covered the landing forces with curtains of fire using 156 field pieces. Also, from the airfield, planes flew sorties to support attacking Marines. Tinian was smaller and not as rugged as Saipan, but it still was daunting to conquer. Thousands of Marines engaged in fierce fighting, sealing off caves, shooting Japanese soldiers, and fending off *Banzais*.[1081] Although the Japanese commanders on Tinian knew Saipan had been lost and that overwhelming numerical superior forces were bearing down on them, they refused to spare themselves and their men useless deaths, making the island "a *Kamikaze* mission on the grand scale," as Tōjō had started to refer to such operations.[1082] The following engagement displayed Japanese tactics that ensured the defenders (or attackers in this case) had no way of surviving. Moreover, once soundly defeated, most Japanese refused to be taken alive as POWs.

Several hours after the landings on 24 July, Gunnery Sergeant Keith Renstrom had been placed in another unit from the one he had served in at Saipan. Late in the day, he took charge of the 2nd platoon of F Company, 2nd Battalion, 25th Marines, 4th MarDiv after its platoon leader and sergeant had been wounded. This platoon was in the forward elements of the attack down the center of the island along one of the main roads. The Gunny's platoon had made progress and was a few miles away from Tinian Town, heading south on the right side of the isle.[1083]

When he took over these Marines, he found they had made some poor decisions. He ordered them to remove themselves from their hard-to-dig foxholes because they had placed them at the edge of a thick sugarcane field with stalks taller than six feet. Barking orders, Renstrom told them to move to the defensive line hundreds of yards behind them. Cursing the Gunny, his Jarheads grudgingly obeyed and pulled back behind some trees near a road they had used before they had come to the clearing and fields. From these trees, they had good concealment, and they had put considerable distance between them and any force that might appear out of the sugarcane field. Although Renstrom reasoned with them about this decision, his Marines still felt he had made them do unnecessary work to re-establish their lines since they had the Japanese on the run.[1084]

Renstrom's men hunkered down into their new positions, and as evening fell, the front seemed uncannily silent. Renstrom told them if they had any visitors during the night or morning to wait for the sound of his tommy gun before they fired. In the early hours, around 0330, some on watch noticed movement and then ensured everyone woke up. From their positions, they saw six Japanese appear suddenly walking down the road. His men listened for the Gunny's tommy gun. The Gunny did not fire. He knew these soldiers were forward elements only and were part of a larger unit. The six enemy walked to Renstrom's platoon's position, but they did not see any of his men and continued down the road toward another platoon in the rear. After several minutes, that rear echelon platoon opened up on the enemy. Renstrom and his men heard the screams and witnessed the small arms fire tear into the squad. As they gazed north listening to the skirmish unfold, they noticed a lone IJA survivor from this attack running back to their position. He stopped a few yards in front of the Gunny's foxhole. The Gunny's men listened for him for direction. Should they kill the last one or not? Definitely not. Renstrom wanted this soldier to survive and go back to his larger group and tell them what he knew the Japanese man believed—the Marines lines were behind where Renstrom was. The soldier panted for a few seconds, found a pool of water, kneeled down, and drank from it, then stood up and continued running down the road. "I was so proud of my men for maintaining fire discipline. No one shot at the lone survivor. Always let one Jap live to go back and sow confusion and fear was our motto," Renstrom said with a grin.[1085]

After several minutes of nothing happening, the dull roar of engines started to pierce the air. Renstrom knew exactly what was coming: tanks. There is nothing more disheartening for infantry than to hear the rumble of iron monsters coming at them when they do not have their own in support. Disregarding such obvious danger, Renstrom jumped into action and directed his men on how they could destroy this enemy force.[1086] Renstrom instructed his Leathernecks to let the tanks pass their position to be attacked by the other platoon in the rear who he had informed on the radio that an armor attack was underway:

> Moving north along the coastal road, the enemy force consisted of...six light tanks with infantrymen riding and following on foot. First warning of the enemy move came when Marine listening posts stationed along the road a short distance forward of the lines reported enemy tanks rumbling in from the south.[1087]

Renstrom knew a lot of Japanese soldiers would trail the reconnaissance force of armored fighting vehicles and he wanted to attack this group.[1088]

When the advance guard of six IJA tanks appeared, driving north, Renstrom's men stared at them as they approached. They rolled nearer. Suddenly, the tanks stopped near Renstrom's foxhole. The Gunny knew they were outgunned.

"That terrified me to death," the Gunny said. "Had they seen us?" Renstrom thought. He grabbed one of his grenades and held it firmly. Suddenly, a hatch flipped open on the lead tank and an officer jumped out, oblivious that over 30 Marines had him triangulated in a perfect kill zone. The officer looked around, lit a cigarette, talked to his men, and then gazed down the road. He finished his cigarette and threw it away and jumped back into his tank and slammed the hatch shut with a metallic clang.[1089]

The tanks then lumbered by, one by one, along the road with none of them noticing the Marines, covered by a nice blanket of darkness. As the tanks left, the Marines peered back toward the sugarcane field. They took in deep breaths tainted with the scent of diesel exhaust. For now, things seemed quiet, but everyone knew that would not last.[1090]

After minutes of uneasy quiet, from down the road, they gradually saw a column of IJA soldiers. The pounding of boots against the road and the jangling of metal weapons rubbing against combat gear ricocheted throughout the air. Three-man machinegun teams carried their heavy weapons surrounded by men armed with rifles, bayonets, "knee-fired" grenade launchers, and grenades. Like clockwork, Renstrom knew these troops would be coming, having studied Japanese tactics when he had been on ship a few weeks before reading about the IJA in the vessel's library. Around 35 men approached them. Men thought to themselves, "Why is the Gunny waiting so long?" Renstrom was waiting for the sign of "seeing the whites of his enemy's eyes" before he attacked. When the enemy was 10 yards away, Renstrom gave his Marines the signal, firing his tommy gun. As he squeezed his trigger, the field erupted with thousands of rounds being fired in a matter of seconds. Renstrom's men waylaid the attacking soldiers, killing all of them—since they were on flat land, the enemy had no cover and did not have a chance to survive the onslaught. As the enemy force lay on the ground, Renstrom's machineguns fired into the IJA soldiers along the whole front.[1091] The Marine Corps official history noted: "At this juncture the… machine guns…levelled a heavy volume of enfilading fire into the area…This fire, in the words of the battalion executive officer, 'literally tore the Japanese… to pieces.'"[1092]

As Renstrom's men annihilated this unit, over the horizon, the other platoon now engaged the enemy tanks with grenades, bazookas, and satchel charges supported by "75mm half-tracks, and 37mm guns." Ships near the shore "began firing illuminating shells over the area, virtually turning night into day." Explosions echoed throughout the land.[1093] Lieutenant Jim Lucas witnessed this attack:

The three lead tanks broke through our wall of fire. One began to glow blood-red, turned crazily on its tracks and careened into a ditch. A second, mortally wounded, turned its machine guns on its tormentors, firing into the ditches in a last desperate effort to fight its way free. One hundred yards more and it stopped dead in its tracks. The third tried frantically to turn and then retreat, but our men closed in, literally blasting it apart… Bazookas knocked out a fourth tank with a direct hit which killed the driver. The rest of the crew piled out of the turret screaming. The fifth tank, completely surrounded, attempted to flee. Bazookas made short work of it. Another hit set it afire and its crew was cremated.[1094]

Out of the clouds of dust and chaos, a lone tank had disengaged and was retreating south, toward Renstrom's platoon. Then, once again, the tank stopped right in front of the Gunny. Without hesitation, Renstrom's bazooka man shot a round at the treads, knocking it out. As its officer exited the tank, Renstrom unleashed a spread of bullets, killing the commander. Looking around, the Gunny did not see any more threats, but he felt uneasy and it was still dark. Unsure whether there were more Japanese or not coming, he had his men reconsolidate their lines, check their guns and re-load their weapons. Then they waited. After at least 40 minutes, things started changing on the horizon to the south.[1095]

Sluggishly, eerie forms started to emerge between the waving, long stalks of sugarcane until dozens of follow-on Japanese infantry emerged in their skirmish line walking into the field past the line of abandoned foxholes. Instead of the enemy coming in a column, slowly and methodically, the figures emerging from the field suddenly started to run and scream *"Banzai!"* in a phalanx attack. Some wielded swords while others held their rifles low in a fixed, bayonet charge. Before the Gunny knew it, around another 35 Japanese rushed them. When they closed within 30 yards, Renstrom gave his men the sign, once again, by firing his tommy gun and then his Leathernecks unleashed hellfire against the suicidal wave. Thousands of rounds were expended until the field fell quiet and no more Japanese were standing. The groans of the injured and dying echoed across the field and then suddenly, grenade explosions lit up the combat zone. The wounded Japanese were killing themselves—committing *jiketsu*. The yells of *"Banzai"* continued to ring out from the enemy's battleground punctuated by grenade blasts. Renstrom said, "That made our job later easier and I was glad they were killing themselves."[1096]

Sometimes, the Marines would hear an explosion and then see "Jap bodies… fly ten to fifteen feet in the air." Leathernecks nearby shook their heads as they witnessed these soldiers flipping and flying into the air, often in pieces. Later, after the Marines mopped-up the area, they found many of the Japanese had been carrying magnetic mines. "The Japs who were wounded and unable to flee were placing the tank mines under their bodies and tapping the detonators," sending themselves into thunderous spouts of blood, guts, and body parts.[1097]

As the sun rose around 0550, Renstrom and his men observed the destruction they had dished out against the enemy. They had not lost one of their own but they had killed at least 70 IJA soldiers in the two attacks. As they left their positions, Renstrom's men, when they found Japanese who had botched their suicides and were still alive, shot them in the back of their heads. After they made sure the IJA soldiers were dead, Renstrom's men then slowly gathered the dead for burial, and the Japanese weapons for the logistics groups behind the lines.[1098] This one Gunny had just organized the total destruction of an armored-reinforced-infantry company comprising of six tanks and 267 enemy soldiers.[1099] Although the attacking Japanese knew their assaults would lead to their deaths, they continued them without hesitation.[1100]

A few days later, after the Marines had cornered the Japanese to the south of the island, the Americans again were faced with Japanese who refused to surrender, and they gathered for a mass charge—possibly 3,000 strong but occurring in broken waves. As the *Banzais* launched on 31 July, the Marines were ready having learned of this tactic on Saipan and they slaughtered almost all the attacking, suicidal Japanese, suffering few causalities themselves. One Marine Corps officer later said, "You don't need tanks. You need undertakers. I never saw so many dead Japs."[1101] Once again, when the Japanese had the ability to surrender, they chose death.

Like at Saipan, the Tinian commanders, IJN Captain Oya and IJA Colonel Ogata, committed suicide. Furthermore, Imperial servicemen, often after helping citizens take their own lives, killed themselves by either jumping off cliffs or shooting themselves (*jiketsu* once again).[1102] Only around 250 of the originally 9,000 garrison force surrendered. The battle officially came to an end on 1 August 1944.

GUAM

America landed tens of thousands of Marines on 21 July 1944 to retake Guam and liberate its people from the Japanese. Like at Saipan, it committed around 60,000 Marines and soldiers to the battle attached to the III Amphibious Corps under Major General Roy S. Geiger (the 3d MarDiv, the 1st Provisional Marine Brigade and the 77th Army Division). The Japanese organized Guam's defense around the 29th Infantry Division, an outfit seasoned in Manchuria, commanded by Lieutenant General Takeshi Takashina. The Naval Guard was increased to 3,000 and there were 5,100 men in the IJA 6th Expeditionary Force, which upon arriving on Guam, was divided up and redesignated 48th Independent Mixed Brigade and the 10th Independent Mixed Regiment. Including naval, ground, and air force personnel, there were around 18,500 Japanese planning defenses, constructing fortifications and lying in wait for the Americans.[1103] Early in 1944, the Japanese knew the Americans were coming, so they closed the schools and had every Chamorra man, woman, and child construct defenses around the clock.[1104] In addition to these laborers, probably over 1,000 Korean forced laborers were among Takashina's ranks and they fought alongside his men—once again, most did not want to be there, but were forced by the empire to serve.[1105]

After several days of fighting, the Marines pushed the Japanese back to the mountain ridges in the island's middle by 25 July, an area now called Nimitz Hill or *Banzai* Ridge (at the time, it was Fonte Ridge). Seeing they were about to face defeat, Takashina ordered an all-out counterattack, in effect a *Banzai*, that in addition to focusing on a worthwhile Japanese activity to provide soldiers a worthy death, also would push the Marines into the sea while doing so. At best, it would be a Pyrrhic victory.

On 25 July, eyes were open and minds sharp once the Marines entrenched themselves on the heights above the beach. Many dangers came with evening because the Japanese proved both adroit and active in night fighting.

The Marines continued to probe for enemy weaknesses in the front doing their best to deploy their armor. Right up until the day before the Japanese massive counterattack, the Marines used tanks that had navigated the difficult terrain to blast enemy positions. The tanks were cumbersome and could not be used freely due to the difficulty in attacking higher ground.[1106] Before evening fell on the 25th, most tanks had pulled back into defensive positions.

During the night on the ridgeline under pelting rain, the Marines experienced a serious counterattack against the northern beachhead of Asan. Toward midnight, the enemy began probing for weaknesses in Marine lines. The 3d MarDiv reported "the probing attacks, at first, were so small and unrelated that it was not realized that this was the prelude to the enemy's supreme attempt to drive our forces into the sea."[1107]

Before the *Banzai*, the Japanese assigned to the attack had gotten drunk on sake (Japanese rice wine).[1108] "The attitude of the enemy…had indicated many of them were drunk—insanely so. A number of canteens containing liquor were found on the enemy dead, and empty sake bottles were strewn in front of the regiment's lines."[1109] Japanese on Guam often fought in a drunken state since the island housed the alcohol depot for Imperial Pacific forces.[1110] This is one clue the Japanese knew they could not win this battle and were about to die.

What may have started as another evening in the trenches shifted to heavy mortar fire onto the Marines' left flank of Fonte Ridge accompanied by a massive *Banzai* around midnight. The Japanese massed their forces, whipped up their troops to an emotional frenzy, stealthily probed the American lines for weaknesses, and then, led by sword-wielding officers, conducted one of the largest charges of the Pacific War, screaming, throwing grenades, and shooting. This was Takashina's audacious move to push the Marines back into the ocean. After the initial hit, the Japanese tried to capitalize upon the advantage of the surprise and at several points they pushed through Marine lines. After the initial shock, the American lines suffered several openings and small bands of enemy crept down the Asan River valley into the 21st Regiment's area, moving toward the 3d MarDiv artillery's command post (CP). Several hundred reached the rice paddies and fought hand to hand with Marines.[1111] Since flares failed to illuminate the infiltrating Japanese, ships broke protocol, drew near the beach, and shone their searchlights over the battle lines.[1112]

The Japanese attacked with an initial wave of at least 4,100 men on the 9,000-yard front of Nimitz's Hill. Follow-on attacks would bring the total to around 5,000. Due to the massing of forces and the obvious direction of their attack, the Marines killed more of the Japanese than the Japanese did Americans. Marines quickly learned this night attack was indeed "more than a mere reconnaissance in force."[1113] Reinforcements rapidly plugged the holes in the broken lines.

Around 2330 the 1st Battalion, 21st Marines' CP at the bottom of Fonte Ridge heard a "cacophony of machinegun fire and explosive bursts" coming from atop the cliff. Reports poured over the airways, many of them mixed and confused. One forward observer stumbled down the cliff to the CP declaring the enemy had attacked in force and "all hell had broken loose."[1114] Neighboring 3rd Battalion, 21st Marines, reported, "After probing in the dark, Nips launched a terrific attack in force."[1115] Men started to fall everywhere.

Things were getting dire on the front lines, and many were dying. Numerous Marines frantically fired away at charging Japanese as flares illuminated the threats.[1116] Japanese screams were heard giving orders or shrieking in pain mixed with the sound of Marines yelling to plug holes, hollering for Corpsmen, and shouting out their fierce wish to kill the "yellow bastards." Medal of Honor recipient Woody Williams observed: "No one can imagine how the noise of battle creates the most bizarre combination of sounds that no one has ever heard other human beings make."[1117] *"Banzai!* Where are you? Over here!

Corpsman, I'm hit! Kaboom. To your right, watch out! Rat-a-tat-a-tat-tat-tat-tat. *Banzai!* Ping. Ahhhhhhhhhhhhhh! Help me! Holy fuck! Fuck you! Ching. Ching. Ching. Stupid Nip! Brrrrrrrrrr. *Banzai! San Nen Kire* (Cut a thousand men!), *Vompp. You Marine Die!!*' One could say the Marines this night "heard all things in heaven and in the earth…[and] heard many things in hell."[1118] In addition to the sounds, the smell of cordite, sweat, decay, and smoke permeated the air while the taste of adrenaline seeped into their mouths, making their tongues and lips dry.

First Battalion commander of the 21st Marines, Lieutenant Colonel Marlowe Williams did not know what was going on as reports flooded in that men were dying, positions overrun and ammunition needed. Looking at his XO (executive officer), Lieutenant Colonel Ronald Reginald Van Stockum, Williams said, "Van, get up there and see what's going on." Stockum said that with this order, "the most hazardous mission of my Marine career" commenced. He grabbed his radio operator and started to scale the cliff where the battle raged.[1119]

Artillery rounds rained overhead sent by the batteries behind Stockum trying to stop the *Banzai.* Simultaneously, Japanese mortars cascaded onto the CP and the front lines. In the confusion, Stockum looked around to locate his radioman, but he had gotten lost in the mayhem and was nowhere to be found. Stockum continued forward.[1120]

Just before dawn at 0400 the *Banzai* pushed through the Marines' rear echelons—it was nothing like what the Marines had already seen. Charles Meacham described the thick enemy crowd charging them, illuminated by flares as resembling "brown maggots wriggling through the grass."[1121] In some places the Japanese infiltrated so quickly the fighting descended to hand-to-hand combat. Allen Shively, after almost being stabbed with a *samurai* sword and shot with a pistol by an opposing officer, threw the man down and beat him to death. The lines got mixed and bodies were bouncing into one another.[1122] The battalion said that at 0330 the enemy had "penetrated between" B Company and C Company and by 0400 were overrunning the battalion's CP and rear mortar positions.[1123] The 3d MarDiv noted that when the main thrust at 0400 hit the Marines, the Japanese shouted strange words with one English speaker yelling, "Wake up, American, and die!"[1124]

Right at the battle's apex, Stockum arrived at the front. He saw the "enraged" company gunnery sergeant, Albert Hemphill, "pick up a discarded *Samurai* sword" and kill a wounded enemy soldier near him who was trying to rise and fight. Screams, shouting, firing, and explosions echoed over the ridges. "It was apparent that [the Japanese] objective was to reach the beach in the rear in order to destroy our artillery and the supply dumps." They had penetrated the lines at several points.[1125] Stockum borrowed a company radio and reported to headquarters that their line had held, barely, however, the rudimentary radios were not designed to handle the jumble of traffic generated by the attack and it was doubtful Stockum's message got through.[1126]

The attack's main thrust hit B Company head-on, commanded by Captain Donald Beck, which had already been reduced from 200 to 50 men. Against heavy odds and although wounded, he held the lines and called in mortar and artillery shells to stave off the Japanese. He and a few of his men survived the onslaught.[1127] The enemy streamed through the gaps, following a draw to the cliff. The right flank of A Company on the left and the left of C Company on the right pulled back to counter the breakthrough. Tanks parked in the rear killed many "Japs" with their machineguns as the enemy reached and overran them. The enemy's rush upon the tanks resembled a horde of ants. They swarmed over the vehicles savagely, disregarding the machinegun fire, and frantically pounded, kicked, and beat against the turrets to get around them and continue their wild rush down the draw to the rear areas of field hospitals, supply depots, and staging areas. Most even forgot to use the demolition charges attached to their belts. One Japanese tripped as he ran, igniting his mine and blowing his body into a thousand pieces.[1128] A crazed officer slashed at the tank with his sword, breaking it and dying under a hail of bullets.[1129] In the chaos, the lines between defending Marines and attacking Japanese became blended and tangled, looking like snakes wrestling each other. The 21st Regiment noted the "situation [was] not clear."[1130] And Baker Company's captain, Beck, noted this "banzai...did away with my Company."[1131]

The Japanese wave made it to the beach and bypassed the 1st Battalion's CP at the cliff's base. Now behind the lines, the Japanese slaughtered several unarmed medical staff and wounded in aid stations.[1132]

The Japanese continued their advance, but the Marines rallied and counterattacked. The 21st Regiment reported elements of the 9th Marines "arrived in the nick of time" and were driving the "Japs away from the Command Post toward rear of right flank."[1133] Many Japanese, seeing their attack had lost momentum and "that they were cut off," blew "themselves up with grenades."[1134]

When one Japanese column attacked the CP of 3rd Battalion, 21st Marines, everyone grabbed their rifles and repelled the attackers. Another group tried to blow up the artillery but were caught by daylight in front of the division field hospital. "In addition to the corpsmen, ambulatory cases turned out in underwear and pajamas to fight with any weapon they could get hold of; patients fired right from their cots in the tents..."[1135] The Japanese lost most of their officers in the first assault and could not move up reinforcements because they had none. They reached the artillery positions and supply dumps below *Banzai* Ridge, but it was a Pyrrhic victory. Their advance lost momentum, and the Marines killed almost all of them.[1136]

Captain Beck kept his men busy on the ridge fighting off the Japanese flanking attacks. Although surrounded, he rallied his depleted force and kept radio communication with his commander. The reports he sent "enabled his battalion commander to locate the break-through and localize it." During this chaos, Beck's men took a heavy "toll from the enemy." One report claimed 200 dead were later found within Beck's CP area alone.[1137] After the battle, the commander of the 2nd Battalion, 9th Marines, Lieutenant Colonel Robert E. Cushman Jr., said he needed a bulldozer to go over the battlefield to bury 800 dead Japanese near their lines because they had started to reek.[1138]

After a full night and tough morning of hard fighting, the Marines retook their positions and 1st Battalion, 21st Marines, noted by 0630 the enemy charge had been broken.[1139] This battalion closed the breach the Japanese had opened.[1140] Lieutenant Colonel Williams received the Silver Star for his actions that evening. He kept control of his men under this assault and "with mortar and artillery fire falling within his position at the risk of his life, he repeatedly moved along his lines encouraging his men." After the engagement, "forty-three enemy dead and several machine guns were found" within his CP. His battalion killed hundreds of the attacking Japanese.[1141]

The Marines claimed victory, having all but annihilated the attacking Japanese, though it had taken hours of fighting. Lieutenant Colonel Cushman Jr. (later, the 25th commandant of the Marine Corps), commented, "In the large picture, the defeat of the large counterattack on the 26th by many battalions of the 3rd Division who fought valiantly through the bloody night finished the Jap on Guam."[1142] Stockum said it more dramatically, "In absorbing this blow, our Marines had broken the enemy's back."[1143]

It is unknown how many enemy participated in the attack. It probably numbered over 5,000 according to accounts: "The wild screams of the charging Japs gave the impression of a wild *Banzai*, but it was far from that type of unorganized suicidal charge. This was a part of an assault in force, planned with care…to drive the Marines from their beachhead."[1144] By noon on 26 July, the Marines had rendered the Japanese unable to attack, and what was left of their units pulled back. As 3rd Battalion of the 21st Marines noted: "Nips are in flight to the north."[1145]

This *Banzai* was Guam's decisive battle.[1146] The front line of the Marines of the 21st and 9th Regiments that turned back the Japanese covered the main thrust of the Japanese, and although they gave up some territory, they held the front.[1147]

That same night of the 25th and 26th of July, a few miles away on Orote Peninsula, the Japanese launched another attack of 3,500 men. Again, the Japanese first got drunk and prepared for their assault. Like their brother soldiers who fought at Fonte Hill (*Banzai* Ridge), they were so intoxicated the Marines facing them described the ruckus they made as akin to a pack of animals on "New Year's Eve in the zoo."[1148] Obviously, this one was not a surprise attack. When they stepped off in the assault between midnight and 0200, many did not have rifles, so they charged with baseball bats, sticks, broken bottles, and pitchforks. The yelling, screaming surge made it into the Marine lines, although many perished as artillery and mortar fire sent "arms and legs" in the air like "snowflakes." The enemy "screamed in terror until they died."[1149] Observers described this Japanese tactic as "veritable war hysteria."[1150] In three hours, U.S. artillerymen fired 26,000 rounds.[1151] That bombardment ended the other large *Banzai* on Guam, convincing most the end of the Japanese was near. Most likely USMC Major Frank Hough includes this second charge when he notes the *Banzai* during 25–26 July was twice as large as the one on Saipan.[1152] More fighting was necessary, although it was largely "mopping-up," with small units engaging one another. Many Japanese who had not died in the charges either retreated to caves or took their own lives, refusing to retreat or surrender.[1153] Hough described the charges:

> The [Jap] attack of 26 July was an extraordinary performance, even by the standards of those unpredictable little men. It combined the best—or worst—features of virtually every attack they had ever put on during the entire Pacific war, plus a few new wrinkles apparently dreamed up for the occasion. There were Banzai charges and infiltration, sharp power thrusts and sneaks through the gullies that separated units; there was high courage and hysteria, fanaticism and stupidity; the whole was supported by artillery, mortars, tanks, flares, whiskey and saki. There is evidence that the attack was carefully planned; that the enemy fully expected it to be decisive. The initial phase can justly be termed successful on several counts. Yet the whole petered out in the abject futility as even the Japanese have been able to achieve.[1154]

Hough's description sums up the different elements that comprised this mad dash against the Marine lines that many today lump together as the *Banzai* on Guam. It was a broken wave hitting many sectors. It killed many and the few minor victories the Japanese did achieve could not sustain their advantage.

After this all-out attack on 25 July, Lieutenant General Takashina's forces were by and large defeated. He immediately thereafter ordered a staged withdrawal headed to the north of the island. During one of these withdrawals, Takashina was caught in an artillery barrage and killed on 28 July. After his death, Lieutenant General Hideyoshi Obata, who was stuck on the island while making an inspection tour when Saipan's invasion began, took over.

Obata did not have much more success once assuming command. He also ordered counterattacks rather than holding actions, and he organized retreats, both tactics expending his men since Marines pursued him relentlessly. Surrender for him was never an option. By August 8th, Marines had pushed within a mile and a half of the northern coast, and the 1st Provisional Marine Brigade along with the 77th Army Division had taken Guam's entire northwestern tip. That night, even Radio Tokyo conceded that nine-tenths of Guam had fallen to American troops.[1155] Taking up his last headquarters, Obata took 55 Chamorro men who had built his bunker complex and executed them to prevent them from telling the Americans the whereabouts of his CP.[1156] It appears Japanese units all over the island were using small Chamorro details to move their supplies and weapons, and thereafter, would execute them.[1157] On 11 August, Obata issued his last order admonishing his troops to fight to the end, and then killed himself.

On that same day, Admiral Nimitz and USMC commandant, General Alexander Archer Vandegrift, steamed into Apra Harbor on the heavy cruiser USS *Indianapolis* and surveyed the battlefield, handed out promotions and decorations, and then continued planning the next phase of the war. By January 1945, Nimitz set up his CP on Guam from where he directed the Pacific Fleet for the rest of the war.[1158] The freedom that came to Guam did so much faster than probably would have happened had Takashina not ordered his massive *Banzai*. For America, these attacks ended battles earlier than had the enemy focused more on defense in depth and holding actions. Although hair-raising and terrifying, *Banzais* were looked upon by American leaders as a useless waste of human materiel by the Japanese. But the Japanese viewed them as a wonderful way to die. Around 473 IJA and Korean forced-laborer personnel were taken prisoner throughout this campaign, with a majority of them being Korean.

IWO JIMA

Unlike Saipan and Tinian, where the massive *Banzais* were done at the battles' end, and unlike on Guam, where the massive *Banzais* were done at the beginning, and one could add at its apex, the *Banzais* on Iwo Jima were done throughout the battle and were small, and limited compared to the ones on the previous islands already studied. Like on Saipan, Tinian, and Guam, Japanese rarely on Iwo surrendered. They committed suicide everywhere and in bizarre ways by conducting *Banzais*, *Kamikaze*-attacks, *jiketsus*, and *seppukus*. Before exploring the battle, we should look at a short history of the *Kamikazes* because they would show up at Iwo and become part of the combat on and around the island landscape, unlike at Saipan, Tinian, and Guam.

BRIEF HISTORY ON *KAMIKAZES* AND THEIR ATTACKS AT IWO JIMA

By October 1944, General MacArthur's troops had invaded the islands of Morotai and Leyte in the Philippines during the largest naval battle in history in the seas surrounding these islands.[1159] By now, American pilots had demolished the Japanese air and naval forces. Nevertheless, Japan would not abandon the fight in the air, and the Empire improvised in a fiendishly clever way with *Kamikazes* in the Divine Wind Special Attack Corps flying planes as human-guided missiles. It was difficult to prevent *Kamikazes* from hitting targets and causing damage and loss of life because the only defense was shooting them out of the sky sufficiently far from the intended goal that they could not reach the target in their descent. "For a steeply diving suicide plane a ship is practically helpless."[1160]

Kamikazes began to appear in battle starting in the autumn of 1944 at Leyte Gulf. Almost 2,300 *Kamikazes* would be launched in the following nine months, often encouraged and blessed by Buddhist and Shintō priests exhorting their flocks of suicide bombers to "abandon the cares of this world and adopt a policy of prostration at the feet of a homicidal dictator [Hirohito]."[1161] Pilots were given sake to drink before their flights, often laced with amphetamines to embolden them on their last crusades. The drugged sake came from none other than Unit 731 to suppress "fear and agitate…the pilots to throw themselves into the attack."[1162] Admiral William "Bull" Halsey said the *Kamikazes* were the most feared weapon he ever faced.

Kamikaze personnel often talked about meeting again in a heavenly bliss at the Yasukuni shrine to regale each other about their exploits in a *Valhalla*-like manner with Valhalla being a hall of heroes killed in battle. No amount of training prepared the Allies for *Kamikazes* and *Banzais*. Nimitz said, "*Kamikazes* took the Navy by surprise since designed suicide had not been a part of American air doctrine."[1163] "There was a hypnotic fascination to a sight so alien to our Western philosophy," observed later Vice Admiral Charles R. Brown. "We watched each plunging *kamikaze* with the detached horror of one witnessing a terrible spectacle rather than as the intended victim. We forgot self for the moment as we groped hopelessly for the thought of that other man up there."[1164] Historian Lee Mandel said, "These suicide aircraft attacks added a new dimension of terror to an already extremely dangerous, stressful environment."[1165] Historian John Toland put it another way: "It was blood-curdling to watch a plane aim relentlessly at your ship, its pilot resolved to blast you and himself to hell."[1166] For Americans, *Kamikazes* expressed an "insane martial spirit."[1167]

Japanese families rallied around these men. *Kamikaze* flight instructor Major Hajime Fuji requested his command to allow him to fly with his students on their one-way missions. His command refused, explaining he had a wife and two young daughters to take care of whereas most of the *Kamikazes* he trained were single, and if married, were without children. Fuji's wife Fukuko saw how much this tormented her husband, so one day when he was away on duty, she killed their daughters and herself to release him for the mission he so passionately desired. Liberated from the burden of taking care of his women, his command then granted his wish to fly his plane into an American ship. A few months later, Fuji flew his aircraft, along with another *Kamikaze*, into the USS *Drexler* off of Okinawa's coast, sinking the vessel and killing 158 Americans. He had fulfilled his greatest quest for his life.[1168]

The Japanese never stopped improvising ways to conduct "straight to heaven" attacks. A Japanese officer explained no one in the IJA thought of death as suffering, but in a divine way, felt martial deaths allowed their spirits to be "further purified."[1169] *Kamikaze* Haruo Araki wrote in his will to his wife Shigeko, "Tomorrow I will dive my plane into an enemy ship. I will cross the river into the other world, taking some Yankees with me. I…will forever protect this nation from [its] enemies."[1170] Haruo believed the gods would give him eternal life, which granted his death meaning. These beliefs gave Japanese confidence to face death with courage, especially *Kamikazes*. As IJN Captain Rikibei Inoguchi, chief of staff of the First Air Fleet, explained:

> We Japanese base our lives on obedience to Emperor and Country… [W]e wish for the best place in death, according to *Bushido*. *Kamikaze* originates from these feelings…By this means we can accomplish peace….from this standpoint, the *Kamikaze* deserved the consideration of the whole world.[1171]

Although Inoguchi's request for respect for Japanese spiritual feelings for *Kamikazes* is difficult to accept, their missions were indeed feared. Ships could do little to prepare for suicide attacks other than to learn when they were coming and produce as much antiaircraft fire as possible, and maneuver at high speed, trying to keep as many guns bearing on the approaching *Kamikaze* as possible. Throughout the war, neither "radar detection, nor seaplane search, nor American fighter interception, nor the picket line of destroyers and other vessels posted" between the fleets and the attacking planes "were sufficient to keep these planes" from finding targets.[1172]

In November 1944, the U.S. Navy began bombarding Iwo Jima. That same month, the first B-29 raids from the Marianas on Japan's pre-war homeland islands began. One month before, Americans started to push their advance for the Philippines' Leyte Island. By January 1945, the U.S. 6th Army invaded Luzon in the Philippines, and carrier forces bombed Japanese-held Indochina. From 25 October 1944 until the end of January 1945, for the price of 378 *Kamikazes* sent into battle for the Philippines, Japan sank 22 warships, including 2 escort carriers and 3 destroyers, and damaged 110 ships, including 5 battleships, 8 fleet carriers, and 16 light and escort carriers. "Success encouraged repetition" so the Japanese sent *Kamikazes* to Iwo Jima when battle broke out.[1173] Almost 2,000 *Kamikazes* would hit ships off Okinawa a few months later and sink 26 and damage an additional 164.[1174] No one knew how many were earmarked for Iwo, but the navy knew they were coming.

The full-out focus on slaughtering oneself knew no bounds in Japanese culture and the nation was willing to sacrifice its people and young men in these suicidal acts to prolong a war obviously over for Japan. However, they were more than willing to commit murder against their own soldiers and airmen if it would murder some of their enemies. It does not make sense to a modern, rational person of the 21st century.

LIEUTENANT GENERAL TADAMICHI KURIBAYASHI AND THE QUESTION OF SURRENDER

One could argue the island defense that Lieutenant General Kuribayashi organized at Iwo Jima was a large-scale *Kamikaze* land operation. He could have spared his men certain death had he surrendered right before the battle began in February 1945 knowing full well he was going to lose, but he did not. Realizing he was going to die seemed to spur him on to even more energetic activity.

We do know that General Yamashita did what Kuribayashi should have done. When Yamashita abandoned Manila, he took his 275,000-man army (14th Area IJA Army) away and disappeared in the mountains. He did conduct guerilla activities and some counterattacks, but by and large, he kept his force away from any major engagements with the Americans for the rest of the war and prevented it from mounting any massive *Banzais*. These actions were done somewhat to spare his men certain death, but overwhelmingly, they were done to tie down American forces to give Japan more time to prepare for the coming large-scale invasion of its home islands. Also, since his men had to live off the land, their logistics would not allow any protracted combat operations. Even so, some units became so starved and "mad," that they hunted stragglers "from other units and ate their flesh. [In some areas], the Imperial Army was reduced to squads of cannibals."[1175] Many Japanese civilians left the cities and went into the mountains with the troops, with thousands dying due to starvation and hardships.[1176] So, although Yamashita did not care about these deaths *per se*, he did conduct an operation that at least had some logic to it when sparing his men useless death in futile operations for a holding action that would buy more time for his countrymen in the homeland to build out their defense to counter the massive invasion coming.

So, unlike Kuribayashi, Yamashita refused to send his men on suicidal attacks. He also refused to allow most of his men during the last six months of his command to do what Kuribayashi, Rear Admiral Iwabuchi, or General Matsui ordered their men to do in Hong Kong, Manila, and Nanking of wholesale rape and slaughter. Shockingly, in the face of defeat, he refused to commit *seppuku*, thinking if he did so he would abdicate his responsibility to his men— very unorthodox for a Japanese general. Remarkably, *he would surrender himself and his staff* to the Americans "to halt the deaths of his men from starvation and disease."[1177] This last act so analyzed saved tens of thousands of his men. Kuribayashi could have also exercised this option and spared himself and his men unnecessary death, but that was not in his DNA, showing his weakness in not recognizing which moral decision he should have made. Of course, Yamashita surrendered after Hirohito had commanded his forces to do so on 15 August 1945—so this is not a 100% equal comparison for Kuribayashi. Nonetheless, Kuribayashi never entertained some of the actions that Yamashita did when everyone knew all was lost.

THE BATTLE FOR IWO JIMA

During the war's early years, the Japanese were uncertain where America would strike; controlling so much of the world's surface, there were many possible points of attack its enemies might try. General Douglas MacArthur had surprised the Japanese repeatedly by attacking in unexpected places, which left large numbers of isolated Japanese stranded, impotent on islands. As Americans fought the war closer to Japan's home islands, the likely points of attack became obvious. Americans looked for harbors for their fleets, airfields for their bombers, and staging areas for the coming invasion of Japan proper. The location of Iwo Jima on air routes to Japan made it a clear target, so Japanese leaders prepared in advance for an effective defense of the island. There would be no surprise attack; only the exact date for invasion was unknown.

In 1944, eight months before the battle, Emperor Hirohito chose Lieutenant General Tadamichi Kuribayashi to prepare Iwo Jima's defenses 650 miles off Japan's shore. Kuribayashi did his best to make Iwo a costly piece of real-estate for Americans to acquire, turning what U.S. commanders thought would be a short campaign into a several-week slugfest.

Lieutenant General Tadamichi Kuribayashi, commander at Iwo. Unfortunately, he also was responsible for horrible war crimes in China, especially at Hong Kong where he was chief of staff of the 23rd Army. Tens of thousands of murders and rapes happened within only a few months of taking over the city in December 1941 with his knowledge and possibly full approval. *USMC Photo*

Before the battle, the Japanese built a fortress on Iwo, the likes of which America had never seen. They did this on a hot and sulfurous island with limited supplies. They stayed filthy since there was insufficient water with which to wash, and rarely had they any downtime. At night, they crawled into their bedrolls in dank tunnels and did not enjoy much in the way of entertainment unlike their American counterparts. Rats and insects infested the tunnels and body lice covered the men.[1178] Yet, they remained committed to their task, although they knew they were building out and living in their future tombs. While Kuribayashi understood that defending Iwo was one of the most important responsibilities of the war, his actions were also, ironically, ensuring that his warriors would die in their youth for a cause already lost.

Most Japanese on Iwo had similar beliefs to Kuribayashi. U.S. Marines faced an island of thousands who believed they owed a sacred duty to their divine monarch and legions of Japanese dead ancestors to honor them in heroic acts that would lead to their own deaths.[1179] They derided Americans for going into battle without "spiritual incentive" strictly relying "on material superiority."[1180] The majority believed there was an inherent "spiritual power" in Japanese civilization (*seishin-shugi*) that would grant them victory.[1181] But for all the talk about religious superiority, America's material power worried Kuribayashi, and it did not go unnoticed by his soldiers.

Kuribayashi's innovative way of defending the island departed from orthodox strategies.[1182] He did not tolerate insubordination nor questioning the new strategy although he had received orders to meet the Marines at the shore like his counterparts had done on Saipan, Tinian, and Guam, an order he himself refused to obey.[1183] He felt those rules on how to defend islands outdated and ineffective. "One may appeal to genius, which is above all rules: which amount to admitting that rules are not only made for idiots, but are idiotic in themselves."[1184] In order to break with the old rules of defending at the beach, he needed to train his men in new and more effective tactics, all of which would ensure their deaths. He felt many of his soldiers "untrained recruits" led by officers who were "superannuated scarecrows."[1185] He would need to harden them into even more fanatical warriors.

He had conflicts with navy commanders, most notably his highest-ranking subordinate, Rear Admiral Toshinosuke Ichimaru. He secured a "truce" with Ichimaru, giving him some material to build a beach defense since Ichimaru believed in the "prevent the landing of the enemy strategy" that had proved unsuccessful on every island battle to date and ensured everyone would die a quick, and by and large, useless death. To keep peace with his navy colleagues, something difficult to do in the Imperial military, Kuribayashi negotiated "terms whereby half of the munitions and material supplied by the navy would go into building pillboxes on the beach, while the rest would be for the use of the army."[1186] He had also reached an agreement at Imperial Headquarters in August 1944 that once they shifted to a ground operation, units and artillery pieces would revert to his command.[1187] Even with this diversion, Kuribayashi believed he would inflict a higher kill ratio on the Americans than any other commander. This innovative approach created a defensive strategy rare among his fellow generals who relied upon massive *Banzais*. Kuribayashi harnessed his soldiers' fanatical fighting spirit to a sound strategy. It would be a prolonged, and effective, *Kamikaze*-like operation.

He constantly walked the island, learned its terrain, and offered instruction at unannounced inspections.[1188] The Tokyo radio described him knowing Iwo so thoroughly "that even should he be asked where a certain hole made by the rats is to be found, he would answer quickly without any hesitation."[1189] Not surprisingly, others felt he was too much of a "slave driver" and "despised [his] harsh discipline."[1190]

One may wonder how Kuribayashi and his men felt being on a death mission. Simply, they felt by protecting Iwo, they defended loved ones. Kuribayashi's grandson, Yoshitaka Shindo, explained:

> Human beings draw great strength when they know they're protecting something sacred. It unites them...and gives them a cause that's worthy to die for....[The] men went to their jobs on Iwo...with joy and determination. It was to keep mainland Japan intact and keep our collective spirit surviving. I don't think they felt forlorn.[1191]

Kuribayashi used this sentiment well and his men labored around the clock to build his fortress.

Studying previous battles, Kuribayashi concluded beachhead defense and massed *Banzais* were ineffective. As a result, he devised a plan to fight from underground fortifications, tunnels, and pillboxes. He would build defensive positions, many of which could survive the battleships' big guns. To execute this defense, he needed a unique type of warrior. First, he forbade massive *Banzais*. Soldiers would not waste lives this way. Second, to prepare the tunnels and fortifications that would be his defense's backbone, he needed engineers.

In March, the First Company of the 9th Engineers stationed in Manchuria was preparing to deploy to Truk Island. Using his contacts and skills as an administrator, Kuribayashi diverted 300 engineers from going to Truk, creating the foundation of his new strategy. He obtained an additional 700 engineers from various commands and mobilized the 1,233 naval engineers already on the island.[1192] As a result, 10% of Kuribayashi's force were engineers who became his new strategy's guiding force—building an underground fortress.

When Kuribayashi took command of Iwo in June of 1944, he felt he could hold the island long enough to provide the navy an opportunity to blindside the U.S. fleet and inflict a terrible blow on the Americans. "When our enemy comes here, we can contain him," he told Major Yoshitaka Horie. "And then our Combined Fleet will come and slap his face. That is to say, our role here is a massive containing action." Horie informed him that much of the fleet had been destroyed and they would not receive naval support. Kuribayashi was shocked; Admiral Nimitz's defeat of the navy in the Marianas had been kept from commanders in the area. After this IJN loss, Kuribayashi realized there was no hope of resupply, reinforcement, or returning to Japan.[1193] He sent his personal effects back home, now fully knowing he would never return.[1194] To maintain morale, he did not tell his staff about this naval defeat.[1195]

He demanded his soldiers work under his engineers around the clock digging trenches and tunnels and constructing pillboxes. He created a new motto: "Every soldier is an engineer."[1196] All his men's activity was devoted into making this island a fortress.[1197]

On 16 June, he found himself taking cover from a U.S. raid:

> [A] massive bomb landed next to the dugout, setting off a huge explosion. I was convinced that [my] dugout…would be blown to bits, but as luck would have it, I didn't even get a scratch. For the duration of the ferocious raid, the only thing I could do was wait in the dugout in a state of extreme anxiety, and pray.[1198]

In three raids that month, the Americans destroyed over 100 airplanes, and during the attack just described, 40 soldiers died. These events "sapped the morale of the Japanese."[1199] They also made Kuribayashi more frantic to get his underground fortress built to avoid the airpower that would leave his personnel vulnerable. He was preparing for a battle that would end in a defeat, but he hoped his nation could negotiate peace as a result. He wrote his wife, "if the island I'm on gets captured, there'll be an increase of several hundred enemy planes, and the air raids on the homeland will be many times more savage than now. In the worst case, the enemy may land on the beaches of Chiba and Kanagawa prefectures and penetrate near to Tokyo."[1200]

After October, Kuribayashi realized the Americans were not moving in his direction as quickly as anticipated. Instead, they diverted west, hitting Peleliu. On 15 November, he issued a new order directing his men spend half the day on building and the other half training.[1201] By 1 December his fortress took on massive proportions. Men now dug tunnels, and built bunkers and pillboxes 30% of the day and trained for 70%.[1202] On 23 December, he switched the men's focus from building shallow tunnel-and-trench systems to now deep underground rooms and passageways 10 meters into the earth, so U.S. Navy guns could not penetrate them.[1203] When not digging, they emphasized cover and concealment, marksmanship, and anti-tank activities.[1204] Kuribayashi continued to refine the routines to perfect his men's behavior: "Constant practice leads to *brisk, precise,* and *reliable* leadership, reducing natural friction and easing the working of the machine."[1205]

Having a defense in depth and letting the Marines land without revealing their positions was key to killing more of them, Kuribayashi reasoned. His defense was like a ju-jitsu move, using the momentum of the opponent's attack to bring an enemy into one's body and then flip him onto the ground. When the enemy is close, he cannot hit the ju-jitsu practitioner and if he is off balance, he can be twisted to the floor.

Close proximity was a factor in this new defense: Kuribayashi knew he had to get Marines close to him before unleashing his firing positions. He adopted "an all-around defense in depth, utilizing rugged ground in the interior of the island." His tactics were a "*distinct* improvement over the tactics on other small islands."[1206] Kuribayashi "had the correct comprehension of reality [and] refused to be awed by precedent."[1207]

The American delay in attacking gave Kuribayashi eight months to prepare the defenses and he profited from it. This eight-square-mile island eventually hosted a network of 11 miles of tunnels and thousands of pillboxes and bunkers.[1208] The 3d MarDiv reported, "In the zone of action of one Marine division, 800 pillboxes of various types were found in an area approximately 1000 yards square. Most...pillboxes and emplacements were so well camouflaged that pre-invasion photo interpretations revealed only a fraction of the number actually existing."[1209] The island held at least 15,000 cave entrances and pillboxes.[1210]

Kuribayashi's network housed almost 22,000 troops who learned to live troglodytic lives. The tunnels boasted large supply depots with trucks, tanks, hospitals, and CPs. They had miles of telephone cables, and because they ran underground, it was difficult to sever communications between the Japanese units during battle. Some areas traversed almost one hundred feet underground, far below where shells from battleships' big guns could penetrate. "One Brigade headquarters, located near Motoyama, could hold 2,000 troops; it was 75 feet deep and had a dozen entrances." In addition to everything described, millions of cockroaches and ants also resided in the tunnels, crawling over the men as they slept. Because there was no regular bathing, parasites covered them.[1211] Kuribayashi shared in their deprivation, writing: "These caves are airless and humid, and they really are—really truly-awful."[1212] But since the island received regular attacks, it was safer to live underground than above it.

In some areas, the geothermal heat was so intense the soles of the troops' *juktabi* "(split-toed rubber-soled shoes) melted, and the sulfur gas gave them headaches and made breathing difficult." Sometimes they wore their cumbersome gas masks for protection from sulfur fumes. "Dressed in only loincloths, they would work in five- or ten-minute shifts because of the intense heat" (sometimes 176° Fahrenheit). Kuribayashi turned "his men into supermoles, excavating the hard komhake rock" working in, one could argue, the bowels of Hell.

Kuribayashi wanted no distractions, so he "officially" refused sex slaves. Since there is no record of him opposing his troops using sex slaves in China, he probably did not allow the "Comfort Women" as a whole on Iwo simply because there was not enough food and water for them, although it does appear he kept a small group of women for sexual activities for himself and his officers.[1213] Kuribayashi, nonetheless, pushed his men to the limit with minimum distractions, building out a formidable fortress. The ability "to endure privation is one of the soldier's finest qualities: without it an army cannot be filled with genuine military spirit."[1214] To vanquish the highest number of "heathen Americans," Kuribayashi felt he had to put his men through "living Hell."[1215] Lieutenant General Smith said as of 1945, Iwo was the most "heavily fortified island in the world."[1216]

Sixty percent of Kuribayashi's force of 21,900 came from the traditions and culture of the army while the others stemmed from the navy numbering 7,500 in the 27th Air Flotilla under Ichimaru's command. Within the ranks, there were 1,600 Koreans.[1217]

As the battle neared, Kuribayashi was increasingly cut off from Japan. With each month, the sorties from airfields dwindled as planes failed to return from missions. Ships bringing men and supplies declined as U.S. submarines sank them. "No fewer than 1,500 Japanese troops drowned in the Nanpo Shoto attempting to reach the Bonin Islands" and at least half of Kuribayashi's tanks (28 in total) were sent to the ocean's bottom before reaching his command.[1218] Besides struggling to increase and train his manpower, he continued to grapple with the precarious island he was charged to captain, as the volcanism was active and unstable.

The aptly named Iwo Jima, literally Sulfur Island, was a volcanic island that shot up steam from holes riddling its terrain and had numerous boiling sulfur springs sprinkled throughout the landscape, making their lives miserable. It was a waterless, barren land except for scrubby vegetation. Kuribayashi's adjutant Major Horie said it was as vulnerable as "a pile of eggs" and it would be better for everyone if they sank it to the bottom of the sea.[1219] Kuribayashi and Horie discussed how many sticks of dynamite it would take to sink the first airfield into the sea on the island, but their calculations showed they did not have enough explosives so they gave up on this plan.[1220]

Iwo Jima looked like a pork chop with the meaty end to the north and the handle pointing down to the south, ending in the extinct volcano center cone of Mt. Suribachi, which rose 556 feet above sea level. It was "an ugly, smelly glob of cold lava squatting in a surly ocean."[1221] Although Horie and Kuribayashi had their misgivings about defending Iwo, they would make the Americans pay for every foot of the god-forsaken island. Iwo would be a maze of death, one of only two places during the Pacific War (the other being Angaur) where the Japanese inflicted more overall casualties on the Americans than Americans inflicted on them.[1222]

Kuribayashi set a goal for his men to kill almost a dozen Marines each before they died: "Every man will resist until the end, making his position his tomb."[1223] To prepare his soldiers for this unconventional style of fighting, Kuribayashi composed six "Courageous Battle Vows" which were distributed in January 1945. His "stern code of *Bushido*" read as follows:

1. We shall defend this island with all our strength to the end.
2. We shall fling ourselves against the enemy tanks clutching explosives to destroy them.
3. We shall slaughter the enemy, dashing in among them to kill them.
4. Every one of our shots shall be on target and kill the enemy.
5. We shall not die until we have killed ten of the enemy.
6. We shall continue to harass the enemy with guerrilla tactics even if only one of us remains alive.[1224]

These vows were "basically a collection of slogans outlining a soldier's proper state of mind in which to face battle."[1225] Marines found copies of these vows all over the island, in bunkers and pillboxes, in caves and tunnels, on the beaches, and on the dead.[1226]

Kuribayashi also composed a set of instructions for soldiers of the "Courage Division":

Preparations for Battle.

1. Use every moment you have, whether during air raids or during battle, to build strong positions that enable you to smash the enemy at a ratio of ten to one.
2. Build fortifications that enable you to shoot and attack in any direction without pausing even if your comrades should fall.
3. Be resolute and make rapid preparations to store food and water in your position so that your supplies will last even through intense barrages.

Fighting defensively.

1. Destroy the American devils with heavy fire. Improve your aim and try to hit your target the first time.
2. As we practiced, refrain from reckless charges, but take advantage of the moment when you've smashed the enemy. Watch out for bullets from others of the enemy.
3. When one man dies a hole opens up in your defense. Exploit man-made structures and natural features for your own protection. Take care with camouflage and cover.
4. Destroy enemy tanks with explosives, and several enemy soldiers along with the tank. This is your best chance for meritorious deeds.
5. Do not be alarmed should tanks come toward you with a thunderous rumble. Shoot at them with anti-tank fire and use tanks.
6. Do not be afraid if the enemy penetrates inside your position. Resist stubbornly and shoot them dead.
7. Control is difficult to exercise if you are sparsely dispersed over a wide area. Always tell the officers in charge when you move forward.
8. Even if your commanding officer falls, continue defending your position, by yourself if necessary. Your most important duty is to perform brave deeds.
9. You should be able to defeat the enemy even if you do not have enough food or water. Be brave, O warriors, even if rest and sleep are impossible.
10. The strength of each of you is the cause of our victory. Soldiers of the Courage Division, do not crack at the harshness of the battle and try to hasten your death.
11. We will finally prevail if you make the effort to kill just one man more. Die after killing ten men and yours is a glorious death on the battlefield.
12. Keep on fighting even if you are wounded in the battle. Do not get taken prisoner. At the end, stab the enemy as he stabs you.[1227]

His philosophy was simple: Every soldier must be a focused, killing machine without regard for himself or his comrades' welfare, and obey *all* his orders without question. Most would posit that if a leader motivated his troops by telling them they were all going to die, it would not cause them to fight more effectively, but the Japanese were different. Kuribayashi knew his men, and when he explained their goal was to do more than any Japanese soldier had been commanded by killing ten Americans before taking their last breath, they realized how seriously their nation viewed their mission. They took his new oath "of violence and revenge"[1228] to heart, knowing their deaths were inevitable, and they willingly obeyed Kuribayashi's mandates.

Kuribayashi and his command embodied military philosopher Carl von Clausewitz's dictum, "War is merely the continuation of policy by other means."[1229] He believed "exacting the maximum bloodshed from the U.S. forces on Iwo…would work in Japan's advantage in negotiating an end to the war."[1230] Japan's culture afforded Kuribayashi men able to be formed in such a way as to buy into the "enormous exertions and great hardship" and ultimate cruel death all his men faced following his will and orders.[1231]

One may find Kuribayashi's motivation for his troops to embrace their coming deaths as strange, but as has already been seen on other islands, it was simply the Japanese way of doing things. Japanese filmmakers sponsored a newsreel before Iwo Jima, describing the conflict "as a suitable place to slaughter the American devils" and do *their* gods' work knowing they would all die doing so. The Japanese believed "to extirpate evil required the mass death of the Other, just as purifying the Self required acceptance of mass self-slaughter."[1232] Long before America's fleet reached Iwo Jima, Kuribayashi "introduced the *Kamikaze* suicide doctrine…Men took oaths to undertake suicide missions if… necessary…Scarves with the *Kamikaze* symbol [神風]…were distributed" to his troops.[1233]

Kuribayashi refused to entertain the thought of unconditional surrender although he knew that might happen if they continued to suffer defeats. He knew his emperor and high command expected him to lose, but they wanted him to do so in a manner that would frame the loss as a Pyrrhic victory for the "heathen" Americans whom he called "devils."

Kuribayashi not only gave orders to condition his men they were going to die, but he also did things to ensure they knew what he expected of them such as blocking their emplacements' exits. After entering pillboxes, many of which were sealed from the outside, the men defending Iwo realized this pillbox was to be their sarcophagus. Once inside, they were *never* leaving.[1234] To this day, many are still in those pillboxes, buried under sand and vegetation (some estimate there are over 11,000 undiscovered bodies still there).[1235] From a military perspective, maybe sealing them inside also camouflaged their dwellings since many structures were buried underground, so this might have been a tactic to prevent Marines from identifying the structures and/or attacking them from a vulnerable rear. There were thousands of cave dwellings and pillboxes organized into a phantasmagoric labyrinth. If many of his soldiers had no way to escape the fortifications, then Kuribayashi probably locked thousands into these concrete sarcophagi before one Marine put a boot on shore. His men went "contentedly, like a quiet ghost with a clean conscience sitting inside the bars of a snug family vault."[1236]

Kuribayashi was "hopelessly holding up hope in the midst of despair."[1237] He was one of the most ruthless commanders of all time, proving indeed that "some dying men are the most tyrannical."[1238] Kuribayashi conducted his battle with skill, knowing that within weeks he would die fighting or commit suicide after almost all his soldiers lay dead. He wrote, "What a pity I have to bring the curtains down on my life in a place like this because of the United States."[1239]

Most Japanese seemed to not lose any faith in their Shintō gods, but this may have been because some Japanese gods are war-gods like *Hachiman Daimyōjin* and *Takemikazuchi-no-kami* or Hirohito, a man-god, who ordered this carnage in the first place.[1240] Many Japanese were in a stage of religious development similar to the ancients who worshiped *Ares* (the Greek god of war), *Mars* (the Roman god of war), *Thor* or *Odin* (Norse gods of war and revenge). Hirohito furthered the human tradition of deification as did ancient Egyptian pharaohs like Tutankhamun or Ramesses II (revered as the offspring of a sun god named *Ra*), and as did Greek leaders like Alexander the Great (son of Ammon-Zeus) or Roman Emperors like Caligula, Nero, and Domitian.[1241] In all cases, these men were not only seen as gods, but also were their nations' supreme military commanders. Transcendentalist Ralph Waldo Emerson wrote, "That which dominates our imagination and our thoughts will determine our lives, and character. Therefore, it behooves us to be careful what we worship, for what we are worshipping we are becoming."[1242] Religious commentator Sam Harris could be describing the average Japanese belief in Hirohito and these Shintō gods when writing: "The only demons we must fear are those that lurk inside every human mind; ignorance, hatred, greed, and *faith*, which is surely the devil's masterpiece."[1243] These beliefs are indeed an oversimplified metaphorical view, but the fact remains the Shintō religion seemed to reinforce the Imperial soldier's will to fight tenaciously, and either die for a merciless empire or commit suicide rather than surrender.[1244] Shintōism also reinforced the belief that if they died honorably, they could become gods themselves "eternally to protect" their families and clans.[1245] In short, the war was *seisen*, "sacred war."[1246] Japanese myths motivated Japan's soldiers to kill without remorse and die with reckless abandon.

As the Marines approached Iwo, thousands of Japanese on Iwo donned their thousand-stitch belts (*senninbari*) to spiritually "ward off bullets."[1247] These three-feet-long and six-inch-wide belts were made by their womenfolk who brought it around their neighborhoods, asking 1,000 women to each put in a stitch to create a belt that would defend a man from the enemy.

Once the battle commenced, the Marines constantly witnessed Japanese soldiers killing themselves in murder-suicide tactics. For instance, the Japanese used smoke grenades to blind assaulting tanks and surrounding Marines and then attacked them with prepared charges, killing themselves as they ran into the tanks holding the charges like footballs (a mini-*Banzai*).[1248] In a field of dead Marines, Sherman tank driver Corporal Leighton Willhite almost got taken out by such a crazed Japanese suicide runner. As this enemy neared his tank carrying a mine, its .30-caliber machinegun opened up and hit the *Kamikaze* sprinter 25 feet away, exploding the mine and blowing it and the "Nip" into a rainbow of debris that covered the tank. Later, Willhite and his buddies scraped off their attacker's flesh, bone, and skull from the tank's outer skin.[1249]

On 21 February, two days after the landings, Japan's suicide pilots started showing up. During this day, the sky would be full of U.S. planes bombing targets and defending against 32 *Kamikazes*. A few got through and damaged the aircraft carrier *Saratoga*, the escort carrier *Lunga Point*, and the anti-torpedo net tender *Keokuk*. One plane sank the escort carrier *Bismarck Sea*, taking 218 crewmen to a saltwater grave. Marines found it disconcerting to see *Kamikazes* dropping from the sky plunging themselves into their targets and transforming ships into giant explosions.[1250]

Immediately after Marines seized Suribachi on 23 February, they saw the devastating psychological impact on the Japanese. A suicide ritual all over the Pacific was for a defeated Japanese soldier to lie down, with his rifle muzzle in his mouth, and squeeze the trigger with his big toe or to hold a live grenade next to his head or heart and commit *jiketsu*. In one cave, Marines found 150 Japanese who had committed *jiketsu* because they had lost Suribachi.[1251] Those who had not decided to kill themselves launched a mini-*Banzai*, all dying in the process.[1252] On being taken over on the same day, a unit near the base of the mountain near Minami Village launched *Banzai* "charges in succession, screaming a battle cry."[1253] Before the Marines landed on Iwo, the Japanese flew a flag with the characters of *Namu Hachiman Daibosatsu* on it, meaning "We Believe in the Merciful God of War."[1254] Well, no god of war showed mercy to these warriors.

The day before Suribachi fell, elements of the 3d MarDiv were attacked by Captain Masao Hayauchi's 12th Independent Anti-Tank Battalion's cannons. In a few hours, Hayauchi destroyed several tanks with rapid-fire artillery pieces, the 47mm cannon. After his cannons had been rendered useless, he led a charge against the remaining Shermans. "Clutching to his chest a charge with the fuse lit, he splayed himself against a tank and blew himself up."[1255] On 24 February, Kuribayashi wrote a *Kanjo* for Hayauchi and it was soon read before the emperor making it a *Jōbun*, the Japanese version of a Medal of Honor.[1256] He also requested a "two-rank promotion" for him.[1257]

Before such attacks like Hayauchi's were performed, soldiers would tell one another they would wait for each other at the *Sunzu* River, the river that Buddhists believe separates the living from the dead, like the river Styx in Greek mythology.[1258] The spiritual rewards Japanese believed they would inherit by dying for such beliefs "created a remarkable combat ideology."[1259] Neuroscientist Sam Harris wrote, "Without death, the influence of faith-based religion would be unthinkable. Clearly, the fact of death is intolerable to us, and faith is little more than the shadow cast by our hope for a better life beyond the grave."[1260] If a Japanese soldier leaned more toward Zen Buddhism than Shintōism, then his spiritual leaders told him that if he were to die, "corporeal annihilation really means a rebirth of [the] soul, not in heaven, indeed, but here among ourselves."[1261] So, if one were to die, he had the chance to either become a god with Shintō beliefs or be reborn and reincarnated with Buddhist ones. A Japanese youth had many options to ease his anxiety. He really would never die even if his physical body was annihilated on the battlefield.

On 4 March, Kuribayashi radioed the Army vice chief of staff Lieutenant General Hata Hikosaburō a report, apologizing for his inability to hold off the Marines. He feared the U.S. would soon use Iwo to mount an invasion of Japan:

> Our forces are making every effort to annihilate the enemy. But we have already lost most guns and tanks and two-thirds of officers...We may have some difficulties in future engagements... Now I, Kuribayashi, believe that the enemy will invade Japan proper from this island...I am very sorry because I can imagine the scenes of disaster in our Empire... Although my own death approaches, I calmly pray to God for a good future for my motherland...I would like now to apologize to my senior and fellow officers for not being strong enough to stop the enemy invasion...My soul will always assault the dastardly enemy and defend the lands of the Empire forever.[1262]

Kuribayashi had become fatalistic and was confronting the seemingly inevitable with his command. He feared what his countrymen on the mainland would soon face, especially after personally seeing how powerful and relentless the U.S. military wave of attack was. In a rare but expected act of humility, he apologized to his commanders for not stopping the enemy although he and his command knew such a fate awaited him and his men even before his boots ever crushed Iwo earth in June 1944. Even Lieutenant General Hikosaburō, who Kuribayashi was reporting to directly, admitted the entire "General Staff Headquarters was firmly determined to fight to the last man" on the mainland, so nothing happening to the Iwo garrison could have come as a surprise to Kuribayashi—they all were conducting "death-defying" actions.[1263] Kuribayashi must have realized that instead of being a major dam stopping the flow of American forces, his *Kamikaze* island strategy served to the Americans to be actually just a downed tree limb forcefully pushed aside. His hope for an *Ermattungsstrategie*, a strategy of attrition (*jikyusen*), although somewhat effective in killing more Marines than the Corps thought possible, still did not achieve his desire to deter the U.S. from marching forward toward Japan.[1264] As Kuribayashi reported to Lieutenant General Hikosaburō, "I, here, apologize to my seniors and fellow members that my power was too small to stop the enemy's invasion."[1265] America would continue to build out massive amphibious forces to attack Japan. Interestingly, Kuribayashi felt heaven could be pleaded with to change events. Furthermore, he felt his own death would not bring eternal rest. Instead, once dead, there would be a spiritual realm where he would continue to battle the Americans.[1266]

Determined to go out in a blaze of glory, naval commander Captain Samaji Inouye ignored Kuribayashi's orders and led a large 1,000-man *Banzai* on 8 March. They attacked elements of the 2nd Battalion, 23rd Marines. The Leathernecks killed 784 Imperial Naval Landing Sailors. The Marine casualties included 90 killed and 257 wounded. The almost 800 Japanese dead from this engagement was the "largest single-day enemy death toll recorded on Iwo."[1267] Also on this day, the remnants of the 2nd Mixed Brigade (under Major General Senda's command) launched a *Banzai* although Kuribayashi had ordered it not to.[1268] A week later, Rear Admiral Ichimaru launched a *Banzai* charge with his staff and some of his men on 16 March. According to an eyewitness, he made it all the way down to a supply depot on the southern beach, throwing grenades and fighting as hard as he could. He was never heard of again.[1269] On 17 March, what was left of Colonel Ikeda's 145th Regiment also launched a *Banzai*.[1270] Toward the battle's end, probably around 22 or 23 March, the radiomen operating communications from the island destroyed their codebooks, smashed their radios, and conducted a mini-*Banzai*.[1271]

In the few cases when a Japanese did surrender, the Marines had to be careful. There was a case in the 3d MarDiv lines when the enemy tried to use a "suicide surrenderer" to draw in Marines to place them in a kill zone, but his act was noticed and the surrendering man was shot dead.[1272] Even after becoming a prisoner, there were times it was a ruse. After one wounded Japanese was taken to a hospital, he escaped, commandeered a weapon, and shot several patients before Marines killed him.[1273] Most continued to fight to the death or commit *seppuku* or *jiketsu*. There were some who gave up, though very few. Some who had not made the decision to kill themselves when faced with surrender were forced by their superiors to do so. One prisoner who emerged from a cave that had been blown up by Seabees told his captors the explosion caused so much confusion it allowed him to leave the cave, preventing "his officers from killing him."[1274]

As Marines continued to prevail in battle and destroy underground bunkers, Japanese continued their *jiketsus*. Most notable was the suicide of Major General Sadasue Senda according to another report. By 14 March, his 2nd Mixed Brigade, initially 4,600 strong, had been reduced to dozens. On that day, Senda gathered together 50 men, almost the entirety of those remaining in his brigade, and said he was going to commit *jiketsu* rather than "surrender to the heathen Marines." He declared, "Let us all meet again at Yasukuni Shrine." He distributed grenades to his men, who then placed them next to their stomachs and blew themselves inside out. During this death ritual, Senda blew out his brains with his pistol.[1275]

As war dragged on, some Japanese realized they were not invincible and the gods would not save them. Contrary to their government's propaganda, the Americans were brave, tough, and relentless. A few IJA servicemen started to change their views, a hard task for religious fanatics. Lieutenant Satoru Omagari was such a man. He ventured out of his cave in the north carrying dynamite for his final mission. He waited for nightfall, crept out until he found several dead Japanese near a logical route for the Americans, and then lay down with the cadavers so he could kill more Marines. He took out his bayonet, sliced open a dead comrade, and smeared his intestines over his own body. He then feigned death and awaited his prey.[1276] Another corpse lying nearby had his mouth open, filled with what looked like rice, "but was a pile of fly larvae." Large bottle-blue flies buzzed around his head like mad hornets. The Marines never arrived yet Omagari waited, sweating in the sun, experiencing the horrifying rot of his dead countrymen with whom he had lain down. Thoughts penetrated his mind about duty, country, and death. Was this what he had been "trained for?" His elders had ingrained in him that it was glorious, honorable, spiritual, and expected to die for the emperor.

Omagari revered the 47 *rōnin* tale, believing they exemplified qualities of a fighting man. The legend of the 47 *rōnin*, also known as the *Akō* vendetta or the *Genroku Akō* incident, is a tale describing a band of *rōnin* (leaderless *samurai*) who avenged their feudal lord's death. Plotting for a year, they finally kill the man who murdered their master. Then, they all commit *seppuku*. Some believe this is the best-known example of the *samurai* code of *Bushidō*. As Omagari lay among the corpses planning the death of Marines, he believed the 47 *rōnin* legend was emblematic of the devotion, sacrifice, and honor people should follow. That was what he had been taught, but by degree, he began to question it.

When darkness fell, he broke the strings of now-hardened intestines that bound him to the bodies and crawled back to his cave. The next day, he again half-buried himself among the dead awaiting the Marines, who again did not come. While there, he agonized about the meaning of life and Japanese culture. When darkness came again, he changed his mind about Japanese beliefs and swore he would never again try to be a human bomb. The battle had changed him, and he started to see the weakness of his religious creeds.[1277] Omagari was rare in questioning his fanatic upbringing. He was raised with a faith that despised the "mind and free individual" and preached "submission and resignation, and that regard[ed] life as a poor and transient thing" preventing him and comrades from "self-criticism."[1278] Luckily for Omagari, he started to question it all.

Omagari saw the inhumanity among his countrymen as they fought each other over water and refused to tend to the wounded, thereby making their environment devolve into a world of "every man for himself." The chain of command broke down and many struck out alone instead of taking orders.[1279] Some killed others for water. Omagari lost his faith in humanity as his comrades killed one another during a losing battle.[1280] As often happens, cultural norms, religious creeds, and moral codes break down under extreme physical and mental stress. The murderous martial discipline inculcated in these men and the barbaric religious creeds of superiority, military domination, and invincibility withered away under the strain of military defeat.

It is unclear what would have happened had the Marines stumbled on the pile of corpses where Omagari lay. Often, when Marines found heaps of seemingly dead enemy, they fired into the bodies and burned them with a flamethrower to ensure there were no suicide sleepers, having learned the hard way to be careful.[1281] For instance, a group of five Japanese had played possum in 3d MarDiv's area of operations and suddenly "sprung to life," shooting two officers before they were killed.[1282] Almost all procedures in the Marine manual about fighting techniques are written in blood. One rule they had learned to follow was, "If it's possible a dead Japanese soldier is really alive, act as if he is." A 3d MarDiv report concluded: "The Japanese probably have used more deception in the present war than has ever been practiced in any other campaign in history."[1283] San Diego boot camp instructors had exclaimed: "If it don't stink, stick it."[1284] In the end, American leaders' "responses [to the Japanese] were conditioned by fear and incomprehension."[1285]

Omagari's reflection during the battle was not unique. On Iwo, a few Japanese came to realize the futility of their beliefs about the cult of death and their unquestioning devotion to the emperor, so they started to change like Omagari. Evidently rejecting his indoctrination, Omagari surrendered, something almost unheard-of for officers. "I became a hostage, but I felt nothing; no shame, sadness or any other emotion. I was an empty, worn-out husk."[1286] The war's horror made him realize that, to use a phrase from Melville, "a man's religion is one thing, and the practical world quite another."[1287] Omagari realized he made himself a *musekimono* (an outcast) by disgracing his family, military, and nation by surrendering.[1288]

Although Marines had been ordered to "take no prisoners," there was still considerable effort to get the Japanese to surrender when they were discovered in caves. In one instance, the Marines pleaded with around 15 Japanese to exit. They responded with a request to give them 15 minutes to discuss it.[1289] The men could hear the enemy speaking loudly with one another. Hearing their vociferous conversation, one Marine said, "When the war is over we must abolish the [Japanese] language: it's an ugly one."[1290] Eventually the enemy stopped speaking and instead of surrendering, they blew themselves up with grenades. Sometimes, the Marines set up loudspeakers and had native speakers plead with those inside to come out. In one case, they used a captured officer as their spokesman. Marines met with little success using these methods and explosive experts had to blow the caves shut because the Japanese, if left alive, would do all within their power to kill Americans.[1291] Also, when the Japanese refused to come out, Marines used flamethrowers on them.[1292]

In a few cases, *nisei* (second generation Japanese Americans) interpreters assigned to the U.S. Army tried to help the Marines save some before they committed suicide or before Marines ran out of patience and sealed them in their caves for eternity. Bravely—insanely—they entered the caves, calling out to their "blood brothers" to lay down arms. Although the report noted that surprisingly, none of the *nisei* died this way, they also met with little success and many Japanese blew themselves up after allowing their *nisei* cousins to leave.[1293]

On many occasions, as the battle slowly rolled to an end, the Japanese were found to be in unfit fighting shape due to substance abuse. In the few weeks leading to the end of Iwo's defense, the Japanese often engaged the Marines while drunk. Knowing imminent defeat awaited them, many killed themselves with grenades while others got wildly intoxicated and conducted uncoordinated attacks or ventured on one-man *Banzai* missions to commit "suicide by Marine."[1294]

As I walked in many of the caves in 2015, my feet often crunched the broken glass of sake bottles. According to Don Graves of the 28th Marines, 5th MarDiv:

> The Japs were so liquored up...that it took several bullets to bring them down. One Nip came at us and I unloaded my entire clip of my M1 in him and he still kept running at us. His heart must have stopped by then, but the adrenaline pushed him forward and guys in a foxhole near me finally brought him down. When the Japanese got drunk on sake...they behaved as if we could not shoot them, but when we did, they continued to fight until they bled out. These people were...nuts.[1295]

Graves remembered seeing two Japanese walking out of their cave in their G-string underwear with sake bottles in their hands, laughing; Dick Dashiell reported on a small *Banzai* where the enemy soldiers were howling hysterically as they charged. Were they drunk or just crazed in the knowledge they were conducting a suicide attack?[1296]

On 16 March, Kuribayashi sent his final message to Imperial Headquarters:

> So sad to fall (in battle), our ammunition is exhausted, we are unable to fulfill the heavy duty for the Nation. I will pick up my sword, though my body lay decaying in the field, I shall reincarnate seven times to seek revenge. My earnest thoughts will go to the Empire long after this island is overgrown with ugly vines.[1297]

Kuribayashi wrote about being reincarnated seven times to continue to fight, a religious concept of the afterlife common to Japanese.[1298] In Judeo-Christian dogma, individuals on the brink of death may take a summation of their lives, often asking for forgiveness for sins and affirming the Almighty in the hope they will enter heaven. In contrast, Kuribayashi yearned to avenge his country for seven different lifetimes, a significant number in Buddhism leading to a state of Nirvana. The word for revenge in Japanese is *katakiuchi* which means "attack enemy." These were Kuribayashi's last thoughts—never view your enemy as worthy of anything less than death even in the face of your own demise.[1299] The day that Kuribayashi made these declarations, 16 March, the government decided to promote him to full general.[1300]

On 21 March, Imperial General Headquarters in Japan announced over the radio the Iwo Jima defenders had all died glorious *samurai* deaths on 17 March. As usual, the Japanese government continued to lie to its people; the *samurai* troops were starving, thirsty, and killing each other. Having run out of ammunition, they were incapable of offering resistance. To feed themselves, they stole and scavenged food from the enemy. They reverted to a primitive state to survive for another day. The glory, if there was any, was found in *Banzais* and *jiketsus* because surrender was not glorious in their belief systems. To those who rejected those beliefs, the end of the Japanese resistance on Iwo was anything but glorious—it was, as Omagari noted, "shameful" and "disgusting."[1301] Kuribayashi reported on 21 March to the Chichi Jima garrison, "My officers and men are still fighting. The enemy front line is 200 to 300 meters from us and they are attacking by tank…They advised us to surrender by loudspeaker, but we only laughed at this childish trick."[1302] He then wrote the emperor, "We have not eaten or drunk for five days. But our fighting spirit is still high."[1303] On 21 March, Prime Minister Kuniaki Koiso issued a radio broadcast about the effort their countrymen made on Iwo. He praised Kuribayashi and his men for their "heroic resistance," embodying the "Japanese spirit."[1304]

From 20 to 26 March, 21st Marine Regiment patrolled the north, securing the areas they had won.[1305] Major General Erskine ordered them on 19 March to "maintain contact with the…enemy encountered until he is annihilated."[1306] Marines now fought Japanese soldiers dressed in Marine uniforms, so attired partly because they wanted to practice subterfuge, and partly because their own tattered uniforms had rotted off their bodies.[1307] As the end neared, the Japanese continued their suicide. Marines started to hear explosions throughout the night from caves as the Japanese blew themselves up.[1308] So many rotting bodies covered the island producing millions of flies that it was sprayed with DDT with "crop-dusters," or better said, "corpse-dusters," to cut down on disease from spreading to healthy personnel.[1309]

During the battle's final days, there was a lot of "mopping-up" or sporadic fighting. Marine demolition experts continued to discover caves full of Japanese enemy. After they failed in convincing the contingent in a certain cave to surrender, they would blow the cave shut. If groups of Japanese offered resistance, they immediately killed them without the offer for surrender being given. Marines often found caves previously sealed were "re-opened by the Japanese" days later. Marines resealed them using more explosives than necessary to ensure no escape was possible. They often heard the faint groans of the dying and muffled explosions of grenades from deep inside the earth as men committed *jiketsu* when it dawned on them the cave was a tomb from which they would never escape.[1310] One such cave caused a horrific night for nearby Marines as the entombed Japanese "hollered" and "squealed" under their feet until dawn. Eventually, the cacophony dwindled to occasional "moans," and by morning, only an eerie silence.[1311] For decades, Japanese had been indoctrinated with the belief their fighting spirit could overcome any enemy's material superiority, which seemed to have been proven during the Russo-Japanese War of 1904–05 and during the first year of WWII when the Japanese defeated superior Allied forces.[1312] On Iwo that belief was shattered and many died probably with broken hearts having realized the lessons their leaders had given them were fallacious.

By the battle's end, the Japanese were out of provisions, had no functional supply chain, and were starving, without water. If Marines had not killed those they found, the Japanese would have died from lack of hydration.[1313]

On 26 March, while Marines covered ground along the northern shoreline, a hidden underground barracks behind their lines and north of Airfield No. 2 housed almost 300 Japanese plotting a sneak attack. They had used their underground tunnel system to travel from the north to infiltrate the rear echelons. From their position behind the lines, they had the element of surprise and were poised to hit the Americans.

In the early morning around 0200, a Japanese commander (some think Kuribayashi) cunningly picked an area west of the second airfield in the island's middle where there were many non-combat U.S. troops in the rear. Sleeping comfortably in their tents were pilots, crewmen, supply troops, shore parties, antiaircraft gunners, and Seabees. Emerging from underground, the Japanese sliced through tents, killing many who were not armed for or accustomed to this type of warfare. Most pilots carried only pistols, and many died in their cots not knowing what hit them. Unlike concurrent *Banzais* in areas that were not behind enemy lines, these Japanese were silent and sober when they struck. As they attacked, they screamed, slashed, fired, and threw grenades to kill as many Americans as possible. The spearhead of this attack also hit the 5th Pioneer Battalion, full of African-Americans. Marines have always been trained as combat troops, epitomized by the 29th commandant of the Marine Corps Al Gray's declaration: "*Every Marine is, first and foremost, a rifleman. All other conditions are secondary.*" Even though the "Negro" units were often relegated to support roles, these Marines knew fire team tactics and proper weapon handling. Thus, 1st Lieutenant Harry L. Martin was able to organize a skirmish line manned by these African-American Marines who had mainly come from the 8th Field Depot (Supply Service, FMF-PAC). Martin, a 34-year-old White reserve officer, counterattacked along with the Black Marines beside him, overrunning a machinegun position and killing four Japanese with his pistol while "yelling abuse at them." Seeing the Japanese using a ridge to hide to mass another charge, Lieutenant Norris Bowen Jr. said that Martin "let out a yell to 'Follow me; I can hold the bastards for a while.' Then I heard him yell, 'Come on out you little yellow bastards or I'm coming in and get you,' and before any of us below could move, he had run down towards the rear of the ridge."[1314] Several Leathernecks followed Martin in his charge attacking and killing the stunned Japanese, many of whom were wielding swords.[1315] Although he had been hit in the head and buttocks with shrapnel, he refused to leave the battle.[1316] A grenade finally killed Martin while leading his men from the front. He received the Medal of Honor posthumously. His Black compatriots fought tenaciously and the Corps shore party commander "was highly gratified with the performance of these colored troops…while in direct action against the enemy for the first time. Proper security prevented their being taken unawares, and they conducted themselves with marked coolness and courage."[1317] As one sees, occasionally in war, racism disappears and merit trumps all, especially in the moments of life and death.

This was the last "major" enemy attack on Iwo. In this *Banzai*, almost all the Japanese died, the U.S. Air Corps suffered 44 dead and 88 wounded, and the Marines suffered 9 dead and 31 wounded.[1318] Kuribayashi's biographer Kumiko Kakehashi, has argued that this last all-out attack was particularly skillful because it was led by the general.[1319] According to a Japanese survivor, Kuribayashi led this attack, and addressed his men beforehand:

> Even if I should perish before you in the battle, the glorious exploits that you have carried out will never be forgotten. Japan may now be losing this battle, but the people of Japan are burning at your loyalty and your patriotism; they are praising your glorious deeds; and the day will come when they offer silent prayers for your ghosts. Be easy in your minds and sacrifice yourself for your country.[1320]

According to this witness, Kuribayashi inspired his men to fight heroically although there was no prospect for victory or survival. As he acknowledged, they had lost the battle. Even so, he took pride they had fought well. His goal to inflict maximum destruction on the Marines had succeeded beyond anything his predecessors had accomplished.

And in researching yet another report, on 27 March Kuribayashi moved to another cave on the northern shore with his staff officer, Colonel Kaneji Nakane. Kuribayashi faced north in the direction of Hirohito's palace, knelt and solemnly bowed three times to the man-god. He then pulled his sword, thrust it in his stomach, and bowed his head. Nakane raised his sword, taking on the role as Kuribayashi's "Second," and sliced off the general's head in ritualistic *seppuku*, *samurai*-fashion. The colonel then buried his commander's body in an unmarked grave, placing his head next to his own headless corpse.[1321] Other stories about Kuribayashi's demise include shellfire blowing the general to bits or a sniper shooting him.[1322] Out of his original garrison of 21,900 men, a little over 1,000 surrendered or were taken prisoner, most of whom were Korean.

After Iwo, Japan prepared its citizens to psychologically embrace *gyokusai*—the conviction to die heroically in battle rather than surrender. The government produced a slogan *ichioku gyokusai*, meaning "the shattering of the hundred million like a beautiful jewel." Leaders taught their citizens to embrace their own extermination, feeling it would provide spiritual purification.[1323] Fighter ace Saburō Sakai wrote, "There was no doubt in anyone's mind that the end was near, that soon the fighting would be transferred to our soil. There was no possibility of surrender. We would fight to the last man."[1324] His wife Hatsuyo carried a knife she would have used on herself instead of falling into American hands.[1325] At the highest levels of government, leaders believed "Japan must fight to the finish and choose extinction before surrender."[1326] This mentality permeated the Japanese strategic vision (Japan must be defended at all costs) and emotional bearing (Japan is worthy to die for even in the face of defeat). Had the war continued, the entire nation was being conditioned to perform *Banzais*, *jiketsus*, *Kamikaze* raids, and *seppukus*. Such was the philosophy of *ichioku gyokusai*.

CONCLUSION

In analyzing the battles of Saipan, Tinian, Guam, and Iwo Jima, one comes away with a profound respect and an overwhelming feeling of terror when exploring how Japanese military leaders expected their troops to behave and how actual soldiers viewed battle and surrender. Analyzing the massive *Banzais* on Saipan (circa 4,300), Tinian (circa 3,000), Guam (circa 8,500) and Iwo Jima (circa 1,300 in two major ones), and the minor-*Banzais* on these islands as well, the widespread performance of *seppuku* and *jiketsu*, the use of pilots in *Kamikaze* raids, and the utter refusal to allow anyone to surrender illustrate that the Japanese military promoted policies that, in the end, did not take care of its troops. As Major Horie wrote, "With Japan already greatly weakened and desperate, *the war made us semi-insane* and led us to drive the soldiers like this [author's italics]."[1327] One could categorically say Horie's statement is a dramatic understatement.

These military policies and religious convictions were detrimental and suicidal in the extreme to the welfare of military personnel incapable of offering any meaningful further resistance. The fanaticism one witnessed on these islands was later seen in droves on Okinawa and would have happened by the hundreds of thousands had Japan been invaded. To develop a military that trained men to kill themselves if they could not fight any longer or were faced with surrender was sadistic. To develop leaders who would kill themselves in ritual suicide in the face of defeat and make sure their men would kill themselves too was psychopathic. To develop a society where the predominant religious, political, and ideological beliefs would lead soldiers to believe mass suicide was honorable and moral displays Japanese society was perverted in its willingness to declare losers should die regardless of the odds against them. They created a genocide against their leaders and their subordinates who failed to secure victory. Ironically, probably the second largest killer of Japanese *during combat* (from 1931 to 1945, disease and starvation killed most Japanese deployed),[1328] besides the Chinese and Americans, were the Japanese as they killed themselves or created situations like during *Banzais* where they would die by conducting such actions. Such deaths were not honorable and courageous, they were wasteful and stupid. This aspect of Japan's mass murder against itself has rarely been explored. Once again, the Japanese in general were excellent at following immoral orders, but not moral ones by Western standards, especially when conditioned to kill themselves in the way they did during the Asian and Pacific Wars.

CHAPTER 20

KNOWLEDGE OF JAPAN'S CRIMES OUTSIDE AND INSIDE THE COUNTRY AND ALLIED REACTION TO JAPAN'S ATROCITIES

"To remember is to create links between past and present, between past and future. To remember is to affirm man's faith in humanity and to convey meaning to our fleeting endeavors."

—Holocaust survivor and writer **Elie Wiesel**[1329]

"If you delight in senseless valor and make a display of violence, the world will in the end detest you and will look upon you as wild beasts. Of this you should take heed."

—**The Emperor Meiji**, a declaration made to the soldiers and sailors of Japan, 4 January 1882[1330]

THROUGHOUT THE 1930S AND 1940S, many knew of Japan's crimes by watching newsreels at the theater and reading newspapers. They especially learned about the Rape of Nanking and the Rape of Shanghai.[1331] Learning about such atrocities, Roosevelt gave a speech on 5 October 1937 calling Japan a "warmaker" and a carrier "of dreaded disease" and called on the world to quarantine it.[1332]

Marine Sergeant John Warner, a China Marine, assigned to the Peking (now Beijing) and Shanghai units in 1937, described how Japanese raped and murdered Chinese civilians everywhere.[1333]Supporting Warner's testimony, General Clifton B. Cates, 4th MarDiv commander on Iwo Jima and later the 19th commandant of the Marine Corps (1948–1951), said the Japanese "were as cruel as could be. We…saw that in Shanghai…[saw] them shoot civilians and run a bayonet through them." Cates witnessed "beheadings" saying the Japanese mind is not the same as an American.[1334] General Lewis William Walt, assistant commandant of the Marine Corps (1968–1971), like Cates, was also stationed in Shanghai in 1937 and witnessed two Japanese soldiers, out in the open, rape a young girl, tie her up to a pole, "and took turns bayonetting her as she screamed." Still alive and bleeding from several wounds, they finally clubbed her to death, and she slumped over, hanging from the wooden post like a macabre Christmas ornament.[1335] During the Rape of Nanking, the American Embassy there gave numerous reports to the American ambassador in Tokyo, Joseph Grew, who in turn took it up with his Japanese counterparts.[1336]

Japanese Foreign Minister Kōki Hirota learned of these crimes, especially from Ambassador Grew and his own personal trip to China, and asked the War Ministry to investigate the matter. The War Ministry eventually replied that they would make sure the atrocities would cease, something history has proven *never happened.*[1337] Hirota never followed up to made sure things would change even though he had personally made the following report about Nanking: "[The] Japanese Army behaved...in [a] fashion reminiscent [of]Attila [and] his Huns. [Not] less than three 300,000 Chinese civilians slaughtered, many cases [in] cold blood."[1338] After the war, he would be hung as a war criminal.[1339] Daily reports of the madness going on in Nanking were made to Japanese diplomatic representatives in the city "who, in turn, reported them to Tokyo."[1340] Hirohito and his underlings did nothing on hearing these reports.

Even after the atrocities of the Rape of Nanking became known throughout Japan, the leaders of these atrocities were still honored and revered. At a Japanese-Christian gathering in November 1939, General Matsui was present, and the entire congregation honored him and his deeds during the Sino-Japanese War. Tadao Yanaihara, an expert on colonial policies, disgusted with these Christians' reverence of Matsui, wrote in the Christian pacifistic magazine *Kashin*: "Would it not have been more appropriate for Christians to have demanded an expression of regret for those [Nanking] actions? Could anything have been less appropriate than for them to have stood up and honored him [for slaughtering and raping innocent civilians]?"[1341] Bravely, Yanaihara was one of the few Japanese at the time trying to do the right thing. Unfortunately, he was part of a tiny minority, and despite his protest in his writing, Matsui continued to be honored by the majority of the Japanese, Shintō/Buddhists and Christian alike, although his deeds were known far and wide within society, the military, and government.

After the Rape of Nanking, U.S. governmental officials became so disgusted with Japan, that by the autumn of 1938 America had stopped all sales of aircraft to Japan and many British firms stopped accepting orders from Japan. "Moral embargos" started spreading throughout the West against Japan as its reputation decayed.[1342] In 1938, U.S. Secretary of State Cordell Hull condemned Japan's focus on bombing Chinese cities with the sole goal to kill civilians.[1343] Due to the butchery going on in China becoming common knowledge, in June 1939, the United States revoked the commercial treaty between the nations laying Japan wide open for further punitive tariffs on imports and exports. Thereafter, Wall Street money stopped flowing into Japan's Manchuria operation.[1344] Throughout 1940, America further placed aviation fuel and limited scrap metal embargos on Japan. In September, the U.S. escalated the iron embargo from a limited restriction to a comprehensive one, further debilitating Japan's industrial capacity. When the Japanese ambassador complained to Secretary of State Cordell Hull, Hull in turn gave him a tongue lashing accusing the Japanese of returning "the world to the Dark Ages."[1345]

After the war began with the U.S., people knew what to expect of the Japanese military. Female nurses on Hawaii, fearing an imminent invasion in 1941 after Pearl Harbor and knowing how the Japanese treated women in foreign lands, carried "pocketknives" and resolved "to slash their wrists if the hospital was taken."[1346] FDR claimed the Pearl Harbor attack provided the "climax of a decade of international immorality."[1347] After the Doolittle raid in April 1942, the Japanese slaughtered 250,000 innocent Chinese civilians around Chekiang which was reported to the world through radio and newspaper channels.[1348] Chiang Kai-Shek personally informed FDR of this mass murder.[1349] When the Japanese committed evil, they did so with "joyous zeal"[1350] and often, with much fanfare making the news of their exploits travel far and wide. In 1944, U.S. Office of Strategic Services called the Japanese headquarters of the Gendarmerie in China a "holy terror."[1351] The leadership of the free world, starting with FDR, knew very well what type of enemy they were fighting. To illustrate this fact in dramatic fashion, the magazine *Collier's*, with a circulation of over 2,800,000, published the following in America in February 1944:

> The horrors of Nanking, Hong Kong and Shanghai did not proceed from the sudden fury of wild beats excited by the smell of blood. Japanese troops acted under the direct orders of Tōjō himself, conveyed in these precise words: 'In pursuit, be thorough and *inexorable*.' The bayoneting of British and Canadian captured and wounded, the rape and murder of hospital nurses, the torture of prisoners, the beheading of Chinese noncombatants until the very gutters ran blood—all of these bestialities trace back to…Tōjō, insane with his hate of 'foreign devils' and infatuated with the German theory of *Schrecklichkeit*.[1352]

From the common man on the streets of America to the leaders in the White House, everyone in the U.S. learned of the atrocities Imperial Japan had conducted throughout its rule almost in real time. It appeared that the Japanese wanted the world to know about what they were doing with how easy it was for the common man to learn of their misdeeds.

Besides knowing about the countless poison gas attacks Japan conducted against the Chinese throughout the 1930s, America also learned of its biological warfare in the 1940s. Chief of the United States Intelligence Branch of the Chemical Warfare Services, Lieutenant Colonel Howard Cole, wrote the U.S. Army's 14th Air Force Intelligence in 1944 that "the Japanese are cultivating large quantities of virus for spreading bubonic plague, pneumonia, relapsing fever, cholera and other epidemics among Chinese or Allied troops."[1353] Unit 731's activities were being learned about far and wide. For instance, in 1942, British military officials had learned of an "aerial plague attack" by the Japanese at Changde in 1942 by Cambridge University professor and scientist, Joseph Needham, who documented everything. Two years later, Dr. Leonard Short, a medical doctor attached to the British 14th Army's Joint Intelligence Collective Agency, documented "live human prisoners in grisly medical experiments" while inspecting former Japanese research and military facilities overrun by Allied troops.[1354]

Japan's military and political leadership clearly knew what it was doing throughout the world, especially if the whole world in turn knew about its crimes. One can surmise that if every Japanese combatant stationed throughout Asia either indirectly or directly committed or supported the crimes against the Asians as seen from 1931 to 1945, then the majority of over five million soldiers stationed in Asia during these years probably participated in or at least obliquely supported the killings.[1355] As a result, *everyone knew in Japan* what was going on since the vast majority of their sons were committing the crimes and talking about them. One corporal at a welcome-home party bragged to his friends and family about bayonetting a pregnant woman to death and cutting off a defenseless Chinese coolie's head.[1356] Other soldiers sent pictures to their families of themselves standing next to naked women they had raped or carrying the severed heads of their enemies all accompanied by proud and macabre declarations of their exploits.[1357] Similar braggadocious stories of numerous officers and men like this corporal mentioned above made made it into the offices and conference rooms of the military authorities' departments.[1358] In January 1938, Imperial Headquarters in the name of Field Marshal Prince Kan'in Kotohito, Hirohito's uncle, wrote General Matsui, "If we look at actual conditions in the army, we must admit that much is less than blemish-free. Invidious incidents, especially as to troop discipline and morality, have occurred with increasing frequency of late."[1359] By August 1938, Lieutenant General

Yasuji Okamura, who replaced Matsui as the commander of the Central Japanese Expeditionary Army, declared, "It is true that tens of thousands of acts of violence, such as looting and rape, took place against civilians during the assault on Nanking. Second, front-line troops indulged in the evil practice of executing POWs on the pretext of [lacking] rations."[1360] And head of the War Ministry (1938–1939), Lieutenant General Seishirō Itagaki, had a top secret memorandum circulated throughout the IJA in 1939 stating, "If the army men who participated in the war [throughout all of China] were investigated individually, they would probably all be guilty of murder, robbery or rape."[1361] For instance, one Japanese soldier experience supported Itagaki's document when he wrote: "The only skills I picked up after half a year in combat were how to rape and loot."[1362] Since Itagaki was the commanding general of the 5th IJA Division that took part in several key battles from 1937 to 1938 in northern China, he knew what his men did to civilians because he allowed it or directly ordered it. For encouraging these acts against humanity, *never ever trying to stop any of the rape and murder his troops committed*, Itagaki would be hanged as a war criminal in 1948.[1363] Itagaki was good friends with Lieutenant Tsuji and protected him when he was insubordinate to his superiors (*gekokujō*) during the Nomonhan battle in 1939 against the Soviet Union. Itagaki was able to prevent the emperor from discharging Tsuji.[1364] Besides the fact that Itagaki allowed his troops to rape and murder in north China, especially in the region around Hankow, the evidence that he was also such good friends and comrades with Tsuji, one of the vilest officers documented in this study, bespeaks of an immoral character and a poor judge of leadership. However, Itagaki was not alone in liking Tsuji. Hirohito, knowing who Tsuji was, allowed him "to be promoted and to serve in important positions on the Army General Staff."[1365]

Hirohito also knew of the Nanking atrocities being so involved with "every Japanese military move" and always reading every "diplomatic telegram." His granduncle, Lieutenant General Prince Yasuhiko Asaka, had led the attack on Nanking under General Matsui's supervision and was the highest-ranking officer during the Rape of Nanking. Reports from Asaka, as well as his uncle Field Marshal Prince Kan'in Kotohito, would have been debriefing Hirohito on everything they saw and did. Hirohito would have also known about and read Lieutenant General Itagaki's top-secret report from 1939 on the criminal behavior of Japanese soldiers throughout China. As historian Herbert P. Bix wrote,

> As the commander in chief who had sanctioned the capture and occupation of Nanking, and as the spiritual leader of the nation—the individual who gave legitimacy to the "chastisement" of China—he bore a minimal moral as well as constitutional duty to project—even if not

publicly—some concern for the breakdown of discipline. He never seems to have done so.[1366]

That Hirohito *did nothing*, with the knowledge he had, not only about the Rape of Nanking, but also of the atrocities going on throughout Asia and the Pacific *in his holy name*, bespeaks of a depraved mind that tacitly approved of everything happening when Japan appeared to have the upper hand and conquering power when fighting China. That he never spoke privately with his commanders to curtail the behavior indicates he welcomed it and approved of what his men were doing to innocent civilians. "[R]ather than do anything *publicly* to show his displeasure, anger, or remorse, he energetically spurred his generals and admirals on to greater victories in the national project to induce Chinese 'self-reflection.'"[1367]

In September 1940, Colonel Naoichi Kawara, adjutant of the Army Ministry, circulated a document with a list of crimes (Kawara used *hanzai* [犯罪], denoting he knew what they were doing was wrong!) and analysis of why they were happening for leaders of the Imperial Army to consider. Among many other things, it discussed how Japanese often murdered and raped while drunk, that crimes were often performed by reservists (the common man if you will), atrocities often were conducted by rear-echelon troops, and that the military personnel felt they were permitted to assault the Chinese because they were racially inferior. Most shockingly, Kawara's report documented that the longer a soldier remained in China, the more "perverse and skillful" he became in conducting his violation of women and slaughter of civilians. In a very astute, and Freudian way, he concluded his document with a sordid analysis that many of the incidents he had studied stemmed from mental illness and depression from the weather.[1368] Maybe one could more accurately argue that these crimes, especially since they were committed by the average Japanese man, denoted that Japan's society was mentally deranged.

Kotohito's, Okamura's, Itagaki's, Hirohito's, and Kawara's statements display that most troops stationed in China committed atrocities. And Hirohito's actions show he did not care that the men he sent into battle became criminals. Unlike the Nazis, the Japanese did not utilize factories of industrialized death with gas chambers, poison chemicals, and crematoria to kill and dispose of their victims. They used knives, bayonets, swords, and bullets, which required more personnel than the Nazis used in their slaughters. The Japanese stationed throughout Asia, Japan, and the Pacific had knowledge of what their nation did from hearing accounts and/or because they did the killing themselves.[1369] This did not make the Japanese Holocaust any less gruesome than the Nazi genocide; it did, however, leave no large-scale evidence. Everyone in the IJA and IJN who served in China had blood on their hands. The Japanese military more broadly participated in individual acts of crimes against humanity than the Nazi *Wehrmacht*.

The Japanese also pillaged and plundered, reaping a harvest of spoils in raw materials of rubber, steel, foodstuffs, and oil. By 1942, Japan seized "all of the world's supply of quinine, most of its rubber and the greatest sources of oil in the Far East."[1370] Slave labor was used throughout the Empire, benefiting the Japanese economy, especially from Korea and China. For example, under Kuribayashi's Hong Kong command, the Kinkaseki Mining Company utilized POW "labor in inhuman, slave-like conditions."[1371] In fact, 25% of all miners were Korean slave laborers.[1372] Therefore, Japan's business community knew where their profits came from.

So, although the Allied leaders knew what Japan was doing throughout its rule, it was only with the Pearl Harbor attack that the full force of their forces were brought to bear to fight against it. Just like one saw with Hitler's persecution of the Jews, only when America was brought into the war in December 1941 when both Japan and Germany declared war against the United States, did the U.S. start mobilizing to defeat the Axis powers. When this happened, America started fighting, thereby, helping stop Hitler's genocide and Japan's Holocaust by 1945. Unfortunately, violations of human rights were not enough justification to mobilize against Hitler and Hirohito militarily in the 1930s when it would have been easy to do so.

Japan's leaders knew about the atrocities their men were committing throughout Asia and the Pacific, but they simply did not care. There was no moral resolve within the IJA and IJN, or the Imperial government, or with Hirohito, to reign in their men from conducting wholesale rape and murder everywhere they went. That there was no counterbalance to this behavior only emboldened Japanese commanders to continue to act without ethics.

Although the Allies should have had mandates against countries that committed crimes against humanity, it was only when they were attacked by these violators of human rights that the Allies actually did rise up to defeat these evil powers. They did so for self-preservation, not for human rights. As history has shown, they waited way too long to act against the Axis nations, and thus, lost opportunities to save millions of peoples' lives. This history shows that when countries allow dictatorships to run amok throughout the world, it is just a matter of time before the neutral countries will be forced to interact with the aggressive forces out there (as Putin's attack on Ukraine displayed in 2022). History has taught that freedom-loving nations would be wise to declare war against any nation that violates human rights, and that practices reckless expansionist goals that especially entail oppression, rape, and mass murder.

CHAPTER 21

JAPAN'S HONORING OF THEIR CRIMINALS AND DEATH UNITS

"Know one another? We'd have to crack open our skulls
and drag each other's thoughts out by the tails."

—**Georg Büchner**, *Danton's Death*[1373]

FEW JAPANESE THEN OR NOW admit openly their country did anything wrong
during the Asian and Pacific Wars. What remains elusive is what Japanese think
privately about these events but are deterred socially or otherwise from speaking
their real views aloud. As I learned, what they may think personally after Japan's
war but do not express aloud customarily may shock. While studying at the
Goethe Institute in Freiburg, Germany, in 1995, I had several discussions with
two Japanese classmates, Takayuki Matsumoto and Tatsu Kashiwabara, about
Japan's horrible behavior from 1931 to 1945. To my surprise, Kashiwabara had
been researching his country's past in Freiburg's libraries since the information
he was finding had not been disclosed to him during his high school and college
studies. Matsumoto was also surprised by the information Kashiwabara had
uncovered. Under a shelf full of pornography and history books, we talked
about the past, Japan's misdeeds during the Asian War, the Nazi Holocaust, and
women. I continually found the conversation odd as it bounced between serious
historical topics to how beautiful Caucasian women were. He was obsessed with
naked white women, claiming Japan did not show the women's private parts
with hair whereas Germany was full of such magazines and books. He displayed
this "literature" with pride and discussed with his excellent memory the facts
from the past and how he understood them. During this discussion, he told me
something I will never forget when discussing the Rape of Nanking. He said,

Bryan-san, you must know something that is different from you Americans and different from the Germans from us Japanese. And that is if Japan asked me to serve in the army and do another Rape of Nanking, as a Japanese male, I would do so without question. That is the Japanese-way. And all leaders who participated in the Rape of Nanking were due respect and honor to be worshipped and remembered in shrines in Japan.[1374]

When Kashiwabara said this, Matsumoto nodded in agreement. I was shocked by this declaration, although I had to respect the honesty of it. If a German today said, "If my country asked me to re-build Auschwitz and kill Jews, I would do so. That is the German way. And all Nazi leaders are due to be honored and remembered," how do you think people would respond? To ask such an absurd question is to answer it outright. Any ethical person would declare this person is mad and dangerous. I was impressed by Kashiwabara's search for the truth, but horrified by what he did with the facts he found. This discussion illustrated to me how far Japan has to go until it is even halfway close to being where Germany is today on the road of ethical behavior and historical research when it comes to learning from the misdeeds of the past.

Whereas Germany has gone to great lengths to erect monuments to honor the victims of the Third Reich domestically, Japan has only erected monuments to its war dead and evil leaders in its country.[1375] Their lack of remorse continues in overt ways: Pilgrims *today* go to the graves of notorious criminals like Prime Minister and General Hideki Tōjō and Emperor Hirohito to worship their spirits. It is analogous to Germans laying wreaths at *SS-Reichsführer* Heinrich Himmler's and Hitler's graves (if there were ones), yet this is what some do— even elected leaders like Prime Minister Shinzo Abe and his cabinet member Minister of Internal Affairs and Communication Yoshitaka Shindo. This is most notable at Tokyo's Yasukuni Shintō shrine where 1,068 war criminals' "souls" are enshrined including those of Prime Minister and General Tōjō, General Yamashita, Prime Minister Kōki Hirota, General Doihara, General Itagaki, General Matsui, and Colonel Mutō (Matsui's adjutant to his chief of staff and Yamashita's chief of staff) just to name a few highlighted in this book.[1376] In fact, Japan awarded the families of these war criminals pensions in 1956— can one imagine the family members of Hitler or Himmler getting German pensions at the same time?[1377]

Before Hirohito died, he often worshiped at the Yasukuni shrine honoring those under his command who committed *his* atrocities.[1378] In fact, starting in 1959, Hirohito would meet family members of executed war criminals, called *The Society of the White Chrysanthemum*, at the Yasukuni shrine to honor their spirits and then, thereafter, have those family members for tea at the Imperial

Palace as his guests.[1379] The fact these people, and the emperor, did not realize that this "controversial" shrine is not holy, but a "place of horror," revels a sick psychology concerning their understanding of human nature and World War II history.[1380]

This shrine would be akin to Germans "erecting a cathedral to Hitler in the middle of Berlin" or a monument to Deathhead-*SS* members where heads of state gather and praise their deeds.[1381] On 5 May 1985, when West German Chancellor Helmut Kohl and President Ronald Reagan commemorated the 40th anniversary of the end of WWII by visiting the German War Cemetery in Bitburg, Germany, where 49 of the 2,000 soldiers buried there were *Waffen-SS* personnel, there was worldwide condemnation of both leaders, especially inside Germany.[1382] Nothing like this happens inside Japan concerning Yasukuni. Maybe one should not find this that surprising when one knows Japan has also erected a Unit 731 monument called *The Seikon Tower* in Tama cemetery outside of Tokyo where some of Lieutenant General Ishii's ashes are also buried. *Sutras* are even chanted for Ishii as Unit 731's founder "War God."[1383] And some of Tōjō's ashes, mixed with those of other war criminals, were thought to be snuck out in an urn to his widow and eventually made its way to the Zoshigaya Cemetery in Tokyo's Toshima Ward. The other ashes of the executed leaders included those of General Doihara, General Itagaki, and General Matsui. The tombstone inscription for the interred men reads, "The Tomb of Seven Martyrs."[1384] To the western eye, there is a symbol under the inscription that resembles a pentagram, the mark of Satan—one could say, how ironic. And last, a little over a decade ago, Japan erected a bronze statue of Lieutenant Colonel Tsuji in his home prefecture, one of the most sadistic war criminals Japan produced. People go there today and worship at this site. As one can see, Japanese society openly parades its crimes and publicly honors its butchers.

Returning to the Yasukuni Shrine, it is 150 years old and serves many purposes for the Japanese. In addition to the 1,068 "souls" of criminals registered there, there are 2,465,138 soldiers' "souls" interred there as well, many of whom fought for the Fascist regime of WWII.[1385] Eight million worshipers visit it annually.[1386] It not only honors those who have served the nation, but is also viewed as a place of good luck where people go to ask the Shintō gods "for help in passing college entrance exams, to get a good job, for healing from an illness, etc…"[1387] So although war criminals are enshrined there, many others were decent citizens thus causing confusion about the shrine's meaning. Kuribayashi often went there and even took his children. His grandson, LDP politician Shindo, goes there regularly:

This is the final resting place for my other grandfather and my uncle's souls. When I go there, I go there to visit them. I've brought my children there. I like the cherry blossoms and the place is…familiar to me. That other nations get upset that people go there is political. In short, we go there to console the souls of our ancestors.[1388]

Since the entire nation of Japan mobilized for war during WWII, this shrine has a heavy emphasis on the years from 1931 to 1945 when Japan offered up millions of souls to this shrine. Many in Japan due to their beliefs feel attached to this shrine which causes confusion and controversy. When Shindo visited it recently, China's government denounced him.[1389] But Shindo snubbed the Chinese believing it is his religious right to honor the "spirits" of the war dead in general and of his family in particular. He is following in the footsteps of his grandfather General Kuribayashi when he worships there. His actions, and those of thousands of other Japanese, sanction the continued christening of declaring men enshrined there as sacred because all souls in the shrine are apotheosized. Likewise, tens of thousands of Japanese worship Hirohito at his grave at Musashi Imperial Graveyard, Hachiōji, Tokyo. This gigantic mausoleum, mirroring a small, round pyramid that is several stories high and encompasses several acres of land, houses his uncremated body. Citizens offer daily prayers to him and revere him as a god—they are worshiping a mass-murdering criminal.

Steeped in ancestor worship, Japan's citizenry refuses to question or interrogate one's past once his soul becomes "sacred" and takes up residence in a shrine, like at Yasukuni. The shrine impedes mankind's struggle to honestly document the past because it prevents many from critically questioning a person's past.[1390] Honorable Justice Liu Daqun, judge of the Appeals Chamber of the International Criminal Tribunals for the Former Yugoslavia and Rwanda Genocide Trials said, "Those visits [to Yasukuni] have prompted many to allege that the country's official stance is one of defiance," and many of Shindo and Abe's acts, claims, and associations attest to this opinion.[1391]

Japan's society shows its immorality with its inability to see that worshiping mass-murdering, raping thugs is disgusting. It further extends the pain of the events for the victim nations and the victims themselves in that Japan displays its overt sanction of these acts by honoring the very men who committed the crimes against humanity. One sees that in the respect of how to deal with crimes and the past, Japan is a diseased and sick nation.

Author Bryan Rigg at the Yasukuni Shintō Shrine, Tokyo, Japan. This is where Japanese politicians and citizens honor their war dead, some of whom were war criminals.
This would be like Germans honoring graves of *SS* officers. 9 April 2018. *Author's Collection*

CHAPTER 22

THE ATOMIC BOMBS AND STOPPING JAPAN'S MASS MURDER

"Truth is the daughter of time."
—**Gordon W. Prange**, *At Dawn We Slept*[1392]

"The Japanese are a people of paradoxes. That is why they
could cling to the idea of victory in the midst of the fact of
defeat. Even though some had come to accept defeat as likely,
a companion conclusion was that it would come only after
Japan had gone down gloriously fighting to the last man."

—**Masuo Kato**, Editor of the Japanese News Agency, *Kyodo*[1393]

ALMOST 80 YEARS AGO, THE first atomic bomb was being prepared to be dropped
on the Japanese city of Hiroshima. Many have asked whether it was necessary
to drop the bomb, and from studying this period for 25 years, I would say
without this bomb, an invasion of Japan in November 1945 would most likely
have gone forward and cost the lives of millions. Indeed, in August 1945, Fleet
Admiral Ernest King was planning on confronting the U.S. Army's planned
invasion, thinking starving and bombing the Japanese to be a better strategy
than losing men in a land war. If King had been able to alter the planned
Olympic invasion, there probably would have been a northern invasion of Japan
to block Russia from taking over any of the nation, fearing the Soviet penchant
for spreading its rule and Communism throughout the world. In the end, all
three of these options would have cost millions of lives, primarily Japanese ones,
so it was a fortunate move on Hirohito's part for Japan that he decided when
he did to surrender. So, the number of people killed by the two atomic bombs

pales in comparison to what could have been, and, in many respects, to what Japan had already been doing throughout its rule.

For instance, Japan exacted a higher cost in human lives during just two operations out of hundreds while destroying China (approximately 300,000 dead in the Nanking/Shanghai region in 1937–1938, and 250,000 in the Chekiang region in 1942) than the number of Japanese who died from the atomic bombs (Hiroshima claimed 140,000 and Nagasaki 70,000). Also unacknowledged are the 30 million Asians slaughtered by Japan, the millions of rape victims (including women, girls, and young boys) and the desolation that has come to be known as the Rape of Shanghai, the Rape of Nanking, the Rape of Hong Kong, the Rape of Malaya and Singapore, the Rape of the Philippines, the Rape of Manila, the Rape of Guam, the Rape of Canton, and the Rape of Beijing just to name a few. In spite of Imperial Japan having started both the Asian and Pacific Wars, targeted civilians in the bombing of Chinese cities, and forged a path of death, rape, and destruction across Asia, some Japanese maintain the illusion of victimhood and demand apologies from America focusing on the atomic bomb being proof the Allies were racist in dropping it on them, never minding the fact that the bomb was initially earmarked for Nazi Germany, a White nation.

Conquering Japan's 146,000 square miles with 71 million citizens would have been a nightmare had *Olympic* been implemented.[1394] Over 10,000 *Kamikaze* airplanes were held in reserve to fly into our forces and ships on and around the mainland.[1395] Naval warfare around Japan's main islands and land war on its main island would have seen some of the bloodiest battles in history. It's essential to remember that the Allies had to engage in ground warfare within Germany. The German surrender only occurred after significant portions of the country had been occupied, Germany was divided into two zones, and Adolf Hitler had taken his own life. The Japanese were more fanatic than the Nazis and they were fighting for their god in the person of Hirohito. One must imagine what it would have taken to conquer Japan if that invasion planned for November 1945 transpired.

Secretary of War Henry Stimson's staff estimated conquering Japan would cost 1.7 to 4 million casualties, including 800,000 dead, double what the U.S. had already experienced. It would have cost the Japanese between 5 to 10 million dead. To understand the Japanese willingness to die for the emperor, consider that half of the 381,550 Japanese in the Philippines, and more than a third if not half of the 300,000 civilians on Okinawa and 40,000 on Saipan/Tinian, died or killed themselves during these battles.[1396] American leaders were so convinced of the toll an invasion would cost, the country produced 500,000

Purple Hearts. After all the bloody wars since WWII, there are still 120,000 of them left in stock after thousands were awarded to personnel from campaigns in Korea, Vietnam, Iraq, Afghanistan, and Syria.[1397]

Thankfully, these medals were not needed because the bombing campaign launched from the Marianas culminated in the detonation of two atomic bombs that ended the war. These massive attacks convinced Hirohito to command his subjects to lay down arms. Before the bombs dropped, Hirohito was not anywhere close to accepting the Potsdam Declaration, which was required to bring the war to an end. The atomic weapon's destructiveness had the necessary psychological impact to make the emperor alter his thinking. He said on 8 August, "we should lose no time in ending the war so as not to have another tragedy like this."[1398]

After the first bomb's deployment, the might of the Soviet Union bore down on Japanese forces in Manchuria with 1.5 million troops, killing thousands of Japanese after Stalin officially declared war on Japan on 8 August. He had planned the invasion for mid-August, but the bomb made him launch the attack prematurely to seize as much Japanese territory as possible. This forced Hirohito to move more quickly on the surrender agreement. With the explosion of the second bomb on 9 August, Hirohito knew he needed to act. While he had waited to address his nation, thousands of his 1,500,000 citizens in Manchuria started to kill themselves out of fear of the enemy, as those on Saipan, Tinian, and Okinawa had already done. The method of their destruction was grenades and cyanide handed out by IJA soldiers and medical staff. Some 665,000 IJA servicemen in Manchuria disappeared by the thousands under the red wave of Soviet superior forces. The IJA offered mad, useless resistance while still in loyal service to their nation, just as they would have done on the mainland against overwhelming Allied firepower and numbers.[1399] The Soviets suffered over 12,000 killed and 22,264 wounded while Japan suffered 80,000 KIAs and tens of thousands of wounded. Confirmed civilian deaths due to the Soviet advance were 180,000 in Manchuria and 32,000 in Korea.[1400]

The Japanese who survived the Manchurian battles became Soviet POWs. Though few returned home, two who did in 1956 were the acting Kwantung Army commander, General Otozō Yamada and his chief of operations, Major General Tomokatsu Matsumura, both of whom committed untold atrocities in China and authorized the use of Lieutenant General Ishii's bacteriological bombs made at Unit 731. Yamada had even visited Unit 731 and was impressed by its weapons and science, and they both strongly supported Ishii's activities. From July 1944 until the war's end, Yamada directed all Unit 731's activities.[1401]

These leaders were lucky they were not executed, and their testimonies have helped document many facts found in this book.

Hirohito knew if an entire Japanese military force of almost 700,000 could not stop the Soviets' superior martial forces, he needed to act quickly before they reached northern Japan. He knew the Soviets now had some of the evilest perpetrators of his biological warfare program in their hands, probably convincing him more that he did not want Japan to come under the authority of Stalin's legions. They were in possession of men who could be strong witnesses against him as a war criminal. Weakening Stalin's role in post-WWII world justice might ensure his power and nation in a way that was best hoped for given the circumstances. Hirohito felt it was better his country be occupied by the Americans than the Russians, and that the Americans' rule of law and sense of justice would be more "gentle" with him than the Soviet versions.[1402]

All these events (i.e. America's blockade, the atomic bombs and the Soviet invasion) stoked fears of Hirohito and other top leaders that the civilian population would revolt and overthrow the government and the imperial institution. Prime Minister in 1945 Admiral Mitsumasa Yonai claimed at the time that this was the "real reason" why Hirohito wanted to surrender.[1403] As one soon learns when studying this time period, Hirohito had many considerations to make concerning the war, all leading him to one conclusion—continued fighting meant national suicide.

These events of Soviet power and possible rule and the "domestic issues" caused by it and American military power prompted Hirohito to sue for peace even more quickly after the bombs were dropped, saying, "I have given serious thought to the situation prevailing at home and abroad and have concluded that continuing the war can only mean destruction for the nation and prolongation of bloodshed and cruelty in the world…the time has come when we must bear the unbearable."[1404] Even with an imminent invasion of Japan by two major powers and with no chance of a "negotiated peace" through Russian diplomats, Hirohito waited days to address his nation due to fear of retribution from military diehards who wanted to continue fighting.[1405] Even after the U.S. Navy's submarines had tightened their coil around Japan, sinking most supply ships coming and going from Asia, and B-29 bombers had continued to run destructive bombing raids after atomic bombs devastated two cities, IJA reactionaries attempted to capture Hirohito, destroy his recorded surrender message, and kill his advisors to prevent capitulation. They stormed the Imperial Palace, shooting and beheading those opposing them. They searched fruitlessly for the unreleased phonograph recording of Hirohito's surrender announcement. The coup failed on the day of the broadcast, but had it succeeded, war would have continued. The conspirators, seeing they had failed, committed suicide in front of the palace.[1406] After this threat was eliminated, Hirohito announced Japan's surrender on 15 August over the radio to a weeping nation. It was the first time his people had ever heard him speak.[1407] Many Japanese bowed in shame, others fainted and many cried.[1408] After signing the official document for Hirohito, War Minister General Korechika Anami wrote a death poem: "I—with my death—humbly apologize to the Emperor for the great crime." He then committed *seppuku*.[1409] What was his crime? It was not convincing Hirohito to fight on even in the face of the destruction the atomic bombs had wrought. By the end of August, over 1,000 officers, many of them generals and admirals, committed suicide like Anami because of the surrender, but Hirohito stuck to his guns.[1410]

Hirohito's risky and bold move worked. The bombs turned his thinking around, and he was the only one who could persuade his people to lay down arms. Weeks later, on 2 September 1945, a Japanese delegation signed the surrender on the USS *Missouri* in Tokyo Bay. Since his subjects believed he was a god, only such authority could end the 2,600-year span from Japan's origins of never surrendering to a foreign power. They accepted the decision because "His Majesty's orders come before anything else" according to Japanese fighter ace Saburō Sakai.[1411] Hirohito's surrender, according to historian Saburō Ienaga, "avoided the mass violence and slaughter of an [gigantic] invasion."[1412]

Knowing that the Nagasaki and Hiroshima bombings changed the mind of a Japanese god to surrender and prevent a staggering death toll, millions of weary GIs, Marines, and their families thanked their God for the atomic bombs. Had Japan not surrendered, the U.S. had more atomic bombs prepared. As Truman said after Hiroshima, "If [the Japanese] do not now accept our terms, they may expect a rain of ruin from the air, the like of which has never been seen on this earth."[1413] This was not presidential bravado. According to historian Richard Frank, one more bomb, and according to historian John Toland, two more bombs were being readied on Tinian to be dropped on Japan by mid- to late August.[1414] America had also planned to drop 115,000 tons of incendiaries per month on Japan starting in September.[1415] America wanted to avoid facing massive armies of soldiers and civilians who would fight to the very last death. Luckily for the Japanese citizenry, it took only two atomic bombs to do the trick. "Political objects can greatly alter during the course of the war and may finally change entirely since they are influenced by events and their probable consequences," according to military philosopher Carl von Clausewitz, which the atomic bombs accomplished. These bombs exhausted Japan's "physical and moral resistance" and allowed the world to establish peace.[1416] Another reason for Hirohito and his forces to surrender was their belief that continuing the struggle would either lead to a devastating defeat in a counter-attack or result in massive losses so severe that the U.S. would be compelled to seek a negotiated end to the war. However, the bombings clearly communicated that the U.S. would not need to pursue an invasion. If there was no invasion, the Japanese had *nothing to offer by national suicide.*[1417] And last, without the bombs, Japan would have continued its mass murder in the areas it still controlled. As Historian Richard Frank wrote:

> What is clear beyond dispute is that the minimum plausible range for deaths of Asian noncombatants each month in 1945 was over 100,000 and more probably reached or even exceeded 250,000. Any moral assessment of how the Pacific war did or could have ended must consider the fate of these Asian noncombatants and the POWs.[1418]

All those would-be victims had plenty of justification to thank their gods and the Americans for allowing the bombs to be dropped on Japan so that the war would end when it did. Lieutenant Colonel and Dr. Donald Bowie, former head of the British Military Hospital in Hong Kong and POW, felt that had the bombs not been dropped and an invasion proceeded of Japan, he and his staff, and all remaining POWs, would have been slaughtered by the Japanese, echoing Frank's analysis above that the bombs, by bringing about a quick victory, spared thousands if not millions from death.[1419] As Bowie said, the bombs created a "wonderful outcome."[1420] Frank further notes that by April 1945, Japan had diverted all rice from Korea for Japan to prevent widespread famine within the home country, which caused untold starvation in Korea and had the war not ended when it did, would have caused *widespread famine within Korea.*[1421]

For those who still feel the atomic bombs were immoral or against the laws of war, General Curtis E. LeMay had some further interesting analysis. All who denounce the use of atomic bombs usually do not denounce the use of conventional bombs. They also in general do not denounce the use of machineguns, rifles, and grenades. Japanese bayonets and *samurai* swords slaughtered more during the Asian and Pacific Wars than the atomic bombs, but they are not denounced and banned as immoral weapons.[1422] So, LeMay posited, what is more wicked, "to kill people with a nuclear bomb" or "to kill people by busting their heads with rocks."[1423] Yes, there are those who say that without the bombs, Japan would have eventually surrendered, but how much longer would they have waited to do so? When people ask of our leaders in retrospect to not have dropped the bombs, they also are wishing that millions of Americans and Japanese had also been slaughtered by traditional means for a more prolonged war. Historian Richard Frank stated, every day the Japanese continued their occupations of Pacific islands and Asian lands, tens of thousands of civilians were dying under their "care" (not to mention the continued rape of women as well!).[1424] Only the shock of the atomic bombs got the Japanese to make the logical decision to surrender. Even General Kuribayashi acknowledged "Japan could never win [the war] against the United States" and knew this years before he ever stepped one foot on Iwo.[1425] The American people's moral resolve and their industrial capabilities were something Japan could never match, he concluded. Yet, although Japanese leaders knew this reality, they continued a war they could never hope to win. Their mindsets were as insane as they were illogical. As Kuribayashi's staff member, Major Yoshitaka Horie, wrote: "Our inability to judge the situation clearly was appalling."[1426] The atomic bombs finally shocked them into clear thinking.

CHAPTER 23

AMPHIBIOUS WARFARE:
THE MARINE CORPS' *FORTE* AND HOW IT STOPPED
HITLER'S GENOCIDE AND JAPAN'S HOLOCAUST

"No one who has not experienced it can realize how difficult
it is to track the shadow of truth through the fog of war."
—**Wilfred J. "Jasper" Holmes**, U.S. Naval Intelligence Officer[1427]

BESIDES STUDYING HOW THE ATOMIC bombs brought WWII to an end and
the termination of Japan's Holocaust, one must know how the Allies were able
to defeat Hitler's and Hirohito's regimes so quickly; namely, by amphibious
warfare. Without it, Hitler and Hirohito would have enjoyed years more of
slaughtering people they deemed inferior and consolidating their conquered
regions into powerful empires. It is important to learn about this facet of the
Second World War because amphibious warfare, more than anything else,
brought the manpower, machines, and weapons to the shores of Nazi Europe
and Imperial Japan to engage them in battle and defeat them, thereby saving
millions more from being murdered.

Japan's outer defense perimeter began to shrink throughout 1942 and 1943
due to the Americans gaining experience and momentum with their amphibious
warfare. By 1944, cracks in Japan's armor appeared. In 1942, America won
battles at Midway and Guadalcanal. In 1943, America killed Admiral
Yamamoto in an air interception raid, taking out one of Japan's most brilliant
military minds, then followed by conquering the rest of the Solomon Islands
and with Australian troops, made advances in Papua New Guinea. In 1944, the
U.S. was finally able to conduct large-scale operations against Japan itself.[1428]

It was hoped that once Saipan, Tinian, and Guam fell, the U.S. could heavily target Japan's home islands from the air. Hirohito understood this and issued a proclamation to troops on Saipan that they must be victorious so the bombing of Tokyo would not increase.[1429] In order to get the bases for these planes, one had to secure islands from the sea, a laborious procedure technologically and logistically.

To accomplish this feat, the U.S. entrusted much of the preparation for their Pacific campaign to one of the most tough, hot-tempered Marine generals in history, Lieutenant General Holland M. "Howlin' Mad" Smith. He was one of the fathers of Marine Corps amphibious warfare, one of the most perilous forms of operations.[1430] His ideas and foresight with the Higgins boats and ship-to-shore tactics were critical for victory.[1431]

Born on 20 April 1882, Smith grew up in Alabama, was the grandson of two Confederate veterans and knew how to hunt and live off the land. He attended Auburn University (at the time, called Alabama Polytechnic Institute) and after graduating with a Bachelor of Science in 1901, he entered Law School at the University of Alabama graduating in 1903. During this time, he had become a first sergeant in the Alabama National Guard and liked soldiering. Instead of joining the Protestant clergy like his mother hoped or the family law firm like his father desired, he dedicated his life to the military. He began his service in the Corps in 1905 and served against Dominican Republican rebels in 1916–17. During WWI, Captain Smith and other Marines were shipped to France to fight the "*Krauts*." Later, Smith fought at Château-Thierry, St. Mihiel, and Belleau Wood in 1918.[1432] For his combat actions, he received "the *Croix de Guerre* [French "War Cross" for valor]...for services in action against the enemy."[1433]

In Captain Smith's first 13 years of service, he experienced much of the world, ending with combat against the Germans on the Western Front. Since his WWI combat experiences were some of the most dramatic in his life up to this point, he began to study tactical, operational, and strategic lessons from the Great War. He was appointed as a general staff officer in December 1918 and then the assistant to the U.S. 3rd Army's G-3 (operations).[1434] He drew many insights from his studies, thinking always about how he could use them to strengthen "*his*" Corps. Before returning home in March 1919, he obtained the rank of major.

During this time, Smith and other Marines took an acute interest in the major amphibious operations of the Great War, led by the First Lord of the Admiralty Winston Churchill. These amphibious landings against the Ottomans at Gallipoli from 1915 to 1916 were disasters. The poorly-equipped,

-supported, and -trained Commonwealth attackers suffered 97,000 wounded and 44,000 dead in a losing effort. The Marines learned from studying Gallipoli how not to attack from the sea. Consequently, after 1918, Captain Smith and other Marines took a "keen, active and progressive interest in amphibious operations" to justify themselves as a separate entity from the army. "The result of their efforts was to be seen in a combination of convincing warfare doctrine, improved technological and logistical assets, and well-trained specialist units that forever identified the Corps with massive and effective assault from the sea."[1435] Although Marines had practiced this throughout the Corps' existence, conducting 160 assault landings before WWII, these operations needed new equipment and tactics.[1436] While the Corps focused on amphibious operations, it had a long way to go to perfect techniques to assault heavily fortified enemy beaches. Few nations focused on this at the time, making Marines unique.[1437]

Before Pearl Harbor, under now Brigadier General Smith's leadership, the Marines conducted several landings on the East Coast from destroyers. Those early landings were fiascos, but the Marines learned valuable lessons, particularly regarding problems with ship-to-shore troop deployment.[1438] Andrew Jackson Higgins, an inventor from New Orleans and a friend of "Howlin' Mad" Smith, had the solution for conducting ship-to-shore operations that were fast, efficient, and simple. His main solution was the Higgins boat, an amphibious craft designed to move men and supplies from large ships to the beach. It was 36 feet long with a crew of four. It could carry 36 and had a forward ramp allowing troops to run out of the boat instead of climbing over its sides, a development strongly influenced by Smith's subordinate, 1st Lieutenant Victor H. Krulak.[1439] USMC Commandant and General Charles C. Krulak (the godson of General "Howlin' Mad" Smith), commenting on his father's work with Higgins, said, "It was my father who brought to light the importance of the bow launch landing craft and the ability to back off the beach."[1440] Krulak's reports about similar boats he observed the Japanese use outside of Shanghai in 1937 submitted to Smith were the deciding factor in educating the by then "Full-Bird" Colonel Smith about the importance of Higgins' boat design and how it could shape amphibious warfare.[1441] With Krulak's and Higgins' prodding and education, Smith realized the Higgins boat was critical to the Marines' future success so he, in turn, educated and then convinced Admiral Ernest King that the Marines and U.S. Navy needed those boats. America built 23,358 of these crafts and they carried the bulk of the burden for successful amphibious operations around the globe.[1442] Smith said without this boat, "landings on Japanese-held beaches in large numbers would have been unthinkable."[1443] So, without the Higgins crafts and Smith's push for them, island invasions would have been difficult if not impossible. The Marines brought this craft to the U.S. Armed Forces which was one of the most important pieces of technology used in WWII.

By 1942, General Smith had served throughout the world, from the Philippines, to Haiti and Cuba in the West Indies, and at home in Washington, D.C., Norfolk, Virginia, and at the Naval War College in Newport, Rhode Island. His background helped him develop the contacts he needed to get many of the boats and operations approved he needed to develop ship-to-shore techniques. And thus, during the crucial years from 1935 to Pearl Harbor, Smith led the Corps' development of amphibious warfare in *all its forms*, not just with the Higgins boats.

Colonel Smith was director of the Division of Operations and Training from 1937 to 1939, after which he was assistant commandant. In 1939, he commanded the 1st Marine Brigade, which became the 1st MarDiv in 1941. After hostilities commenced, now Major General Smith trained the army and the Marine Corps in amphibious warfare, taking command in August 1942 of the Pacific Fleet's department of the Amphibious Corps. Because of the Marines' innovative tactics of sea assaults and their knowledge of both the machinery and how to implement such combat, Smith made amphibious warfare the Corps' "main *raison d'être*."[1444]

Under Smith's leadership, the Corps understood its role as the principal force for the *entire U.S. military* responsible for amphibious warfare—the very justification for its existence. Through Smith and other Marine officers' efforts, they demonstrated to the navy amphibious landings were critical, greatly impacting America's way of conducting war. The Marine doctrine was adopted by the U.S. Army, which republished it in manuals, having never developed an amphibious warfare doctrine of its own. The Marines trained army officers as well, and they spread around the world conducting landings in Alaska, North Africa, Italy, France, and the Philippines. Commandant and General Alexander A. Vandegrift said after the war,

> Despite its outstanding record as a combat force in the past war, the Marine Corps' far greater contribution to victory was doctrinal: that is, the fact that the basic amphibious doctrines which carried Allied troops over every beachhead of World War II had been largely shaped—often in the face of uninterested or doubting military orthodoxy—by U.S. Marines.[1445]

The later Lieutenant General Victor H. Krulak, as a member of Smith's staff in the late 1930s and early 1940s, not only helped in the development of the Higgins Boats, but also with amtracs. These landing crafts, called "alligators," were floating tanks or armored treaded vehicles that could land on beaches and *drive* inland after being dropped into the sea via a ship offshore. These two "boats" carried the bulk of the burden for amphibious warfare. You could not have one without the other when conducting landings because amtracs protected Higgins boats, and Higgins boats brought the riflemen necessary to provide amtracs the support they needed once ground combat commenced (which, when hitting an enemy beach, happened almost immediately). Indeed, there were other versions of amtracs that also carried troops to the beach as well since they were superior to Higgins boats at driving over reefs and other obstacles. So, there were multi-uses and versions of amtracs that ensured a beach was hit quickly and secured by Marines before supplies and other troops were brought on by Higgins boats and LSTs (Landing Ship, Tank—382-foot vessels). After the war, Krulak commented on the Marines' main mission throughout the 1920s and 1930s, writing,

> Had the Marine Corps not so devoted itself [to amphibious warfare], there would have been no amphibious doctrine for the Army to follow when the threat of war appeared and the Army, when it evidenced its first sustained interest in the amphibious problem in 1940, would have found itself twenty years late.[1446]

Krulak was making the point that the U.S. Army would have been in a disastrous position in projecting its power against Hitler and Hirohito had it not been for the Marine Corps. It was men like Smith and members on his staff like 1st Lieutenant Victor H. Krulak, his chief of staff Colonel Graves B. Erskine and many others who perfected useable and strategically deadly procedures for large naval and land forces to attack from the sea.

Although Smith was this type of warfare's visionary, it was his chief of staff, Colonel Erskine, who developed much of the guts of how one should conduct it. Erskine explored the details of how Marines should be berthed on a ship before an assault, how amphibious tractors (amtracs) should be used ahead of Higgins boat landings, and how the men should deploy on the beach once leaving their crafts. He developed the procedures on how to ascertain when the beachhead was secured enough by the amtracs and Higgins-borne troops ashore in order to then bring to the beaches the LCIs (Landing Craft, Infantry—158-foot vessels) that could deploy 200 troops and their equipment and LSTs that could land tanks, jeeps, artillery batteries, and trucks from their bow-butterfly doors to provide a second wave of overwhelming power against the enemy. Erskine was Smith's "right-hand-man." As chief of staff, Erskine ran "the outfit" behind the scenes, allowing Smith to keep amphibious operations in Marine hands by looking "after the politics." If Smith was one of the fathers of amphibious warfare, then Erskine was his godfather to develop it.[1447]

Graves Blanchard Erskine (the "Big E" or "Blood and Guts")[1448] was born on 28 June 1897 in Columbia, Louisiana and, like Smith, also descended from strong Southern roots—his maternal grandfather had fought for the Confederacy. Before WWI, he served in the Louisiana State Guard as a sergeant while studying for his bachelor's, which he received from Louisiana State University in 1917. In that year, he entered the Marines and in 1918, he deployed to France and fought at Belleau Wood, Château-Thierry, and St. Mihiel, and he would receive the Silver Star and a Purple Heart for his heroics. After the war, he rose through the ranks. He spent time overseas in Haiti, Nicaragua, Japan, and China (American Legation in Beijing 1935–37). He received the Legion of Merit for his roles in planning the Saipan and Tinian assaults, which he received from Nimitz.[1449] This was one piece of evidence out of many as to Erskine's roles in helping Smith and others develop and then utilize amphibious warfare.

As Smith's chief of staff, Erskine had one of the most important jobs in the Corps. When Brigadier General Mike Edson took over Erskine's role as chief of staff of Amphibious Warfare Operations once Erskine took over the 3d MarDiv in late 1944 earmarked for Iwo, Edson wrote of this billet that it "was easily the fourth, and maybe the third, most important post in the entire Marine Corps and the success or failure of the Corps [resided in this position]."[1450] Erskine was largely responsible for developing the operational warfare for the new and more powerful Marine Corps that destroyed Japanese-held islands—his fingerprints were on most of the major island campaigns.

Amphibious warfare brought the death grip around Japan, accomplishing its "basic mission on the most vital front."[1451] There was no other way to take those islands without hitting the beach fast and unloading quickly, which the Higgins boat and a host of other craft like amtracs, LCIs, and LSTs allowed the Marines to do. In the end, as historians Philip A. Crowl and Jeter A. Isely concluded: "The most important contribution of the United States Marines to the history of modern warfare rests in their having perfected the doctrine and techniques of amphibious warfare to such a degree as to be able to cross and secure a very energetically defended beach."[1452] One could argue the only way anyone was going to destroy Hirohito's regime was to assault its islands, and the Marine Corps had developed such operations that would shock Japanese leaders with how effective they were in bringing the full force of American fighting men deep into the empire.

It is imperative to understand something important when one studies Hitler's genocide and Hirohito's Holocaust; namely, these men and their legions would have never stopped their mass murder had they not been militarily destroyed. Knowing what it took to defeat these regimes and the importance of amphibious warfare, one must never forget the language all nations understand is force. If America, and other freedom-loving countries, want to remain a force to be feared and one able to stop genocide and mass murder, we must always be able to reach such places by the sea, and thus, one part of preventing genocide and mass murder, besides having strong, standing armies, is to also be able to project power from the oceans. This is a lesson few Holocaust historians focus on, and thus, it has been highlighted here. When one studies the history of mass murder in WWII, one should be thanking men like Smith, Erskine, and Krulak, and organizations like the Marine Corps, for helping the world end Hitler's genocide and Hirohito's Holocaust years before they otherwise would have been had amphibious warfare not been developed.

CONCLUSION

"*Optime qui ultime ridet* (He laughs best who laughs last)."

—**Sign** at one of the Japanese Singapore POW camps' portals made by the Allied inmates to secretly ridicule their Japanese overseers[1453]

THE JAPANESE EMPIRE UNDER HIROHITO, spanning from 1927 to 1945, stands as one of the most abhorrent regimes to ever arise on the face of the earth. Only through the collective efforts of the Allied powers, with the United States leading the way using amphibious warfare and atomic bombs, was this repulsive nation brought to its knees. Studying the origins of its Fascist rule, one uncovers a dark web of complicity, where the monarchy, government, military, and religions of Japan all played their part in reinforcing totalitarianism, fanaticism, and the perpetration of mass murder.

As Japan embarked on its imperialistic endeavors, particularly its desire to conquer the entirety of China and enslave and butcher its people, it revealed a medieval, plebian approach to dealing with conquered territories. In the wake of their conquests, one sees a flotsam of economic ruin, widespread rape, and wholesale mass slaughter wherever the Japanese ruled. As the International Military Tribunal at Tokyo wrote in its final judgement in 1948:

> During a period of several months the Tribunal heard evidence from witnesses who testified in detail to atrocities committed in all theatres of war on a scale so vast, yet following so common a pattern, that only one conclusion is possible. The atrocities were either secretly ordered, or willfully permitted by the Japanese Government, or individual members thereof, and by the leaders of the armed forces.[1454]

Back in 1938, Bengali poet Rabindranath Tagore confronted writer Yonejiro Noguchi in Japan, astutely observing that Hirohito and his legions were building their "conception of an Asia" on a foundation of "a tower of skulls."[1455] Mass murder was Japan's *modus operandi*, and it was only through the resolute defeat of Hirohito and his legions by the Allied powers that this reign of terror came to an end.

The different ways the U.S. and Japan conducted war vividly demonstrated the clash of two fundamentally irreconcilable cultures. Japan adhered to a ruthless philosophy of "kill all, burn all, destroy all," exemplified by its unbridled aggression and inhumane actions during the war. In stark contrast, President Roosevelt, with the support of the British, Russians, and Chinese, rallied the Allies to sign the "Declaration of the United Nations" in 1942. This declaration "pledged the Allies to pursue total victory (no separate peace treaties)...in order 'to defend life, liberty, and religious freedom, and to preserve human rights and justice.'"[1456] The Allies were prepared to make great sacrifices to uphold this solemn pledge. Japan's unprovoked attacks and aggression incited the full fury of the Allies, who were united in their determination to defeat such tyranny. By 1945, Japan was drowning in a flood of enemies.

The intervention of the U.S. and its allies spared Asia from unimaginable suffering by not allowing Japan's oppressive rule to go unchallenged. The Allied Tribunal, the Asian Nuremburg Trials, noted Japanese leaders:

> ...engaged in a conspiracy to commit atrocities that led to the 'wholesale destruction of human life, not alone on the field of battle...but in homes, hospitals, and orphanages, in factories and fields; and the victims would be the young and the old, the well and the infirm—men, women and children alike.'[1457]

The Allies' insistence on unconditional surrender was crucial in liberating oppressed peoples and protecting those under threat. This commitment came at a cost, as the Pacific War evolved into "one of the most brutal ever fought, on both sides."[1458]

Upon examining this Japanese history, one cannot help but notice Hirohito held a unique position of authority and influence over his troops. As a revered living god, he possessed the power to not only halt the war but also prevent it from occurring in the first place. Prime Minister and General Tōjō confirmed at his trial "that Hirohito had been responsible for the war, because he could have stopped it if he wished."[1459] Given the unwavering obedience of Hirohito's subjects, it stands to reason that if he had commanded his troops to cease their brutal actions of raping and killing those they ruled over, they would have complied, just as they did when he commanded them to lay down arms. Similarly, he could have directed his citizens and military leaders not to resort to suicide and instead surrender when faced with defeat. Hirohito's authority was so profound that his word held significant sway over the actions of the Japanese people. Thus, he possessed the capability to prevent the worst atrocities committed during the war and could have steered the nation towards a different path. The fact that he did not exercise this power has led to significant controversy and debate over his role in Japan's war crimes and the tragic events that unfolded under his rule.

With these facts in mind, Hirohito should have been brought up on war crimes after the war and hung as a common war criminal. MacArthur should not have spared him. How could he have done so and prevented widespread revolt? This is the main argument used to justify sparing him. I think it could have been done easily. In a public presentation, General of the Army MacArthur could have invoked traditional Japanese customs and asked the emperor to do to himself what he required of all his men to do when they suffered defeat in battle; namely, he should commit *seppuku* or *jiketsu* to atone for Japan's defeat, as all honorable Japanese warriors were required to do. MacArthur could have placed a sword on a table in front of Hirohito and called into question his leadership, manhood, and honor. With my understanding of Japanese culture, I think Hirohito, although a coward in many respects, would have felt the pressure so much he would have killed himself. That would have rid the world of one of the most despicable dictators ever to be seen, and he would have done so according to Japanese traditions. And of course, MacArthur could have simply put Hirohito on trial and not made an exception for him and told the Japanese to deal with it. If Hitler had survived, you better believe the world would have demanded he stand trial and be executed. Although MacArthur's decision to keep Hirohito on "his throne" can be understood, in retrospect, it was wrong from a moral and ethical point of view. Historian Yuma Totani wrote, "The failure to address the culpability of the Japanese head of state [for World War II crimes] continues to cast a dark shadow over the Tokyo Trial and its legacy."[1460] Ultimately, it is crucial to understand that this was a complex historical moment with no easy answers. Different perspectives exist on how Hirohito's role should have been addressed, and the implications of those decisions continue to be debated in the realm of historical analysis and moral judgments.

Aside from discussing Hirohito's ability to stop Japan's massacres and the arguments for his execution as a war criminal, it is crucial to recognize that Hirohito was one of the major players, if not *the central actor*, in Japan's Holocaust. He not only knew about Japanese atrocities and did nothing, but he also actively allowed them to happen, encouraging his leaders to continue their despicable behavior in the lands they conquered by rewarding them with rescripts, medals, and promotions. A significant example of his involvement can be found in the approval he gave on 5 August 1937 for his generals and admirals to ignore international law while invading China. He personally sanctioned a directive that read, in part, as follows:

> In the present situation, in order to wage total war in China, the empire will neither apply, nor act in accordance with, all the concrete articles of the Treaty Concerning the Laws and Customs of Land Warfare and Other Treaties Concerning the Laws and Regulations of Belligerency.[1461]

In other words, Hirohito told his men not to adhere to the Hague Convention (1907), Kellogg-Briand Pact (1928), and the Geneva Convention (1929). With this edict, he gave permission to all Japanese to behave recklessly and criminally, giving this *carte blanche* to his soldiers and sailors to behave the way they did, with evil and malicious intent. Telling his men they had license to behave as they saw fit without any legal or ethical consequences presents us with strong evidence Hirohito knew what he needed to do in order to encourage his men to rape and murder wherever they marched without questioning whether or not they were acting immorally or not. Historian Herbert P. Bix rightly noted, "At the end of the war as at its beginning, and through every stage of its unfolding, Emperor Hirohito played a highly active role in supporting the actions carried out in his name."[1462]

Japan's reprehensible actions during the period from 1927 to 1945 were not limited to a few instances but spread throughout numerous cities and islands—basically, everywhere Japan deployed their Imperial military personnel. If an exhaustive documentation were to be made of all the places Japan destroyed and criminally ruled over during that time, it would fill volumes. The scope of their atrocities was vast, and their conduct extended far and wide. When one knows that 5.2 million Japanese troops were still stationed in China when the war ended in 1945, and that most IJA soldiers and sailors were apt to commit crimes when they could, there remains much to be uncovered and documented about their sordid deeds.[1463]

When the Japanese had an opportunity to act morally, they rarely did whether in China, Manchuria, Malaya, Singapore, the Philippines, Guam, Wake Island, Burma, Indonesia, or on the High Seas. In all these regions, they exported chaos, death, crime, rape, and disorder. This conduct persisted regardless of the people they ruled or the circumstance they faced, whether in victory, occupation, or defeat. Ironically, generals like General Matsui, General Yamashita, Lieutenant General Sakai, Lieutenant General Kuribayashi, and Lieutenant General Sakurai did issue orders not to rape, murder, and pillage, but these orders were *never followed, ever* by most of the soldiers so ordered. Conversely, when commanders turned a blind eye to illegal orders by subordinates, gave tacit approval for bad behavior, or even gave explicit orders to commit crimes, *they were always followed* and often done so with enthusiasm. This study has documented only one rare case where a flag officer did something moral during combat. In a rare case of justice, Lieutenant General Yamashita brought some of his lower-level soldiers to trial for crimes against people in Malaya, found them guilty, and executed them.[1464] However, he let his operations officer, Lieutenant Colonel Tsuji, and two of his subordinate commanders, Lieutenant General Nishimura and Major General Kawamura, collect Chinese civilians and Allied POWs during the Malaya and Singapore campaigns and slaughter them by the thousands. Yamashita did nothing to prosecute these criminals. Additionally, he never once tried to punish Rear Admiral Iwabuchi for his crimes in Manila or stop him from destroying the Filipinos under his control. So, Yamashita's minor moral act to punish a few low-ranking subordinates in Malaya was a drop in the bucket of what he should, and could, have done. There does seem to be another case like this one when a few rapists were arrested after the fall of Hong Kong by Lieutenant General Sakai and Lieutenant General Kuribayashi. However, the outcomes of these arrests remain unknown. Unlike Yamashita's case, it appears that these men were not executed, but only punished to some extent.[1465]

In the midst of the darkness that shrouded Japan's actions during WWII, there were a few more glimmers of humanity that emerged from the shadows besides the ones just mentioned. One such incident happened when a POW prison guard became so disgusted by how his command treated prisoners that he took decisive action. In an act of extreme courage and remorse, he attacked his superiors and shot them, killing one and wounding three others, including Captain Takuo Takakuwa, who ordered the death march from Sandakan to Ranua in Indonesia mentioned earlier. It is worth noting that this guard had previously committed horrible crimes, and he was disgusted with himself and his command. After his attack, he turned his rifle on himself and blew out his brains.[1466]

Another case where a Japanese acted nobly happened when IJN Captain Shunsaku Kudō, commander of the destroyer *Ikazuchi*, defied the prevailing brutality by rescuing 442 British and American sailors instead of killing them in 1942.[1467] Similarly, and in the last case of morality, there was a Japanese soldier who refused to slaughter an injured American. Instead, upon discovering that the wounded man was a fellow Boy Scout, he saw a bond of brotherhood that transcended national borders, claiming: "I understand you are a brother Scout. I was a Japanese Boy Scout. We are brothers. I cannot kill my Scout brother."[1468]

Regrettably, these instances were the exception rather than the norm. The overwhelming reality remains that, besides these minor cases, this study has found that *no major leader or group rebelled against* his or their command to stop military personnel from raping and killing innocent civilians and POWs. The Rapes of Nanking, Hong Kong, Singapore, Guam, the Philippines, and Manila stand as harrowing examples of the utter lack of intervention by those in positions of power. When the world needed moral men to protect the innocent and vulnerable, especially young women and defenseless POWs, *no one in responsible positions in the Japanese military ever lifted a finger to help anyone.*

Contrasting with Germany, where some individuals attempted to rebel against Hitler and the Nazis, Japan lacked equivalent figures willing to challenge the pervasive evil that had engulfed their nation. The absence of leaders like Colonel Claus von Stauffenberg, General Ludwig Beck, and Pastor Martin Niemöller who all tried to kill Hitler and remove the Nazis from power, or Lieutenant General Dietrich von Choltitz, who defied Hitler's order to destroy Paris and kill innocent civilians, underscored Japan's surrender to a culture tainted by malevolence. Japan had embraced evil, and the men who perpetrated this evil often did so while laughing at the expense of others who were suffering and dying in their midst. Their deeply ingrained *Schadenfreude* took on a sadistic, macabre tenor that infected the whole military community, a telltale sign of an atrocious and inhuman nature that had taken root in Japanese society.

Throughout the Asian and Pacific Wars, a troubling pattern emerges within the Japanese military. Men seemed to reserve their loyalty solely for commanders who condoned horrendous acts of murder, rape, and destruction. In cases where moral orders were issued, even if genuinely intended, the widespread crimes committed by all ranks "showed that the services were completely unable to control their own officers and men" and prevent them from disobeying lawful and ethical orders.[1469] The lack of restraint and the prevailing culture of violence and brutality within the military further exacerbate this grim reality.

When exploring the barbaric behavior displayed by the Japanese during Japan's Holocaust, countless cases studied reveal that while victims pleaded for their lives and cried out in pain during beatings, bayonetting, raping, and killing, that instead of eliciting revolt in the average soldier, such scenes often *just prompted laughter*. It is both puzzling and deeply disturbing to witness people laughing in the midst of such unspeakable atrocities of murder, rape, and debasement. However, understanding the psychology behind this laughter provides some insight. Laughter, in many cases, serves as an overt social signal to connect with others. In the context of these atrocious acts, soldiers' laughter indicated alignment with their comrades, a chilling demonstration that their barbaric actions were considered socially acceptable within their group. This twisted form of camaraderie, reinforced by laughter, perpetuated and normalized this despicable behavior so witnessed. Research indicates that "when we genuinely laugh, we signal that we are comfortable and feel like we belong."[1470] In the context of Japan's Holocaust, this disturbing laughter served as a mechanism for soldiers and sailors to feel at ease with their actions, signaling a disturbing level of cooperation in carrying out these atrocities. Throughout this book, one has read how the Japanese soldiers and sailors continually laughed at what they were doing, proving they were *comfortable* with their behavior since laughter, at its core, "signals cooperation."[1471]

When pondering the unsettling question "What did the average Japanese soldier think when he shot an elderly woman or when he raped a young girl, and thereafter, cut off her head?", the chilling answer emerges, "He laughed and was enjoying himself when he did so." The atrocious behavior displayed by Japanese military personnel provides undeniable evidence of how critical it is for a society to raise its children with good historical studies and ethical teachings, instilling empathy and compassion into the very fabric of the community. By 1941, Japan had set loose a deplorable generation of young men onto the world. In juxtaposition, America had deployed a generation of boys who did not enjoy raping and slaughtering and had a legal code both civilian- and military-wise, that prevented such behaviors. This stark difference stands as a testament to how far America had come in its pursuit of justice, morals, and democracy. The actions of American soldiers, who were often moved to tears upon liberating Nazi concentration camps or Japanese POW camps, and their humane treatment of prisoners and civilians in occupied territories, exemplify the moral fabric instilled in American society. Conversely, Japan's legal system and military culture actively supported violent crimes as being its *modus operandi* during deployments, revealing a dangerous nation deserving of opposition and defeat. Moreover, the fact that most modern Japanese citizens remain unaware of the Rape of Nanking exhibits a concerning trend in societies like Japan that refuse to acknowledge their dark history. This refusal to embrace past crimes hinders efforts to prevent their repetition, an issue that demands serious attention and change. That, to be sure, is no laughing matter.

The exploration of sexual crimes in this book inevitably raises the question: Why did the Japanese engage in such widespread and systematic rape during WWII? Psychologists offer one explanation for this behavior, rooted in Japan's historical and cultural views of women. For generations, Japanese society considered women as inferior, a perspective not entirely unique to their culture. During Hirohito's reign, societal norms dictated that women's primary role was to raise children, often employing corporal discipline in doing so. This upbringing instilled in boys the perception of women as weak, stupid, and emotional, leading to subconscious resentment towards the very half of society responsible for raising them. Ironically, Japan subjugated the very segment of its population responsible for nurturing the next generation. In Japanese culture, women were often regarded as inferior, even sub-human beings, with "their thoughts and feelings totally disregarded, their rights not even conceived of." Rapists' childhoods are "typified by neglect alternating with harsh punishment and deprivation" which most Japanese children experienced.[1472] Also, rapists are "likely to have been raised by a…single…parent," all of which many Japanese experienced because absentee fathers were common.[1473] Japanese were raised in a culture marked by despair, force, and violence, leading to the belief that physical aggression was acceptable and necessary.[1474] Throughout WWII, Japanese servicemen demonstrated "an aggression toward women syndrome."[1475] This deeply ingrained aggression, combined with the stress of facing certain death on the battlefield, partly explains their persistent predilection for rape. Moreover, as they conquered foreign lands, they raped many women they encountered, viewing them "as adversaries to be attacked and subdued," further fueling their violent actions.[1476] Combining these views about women with their reactions of knowing they often were facing certain death also explains, in part, "their persistent predilection for rape,"[1477] yet, while this explanation accounts for their behavior during wartime, it does not fully address their actions during garrison and occupational duties, where the imminent threat of death was not present, yet they continued to "rape and loot at will."[1478] This suggests that factors beyond wartime stress played a role in the perpetuation of this abhorrent behavior. An example illustrating the extent of this problem can be found in a small pamphlet issued by Colonel Naoichi Kawara, Adjutant of the Army Ministry, from September 1940. In it, Kawara explained that most of the raping and murdering done by Japanese troops was done by those mostly "on guard duty and rear-area duty."[1479] This finding suggests that the fear of facing death on the battlefield was only one of the many excuses a Japanese soldier could use to justify raping a foreign woman. The existence of other underlying factors indicates a deep-rooted issue within the military culture that allowed such atrocities to occur.

In *every region* Japan conquered, it spawned a nation of men who took their psychotic drive to conquer to a whole different level of diabolical, particularly when exploring their sexual crimes. They were what psychologists Robert Prentky and Ann Burgess called *enraged* and *sadistic* rapists who "hate their victims" and want to "humiliate and dominate women."[1480] They often made "unusual and painful sexual demands and many seem to be acting out a bizarre fantasy." Frequently they "fatally injure their victims"; the Japanese did this by the millions.[1481] Disturbingly, many officers even believed that rape could enhance their soldiers' "fighting spirit" and thus encouraged and permitted such behavior. Lieutenant General Kuribayashi, for example, apparently condoned rape while serving as second in command of the 32nd Imperial Japanese Army.[1482] Historians Meirion and Susie Harries wrote, quoting a liberal Japanese professor from 1934, "While a Japanese woman or child is practically helpless before the power of a male, it can be imagined that in the case of millions who are not of the race, the result is even more terrible. The young Korean girls and those of Formosa [and Hong Kong and China] are absolutely beyond help."[1483] That it was not universally held in Japan during the Asian and Pacific Wars that it was wrong to rape is deeply troubling and reflects a society that was barbaric and unethical.[1484] To support this analysis, head of the Hong Kong Sanatorium and Hospital during the Rape of Hong Kong, Dr. Shu-Fan Li, had this further analysis about this phenomenon: "Anyone who witnessed the tidal wave of Japanese sex crimes...in any...city they captured could be excused for thinking that the Japanese were by nature a race of sexual criminals...I had a strong suspicion that the Japanese government and...military...condoned rape with the tacit understanding that it was one of the rewards if not the right of the conqueror."[1485]

The atrocities committed by Japanese military personnel during their rule raise another troubling question about their excessive and sadistic behavior towards their victims' bodies. Throughout their areas of operation, Japanese servicemen demonstrated a disturbing penchant for desecrating the bodies of their victims. Whether it was sticking twigs into raped and dead women's vaginas, or cutting out tongues, slicing off ears, beheading defenseless POWs, hacking off women's breasts, stuffing the severed testicles and penises of alive and dead prisoners into their own mouths, or butchering bodies for torture and then food, the Japanese never tired of defiling the bodies of their enemies seen in *all their areas of operations*. Murderers who take pleasure in dismembering bodies exhibit "other deviant behavior and a tendency towards excessive cruelty."[1486] These types of killers, which Japan was full of at that time, lacked "empathy and [the] inability to properly experience emotions," evidencing that these offenders' self-image was "disturbed and negative."[1487] Such behavior is usually extremely rare in society, with only around 2% of murderers engaging in dismemberment. However, among the Imperial Japanese military, it was disturbingly prevalent, approaching 100% of the murdering population. Psychologists call this type of death "offensive mutilation" where the real purpose of the slaughter "include[s] lust and necro-sadistic" tendencies.[1488] Another category of this type of killing is called "aggressive mutilation," brought on by strong emotions. In the case of Japanese soldiers, it probably stemmed from being in combat, from having been indoctrinated to hate their enemies and viewing them as non-human, and from wanting to show their manliness (according to their version of *Bushido-samurai*-toughness).[1489] These notions of "being a tough Japanese guy" may also define many of these Imperial "warriors" as "psychotic murderers" where they had "lost touch with reasoning and perceptual reality in the conventional sense, so that they may be hearing voices or they suffer from bizarre delusions."[1490] Another form of dismemberment is used by a group, often seen today with the Mafia, as a way of creating a "warning or threat."[1491] The Japanese wanted to also communicate to those who would resist them that such fates awaited them as seen with those they dismembered. The tendency of the Japanese to not only kill innocent people, but also to take pleasure with treating their bodies as toys to be cut up, violated, displayed as trophies, and mocked, bespeaks of a collective criminality that Japanese society produced which, in the end, became common, *normal* behavior for Japanese men. Japan produced not only killing machines with their servicemen, but also, they produced sadistic, joyful, inventive, and demonic murdering automatons.

The inability of officers, who were Japan's educated elite, to recognize the wrongness of the atrocities they witnessed and committed speaks to a lack of moral discernment and self-reflection. This fundamental human principle, as articulated by the Jewish sage Hillel, stated, "What is hateful to you, do not do to others,"[1492] seems to have been disregarded by most Japanese men who engaged in rape and murder "without feeling guilt or remorse."[1493] This behavior was further supported and enabled by their officers, creating a deeply disturbing culture of violence. In a rare instance of an officer critically analyzing the acts of his fellow comrades, Colonel Kazuo Horiba claimed:

> Most of the officers in responsible positions were incapable of an objective assessment of their own actions…individuals prone to vacillation, evading responsibility, and a lack of perspective tended to end up in the important posts [and] decided government policy, but not accept ultimate responsibility is a crime, to ignore previous mistakes and repeat errors of national policy is a crime [sic].[1494]

As the philosopher Socrates emphasized, self-awareness is crucial for cultivating enduring and respectful relationships with others.[1495] The Japanese, unfortunately, demonstrated a lack of self-awareness, failing to recognize that we are part of one race, the human race, and are part of one humanity. To violate others violates oneself, and as they practiced atrocities, they dehumanized themselves and disgraced their culture. Their crimes against humanity displayed a dangerous disregard for the progress of humankind, making them a menace to the world. As historian Saburō Ienaga wrote, the mistreatment of the people under the rule of Japan during its Holocaust has "eternally blemished Japan's record as a civilized nation."[1496]

It should not be surprising that the oppressed citizens and victims of Hirohito's tyrannical policies sought revenge on the Japanese in their respectful regions at the end of the war. There were countless cases of the common man who had suffered under the Japanese oppression, who, when he could, took the opportunity at the war's end to kill IJA and IJN servicemen and *Nipponese* citizens. Armed with pitchforks, clubs, and their bare fists, these people sought justice when the tables turned on their former oppressors. Whether they were Chinese peasants in Manchuria, Borneo tribesmen in Indonesia, observant Catholic Filipino teenagers in the Philippines, or peaceful, loving, and kind Chamorros on Guam, they felt great satisfaction in exacting retribution against the *Nipponese*.[1497] Having personally met hundreds of individuals from these regions, I can attest that the fact Japan could incite such revengeful and murderous responses from otherwise gentle Chamorros is saying something about who the Japanese were—Chamorros are some of the nicest, kindest, and most peaceful people I have ever met. That they rose up the way they did when the war ended to kill *all Japanese they could get their hands on* is a dramatic condemnation of Japanese behavior. The hatred for Japan and its culture still persists today. During my trip to China in 2019, countless Chinese expressed their wish that the United States had bombed Japan with more atomic bombs and despise the Japanese today, teaching this hatred to their children and children's children, especially since Japan refuses to acknowledge what it did to China. Ironically, something that would literally take little of a nation to do like with admitting its crimes fully, paying appropriate levels of reparations, and building a few honest museums in its capital is something Japan refuses to do. When one explores how much treasure, gold, effort, and time Japan spent in raping Asia compared to how little they have put into trying to atone for those sins committed there shows what Japan enjoys putting their time and energy into. In comparison, Germany has put the proper time and energy into their atonement for the Third Reich, and it is the superior nation because of it. Japan's failure to follow suit raises questions about its priorities and values. The path to reconciliation and redemption remains open to Japan, but until it takes concrete steps towards acknowledging and atoning for its past, its reputation will continue to be marred by the ghosts of its history.

While exploring the tragic events of Japan's Holocaust, this study closely explored the life of one of the most renowned Japanese generals from the Asian and Pacific Wars, General Tadamichi Kuribayashi. Clint Eastwood's films about Kuribayashi brought him fame, but they unfortunately only highlighted the positive aspects of his personality, portraying him as a "diplomate" in the United States before the war and a military leader in 1945. However, a closer examination of Kuribayashi's biography is necessary to understand his actions more clearly, especially considering his role as chief of staff of the 23rd Army and his garrison activities in Hong Kong and the surrounding region thereafter. Moreover, a thorough exploration of his entire command history on Iwo Jima, analyzing all facets of his leadership, is necessary to understand the complexities and contradictions of his character fully. In reviewing Kuribayashi's career, a former Marine Corps Lieutenant Colonel, Japanese-language expert and relative by marriage to the general's family, has praised the general, arguing that during his time as a commanding officer, he did not engage in any atrocities.[1498] According to this "expert," Kuribayashi really did not have any power while in second-of-command at Hong Kong to change his troops' horrible behavior (an assertion hard to believe, but nonetheless claimed by this expert), but while in command of the Iwo garrison, he behaved more morally since he was in full control.[1499] However, it cannot be emphasized enough that as chief of staff of the 23rd Army under Lieutenant General Sakai, Kuribayashi was guilty of crimes against humanity and would have most likely been charged with it by the International Military Tribunal had he survived the battle at Iwo Jima.

To explore one fact of Kuribayashi's criminal behavior while in control of Iwo Jima, it is crucial to note that every time a Marine was taken prisoner by the Japanese on the island, historical documentation confirms that he was subjected to torture and executed.[1500] These disturbing acts blatantly violated the Hague Convention, which Japan signed, making Kuribayashi and his troops guilty of war crimes. Despite the clear violation of international law, no documentation has been found to suggest that Kuribayashi issued orders to prevent this type of behavior. Yet, this should not be surprising, since he commanded and witnessed this during the battle for Hong Kong. He knew his men on Iwo Jima would do the same thing if not ordered to do otherwise while stationed on Iwo. The killing of prisoners was a flagrant violation of international law, and regrettably, Kuribayashi's troops never hesitated to mercilessly slaughter defenseless prisoners during both conflicts. This deplorable behavior not only underscores the horrific actions of the soldiers but also sheds light on Kuribayashi's command style and the expectations he set for his troops. His failure to prevent and condemn such atrocities reflects a disturbing lack of regard for human rights and the rule of law within the ranks.

During his tenure as chief of staff of the 23rd Army and later as the commander at Iwo Jima, Kuribayashi made used of approximately 1,600 Korean slave laborers, a clear violation of international law.[1501] The British *Manual of Military Law* defines such actions as war crimes, stating "acts which both violate the unchallenged rules of warfare and outrage the general sentiments of humanity" make one culpable.[1502] Forcing individuals from a country that has suffered under Japanese occupation to perform slave labor against their will undoubtedly contravened the accepted "rules of warfare" and generated "outrage from humanity." These were undeniably war crimes committed by Kuribayashi during his time on Iwo Jima. The Korean laborers had rights under international law, and Kuribayashi's coercion of their involvement in military duties and their subsequent deaths in service of a country to which they owed no loyalty violated his duty to "abide by the laws and customs of war governing… conduct towards the inhabitants [of an occupation—in this case, Korea]."[1503]

Claims that Kuribayashi behaved differently as a commander at Iwo Jima, compared to other leaders who allowed their troops to commit atrocities, need careful analysis in light of universally accepted rules and laws of warfare during that time besides what has already been discussed. During the post-World War II war trials, many Japanese commanders attempted to justify their criminal acts by claiming they were simply following superior orders. However, this defense does not hold if the individual knew the order to be a "contravention of the law, in this case International Law." If this is the case, he cannot hide behind the claim that he "was just following orders."[1504] In the case of Kuribayashi, his actions in fulfilling Lieutenant General Sakai's orders or his complacency towards the rape and destruction of Hong Kong could not be justified as "enacting superior orders." Raping and killing "defenseless people" were clear breaches of the law, and these crimes were perpetrated on a massive scale during the Rape of Hong Kong.[1505] Even if there were no explicit written orders to commit these crimes, once they began, Kuribayashi was duty-bound to intervene and stop them—something *he never did*. Given these facts, it becomes difficult to praise Kuribayashi for not conducting similar acts against civilians on Iwo Jima as there was no foreign civilian population to dominate on the island. Iwo Jima was a Japanese territory, and therefore, Kuribayashi was not faced with the same dilemmas of dealing with foreign populations. It is reasonable to assume that he probably would have allowed his troops to do what his troops did in Hong Kong, or General Yamashita's troops did in Malaya, Singapore, and Manila, or General Matsui's troops did in Nanking, had there been a foreign citizenry there. Luckily for humanity, there was not such a population on the island.

When considering superior orders, it's important to note that Prime Minister and General Tōjō instructed Kuribayashi to conduct the battle similarly to how his counterparts had conducted the Attu battle in 1943, advocating to go down in a blaze of glory in a massive *Banzai*. This order clearly violates "the unchallenged rules of warfare" and outrages "the general sentiments of humanity."[1506] Sacrificing troops in battle where there was no hope of survival or success cannot be seen as a moral act. Even if one could possibly have argued back then that the defense of Iwo Jima could potentially have made the U.S. sue for peace, Kuribayashi's leadership did not justify the needless sacrifice of his men in a futile attempt to halt America's juggernaut heading for Japan. Kuribayashi followed Tōjō's mandate in an effective way, but one that sacrificed his men needlessly. It was a waste of men and time. As historian Saburō Ienaga wrote of such plans Kuribayashi was enacting on Iwo: "It was a defense strategy worthy of little boys playing *Samurai*."[1507]

Kuribayashi undoubtedly demonstrated brilliance in evolving Japanese tactics and disobeying superior orders that he deemed obstructive while preparing the defenses of Iwo Jima. Departing from traditional strategies like beach defense and massive *Banzai* attacks, he displayed innovative thinking. However, his ingenuity was disappointing in not using those "thinking out of the box" skills he had for moral purposes, such as protecting Hong Kong civilians in 1941 or preserving the lives and dignity of his men, including the few prostitutes and/or "sex slaves" on Iwo Jima in 1945. In this respect, his violation of orders only helped him to inflict more death on the enemy and his own men, never to make this world a better and more moral place. In contrast to courageous German figures like Colonel Claus von Stauffenberg or General Ludwig Beck, who recognized Hitler's evil and tried to kill him in July 1944, Kuribayashi did not show the same moral conviction to challenge his immoral leaders. While we know a brave officer, Major Tomoshige Tsunoda, tried to assassinate Tōjō in 1944, but failed,[1508] Kuribayashi did not make such attempts when he had an opportunity to do so. It would have been a more honorable and visionary act if he had tried to eliminate Hirohito or Tōjō during his meetings with them in 1944 rather than obeying their orders, orders he had seen for years to be immoral. In this respect, his command on Iwo Jima was anything but honorable. From a military perspective, Kuribayashi's command on Iwo Jima was indeed a remarkable martial feat, exemplified by his dedication to defend the island until the last man. Nevertheless, from a sociological perspective, it was a moral disgrace. Ultimately, his legacy remains tainted by his inability to use his ingenuity for the greater good and create a more moral world.

And there were indeed other actions Kuribayashi could have taken besides assassinating his leaders that could have sent a strong message to Tokyo that it was on the wrong path. For example, Kuribayashi could have taken a radical departure from the norm by surrendering his entire garrison before the battle for Iwo Jima ever began. Such a decision would have had profound implications; it would have saved thousands of lives and sent a strong message to Emperor Hirohito and Japan about the immorality and futility of the war. Despite the prevailing propaganda that led the rank and file to believe that surrendering to the Americans would result in violation and torture, Kuribayashi knew from his personal experiences in America, studying at its universities (Harvard University, for God's sake), and training with its soldiers, that the opposite was true. He had firsthand knowledge that United States soldiers and Marines would treat his men in accordance with the Geneva Convention and American values. As the 32nd Army's operations officer on Okinawa, Colonel Hiromichi Yahara, who, like Kuribayashi, had spent years in the U.S., wrote:

> The refugees [on Okinawa] were in mortal terror of being raped and murdered if they fell into enemy hands. From my two years of experience in the United States, I knew that Americans were not at all brutal. The refugees would be safe in American hands...*I knew we would not be mistreated* [author's italics].[1509]

Yahara would indeed witness how kind and friendly the Americans were to his surrendered troops and citizens.[1510] Hirohito would just five months later after the defeat at Iwo Jima come to the same conclusion that he could, and must, surrender his nation to the Americans, who he knew would treat his nation according to international law; hence, why he did not surrender to the Russians. Had Kuribayashi chosen the path of surrender, he could have beaten Hirohito to the punch in realizing the necessity of surrendering to the Americans. However, he did not, and thus, he consigned his men to a cruel and useless battle where their deaths had little effect on the overall outcome of the war and deprived them of years of life. Had Kuribayashi made this courageous decision, he would have been held as a true hero of the war, rather than remembered as a brutal military commander solely focused on killing Americans. In many respects, former Naval Intelligence officer and Japanese expert, Frank B. Gibney, could have been discussing Kuribayashi when he wrote about Japanese flag officers: "No modern army was crueler than the Japanese, but in no high command did *the capacity for self-delusion flourish so abundantly* [author's italics]."[1511] In the end, had Kuribayashi broken away from this self-delusion and prioritized human lives over futile battle operations, he would be dramatically more famous than he is now for such a remarkable act of heroism and moral clarity instead of battlefield feats.

There is some evidence to suggest that Kuribayashi had planned to surrender himself and his remaining men at the battle's end, but he was allegedly murdered by a subordinate for even considering such a move.[1512] In contrast to Yamashita, who did not sacrifice all his soldiers in battle before contemplating surrender, Kuribayashi did seem to consign his men to a losing struggle before he did so. It was only when he realized that further resistance was futile that he appeared to consider surrendering himself and his garrison, which likely numbered only a few thousand. While this may have been a better move than what other commanders had displayed on different islands, some may argue that it was too little too late to save most of his men if indeed he had such thoughts. Perhaps one reason he did not surrender early in the campaign was the fear of what eventually did happen to him when he finally decided to do so, according to this report—he knew that surrendering might be his death sentence, as it could have turned his entire staff against him.

Many claim Kuribayashi was moral to remove the bulk of the 1,150 civilians from Iwo before the battle started, something the Saipan and Tinian commanders did not do (he only kept 30 military-age men).[1513] However, it seems he did not evacuate all the female civilians. Countless U.S. Marine and sailor witnesses found women on the island during the battle, and firmly believed these women were there for the sexual pleasure of the officers. It was likely that Kuribayashi and others kept their favorite prostitutes or "Comfort Women" with them and denied them safe passage to Japan.[1514] Unfortunately, it was not uncommon for Japanese officers to keep such women within the front lines, subjecting them to combat conditions where they often died alongside the troops who were also abusing them.[1515]

According to Marine veteran Don Graves from the 5th MarDiv, as they neared the island's northern end, he discovered women among the dead Japanese.[1516] This account has been corroborated by at least six other Iwo veterans who also found women on Iwo.[1517] In one of the earliest histories of the battle, written in 1945 by Marine correspondents and Iwo veterans, two women were found in the wreckage of Motoyama after artillery and ship "guns had smashed it."[1518] George Bernstein of the 4th MarDiv witnessed women jumping off cliffs on the northern shore.[1519] One Japanese officer said many officers kept their Korean mistresses or "Comfort Women" on the island.[1520] In fact, some of the women may have been like the "Comfort Women" and prostitutes on Okinawa who willingly chose to stay with the officers who kept them like pets (possibly a result of Stockholm syndrome).[1521] Some of the nurses, "Comfort Women," and geishas on Okinawa declared when the 32nd Army operations officer, Colonel Yahara, ordered them to leave headquarters: "You order us out because you think of us only as women. We are no longer just women. We are soldiers, and we wish to die with you."[1522] Considering that Graves found many women dressed in Japanese uniforms on Iwo, it is possible that they, too, expressed their desire to stay and fight alongside Kuribayashi and his staff even in the face of death. Kuribayashi could not have been unaware many women were on the island and probably had his own concubine with him. Keeping them on the island, knowing that they would die in battle, was a clear violation of international law. While the abuse of women was not as widespread under Kuribayashi's command on Iwo as it had been under his command in Hong Kong, it still showed his insensitivity to the welfare of women and their security. Kuribayashi was probably no different from other officers when he moved his command to Iwo Jima, importing his "sex toys" there as well as military supplies.[1523] These women were kept on the island for selfish reasons, and their deaths serve as further evidence of Kuribayashi's crimes against humanity. All women found on Iwo, as documented by witnesses, were either dead or in in the act of killing themselves. As historian Saburō Ienaga wrote, "'Comfort girls' [in the front lines who were] wounded in the fighting were apparently sometimes abandoned or shot to prevent capture."[1524]

This study shows Japanese men, the bulk of whom had wives back in Japan, were not the only sexually immoral ones in their nation. Yes, they had Japanese mistresses, visited prostitutes, and raped countless "Comfort Women" and Asian civilians throughout their garrison and combat operations. But apparently, their wives back in Japan enjoyed committing adultery just as much as them since a governmental Police Bureau report documented *widespread* adultery by wives of soldiers away at the front."[1525] Monogamy and loyalty within marriage was not something Japanese men or women seemed to honor although they then, as now, give it much lip service. So, condemning the millions of men for the immoral act of adultery while on campaigns without knowing that many, if not most, of their wives were doing the same is to fail to acknowledge Japanese society did not lay much worth on loyalty within marriage during its past. However, at least their wives were not raping and slaughtering the people they were having affairs with (these adulterers were Japanese citizens after all), so in the scale of morality, their cheating wives were living more morally upright lives.

Kuribayashi, like many other Japanese leaders, perpetuated the dark tradition of committing war crimes. His men murdered POWs, utilized slave labor from Korea, obeyed orders that ensured their own destruction, sexually violated women, and murdered innocent civilians. While his command on Iwo Jima displayed unique tactics and operations, it was not unique in terms of its barbarity and disregard for the law. Kuribayashi was undoubtedly a brave and tactically intelligent general while on Iwo Jima, but his actions also reveal an evil, corrupt, and disgraceful side of his character. While Kuribayashi displayed tactical brilliance, he seemed to lack the strategic vision necessary to anticipate the broader implications of the battle on the American forces at that time. His focus seemed to only be on immediate military objectives rather than considering the broader strategic consequences and repercussions of his actions on American leadership. In other words, his efforts achieved the exact opposite of what he hoped. Instead of weakening the resolve of the United States, the bloody battle for Iwo Jima further convinced America to pursue unconditional surrender and intensify its efforts to destroy Imperial Japan.

Kuribayashi was the example of Japan's educated *crème de la crème* and was symbolic of many leaders explored throughout this book like Emperor Hirohito, Prime Minister and General Tōjō, General Matsui, General Yamashita, General Doihara, Lieutenant General Sakai, Lieutenant General Ishii, Lieutenant General Homma, Rear Admiral Iwabuchi, and Lieutenant Colonel Tsuji. These sophisticated men were well-traveled and well-educated, and had diverse backgrounds as medical doctors, Buddhist scholars, Harvard alumni, poets, writers, college graduates, and multilingual individuals. They had befriended countless people in England and America long before they started to demonize these nations and murder their citizens. Their actions raise the disheartening question: If such sophisticated men can conduct such diabolical acts documented in this book, what hope is there for the general mass of humankind, who are far less educated and intelligent then these men, especially when under an immoral regime? Since a majority of humankind is still currently under evil regimes, like Russia, Iran, Afghanistan, Pakistan, China, and North Korea, we have much to fear and more work to do to make this world safe. In passing judgement on these leaders of Imperial Japan, the Tokyo Tribunal on 16 April 1948 had this eloquent conclusion:

> These defendants were not automatons; they were not replaceable cogs in a machine; they were not playthings of fate caught in a maelstrom of destiny from which there was no extrication. These men were the brains of an empire…It was theirs to choose whether their nation would lead an honored life…or…would become a symbol of evil throughout the world. They made their choice. For this choice they must bear the guilt—a guilt which is perhaps greater than that of any group of men who have stood

before the bar of justice in the entire history of the world. These men were not the hoodlums who were the powerful part of the group which stood before the Tribunal in Nuremberg, dregs of a criminal environment thoroughly schooled in the ways of crime and knowing no other methods but those of crime. These men were supposed to be the elite of the nation, the honest and trusted leaders to whom fate of the nation had been confidently entrusted...These men knew the difference between good and evil. They knew the obligations to which they had solemnly pledged their nation. With full knowledge they voluntarily made their choice for evil, to disregard the obligations and to betray the faith which their own people and others had in them! With full knowledge they voluntarily elected to follow the path of war bringing death and injury to millions of human beings and destruction and hate wherever their forces went. They gambled with the destiny of the people of their nation and like common felons everywhere brought only death and hurt and destruction and chaos to those whose care had been entrusted to them...They made their choice for aggression and for war and they made it freely and voluntarily. For this choice they must bear the guilt.[1526]

This judgment should inspire hope, as it demonstrates that good can, and often does, triumph over evil. The Allies did bring many Japanese leaders to justice, and the analysis of these trials was powerful. These Japanese leaders knew better than to commit the atrocities they did, but they allowed hate, greed, peer-pressure, bigoted religious convictions, and social conditioning to guide their actions. Instead of choosing a different path, they recklessly pursued empire and control, focused on grabbing and dominating without considering the consequences. They failed to reflect on how their actions would be perceived by cultures outside their own or how their deeds would be judged if done by another nation within Japan. The absence of such contemplation led to their downfall when their actions were brought to light in a courtroom. The guilty verdicts were inevitable, and the Allies handed out justice through the executions of over 900 Japanese war criminals. This serves as a reminder that no matter how powerful or influential one may be, there are universal moral standards that apply to all.

Upon reviewing the information presented in this study, it remains perplexing how Japan continues to conceal its history from its own people. It is disheartening to observe that when confronted with the misdeeds of their fathers or grandfathers, many family members resort to childish and unethical responses. One striking example is Captain Yoshitsugu Akamatsu, who forced hundreds of Okinawan civilians to commit suicide (killing some himself) during his command in 1945. Shockingly, Akamatsu did not take his own life in the face of defeat, although he ordered the Japanese civilians under his care to do so. In an audacious display, Akamatsu even revisited the island in 1970 to relive his once fame as an officer. When books documenting his misdeeds were published, his family filed a libel lawsuit against the authors, displaying a refusal to acknowledge the truth. Although the court eventually dismissed their lawsuit, it once again illustrates the Japanese's inability to confront their criminal past and the shameful behavior they displayed when faced with historical evidence.[1527] This behavior of Akamatsu's family reminds me of how the "Honorable" Shindo behaved when presented with the undeniable facts about his grandfather, Kuribayashi, and his unwillingness to recognize the general's atrocities and disgraceful behavior. This pattern of denial and evasion only perpetuates a cycle of ignorance and hinders genuine reconciliation with Japan's past within Japan itself.

In the end, Hirohito's followers would have continued their Holocaust had the free world not risen up and smashed them to the ground. The only thing that spoke to the Fascist leader Hirohito to lay down arms and to stop his mass murder were the atomic bombs. Without these bombs, Japan would have continued racking up large tallies of dead in the lands under its control. And the only way those bombs got dropped on Japan was through the development of amphibious warfare that created a chain of bases through the Pacific Ocean right up to Japan's doorstep. This strategic progress laid the groundwork for the ultimate confrontation and forced Hirohito's hand to put an end to the bloodshed.

It took millions of Allied servicemen to defeat Imperial Japan. By defeating Hirohito and his military legions, the Allies saved untold millions from further bloodbaths. This Holocaust "will forever haunt the old" Japanese military.[1528] Paul Berman, author of *Terror and Liberalism*, wrote a "primer on totalitarianism" stating that such "pathological" regimes like Imperial Japan contain "a genocidal, and even suicidal, dimension…that get drunk on slaughter."[1529] XIV U.S. Army Corps, after investigating Japanese atrocities at Manila, summed up what the Empire of the Sun was: "Japan…is truly an enemy of the civilized world."[1530] Everywhere Japanese soldiers went, they built a "nest of wickedness."[1531] "The world has long since called them blind, a people presumptuous, avaricious, envious; be sure to cleanse yourself of their foul ways."[1532] By 1945, America and her Allies cleansed the world of Japan's filth and ended its "mad ambition" for world domination.[1533] Chief of counsel for the International Military Tribunal for the Far East, Joseph B. Keenan, wrote in 1946:

A very few throughout the world, including these accused [Japanese Class-A War Criminals like Tōjō, Matsui, Sakai], decided to take the law into their own hands and to force their individual will upon mankind. They declared war upon civilization. They made the rules and defined the issues. They were determined to destroy democracy and its essential basis—freedom and respect of human personality; they were determined that the system of government of and by and for the people should be eradicated and what they called the 'New Order' established instead. And to this end they joined hands with the Hitlerite group; they did formally, by way of treaty, and were proud of their confederacy. Together they planned, prepared and initiated aggressive wars against the great democracies [throughout the world]. They willingly dealt with human beings as chattels and pawns. That it meant murder and the murder and the subjugation and enslavement of millions was of no moment to them. That it encompassed a plan or design for the murder in all parts of the world of children and aged, that it envisaged the entire obliteration of whole communities, was to them a matter of complete indifference. That it should cause the premature end of the very flower of the youth of the world—their own included—was entirely beside the point. Treaties, agreements and assurances were treated as mere words—bits of paper— in their minds, and constituted no deterring influence on their efforts. Their purpose was that force should be unloosed upon the world. They thought in terms of force and domination and entirely obscured the end of justice. In this enterprise millions could die; the resources of nations could be destroyed. All of this was of no import in their mad scheme for domination and control of Eastern Asia, and as they advanced, ultimately the entire world. This was the purport of their conspiracy.[1534]

The gravity of this indictment provides ample justification for all living free men and women in the Allied nations to be grateful for the use of the atomic bombs. For all the nameless and named victims of Japan's Holocaust, from Nanking to Canton, to Shanghai to Hong Kong, to Bataan to Singapore, to Harbin to Manila, they too, if they could still have spoken, would have thanked those who dropped the atomic bombs. With the resounding impacts and explosions of these atomic bombs, their cries were heard across the vast ocean. In a rare moment of honesty for a Japanese field commander, the former Kwantung commander, General Yamada, who commanded not only troops who raped and killed throughout Manchuria, but also was responsible for Units 731's and 100's activities from 1944 to 1945, admitted at his trial in Russia in 1949: "I must say that I consider all that I did an evil thing—I want to correct myself: I consider it a *very evil thing* [author's italics]."[1535] Almost every field commander in the Japanese army could have echoed this sentiment, not only for their own deeds, but also for those of their men. Sadly, such remorse was a rarity among them.

During his trial on Guam, Lieutenant General Yoshio Tachibana, the commander of Chichi Jima, who was guilty of killing American POWs and eating many of them, would yell at Major Yoshitaka Horie, who gave testimony against him, calling him an "American dog" and that he was "not Japanese."[1536] This lack of remorse was not unique to Tachibana; most Japanese commanders on trial after the war showed defiance and remained unrepentant. As Horie observed after the war, Japanese men had been raised with the "wrong type of education," which led them to a despising of foreigners and a lack of respect for the "value of human life."[1537] However, in typical Japanese fashion, Horie likely also showed his incredible hypocrisy after the war by presenting himself without blemish while condemning others like Tachibana, and the "Tiger of Chichi," Major Sueo Matoba, the notorious sadist and cannibal of American airmen and who was brought to trial on Guam for his crimes on Chichi Jima. Horie was a hypocrite because he participated in aggressive operations in Northern China from 1937 until 1939, taking part in 27 battles as a first lieutenant, so he helped conduct some of the atrocities detailed throughout this book. As a communications officer, he had a role in coordinating units that committed these crimes.[1538] As head of the War Ministry (1938–1939), Lieutenant General Seishirō Itagaki, had documented in 1939, all IJA men in China during this time were guilty of "murder, robbery or rape."[1539] As an officer, Horie was thus overseeing soldiers involved in these criminal actions. In showing his two-faced nature during the war and thereafter, Tachibana was wrong in calling Horie "not Japanese." He actually was very Japanese for this time period having a typical Japanese-Janus face. In a Freudian moment, Horie noted: "Thinking about the war criminals and their families, I had to be disappointed by the tragedy deriving from the failure to teach international law in the schools and colleges and the general tendency in Japan to mistreat the individual."[1540]

In analyzing how Japan treated its own citizens in combat zones as well as its own military personnel during times of defeat bespeaks of an extreme inhumanity with how a country deals with its fellow human beings and national citizens. While mistreatment of enemy combatants and civilians is, to some extent, comprehensible, though not justifiable, the utter lack of mercy for one's own people is insane and deeply unsettling. Convincing people that it was honorable to kill themselves when they lost a battle or had no way of further fighting a superior foe ensured that Japanese society would have exterminated itself had the war continued not in its favor. The Japanese were very bad losers indeed.

Returning to the realities of modern-day Japan, its weakness in confronting the past, especially when teaching its future generations the truth, makes it a threat to the pursuit of democracy and human rights for the future. The lengths the Japanese go to in order to fabricate historical truths show that Japan, ironically, is still a nation to be leery of when it comes to human rights. A country that fails to acknowledge and atone for past crimes risks repeating such acts in the future. Since the Japanese obviously have failed to acknowledge that such criminal acts gave them a society no respectable country would ever want (a society that even slaughtered its own people), they show that it is still possibly *a society its people might still desire having.* Let us hope this is not the case. In stark contrast to Germany, which is a thriving democracy and a voice for morality in the world, Japan is a defective democracy. It serves as a cautionary example to the world, showing what "enlightened" countries should not aspire to be like. Many aspects of Japan's academic world and political structure should not be emulated since they both have failed in being honest about its past. Since it does not open its archives fully to scholars, and it has not built monuments and museums to tell the honest rendition of history inside or outside its country, it is a society that gives a profound example to the world of a morally bankrupt citizenry who are weak and cowardly in how they deal with crimes and problems.

In conclusion, the book has shed light on the deeply troubling issue of Japanese society's reluctance to acknowledge its past crimes, *its Holocaust,* revealing a disgraceful aspect of their collective identity. As a global community, we should stand united when proclaiming "Never Again," but for this pledge to hold true, we must confront and understand the historical events we are vowing never to repeat. When Americans say "Never Again" to slavery, they understand what is being discussed. Similarly, when Germans say "Never Again," they know they are stating they will never allow a Hitler-type or the Nazis to take control of their country ever again or commit another genocide. However, when the Japanese say "Never Again," they often mean they will never be defeated in war again or have atomic bombs dropped on them, not that they will never again commit mass murder and mass rape. It is crucial for Japanese citizens and politicians alike to grasp the true meaning behind "Never Again," and give it a new answer so that they can better learn from history in the desire to avoid repeating grave mistakes. We can only hope the Japanese citizens in general, and the Japanese politicians in particular, start to learn this lesson that history needs to become known if it is not going to be repeated. May this book, in its own small way, contribute to this vital endeavor and raise awareness about events that must never be allowed to recur in human society. Together, let us strive for a future where "Never Again" becomes a reality for all of humankind.

WHAT DOES ALL THIS HISTORY MEAN?

Leaving the micro-level with modern Japan's pathetic behavior concerning its Holocaust and returning to the macro-level of this study, one sees this history has explored socio-religious issues that led to mass murder, racism, and intolerance so we may do a better job in the future of recognizing these dangers sooner and destroy them. In particular, this book has examined Shintōists' and Zen Buddhists' beliefs under their High Priest and god, Hirohito, which led the Japanese to embrace Fascist beliefs that fueled their rape and conquest in the hope of helping prevent such things from happening again. Young American boys' and girls' lives should not be interrupted or destroyed to prevent the plagues of murderous regimes like Hitler's and Hirohito's (16.3 million Americans served during WWII alone with 400,000 dying in the process).[1541] American boys and girls helped bring to an end World War II, that all told, cost 60 million lives (over half of which were slaughtered in cold blood by Japan [30 million][1542] and Germany [11.7 million]).[1543] American lives should instead focus on making this world a better place through science, industry, education, and invention, not on how to kill people. Yes, we should always have a portion of our population trained as willing warriors, but the majority of each generation should focus on more productive and useful activities like curing cancer, Parkinson's disease, or Alzheimer's. In recent times, it truly does just take a small percentage of America's population to fight its wars. The victory our men and women secured in WWII has likely ensured that reality to date. Let us hope that we never again have to mobilize our entire population to focus on war and killing millions to preserve democracy. However, we must always be willing to do so if that democracy is to survive the ages.

Apart from studying Japan's Holocaust and to show how evil Matsui, Sakai, Tsuji, Kuribayashi, Yamashita, Ushijima, Takashina, Tōjō and many others were in furthering Hirohito's lust for empire, and that the Rape of Nanking-like actions were commonplace, this book has another mission: to challenge readers to think about their beliefs, education, society, and actions and whether they are making the world better. Since I began this research, mass murder and genocide continue to be a recurring event, evidenced by Northern Iraq under ISIS, Afghanistan under the Taliban, Gaza under Hamas, and occupied regions of the Ukraine by Russian forces. Violence against women is widespread, particularly in territory controlled by fundamentalist Muslims or Putin's military thugs, who would have made many Imperial Japanese commanders proud. America is still at war against various groups of viciously intolerant Islamic radicals in a global war on terror, one of the most protracted and complicated conflicts in world history. And Ukraine's democracy is defending itself bravely against Russia's brutal and criminal dictator, Vladimir Putin, who launched an unprovoked war against this country in 2022, indiscriminately killing women and children, in his quest for empire. Many problems that faced humanity from 1927 to 1945 still remain. This book explores how a nation founded on freedom of religion responded to religious fanaticism and destroyed Imperial Japan, thereby preventing its protracted and continued mass murder throughout the world. When looking at WWII, we get high marks in these areas: We destroyed Hirohito's religious fanatics; we saved millions of additional Asians from being added to the list of Japan's Holocaust victims; we adhered to the laws of war; and we re-built Japan's country in a massive, postwar humanitarian effort and *actually gave* the territory back to them once transformed into a democracy so that they could rule themselves again! We fought the good fight, but we still have more to do.

In recent years, the world has become more dangerous and unstable. Maybe this has been the case since history began, but most of the world throughout time did not have nuclear weapons spread out over the Earth as it does now. I hope this work will get more people interested in the issues threatening us and make them more ready to act against the criminals who are making this world worse. Moreover, I hope this book will help people fight against the bad ideas that motivate the wicked. This book explores deeper and more enduring issues of humanity such as: How do we create a good society?

Reflecting on the U.S.'s Imperial Japanese enemy in light of religious fundamentalism, I realize that fundamentalist groups, regardless of who they are, tend to suppress and disregard information when it conflicts with their dogmas and often kill those who bring such information to light. People who claimed Hirohito was evil/not a god in 1940 Japan got their heads cut off, and people in radical Islamic lands who claim Mohammed is a murderer/not Allah's messenger get slaughtered. Those who protest Putin's autocratic rule in Russia and his illegal war in Ukraine get arrested, persecuted, and sometimes murdered. Getting rid of the types of people who commit such crimes against free thought and expression is one way to "create a good society." I have come to admire America's founding fathers' wisdom that recognized the danger of combining religion with civil government, as the fusion is harmful to both religious freedom and good governance. And I appreciate our founding fathers' desire to set up a government that prevents dictatorships.

America's colonies were overwhelmingly Protestant, from a variety of denominations. "Typically the proponents of all these forms of Protestantism saw a high regard for natural science, reason, common sense, self-evident rights, and ideals of liberty as fully compatible with their Protestant heritage" although they looked at each other with skepticism. The founding fathers' task was to build a cohesive, voluntary civilization out of competing subgroups. America is fortunate that Thomas Jefferson, Benjamin Franklin, George Washington, and James Madison, to name a few, were the architects of the religious and political freedoms that prevented government entanglement with religious beliefs as expressed in the First Amendment. They recognized that the separation of church and state is a cornerstone of democracy, laying a foundation to prevent government from restricting people's rights to follow their spiritual convictions and/or political beliefs. The freedom and tolerance in America, where so many had come to escape Old World religious and ethnic persecution as well as monarchist oppression, were a nurturing environment for religious minorities and people holding diverse political thought.[1544] President George Washington pledged to the Jews of Newport, Rhode Island: "To bigotry no sanction; to persecution no assistance."[1545] To prevent bigotry and persecution, Washington knew no religious institution should be permitted to hold power in government. One could interpret Washington as also saying that fanaticism has no part in governance. This doctrine is a foundational tenet of American civics. American beliefs about how government should rule were bequeathed to the post-WWII Japanese and German governments, and demonstrate that such mandates create democratic, non-Fascistic, and anti-theocratic regimes.

This history is much more than a narration of Japan's Holocaust and its many atrocities. It explores how history is documented, how ideas shape action, and how knowledge is preserved. To explore such themes, authors rely on the freedom of speech and of the press. Ironically, one of the biggest fights I had in writing this work was with Kuribayashi's grandson, the "honorable" Shindo himself, who tried to suppress this work through threats, demanding the right to approve what I could and could not write. He failed to realize history should not be censored and this book is not *solely about him*. Fortunately for history and this work, the U.S.'s First Amendment won out and the publication of this book has not been suppressed. Freedom of speech triumphs again. As historian Colin Heaton explains, if Shindo was a "truly intelligent specimen, he would know that the honest historian favors no one, takes no unreasonable position, just educates, illuminates, and presents evidence. Perhaps this evidence is controversial, but hopefully irrefutable, just as an honest attorney in a court of law would do."[1546]

I was saddened by the obstruction I encountered; Shindo is indeed one who supposedly has taken oaths to uphold the Japanese Constitution which guarantees the freedom of the press and the freedom of speech (we Americans wrote it for the Japanese, after all!). My experience with him makes me realize that when a historian gathers the truth from history, he should never make a Faustian arrangement with any of his subjects nor give them the final word on the research. If this became the norm, we would have limited ourselves to censored history, not truthful history.

In returning to how we may make this world better, this book hopefully helps us see that we need to be ever vigilant against dangerous religions and political movements (which often mirror religious organizations). As ex-evangelical Dan Barker writes, "If we consider ourselves to be moral (or ethical), we ought not to refrain from denouncing religious teachings and practices that cause harm."[1547] In his novel, *The Plague*, Albert Camus described not only many religions, but also dangerous ideologies, as having much intolerance buried away in their foundational creeds. Camus wrote using the disease as a symbol of hateful ideas:

> The plague bacillus never dies or disappears for good; that it can lie dormant for years and years in furniture and linen-chests; that it bides its time in bedrooms, cellars, trunks, and bookshelves; and that perhaps the day would come when, for the bane and the enlightening of men, it would rouse up its rats again and send them forth to die in a happy city.[1548]

In other words, we should guard against malevolent ideas, both political and religious, that find their breeding ground in holy books and hate groups and shun those elements before they infect society and emerge with terrible violence in times of social strain as seen with Imperial Japan and Nazi Germany. "We must keep *ourselves* in check, remaining ever vigilant against the darker side of our natures by which we are constantly threatened."[1549] We need to remember that what a person believes is not private because beliefs are a "fount of action *in potentia*."[1550] Some beliefs, like "Jews are bad" or "infidels should die" or "non-believers go to Hell" or "Gentiles are inferior" or "homosexuals are deviant and sinners" or "the gods say Japanese should rule everyone" or "Chinks are bad" or "conquered women are only good for raping" are beliefs that can give birth to dangerous movements, as history attests.

Imperial Japan continued a human tradition of religious and ethnic prejudice expressed in mass slaughter which is not unique. Consider the Biblical story of 12,000 Israelites killing probably over 300,000 Midianites and raping 32,000 "virgins" in a divinely ordered orgy of ethnic cleansing (see Numbers 31)[1551] for enticing Israelites to be unfaithful to the Lord, or the Christians killing Jews and Muslims during the Crusades for not being Christian.[1552] Consider the one million Christian Armenians slaughtered by the Ottoman Muslim Turks from 1915 to 1917.[1553] Consider the Nazis or Maoists who massacred millions in the name of ideology, which was just a replacement for religion. Hitler or Mao Zedong were stand-ins for the Messiah or leader chosen by Providence, and both were creating a "utopia/heaven" on Earth—for Hitler, the thousand-year *Reich*, and for Mao, the new China reborn through Marxism.[1554]

Historian Jonathan Steinberg warns that when followers of men like Hitler, Mao or Hirohito make gods out of them, they will suffer dire consequences.[1555] Mao is possibly the greatest slaughterer of all times, exceeding Hirohito, Hitler, and Stalin combined, with a likely total of 70 million dead, largely because his reign as "god" lasted for five decades.[1556] In these examples, we have people motivated by their misguided convictions to act with complete disregard for individual freedom and well-being and do harm to specific religious, ethnic, and political groups.

Thus, political or religious fanaticism destroys everything it touches. But these movements can only take hold if the organization that gives birth to this fanaticism remains unchallenged. Ideas, leaders, and movements should always be questioned—in fact, every society or government should preserve this ability to challenge, through the press or through oppositional parties, so that no one person or group obtains unquestioned authority. Fanatics like Hitler, Hirohito, Stalin, and Mao remained in power for so long because they could not be questioned. This absolute power allowed them to turn into monsters. Jonathan Steinberg writes:

> Nobody is always right. No arguments are 'unanswerable.'… Unreason knows no limits. It cannot measure profit against loss or assess means and ends. It rejects liberty of the mind and threatens the person of the thinker. It cannot tolerate free speech, blasphemous books, satire and irreverence. It mobilizes the turbulent energies, emotions and wishes inside each of us and hurls them against the limits of the human condition. In doing so it destroys itself and lays waste its surroundings.[1557]

To explore such truths, this book highlights the results of extreme forms of religious and political rule by men like Hirohito and his "Zen-obedient zombies."[1558] Shintōist-Zen Buddhist-Imperial Japan prevented its adherents from seeing their own atrocities and biases. Blaise Pascal said, "Men never do evil so completely and cheerfully as when they do it from religious conviction."[1559] Fanatical beliefs, whether religious or political, prevent their adherents from seeing injustices around them so they may correct them.

Fighting genocide and religious totalitarianism should be two focuses of enlightened and democratic societies. In our battle against the Axis fanatics, America became what Roosevelt called "the arsenal of democracy,"[1560] beginning in the period while we were still neutral, and eventually playing a crucial military role in bringing Hitler's and Hirohito's regimes to their knees. Germany and Japan could have been defeated earlier if the U.S. had acted expeditiously against them instead of waiting for them to arm, militarize, threaten, and attack.

Long before his rise to power, Hitler revealed in *Mein Kampf* a murderous intolerance, and he continued preaching his hate in the diatribes he made to anyone who would listen. Starting as early as 1927, Hirohito's regime committed atrocities in its rampage across Asia. The lack of any major international condemnation only emboldened both of these obsessive leaders. Although the U.S. played one of the most important roles in WWII to defeat Hitler and Hirohito, it was disastrously slow to pick up the sword, and did so not on moral grounds, but for the sake of self-preservation.

Other democracies also made mistakes. British Prime Minister Neville Chamberlain sold out Europe with his policy of appeasement when he signed the Munich Agreement in September 1938. The Allies allowed Hitler to violate numerous border and treaty obligations from 1935 to 1938 without any serious repercussions. Several Allied nations knew about the Rape of Nanking and of Japanese atrocities in cities like Beijing, Canton, Shanghai, and Tientsin, yet they were unwilling to risk war to help prevent China from falling under Japan's cruel shadow. As WWII MOH recipient and later Vice Admiral John D. Bulkeley, who had personally witnessed Japanese atrocities, wrote, "Official Washington and the American people could stick their heads in the sand and ignore the holocaust that the empire of Japan was inflicting on the Chinese people."[1561] Similarly, the U.S. and her Allies continually turned a blind eye to the Nazis' escalating violence against Jews as seen in the Night of Broken Glass (*Kristallnacht*: 9–10 November 1938), the MS *St. Louis* refugees (May 1939), the ghetto system in Poland (1939–40) and then the full slaughter of Jews once the Soviet Union was invaded (21 June 1941). These failures of action by the Allies in response to these Fascist deeds told Hitler and Hirohito that they held the political and military high ground. There was a tragically high price in blood and treasure that was paid for years of neutrality in the face of the evil displayed in events around the world. This dangerous inaction in the face of injustice remains a lesson to enlightened and democratic nations that when they see an evil regime or dictator, they would be wise to destroy it or him *immediately*. More importantly, they must maintain militaries that can and will be able to destroy such immorality.

We need to do our best to punish those who persecute and exterminate others for their thoughts, ethnicity, and religions and when possible, defeat these fanatical groups as we did with the Nazi Germans and Imperialistic Japanese, and as we are currently doing with Muslim fanatics in the Taliban, Al-Qaida, Hamas, or ISIS, and as we are helping Ukrainian forces do to Putin's autocratic legions who are wreaking havoc in Europe.

In conclusion, besides reading about remarkable and disturbing WWII events, I hope the reader thinks about the ideas and motivations that set the stage for the events between 1927 and 1945. In addition to being interested in the varied subject matters explored, I hope you are challenged to think about how you live your life and whether you would have the courage to stand up to evil. History shows we need more citizens like the Allied leaders and military men documented in this book who acted with a high sense of moral integrity to save lives and preserve democracy. Michael Berenbaum wrote about a prisoner in the Sachsenhausen concentration camp who would tell the new arrivals about "the darkness that awaited them. He told them what was to be—honestly, directly, and without adornment." He would end with the admonition: "I have told you this story not to weaken you. But to strengthen you. Now it is up to you!"[1562] In the end, I hope this book will make you a more open-minded person, a more aggressive champion of justice, and a more resolute defender of the helpless. We must constantly remind ourselves, as Socrates taught, that "the unexamined life is not worth living" and it is in the pursuit of truth that we achieve enlightenment rather than in the attainment of it.[1563] Because once one thinks he has the truth, then he stops growing and learning. And those who think they know everything are the most ruthless and dangerous men amongst us.

INTERVIEWS BY BRYAN MARK RIGG

Roger Cirillo, 12 May 2018
Mary Dalbey-Rigg, Summer 1996
Edward J. Drea, 17 Dec. 2017
Don Graves, 7 May 2017, 8 May 2017, 23 May 2017,
14 June 2017, 3 April 2018, 4 April 2018, 2 May
2018, 7 May 2018, 4 July 2018, 11 Jan. 2020
James Oelke Farley, 23 March 2015, 8 Nov.
2017, 17 March 2018, 25 March 2018
Richard Frank, 20 July 2017, 22 March 2018, 23 March 2018
Fiske Hanley, 20 March 2015
Bonnie Haynes, 27 Feb. 2019
Mant Hawkins, 16 Feb. 2019
Colin Heaton, 17 Dec. 2017, 8 June 2018, 16 Feb. 2019
Shayne Jarosz, 12 May 2017, 25 March 2018
Charles C. Krulak, 6 Dec. 2019
Master Johnny Kwong Ming Lee, 10 April 2019
Laura Leppert, 13 May 2017, 24 May 2019
Sigmund L. Liberman, 10 June 2013
Tommy Lofton, 30 April 2018
Ann R. Mandel, 17 June 2019
Lee Mandel, 17 June 2019
Dwight Mears, 10 May 2018
Martin K.A. Morgan, 10 Dec. 2017
John Mountcastle, 14 Jan. 2018
Charles Neimeyer, 15 Dec. 2017
Keith Renstrom, 22 March 2018
Ken Roseman, 23 Feb. 2015
Tatsushi Saito, 9-10 April 2018
Jinghua Shi, 22 May 2019
Yoshitaka Shindo, 9 April 2018

Dennis Showalter, 18 May 2019
Gerhard Weinberg, 2 Sept. 2005
Edgar Weinsberg, 6 Dec. 2019
Glenna Whitley, 7 Jan. 2020
Yukio Yasunaga, 10 April 2018.
Jerry Yellin, 22 March 2015, 18 Aug. 2016, 2 June 2017, 6 July 2017

Unrecorded Interviews by historian Colin Heaton
Hans Baur, 1985.
Albert Kerscher, 1985.
Otto Kumm, 1985.
Karl Wolff, 1984.

Interview by John Renstrom
Keith Renstrom 20–23 June 2016.
Interviews By Scott Farber
Generations Broadcast Center, Project SFMedia Consultants,
Inc., WWII Interviews, Jim Reed, 31 Jan. 2013

Movies/Documentaries
Internet Archive:1940 JAPANESE WAR HORSE
FILM "PRAYER AT DAWN" 17184
Military Heritage Institute 2011 film *The Battle for the Marianas.*
A Savage Christmas: The Fall of Hong Kong 1941,
Canadian Documentary, 12 Jan. 1992.

PRIMARY SOURCES:

Bundesarchiv-Militärarchiv (BA-MA), Freiburg, Germany
Bibliothek, *Japan's Eintritt in den Krieg*, Hrsg. v. der
Kaiserlich Japanischen Botschaft, Berlin, 1942.
NS 19/3134
RH 2/ 1848
RM 11/69
RM 11/79
RM 11/81

The Founding Era Collection
Thomas Jefferson Papers, Docs. Jan. 1819-4 July
1836, Jefferson to Henry Lee, 15 May 1826.

University of Georgia School of Law (UGSL)
J. Alton Hosch Papers, Tokyo War Crimes Trials

Harvard School Student Archives
File Tadamichi Kuribayashi

Oral History Division: Marine Corps Historical Division
Bert Banks, George Burledge, Clifton Cates, Robert E. Cushman
Jr., Graves Erskine, Victor H. Krulak, Holland M. Smith

Marine Corps Historical Division, Quantico,
VA. (MCHDQV/MCHDHQ)
HQ, 3d MarDiv
Biographical Correspondent File Donald Beck
Dashiell File (Correspondent File of Frederick "Dick" Dashiell)

Marine Corps Recruit Depot Archive, San Diego (MCRDASD)
C-2 Special Study, Enemy Situation, VAC, 6 Jan. 1945
HQ 8th Marines, 2nd Marine Brigade, July-Aug.
1942, Japanese Tactics, Warfare and Weapons.
MCRD Training Book, File 1-2, 1944, By Sgt. Lawrence Henry Pepin
Soldiers Guide to the Japanese Army, Military Intel Service,
War Dept., Washington D.C., 15 Nov. 1944

Micronesian Area Research Center (MARC), Univ. of Guam
Guam War Reparations Commission (GWRC)
Olivia L.G. Cruz Abell, Box 1, Rec. 2090, Maria T. Abrenilla, Box
1, Rec. 40, Fausto Acfalle, Box 1, Rec. 120, Francisco Acfalle, Box
1, Rec. 2230, Frutuoso S. Aflague, Box 1, Consuelo Aguon, Box
1, 1980, Candelaria Aguon, Box 1, Rec. 1910, Dolores F. Aguon,
Box 1, Rec. 380, Edward L.G. Aguon, Box 1, Felix Aguon, Box
1, Felix Cepeda Aguon, Box 1, Ignacio T. Leon Guerrero, Box 20,
Rec. 39680, Diana Leon Guerrero, Box 20, 39502, Francisco Q.
Leon Guerrero, Box 20, 39620, Jesus Leon Guerrero, Box 20
GC 64 SC 324737

GC 65—80 G 241236, 279846, 279849,301770, 301776,
301784, 324737, 332346, 333809, 356560,490319, 490364
GC 94

National Archives, College Park, Maryland, (NACPM)
Biography Kenji Doihara
Microfilm Room, Roll 1499, #86, #101, #113
RG 127 Box 14 (3d MarDiv)
RG 127 Box 318 (Saipan-Tinian)
RG 127 Box 329 (Saipan-Tinian)
RG 226, Box 368 (Records Off. US Strategic Services)

National Archives, St. Louis Personnel Files, (NASLPR)
Graves Erskine, Holland M. Smith, John Warner,
Hershel Woodrow "Woody" Williams

**National Institute for Defense Studies, Ministry of Defense
Military Archives (NIDSMDMA), Tokyo, Japan**
Akira Fukuda, JDF Civilian Instructor, "Regarding
Army Engineering at Iwo Jima."
Collection Iwo Jima Operation, #1
Collections for Lt. General Kuribayashi, Bio info.
Collections of History Calvary Rgts
Kai-Ko-Sha Kiji, October 1938 Vo1. 769, Kuribayashi,
"Building New Remount Administrative Plan," 83-92.
————, March 2001, "Fund for the Production to
Increase Strength of the Control by the Military."
Kambu Gakko Kigi, (JGSDF Staff College), Col. Fujiwara,
"Commemorating General Kuribayashi," August 1966, Tokyo
Records of Showa Emperor, (ed.) *Kunaichō*, Tokyo, Sept. 2016.
Senshi-Sosho, Operation Central Pacific, Operation
#2, Peleliu, Angaur, Iwo Jima, Vol. 13, 1971
————, "Operations Hong Kong & Chosa,"
War History Series, Vol. 47, 1971.

The Second Historical Archives of China, Nanjing, China
Memory of the World: Documents of Nanjing
Massacre, Vol 1-20 (TSHACNCDNM)
Shanghai Library Historical Archives, China (SLHA)
Far Eastern Illustrated News, No. 1-61 The Young Companion,
1940, 150-155 The Young Companion, 1941-1945, 167-172.

**United States Congress, House, Committee on
Ways and Means, April 18–May 14, 1945**

United Nations Archives
Security Microfilm Programme 1998, UNWCC, PAG-3,
Reel no. 61, Summary Translation of the Proceedings of the
Military Tribunal, Nanking, on the Trial of Takashi Sakai

WEB SITES:

https://www.exeter.edu/about-us/academy-mission
https://www.revolvy.com/page/Yoshitaka-Shind%C5%8D
https://www.nationalww2museum.org/war/
articles/history-through-viewfinder-23
https://www.britannica.com/event/Bataan-Death-March
http://www.kemstone.com/Nonfiction/Philosophy/Thesis/plague.htm

BIBLIOGRAPHY

ARTICLES:

Bartlett, Duncan, "Japan Looks Back on 17th-Century Persecutions," *BBC News*, 24 Nov. 2008.

Black, Richard, "Those Who Deny Auschwitz Would be Ready to Remake it," *Jewish News*, 27 Jan. 2015.

Bowie, Donald C., "Captive Surgeon in Hong Kong: The Story of the British Military Hospital, Hong Kong 1942-1945," *Journal of the Hong Kong Branch of the Royal Asiatic Society*, Vol. 15 (1975).

Crovitz, L. Gordon, "Defending Satire to the Death," *Jewish News*, 12 Jan. 2015.

Daly, Kyle, "The Legacy of Holland M. Smith," *Leatherneck Magazine*, Oct. 2018.

Davis, James Martin, "Operation Olympic: An Invasion not Found in History Books," *Omaha World Herald*, November 1987.

Editorial Board, "A Lesson From the Holocaust: Never Stop Telling the Terrible Stories," *Chicago Tribune*, 12 April 2018.

Gaerlan, Cecilia, "War Crimes in the Philippines during WWII," Arthur D. Simons Center for Interagency Cooperation, Ft. Leavenworth, Kansas, 2019.

Ghosh, Palash, "Germany to Pay Out $1 Billion in Reparations For Care of Aging Holocaust Survivors," *International Business Times*, 29 May 2013.

Glass, Andrew, "Reagan Visits German War Cemetery, May 5, 1985," *Politico*, 5 May 2018.

Glum, Julia, "San Francisco Statue Honoring 'Comfort Women' Sex Slaves from World War II Infuriates Japan," *Newsweek*, 30 Oct. 2017.

Goldman, Stuart D., and Shulatov, Yaroslav A., "The Fanatical Colonel Tsuji," *World War II Magazine*, April 2019.

Heneroty, Kate, "Japanese Court Rules Newspaper Didn't Fabricate 1937 Chinese Killing Game," Jurist Legal News and Research, Univ. of Pittsburgh School of Law, 23 Aug. 2005.

Hogg, Chris, "Victory for Japan's War Critics," *BBC*, 23 Aug. 2005.

Mr. James, "The Untold Story of Captain Kudo Shunsaku and the Destroyer Ikazuchi," *Japan Probe*, 19 May 2007.

"Japan Halts UNESCO Funding Following Nanjing Massacre Row," *The Guardian*, 14 Oct. 2016.

"Japan Withholds UNESCO Funding After Nanjing Massacre Row," *Reuters*, 14 Oct. 2016.

"Japanese Court Rejects Germ Warfare Damages," *NYT*, 20 July 2005.

"Japanese Minister Yoshitaka Shindo Visits Yasukuni Shrine Provoking China's Ire," *South China Morning Post*, 1 Jan. 2014.

Jeans, Roger B., "Victims or Victimizers? Museums, Textbooks, and the War Debate in Contemporary Japan," *The Journal of Military History*, Society for Military History, 69 (1): (January 2005), 149–195.

Jones, Kevin L., "'Comfort Women' Statue Strains 60-Year San Francisco-Osaka Alliance," *Art Wire*, 28 Sept. 2017.

Journal of Nanjing Massacre Studies (JNMS), Vol. 1, No. 1, Nanking, China, 2019.

Kennedy, David M., "The Horror: Should the Japanese atrocities in Nanking be equated with the Nazi Holocaust?," *The Atlantic Monthly*, Vol. 281, No. 4 (April 1998), 110-116.

Knapton, Sarah, "Small Man Syndrome Really Does Exist, US Government Researchers Conclude," *The Telegraph*, 25 Aug. 2015.

Knight, Heather, "Japanese Mayor Cuts Ties Between SF and Osaka Over Comfort Women Statue," *San Francisco Chronicle*, 3 Oct. 2018.

Matthews, Dylan, "Six Times Victims Have Received Reparations—Including Four in the US," *Vox*, 23 May 2014.

McNeill, David, "Even the Dead Were Being Forced to Fight," *The Japan Times*, 13 Aug. 2006.

———. "Reluctant Warrior," World War II Magazine, Special Collector's Edition for the 60th Commemoration of Iwo Jima.

Morris-Suzuki, Tessa, "Who is Responsible? The Yomiuri Project and the Legacy of the Asia-Pacific War in Japan," *Asian Perspective*, Vol. 31, No. 1, 2007, 177-191.

"Nationalist 'Japan Conference' Building Its Clout: Ten Days after the Meeting, Abe Officially Addressed the Issue of Revising the Pacifist Constitution," *Korea JoongAng Daily*, 3 May 2013.

Pennington, Lisa Kelly, "The Pacific War Crimes Trials: The Importance of the 'Small Frey' vs. the 'Big Fish,'" Old Dominion Univ. ODU Digital Commons, History Theses & Dissertations, History, Summer 2012.

Rayner, Gordon, "Sir Winston Churchill May Have Had 'Short Man Syndrome,' Suggest Boris Johnson," *London Telegraph*, 10 Oct 2014.

Researching Japanese War Crimes Records: Introductory Essays by Edward Drea, Greg Bradsher, Robert Hanyok, James Lide, Michael Petersen and Daqing Yang, Washington D.C., 2006 (National Archives, College Park, Maryland).

Robison, Neal, "The Japanese Scouting Unknown Soldier Story," *Vanguard Scouting*, 4 February 2021.

Roland, Charles G., "Massacre and Rape in Hong Kong: Two Case Studies Involving Medical Personnel and Patients," *Journal of Contemporary History*, Vol. 32 (I), 43-61, 1997.

Russell, Shahan, "The Tragic Tale of Hajime Fuji: A Kamikaze Fighter Who Crashed Into & Sunk the USS Drexler," *War History Online*, 16 Sept. 2016.

Sanger, David, "New Tokyo Minister Calls 'Rape of Nanking' Fabrication," *NYT*, 5 May 1994.

Spitzer, Kirk, "Apology Question Hounds Obama's Planned Visit to Hiroshima," *USA Today*, 21 May 2016.

Walters, Joanna, "An Evil Family: Sacklers Condemned as They Refuse to Apologize for Role in Opioid Crisis," *Guardian News*, 17 Dec. 2020.

Yoshida, Reiji, "Japan Withholds UNESCO Funding After Nanjing Massacre Row," *Reuters*, 14 Oct. 2016.

BOOKS:

Ang, Armando A., *Brutal Holocaust: Japan's World War II Atrocities and Their Aftermath*, Manila, 2005.

Astroth, Alexander, *Mass Suicides on Saipan and Tinian, 1944*, Jefferson NC, 2019.

Aurthur, Robert A., and Cohlmia, Kenneth, *The Third Marine Division*, Washington D.C., 1948.

Barker, Dan, *Godless: How an Evangelical Preacher Became One of America's Leading Atheists*, Berkeley, 2008.

Berenbaum, Michael, *The World Must Know: The History of the Holocaust as Told in the United States Holocaust Memorial Museum*, Baltimore, 2007.

Barenblatt, Daniel, *A Plague Upon Humanity: The Secret Genocide of Axis Japan's Germ Warfare Operation*, NY, 2004.

Bingham, *Kenneth E., Black Hell: The Story of the 133rd Navy Seabees on Iwo Jima February 19, 1945*, CreateSpace Publishing, 2011.

Birch, Alan and Cole, Martin, *Captive Years: The Occupation of Hong Kong 1941-45*, Hong Kong, 1982.

Bix, Herbert P., *Hirohito and the Making of Modern Japan*, NY, 2000.

Blair, Bobby C., & DeCioccio, John Peter, *Victory at Peleliu: The 81st Infantry Division's Pacific Campaign (Volume 30) (Campaigns and Commanders Series*, Norman, OK, 2014.

Brackman, Arnold C., *The Other Nuremberg: The Untold Story of the Tokyo War Crimes*, NY, 1987.

Bradley, James and Powers, Ron, *Flags of Our Fathers*, NY, 2000.

Bradley, James, *Flyboys: A True Story of Courage*, NY, 2003.

Breuer, William B., *Sea Wolf: A Biography of John D. Bulkeley, USN*, Novato, CA, 1989.

Browne, Courtney, *Tojo: The Last Banzai*, London, 1967.

Browning, Christopher, *Reserve Police Battalion 101 and the Final Solution in Poland*, NY, 1998.

The Teaching of Buddha, Buddhist Promoting Foundation, Tokyo, Japan, 1992.

Burleigh, Michael, *Moral Combat: Good and Evil in World War II*, NY, 2012.

Burrell, Robert S., *The Ghosts of Iwo Jima*, Bryan, TX, 2006.

Butow, Robert J.C., *Tojo and the Coming of the War*, Princeton, 1961.

Cameron, Meribeth E., Mahoney, Thomas H.D., and McReynolds, George E., *China, Japan and the Powers: A History of the Modern Far East*, NY, 1960.

Camp, Dick, *Leatherneck Legends: Conversations with the Marine Corps' Old Breed*, Minneapolis, MN, 2006.

Ch'êng-ên, Wu, *Monkey*, trans. Arthur Waley, NY, 1943.

Chang, Iris, *The Rape of Nanking: The Forgotten Holocaust of World War II*, NY, 1997.

Chang, Jung and Halliday, Jon, *Mao: The Unknown Story*, London, 2006.

Churchill, Winston S., *The Grand Alliance*, NY, 1950.

———. *Memories of the Second World War: An Abridgement of the Six Volumes of The Second World War*, Boston, 1987.

Cohen, R., *Soldiers and Slaves: American POWs Trapped by the Nazis' Final Gamble*, NY, 2005.

Coogan, Michael D., (ed.), *Eastern Religions: Origins, Beliefs, Practices, Holy Texts, Sacred Places*, Oxford, 2005.

Cook, Haruko Taya and Cook, Theodore F., *Japan at War: An Oral History*, NY, 1992.

Cooper, Matthew, *The German Army, 1933–1945: Its Political and Military Failure*, NY, 1978.

Cornwell, John, *Hitler's Pope: The Secret History of Pius XII*, NY, 1999.

Craig, Gordon A., *Germany, 1866–1945*, NY, 1978.

Crowe, David M., *War Crimes, Genocide, and Justice: A Global History*, NY, 2014.

Crowl, Philip A. and Isely, Jeter A., *The U.S. Marines and Amphibious War Its Theory and Its Practice in the Pacific*, Princeton, 1951.

Crowley, James B., *Japan's Quest or Autonomy: National Security and Foreign Policy 1930-1938*, Princeton, 1966.

Dallin, Alexander, *German Rule in Russia 1941-1945: A Study of Occupation Policies*, NY, 1957.

Dallek, Robert, *Franklin D. Roosevelt: A Political Life*, NY, 2017.

Dante Alighieri, *The Divine Comedy of Dante Alighieri: Inferno*, trans. Allen Mandelbaum, NY, 1980.

Dawkins, Richard, *The God Delusion*, NY, 2006.

Dimont, Max I., *Jews, God and History*, NY, 1964.

Divine, Robert A., Breen, T.H., Fredrickson, George M., and Williams, R. Hal, *America: Past and Present*, London, 1987.

Documents on the Tokyo International Military Tribunal Charter, Indictment and Judgements, Boister, Neil and Cryer, Robert (eds.), Oxford, 2008.

Dower, John W., *War Without Mercy: Race & Power in the Pacific War*, NY, 1986.

Drea, Edward J., *Japan's Imperial Army: Its Rise and Fall, 1853-1945*, Kansas, 2009.

Driscoll, Mark, *Absolute Erotic, Absolute Grotesque: The Living, Dead, and Undead in Japan's Imperialism, 1895-1945*, Chapel Hill, 2010.

Edgerton, Robert B., *Warriors of the Rising Sun*, NY, 1997.

Families in the Face of Survival: World War II Japanese Occupation of Guam 1941-1944, Guam War Survivors Memorial Foundation, Guam, 2015.

Farrell, Don A., *Liberation-1944: The Pictorial History of Guam*, Tinian, 1984.

Felton, Mark, *Slaughter at Sea: The Story of Japan's Naval War Crimes*, South Yorkshire, 2007.

Ferguson, Ted, *Desperate Siege: The Battle of Hong Kong*, Scarborough, Ontario, 1980.

Fogel, Joshua A. (ed.), *The Nanjing Massacre in History and Historiography*, Berkeley, 2000.

Frank, Richard B., *Downfall: The End of the Imperial Japanese Empire*, NY, 1999.

————. *Tower of Skulls: A History of the Asia-Pacific War: July 1937-May 1942*, NY, 2020.

Frankl, Victor, *Man's Search for Meaning: An Introduction to Logotherapy*, NY, 1963.

Garand, George W. & Stobridge, Truman R., *Western Pacific Operations: History of U.S. Marine Corps Operations in World War II*, Quantico, 1971.

Giangreco, Dennis M., *Hell to Pay: Operation Downfall and the Invasion of Japan, 1945–1947*, Annapolis, 2009.

Glantz, David M., and House, Jonathan, *When Titans Clashed: How the Red Army Stopped Hitler*, Kansas, 1995.

The Goebbels Diaries, 1942–43, ed. and trans. by Louis P. Lochner, NY, 1948.

Gold, Hal, *Unit 731 Testimony*, Rutland, 1996.

Goldberg, Harold, *D-Day in the Pacific: The Battle of Saipan*, Indiana Univ. Press, 2007.

Gow, Ian, *Military Intervention in Pre-War Japanese Politics: Admiral Katō Kanji and the 'Washington System'*, London, 2004.

Gruhl, Werner, *Imperial Japan's World War Two: 1931-1945*, London, 2007.

Guam War Claims Review Commission: Report on the Implementation of the Guam Meritorious Claims Act of 1945, Guam, 2004.

Haas, Kurt & Haas, Adelaide, *Understanding Sexuality*, New Paltz, NY, 1993.

Hane, Mikiso, *Modern Japan: A Historical Survey*, Oxford, 2001.

Hanley II, Fiske, *Accused War Criminal: An American Kempei Tai Survivor*, Dallas, TX, 2020.

Hardacre, Helen, *Shintō and the State, 1886-1988*, Princeton Univ. Press, 1991.

Harris, Meirion and Harris, Susie, *Soldiers of the Sun: The Rise and Fall of the Imperial Japanese Army*, NY, 1991.

Harris, Sam, *The End of Faith: Religion, Terror, and the Future of Reason*, NY, 2004.

Harris, Sheldon H., *Factories of Death: Japanese Biological Warfare, 1932-1945, and the American Cover-up*, NY, 2002.

Haynes, Fred & Warren, James A., *The Lions of Iwo Jima: The Story of Combat Team 28 and the Bloodiest Battle in Marine Corps History*, NY, 2008.

Henri, Jim G., Beech, W. Keyes, Dempsey, David K., Josephy, Alvin M., and Dunn, Tom, *The U.S. Marines on Iwo Jima*, NY, 1945.

Hilberg, Raul, *Destruction of the European Jews*, NY, 1961.

Hitchens, Christopher, *god is not Great: How Religion Poisons Everything*, NY, 2007.

Hitchens, Christopher, (ed.), *The Portable Atheist: Essential Readings for the Nonbeliever*, NY, 2007.

Hitler, Adolf, *Mein Kampf*, Boston, 1971.

Hoffman, Jon T., *Chesty: The Story of Lieutenant General Lewis B. Puller*, NY, 2001.

———. *Once A Legend: "Red Mike Edson of the Marine Raiders*, Novato, 1994.

Horie, Yoshitaka, *The Memoirs of Fighting Spirit: Major Yoshitaka Horie and the Battle of Iwo Jima*, edited by Robert D. Eldridge and Charles W. Tatum, Annapolis, 2011.

Hough, Frank O., *The Island War: The United States Marine Corps in the Pacific*, NY, 1947.

Hoyt, Edwin P., *Warlord: Tojo Against the World*, Landam, MD, 1993.

Ienaga, Saburō, *The Pacific War: 1931-1945*, NY, 1978.

Jennings, John M., *The Opium Empire: Japanese Imperialism and Drug Trafficking in Asia, 1895-1945*, Westport, CT, 1997.

Kagan, Robert, *Dangerous Nation: America's Place in the World from Its Earliest Days to the Dawn of the Twentieth Century,* NY, 2006.

Kakehashi, Kumiko, *So Sad to Fall in Battle*, NY, 2007.

Keegan, John, *The Second World War*, NY, 1990.

King, Dan, *A Tomb Called Iwo Jima: Firsthand Accounts From Japanese Survivors*, North Charleston, SC, 2014.

Kennedy, Paul, *Engineers of Victory*, NY, 2013.

———. *The Rise and Fall of the Great Powers: Economic Change and Military Conflict from 1500 to 2000*, NY, 1987.

Kershaw, Ian, *Hitler, 1936–1945: Nemesis*, NY, 2000.

Kertzer, David, *The Pope and Mussolini: The Secret History of Pius XI and the Rise of Fascism in Europe*, Oxford, 2014.

Kirchmann, Hans, *Hirohito: Japans letzter Kaiser Der Tenno*, München, 1989.

Krakauer, Jon, *Where Men win Glory: The Odyssey of Pat Tillman*, NY, 2009.

Krulak, Victor H., *First to Fight: An Inside View of the U.S. Marine Corps*, Annapolis, 1999.

Kuhn, Dieter, *Der Zweite Weltkrieg in China*, Berlin, 1999.

Kwong, Chi Man and Tsoi, Yiu Lun, *Eastern Fortress: A Military History of Hong Kong, 1840-1970*, Hong Kong, 2014.

LaFeber, Walter, *The American Age: United States Foreign Policy at Home and Abroad Since 1750*, NY, 1989.

Lai, Benjamin, *Hong Kong 1941-45; First Strike in the Pacific War*, NY, 2014.

Lauren, Paul Gordon, *Power and Prejudice*, London, 1988.

Law Reports of Trials of War Criminals, Vol. III, The United Nations War Crimes Commission, 1948, Trial of General Takashi Sakai.

Linton, Suzannah (ed.), *Hong Kong's War Crimes Trials*, Oxford, 2013.

Maga, Tim, *Judgement at Tokyo: The Japanese War Crimes Trials*, University of Kentucky, 2001.

Manchester, William, *Goodbye Darkness*, NY, 1979.

Mandel, Lee, *Unlikely Warrior: A Pacifist Rabbi's Journey from the Pulpit to Iwo Jima*, Gretna, 2015.

Mansell, Roger, *Captured: The Forgotten Men of Guam*, Annapolis, 2012.

Marsden, George M., *The Twilight of the American Enlightenment: The 1950s and the Crisis of Liberal Belief*, New York, 2014.

Marsman, Jan Henrik, *I Escaped from Hong Kong*, NY, 1942.

Maser, Werner, *Adolf Hitler. Legende Mythos Wirklichkeit*, München, 1971.

McGlothlin, Frank Emile, *Barksdale to Bataan: History of the 48th Materiel Squadron October 1940-April 1942*, 1984.

Melville, Herman, *Moby Dick*, Oxford, 2008.

Millett, Allan R., and Maslowski, Peter, *For the Common Defense: A Military History of the United States of America*, NY, 1984.

Millett, Allan R., *Semper Fidelis: The History of the United States Marine Corps*, NY, 1991.

Modder, Ralph, *The Singapore Chinese Massacre: 18 February to 4 March 1942 Were 5,000 or 50,000 Civilians Executed by the Japanese Army?*, Singapore, 2004.

Moore, Aaron William, *Writing War: Soldiers Record the Japanese Empire*, Cambridge, 2013.

Moskin, J. Robert, *The U.S. Marine Corps Story*, NY, 1992.

Mosley, Leonard, *Hirohito: Emperor of Japan*, NJ, 1966.

Muggenthaler, Karl August, *German Raiders of World War II: The First Complete History of Germany's Mysterious Naval Marauders*, Suffolk, 1978.

Murphy, R. Taggart, *Japan and the Shackles of the Past*, NY, 2014.

The Memorial Hall of the Victims in Nanjing Massacre by Japanese Invaders, Informational Booklet by Museum, London Editions (LTD), 2010.

Newcomb, Richard F., *Iwo Jima*, NY, 1965.

O'Brien, Cyril J., *Liberation: Marines in the Recapture of Guam*, World War II Commemorative Series, Marine Corps Historical Center, Washington D.C., 1994.

O'Brien, Phillips Payson, *The Second Most Powerful Man in the World: The Life of Admiral William D. Leahy, Roosevelt's Chief of Staff*, NY, 2019.

O'Donnell, Patrick K., *Into the Rising Sun: World War II's Pacific Veterans Reveal the Heart of Combat*, NY, 2002.

Oliver, Robert T., *A History of the Korean People in Modern Times: 1800 to the Present*, Newark, 1993.

Olson, Lyne, *Those Angry Days: Roosevelt, Lindbergh, and America's Fight Over World War II, 1939-1941*, NY 2013.

Owen, Frank, *The Fall of Singapore*, NY, 2001.

Paterson Thomas A. (ed.), *Major Problems in American Foreign Policy: Volume II: Since 1914*, Third Edition, Lexington, MA, 1989.

Patterson, James T., *American in the Twentieth Century: A History—Third Edition*, Orlando, 1976.

Picker, Henry, *Hitlers Tischgespräche im Führerhauptquartier, 1941–42*, ed. Percy Ernst Schramm, Stuttgart, 1976.

Potter, John Deane, *The Life and Death of a Japanese General*, NY, 1962.

Prange, Gordon W., *At Dawn We Slept: The Untold Story of Pearl Harbor*, NY, 1981.

Redlich, Fritz, *Hitler: Diagnosis of a Destructive Prophet*, Oxford, 1998.

Rhodes, Richard, *The Making of the Atomic Bomb*, NY, 1986.

Rigg, Bryan Mark, *Hitler's Jewish Soldiers: The Untold Story of Nazi Racial Laws and Men of Jewish Descent in the German Military*, Kansas, 2002.

———. *Lives of Hitler's Jewish Soldiers: Untold Tales of Men of Jewish Descent Who Fought for the Third Reich*, Kansas, 2009.

———. *The Rabbi Saved by Hitler's Soldiers: Rebbe Joseph Isaac Schneersohn and His Astonishing Rescue*, Kansas, 2016.

Roberts, Andrew, *Churchill: Walking with Destiny*, NY, 2018.

———. *The Storm of War: A New History of World War II*, NY, 2012.

Robertson, Jennifer E., *Politics and Pitfalls of Japan Ethnography: Reflexivity, Responsibility, and Anthropological Ethics*, NY, 2009.

Rodriguez, Robyn L., *Journey to the East: The German Military Mission in China, 1927-1938*, PhD Dissertation, Ohio State University, 2011.

Rogers, Robert F., *Destiny's Landfall: A History of Guam*, Univ. of Hawaii Press, 1995.

Ross, Bill D., *Iwo Jima: Legacy of Valor*, NY, 1985.

Russell, Edward Frederick Langley (known as Lord Russell of Liverpool), *The Knights of Bushido: A History of Japanese Crimes During World War II*, NY, 2016.

Sakai, Saburo with Caidin, Martin and Saito, Fred, *Samurai!: The Unforgettable Saga of Japan's Greatest Fighter Pilot—The Legendary Angel of Death*, NY, 1975.

Samuels, Richard J., *Machiavelli's Children: Leaders and Their Legacies in Italy and Japan*, Cornell Univ. Press, 2005.

Sasser, Charles, *Two Fronts, One War: Dramatic Eyewitness Accounts of Major Events in the European and Pacific Theaters of Operations on Land, Sea and Air in WWII*, London, 2014.

Schappes, Morris U. (ed.), *A Documentary History of the Jews in the United States 1654-1875*, NY, 1950.

Scott, James M., *Rampage: MacArthur, Yamashita, and the Battle of Manila*, NY, 2018.

Shelton, Dinah (ed.), *Encyclopedia of Genocide and Crimes of Humanity*, NY, 2005.

Shu-Fan, Li, *Hong Kong Surgeon*, NY, 1964.

Skya, Walter A., *Japan's Holy War: The Ideology of Radical Shintō Ultranationalism*, Duke Univ. Press, 2009.

Sledge, E. B., *With the Old Breed: At Peleliu and Okinawa*, NY, 1981.

Smith, Holland M., *Coral and Brass*, Arcadia, 2017.

Smith, Larry, *Iwo Jima: World War II Veterans Remember the Greatest Battle of the Pacific*, NY, 2008.

Smith, Seven B., *Spinoza, Liberalism, and the Question of Jewish Identity*, New Haven, 1997.

Snow, Philip, *The Fall of Hong Kong: Britain, China and the Japanese Occupation*, New Haven, 2003.

Snyder, Louis L., *Encyclopedia of the Third Reich*, NY, 1989.

Soldiers Guide to the Japanese Army, Military Intel Service, War Dept., Washington D.C., 15 Nov. 1944.

Spector, Ronald H., *Eagle Against the Sun: The American War Against Japan*, NY, 1985.

Speer, Albert, *Inside the Third Reich*, NY, 1970.

Spence, Jonathan, *The Search for Modern China*, NY, 1990.

Stalecker, Gene E., *Rolling Thunder*, Mechanicsburg, PA, 2008.

Steinberg, Jonathan, *All or Nothing: The Axis and the Holocaust 1941-1943*, NY, 1991.

Steinberg, Rafael, *Island Fighting*, Alexandria Virginia (Time Life Books), 1978.

Stoltzfus, Nathan, *Resistance of the Heart: Intermarriage and the Rosenstrasse Protest in Nazi Germany*, NY, 1996.

Synder, Timothy, *Bloodlands: Between Hitler and Stalin*, NY, 2010.

Tanaka, Yuki, *Hidden Horrors: Japanese War Crimes in World War II*, Lanham, MD, 2018.

Thompson, Paul W., Doud, Harold, and Scofield, John, *How the Jap Army Fights*, NY, 1942.

Tokayer, Marvin, *The Fugu Plan*, NY, 1979.

Toland, John, *The Rising Sun: The Decline and Fall of the Japanese Empire 1936-1945, Vol. I-II*, NY, 1970.

Toll, Ian W., *The Conquering Tide: War in the Pacific Islands, 1942-1944*, NY, 2015.

———. *Pacific Crucible: War at Sea in the Pacific, 1941-1942*, NY, 2012.

Totani, Yuma, *The Tokyo War Crimes Trial: The Pursuit of Justice in the Wake of World War II* (Cambridge, MA, 2008).

Trevor-Roper, R., *The Last Days of Hitler*, NY, 1947.

Tsuchiya, Koken, *The Asian Holocaust 1931-1945: Hidden Holocaust of World War II by the Japanese Army*, Tokyo, 1998.

Tuchman, Barbara, *Stilwell and the American Experience in China 1911-45*, NY, 1971.

Van Ness, C. P., *Exploding the Japanese Superman Myth*, Washington D.C., 1942.

Victoria, Brian Daizen, *Zen at War*, NY, 2006.

———. *Zen War Stories*, NY, 2004.

von Clausewitz, Carol, *On War*, (eds.) Howard, Michael & Paret, Peter, Princeton, NJ, 1976.

von Lang, Jochen, *The Secretary: Martin Bornmann*, NY, 1979.

Wakabayashi, Bob Tadashi (edited), *The Nanking Atrocity, 1937-38: Complicating the Picture*, NY, 2017.

Wallace, David and Williams, Peter, *Unit 731: Japan's Secret Biological Warfare in World War II*, NY, 1989.

Weinberg, Gerhard, *A World at Arms: A Global History of World War II*, NY, 1999.

Weiner, Michael (ed.), *Race, Ethnicity and Migration in Modern Japan*, NY, 2004.

Yagami, Kazuo, *Konoe Fumimaro and the Failure of Peace in Japan, 1937-1941: A Critical Appraisal of the Three-time Prime Minister*, Jefferson NC, 2006.

Yahara, Hiromichi, *The Battle for Okinawa*, NY, 1985.

Yahil, Leni, *The Holocaust*, Tel Aviv, 1987.

Yoshida, Takashi, *The Making of the 'Rape of Nanking': History and Memory in Japan, China, and the United States*, Oxford, 2006.

Yoshimi, Yoshiaki and O'Brien, Suzanne, *Comfort Women*, NY, 2002.

Zabel, Mortan Dauwen (Ed.), *The Portable Conrad*, "Heart of Darkness," NY, 1976.

Zeiler, Thomas W., *Unconditional Defeat: Japan, America, and the End of World War II*, Wilmington, DE, 2004.

Zich, Arthur, *The Rising Sun*, Alexandria, Virginia (Time Life Books), 1977.

ENDNOTES

1   "The Academy's Mission and Values." https://www.exeter.edu/about-us/academy-mission.

2   Although Chang did an excellent job of getting this story out about the Rape of Nanking, her book is full of mistakes and needs to be used with caution. See Bob Tadashi Wakabayashi (ed.), *The Nanking Atrocity, 1937-38*: Complicating the Picture," NY, 2017; *The Nanking Atrocity, 1937-38*, Wakabayashi, "Iris Chang Reassessed," xxi-lii & Akira, "The Nanking Atrocity: An Interpretive Overview," 34; Aaron William Moore, *Writing War: Soldiers Record the Japanese Empire*, Cambridge, 2013, 268.

3   *The Memorial Hall of the Victims in Nanjing Massacre by Japanese Invaders*, Informational Booklet by Museum, London Editions (LTD), 2010, Inside Flap.

4   Arnold C. Brackman, *The Other Nuremberg: The Untold Story of the Tokyo War Crimes*, NY, 1987, 171. Amateur historian and former NASA Chief of Cost and Economic Analysis, Werner Gruhl, also uses this term "Holocaust" to describe what Japan did in *Imperial Japan's World War Two: 1931-1945*, London, 2007. Gruhl, 7, 223.

5   Armando A. Ang, *Brutal Holocaust: Japan's World War II Atrocities and Their Aftermath*, Manila, 2005; Koken Tsuchiya, *The Asian Holocaust 1931-1945: Hidden Holocaust of World War II by the Japanese Army*, Tokyo, 1998.

6   United States Congress, House Committee on Ways and Means, April 18-May 14, 1945, p. 1075.

7   Haruko Taya Cook & Theodore F. Cook, *Japan at War: An Oral History*, NY, 1992, 25.

8   Christopher Browning, *Reserve Police Battalion 101 and the Final Solution in Poland*, NY, 1998.

9   Yuki Tanaka, *Hidden Horrors: Japanese War Crimes in World War II*, Lanham, MD, 2018, xii.

10   Cook & Cook, 10-1.

11   IJA was called "Imperial" to connect the army to the emperor. It has also been used as an apologist term, which is not the intent when used here. In

other words, some Japanese today say it was the Imperial warlords who committed crimes during the Pacific War and not Japan to whitewash its crimes. Edward J. Drea, *Japan's Imperial Army: Its Rise and Fall, 1853-1945*, Kansas, 2009, 161; Review of *Flamethrower* by Robert Burrell, 26 Feb. 2018.

12   The Founding Era Collection, Thomas Jefferson Papers, Docs. Jan. 1819–4 July 1836, Jefferson to Henry Lee, 15 May 1826.

13   Editorial Board, "A Lesson From the Holocaust: Never Stop Telling the Terrible Stories," *Chicago Tribune*, 12 April 2018.

14   Barbara Tuchman, *Stilwell and the American Experience in China 1911-45*, NY, 1971, 178; Richard B. Frank, *Tower of Skulls: A History of the Asia-Pacific War: July 1937-May 1942*, NY, 2020, 52. After the battle, many IJA soldiers took their films to Shanghai shops to have them developed. Shop keepers made sure copies of the horrific pictures made their way to western correspondents. Tuchman, 178.

15   Dante Alighieri, *The Divine Comedy of Dante Alighieri: Inferno*, trans. Allen Mandelbaum, NY, 1980, Canto IV 31, 7–8.

16   Dante, *Inferno*, Canto V 45, 90.

17   Ibid., Canto III 23, 56-57.

18   Tanaka, 1.

19   Michael Burleigh, *Moral Combat: Good and Evil in World War II*, NY, 2012, 12; Leonard Mosely, *Hirohito: Emperor of Japan*, NJ, 1966, 95; Herbert P. Bix, *Hirohito and the Making of Modern Japan*, NY, 2000, 171.

20   Robert B. Edgerton, *Warriors of the Rising Sun*, NY, 1997, 271; Drea, 137; Richard B. Frank, *Downfall: The End of the Imperial Japanese Empire*, NY, 1999, 88.

21   Quote is from Drea, vii. See *Researching Japanese War Crimes Records: Introductory Essays*, Edward Drea, Greg Bradsher, Robert Hanyok, James Lide, Michael Petersen and Daqing Yang, Wash. D.C., 2006; *Documents on the Tokyo International Military Tribunal Charter, Indictment and Judgements*, Neil Boister & Robert Cryer (eds.), Oxford, 2008; The Second Historical Archives of China, Nanjing, China, Memory of the World: Documents of Nanjing Massacre (TSHACNCDNM), Vol. 10, 295, Statement Joseph B. Keenan, Chief of Counsel, International Military Tribunal for the Far East, 4 June 1945, 33; Wakabayashi (ed.), *The Nanking Atrocity, 1937-38*, Akira, "The Nanking Atrocity: An Interpretive Overview," 29; Meirion Harries and Susie Harries, *Soldiers of the Sun: The Rise and Fall of the Imperial Japanese Army*, NY, 1991, 142. Often historians start chronicling Japan's aggressive acts with 1931 in Manchuria forgetting it had already deployed troops and committed crimes in China starting in 1927.

22   Quote comes from James B. Crowley, *Japan's Quest or Autonomy: National Security and Foreign Policy 1930-38*, Princeton, 1966, xiii. See Drea, 1; Harries & Harries, 5, 10–11.

23   R. Taggart Murphy, *Japan and the Shackles of the Past*, NY, 2014, 73.

24   Murphy, 53-4; Mark Driscoll, *Absolute Erotic, Absolute Grotesque: The Living, Dead, and Undead in Japan's Imperialism, 1895-45*, Chapel Hill, 2010, x; Jonathan Spence, *The Search for Modern China*, NY, 1990, 155-9; Moore, 5; Harries & Harries, 8.

25   Mikiso Hane, *Modern Japan: A Historical Survey*, Oxford, 2001, 77; Harries & Harries, 8, 18.

26   Paul Kennedy, *Engineers of Victory*, NY, 2013, 284; Drea, 7, 15; Tanaka, 237, 242.

27   Helen Hardacre, *Shintō and the State, 1886-1988*, Princeton, 1991, 123-31.

28   Drea, 38.

29   Murphy, 74; Eugen Weber's *Peasants into Frenchmen: The Modernization of Rural France, 1870-1914*.

30   Quote from Crowley, xiii; 176; Drea, 29; Harries & Harries, 19.

31   Drea, 7–8, 10–34; Harries & Harries, 13–17, 30–1; Moore, 22.

32   Harries & Harries, 19. These missionaries promulgated the "Three Great Principles": 1) "love of country," 2) "reverence for the Emperor," and 3) "obedience to the will of the Court."

33   Quote comes from Meribeth E. Cameron, Thomas H.D. Mahoney, and George E. McReynolds, *China, Japan and the Powers: A History of the Modern Far East*, NY, 1960, 537-8. See also Burleigh, 12; Drea, 134; Interview Morgan, 10 Dec. 2017.

34   Many ideas explored here come from Richard Dawkins and Christopher Hitchens. Richard Dawkins, *The God Delusion*, NY, 2006, 37-9; Christopher Hitchens (ed.), The Portable Atheist: Essential Readings for the Nonbeliever, NY, 2007, Hitchens, "Introduction," xvii-xviii & Introduction to Omar Khayyam by Hitchens, 7. See also Harries & Harries, 4; John Toland, *The Rising Sun: The Decline and Fall of the Japanese Empire 1936-1945, Vol. I*, NY, 1970, 30.

35   Seven B. Smith, *Spinoza, Liberalism, and the Question of Jewish Identity*, New Haven, 1997, 30.

36   Drea, viii, 29.

37   Brian Daizen Victoria, *Zen at War*, NY, 2006, xiv.

38   Tanaka, 237.

39   Leonard Mosley, *Hirohito: Emperor of Japan*, NJ, 1966, 131.

40   Drea, 31; Hardacre, 122; Hane, 33, 66; Crowley, 86; Burleigh, 12; Cook & Cook, 217; NACPM, RG 165, Box 2153, War Dept., 6910 (Japan), Memo on Japanese Vulnerability, Tradition (a); Edward Rice, *Ten Religions of the East*, NY, 1978, 116; Michael D. Coogan (ed.), *Eastern Religions: Origins, Beliefs, Practices, Holy Texts, Sacred Places*, Oxford, 2005, 446; Burleigh, 12; Mosley, 32, 102, 131-3; Bix, xvi, 2, 7, 16.

41   Murphy, 73; Michael D. Coogan (ed.), *Eastern Religions: Origins, Beliefs, Practices, Holy Texts, Sacred Places*, Oxford, 2005, 420-1, 440, 464; Cook & Cook, 232, 309, 328; Drea, 154; Mosley, 17-8, 99; Bix, xv; Smith, *Spinoza*, 31; Saburō Ienaga, *The Pacific War, 1931-1945: A Critical Perspective on Japan's Role in World War II*, NY, 1978, 180., 21-2.

42   NACPM, Microfilm Room, Roll 1499, #86, To: The A.C. of S., G-2, War Dept., Wash. D.C. (26 June 1942), Subj.: 'The Imperial Forces Will Surely Win,' Adm. Kato, 1933; Ian Gow, *Military Intervention in Pre-War Japanese Politics: Admiral Katō Kanji and the 'Washington System,'* London, 2004, 1.

43   NACPM, Microfilm Room, Roll 1499, #86, To: The A.C. of S., G-2, War Dept., Wash. D.C. (26 June 1942), Subj: 'The Imperial Forces Will Surely Win,' Admiral Kato, 1933.

44   Murphy, 75; Coogan, 420-2, 428-9; Crowley, 86; Rice, 122.

45   Coogan, 423; Victoria, *Zen at War*, 11.

46   Victoria, *Zen at War*, 12.

47   Cook & Cook, 238-9.

48   Smith, *Spinoza*, 95.

49   Ibid., 3.

50   Ibid., 20.

51   Victoria, *Zen at War*, 192-3, 223; Ienaga, 123.

52   Victoria, *Zen at War*, xiv.

53   Ibid., 78, 80.

54   Ibid., 82.

55   Ibid., 91, 104-5.

56   James Bradley, *Flyboys: A True Story of Courage*, NY, 2003, 16-7; Edgerton, 310; Coogan, 465; Winston S. Churchill, *The Grand Alliance*, NY, 1950, 579; Duncan Bartlett, "Japan Looks Back on 17th-Century Persecutions," *BBC News*, 24 Nov. 2008; NACPM, Trial of Col. Ryoichi Tazuka (typist in document misspelled Tazuka's name Tozuga), SC 249223, 27 June 1946 & SC 203673-S; Edward Frederick Langley Russell (Lord Russell of Liverpool), *The Knights of Bushido: A History of Japanese Crimes During World War II*, NY, 2016, 260-1; Victoria, *Zen at War*, xiv. A note about James Bradley—he put together two interesting books with *Flyboys* and *Flags of Our Fathers*. However, he is not a trained historian, and he makes numerous mistakes. He does cite interesting facts and when appropriate, he is cited here, but his books need to be used with caution.

57   Victoria, *Zen at War*, 25, 91, 152, 154, 156, 167.

58   Ibid., 88.

59   Ibid.

60   Tanaka, 243.

61   Harries & Harries, 480.

62   Bix, 21. Hirohito took the throne on 25 Dec. 1925. A few days later, he took the name *Shōwa*, meaning "illustrious peace." Burleigh, 12; Mosley, 95; Bix, 171.

63   Bix, 39.

64   Bix, 119-121. Bix's biography is superior to Mosley's whose work needs to be used with caution. Historian Drea says Mosley's work is seriously flawed. Interview Drea, 17 Dec. 2017.

65   The quotes come from Bix, xvi, 8, 12, 387. See also Burleigh, 12; Drea, 52, 164; Cook & Cook, 442.

66   Quote comes from Bix, 8. See also Toland, *The Rising Sun*, Vol. I, 29. Historians Meirion and Susie Harries wrote: "[A]s part of the…constitution, it had been agreed that the Emperor possessed two separate military powers: *gunrei*, the power of command…and *gunsei*, the power of military administration." Harries & Harries, 37; David Wallace and Peter Williams, *Unit 731: Japan's Secret Biological Warfare in World War II*, NY, 1989, 79-80 (While there is a lot of good information in Wallace's and Williams' work, both historians Edward Drea and Richard Frank feel there are several mistakes and sloppy research done for this book. It should be used with caution); *Materials on the Trial of Former Servicemen of the Japanese army Charged with Manufacturing and Employing Bacteriological Weapons*, Foreign Languages Publishing House, Moscow, 1950, 283. Historian Richard Frank cautions researchers to be careful using Soviet material because of how Russian interrogators usually got their confessions from their prisoners. Notes on manuscript by Richard Frank, 3 March 2023.

67   Lord Russell of Liverpool, xv; *Documents on the Tokyo International Military Tribunal Charter*, xlvi.

68   Herbert P. Bix, *Hirohito and the Making of Modern Japan*, NY, 2000, 1-40.

69   Lord Russell of Liverpool, xv.

70   Quote comes from Drea, viii. See also Lord Russell of Liverpool, 38. Drea, "Introduction," in *Researching Japanese War Crimes Records*, 15; Victoria, *Zen at War*, 230; Tanaka, xii.

71   Victoria, *Zen at War*, xi, 3, 10, 13, 30, 81, 134; Hane, 7-9, 14; TSHACNCDNM, Vol. 2, 214, 221-2 from H. J. Timperley, *What War Means: The Japanese Terror in China*, London, 1938, 164. Timperley was a paid propagandist for the Nationalists' International Propaganda Division and may have falsified numbers. However, the crimes in general he described occurred. Wakabayashi (ed.), *The Nanking Atrocity, 1937-38*, Askew, "Part of the Numbers Issue: Demography and Civilian Victims," 97; Harries & Harries, 4, 7, 44; Ian Toll, *Pacific Crucible: War at Sea in the Pacific, 1941-1942*, NY, 2012, 64; Email Drea to Rigg, 17 Jan. 2020.

72   Victoria, *Zen at War*, 3; Hane, 7-9.

73   Victoria, *Zen at War*, 15.

74   John W. Dower, *War Without Mercy: Race & Power in the Pacific War*, NY, 1986, 130; Bix, 10' Victor Frankl, *Man's Search for Meaning: An Introduction to Logotherapy*, NY, 1963, 155; Cook & Cook, 14-5.

75   Hane, 362.

76   Quote from Ralph Modder, *The Singapore Chinese Massacre: 18 February to 4 March 1942 Were 5,000 or 50,000 Civilians Executed by the Japanese Army?*, Singapore, 2004, 28. See also Toll, *Pacific Crucible*, 115.

77   Adolf Hitler, *Mein Kampf*, Boston, 1971, 290–1; Toll, *Pacific Crucible*, 115.

78   Albert Speer's *Inside the Third Reich*, NY, 1970,145.

79   Interview with Hans Baur by Colin Heaton, 1984; *Hitler's Tischgespräche im Führerhauptquartier*, Einführung von Picker, 310, 398 n. 388; *The Goebbels Diaries, 1942–43*, ed. and trans. by Louis P. Lochner, NY, 1948, 51, 60, 77, 79, 86, 91, 138; Raul Hilberg, *Destruction of the European Jews*, NY, 1961, 45; Paul Gordon Lauren, *Power and Prejudice*, London, 1988, 124; Nathan Stoltzfus, *Resistance of the Heart: Intermarriage and the Rosenstrasse Protest in Nazi Germany*, NY, 1996, 42; Leni Yahil, *The Holocaust*, Tel Aviv, 1987, 71; Louis L. Snyder, *Encyclopedia of the Third Reich*, NY, 1989, 170; Gordon A. Craig, *Germany, 1866–1945*, NY, 1978, 696; R. Trevor-Roper, *The Last Days of Hitler*, NY, 1947, 21–2; Otto Klineberg, "Racialism in Nazi Germany," in *The Third Reich*, ed. Maurice Baumont, John H. E. Fried and Edmond Vermeil, NY, 1955, 859; Fritz Redlich, *Hitler: Diagnosis of a Destructive Prophet*, Oxford, 1998, 149; Ian Kershaw, *Hitler, 1936–1945: Nemesis*, NY, 2000, 504; Rigg, *Hitler's Jewish Soldiers*, 184; Burleigh, 13.

80   Interview with Karl Wolff by Colin Heaton, 1984.

81   UGSL, J. Alton Hosch Papers, Tokyo War Crimes Trials, The Military Domination of Japan and Preparation of War (Vol. 2), 519. U.S. Secretary of State Cordell Hull noted the Tripartite Pact created a partnership "enabling Hitler to take charge of one-half of the world and Japan the other half." Toland, Vol. I, 175; Bix, 380.

82   BA-MA, RM 11/69, Deutsche Botschaft, Der Marineattaché an den Chef der Marineleitung z. Hd. Herrn Kapitänleutnant von der Forst Reichswehrministerium, Betrifft: Judenfrage in der japanisschen Marine, 13.05.1935, bl. 1-2; Marvin Tokayer, *The Fugu Plan*, NY, 1979.

83   Bix, 280-1.

84   Ibid., 281.

85   BA-MA, RM 11/69, Deutsche Botschaft, Der Marineattaché an den Chef der Marineleitung z. Hd. Herrn Kapitänleutnant von der Forst Reichswehrministerium, Betrifft: Judenfrage in der japanisschen Marine, 13.05.1935, bl. 1-2; Marvin Tokayer, *The Fugu Plan*, NY, 1979.

86 Tuchman, 186; Robyn L. Rodriguez, *Journey to the East: The German Military Mission in China, 1927-1938*, PhD Dissertation, Ohio State Univ., 2011, 136.

87 BA-MA, BMRS, Interview Elisabeth Borchardt, 18 Feb. 1995.

88 Edgerton, 308-9.

89 Toland, Vol. I, 375; Tanaka, 80; Ienaga, 51-2.

90 Sakai, 3, 8. See also Modder, 21; Tanaka, 243; *Hong Kong's War Crimes Trials*, Daqun, "Forward," vi & Linton, "Major Murray Ormsby: War Crimes Judge and Prosecutor 1919-2012," 226.

91 Tanaka, 239. See also Hiromichi Yahara, *The Battle for Okinawa*, NY, 1985, Commentary by Frank B. Gibney, "Two Views of Battle," xix; Ienaga, 51-2.

92 Cook & Cook, 318.

93 Suzannah Linton (ed.), *Hong Kong War Crimes Trials*, Oxford, 2013, Daqun, "Forward," vi & Linton, "Major Murray Ormsby: War Crimes Judge and Prosecutor 1919-2012," 226; Paul W. Thompson, Harold Doud, and John Scofield, *How the Jap Army Fights*, NY, 1942, 13; Crowley, 86; Kennedy, *Rise and Fall of Great Powers*, 301; James Bradley and Ron Powers, *Flags of Our Fathers*, NY, 2000, 40; Bix, 55.

94 Notes on manuscript from Richard Frank, 25 Feb. 2023. Special thanks to Frank for the concepts and phraseology used above.

95 Quote comes from Saburo Sakai, *Samurai!: The Unforgettable Saga of Japan's Greatest Fighter Pilot—The Legendary Angel of Death*, New York, 1975, 3, 8. See also Harries & Harries, 7.

96 Bradley & Powers, *Flags of Our Fathers*, 137. See also Harries & Harries, 7.

97 Richard B. Frank, *Downfall: The End of the Imperial Japanese Empire*, NY, 1999, 28.

98 Dan King, *A Tomb Called Iwo Jima: Firsthand Accounts From Japanese Survivors*, Charleston, SC, 2014, 68, 70; Burleigh, 20; Cook & Cook, 318; Drea, 33, 68, 134-5, 161; Bix, 51-2; Takashi Yoshida, *The Making of the 'Rape of Nanking': History and Memory in Japan, China, and the United States*, Oxford, 2006, 18; Tanaka, 239; Toll, *Pacific Crucible*, 96; Moore, 189, 194; Frank, *Tower of Skulls*, 57; Modder, 21; Harries & Harries, 421.

99 Mosley, 99. Supposedly teachers who made similar mistakes of stumbling "over the words" of an Imperial rescript as the officer mentioned in the text did also committed suicide. Harries & Harries, 41.

100 Quote is from Edgerton, 310. See also Bradley, *Flyboys*, 16-7; Coogan, 465; Dower, 46. *Gaizin* or *Gaijin* can mean simply foreigner, and today, that is how many Japanese view the term. However, it can also be used as meaning non-human and during Fascist Japan, that is what it meant.

101 Cook & Cook, 153, 155, 325.

102 Dower, 46.

103   Takashi Yoshida, 40.
104   Dower, 126.
105   Cook & Cook 40-4; Toll, *Pacific Crucible*, 112.
106   Cook & Cook, 42, 464.
107   Ibid., 42.
108   Cook & Cook 43; Toll, *Pacific Crucible*, 112.
109   Cook & Cook 43; Toll, *Pacific Crucible*, 112.
110   Cook & Cook, 42.
111   Lord Russell of Liverpool, 239.
112   NACPM, 208-AA-132T-23 & 25 (on the typewritten backs of the photo-graphs cited by the U.S. Authority, see 43150-FA and 43152-FA). On some of the photographs, the reference number is 208-AA-132S-25. Smith, *Coral and Brass*, 104; Moore, 170; Cook & Cook, 44.
113   Toland, Vol. I, 375.
114   Ienaga, 49.
115   Ibid.
116   Edgerton, 241-2; NACPM, 127 Box 14 (3d MarDiv), HQ Div, FMF, Intel Bulletin #4-44, Capt. D. Whipple, Intel Technique on Attu, 3; Drea, 120; Bix, 251; Moore, 77.
117   Bix, 251; Yahara, *The Battle for Okinawa*, NY, 1985, Commentary Frank B. Gibney, "Two Views of Battle,", xxii; Ienaga, 49.
118   Frank, *Tower of Skulls*, 121.
119   Quote from Edgerton, 310; Toland, Vol. I, 375; Yahara, *The Battle for Okinawa*, NY, 1985, Commentary Gibney, "Two Views of Battle," xvi.
120   Lord Russell of Liverpool, 120.
121   Lord Russell of Liverpool, 120. National Archives, College Park Maryland, International Military Tribunal For the Far East, Transcripts of Proceedings 13 Jan. 1947, 14,949-15,106, 14,993-4.
122   Lord Russell of Liverpool, 121; National Archives, College Park Maryland, International Military Tribunal For the Far East, Transcripts of Proceedings 13 Jan. 1947, 14,949-15,106, 14,998-9; Edgerton, 263.
123   R. Cohen, *Soldiers and Slaves: American POWs Trapped by the Nazis' Final Gamble*, NY, 2005; Lord Russell of Liverpool, 57, 72, 76, 235-6.; Interview Marty Morgan, 10 Dec. 2017; Frank, *Tower of Skulls*, 309; Cook & Cook, 110.
124   Bix, 360.
125   Frank, *Tower of Skulls*, 391.
126   Frank, *Tower of Skulls*, 420. The act described here against these POWs put Lt. General Hitoshi Imamura, the 16th Army commander, on trial after the war and he was sentenced to ten years in prison.

127 Mosley, 133; Cook & Cook, 78; Bix, 365; Hans Kirchmann, *Hirohito: Japans letzter Kaiser Der Tenno*, München, 1989, 65.

128 Smith, *Spinoza*, 45.

129 Crowley, 86; Bradley & Powers, 37; Review *Flamethrower*, Burrell, 26 Feb. 2018.

130 Lord Russell of Liverpool, 3-4.

131 *Materials on the Trial of Former Servicemen of the Japanese army Charged with Manufacturing and Employing Bacteriological Weapons*, 8.

132 Toll, *Pacific Crucible*, 109.

133 Toll, *Pacific Crucible*, 109. See also Ienaga, 5 for some history on these ideas.

134 Quote comes from Meribeth E. Cameron, Thomas H.D. Mahoney, and George E. McReynolds, *China, Japan and the Powers: A History of the Modern Far East*, NY, 1960, 537-8. See also Burleigh, 12; Drea, 134; Interview Morgan, 10 Dec. 2017.

135 Quote from Dower, 207, 217, 269. See also Hane, 33; Coogan, 419; Lord Russell of Liverpool, 13; Modder, viii.

136 Crowley, 203; Mosley, 126-9, 131-2; Lord Russell of Liverpool, 286-7. Araki also supported chemical and biological warfare. Wallace & Williams, 8. See also Tuchman, 145.

137 Victoria, *Zen at War*, 117-27.

138 Ibid., 117-9, 121.

139 Hitler, 65; Hilberg, *Destruction of the European Jews*; BA-B, NS 19/3134, Bl. 1-2; Werner Maser, *Adolf Hitler. Legende Mythos Wirklichkeit*, München, 1971, 282; Henry Picker, *Hitlers Tischgespräche im Führerhauptquartier, 1941–42*, ed. Percy Ernst Schramm, Stuttgart, 1976, 45; Jochen von Lang, *The Secretary: Martin Bornmann*, NY, 1979, 156; Max I. Dimont, *Jews, God and History*, NY, 1964, 331-32; Bryan Mark Rigg, *Lives of Hitler's Jewish Soldiers: Untold Tales of Men of Jewish Descent Who Fought for the Third Reich*, Kansas, 2009, 238; Rigg, *Hitler's Jewish Soldiers*, 185; David Kertzer, *The Pope and Mussolini: The Secret History of Pius XI and the Rise of Fascism in Europe*, Oxford, 2014, 50-1, 58, 106, 109, 280, 404; Dawkins, 274; Christopher Hitchens, *god is not Great: How Religion Poisons Everything*, NY, 2007, 240; John Cornwell, *Hitler's Pope: The Secret History of Pius XII*, NY, 1999, 7, 137, 199-215.

140 Victoria, *Zen at War*, 116, 125.

141 Toll, *Pacific Crucible*, 115.

142 Michael Weiner (ed.), *Race, Ethnicity and Migration in Modern Japan*, NY, 2004, Weiner, "Race, Nation and Empire," 8; Toll, *Pacific Crucible*, 115; Cook & Cook, 48.

143 Weiner (ed.), *Race, Ethnicity and Migration in Modern Japan*, Weiner, "Race, Nation and Empire," 8.

144 Weiner (ed.), *Race, Ethnicity and Migration in Modern Japan*, Louise Young, "Rethinking Race for Manchukuo: Self and Other in the Colonial Context," 280; Harries & Harries, 95; Walter LaFeber, *The American Age: United States Foreign Policy at Home and Abroad Since 1750*, NY, 1989, 427; Phillips Payson O'Brien, *The Second Most Powerful Man in the World: The Life of Admiral William D. Leahy, Roosevelt's Chief of Staff*, NY, 2010, 33.

145 Interview Jerry Yellin, 6 July 2017; Robert Dallek, *Franklin D. Roosevelt: A Political Life*, NY, 2017, 444; NMPWANM, 13 July 2017.

146 Drea, 259.

147 Harries & Harries, 3.

148 Robert J.C. Butow, *Tojo and the Coming of the War*, Princeton, 1961, 41.

149 Bix, 8-10; Robert Kagan, *Dangerous Nation: America's Place in the World from Its Earliest Days to the Dawn of the Twentieth Century*, NY, 2006, 294; Ienaga, 7; Tuchman, 30.

150 Quote comes from Wakabayashi (ed.), *The Nanking Atrocity, 1937-38*, Fogel, "The Nanking Atrocity and Chinese Historical Memory," 282. See also Harries & Harries, 60; Drea, 86.

151 Harries & Harries, 60; Drea, 86.

152 Ienaga, 23.

153 Harries & Harries, 68.

154 Ienaga, 7.

155 Ibid., 159.

156 Drea, 109; Harries & Harries, 89, 91. Steam-powered ships were also used at the Manila and Santiago battles during the Spanish-American War in 1898, but these were near land and in ports and not in an open ocean conflict.

157 Drea, 109; Mosley, 14; Bix, 9; Kagan, 294-5; Churchill, *The Grand Alliance*, 580.

158 Harries & Harries, 92, 99-100; Bradley, *Flyboys*, 31.

159 Ienaga, 156.

160 Ienaga, 158; Harries & Harries, 309.

161 Ienaga, 8.

162 Cook & Cook, 173; Harries & Harries, 99-100, 127, 235; Drea, 232; Ienaga, 158-9; John Toland, *The Rising Sun: The Decline and Fall of the Japanese Empire 1936-1945, Vol. II*, NY, 1970, 898.

163 Ienaga, 158.

164 Cook & Cook, 173, 387.

165 Ibid., 192-3.

166 Harries & Harries, 309.

167 Ibid., 75.

168 Tuchman, 46, 48.

169 Kennedy, *Engineers of Victory*, 284; Frank, "Review *Flamethrower*," 25 May 2017.

170 O'Brien, 33-4.

171 Ibid., 33-4, 40, 77, 104-7, 113-4, 118-9, 170, 192, 202, 206-7, 214-5, 217, 226, 237, 268, 281, 284–5.

172 Philip A. Crowl and Jetek A. Isely, *The U.S. Marines and Amphibious War Its Theory and Its Practice in the Pacific*, Princeton, 1951, 25-7 (loc. 696-748); Victor H. Krulak, *First to Fight: An Inside View of the U.S. Marine Corps*, Annapolis, 1999, 76-8; Holland M. Smith, *Coral and Brass*, Arcadia Press, 2017, 37.

173 Walter A. Skya, *Japan's Holy War: The Ideology of Radical Shintō Ultranationalism*, Duke Univ., 2009, 190.

174 Burleigh, 12; Mosley, 5-6, 94; Bix, xv, 21-2, 88.

175 Drea, 128, 140, 147, 150-1, 153, 175.

176 Bix, 214–5.

177 Cook & Cook, 23; Tuchman, 119-120, 131.

178 Bix, 207.

179 Tuchman, 155; Harries & Harries, 179, 243, 480; Bix, 235; Ienaga, 60.

180 Ienaga, 37.

181 Ibid., 61.

182 Ibid., 62.

183 Ibid., 63.

184 Tuchman, 155; Harries & Harries, 179, 243, 480; Bix, 235.

185 Ienaga, 64.

186 Robert A. Divine, T.H. Breen, George Fredrickson and Hal Williams, *America: Past and Present*, NY, 1987, 782; Burleigh, 18; Bix, 261; TSHACNCDNM, Vol. 10, 295, Statement Keenan, Chief of Counsel, International Military Tribunal Far East, 4 June 1945, 33; Harries & Harries, 141, 150; Ian W. Toll, *Pacific Crucible: War at Sea in the Pacific, 1941-1942*, NY, 2012, 89; LaFeber, 339; Tuchman, 118; Crowley, 182; Gerhard Weinberg, *A World at Arms: A Global History of World War II*, NY, 1999, 79; Burleigh, 17; Driscoll, x, xiv; Cook & Cook, 23, 33-4, 56, 125, 156; NACPM, Microfilm Room, Roll 1499, #101, 19557, U.S. Intel Report Ref. Div., 7 July 1942, Regarding: Economy of Manchuria, Population Oct. 1940; Drea, 168; Burleigh, 15-6; Lord Russell of Liverpool, 7; Edgerton, 311; Ienaga, 63-4. Info from the National Museum of the Pacific War's display, Home of Adm. Nimitz Museum (NMPWANM, 13 July 2017). In this book, info collected from this museum will be cited. Although it is unorthodox, Michael Berenbaum encouraged the use of such data since from his experience at the Holocaust Museum in D.C., most information displayed is put together using committees of experts.

187 Drea, 251; Cook & Cook, 56, 403, 407-9; Dieter Kuhn, *Der Zweite Weltkrieg in China*, Berlin, 1999, Epilog; James T. Patterson, *American in the Twentieth Century: A History—Third Edition*, Orlando, 1976, 256-7, 296; Bix, 508; Toland, Vol. II, 998; Moore, 242; Tanaka, 42-3; Harries & Harries, 203.
188 Harries & Harries, 230.
189 Quote from Bix, 247; Frank, *Tower of Skulls*, 130.
190 Bix, 247.
191 Harries & Harries, 156.
192 Ibid., 161.
193 Crowley, 186.
194 Ibid.
195 Robert A. Divine, T.H. Breen, George Fredrickson and Hal Williams, *America: Past and Present*, NY, 1987, 782; Burleigh, 18; Bix, 261; TSHACNCDNM, Vol. 10, 295, Statement Keenan, Chief Counsel, International Military Tribunal Far East, 4 June 1945, 33; Harries & Harries, 141, 150, 161; Ian W. Toll, *Pacific Crucible: War at Sea in the Pacific, 1941-1942*, NY, 2012, 89; LaFeber, 339; Harries & Harries, 203; Bix, 261; Ienaga, 66; Tuchman, 134.
196 Crowley, 90-1, 203.
197 Ienaga, 141.
198 Tuchman, 134.
199 Ibid., 138.
200 Ibid., 142.
201 Drea, 194; Bix, 357; O'Brien, *The Second Most Powerful Man in the World*, 106; Crowley, 186, 350.
202 Quote comes from Wakabayashi (ed.), *The Nanking Atrocity, 1937-38*, Akira, "The Nanking Atrocity: An Interpretive Overview," 30. See also Bix, 359-60; Tanaka, xvi.
203 Harries & Harries, 207.
204 Hitler at first saw his union with China as a way to fight communism, but as his alliance shifted to Japan, especially with the 1936 anti-Comintern Pact, he slowly, but surely pulled out his advisors and focused on building good relations with Japan ending his support of China by July 1938. Wakabayashi (ed.), *The Nanking Atrocity, 1937-38*, Wakabayashi, "The Messiness of Historical Reality," 17; Tuchman, 141.
205 Tuchman, 47, 67, 81, 95, 102, 105, 131-2, 141, 144, 152, 156, 167; Wakabayashi (ed.), *The Nanking Atrocity, 1937-38*, Akira, "The Nanking Atrocity: An Interpretive Overview," 34; Harries & Harries, 204, 207-8; Zeiler, 24; Moore, 6, 38-9, 46; LaFeber, 336, 393; Ienaga, 58, 76.
206 Lord Russell of Liverpool, 40.
207 Ibid., 39.
208 Mosley, 170.

209   Rodriguez, 263.

210   BA-MA, RH 2/1848, OKH, Anliegend wird eine Ausarbeitung Erfahrungen und Netrachtungen aus dem japanisch-chinesischen Feldzug 1937-38 übersandt, 15.3.1938.

211   Cook & Cook, 2.

212   Interview Karl Wolff by Colin Heaton, 1984.

213   Harries & Harries, 241.

214   Ienaga, 107; Bradley, *Flyboys*, 36.

215   Divine, Breen, Fredrickson and Williams, 789; Drea, 213; Bix, 380.

216   Bix, 383.

217   Drea, 212, 217-8; LaFeber, 379. In response to Japan's completion of taking over Indochina in 1941, FDR froze Japanese assets in the U.S. and embargoed oil exports to Japan.

218   Frank Owen, *The Fall of Singapore*, NY, 2001, 65; Toland, Vol. I, 298-303.

219   Divine, Breen, Fredrickson and Williams, 778.

220   Quote comes from Bix, 12. One of the reasons for Japan taking Attu and Kiska in Alaska's Aleutian island chain was to prevent air attacks on the mainland. This is often overlooked and many claim it was just a diversion from the main attack on Midway. Bix, 12. Interestingly, Thailand was already free from colonial rule and independent so the Japanese were not "liberating" it from the "White man." Weinberg, 322.

221   Tanaka, 17; Frank, *Tower of Skulls*, 380.

222   Quote from Rafael Steinberg, *Island Fighting*, Alexandria, Virginia, 1978, 8, 18-21. See also Charles Sasser, *Two Fronts, One War: Dramatic Eyewitness Accounts of Major Events in the European and Pacific Theaters of Operations on Land, Sea and Air in WWII*, London, 2014, 3; Cook & Cook, 55; Weinberg, 3; Toll, *Pacific Crucible*, 254.

223   William Manchester, *Goodbye Darkness*, NY, 1979, 77–8.

224   Crowley, xvii.

225   Dower, 8; Manchester, 78; Crowley, 190.

226   Interview Shindo, 9 April 2018. Special thanks to the translation company SIMUL and translator expert Ms. Mariko Uo who helped screen and formulate my questions for Shindo and then reviewed his answers for accuracy after the interview.

227   Crowley, xiii; Bix, 176; Toland, Vol. II, 566.

228   Ienaga, 180.

229   Don A. Farrell, *Liberation-1944: The Pictorial History of Guam*, Tinian, 1984, 10.

230   Bix, 1-3. His younger brother, Prince Mikasa Takahito, said at the war's end to his subordinate Sadao Magami: "Even if Japan were to win this war, do you think the one billion people of Asia would follow Japan after the things

we did in China [i.e.] genocide?" Cook & Cook, 456. He knew about the atrocities. See Ienaga, 170.

231   Cook & Cook, 69; Bix, 1.

232   Robert Burrell, Review *Flamethrower*, 26 Feb. 2018.

233   BA-MA, RM 11/81, Marine-Kriegsberichter-Halbkompanie Kriegsberichter Werner Jörg Lüddecke, "Die glorreiche Ankunft. Aus den Erfahrungen einer Blockadereise nach Japan," 5 June 1942, 298.

234   Ibid., 12 II/250, KTB, T. 38, Marineattachés u. M(Ltr) Grossetappe Japan-China, Sept. 1941, 17, 223.

235   Harries & Harries, 294.

236   Bix, xx; Gordon W. Prange, *At Dawn We Slept: The Untold Story of Pearl Harbor*, NY, 1981, 40. U.S. commanders had failed to learn from the Battle of Taranto 11-2 Nov. 1940 when the British surprised the Italian navy at port and took out several warships. Prange, 40. Japan learned from it and studied it for their Pearl Harbor attack. Churchill, *The Grand Alliance*, 585.

237   Weinberg, xiv; Harries & Harries, 271; Toll, *Pacific Crucible*, 123; Harries & Harries, 271.

238   Edgerton, 312.

239   Mosley, 194; Toland, Vol. I, 76; Tuchman, 199.

240   Toland, Vol. I, 101.

241   Bix, 401, 408; Patterson, *American in the Twentieth Century*, 256-7; Thomas A. Paterson (ed.), *Problems in American Foreign Policy: Vol. II: Since 1914*, Third Ed., Lexington, MA, 1989; Robert Dallek, "Roosevelt's Leadership, Public Opinion, and Playing for Time in Asia," 215; Edgerton, 251, 312; Jon T. Hoffman, *Chesty: The Story of Lieutenant General Lewis B. Puller*, NY, 2001, 127; Cook & Cook, 23, 44-6; NMPWANM, 13 July 2017; Toland, Vol. I, 96, 98; Toll, *Pacific Crucible*, 122; LaFeber, 379, 382; O'Brien, *The Second Most Powerful Man in the World*, 155.

242   Carol von Clausewitz, *On War*, (eds.) Howard, Michael & Paret, Peter, Princeton, NJ, 1976, Commentary by Bernard Brodie, "A Guide to Reading of On War," 690.

243   Tuchman, 264; SLHA, The Young Companion, 1941-45, 167-72, "A Review of 4 Years of War in Figures". The Young Companion here says the Nationalists had 5 million troops, but since Tuchman is a trained scholar and the YC was a propaganda magazine, her figure is used.

244   Quote from SLHA, The Young Companion, 1940, 150-5, "Chin's Another Million". See also Tuchman, 264. By 1942, Chiang Kai-Shek had around 3 million men under arms.

245   Toll, *Pacific Crucible*, 250' O'Brien, *The Second Most Powerful Man in the World*, 255.

246   Wakabayashi (ed.), *The Nanking Atrocity, 1937-38*, Akira, "The Nanking Atrocity: An Interpretive Overview," 32.

247   Toll, *Pacific Crucible*, 271.

248   Ibid., 486.

249   Cook & Cook, 66, 334; Mosley, 68; Bradley, *Flyboys*, 36; Lord Russell of Liverpool, 1.

250   Ibid.

251   Cook & Cook, 71-2.

252   Bix, 436-7, 441.

253   Ibid., 443.

254   Ienaga, 136.

255   Drea, 206; Cook & Cook, 380; Victoria, *Zen at War*, 230; Tanaka, 111.

256   Harries & Harries, 475-6. Cannibalism of one's enemies was commonplace throughout Asia. General Stilwell, as a young officer in 1911, witnessed Chinese militia capture 66 pirates, kill them, and then eat their hearts. Tuchman, 39-40.

257   Armando Ang indeed tried to do this to some degree with his book *Brutal Holocaust*, and should be praised for his efforts. However, the lack of historical documentation and primary research make his work more of a survey book instead of one steeped in solid research.

258   L. Gordon Crovitz, "Defending Satire to the Death," *Jewish News*, 12 Jan. 2015; Hitchens, *god is not Great*, 264.

259   UGSL, J. Alton Hosch Papers, Tokyo War Crimes Trials, Conventional War Crimes (Atrocities), Part B, Ch. VIII, 1011-19; Iris Chang, *The Rape of Nanking: The Forgotten Holocaust of World War II*, NY, 1997, 4, 6, 87, 91, 103, 155, 211; Bradley & Powers, *Flags of Our Fathers*, 65; Burleigh, 19-20; Arthur Zich, *The Rising Sun*, Alexandria, VA (Time Life Books), 1977, 23; Spence, 448; Drea, 197; Edgerton, 14, 246-8; Iriye, 48; Cook & Cook, 39, 206; Conversation with Frank at Iwo, 21 March 2015; Drea, 236-7; Bradley & Powers, *Flags of Our Fathers*, 65; Bix, 334-5; Kuhn, 91; Hane, 297-8; Lord Russell of Liverpool, 41-2, 294; Kirchmann, 78; Weinberg, 322; Brackman, 177; NMPWANM, 13 July 2017; Burleigh, 18, 20; Daqing Yang, "Diary of a Japanese Army Medical Doctor, 1937," in *Researching Japanese War Crimes Records*, x; Toland, Vol. I, 63; Tanaka, 5; *Journal of Nanjing Massacre Studies* (JNMS), Vol. 1, No. 1, Nanking, China, 2019, Sun Zhaiwei, "How Many Chinese Military Personnel Were Among the Nanjing Massacre Victims," 16-7; Moore, 118-24, 144-5. A special note on Chang: Although she has done a good job of bringing public awareness to the Rape of Nanking, her work needs to be used with caution. She was not a trained historian and makes many errors. Wakabayashi (ed.), *The Nanking Atrocity, 1937-38*, Wakabayashi, "Iris Chang Reassessed," xxi-lii & Akira, "The Nanking

Atrocity: An Interpretive Overview," 34; Moore, 268; Frank, *Tower of Skulls*, 55. Since the German representatives in the International Committee in the Free Zone in Nanking estimated 20,000 women were raped during *the first two weeks alone*, this study estimates that at least another 60,000 women must have been raped during the campaign leading up to and during the destruction of Nanking, and hence, I have made the minimum number to be at least 80,000. See Harries & Harries, 225; David M. Crowe, *War Crimes, Genocide, and Justice: A Global History*, NY, 2014, 128.

260   Harries & Harries, 210, 217; Drea, 191; Mosley puts the attacking army's size at 160,000 which was too low. Mosley, 171; Daqing Yang, "Diary of a Japanese Army Medical Doctor, 1937," in *Researching Japanese War Crimes Records*, ix; Toland, Vol. I, 63; JNMS, Vol. 1, No. 1, Sheng, "The Seven Why-Questions in the Writing of History," 14; Wakabayashi (ed.), *The Nanking Atrocity, 1937-38*, Akira, "The Nanking Atrocity: An Interpretive Overview," 32; Lord Russell of Liverpool, 42; Gruhl, 70-1.

261   Frank, *Tower of Skulls*, 42.

262   Ienaga, 166.

263   Ibid.

264   Ibid., 166.

265   Spence 448; Wakabayashi (ed.), *The Nanking Atrocity, 1937-38*, Wakabayashi, "The Messiness of Historical Reality," 18 & Akira, "The Nanking Atrocity: An Interpretive Overview," 37, 43; Harries & Harries, 221. Tang was joined by many fellow officers in abandoning their troops causing much confusion. Moore, 117; Frank, *Tower of Skulls*, 38, 46.

266   Quote from Tuchman, 194. See also LaFeber, 393; O'Brien, *The Second Most Powerful Man in the World*, 301. Regarding Tuchman, she was an excellent historian, but dependent on her sources. In this case, she overly relied on Stilwell's personal archive and his dispatches. Since Chiang's diaries have been released in 2006, there has been a more favorable view of Chiang and his leadership. Notes on manuscript by Richard Frank, 25 Feb. 2023.

267   JNMS, Vol. 1, No. 1, Zhaiwei, "How Many Chinese Military Personnel Were Among the Nanjing Massacre Victims," 16.

268   Frank, *Tower or Skulls*, 32.

269   Ibid., 35.

270   Bix, 332.

271   Gruhl, 70.

272   Dallek, *Franklin D. Roosevelt*, 291; Patterson, 243, 247-8; Robert B. Edgerton, *Warriors of the Rising Sun*, NY, 1997, 246; Akira Iriye, *The Origins of the Second World War: In Asia and The Pacific*, NY, 1987, 48-9; Lee Mandel, *Unlikely Warrior: A Pacifist Rabbi's Journey from the Pulpit to Iwo Jima*, Gretna, 2015, 108; Mosely, 171-4; Bix, 340; Frank, *Tower of Skulls*,

101-2; Mandel, 109; Conrad Black, *Franklin Delano Roosevelt: Champion of Freedom*, NY, 2003, 427-8; BA-MA, RM 11/79, Bericht Marineattachés Deut. Botschaft Tokyo v. 20.12.1937. Zwischenfälle "Panay" u. "Ladybird", 1; Toland, Vol I, 60-1; Tuchman, 179; The Second Historical Archives of China, Nanjing, China, *Kangri Zhanzheng Zhengmian Zhanchang*, Vol. 1., 10; Toll, *Pacific Crucible*, 114; LaFeber, 370; Phillips Payson O'Brien, 113; Frank, *Tower of Skulls*, 102. Historian Bob Tadashi Wakabayashi claims the attack on *Panay* may have been justified since it "furtively escorted Chinese troops and war materiel to safety under U.S." colors. Bob Tadashi Wakabayashi (ed.), *The Nanking Atrocity, 1937-38*: Complicating the Picture," NY, 2017, Wakabayashi, "The Messiness of Historical Reality," 18. Although Wakabayashi has put together a good book of insightful articles by various authors, one must use the articles he wrote with caution. Here are just a few problems with his work: 1. He claims the rapes Japan conducted during WWII were not unique, which from what I have studied about WWII British, U.S., and German troops is absolutely false (xxxviii). One can claim the Soviet troops committed horrible rapes too, but they did not conduct the rapes to the extent of the Japanese. 2. He further states the Japanese did not conduct *Lebensraum* campaigns, but when one looks at the takeover of Manchuria where Japan brought in 1,500,000 settlers, then his argument breaks down (xl). 3. I take offense at his comparison of Chang's use of faulty documents to people using the horribly anti-Semitic *Protocols of the Elders of Zion*, which have been used to persecute and kill Jews throughout the last 115 years since it came out under Tsarist Russia after its defeat in 1905 by the Japanese (xlii). Wakabayashi's insensitivity here bespeaks of a lack of historical knowledge and understanding of the history of antisemitism. 4. Although the U.S. did make major mistakes in its conduct of the Vietnam War, to place our presidents at the time at the level of Tōjō, Matsui, Sakai, or Yamashita in claiming they possibly should have been brought to a war trial speaks of a grotesque attempt to equate our leaders with such unethical and barbaric men just listed, which is so ahistorical one has a hard time believing Wakabayashi could write such nonsense (127). Our leaders did not unleash armies of wholesale rape and mass slaughter like the Japanese government under Hirohito did during WWII. 5. Wakabayashi claims the U.S. killed half of the Okinawans during the island campaign there in 1945 (259). If one studies this battle, one learns many of the islanders killed themselves, were killed by their own IJA personnel, and died during the battle being caught in the crossfire of both Japanese and American forces. To say *America killed half the population* is horribly inaccurate and shows this man has problems of trying to prove too much always in favor of minimizing what Japan did. Although one would not necessarily call him a revisionist historian, his arguments seem to lean toward equivocating Japan's actions often with America's, which is wrong.

273 Tuchman, 179, 198.

274 MCHDQV, Oral History, Robert E. Cushman Jr., 118.

275 Edgerton, 246; Mosley, 171-3; Bix, 340; BA-MA, RM 11/79, Bericht Marineattachés Deut. Botschaft Tokyo v. 20.12.1937. "Panay" und "Ladybird", 1; Cook & Cook, 52; Drea, 201; Toland, Vol. I, 60-1. The *Ladybird* attack was not the first act of Japanese aggression against the British. On 27 Aug. 1937, Japanese planes attacked a car bedecked with a Union Jack driving between Nanking and Shanghai. Inside was British Ambassador Sir Hugh Knatchbull-Hugessen who was "gravely wounded in the back." Mosley, 171.

276 Frank, *Tower of Skulls*, 102; Lord Russell of Liverpool, 287.

277 Victoria, *Zen War Stories*, 12; Wakabayashi (ed.), *The Nanking Atrocity, 1937-38*, Akira, "The Nanking Atrocity: An Interpretive Overview," 37.

278 Victoria, *Zen War Stories*, 12. See also JNMS, Vol. 1, No. 1, Zhaiwei, "How Many Chinese Military Personnel Were Among the Nanjing Massacre Victims," 19-20; Brackman, 178.

279 JNMS, Vol. 1, No. 1, Zhaiwei, "How Many Chinese Military Personnel Were Among the Nanjing Massacre Victims," 16, 25; Wakabayashi (ed.), *The Nanking Atrocity, 1937-38*, Akira, "The Nanking Atrocity: An Interpretive Overview," 38-9, 43-5 & Tokushi, "Massacres Outside Nanking City," 58 & Kenji, "Massacres Near Mufushan," 77-9, 81-2.

280 JNMS, Vol. 1, No. 1, Zhaiwei, "How Many Chinese Military Personnel Were Among the Nanjing Massacre Victims," 18; Tanaka, 18-19; *Hong Kong's War Crimes Trials*, Zahar, "Trial Procedure at the British Military Courts, Hong Kong, 1946-1948," 15.

281 Edgerton, 245.

282 Lord Russell of Liverpool, 294.

283 Edgerton, 245.

284 Ibid.

285 Ibid.

286 Quote from Lord Russell of Liverpool, 295. See also Edgerton, 245-6.

287 Lord Russell of Liverpool, 295.

288 JNMS, Vol. 1, No. 1, Zhaiwei, "How Many Chinese Military Personnel Were Among the Nanjing Massacre Victims," 18; Wakabayashi (ed.), *The Nanking Atrocity, 1937-38*, Akira, "The Nanking Atrocity: An Interpretive Overview," 40.

289 Harries & Harries, 135.

290 Ibid., 229. For information on Hitler's treatment of Soviet POWs, see Alexander Dallin, *German Rule in Russia 1941-1945: A Study of Occupation Policies*, NY, 1957.

291 Tanaka, 88. Matsui was also in control of the Shanghai Expeditionary Army (SEA) or Shanghai Expeditionary Force (SEF), which merged together with the 10th Army to make the Central China Area Army (CCAA) under Matsui's overall command. Wakabayashi (ed.), *The Nanking Atrocity, 1937-38*, Akira, "The Nanking Atrocity: An Interpretive Overview," 31-2.

292 Wu Ch'êng-ên, *Monkey*, trans. Arthur Waley, NY, 1943, 28.

293 Quote from Victoria, *Zen War Stories*, 13, 234 fn.5. See also Bradley, *Flyboys*, 58.

294 Spence, 448.

295 Harries & Harries, 222.

296 Bix, xvii-xviii; NMPWANM, 13 July 2017. The Japanese Ministry of Foreign Affairs calls it the "Nanjing Massacre" and admits its army killed "a large number of noncombatants," and looted their belongings. However, it denies the number of 300,000 dead and denies it committed rape. "History Issues Q&A by the Ministry of Foreign Affairs of Japan" given by Deputy Consul Gen. in Houston Ryuji Iwasaki, 10 Dec. 2017; Bundesarchiv-Militärarchiv (BA-MA), RH 2/1848, OKH, Ausarbeitung Erfahrungen u. Netrachtungen aus dem japanisch-chinesischen Feldzug 1937/1938 übersandt, 15.3.1938, S. 31; Interview Drea, 17 Dec. 2017; Wakabayashi (ed.), *The Nanking Atrocity, 1937-38*, Wakabayashi, "The Messiness of Historical Reality," 3-4 & Akira, "The Nanking Atrocity: An Interpretive Overview," 33-4, 50; Tuchman, 178; Harries & Harries, 229, 241; Edgerton, 245.

297 TSHACNCDNM, Vol. 2, 214, 221-2 from H. J. Timperley, *What War Means*, 91. See also Gruhl, 70.

298 Gruhl, 71.

299 TSHACNCDNM, Vol. 2, 214, 221-2 from H. J. Timperley, *What War Means*, 94-5; Wakabayashi (ed.), *The Nanking Atrocity, 1937-38*, Akira, "The Nanking Atrocity: An Interpretive Overview," 40; Harries & Harries, 228. In many cities, the Chinese "huddled around foreign missionaries in their churches," but it seems without the success like was seen at Nanking. Moore, 82; Brackman, 185-6.

300 Harries & Harries, 228.

301 Hal Gold, *Unit 731 Testimony*, Rutland, 1996, 164.

302 TSHACNCDNM, Vol. 10, 290, Statement Keenan, Chief Counsel, International Military Tribunal Far East, 4 June 1945, 28.

303 Tanaka, 249-50; Wakabayashi (ed.), *The Nanking Atrocity, 1937-38*, Akira, "The Nanking Atrocity: An Interpretive Overview," 32, 36 & Tokushi, "Massacres Outside Nanking City," 58, 64; Harries & Harries, 481.

304 Wakabayashi (ed.), *The Nanking Atrocity, 1937-38*, Tokushi, "Massacres Outside Nanking City," 64.

305 Ienaga, 170.

306 Ibid.

307 「闇に葬られた皇室の軍部批判」、『This   is   読売』、一九九四年八月号57ページ

308 Bradley, *Flyboys*, 59; Chang, 59; Gruhl, 73-4. There has been postwar controversy about the competition and historian Richard Frank claimed he has seen evidence it may not be true. However, a Japanese court reviewed the evidence and concluded it had occurred. Chris Hogg, "Victory for Japan's War Critics," *BBC*, 23 Aug. 2005; Kate Heneroty, "Japanese Court Rules Newspaper Didn't Fabricate 1937 Chinese Killing Game," *Jurist Legal News and Research*, Univ. of Pittsburgh School of Law, 23 Aug. 2005. Both Noda and Mukai were found guilty of war crimes at the Nanking War Crime Trials in 1948 and executed. Historian Bob Tadashi Wakabayashi makes a strong argument though that this competition did not happen. See Wakabayashi (ed.), *The Nanking Atrocity, 1937-38*, Wakabayashi, "The Nanking 100-Man Killing Context Debate, 1971-75," 115-46. It is this study's conclusion that both men probably committed crimes since they were part of the Nanking campaign. Yale University professor Jonathan Spence believes the numbers and the sources for the full competition. Mukai said he played along with the article and lied about killing many to get a "good wife," which his wife admitted to working! The fact these men felt that bragging about killing people was something to be proud of probably denotes that only after the war, did they claim they made it up to try to save their lives. Noda had claimed right after the war that he slaughtered innocent POWs and even told such stories to school children.

309 Conrad, "Heart of Darkness," 586.

310 Gruhl, 74.

311 TSHACNCDNM, Vol. 2, 214, 221-2 from H. J. Timperley, *What War Means*, 92-3.

312 Crowley, 357, 396; Cook & Cook, 23.

313 Butow, 100.

314 Edwin P. Hoyt, *Warlord: Tojo Against the World*, Landam, MD, 1993, 15.

315 Kirchmann, 78; Bix, 339.

316 Bix, 339.

317 Ibid.

318 Ibid.

319 Ibid.

320 JNMS, Vol. 1, No. 1, Meng Guoxiang, "How the Japanese Military Invaders Destroyed and Exploited Buddhism in Nanjing," 97-125; Toll, *Pacific Crucible*, 99; Harries & Harries, 12.

321 JNMS, Vol. 1, No. 1, Zhaiwei, "How Many Chinese Military Personnel Were Among the Nanjing Massacre Victims," 18-9 & Zhu Tianle & Zhu Chengshan, "The Legally Affirmed Chain of Evidence for the Nanjing Massacre, 71.

322 *The Memorial Hall of the Victims in Nanjing Massacre by Japanese Invaders*, Doc. Display, 11 May 2019.

323 Frank, *Tower of Skulls*, 51.

324 Quote from Chang, 91. See also Edgerton, 246; Lord Russell of Liverpool, 45; Bix, 336; Shinsho Hanayama, *The Way of Deliverance: Three Years with the Condemned Japanese War Criminals*, NY, 1950, 185–6. Slicing open young women's vaginas to rape them was common among IJA troops. See James M. Scott, *Rampage: MacArthur, Yamashita, and the Battle of Manila*, NY, 2018, 263, 471.

325 TSHACNCDNM, Vol. 2, 214, 221-2 from H. J. Timperley, *What War Means*, 182.

326 Ibid., 91.

327 Ibid.

328 TSHACNCDNM, Vol. 2, 214, 221-2 from H. J. Timperley, *What War Means*, 174; Wakabayashi (ed.), *The Nanking Atrocity, 1937-38*, Akira, "The Nanking Atrocity: An Interpretive Overview," 49.

329 TSHACNCDNM, Vol. 2, 214, 221-2 from H. J. Timperley, *What War Means*, 178, 181.

330 Ibid., 182-3.

331 Modder, 21.

332 Ibid., 21-2.

333 Ibid., 22.

334 Ibid.

335 TSHACNCDNM, Vol. 2, 214, 221-2 from H. J. Timperley, *What War Means*, 92-3, 181. See also Wakabayashi (ed.), *The Nanking Atrocity, 1937-38*, Akira, "The Nanking Atrocity: An Interpretive Overview," 32, 36; Tuchman, 178; Harries & Harries, 227; Moore, 83.

336 TSHACNCDNM, Vol. 2, 163-4.

337 UGSL, J. Alton Hosch Papers, Tokyo War Crimes Trials, Conventional War Crimes (Atrocities), Part B, Ch. VIII, 10013; Chang, 4, 6, 59, 86, 87-9 91, 94-5, 103, 155; Interview Master Johnny Kwong Ming Lee, 10 April 2019; Scott, 184-5, 260; JNMS, Vol. 1, No. 1, Tianle & Chengshan, "The Legally Affirmed Chain of Evidence for the Nanjing Massacre, 79; TSHACNCDNM, Vol. 2, 214 from H. J. Timperley, *What War Means*,

Chapter II, 61; The Memorial Hall of the Victims in Nanjing Massacre by Japanese Invaders, White Stone Display Wall, Testimony Chang Zhiqiang, 12 May 2019; Tuchman, 178; Frank, *Tower of Skulls*, 49; Harries & Harries, 223-4; Ienaga, 169.

338 TSHACNCDNM, Vol. 3, No. 10, 18-23, Rabe to Japanese Embassy, 18 Dec. 1937.

339 Gruhl, 71.

340 Chang, 4, 6, 59, 86, 87-91, 94-5, 103, 155; Toland, Vol. I, 62 ; Bradley, *Flyboys*, 59. See also Ienaga, 173.

341 Chang, 59.

342 Cook & Cook, 155.

343 BA-MA, BMRS, Interview Elisabeth Borchardt, 18 February 1995. See also Rodriguez, 262.

344 Brackman, 186.

345 Chang, 4, 6, 59, 86, 87-9 91, 94-5, 103, 155; Bradley, *Flyboys*, 58-9, 62, 111-2, 152, 200-1, 225, 228-232, 245, 316; Edgerton, 16, 246-7; Burleigh, 561; Cook & Cook, 273-4, 462; Lord Russel, 41-2, 57; NACPM staff, "Japanese War Crimes Records National Archives: Research Starting Points," in *Researching Japanese War Crimes Records*, 102-3; Bradley, *Flyboys*, 200; Greg Bradsher, "The Exploitation of Captured and Seized Japanese Records Relating to War Crimes, 1942-1945," in *Researching Japanese War Crimes Records*, 152); MCHDQV, Dashiell File, #1, Davis-Filipinos; Mark Felton, *Slaughter at Sea: The Story of Japan's Naval War Crimes*, South Yorkshire, 2007; UGSL, J. Alton Hosch Papers, Tokyo War Crimes Trials, Conventional War Crimes (Atrocities), Part B, Ch. VIII, 1033, 1067; Tanaka, 129, 139; JNMS, Vol. 1, No. 1, Zhang Sheng, "The Seven Why-Questions in the Writing of History," 10 & Zhang Lianhong, "A Hero of Nanjing: Austrian Mechanic Rupert R. Hatz During the Nanjing Massacre," 27; TSHACNCDNM, Vol. 2, 214, 221-2 from H. J. Timperley, *What War Means*, 36, 42-3, 62, 65, 184-5, 189-91 & Vol. 3, 28-49, Cases of Disorder by Japanese Soldiers in the Safety Zone; Moore, 84-107; Frank, *Tower of Skulls*, 43, 48.

346 Butow, 101.

347 Harries & Harries, 227.

348 Ibid., 228.

349 Toland, Vol. I, 62; Bix, 334.

350 Toland, Vol. I, 62; Butow, 102.

351 Butow, 102-3.

352 Ibid., 126-8.

353 Lord Russell of Liverpool, 295.

354 Interivew with Karl Wolff done by historian Colin Heaton, 1984.

355 Brissaud, 157.

356   Levin, 154-5; *The Von Hassell Diaries 1938-1944: The Story of the Forces Against Hitler Inside Germany as Recorded by Ambassador Ulrich von Hassell—A Leader of the Movement*, New York, 1947, 79; Nicolaus von Below, *Als Hitlers Adjutant 1937-1945*, Mainz, 1980, 72-73; Brissaud, *Canaris*, 157; Kershaw, *Hitler: 1936-1945 Nemesis*, 248.

357   Frank, *Tower of Skulls*, 48.

358   Talmud, Tractate of *Shabbat* (the Sabbath), 31a.

359   Harries & Harries, 467.

360   Scott, 323.

361   Stuart D. Goldman and Yaroslav A. Shulatov, "The Fanatical Colonel Tsuji," *World War II Magazine*, April 2019, 34; Harries & Harries, 304, 307; Bradley, *Flyboys*, 200; John Deane Potter, *The Life and Death of a Japanese General*, NY, 1962, 11.

362   Frank, *Tower of Skulls*, 346.

363   Ibid., 350.

364   Ibid., 361.

365   Harries & Harries, 343.

366   Frank, *Tower of Skulls*, 363.

367   Ibid., 366.

368   Scott, 42; Frank, *Tower of Skulls*, 67.

369   Frank, *Tower of Skulls*, 365. See also Brackman, 34-5.

370   Lord Russell of Liverpool, 99.

371   Ibid., 100-2.

372   Frank, *Tower of Skulls*, 374.

373   Scott, 42; Frank, *Tower of Skulls*, 67, 375; Lord Russell of Liverpool, 96; Harries & Harries, 309; Drea, 223; Edgerton, 268; Hoyt, 100.

374   Goldman & Shulatov, 35.

375   Ibid.

376   Frank, *Tower of Skulls*, 380.

377   Edgerton, 263, 269-70; Burleigh, 562; Drea, 223-4; Lord Russell of Liverpool, 242-4, 261; Andrew Roberts, *The Storm of War: A New History of World War II*, NY, 2012, 275-7; "Bataan Death March," Encyclopedia Britannica, https://www.britannica.com/event/Bataan-Death-March, accessed May 28, 2017; Modder, vii. Col. Tsuji was responsible for many crimes done in Singapore. Toland, Vol. I, 367; Ienaga, 173.

378   Tanaka, 69.

379   Frank, *Downfall*, 163; Rahil Ismail, Brian Shaw and Ooi Giok Ling (eds.), *Southeast Asian Culture and Heritage in a Globalizing World: Diverging Identities in a Dynamic Region*, NY, 2016, 97; Scott, 43; Tanaka, 7, 17; Frank, *Tower of Skulls*, 380; Modder, 7, 58.

380   Lord Russell of Liverpool, 278.

381 Tanaka, 7.
382 Lord Russell of Liverpool, 243.
383 Goldman & Shulatov, 34-6; Modder, 78.
384 Frank, *Tower of Skulls*, 346.
385 Goldman & Shulatov, 34-6; Modder, 10.
386 Ienaga, 174.
387 Frank, *Tower of Skulls*, 381.
388 Lord Russell of Liverpool, 213-4, 249, 252.
389 Edgerton, 268.
390 Courtney Browne, *Tojo: The Last Banzai*, London, 1967, 153.
391 Goldman & Shulatov, 34-6; Toland, Vol. I, 367.
392 Modder, 37.
393 Lord Russell of Liverpool, 280-1.
394 Ibid.
395 Ibid.
396 Scott, 9.
397 Toll. 238-40; Frank, *Tower of Skulls*, 440.
398 Wallace & Williams, 115.
399 Scott, 3. See also Roberts, *The Storm of War*, 566.
400 Scott, 3-4.
401 Frank, *Tower of Skulls*, 517.
402 Frank, *Tower of Skulls*, 517; Lord Russell of Liverpool, 138.
403 Frank, *Tower of Skulls*, 517.
404 Frank, *Tower of Skulls*, 517; Harries & Harries, 315.
405 Toll. 299; Goldman & Shulatov, 36; Frank, *Tower of Skulls*, 518; Lord Russell of Liverpool, 142; Harries & Harries, 318; Drea, 224.
406 Quote from Goldman & Shulatov, 35; Toland, Vol. I, 375.
407 Goldman & Shulatov, 36.
408 MCHDQV, Oral History, Bert Banks, 4-5.
409 Frank, *Tower of Skulls*, 518; Toland, Vol. I, 367.
410 Quote from Toland, Vol. I, 372. See also Harries & Harries, 315-6.
411 Frank, *Tower of Skulls*, 518.
412 Frank, *Tower of Skulls*, 518; Lord Russell of Liverpool, 139; Toland, Vol. I, 371.
413 NMPWANM, 13 July 2017.
414 Toland, Vol. I, 376.
415 (NIV—New International Version), 89. The NIV version used throughout is: "The Student Bible: New International Version, Notes by Philip Yancey and Tim Stafford, Zondervan Bible Publishers, Grand Rapids, Michigan, 1987.
416 NACPM, 127 Box 14 (3d MarDiv), HQ, FMF, Intel Bulletin #4-44, Capt. Whipple, American Soldier, 7-8.

417   John E. Olson, *O'Donnell: Andersonville of the Pacific Extermination Camp of American Hostages in the Philippines*, NY, 1985; Frank, *Tower of Skulls*, 519.
418   Tanaka, 8.
419   Lord Russell of Liverpool, 144, 200, 202.
420   Douglas MacArthur, *Reminiscences*, Naval Institute Press, MA, 1964.
421   Lord Russell of Liverpool, 302-3.
422   Harries & Harries, 342.
423   Notes on manuscript by Richard Frank, 23 Feb. 2023.
424   https://www.nationalww2museum.org/war/articles/history-through-viewfinder-23.
425   Samuel Eliot Morison, *History of the United States Naval Operations in World War II, Vol. VIII*, NY, 1975, 149; *Robert F. Rogers, Destiny's Landfall: A History of Guam*, Univ. of Hawaii Press, *1995, 116;* Jon T. Hoffman, *Once A Legend: Red Mike Edson of the Marine Raiders*, Novato, 1994, *38-9.*
426   Toll, *Conquering Tide*, 459.
427   O'Brien, *The Second Most Powerful Man in the World*, 16.
428   Morison, 377; *Families in the Face of Survival: World War II Japanese Occupation of Guam 1941-1944*, Guam War Survivors Memorial Foundation, Guam, 2015, 126.
429   Morison, 151.
430   National Park Service, War in the Pacific: Outbreak of the War accessed 10/22/16 at https://www.nps.gov/parkhistory/online_books/npswapa/extContent/wapa/guides/outbreak/sec6.htm and /sec.3.htm.
431   *Families in the Face of Survival*, 126; Frank O. Hough, *The Island War: The United States Marine Corps in the Pacific*, NY, 1947, 20.
432   *Families in the Face of Survival*, 126; Dick Camp, *Leatherneck Legends: Conversations with the Marine Corps' Old Breed*, St. Paul, 120; Kathleen R. W. Owings (ed.), *The War Years on Guam: Narratives of the Chamorro Experience*, Vol. I, Micronesian Area Research Center (MARC), 1981, 1, 145.
433   Hough, 21; Thomas Wilds, "The Japanese Seizure of Guam," *Marine Corps Gazette*, July, 1955.
434   J. Robert Moskin, *U.S. Marine Corps Story*, NY, 1992, 236; Farrell, *Liberation-1944,* 9.
435   Owings (ed.), *The War Years on Guam:* Vol. I, 100, 103.
436   Farrell, *Liberation-1944,* 9; Edgerton, 294.
437   Roger Mansell, *Captured: The Forgotten Men of Guam*, Annapolis, 2012, vii.
438   MCHDQV, Oral History, George Burledge, 9-11; Toland, Vol. II, 748-9.
439   Mansell, vii.
440   Morison, 373; Hough, 284.
441   Farrell, *Liberation-1944,* 27; *Guam War Claims Review Commission*, 5; Owings (ed.), *The War Years on Guam:* Vol. I, 55-6, 127-8.

442 Hough, 282; MARC, Guam War Reparations Commission (GWRC), Olivia L.G. Cruz Abell, Box 1, Rec. 2090 & Francisco Q. Leon Guerrero, Box 20, 39620 & Ignacio T. Leon Guerrero, Box 20, Rec. 39680; *Families in the Face of Survival*, 127; *Guam War Claims Review Commission*, 5; National Park Service, A Guide to the War in the Pacific; Owings (ed.), *The War Years on Guam:* Vol. I, 127; Tim Maga, *Judgement at Tokyo: The Japanese War Crimes Trials*, University of Kentucky, 2001, 108-9.

443 Owings (ed.), *The War Years on Guam:* Vol. I, 4. See also pp. 132-3.

444 Ibid., 120, 129, 140, 174. See also Maga, 109-110.

445 MARC, The Pacific Command and United States Pacific Fleet, Headquarters of the Commander Naval Forces Marianas, Naval Forces Marshalls-Carolines and Marshalls-Carolines Area, FF12/A17-10(2), 02-JDN-fsk, 1-4; Maga, 108-9.

446 Owings (ed.), *The War Years on Guam:* Vol. I, 128.

447 Ibid., 106.

448 Ibid., 100, 103.

449 Wakabayashi (ed.), *The Nanking Atrocity, 1937-38*, Akira, "The Nanking Atrocity: An Interpretive Overview," 48 & Tokushi, "Massacres Outside Nanking City," 66.

450 Harries & Harries, 225.

451 Hough, 282; MARC, Guam War Reparations Commission (GWRC), Olivia L.G. Cruz Abell, Box 1, Rec. 2090 & Francisco Q. Leon Guerrero, Box 20, 39620 & Ignacio T. Leon Guerrero, Box 20, Rec. 39680; *Families in the Face of Survival*, 127; *Guam War Claims Review Commission*, 5; National Park Service, A Guide to the War in the Pacific; Mansell, 223 fn. 6.

452 MARC, GWRC, Francisco Acfalle, Box 1, Rec. 2230 & Ignacio T. Leon Guerrero, Box 20, Rec. 39680.

453 National Park Service, A Guide to the War in the Pacific.

454 Cook & Cook, 110.

455 MARC, GWRC, Frutuoso S. Aflague, Box 1 & Ignacio T. Leon Guerrero, Box 20, Rec. 39680; National Park Service, A Guide to the War in the Pacific; *Guam War Claims Review Commission*, 6; Owings (ed.), *The War Years on Guam:* Vol. I, 7, 31, 37-8, 50, 75-6 (above quote from here), 112, 166.

456 Owings (ed.), *The War Years on Guam:* Vol. I, 4.

457 MARC, GWRC, Frutuoso S. Aflague, Box 1 & Ignacio T. Leon Guerrero, Box 20, Rec. 39680; National Park Service, A Guide to the War in the Pacific; *Guam War Claims Review Commission*, 6.

458 Owings (ed.), *The War Years on Guam:* Vol. I, 114.

459 Ibid., 2-3.

460 Hough, 284; MARC, GWRC, Edward L.G. Aguon, Box 1 & Felix Aguon, Box 1; Flores, Camacho 2, Palacios 6; National Park Service, A Guide to the War, in the Pacific.

461 MARC, GWRC, Fausto Acfalle, Box 1, Rec. 120.

462 Owings (ed.), *The War Years on Guam:* Vol. I, 150. See also page 155.

463 *Guam War Claims Review Commission*, 5-6; MARC, Guam War Reparations, Jesus Leon Guerrero, Box 20 & Francisco Q. Leon Guerrero, Box 20, 39620 & Diana Leon Guerrero, Box 20, 39502.

464 Owings (ed.), *The War Years on Guam:* Vol. I, 149.

465 *Guam War Claims Review Commission*, 5; Email Farrell to Rigg, 22 Aug. 2016; Farrell, *Liberation-1944*, 3, 27-53; Interview James Farley Oelke, 25 March 2018; MARC, GWRC, Olivia L.G. Cruz Abell, Box 1, Rec. 2090 & Maria T. Abrenilla, Box 1, Rec. 40 & Felix Cepeda Aguon, Box 1 & Dolores F. Aguon, Box 1, Rec. 380; *Families in the Face of Survival*, 151.

466 Farrell, *Liberation-1944*, 27.

467 Hough, 284.

468 Farrell, *Liberation-1944*, 12; Hough, 284.

469 Farrell, *Liberation-1944*, 7, 27-53.

470 Morison, 373; Hough, 284; MARC, GWRC, Olivia L.G. Cruz Abell, Box 1, Rec. 2090; MARC, GWRC, Edward L.G. Aguon, Box 1. The camps were Atate, Malojloj, Mata, Manenggon, Asinan, Maimai and Tai; Notes on manuscript by Richard Frank, 11 March 2023.

471 Moskin, 335.

472 Owings (ed.), *The War Years on Guam:* Vol. I, 136.

473 NACPM, 127 GW-1386, Chamorro Elders to Nimitz, 10 Aug. 1944.

474 NACPM, 127 GW-1381; Owings (ed.), *The War Years on Guam:* Vol. I, 121-2, 135.

475 Interview James Oelke Farley, 25 March 2018; Email from Kina Doreen Lewis, 9 May 2019.

476 Interview with Saburo Sakai by Colin Heaton, Nov. 1990.

477 Lord Russell of Liverpool, 234.

478 Ibid.

479 Ibid., 260.

480 Ibid.

481 Ibid., 261.

482 Ienaga, 172.

483 Scott, 134.

484 *Law Reports of Trials of War Criminals: Selected and Prepared by The United Nations War Crimes Commission*, Volume IV, London, 1948, 5.

485 Ibid., 19-20.

486 Ibid., 20.

487 Lord Russell of Liverpool, 187-90.

488 Potter, 156.

489 *Law Reports of Trials of War Criminals: Selected and Prepared by The United Nations War Crimes Commission*, Volume IV, London, 1948, 18.

490 Scott, 73.
491 NACPM, 208 AA 132R-6; Cook & Cook, 380; Scott, 79; Potter, 156.
492 Scott, 80; Lord Russell of Liverpool, 110-1, 113.
493 Lord Russell of Liverpool, 115.
494 Ibid.
495 Ibid., 116.
496 NACPM, RG 127, Commandant's Office, Box 821, Folder MOH 1740-55-50, Folder (1 Jan. 1944-31 Dec. 1947), Capt. Hamas (USMC) to Supreme Commander Allied Powers, Gen. HQ, 5 Nov. 1946, 2; Frank, *Tower of Skulls*, 310; Maga, 104-105.
497 Maga, 104-105.
498 Notes on manuscript by Richard Frank, 2 March 2023.
499 Thomas M. Huber, "The Battle of Manila," U.S. Combat Studies Institute, 2001.
500 *Law Reports of Trials of War Criminals: Selected and Prepared by The United Nations War Crimes Commission*, Volume IV, London, 1948, 21.
501 Thomas M. Huber, "The Battle of Manila," U.S. Combat Studies Institute, 2001; Scott, 95.
502 Lord Russell of Liverpool, 252-3.
503 Ibid., 252.
504 Scott, 109; Lord Russell of Liverpool, 255, 260.
505 Scott, 259, 382. For other cases of Japanese laughing at the suffering of others, see Lord Russell of Liverpool, 111, 113, 180, 187.
506 Scott, 260.
507 Scott, 386.
508 Ibid., 474.
509 Ibid., 471.
510 Ibid., 210.
511 Ibid.
512 Ibid., 263.
513 Ibid., 401.
514 Ibid., 425. See also Li Shu-Fan, *Hong Kong Surgeon*, NY, 1964, 108, 120.
515 Connaughton, R., Pimlott, J., and Anderson, D., 1995, The Battle for Manila, London: Bloomsbury Publishing. Greg Bradsher, "The Exploitation of Captured and Seized Japanese Records Relating to War Crimes, 1942-1945," *Researching Japanese War Crimes Records*, 153-4; NACPM, Trial of Yamashita, SC 220798, 13 Nov. 1945; NACPM, 208 AA 132T 8 Feb 1945 & SC-2030320-S; Scott, 278-9, 418.
516 Interview James Dowell, 13 May 2018.
517 Scott, 280.
518 Ibid., 282.

519 Ibid., 338.

520 Lord Russell of Liverpool, 254.

521 Ibid., 259.

522 Scott, 422; Edgerton, 293; Dower 44-5; Peter Maslowski, and Allan R. Millett, *For the Common Defense: A Military History of the United States of America*, NY, 1984, 461; Frank, *Downfall*, 26; Gilbert, *Second World War*, 642; Harries & Harries, 436. The 100,000 number first appeared in the U.S. Army's official history compiled by Robert Ross Smith. Recent research has called into question this number with historian Richard Frank thinking it was around 60,000. Frank further states, though, had the Japanese not been defeated in Manila, they would have killed all the civilians under their control. Notes on manuscript by Richard Frank, 25 Feb. 2023.

523 Scott, 251-2.

524 *Law Reports of Trials of War Criminals: Selected and Prepared by The United Nations War Crimes Commission*, Volume IV, London, 1948, 32.

525 Lord Russell of Liverpool, 252-5; Edgerton, 17, 292-3; Connaughton, R., Pimlott, J., and Anderson, D., 1995, The Battle for Manila, London: Bloomsbury Publishing. Greg Bradsher, "The Exploitation of Captured and Seized Japanese Records Relating to War Crimes, 1942-1945," *Researching Japanese War Crimes Records*, 153-4; NACPM, Trial of Yamashita, SC 220798, 13 Nov. 1945; NACPM, 208 AA 132T 8 Feb 1945 & SC-2030320-S; Scott, 278-9, 418.

526 Scott, 386.

527 Ibid., 483.

528 Lord Russell of Liverpool, 253.

529 Thomas M. Huber, "The Battle of Manila," U.S. Combat Studies Institute, 2001.

530 Cecilia Gaerlan, "War Crimes in the Philippines during WWII," Arthur D. Simons Center for Interagency Cooperation, Ft. Leavenworth, Kansas, 2019.

531 Gaerlan, "War Crimes in the Philippines during WWII."; Frank, 162, 325, 329; James Kelly Morningstar, *War and Resistance: The Philippines 1942-1944*, PhD dissertation for the University of Maryland, 2018, 805.

532 Potter, 155.

533 Ibid. 155.

534 Ibid., 155-6.

535 *Law Reports of Trials of War Criminals: Selected and Prepared by The United Nations War Crimes Commission*, Volume IV, London, 1948, 1.

536 Ibid., 37-8.

537 Potter, 169.

538 For a discussion on what Hitler did and did not do in organizing the Holocaust, see Richard J. Evans, *Lying About Hitler: History, Holocaust, and*

the David Irving Trial, NY, 2001. Also, *SS* Lieutenant General Karl Wolff said,"Hitler was smart enough not to put anything in writing to Himmler, and likewise Himmler to Bach-Zelewski, Berger and others. Euphemisms were enough, and they all knew their duties." Interview Karl Wolff by Colin Heaton, 1984.

539   *Law Reports of Trials of War Criminals: Selected and Prepared by The United Nations War Crimes Commission*, Volume IV, London, 1948, 19.

540   Ibid.

541   Ibid.

542   Lord Russell of Liverpool, 95.

543   Williams Shakespeare, *The Tempest*, Act I, Scene 2.

544   Drea, 236; Neil MacPherson, "Death Railway Movements, Australian Government Archives, 6 January 2015; Lord Russell of Liverpool, 91, 93, 95; Cook & Cook, 74, 99; Edgerton, 277; Dower, 47; Gruhl, 112.

545   Harries & Harries, 476.

546   Butow, 520.

547   "The Bridges of the Thailand-Burma Railway," PBS, 26 June 2008.

548   Harries & Harries, 309-10.

549   Lord Russell of Liverpool, 88-9.

550   David Boggett, "Notes on the Thai-Burma Railway, Part II: Asian Romusha; The Silenced Voices of History," Kyoto Seika University, 9 January 2015.

551   Australian Government, Depart of Veterans' Affairs, "The Thai-Burma Railway & Hellfire Pass: Australian Prisoners of War on the Thai-Burma Railway 1942-1945," 20 April 2013.

552   Lord Russell of Liverpool, 303.

553   Ibid., 292-3.

554   Ibid., 293.

555   Australian Government, Depart of Veterans' Affairs, "The Thai-Burma Railway & Hellfire Pass: Australian Prisoners of War on the Thai-Burma Railway 1942-1945," 20 April 2013.

556   Lord Russell of Liverpool, 92.

557   Australian Government, Depart of Veterans' Affairs, "The Thai-Burma Railway…," 20 April 2013.

558   Cook & Cook, 114.

559   Ibid., 116.

560   Ibid., 113.

561   Bix, 140; Ienaga, 8.

562   Cook & Cook, 193.

563   Ibid., 195-6.

564   Larry Smith, *Drill Sergeants*, 29; Henri, et al., 13; Smith, xxi; Wheeler, 41; Richard F. Newcomb, *Iwo Jima*, NY, 1965, 35; Edgerton, 226; Oliver, 110–

24; Cook & Cook, 48, 73, 173, 192-3; Drea, 213-4, 232, 285; "Spit on My Grave," Chosun Ilbo, Seoul, Korea, article no. 104-16, 1998; Weinberg, xiii; NACPM, RG 226, Box 368 (Off. US Strategic Servs.), Y-125, Enemy Troop Movements, 20 June 1944 & Enemy Conscription 10 June 1944; Dower, 285; Interview Graves, 2 May 2018; Victoria, *Zen at War*, 156; Tanaka, 42-3, 77.

565 Lord Russell of Liverpool, 93.

566 Harries & Harries, 309-10; Lord Russell of Liverpool, 252.

567 David McNeill, "Reluctant Warrior," WWII Magazine, Special Collector's Edition for the 60th Commemoration of Iwo Jima, 43.

568 Interview Shindo, 9 April 2018; Interview Tatsushi Saito, 10 April 2018 (Military History Div., National Institute for Defense Studies, Ministry of Def.); Interview Col. Yukio Yasunaga, 10 April 2018 (Sen. Fellow, Military History Div., National Institute for Def. Studies, Ministry of Def.); MCRDSDA, C-2 Special Study, Enemy Situation, VAC, 6 Jan. '45, Unit Commanders, 11.

569 Many sources have Kuribayashi listed as a Deputy Military *attaché* in Washington, but in the Japanese Defense Military archives, there is no evidence he held such a position. Burleigh, 331; Kumiko Kakehashi, *So Sad to Fall in Battle*, NY, 2007, 37, 112. Yamamoto also attended Harvard (although he dropped out after a month in 1920 (Harvard Univ. Student Archives File Yamamoto)). Prange, 111; E. B. Sledge, *With the Old Breed: At Peleliu and Okinawa*, NY, 1981, 304; Cook & Cook, 90-1. Several historians incorrectly list Yamamoto as a "Harvard-educated admiral," which is dead wrong like historian Bob Tadashi Wakabayashi and Ian W. Toll. See Wakabayashi (ed.), *The Nanking Atrocity, 1937-38*, Wakabayashi, "The Messiness of Historical Reality," 17; Toll, *Pacific Crucible*, 69.

570 Harvard Univ. Student Archives, Tadamichi Kuribayashi, Summer 1928; Email King to Rigg, 2 Aug. 2017.

571 Bill D. Ross, *Iwo Jima: Legacy of Valor*, NY, 1985, 20; Newcomb, 8; McNeill, "Reluctant Warrior," 39; Edgerton, 256-7; Kakehashi, 112; Yoshitaka Horie, *The Memoirs of Fighting Spirit: Major Yoshitaka Horie and the Battle of Iwo Jima*, edited by Robert D. Eldridge and Charles W. Tatum, Annapolis, 2011, 51-2.

572 Keith Wheeler, *The Road to Tokyo*, Alexandria, VA (Time Life Books), 1979, 40; McNeill, "Reluctant Warrior," 39; Kakehashi, 113-4.

573 NIDSMDMA, Collections Kuribayashi, Bio info; NIDSMDMA, *Senshi-Sosho*, Central Pacific, Op. #2, Peleliu, Angaur, Iwo, Vol. 13, 278-9; Robert Burrell, *Ghosts of Iwo Jima*, Bryan TX, 2006, 40; Alexander, 6; Henri, et al., 6; MCRDSDA, C-2 Special Study, Enemy Situation, VAC, 6 Jan. '45, Unit

Commanders, 11; Frank, 282; Edgerton, 264-5; Kakehashi, 87; Cook & Cook, 83-4; Drea, 204-5; Weinberg, 6.

574 Philip Snow, *The Fall of Hong Kong: Britain, China and the Japanese Occupation*, New Haven, 2003, 102; Tanaka, 110.

575 Interview Shindo, 9 April 2018.

576 Harries & Harries, 5.

577 Interview Shindo, 9 April 2018; Notes Shindo 3 Oct. 2018. Many of Shindo's thoughts mirror what Zen Buddhists believed back during the Imperial age. See Victoria, *Zen at War*, 58-9; Harries & Harries, 4-5.

578 NIDSMDMA, Collections Kuribayashi, Bio info; NIDSMDMA, History Calvary Rgts, 508, 513, 515; Email Tatsushi Saito to Rigg, 23 April 2018.

579 NIDSMDMA, Kuribayashi, Bio info; MCRDSDA, C-2 Special Study, Enemy Situation, VAC, 6 Jan. 1945, Unit Commanders, 11.

580 NIDSMDMA, *Kai-Ko-Sha Kiji*, Oct. 1938 Vol. 769, Kuribayashi, "Building New Remount Administrative Plan," 83-92; NIDSMDMA, *Kai-Ko-Sha Kiji*, March 2001, "Fund for the Production to Increase Strength of the Control by the Military"; Wakabayashi (ed.), *The Nanking Atrocity, 1937-38*, Akira, "The Nanking Atrocity: An Interpretive Overview," 30; Rigg, *Lives of Hitler's Jewish Soldiers*, 160; Matthew Cooper, *The German Army, 1933–1945: Its Political and Military Failure*, NY, 1978, 279.

581 TSHACNCDNM, Vol. 2, 214, 221-2 from H. J. Timperley, *What War Means*, 36, 75.

582 Jan Henrik Marsman, *I Escaped from Hong Kong*, NY, 1942, 94.

583 Internet Archive:1940 JAPANESE WAR HORSE FEATURE FILM "PRAYER AT DAWN" 17184.

584 Quote from Kakehashi, 36. See also Horie, 40, 52.

585 At the time, the Japanese military did not have a term "chief of staff." The term Deputy Commander was frequently used. However, during the War Trials and many histories, the title and responsibilities of the position were most akin to what we in the West understand as a chief of staff. Interview Lt. Col. W. K., 6 Jan. 2022.

586 Chi Man Kwong and Yiu Lun Tsoi, *Eastern Fortress: A Military History of Hong Kong, 1840-1970*, Hong Kong, 2014, 168; Benjamin Lai, *Hong Kong 1941-45; First Strike in the Pacific War*, NY, 2014, 32, 62.

587 Snow, 78. Such directives were given to many commands, but they were not obeyed. Harries & Harries, 480-1.

588 Snow, 78.

589 Ibid.

590 Ibid.

591 Snow, 82.

592 Frank, *Tower of Skulls*, 58.

593 Email Tatsushi Saito to Rigg, 23 April 2018; NIDSMDMA, *Senshi-Sosho*, "Operations Hong Kong & Chosa," War History Series, Vol. 47, 1971, 53, 180-1, 323; Kwong and Tsoi, 171; Ted Ferguson, *Desperate Siege: The Battle of Hong Kong*, Scarborough, Ontario, 1980, 32, 48; Snow, 53; UGSL, Hosch Papers, Tokyo War Crimes Trials, The Pacific War, Part B, Ch. VII, 984.

594 Andrew Roberts, *Churchill: Walking with Destiny*, NY, 2018, 698; Snow, 63.

595 Snow, 74-5.

596 NIDSMDMA, *Senshi-Sosho*, "Hong Kong & Chosa," War History Series, Vol. 47, 1971, 53, 180-1, 323; Interview Saito, 9-10 April 2018; Kwong and Tsoi, 192, 194, 223; Email Kwong to Rigg, 6 May 2018; Lai, 13, 32; 118-20, 137, 140; Snow, 53, 64-5; Email Tatsushi Saito to Rigg, 18 March 2019.

597 Snow, 82-3; Interview Master Johnny Lee, 9 April 2019; Scott, 66, 266. There was one case documented when a Japanese man found 15-year-old Priscilla Garcia in Manila on her period and refused to rape her so maybe there was some taboo amongst Japanese not to rape someone menstruating. Scott, 262.

598 Snow, 78-9, 82-3; Ferguson, 25, 76, 94, 205, 218; Shu-Fan, 108-9.

599 NIDSMDMA, *Senshi-Sosho*, "Hong Kong & Chosa," War History Series, Vol. 47, 1971, 53, 180-1, 323; Interview Saito, 9-10 April 2018; Kwong and Tsoi, 192, 194, 223; Email Kwong to Rigg, 6 May 2018; Lai, 13, 32; 118-20, 137, 140; Snow, 53, 64-5.

600 Kwong and Tsoi, 177-8; Lai, 13; Snow, 54; Ferguson, 70-2.

601 Snow, 65.

602 NIDSMDMA, *Senshi-Sosho*, "Hong Kong & Chosa," War History Series, Vol. 47, 1971, 53, 180-1, 323; Tanaka, 92.

603 Kwong and Tsoi, 161.

604 Ibid., 222. The breakdown of KIAs and WIAs for the Commonwealth soldiers were 2,113 KIAs and 1,332 WIAs. Donald C. Bowie, "Captive Surgeon in Hong Kong: The Story of the British Military Hospital, Hong Kong 1942-1945," *Journal of the Hong Kong Branch of the Royal Asiatic Society*, Vol. 15 (1975), 267.

605 Ibid., 115.

606 Harries & Harries, 238.

607 Ibid., 223.

608 NIDSMDMA, Kuribayashi, Bio info; Burrell, *Ghosts of Iwo Jima*, 41; George W. Garand & Truman R. Stobridge, *Western Pacific Operations: History of U.S. Marine Corps Operations in World War II*, Quantico, 1971, 451; MCRDSDA, C-2 Special Study, Enemy Situation, VAC, 6 Jan. '45, Unit Commanders, 11.

609 Horie, 49.

610 Ross, 20; Newcomb, 4-5, 7; NIDSMDMA, Records Showa Emperor, (ed.) *Kunaichō*, Tokyo, Sept. 2016, 359; Interview Shindo, 9 April 2018; NIDSMDMA, Collections Kuribayashi, Bio info.

611 Interview Shindo, 9 April 2018.

612 Burrell, *Ghosts of Iwo Jima*, 41.

613 Toland, Vol. II, 797.

614 NIDSMDMA, Kuribayashi, Bio info; Interview Shindo, 9 April 2018; Bradley & Powers, *Flags of Our Fathers*, 148.

615 Ross, 20.

616 Kakehashi, 94.

617 Interview Shindo, 9 April 2018.

618 Cameron, Mahoney and McReynolds, 133.

619 McNeill, "Reluctant Warrior," 39; Herman Melville, *Moby Dick,* Oxford, 2008, 166.

620 Kakehashi, 48; NMPWANM, 13 July 2017; Drea, 246.

621 *Minchas Chinuch,* Com. 37. See also Leviticus 19:16, (NIV), 125 & (KJV), 194. Interview Edgar Weinsberg, 6 Dec. 2019.

622 TSHACNCDNM, Vol. 10, 268-272, Statement Keenan, Chief Counsel, International Military Tribunal Far East, 4 June 1945, 7-10; *Hong Kong's War Crimes Trials*, Linton, "Introduction," 2-3.

623 NIDSMDMA, Collections Kuribayashi, Bio info; NIDSMDMA, *Senshi-Sosho*, Central Pacific, Op. #2, Peleliu, Angaur, Iwo, Vol. 13, 278-9. The Marine history called *The U.S. Marines on Iwo Jima* incorrectly claims Kuribayashi fought at Lake Nomanhan against the Soviets in 1939, but the Tokyo NIDS archives do not support this. Henri, et al., 6.

624 Mosley, 115.

625 UGSL, Hosch Papers, Tokyo War Crimes Trials, Conventional War Crimes (Atrocities), Part B, Ch. VIII, 1008; Lord Russell of Liverpool, 39; Cook & Cook, 5.

626 Tanaka, 4; Ienaga, 164.

627 Lord Russell of Liverpool, 41. See also Gruhl, 68.

628 Wallace & Williams, 182.

629 Ienaga, 164.

630 Snow, 79-80.

631 Marsman, 80–3, 87.

632 Ibid., 93–4.

633 Ibid., 94–5.

634 Snow, 81; Keith Bradsher, "Thousands March in Anti-Japan Protest in Hong Kong," *NYT*, 18 April 2005; Suzannah Linton, "Rediscovering the War Crimes Trials in Hong Kong, 1946-48," Melbourne Journal of International Law, Vol. 13, No. 2, 2012, 22-3; Ferguson, 54, 76, 94, 211-2,

217-8; UGSL, Hosch Papers, Tokyo War Crimes Trials, Conventional War Crimes (Atrocities), Part B, Ch. VIII, 1033, 1038; Drea, 224; *Hong Kong's War Crimes Trials*, Daqun, "Foreword," vi; Frank, *Tower of Skulls*, 315; *Law Reports of Trials of War Criminals: Selected and Prepared by The United Nations War Crimes Commission*, Volume XIV, London, 1948, 1-2.

635 Shu-Fan, 111.

636 Dower, 42; Fred Haynes & James A. Warren, *The Lions of Iwo Jima: The Story of Combat Team 28 and the Bloodiest Battle in Marine Corps History*, NY, 2008, 147; Harries & Harries, 313. Nuns were also raped and focused on when Japan conquered Guadalcanal in 1942. See Lord Russell of Liverpool, 269.

637 Interview Mary Dalbey-Rigg, Summer 1996. The interview with the nurse was conducted at Yale Univ. School of Nursing circa 1957.

638 Ferguson, 216.

639 Wakabayashi (ed.), *The Nanking Atrocity, 1937-38*, Tokushi, "Massacres Outside Nanking City," 58.

640 Shu-Fan, 111.

641 Ferguson, 211; Toland, Vol. I, 316; Snow, 80; Tanaka, 91-2; Hong *Kong's War Crimes Trials*, Daqun, "Foreword," v; Haynes & Warren, 147; Frank, *Tower of Skulls*, 314; Lord Russell of Liverpool, 97-8; Alan Birch and Martin Cole, *Captive Years: The Occupation of Hong Kong 1941-45*, Hong Kong, 1982, 16, 23, 29; Hoyt, 100.

642 Snow, 80.

643 Ibid.

644 Ferguson, 212.

645 Ferguson, 216; Interview Dalbey-Rigg, Summer 1996; Tanaka, 97. In numerous sources, the Japanese were found to laugh when torturing their victims. See Scott, 80, 261, 382.

646 Lord Russell of Liverpool, 98.

647 Strangely enough, Dr. Donald Bowie, who was a Lt. Colonel in the British Army and head of the British Military Hospital in Hong Kong, documented his hospital was spared the common treatment "in Japanese hands." So, not all Hong Kong hospitals were treated as roughly as St. Stephen's College. Bowie, 275.

648 Ferguson, 217. Japanese often enjoyed raping wives in front of their husbands. See Scott, 210.

649 Email Chi Man Kwong, Hong to Rigg, 30 April & 5 May 2018; Ferguson, 101, 218; Kwong and Tsoi, 181, 184; Snow, 80; *Hong Kong's War Crimes Trials*, Daqun, "Foreword," vi.

650 Snow, 82; *Hong Kong's War Crimes Trials*, Daqun, "Foreword," v.

651   *A Savage Christmas: The Fall of Hong Kong 1941*, Canadian Documentary, 12 Jan. 1992.

652   Browne, 154.

653   Dower, 44; Lord Russell of Liverpool, 63; Browne, 154.

654   Ferguson, 80, 144-7, 158, 166, 170, 176, 199, 210-1; Kwong and Tsoi, 218; Lai, 56, 79, 89; UGSL, Hosch Papers, Tokyo War Crimes Trials, Conventional War Crimes (Atrocities), Part B, Ch. VIII, 1033, 1038; Drea, 224; Snow 79–80; *Hong Kong's War Crimes Trials*, Daqun, "Foreword," v & Linton, "War Crimes," 96.

655   Ferguson, 211.

656   *Hong Kong's War Crimes Trials*, Daqun, "Foreword," v.

657   Bradsher, "Thousands March in Anti-Japan Protest in Hong Kong"; Ferguson, 25; Snow, 79; *Hong Kong's War Crimes Trials*, Daqun, "Foreword," vi & Linton, "War Crimes," 107-9, 113-4; Birch & Cole, 118-127; Shu-Fan, 103-4, 160-1; Bowie, 222, 227.

658   Snow, 86.

659   Ibid., 105.

660   Ibid., 86.

661   *Hong Kong's War Crimes Trials*, Daqun, "Foreword," vi.

662   Snow, 87.

663   Snow, 94-5.

664   Lord Russell of Liverpool, 121-5, 134; Birch & Cole, 78-88.

665   Kakehashi's biography *So Sad to Fall in Battle*, cited throughout this book. Burrell, *Ghosts of Iwo Jima*, 43; Email Tatsushi Saito to Rigg, 18 March 2019; Toland, Vol. II, 797; Crowl & Isley, 468; Horie, 50.

666   Kwong and Tsoi, 177-8. Kwong writes Kuribayashi was removed from "active staff duty" when he confronted Sakai over the treatment of Col. Doi, but this is wrong. He just moved from the front and returned to the 23rd Army's headquarters to the north. It was unclear whether this was punishment or just a normal re-deployment for Kuribayashi. Interview Tatsushi Saito, NIDS, 9 April 2018; Email Chi Man Kwong to Rigg, 10 March 2019 & 18 March 2019; Email Tatsushi Saito to Rigg, 17 March 2019.

667   *Hong Kong's War Crimes Trials*, Zahar, "Trial Procedure at the British Military Courts, Hong Kong, 1946-48," 15 & Linton, "War Crimes," 133.

668   Charles G. Roland, "Massacre and Rape in Hong Kong: Two Case Studies Involving Medical Personnel and Patients," *Journal of Contemporary History*, Vol. 32 (I), 43-61, 1997. However, historian Chi Man Kwong defends Kuribayashi saying he was on the Kowloon side and most of the atrocities took place "on the island side," but nonetheless, atrocities also took place in Kowloon. Email Chi Man Kwong to Rigg, 5 May 2018; *Hong Kong's War Crimes Trials*, Linton, "War Crimes," 133.

669 Linton, "Rediscovering the War Crimes Trials in Hong Kong, 1946-48," 56-8; Carroll, John Mark. (2007). A concise history of Hong Kong, 123; Alexander, 6; Edgerton, 264-5; Burleigh, 331; Kakehashi, xi, 3-4; *Law Reports of Trials of War Criminals*. Vol. III. The UN War Crimes Commission, 1948, Trial Gen. Takashi Sakai; NACPM, RG 165, Box 2151, War Dept., 6900-5 (Japan), memorandum Consul Gen. Robert S. Ward: Japanese attack on and Capture of…Hong Kong, 17; NACPM, Microfilm Room, Roll 1499, #144, 23838, Current Intel Sec. A-2, Interview Charles Schaefer, Dist. Manager, Hong Kong—PAM Airlines, 28 Aug. 1942; UN Archives (UNA), Security Microfilm Programme 1998, UNWCC, PAG-3, Reel no. 61, Summary Translation of the Proceedings of the Military Tribunal, Nanking, Trial of Takashi Sakai, 3; *Hong Kong's War Crimes Trials*, Honorable Justice Liu Daqun, "Foreword," vi & Linton, "War Crimes," 96.

670 Linton, 58.

671 UNA, Security Microfilm Programme 1998, UNWCC, PAG-3, Reel no. 61, Summary Translation of the Proceedings of the Military Tribunal, Nanking, Trial Takashi Sakai, 1.

672 Ibid., 3.

673 Snow, 81; Shu-Fan, 109-111.

674 Snow, 82.

675 Linton (ed.), Linton, "Introduction," 1.

676 Interview Dennis Showalter, 18 May 2019.

677 Snow, 80. It seems there was only one case where the Japanese command tried to re-instate some semblance of justice. According to historian Snow, three days after the fall of Hong Kong, nine IJA troops who had raped British nurses in Happy Valley were executed. However, this study has seen no evidence that IJA personnel were ever punished for harming and killing Chinese civilians in Hong Kong. Snow, 81.

678 Hong Kong's War Crimes Trials Collection, Case No. W0235/1030, Maj. Gen. Ryossaburo Tanaka & Lt. Gen. Takeo Ito, Case No. W0235/1107; Lai, 32, 89; Snow, 80; *Hong Kong's War Crimes Trials*, Linton, "War Crimes," 99.

679 Snow, 80.

680 *Hong Kong's War Crimes Trials*, Totani, "The Prisoner of War Camp Trials," 75, 78-9.

681 Bowie, 197, 203-4.

682 *Hong Kong's War Crimes Trials*, Totani, "The Prisoner of War Camp Trials," 78.

683 Ibid., Daqun, "Foreword," vi & Linton, "Major Murray Ormsby," 231-2, 240-1.

684 Interview Mant Hawkins, 16 Feb. 2019.

685 Scott, 489.

686 Information and quote from Scott, 501. See also Lord Russell of Liverpool, 295.

687 Interview Lt. Col. W. K., 6 Jan. 2022.

688 Lord Russell of Liverpool, 296.

689 Ibid.

690 Scott, 502.

691 Sheldon H. Harris, *Factories of Death: Japanese Biological Warfare, 1932-45, and the American Cover-up*, NY, 2002, 86-7, 127, 229; Sheldon H. Harris, Ch. 16, "Japanese Biomedical Experimentation During the World War II Era," 477, 481, LaGuardia Community College Files; Email Saito to Rigg, 4 April 2019; *People's Daily Online*, New Proof of Japan's WWII Invasion Found in Guangzhou, 17 April 2005.

692 Email Saito to Rigg, 4 April 2019; ［以下、栗林が参謀長の時の第23軍の話です。(1941.9-1943.6)
第23軍司令部は、この間、"広東"にありました。
まず、香港攻略以後、栗林のいる間は大きな作戦は実施していません。
そして、香港の占領地行政は、陸軍大臣直轄の香港占領地総督部が行います。
香港の占領地行政には第23軍は、ほとんど関与しません。
香港攻略戦の後、第23軍が何をていたかという史料は少なく、詳しくはわかりません。
しかし、ここには、いくつかの参謀長名の電報と、レポートがあります。
この史料から推測すると、占領地域（広東、香港地域など）の治安維持、飛行場などの施設整備、経済対策（金融、通貨、物資配給・統制）などである。
その他、当然ながら、軍隊の教育訓練、維持管理、兵站基地としての機能もあったと思われる。
上記の参考となった史料名、以下2点です。］
①南支那方面第23軍関係電報綴（中央―作戦指導重要電報―42）
②波集団司令部「波集団経済封鎖情報月報」（支那―大東亜戦争南支―3）See also Moore, 219.

693 Ibid.

694 Burrell, *Ghosts of Iwo Jima*, 41.

695 Snow, 102.

696 Tanaka, 105.

697 Shu-Fan, 114.

698 Quote from Tanaka, 106. See also Bowie, 208.

699 Snow, 102; Tanaka, 110; Shu-Fan, 116.

700 Marsman, 90-1.

701 Tanaka, 107; Shu-Fan, 119. See also Ienaga, 190.

702 Tanaka, 110.

703 Shu-Fan, 121.
704 Snow, 131.
705 Ibid., 132.
706 Quote from Snow, 133-4. See also Bowie, 196.
707 Crowl & Isely, 468; Henri, et al., 6.
708 Snow, 159. Renaming landmarks and cities after Japanese names was common throughout Japan's conquered empire. See Scott, 62; Shu-Fan, 147.
709 Snow, 160.
710 Ibid., 163-4.
711 Ibid., 106, 114, 118.
712 *Law Reports of Trials of War Criminals: Selected and Prepared by The United Nations War Crimes Commission*, Volume XIV, London, 1948, 2.
713 Ibid., 7.
714 Ibid.
715 NIDSMDMA, *Senshi-Sosho*, Central Pacific, Op. #2, Peleliu, Angaur, Iwo, Vol. 13, 391; MōDQV, Dashiell File, #196, Iwo Items; Larry Smith, *Drill Sergeants*, 29; Henri, et al., 13; Smith, *Iwo Jima*, xxi; Wheeler, 41; Newcomb, 35; Edgerton, 226; Robert T. Oliver, *A History of the Korean People in Modern Times: 1800 to the Present*, Newark, 1993, 110–24; Cook & Cook, 48; Drea, 232. Thanks to Dr. Kwan-sa You for translating this info from Kap-jae Cho: "Spit on My Grave—The Life of Park Chung-hee," Chosun Ilbo, Seoul, Korea, No. 104-16, 1998; Snow, 95.
716 Interview Shindo, 9 April 2018.
717 Samuel Beckett, *Waiting for Godot*, NY, 1954, Act II, 52.
718 Yoshiaki Yoshimi and Suzanne O'Brien, *Comfort Women*, NY, 2002; Lord Russell of Liverpool, 43, 243, 257, 266, 294; Jones, "Comfort Women," *Art Wire*, 28 Sept. 2017; Julia Glum, "San Francisco Statue Honoring 'Comfort Women' Sex Slaves from WWII Infuriates Japan," *Newsweek*, 30 Oct. 2017; Tanaka, 5, 102; Scott, 263-4, 280; TSHACNCDNM, Vol. 2, 240 from H. J. Timperley, *What War Means*, 64-5, 188-9, 192; Moore, 134, 148-153; Ienaga, 158-9, 184 ; Bradley, *Flyboys*, 61; Crowe, 130-1.
719 Tanaka, 102.
720 Bradley, *Flyboys*, 61.
721 Tanaka, 104.
722 UGSL, Hosch Papers, Tokyo War Crimes Trials, Conventional War Crimes (Atrocities), Part B, Ch. VIII, 1023; Modder, 23.
723 The Soviet military raped millions of German women, but they usually did not force them into brothels and/or also kill them thereafter like was seen in the Japanese military. See Beevor, 28, 31, 107-8, 300, 410; Sajer, 415-6, 421; Ienaga, 233-4. For an excellent book on the sexual crimes of the Soviet Army raping over two million women in 1944/1945, see Ingo von Münch, *Frau,*

komm!: Die Massenvergewaltigungen deutscher Frauen und Mädchen 1944/45, Graz, 2009.

724 Bradley, *Flyboys*, 61.

725 Scott, 11.

726 Harris, *Factories of Death*; Sheldon H. Harris, Ch. 16, "Japanese Biomedical Experimentation During the World War II Era," 477, 481, LaGuardia Community College Files.

727 Ienaga, 188; Wallace & Williams, 16.

728 Harris, 14; Gold, 23.

729 Harris, 14-5, 17, 32-3; Wallace & Williams, 5-11.

730 Harries, 18-19; Gold, 25.

731 Notes on manuscript by Richard Frank, 3 March 2023.

732 Harris, 22-8; Wallace & Williams, 32; *Materials on the Trial of Former Servicemen of the Japanese army Charged with Manufacturing and Employing Bacteriological Weapons*, 17; Gold, 26.

733 Harris, 52; Wallace & Williams, 13-16.

734 Harris, 31-3; Wallace & Williams, 16.

735 Harris, 52.

736 Wallace & Williams, 223. Hirohito biography Herbert Bix documents that the emperor knew everything about Unit 731. Bix, 364.

737 Ibid., 79-80.

738 *Materials on the Trial of Former Servicemen of the Japanese army Charged with Manufacturing and Employing Bacteriological Weapons*, 283.

739 Ibid., 10.

740 Wallace & Williams, 79-80.

741 Bix, 364. Historian Sheldon Harris claims Hirohito probably did not know everything about Unit 731 (Harris, 144-6). However, Bix's research is more thorough and he claims Hirohito knew about it in its entirety.

742 Harris, 47; Wallace & Williams, 20.

743 Wallace & Williams, 20.

744 Ibid., 31.

745 Nicholas D. Kristof, "Unmasking Horror—As Special Report. Japan Confronting Gruesome War Atrocity," *The New York Times*, 17 March 1995; Daniel Barenblatt, *A Plague Upon Humanity: The Secret Genocide of Axis Japan's Germ Warfare Operation*, NY, 2004, xii, 173-4; (Rare) Unit 731 surgeon Okawa Fukumatsu (interview footage) see https://vimeo.com/625179260; Harris, *Factories of Death*, 51, 86-7, 127, 229; Sheldon H. Harris, Ch. 16, "Japanese Biomedical Experimentation During the World War II Era," 477, 481, LaGuardia Community College Files; Wallace & Williams, 35; *Materials on the Trial of Former Servicemen of the Japanese army*

Charged with Manufacturing and Employing Bacteriological Weapons, 20; Crowe, 135.

746 Crowe, 135.

747 Cook & Cook, 44-5, 162-5, 199-202; Drea, 203; Bix, 361-4; Takashi Yoshida, 29-30; Moore, 127-9, 227; Harris, 78.

748 Gruhl, 83.

749 Ibid.

750 Ibid.

751 Cook & Cook, 163; Edgerton, 284; Wallace & Williams, 24.

752 Cook & Cook, 44-5, 162-5, 199-202; Drea, 203; Bix, 361-4; Takashi Yoshida, 29-30; Moore, 127-9, 227; Frank, *Tower of Skulls*, 79, 161.

753 Cook & Cook, 44-5. See also Harris, 73.

754 Bix, 362.

755 Harris, 49; Wallace & Williams, 35.

756 Wallace & Williams, 46.

757 Cook & Cook, 149, 151.

758 Bix, 361.

759 Gold, 157-8, 163, 198-9; Cook & Cook, 162; Harries & Harries, 360; Wallace & Williams, 41.

760 Harris, 49; Harries & Harries, 360-1.

761 Harries & Harries, 360-1.

762 Gold, 165-6.

763 *Materials on the Trial of Former Servicemen of the Japanese army Charged with Manufacturing and Employing Bacteriological Weapons*, 279-80.

764 Harris, 83-5; Wallace & Williams, 200 203, 221; Edgerton, 284; Gold, 49.

765 Wallace & Williams, 178-9.

766 Harris, 138; Harries & Harries, 360.

767 Christopher W. George, Theodore J. Cieslak, Julie A. Pavlin, and Edward M. Eitzen, "Biological Warfare: A Historical Perspective," *The Journal of the American Medical Association*, 278 (5), 412-17; Wallace & Williams, 68-70; Barenblatt, 58.

768 Harries & Harries, 360; Barenblatt, 58; Wallace & Williams, 68-70.

769 Barenblatt, 58.

770 Harris, 80; Wallace & Williams, 176.

771 Harris, 80, 110-1.

772 Wallace & Williams, 21, 26.

773 Harris, 77-8; Ienaga, 188.

774 Doug Hickey, Scarllet Sijia Li, Ceila Morrison, Richard Schulz, Michelle Thiry, and Kelly Sorensen, "Unit 731 and Moral Report," *Journal of Medical Ethics*, 43 (4), April 2017, 270-6; Harris, *Factories of Death*; Sheldon H.

Harris, Ch. 16, "Japanese Biomedical Experimentation During the World War II Era," 477, 481, LaGuardia Community College Files.

775 Wallace & Williams, 42; *Materials on the Trial of Former Servicemen of the Japanese army Charged with Manufacturing and Employing Bacteriological Weapons*, 17; Ienaga, 188; Gold, 49.

776 Harris, 62; "Asia's Auschwitz," The Sydney Morning Herald, 17 December 1994.

777 Wallace & Williams, 44; *Materials on the Trial of Former Servicemen of the Japanese army Charged with Manufacturing and Employing Bacteriological Weapons*, 17-18; Ienaga, 188.

778 Bix, 364; Edgerton, 284; Wallace & Williams, 23, 49, 81; Justin McCurry, "Japan Unearths Site Linked to Human Experiments," *The Guardian*, 21 Feb. 2011; Bradley, *Flyboys*, 113; Bradley & Powers, *Flags of Our Fathers*, 59-60; Frank, 324-5; Toland Vol. II, 612-3; Crowl & Isely, 336; Hallas, *Saipan*, 60-1; *Documents on the Tokyo International Military Tribunal Charter*, 539-40.

779 Wallace & Williams, 49.
780 Harris, 63.
781 Wallace & Williams, 51-62.
782 Ibid., 23.
783 Ibid., 30.
784 Wallace & Williams, 253.
785 Harris, 66-7; Wallace & Williams, 86.
786 Wallace & Williams, 49.
787 Ibid., 137, 141.
788 Gold, 109. See also Harris 178-9; Wallace & Williams, 133; Tanaka, 174.
789 Wallace & Williams, 138; Lisa Kelly Pennington, "The Pacific War Crimes Trials: The Importance of the 'Small Frey' vs. the 'Big Fish,'"Old Dominion University ODU Digital Commons, History Theses & Dissertations, History, Summer 2012, 112.
790 Drea, 261; Barenblatt, 207; Wallace & Williams, 165.
791 Wallace & Williams, 228-9.
792 Ibid., 230.
793 Timothy Synder, *Bloodlands: Between Hitler and Stalin*, NY, 2010.
794 Harris, 114-5, 118, 121; Wallace & Williams, 246; Barenblatt, 226.
795 Wallace & Williams, 247; Barenblatt, 226.
796 Barenblatt, 226.
797 Ibid., 235-6.
798 Ibid., 235.
799 Ibid., 236.
800 "Japanese Court Rejects Germ Warfare Damages," *NYT*, 20 July 2005.

801 Ibid.

802 NACPM, General Kenji Doihara, OSS Report, F.E.E. of X-2, June 1943.

803 John M. Jennings, *The Opium Empire: Japanese Imperialism and Drug Trafficking in Asia, 1895-1945*, Westport, CT, 1997, 82.

804 John King Fairbank and Merle Goldman, *China: A New History*, Harvard, 320; Bix, 257.

805 United Nations War Crimes Commission, War Crimes Trials in the Far East, The Trial of the Major Japanese War Criminals, December 1947, p. 4; NACPM, General Kenji Doihara, OSS Report, F.E.E. of X-2, June 1943.

806 See article by Chen Yung-Fa in *New Perspectives on the Chinese Communist Revolution*. Chen Young-Fa, *Zhongguo Gongchan Geming Qishi Nian*, Taiwan, Lianjing Chuban Shiye Gongsi, 1st Ed., 1998, 2nd Ed., 2001.

807 Tanaka, xvi; Drea, 168; Cook & Cook, 23; Burleigh, 15-6; Lord Russell of Liverpool, 7; Edgerton, 311; LaFeber, 337-8; Harries & Harries, 145. Hitler did the same thing with Poland in 1939. He created a false attack and then countered with an invasion. Bryan Mark Rigg, *The Rabbi Saved by Hitler's Soldiers: Rebbe Joseph Isaac Schneersohn and His Astonishing Rescue*, Kansas, 2016, 11-8. Mukden today is Shenyang. *Manchukuo* was the name the Japanese gave the occupied land and their puppet government in Manchuria (1931-45) which was 600,000 square miles. Japan took over this area that had a population of 43,233,954. In 1933, Japan sent 1,500,000 colonists there. Drea, 251; NACPM, Microfilm Room, Roll 1499, #101, 19557, U.S. Intelligence Report from Reference Division, 7 July 1942, Regarding: The Economy of Manchuria, Population Oct. 1940; Cook & Cook, 33-4, 125, 156; Information from the display of the National Museum of the Pacific War, Home of Admiral Nimitz Museum (NMPWANM), Fredericksburg, TX, 13 July 2017; Ienaga, 60; Crowley, 96, 114-7.

808 MCHDQV, Oral History, Erskine from 1969-70, 149.

809 Univ. of Georgia School of Law (UGSL), J. Alton Hosch Papers, Tokyo War Crimes Trials, Japanese Aggression Against China, Part B, Ch. V, 644-7; Tuchman, 141; Harries & Harries, vii, 230, 246; Ienaga, 165; Jennings, 107.

810 Harries & Harries, vii.

811 Jennings, 91.

812 Ronald Sydney Seth, *Secret Servants: A History of Japanese Espionage*, NY, 1957, 128.

813 Ronald Sydney Seth, *Encyclopedia of Espionage*, NY, 1974, 315.

814 Seth, *Encyclopedia of Espionage*, 316; Harries & Harries, 332-3; Ienaga, 101-2.

815 Cook & Cook, 153.

816 Harries & Harries, 246, 261.

817 Ibid., 246.

818 Patrick Knox, "'Kill, Steal, Rape, Control'; How the Murderous MS-13 Gang Has Become a Multi-Million-Pound Crime Cartel Rivalling the Mafia that Trump Has Vowed to Rid from America," The Sun, 20 April 2017.
819 Dower, 8; Manchester, 78; Crowley, 190.
820 Harries & Harries, 246.
821 Edgerton, 244.
822 See Tuchman, 78, 81, 154-5.
823 Harries & Harries, 245.
824 Ibid., 246. See also Brackman, 191,
825 Ibid. See also Brackman, 191.
826 Shu-Fan, 117.
827 Brackman, 193.
828 Ibid., 195.
829 Jennings, 106-7.
830 Pennington, 56.
831 Dina Gusovsky, "Americans Consume Vast Majority of the World's Opioids," CNBC, 27 April 2016.
832 Natalie Sherman, "Purdue Pharma to Plead Guilty in $8bn Opioid Settlement," BBC, 21 Oct. 2020; Joanna Walters, "An Evil Family: Sacklers Condemned as They Refuse to Apologize for Role in Opioid Crisis," Guardian News, 17 Dec. 2020.
833 Maggie Fox, "Drug Overdose Deaths Hit Highest Number Ever Recorded, CDC Data Shows," CNN, 14 July 2021.
834 Conrad, "Heart of Darkness," 543.
835 Lord Russell of Liverpool, 39.
836 Harries & Harries, 4.
837 Lord Russell of Liverpool, 51.
838 Tuchman, 168; Moore, 84-5; Gruhl, 68.
839 Tuchman, 171.
840 Ienaga, 167.
841 Ibid.
842 Frank, Tower of Skulls, 80.
843 Bix, 348.
844 Ibid., 61.
845 Ienaga, 167.
846 Harries & Harries, 235; Frank, Tower of Skulls, 69–72.
847 NACPM, General Kenji Doihara, OSS Report, F.E.E. of X-2, June 1943.
848 Frank, Tower of Skulls, 111.
849 Cook & Cook, 44.
850 Ibid., 464.
851 Ibid., 462.

852 Ibid., 466-7.

853 Frank, *Tower of Skulls*, 462, 478.

854 Harries & Harries, 310, 312. Of course, many refugees were Indians who had come to Burma with the British to control this region. These Indians were not only worried about the Japanese, but they also were worried about Burmese retribution against them for helping the British colonize their country.

855 Lord Russell of Liverpool, 325.

856 Ibid., 270.

857 Bradley, *Flyboys*, 111.

858 Quote from James M. Scott, "The Untold Story of the Vengeful Japanese Attack After the Doolittle Raid," *Smithsonian Magazine*, 15 April 2015; Edgerton, 275; Scott, 510; Toll, *Pacific Crucible*, 300.

859 Quote from Edgerton, 275; Scott, 510; Toll, *Pacific Crucible*, 300; James M. Scott, "The Untold Story of the Vengeful Japanese Attack After the Doolittle Raid," *Smithsonian Magazine*, 15 April 2015; Bradley, *Flyboys*, 111, 113.

860 Toll, *Pacific Crucible*, 300.

861 Harris, 80-1, 139, 181-9; Lord Russell of Liverpool, 288.

862 Lord Russell of Liverpool, 213-4.

863 Ibid., 214-5.

864 Ibid., 266.

865 Ibid., 212.

866 Chang, 4, 6, 59, 86, 87-9 91, 94-5, 103, 155; Bradley, *Flyboys*, 58-9, 62, 111-2, 152, 200-1, 225, 228-232, 245, 316; Edgerton, 16, 246-7; Burleigh, 561; Cook & Cook, 155, 273-4, 462; Lord Russel, 41-2, 57, 240; NACPM staff, "Japanese War Crimes Records National Archives: Research Starting Points," in *Researching Japanese War Crimes Records*, 102-3; Bradley, *Flyboys*, 200; Greg Bradsher, "The Exploitation of Captured and Seized Japanese Records Relating to War Crimes, 1942-1945," in *Researching Japanese War Crimes Records*, 152); MCHDQV, Dashiell File, #1, Davis-Filipinos; Mark Felton, *Slaughter at Sea: The Story of Japan's Naval War Crimes*, South Yorkshire, 2007; UGSL, J. Alton Hosch Papers, Tokyo War Crimes Trials, Conventional War Crimes (Atrocities), Part B, Ch. VIII, 1033, 1067; Tanaka, 129, 139; JNMS, Vol. 1, No. 1, Zhang Sheng, "The Seven Why-Questions in the Writing of History," 10 & Zhang Lianhong, "A Hero of Nanjing: Austrian Mechanic Rupert R. Hatz During the Nanjing Massacre," 27; Dante, *Inferno*, Canto XXXIV, 115; TSHACNCDNM, Vol. 2, 214, 221-2 from H. J. Timperley, *What War Means*, 36, 42-3, 62, 65, 184-5, 189-91 & Vol. 3, 28-49, Cases of Disorder by Japanese Soldiers in the Safety Zone; Moore, 210; Harries & Harries, 405, 484.

867 Goldman & Shulatov, 38.

868 Bradley, *Flyboys*, 200.

869 Wu Ch'êng-ên, 284.

870 Harries & Harries, 405.

871 *Silence of the Lambs* is a 1991 horror film about a serial killer who tortures and eats his victims.

872 Conrad, "Heart of Darkness," 495. Conrad is describing Belgium King Leopold II's brutal Congo rule from the 1890s until 1908.

873 Cook & Cook, 40-4; Victoria, *Zen at War*, 76-7; Toll, *Pacific Crucible*, 112.

874 Bix, 15. See also Bix, 336–8.

875 Weinberg, 894; Dower, 47, 295-7; Bix, 4; Interview Gerhard Weinberg, 2 Sept. 2005; Edgerton, 250, 272, 284; Frank, 162-3, 325, 329; Hane, 361-2; Karl August Muggenthaler, *German Raiders of World War II: The First Complete History of Germany's Mysterious Naval Marauders*, Suffolk, 1978, 270; Cook & Cook, 74, 99; Drea, 236; Robert Hanyok, "Wartime COMINT Records National Archives about Japanese War Crimes in the Asia and Pacific Theaters, 1978-1997," in *Researching Japanese War Crimes Records*, 142; Spence, 496. Frank writes that recent scholarship puts the number at 18 million civilian deaths under the Japanese alone. Here is the breakdown of death by the Japanese from 1931-45 by country using historian Robert Newman's data: China (10,000,000); Java (Dutch West Indies Indonesia) (3,000,000); Outer Islands (Dutch Indies) (1,000,000); Philippines (120,000); India (180,000); Bengal Famine (1,500,000); Korea (70,000); Burma-Siam railroad (82,500)*; Indonesian, Europeans (30,000); Malaya (100,000); Vietnam (1,000,000)**; Australia (30,000); New Zealand (10,000); U.S. (100,000). Altogether, Frank cites 17,222,500 killed by the Japanese during WWII. Frank, 163. Frank also notes these numbers would be higher if one also included the deaths that happened after 1945 when the effects of the Japanese medical experiments and famine on the populations they controlled were tabulated. Frank, 162, 325, 329. *Sources listed in the chapter on the Siam-Burma railroad indicate that closer to 350,000 total were slaughtered by the Japanese conducting this project. **A special note on Vietnam, according to the National Archives, 1,000,000 Vietnamese starved alone from 1944-45 due to Japanese policies, so this nation probably lost more than what is cited in Frank's work. Robert Hanyok, "Wartime COMINT Records in the National Archives about Japanese War Crimes in the Asia and Pacific Theaters, 1978-97," in *Researching Japanese War Crimes Records*, 142. Historian Yuki Tanaka puts the number even higher to 2 million Vietnamese. Tanaka, 250. See also Ienaga, 178. Former NASA Chief of Cost and Economic Analysis, Werner Gruhl, used used his experience in calculating statistics to come up with a minimum of 24 million deaths caused by Imperial Japan during WWII. See Gruhl, 19.

876   NMPWANM, 13 July 2017; The breakdown follows of those citizens killed by the Japanese: U.S. 1,542 , Malaya 100,000, Indonesia (Europeans) 30,000, Korea 378,000-533,000 (includes forced laborers and IJA soldiers), Philippines (Manila 1945) 120,000, Philippines 1 million, Indo China (Vietnam) 500,000, India 26,000, Dutch East Indies 4 million, Burma 250,000, China 10-17 million and Australia 700. Bix, 4; Tanaka, xix, 8-9, 251; Gaerlan, "War Crimes in the Philippines during WWII," Arthur D. Simons Center for Interagency Cooperation, Ft. Leavenworth, Kansas, 2019; Morningstar, *War and Resistance: The Philippines 1942-1944*, 805.

877   Dinah Shelton, ed. *Encyclopedia of Genocide and Crimes of Humanity*, NY, 2005, 171; Dower, 295-7; Chang, 8; Spence, 464; Drea, 245; NMPWANM, 13 July 2017; Kuhn, 30; Interview Morgan, 10 Dec. 2017; Interview Heaton, 17 Dec. 2017; Burleigh, 562. Chang has the number between 10-19 million. Considering how the Japanese behaved, this study finds 10 million low. The general consensus is that Japanese killed many more in China than can be documented because they murdered everywhere they went for 15 years unlike the Nazis who only murdered intensively for four years from 1941-4. This study believes the Japanese murdered over 30 million. Renowned Yale Univ. historian Jonathan Spence claims in one region in Communist Mao-held lands, due to Japanese "counterattacks" and their "immense cruelty," the population dropped from 44 million to 24 million, with many if not most dying. In fact, the Japanese often destroyed "whole villages" during their operations. Spence, 464. Drea writes 10 million Chinese soldiers died fighting the Japanese and "civilian casualties certainly surpassed that number." Drea, 245. Dieter Kuhn writes that between 1937-45, the Japanese murdered over 19 million. Kuhn, 30. Marty Morgan and Colin Heaton say the Japanese probably murdered over 40 million. Interview Morgan, 10 Dec. 2017; Interview Heaton, 17 Dec. 2017.

878   NMPWANM, 13 July 2017.

879   Frank, 162; Edgerton, 14.

880   Driscoll, 5.

881   Interview Morgan, 10 Dec. 2017; Weiner (ed.), *Race, Ethnicity and Migration in Modern Japan*, Weiner, "Introduction," 3. Wakabayashi quotes sources that 35 million died during the Second Sino-Japanese War, but does not delineate how many were due to atrocities and how many were due to battle. Wakabayashi (ed.), *The Nanking Atrocity, 1937-38*, Wakabayashi, "The Messiness of Historical Reality," 9; Dower, 43; Spence, 469; Frank, 109, 160; Edgerton, 249-50; Drea, 214; Weinberg, 2, 20-1, 28; Patterson, 254-5; Zeiler, 3.

882   Drea, 214; Bix, 365.

883   Some literature out there tries to pin the responsibility of this famine on the shoulders of the British colonial government. The problem with this opinion is that the British had dealt with previous famines and provided relief to the starving populations before. So, one could argue, why stop it now? The places the British often went to in order to aid the Bengal population were Burma, Thailand, and southern Indochina (Vietnam). During this famine, these regions were under Japanese control and the Japanese did nothing to stop this famine.

884   Quote from Hane, 361. See also Cook & Cook, 2.

885   Lord Russell of Liverpool, 52.

886   Spence, 448.

887   Statement Prime Minister Junichiro Koizumi, 15 Aug. 2005.

888   Interview, Japanese Deputy Consul Gen. Ryuji Iwasaki, 12 Dec. 2017; Ministry of Foreign Affairs of Japan's take on "What is the view of the Government of Japan on the incident known as the "Nanjing Massacre"?" It answers some of this question with "…there are numerous theories as to the actual number of victims, and the Government of Japan believes it is difficult to determine which the correct number is." In Prime Minister Shinzo Abe's statement on WWII from 14 Aug. 2017, he never mentioned his country murdered millions. Statement PM Abe on 70th commemoration of WWII's end.

889   *The Teaching of Buddha*, Buddhist Promoting Foundation, Tokyo, Japan, 1992, DHAMMAPADA (103).

890   Note by Colin Heaton, 28 May 2017.

891   Cook & Cook, 10; Interview Drea, 17 Dec. 2017; Weiner (ed.), *Race, Ethnicity and Migration in Modern Japan*, Weiner, "Introduction," 2. Historians Meirion and Susie Harries write about Japan's Holocaust: "The exhaustive and cathartic examination of the Holocaust by Germans in recent years has no Japanese equivalent. There has been no easy explanation of Japanese atrocities, no Nazi party to act as the scapegoat for collective war guilt. Because the Japanese have not come to terms with their own past, neither have others." Harries & Harries, ix.

892   Harries & Harries, viii.

893   For an interesting articles about these issues, and which shows that there is indeed a movement within Japan, albeit small, to document the past truthfully, see Roger B. Jeans, "Victims or Victimizers? Museums, Textbooks, and the War Debate in Contemporary Japan." *The Journal of Military History*. Society for Military History. 69 (1): (January 2005), 149–195.

894   Honda Katsuichi, *The Nanjing Massacre: A Japanese Journalist Confronts Japan's National Shame*, London, 1999, 287 (Nanjing and Nanking are two spellings for the same city); Bradley, *Flyboys*, 61; Edgerton, 16; Cook

& Cook, 116, 446-7; Drea, vii; Interview Morgan, 10 Dec. 2017. See also *Hong Kong's War Crimes Trials*, Daqun, "Foreword," viii. See also Tanaka, xv; Brackman, 27.

895 Quote from Cook & Cook, 441; Edward J. Drea, "Introduction," in *Researching Japanese War Crimes Records*, 6; Interview Drea, 10 Dec. 2017; Tanaka, xv; Wakabayashi (ed.), *The Nanking Atrocity, 1937-38*, Akira, "The Nanking Atrocity: An Interpretive Overview," 39, 51.

896 Tanaka, xi.

897 Chang, xii, (Foreword William C. Kirby); Bradley & Powers, *Flags of Our Fathers*, 62; Drea, "Introduction," in *Researching Japanese War Crimes Records*, 5.

898 Edgerton, 249. David Sanger, "New Tokyo Minister Calls 'Rape of Nanking' Fabrication," *NYT*, 5 May 1994.

899 Yashukan War Museum in Tokyo, Japan, 9 April 2018.

900 Yahara, 197.

901 Ibid., 105.

902 Yahara, 106 fn. 2, 173, 179, 186.

903 Gruhl, 81.

904 *Documents on the Tokyo International Military Tribunal Charter*, 36; Bix, xvii, 364; Tanaka, xvii, 5-6; SLHA, Young Companion, 1941-1945, 167-72, "A Review of 4 Years of War in Figures" & 1940, 150-5, "Air Raids in Lanchow"; Tuchman, 136, 166; Interview Fiske Hanley, 20 March 2015; LaFeber, 426; O'Brien, *The Second Most Powerful Man in the World*, 107; Tanaka, xvii, 5-6; Frank, *Tower of Skulls*, 133, 136; Cook & Cook, 199-201; Harries & Harries, 247; Ienaga, 187; Bradley, *Flyboys*, 296; Tuchman, 136, 166-7.

905 Maga, 51.

906 BA-MA, RM 11/79, Mitteilung d. chinesischen Delegation an den Generalsekretär (Société des Nations), 21 Sept. 1937, 26 & RM 11/74, Marineattaché Tokyo an OKM, Auszug 31 Okt. 1938, 26.

907 Toland, Vol. II, 839.

908 Tanaka, xvi.

909 Interview Lt. Col. W. K., 6 Jan. 2022.

910 Tanaka, xvii.

911 Richard Black, "Those Who Deny Auschwitz Would be Ready to Remake it," *Jewish News*, 27 Jan. 2015.

912 Harries & Harries, 491.

913 "Another Attempt to Deny Japan's History," NY Times, 2 Jan. 2013; Justin McCurry, "Shinzo Abe, an Outspoken Nationalist, Takes Reins at Japan's LDP, Risking Tensions with China, South Korea," Global Post, 28 Sept. 2012; Norimitsu Onishi, "Abe Rejects Japan's Files on War Sex, *NYTimes*, 22

July 2018; "Japan PM Abe Demands Apology for South Korean Comments on Emperor Akihito," The Straits Times, 12 Feb. 2019; Tanaka, xv, xxii, xvii.

914   Hitchens (ed.), *The Portable Atheist*, George Eliot, "Evangelical Teaching," 76; Tanaka, xi.

915   Driscoll, 266-77; Richard Samuels, "Kishi and Corruption: An Anatomy of the 955 System," Working Paper No. 83, Dec. 2001, Japan Policy Research Institute; Bright, 517.

916   Crowl & Isely, 500-1.

917   Letter Shindo to IJAA, DD Dec. 2018.

918   "Nationalist 'Japan Conference' Building Its Clout: Ten Days after the Meeting, Abe Officially Addressed the Issue of Revising the Pacifist Constitution," *Korea JoongAng Daily*, 3 May 2013; "Japanese Minister Yoshitaka Shindo Visits Yasukuni Shrine Provoking China's Ire," *South China Morning Post*, 1 Jan. 2014; https://www.revolvy.com/page/Yoshitaka-Shind%C5%8D.

919   "Behavioral Principle of the Right Wing Organization 'Japan Conference' Supporting the Abe Administration: Interview with Mr. Sueno, author of 'Japanese Conference Research'", Diamond Online, 20 May 2016; Josh Gelernter, "Japan Reverts to Fascism," National Review, 16 July 2016.

920   Norihiro Kato, "Tea Party Politics in Japan," NY Times, 12 Sept. 2014; Jennifer E. Robertson, *Politics and Pitfalls of Japan Ethnography: Reflexivity, Responsibility, and Anthropological Ethics*, NY, 2009, 66; Emma Chanlett-Avery, Mark E. Manyin, Rebecca M. Nelson, Brock R. Williams and Taishu Yamakawa, *Japan-U.S. Relations: Issues for Congress*, Congressional Research Service, 16 Feb. 2017, 8-10; Tanaka, xxi-xxii, 257; JNMS, Vol. 1, No. 1, Sheng, "The Seven Why-Questions in the Writing of History," 10. Article 11 of the Japanese Constitution clearly states: "Japan accepts the judgements of the International Military Tribunal for the Far East and of other Allied War Crimes Courts both within and outside Japan, and will carry out the sentences imposed thereby upon Japanese nationals imprisoned in Japan." Wakabayashi (ed.), *The Nanking Atrocity, 1937-38*, Wakabayashi, "The Messiness of Historical Reality," 8.

921   JNMS, Vol. 1, No. 1, Sheng, "The Seven Wh-Questions in the Writing of History," 3.

922   TSHACNCDNM, Vol. 10, 267, Statement Keenan, Chief Counsel, Inter. Military Tribunal Far East, 4 June 1945, 5.

923   Takashi Yoshida, 5.

924   Ibid., 5.

925   JNMS, Vol. 1, No. 1, Sheng, "The Seven Wh-Questions in the Writing of History," 3. See also *Hong Kong's War Crimes Trials*, Daqun, "Foreword," viii.

926   Toland, Vol. II, 1078.

927 Weiner (ed.), *Race, Ethnicity and Migration in Modern Japan*, Weiner, "Introduction," 2.

928 Meeting at AJC's Dallas office with Consul-General of Japan Houston, Tetsuro Amano, 30 Jan. 2018.

929 Crowe, 130-1, 225.

930 Tessa Morris-Suzuki, "Who is Responsible? The Yomiuri Project and the Legacy of the Asia-Pacific War in Japan," *Asian Perspective*, Vol. 31, No. 1, 2007, 177–191.

931 The 11.7 million number was given to me by my Yale University professor, Henry Turner, and my Cambridge University PhD advisor, Jonathan Steinberg. Recent research seems to indicate this number was more likely 14 million. See Synder's book *Bloodlands* for an analysis of this figure.

932 Chang, 12, 222. As of 2012, Germany has given $90 billion in reparations. Dylan Matthews, "Six Times Victims Have Received Reparations— Including Four in the US," *Vox*, 23 May 2014; Palash Ghosh, "Germany to Pay Out $1 Billion in Reparations For Care of Aging Holocaust Survivors," *International Business Times*, 29 May 2013; Source Minister of Foreign Affairs of Japan given to author by Ryuji Iwasaki, 12 Dec. 2017. Lord Russell of Liverpool, 41. Although, Japan's reparations are miserly, there has been some economic activity that supposedly Japan has used as a form of reparation in China that needs further exploration. See Wakabayashi (ed.), *The Nanking Atrocity, 1937-38*, Wakabayashi, "The Messiness of Historical Reality," 11 & Wakabayashi, "The Nanking 100-Man Killing Context Debate, 1971-75," 116 & Yamamoto, "A Tale of Two Atrocities: Critical Appraisal of American Historiography," 294; Alexander Dallin, *German Rule in Russia 1941-1945: A Study of Occupation Policies*, NY, 1957, 427.

933 Wakabayashi (ed.), *The Nanking Atrocity, 1937-38*, Wakabayashi, "The Messiness of Historical Reality," 10.

934 Moreover, most Japanese war criminals showed no remorse for what they had done. *Hong Kong's War Crimes Trials*, Linton, "Major Murray Ormsby: War Crimes Judge and Prosecutor 1919-2012," 226, 236; Harries & Harries, 478.

935 Bradley & Powers, *Flags of Our Fathers*, 65-6; Richard Rhodes, *The Making of the Atomic Bomb*, NY, 1986, 734-43; John Keegan, *The Second World War*, NY, 1990, 584; Cook & Cook, 383; Scott, 510.

936 Weiner (ed.), *Race, Ethnicity and Migration in Modern Japan*, Weiner, "Introduction," 2-3; Tanaka, xv, xvii, xxii.

937 Kevin L. Jones, "'Comfort Women' Statue Strains 60-Year San Francisco-Osaka Alliance," *Art Wire*, 28 Sept. 2017; Julia Glum, "San Francisco Statue Honoring 'Comfort Women' Sex Slaves from WWII Infuriates Japan," *Newsweek*, 30 Oct. 2017; Heather Knight, "Japanese Mayor Cuts

Ties Between SF and Osaka Over Comfort Women Statue," *San Francisco Chronicle*, 3 Oct. 2018.

938 Interview Yukio Yasunaga, 10 April 2018.

939 UNESCO Nomination Form, International Memory of the World Register, Documents of Nanjing Massacre, 2014-50; "Japan Halts UNESCO Funding Following Nanjing Massacre Row," *The Guardian*, 14 Oct. 2016; Reiji Yoshida, "UNESCO Strikes Political Nerve with Nanking Massacre Documents," *The Japan Times*, 19 Oct. 2015; "Japan Withholds UNESCO Funding After Nanjing Massacre Row," *Reuters*, 14 Oct. 2016.

940 Quote from Wakabayashi (ed.), *The Nanking Atrocity, 1937-38*, Wakabayashi, "The Messiness of Historical Reality," 11. Cook & Cook, 10. Historian Noriko Kawamura of Washington State University has uncovered sources that indicate Hirohito was haunted by post war guilt. During the World War II Museum international conference in 2022, she presented her facts. In the 1950s, Hirohito even wanted to issue a public apology for his part in Japan's atrocities, but the prime minister at the time talked him out of it. However, one could argue, if he was moral and wanted to atone for what he and his nation had done, he shouldn't have allowed a prime minister to convince him to not do what was honorable or moral. To the outside observer, Hirohito allowed people to think he was living a life of privilege and leisure without any second thoughts about what had happened under his leadership.

941 Bix, 16–7.

942 Cook & Cook, 15.

943 Interview Walter Frank, 18 April 1997; Kirchmann, 180.

944 Bix, 6; Cook & Cook, 16.

945 Quote from Cook & Cook, 16; Lord Russell of Liverpool, xiii; Gruhl, 221.

946 Interview Ryuji Iwasaki, 12 Dec. 2017.

947 *Documents on the Tokyo International Military Tribunal Charter*, xlvi.

948 Pennington, 16.

949 Interview LeMay by Colin Heaton June 1986.

950 Pennington, 16.

951 Cook & Cook, 6–7.

952 Ibid.

953 Bix, 5, 16–7.

954 Kirk Spitzer, "Apology Question Hounds Obama's Planned Visit to Hiroshima," *USA Today*, 21 May 2016.

955 Tanaka, xvii.

956 Ibid., xi.

957 Spitzer, "Apology Question Hounds Obama's Planned Visit to Hiroshima."

958 Ibid.

959 Burleigh, 562.

960 Bradley, *Flyboys*, 316.

961 Wallace & Williams, 235.

962 Goldman & Shulatov, 38-9.

963 Lord Russell of Liverpool, 309.

964 For helping me understand these concepts about Japanese culture above, many thanks to (USMC) Lt. Col. W. K.

965 Harries & Harries, 467.

966 Ienage, 158, 239.

967 Ibid., 239.

968 Browne, 247.

969 Ibid., 250.

970 Ibid., 257.

971 Butow, 103.

972 Ibid., 105

973 Butow, 522.

974 Browne, 257.

975 Jon Krakauer, *Where Men win Glory: The Odyssey of Pat Tillman*, NY, 2009, xxiii.

976 NACPM, RG 127 Box 329 (Saipan-Tinian), RCT 23 Report Forager Phase I Saipan, Enclosure (A)., 10, 12.

977 RG 127 Box 318 (Saipan-Tinian) HQ Northern Troops Landing Force, Marianas Phase I (Saipan) 1. Civ. Affairs Report 2. Liaison Off. Report 2. Public Rel. Report, 9 Nov. 1944, HQ VAC, Corps Civ. Affairs Off. to Com. Gen., 13 Aug. 1944, Donald T. Winder, 3; Hoffman, *Once a Legend*, 220. According to historian Alexander Astroth, the civilian population on Saipan was 28,663. The internment camp populations and the number of civilians killed during battle recorded by July 1944 may suggest a smaller number remaining in the north. Email Astroth to Rigg, 26 March 2023. I have cited numbers of civilian deaths and population numbers from the Marine Corps files from the National Archives. Astroth has done more extensive research in this area than I have, so I have noted his different numbers within the footnotes.

978 According to historian Alexander Astroth, he did not find any orders by Saitō showing he gave the order listed above to lower-level officers. A Japanese POW claimed after the battle that Admiral Nagumo had given such an order to his chain of command. There were indeed some IJA officers who did allow civilians to surrender and others cared for them. See Alexander Astroth, *Mass Suicides on Saipan and Tinian, 1944*, Jefferson NC, 2019, 119, 123.

979 Quote from Manchester, 270-1; Toland, Vol. II, 640; Yahara, *The Battle for Okinawa*, NY, 1985, Commentary given by Frank B. Gibney, "Two Views of Battle," xvii; Yahara, 173.

980 NACPM, 127 Box 14 (3d MarDiv), HQ, FMF, Intel Bulletin #4-44, Capt. Whipple, <u>American Soldier</u>, 3, 6-7.

981 Burrell, *Ghosts of Iwo Jima*, 47.

982 NACPM, RG 127 Box 329 (Saipan-Tinian), RCT 23 Report Forager Phase I Saipan, Enclosure (A), D. Propaganda Sec. 2; Cook & Cook, 359-65; Hallas, *Saipan*, 429.

983 NACPM, RG 127 Box 329 (Saipan-Tinian), A14-1, 4th MarDiv Report 15 June to 9 July, HQ 24th Marines, 4th MarDiv, FMF, Brig. Gen., F.A. Hart, 28 Aug. 1944 & RCT 23 Report Forager Phase I Saipan, Enclosure (A)., 7.

984 Moskin, 329; Dower, 45; Toland, Vol. II, 640; Steinberg, *Island Fighting*, 170-1; Frank, 29; Melville, 19; Hane, 345; Cook & Cook, 289-92; Smith, *Coral and Brass*, 107; Hough, 246; Toland, Vol. II, 647-8; Ienaga, 185.

985 Ienaga, 198.

986 NACPM, RG 127 Box 329 (Saipan-Tinian), RCT 23 Report Forager Phase I Saipan, Enc. (A)., 9-10.

987 Spector, 317; Frank, 29; Toland, Vol. II, 648; Ienaga, 198.

988 Interview Keith Renstrom by John Renstrom, 20-23 June 2016.

989 Spector, 317-8.

990 Cook & Cook, 289, 342; Toland, Vol. II, 648.

991 NACPM, RG 127 Box 329 (Saipan-Tinian), A14-1, 4th MarDiv Report 15 June to 9 July, HQ 24th Marines, 4th MarDiv, FMF, Subj.: Report Saipan Op., Com. Off. to Com. Gen., 4th MarDiv, Brig. Gen., F.A. Hart, 28 Aug. 1944.

992 Interview Keith Renstrom, 22 March 2018; Interview Keith Renstrom by John Renstrom, 20-23 June 2016.

993 Toll, *Conquering Tide*, 535; Cook & Cook, 339.

994 Drea, 240.

995 Frank, 29-30; Drea, 240; Keegan, 307. Military Heritage Institute 2011 film *The Battle for the Marianas*.

996 NACPM, RG 127 Box 318 (Saipan-Tinian) HQ Northern Troops Landing Force, Marianas Phase I (Saipan) 1. Civ. Affairs Report 2. Liaison Offs. Report 2. Public Rel. Report, 9 Nov. 1944, HQ VAC, Corps Civ. Affairs Off. to Com. Gen., 13 Aug. 1944, Donald Winder, 3; Interview Frank, 21 July 2017; Keegan, 307; Interview Frank, 20 July 2017; Toland, Vol. II, 650.

997 Cook & Cook, 291-2.

998 *Hong Kong's War Crimes Trials*, Linton, "War Crimes," 104.

999 NACPM, RG 127 Box 329 (Saipan-Tinian), HQ, 25th Marines, 4th MarDiv, FMF, San Francisco, CA, Enc. A, Report Saipan, 6 & 7 July 1944

D Plus 21 & 22 day & Box 328 (Saipan-Tinian), 4th MarDiv Report Saipan 15 June to 9 July 1944, Subseq. Ops. (10 July to 16 July), 37.

1000 NACPM, RG 127 Box 329 (Saipan-Tinian), RCT 23 Report Forager Phase I Saipan, Encl. (A)., 9 & Enc. (A)., II. (g); Hallas, *Uncommon Valor on Iwo Jima*, 332.

1001 According to historian Alexander Astroth, he found different numbers from my sources. He found that 10,436 civilians died due to the causes listed above and that 18,227 survived. See Astroth, 5, 164-7.

1002 NACPM, RG 127 Box 329 (Saipan-Tinian), RCT 23 Report Forager Phase I Saipan, Encl. (A)., II. (f.); See also Drea, 240. For an excellent overview of the civilians on Saipan and Tinian and the battles at these places, see Alexander Astroth, *Mass Suicides on Saipan and Tinian, 1944*, Jefferson NC, 2019.

1003 Dower, 144.

1004 Sledge, 31; MCRDSDA, MCRD Training Book, File 1, <u>Miscellaneous</u>.

1005 Drea, 173.

1006 Generations Broadcast Center, Project SFMedia Consultants, Inc., WWII Interviews, Jim Reed, 31 Jan. 2013.

1007 Ibid.

1008 Interview Keith A. Renstrom, 22 March 2018; Interview Keith Renstrom by John Renstrom, 20-23 June 2016; Email John Renstrom to Rigg, 9 Jan. 2020 (11:53 CT); Email John Renstrom to Rigg, 9 Jan. 2020 (12:57 CT).

1009 Ibid.

1010 Ibid. In 2016, during the interview about this event, Renstrom said with tears streaming from his eyes, "I often wonder whatever happened to her."

1011 Indeed, some civilians were evacuated from Saipan before the battle. According to historian Alexander Astroth, 2,580 people were removed from the island so "there was some care somewhere in the Empire of Japan to keep some imperial subjects...alive." Email Astroth to Rigg, 26 March 2023. See Astroth, 164-5. However, Astroth also found, like me, that many Japanese leaders did not concern themselves with civilians. See Astroth, 126.

1012 Gold, 86.

1013 Linda Sieg, "Historians Battle Over Okinawa WW2 Mass Suicides," *Reuters*, 6 April 2007.

1014 Frank, "Review *Flamethrower*," 25 May 2017.

1015 Potter, 313–4.

1016 Toland, Vol. II, 641.

1017 Ibid., 640.

1018 Smith, *Coral and Brass*, 107; Toland, Vol. II, 642.

1019 Frank, 29; Hough, 247.

1020 Smith, *Coral and Brass*, 107; Hough, 244; MCHDQV, Oral History, Erskine, 165; Mosley, 68.

1021 NACPM, RG 127 Box 318 (Saipan-Tinian) HQ Northern Troops Landing Force, Marianas Phase I (Saipan) 1. Civ. Affairs Report 2. Liaison Offs. Report 2. Public Rel. Report, 9 Nov. 1944, HQ VAC, Corps Civ. Affairs Off. to Com. Gen., 13 Aug. 1944, Donald Winder, 1.

1022 Ibid., 6.

1023 NACPM, RG 127 Box 318 (Saipan-Tinian) HQ Northern Troops Landing Force, Marianas Phase I (Saipan) 1. Civ. Affairs Report 2. Liaison Offs. Report 2. Public Rel. Report, 9 Nov. 1944, HQ VAC, Corps Civ. Affairs Off. to Com. Gen., 13 Aug. 1944, Donald Winder, 3; Drea, 240.

1024 RG 127 Box 318 (Saipan-Tinian) HQ Northern Troops Landing Force, Marianas Phase I (Saipan) 1. Civ. Affairs Report 2. Liaison Offs. Report 2. Public Rel. Report, 9 Nov. 1944, HQ VAC, Corps Civ. Affairs Off. to Com. Gen., 13 Aug. 1944, Donald Winder, 4.

1025 Steinberg, *Island Fighting*, 194; Smith, *Coral and Brass*, 112-3; Hough, 259.

1026 Harwood, 29.

1027 Harwood, 29; Hough, 259. According to historian Alexander Astroth, his research on the Tinian civilian population found that 2,610 died during the battle and 11,761 survived it. See Astroth, 5, 164–7.

1028 Steinberg, *Island Fighting*, 194; Smith, *Coral and Brass*, 112-3; Hough, 259.

1029 Frank, 188, 243, 257, 340, 351-2, 472-3; Davis, "Operation Olympic," 18; Hane, 353; Cook & Cook, 341-2, 367, 459-60; Drea, 247-8, 250; Sledge, 312; Bix, 485; Sieg, "Historians Battle Over Okinawa WW2 Mass Suicides"; James Brooke, "Okinawa Suicides and Japan's Army: Burying the Truth?", *NYT*, 20 June '05; Toland, Vol. II, 897-8; NACPM, RG 127 Box 318 (Saipan-Tinian) HQ Northern Troops Landing Force, Marianas Phase I (Saipan) 1. Civ. Affairs Report 2. Liaison Offs. Report 2. Public Rel. Report, 9 Nov. 1944, HQ VAC, Corps Civ. Affairs Off. to Com. Gen., 13 Aug. 1944, Donald Winder, 3; Harwood, 29; Hough, 259; O'Brien, *The Second Most Powerful Man in the World*, 347-8; Ienaga, 199.

1030 Ienaga, 185.

1031 Quote from Yohara, 186. See also Yahara, 179.

1032 Yahara, 170.

1033 Quote from Drea, 247. See also Ienaga, 185.

1034 Drea, 248.

1035 Yahara, 123.

1036 Yahara, *The Battle for Okinawa*, NY, 1985, Commentary by Gibney, "Epilogue: The Battle Ended—Capture and Reutrn," 200.

1037 Yahara, 173.

1038 Cook & Cook, 460; Toland, Vol. II, 895; Yahara, *The Battle for Okinawa*, NY, 1985, Commentary given by Frank B. Gibney, "Two Views of Battle," xviii.

1039 Yahara, 154.

1040 Cook & Cook, 460; Yahara, 134.

1041 Quote from Toland, Vol. II, 895; Yahara, 156.

1042 Yahara, 230-1.

1043 Yahara, *The Battle for Okinawa*, NY, 1985, Commentary given by Frank B. Gibney, "Epilogue: The Battle Ended—Capture and Reutrn," 199–200.

1044 Yahara, 195–6.

1045 Harries & Harries, 443; Sledge, 312; Hane, 352–3.

1046 Gold, 87–8.

1047 Yahara, *The Battle for Okinawa*, NY, 1985, Commentary given by Frank B. Gibney, "Epilogue: The Battle Ended—Capture and Return," 201.

1048 Millet, 462; Davis, "Operation Olympic," 18; Frank, 232-4; Hoffman, *Once a Legend*, 315.

1049 Frank, 239.

1050 Frank, 311; Rhodes, 744; Edgerton, 298. The number of 7,500 *Kamikaze* aircraft defending the mainland comes from the *Yushukan* War Museum in Tokyo in its displayed labelled: "Available Military Strength for Defense of the Homeland." Richard Frank says the number was more like 10,000. Frank, Review *Flamethrower*, 8 Aug. 2018. Toland agrees with Frank. Toland, Vol. II, 934, 1025.

1051 Victoria, *Zen at War*, 138–9.

1052 Ibid., 138.

1053 Toland, Vol. II, 929–30.

1054 Frank, 190.

1055 Toland, Vol. II, 934.

1056 Ienaga, 231.

1057 Dower, 232-3; Bradley, *Flyboys*, 5, 293; Cook & Cook, 172, 184, 324-5, 375; James Martin Davis, "Operation Olympic: An Invasion not Found in History Books," *Omaha World Herald*, Nov. 1987, 20-1; Miller, "Deathtrap Island," 10; Edgerton, 300; Bix, 480, 482; Frank, 188; Frank, Review *Flamethrower*, 8 Aug. 2018; Toland, Vol. II, 934-5; Victoria, *Zen at War*, 138.

1058 Ienaga, 182.

1059 Ibid.

1060 Frank, *Downfall*, 190.

1061 Ibid., 321.

1062 Harries & Harries, 444-5. For information on Aikawa, see Warren Ivan Hilliard, *The Seventh-day Adventist Family in Japan*, Andrews University, 1977.

1063 Harries & Harries, 25.

1064 Hane, 362; Hardacre, 133; Coogan, 439; Cook & Cook, 4, 33, 307; Harries & Harries, 258.

1065 Christopher Hitchens, *Mortality*, NY, 2012, 90.

1066 NACPM, 208-AA-132T-23 & 25 (on the typewritten backs of the two photographs cited by the U.S. Authority, see 43150-FA and 43152-FA). On some of the photographs, the reference number is 208-AA-132S-25.

1067 Ibid.; See also Smith, *Coral and Brass*, 104; Moore, 170; Cook & Cook, 44.

1068 Cook & Cook, 271-2, 278; *Soldiers Guide to the Japanese Army*, Military Intel. Service, War Dept., Wash. D.C., 15 Nov. 1944, 12; Harries & Harries, 374, 427; Yahara, 109.

1069 Frank, 29; Drea, 17-8, 45, 119-20, 172-3; Interview Drea, 17 Dec. 2017.

1070 Kennedy, *Rise and Fall of Great Powers*, 298.

1071 Toll, *The Conquering Tide*, 459; Smith, *Coral and Brass*, 88; NACPM, RG 127 Box 328 (Saipan-Tinian), 4th MarDiv Ops. Report—Saipan, Annex B, Intel, E. Enemy, 23; NASLPR, Gen. Erskine, Record Graves Blanchard Erskine, #0268, Card #11 or 12, Note Jan. 1945; Toland, Vol. II, 611; Hallas, *Saipan*, 55.

1072 Edgerton, 284; Cook & Cook, 288, 329; Smith, *Coral and Brass*, 106.

1073 MCHDQV, HQ, 3d MarDiv, FMF, In Field, Report Turton (D-3), 19 Aug. 1944, 8; Harold Goldberg, *D-Day in the Pacific: The Battle of Saipan*, Indiana Univ., 2007, 167–94; Moskin, 329; Spector, 316-20; Aurthur and Cohlmia, 152, 154; Edgerton, 289; Toll, 506; Hough, 244-5; O'Brien, *Liberation*, 27-8; Toland, Vol. II, 643; Millett, 414.

1074 Hough, 245; Cook & Cook, 357.

1075 Toll, *Conquering Tide,* 505.

1076 Toland, Vol. II, 642.

1077 Ibid., 643.

1078 Hough, 245.

1079 Horie, 22.

1080 Smith, *Coral and Brass*, 107; Hough, 244; MCHDQV, Oral History, Erskine, 165; Mosley, 68.

1081 Moskin, 334; Spector, 319; USMC Publication, "Intel," MCDP 3, 16 April 1998, 85; Hough, 248; Hoffman, *Once a Legend,* 298; Crowl & Isely, 356, 363; Millett, 416; Richard Harwood, "A Close Encounter: The Marine Landing on Tinian," Final Days, Marines in WWII Commemorative Services, Washington D.C., 1994, 6, 9.

1082 Harries & Harries, 429.

1083 NASLPR, Keith Arnold Renstrom, Gold Star in lieu of a second Bronze Star Medal for actions on Tinian; Interview John Renstrom, 17 Nov. 2019; Keith A. Renstrom, *Keith A. Renstrom Recounts Battle in Tinian and Awards*, 30 Aug. 2017; Interview Keith Renstrom by John Renstrom, 20-23 June 2016; Interview John Renstrom, 16 Jan. 2020; Interview John Renstrom, 22-23 Jan. 2020; https://www.ww2online.org/view/keith-renstrom; Harwood, 17.

1084 Ibid.

1085 NASLPR, Keith Arnold Renstrom, Gold Star in lieu of a second Bronze Star Medal for actions on Tinian; Keith A. Renstrom, *Keith A. Renstrom Recounts Battle in Tinian and Awards*, 30 Aug. 2017; Interview Keith Renstrom by John Renstrom, 20-23 June 2016; Interview John Renstrom, 16 Jan. 2020; Interview John Renstrom, 22-23 Jan. 2020; https://www.ww2online.org/view/keith-renstrom; Harwood, 17.

1086 Ibid.

1087 Ibid.; Quote comes from Hoffman, *The Seizure of Tinian*, 65.

1088 Keith A. Renstrom, *Keith A. Renstrom Recounts Battle in Tinian and Awards*, 30 Aug. 2017; Interview Keith Renstrom by John Renstrom, 20-23 June 2016; Interview John Renstrom, 16 Jan. 2020; Interview John Renstrom, 22-23 Jan. 2020; https://www.ww2online.org/view/keith-renstrom.

1089 Renstrom, *Keith A. Renstrom Recounts Battle in Tinian and Awards*, 30 Aug. 2017; Interview Keith Renstrom by John Renstrom, 20-23 June 2016; Interview John Renstrom, 16 Jan. 2020; Interview John Renstrom, 22-23 Jan. 2020; https://www.ww2online.org/view/keith-renstrom; Hoffman, *The Seizure of Tinian*, 67.

1090 Renstrom, *Keith A. Renstrom Recounts Battle in Tinian and Awards*, 30 Aug. 2017; Interview Keith Renstrom by John Renstrom, 20-23 June 2016; Interview John Renstrom, 16 Jan. 2020; Interview John Renstrom, 22-23 Jan. 2020; https://www.ww2online.org/view/keith-renstrom.

1091 Renstrom, *Keith A. Renstrom Recounts Battle in Tinian and Awards*, 30 Aug. 2017; Interview Keith Renstrom by John Renstrom, 20-23 June 2016; Interview John Renstrom, 16 Jan. 2020; Interview John Renstrom, 22-23 Jan. 2020; https://www.ww2online.org/view/keith-renstrom.

1092 Hoffman, *The Seizure of Tinian*, 64.

1093 Renstrom, *Keith A. Renstrom Recounts Battle in Tinian and Awards*, 30 Aug. 2017; Interview Keith Renstrom by John Renstrom, 20-23 June 2016; Interview John Renstrom, 16 Jan. 2020; Interview John Renstrom, 22-23 Jan. 2020; https://www.ww2online.org/view/keith-renstrom; Harwood, 17; Hoffman, *The Seizure of Tinian*, 65.

1094 Harwood, 17; Hoffman, *The Seizure of Tinian*, 65.

1095 NASLPR, Keith Arnold Renstrom, Gold Star in lieu of a second Bronze Star Medal for actions on Tinian; Keith A. Renstrom, *Keith A. Renstrom Recounts Battle in Tinian and Awards*, 30 Aug. 2017; Interview Keith Renstrom by John Renstrom, 20-23 June 2016; Interview John Renstrom, 16 Jan. 2020; Interview John Renstrom, 22 Jan. 2020; https://www.ww2online.org/view/keith-renstrom; Harwood, 17.

1096 Ibid.

1097 Hoffman, *The Seizure of Tinian*, 66; Interview Don Graves, 24 Jan. 2020.

1098 Renstrom, *Keith A. Renstrom Recounts Battle in Tinian and Awards*, 30 Aug. 2017; Interview Keith Renstrom by John Renstrom, 20-23 June 2016; Interview John Renstrom, 16 Jan. 2020; Interview John Renstrom, 22 Jan. 2020; https://www.ww2online.org/view/keith-renstrom; Harwood, 17.

1099 Hoffman, *The Seizure of Tinian*, 66.

1100 In a WWII museum interview, Renstrom explained why they killed the injured: "Well, you barely have time to care for your own wounded let along the enemy's wounded. If you did leave them there alive then you're leaving yourself open to the possibility of them being able to snipe someone else later." As historian Colonel Carl Hoffman wrote of the battlefield where Renstrom was at: "Another tank incurred minor damage when a Japanese rose from the dead around him [holding] a magnetic mine. A hail of Marine fire dropped him almost where he had lain before." Hoffman, *The Seizure of Tinian*, 66.

1101 USMC Museum, Quantico VA, display Marines during WWII; Hough, 258; Crowl & Isely, 357.

1102 Steinberg, *Island Fighting*, 194; Smith, *Coral and Brass*, 112-3; Hough, 259.

1103 Morison, 373; Hough, 262; Interview James Oelke Farley, 8 Nov. 2017; O'Brien, *Liberation*, 7; MCHDHQ, Woody Williams, unpublished article, "Leaving Guadalcanal June 1944," 1.

1104 *Guam War Claims Review Commission*, 6.

1105 NACPM, RG 127 Box 50 (Guam), HQ 21st Marines, 3d MarDiv, FMF, In Field, Com. Off. 21st Marines to Com. Gen. 3d MarDiv, Report, Forager Operation, Butler, 16 Aug. 1944, 10.

1106 NACPM, RG 127 Box 51 (20th, 21st & 22nd Rgts), 1st Btl., 21st Rgt Log, 25 July 1944.

1107 MCHDQV, HQ, 3d MarDiv, FMF, In Field, Report Lt. Col. Turton (D-3), 19 Aug. 1944, 7.

1108 MCHDQV, Dashiell File, #82, Wagoner; Interview Lee, 21 July 2016.

1109 Aurthur and Cholmia, 154; NACPM, RG 127 Box 50 (Guam), HQ 21st Marines, 3d MarDiv, FMF, In Field, Com. officer 21st Marines to Com. Gen. 3d MarDiv, Report, *Forager*, A.H. Butler, 16 Aug. 1944, 5, 14; Hough, 274.

1110 Farrell, *Liberation-1944*, 21-2; Spector, 320; Hough, 260.

1111 O'Brien, *Liberation*, 9, 22-5; Aurthur and Cholmia, 151; Woody Williams, unpublished article, "Leaving Guam in June 1944," 1; Interview Woody, 21 July 2016; Farrell, *Liberation-1944*, 102-3.

1112 Farrell, *Liberation-1944*, 98.

1113 MCHDQV, HQ, 3d MarDiv, FMF, In Field, Report Lt. Col. Turton (D-3), 19 Aug. 1944, 8.

1114 Van Stockum, "Japanese Counterattack Plan," 3.

1115 NACPM, RG 127 Box 51 (20th, 21st & 22nd Rgts), 3rd Btl., 21st Rgt. Log, 25 July 1944 (3rd notation of date).

1116 Van Stockum, "Japanese Counterattack Plan," 3.

1117 Interview Woody, 22 July 2016; MCHDQV, HQ, 3d MarDiv, FMF, In Field, Report Lt. Col. Turton (D-3), 19 Aug. 1944, 8.

1118 Poe, "The Tell-Tale Heart," 555.

1119 Van Stockum, "Japanese Counterattack Plan," 4; MCHDHQ, Letter Beck to Ruth Beck, 23 April 1943.

1120 Ibid., 4-5.

1121 O'Brien, Liberation, 24; Patrick K. O'Donnell, Into the Rising Sun: World War II's Pacific Veterans Reveal the Heart of Combat, NY, 2002, 139.

1122 O'Donnell, 138.

1123 NACPM, RG 127 Box 51 (20th, 21st & 22nd Rgts), 1st Btl., 21st Rgt. Log, 26 July 1944; NACPM, RG 127 Box 50 (Guam), HQ 21st Marines, 3d MarDiv, FMF, In Field, Com.off. 21st Marines to Com. Gen. 3d MarDiv, Report, Forager, Butler, 16 Aug. 1944, 4-5.

1124 NACPM, RG 127 Box 50 (Guam), HQ 21st Marines, 3d MarDiv, FMF, In Field, Com. Off. 21st Marines to Com. Gen. 3d MarDiv, Report, Forager, Butler, 16 Aug. 1944, 4.

1125 Van Stockum, "Japanese Counterattack Plan," 4-5; Email Van Stockum to Rigg, 18 June 2017.

1126 Commentary Van Stockum on Flamethrower, 23 June 2017.

1127 Van Stockum, "Japanese Counterattack Plan," 6-7; NACPM, RG 127 Box 50 (Guam), HQ 21st Marines, 3d MarDiv, FMF, In Field, Com. Off. 21st Marines to Com. Gen. 3d MarDiv, Report, Forager, Butler, 16 Aug. 1944, 4.

1128 Aurthur and Cholmia, 153; Sulzberger, 541.

1129 MCHDQV, August Larson, 86.

1130 NACPM, RG 127 Box 60 (Guam) A31-1 3rdBtl. 21stRegt. Reports 21 July-1 Nov., 2400 25 July-2400 26 July, 1.

1131 MCHDHQ, Letter Beck to Ruth Beck, 18 Jan. 1945.

1132 Interview Woody, 21 July 2016.

1133 NACPM, RG 127 Box 60 (Guam) A31-1 3rdBtl. 21stRegt. Reports 21 July-1 Nov., 2400 25 July-2400 26 July, 1.

1134 NACPM, RG 127 Box 50 (Guam), HQ 21st Marines, 3d MarDiv, FMF, In Field, Com. Off. 21st Marines to Com.Gen. 3d MarDiv, Report, Forager, Butler, 16 Aug. 1944, 5.

1135 Morison, 387-8.

1136 Van Stockum, "Japanese Counterattack Plan," 6-7; Aurthur and Cholmia, 153; 541; Sulzberger, 541.

1137 NASLPR, Beck, Silver Star Citation.

1138 MCHDQV, Oral History, Robert E. Cushman Jr., 167.

1139 NACPM, RG 127 Box 51 (20th, 21st & 22nd Marine Rgts), 1st Btl., 21st Rgt. Log, 26 July 1944.

1140 Hough, 274.

1141 MCHDQV, Dashiell File, #159, Williams-Silver Star; NASLPR, Marlowe Williams, Silver Star Citation.

1142 O'Brien, *Liberation*, 24, 26.

1143 Van Stockum, "The Battle for Guam," 1.

1144 Aurthur and Cholmia, 152, 154; Steinberg, *Island Fighting*, 174; Spector, 320; MCHDQV, HQ, 3d MarDiv, FMF, In Field, Report Lt. Col. Turton (D-3), 19 Aug. 1944, 8; Hough, 274.

1145 NACPM, RG 127 Box 51 (20th, 21st & 22nd Rgts), 3rd Btl., 21st Rgt. Log, 27 July 1944.

1146 Morison, vol. XIII, 388.

1147 O'Brien, *Liberation*, 25.

1148 Hough, 279; Farrell, *Liberation-1944*, 112-3; Steinberg, *Island Fighting*, 173.

1149 Hough, 279; Farrell, *Liberation-1944*, 112-3; Steinberg, *Island Fighting*, 173; MCHDQV, Oral History, August Larson, 84-5.

1150 Thompson, Doud & Scofield, 16.

1151 O'Brien, *Liberation*, 28.

1152 Hough, 274.

1153 Ibid., 274.

1154 Ibid., 271-2.

1155 Gene E. Stalecker, *Rolling Thunder*, Mechanicsburg, PA, 2008, 207; Newcomb, 6, 18; Kakehashi, 49.

1156 Interview James Oelke Farley, 25 March 2018.

1157 Owings (ed.), *The War Years on Guam:* Vol. I, 137.

1158 O'Brien, *Liberation*, 42-3; Frank 3-19.

1159 Hane, 350.

1160 Frank, 181.

1161 Hitchens, *god is not Great*, 203. See also Drea, 248; Hane, 353; Mandel, "Combat Fatigue," 24; NACPM, RG 127 Container 14, R.N. Davis, Report #688.

1162 Gold, 170-1.

1163 Maslowski, and Millett, 445; Rice, 122-3; Cook & Cook, 353; Robert Gandt, *The Twilight Warriors: The Deadliest Naval Battle of World War II and the Men Who Fought It*, NY, 2010, 42.

1164 Toland, Vol. II, 883.

1165 Mandel, "Combat Fatigue," 24.

1166 Toland, Vol. II, 883.

1167 Blum, 46.

1168 Shahan Russell, "The Tragic Tale of Hajime Fuji: A Kamikaze Fighter Who Crashed Into & Sunk the USS Drexler," *War History Online*, 16 Sept. 2016.

1169 Dower, 232; Maslowski, and Millett, 445.

1170 Cook & Cook, 327.

1171 Crowl & Isely, 536.

1172 Ibid., 558.

1173 Cook & Cook, 265.

1174 Crowl & Isely, 539, 558.

1175 Ienaga, 192.

1176 Ibid., 234–5.

1177 Harries & Harries, 436–7.

1178 NACPM, RG 127, Box 83, (Iwo), AB-1, Com. Gen. 3d MarDiv Erskine to Commandant, 3 June 1945, 79.

1179 Cameron, Mahoney and McReynolds, 133, 537; Bradley & Powers, *Flags of Our Fathers*, 140; Interview Shindo, 9 April 2018; Henri, et al., 13; Hough, 328); Rice, 120 & Coogan, 421, 435–7.

1180 Toland, Vol. II, 808.

1181 Crowley, 89–90; Drea, 132–3, 147–8, 151, 157; Bix, 533–4.

1182 Alexander, 6; Newcomb, 19; McNeill, "Reluctant Warrior," 40; Kakehashi, 62; Garand & Stobridge, 458; Horie, 83.

1183 John W. Dower, "Lessons from Iwo Jima," Perspectives on History, Sept. 2007.

1184 Clausewitz, *On War*, 184.

1185 Burrell, *Ghosts of Iwo Jima*, 43.

1186 Kakehashi, 55; Burrell, *Ghosts of Iwo Jima*, 43–5.

1187 NIDSMDMA, *Senshi-Sosho*, Central Pacific, Op. #2, Peleliu, Angaur, Iwo, Vol. 13, 308.

1188 NIDSMDMA, *Kambu Gakko Kigi*, (JGSDF Staff College), Col. Fujiwara, "Commemorating Gen. Kuribayashi," Aug. 1966, Tokyo, 63.

1189 Crowl & Isely, 468.

1190 Quote from Burrell, *Ghosts of Iwo Jima*, 43. See also Horie, 50.

1191 Interview Shindo, 9 April 2018.

1192 NIDSMDMA, Akira Fukuda, JDF Instructor, "Regarding Army Engineering at Iwo Jima," 3–5.

1193 Toland, Vol. II, 796-8; Wheeler, 41; Burrell, *Ghosts of Iwo Jima*, 41; Horie, 40, 52.

1194 Kakehashi, 10.

1195 Burrell, *Ghosts of Iwo Jima*, 45.

1196 NIDSMDMA, *Senshi-Sosho*, Central Pacific, Op. #2, Peleliu, Angaur, Iwo, Vol. 13, 320-1.

1197 Alexander, 4; Bradley & Powers, *Flags of Our Fathers*, 141; King, 76; Hough, 257; Kakehashi, 65.

1198 Kakehashi, 8.

1199 Ibid., 8.

1200 Ibid., 43-4.

1201 NIDSMDMA, *Senshi-Sosho*, Central Pacific, Op. #2, Peleliu, Angaur, Iwo, Vol. 13, 329-30.

1202 Ibid., 335.

1203 Ibid.

1204 Ibid., 329.

1205 Clausewitz, *On War*, 153.

1206 NACPM, 127 Box 14 (3d MarDiv), Intel. Bulletin: Japanese Tactics and Strategy, 29 Oct 1942-29 May 1945 Folder 7, Col. Robert E. Hogaboom, 29 May 1945, 1, 7, Section (1) (a) and (3) (b) (2); Kakehashi, 60, 64.

1207 Kakehashi, 65.

1208 Interview Shindo, 9 April 2018; Interview King, 21 July 2016; Henri, et al., 92; Wheeler, 42-3; Garand & Stobridge, 456; NACPM, 127 Box 14 (3d MarDiv), Intel. Bulletin: Recent Trends Japanese Defenses, 29 Oct 1942-29 May 1945 Folder 7, Col. R. E. Hogaboom, 4 May 1945, 1, Sec. (1.) Emplacements; Smith, *Coral and Brass*, 142; Kakehashi, 123; McNeill, "Reluctant Warrior," 40; Interview Oelke Farley, 8 Nov. 2017.

1209 NACPM, 127 Box 14 (3d MarDiv), Intel. Bulletin: Recent Trends in Japanese Defenses, 29 Oct 1942-29 May 1945 Folder 7, Col. R. E. Hogaboom, 4 May 1945, 1, Sec. (2.) Emplacements.; Hough, 345; Interview Oelke Farley, 8 Nov. 2017; Crowl & Isely, 485.

1210 Burrell, *Ghosts of Iwo Jima*, 47; NIDSMDMA, *Senshi-Sosho*, Cen. Pacific, Op. #2, Peleliu, Angaur, Iwo, Vol. 13, 348.

1211 Toland, Vol. II, 801-2; McNeill, "Reluctant Warrior," 40; Kakehashi, 7, 17, 156.

1212 Kakehashi, 8.

1213 King, 31, 59-60; Burrell, *Ghosts of Iwo Jima*, 39; McNeill, "Reluctant Warrior," 40; Burleigh, 330; Kakehashi, 34, 66, 125; Harries & Harries, 245; Snow, 102; Tanaka, 110. Dan King doubts women were on Iwo. Email King to Rigg, 9 May 2017. However, veteran Don Graves says he saw women on Iwo. Interview Graves, 7 May 2017. Shayne Jarosz, Ex. Dir. of the IJAA, says Iwo veterans George Alden and Jack Lazarus claimed the same thing and that they found these women "dressed in uniforms wearing thousand stitch belts." Email Jarosz to Don Farrell, 11 May 2017; Interview Shayne Jarosz, 12 May 2017. In *Black Hell*, Bingham writes veteran Earl Stephenson saw women in the tunnels, and had been used for sexual reasons. Bingham, 159. Historian Jeffrey Ethell interviewed a Japanese Iwo veteran who said some officers had brought their Korean mistresses/comfort women with them to Iwo. Conversation with Heaton, 27 May 2017. Historian James Oelke Farley believes the stories of women being on the island. He said it was common for IJA officers to bring their prostitutes and comfort women with them in combat zones. Interview Farley, 8 Nov. 2017; IJAA symposium lecture by Iwo veteran Ira Rigger, 17 Feb. 2018. Rigger was a Seabee on the island and personally found a woman in the tunnels. Iwo veteran George Bernstein also claimed he found women on the island. Interview George Bernstein, 22 March 2018. On other battlefronts, Japanese females were also found to have fought against the Marines. See Moore, 209.

1214 Clausewitz, *On War*, 331.

1215 McNeill, "Reluctant Warrior," 40.

1216 Henri, et al., vii.

1217 NIDSMDMA, *Senshi-Sosho*, Central Pacific, Op. #2, Peleliu, Angaur, Iwo, Vol. 13, 391; Crowl & Isely, 483 (loc. 10526); Newcomb, 12, 35; McNeill, "Reluctant Warrior," 40. Crowl & Isely write that 700 Koreans were on the island, but NIDSMDMA write 1,600 were garrisoned there.

1218 Burrell, *Ghosts of Iwo Jima*, 48; Toland, Vol. II, 799. There were around 23 IJA tanks on Iwo. See Horie, 82.

1219 Burrell, *Ghosts of Iwo Jima*, 4; Wheeler, 40. See also Henri, et al., 97.

1220 Horie, 79, 83.

1221 Manchester, 337; Toland, Vol. II, 795.

1222 Bobby C. Blair, and John Peter DeCioccio, *Victory at Peleliu: The 81st Infantry Division's Pacific Campaign (Volume 30) (Campaigns and Commanders Series*, Norman, OK, 2014, 255.

1223 Toland, Vol. II, 800-1; Henri, et al., 8; Bingham, 7. According to Kuribayashi's staff officer, Major Horie, this idea of killing "enemy troops per man" was his idea. He argued if they did this, then "when we die the mathematics will tell the people of the world that we actually won the war." Horie, 56.

1224 Ross, 151; Kakehashi, 39.

1225 Kakehashi, 39.

1226 NIDSMDMA, *Senshi-Sosho*, Cen. Pacific, Op. #2, Peleliu, Angaur, Iwo, Vol. 13, 351; Ross, 150; Kakehashi, 40.

1227 Kakehashi, 159-60; NIDSMDMA, *Senshi-Sosho*, Cen. Pacific, Op. #2, Peleliu, Angaur, Iwo, Vol. 13, 350-1.

1228 Melville, 159.

1229 Clausewitz, *On War*, 69, 87 & Brodie, "A Guide to Reading of On War," 645.

1230 Kakehashi, 45.

1231 Clausewitz, *On War*, 180.

1232 Dower, 248-9; Cook & Cook, 17.

1233 Jim G. Henri, W. Keyes Beech, David K. Dempsey, Alvin M. Josephy, and Tom Dunn, *The U.S. Marines on Iwo Jima*, NY, 1945, 8; Newcomb, 41; Hane, 10.
1234 Interview Woody, 23 July 2016. See also Harries & Harries 392.
1235 Interview Shindo, 9 April 2018; Notes by Shindo, 3 Oct. 2018.
1236 Melville, 205.
1237 Ibid., 203.
1238 Ibid., 427.
1239 Kakehashi, 90.
1240 Hane, 12; Edgerton, 253; King, 149; McNeill, "Reluctant Warrior," 40.
1241 Paul Johnson, *A History of Christianity*, NY, 1995, 6; George Hart, *A Dictionary of Egyptian Gods and Goddesses*, NY, 1986, 179-82.
1242 *Singing the Living Tradition*, Univ.-Unitarian Song Book, Meditations, 563.
1243 Sam Harris, *The End of Faith: Religion, Terror, and the Future of Reason*, NY, 2004, 226.
1244 Hane, 12.
1245 Edgerton, 323.
1246 Quote from Cook & Cook, 26, 78; Toland, Vol. I, 376; Moore, 64.
1247 Cook & Cook, 5, 124; Newcomb, 41.
1248 NACPM, RG 127, Box 83, (Iwo), AB-1, Com Gen. 3d MarDiv Erskine to Commandant, Report, 3 June 1945, 34.
1249 Interview Leighton Willhite, 30 Nov. 2019; Henri, et al., 100.
1250 Moskin, 364; Toland, *The Rising Sun, Vol. 2*, 813; Newcomb, 136-7; Burrell, *Ghosts of Iwo Jima*, 68.
1251 Bradley & Powers, *Flags of Our Fathers*, 206-7.
1252 Horie, 110.
1253 Ibid.
1254 Sakai, 253; King, 33.
1255 NIDSMDMA, *Senshi-Sosho*, Cen. Pacific, Op. #2, Peleliu, Angaur, Iwo, Vol. 13, 381-2; Newcomb, 105, 170.
1256 Ibid.
1257 Horie, 100. There are other spellings out there for Hayauchi. In Horie's memoir, he writes Hayakawa.
1258 Newcomb, 139.
1259 Crowley, 86.
1260 Harris, *The End of Faith*, 39.
1261 Victoria, *Zen at War*, 26.
1262 Toland, Vol. II, 821.
1263 University of Virginia Law Library, The International Military Tribunal for the Far East, Tavenner Papers & IMTFE Official Records, Box 2,

General Reports and Memoranda April 1946, Statement of Gen. Hata Hikosaburo, 2-3.

1264 Clausewitz, *On War*, Howard, "The Influence of Clausewitz," 35.

1265 Horie, 103.

1266 Toland, Vol. II, 821.

1267 Essay in Woody's archive, "No Word From Jim Hamilton Following Battle of Iwo Jima," 1; Wheeler, 56; Hallas, *Uncommon Valor on Iwo Jima*, 318; Burrell, *Ghosts of Iwo Jima*, 74.

1268 Horie, 103.

1269 Ibid., 153.

1270 Ibid., 113.

1271 Ibid., 151

1272 MCHDQV, HQ, 1st Btl., 21st Rgt., 3d MarDiv, FMF, In Field, 6 April 1945, Report Lt. Col. Williams, 13.

1273 Mandel, 289.

1274 Bingham, 76.

1275 Ross, 344; Toland, Vol. II, 822-30; Keegan, *Second World War*, 566; Rhodes, 594; Frank, 61; Raymond Henri, 91-3.

1276 King, 147-8, 152-6; Toland, Vol. II, 824-5; David McNeill, "Even the Dead Were Being Forced to Fight," Japan Times, 13 Aug. 2006.

1277 King, 147-8, 152-6; Toland, Vol. II, 824-5; McNeill, "Even the Dead Were Being Forced to Fight"; Wheeler, 56; Mosley, 31; *Japan at War*, 139.

1278 Hitchens, *god is not Great*, 204.

1279 McNeill, "Even the Dead Were Being Forced to Fight"; Wheeler, 56.

1280 King, 156.

1281 McNeill, "Even the Dead Were Being Forced to Fight."

1282 NACPM, RG 127 Container 14, Dashiell, #300; NACPM, 127 Box 14 (3d MarDiv), HQ, FMF, Camp Elliott, Subj: Japanese Military Org., 29 Oct. 1942, By Command of Maj. Gen. Barrett, Col. Noble, CoS, (9.) Deception as practiced by Japanese (7).

1283 NACPM, 127 Box 14 (3d MarDiv), HQ, FMF, Camp Elliott, Subj.: Japanese Military Org., 29 Oct. 1942, By Command of Maj. Gen. Barrett, Col. Noble, CoS, (9.) Deception as practiced by Japanese; Hallas, *Uncommon Valor on Iwo Jima*, 294.

1284 MCRDSDA, MCRD Training Book, File 1, Jungle Warfare.

1285 Harries & Harries, 325.

1286 McNeill, "Even the Dead Were Being Forced to Fight."

1287 Melville, 66.

1288 Toland, Vol. II, 909.

1289 NACPM, RG 127 Box 96 (Iwo) A45-2, 21st Marine Rgt. Journal Iwo, 16 March 1945, R-3 Log, Time 1200; NACPM, RG 127 Container 14, Dashiell (Report in mid 200s).

1290 Excerpts of letter by SSG Joe Franklin, a 21st Marines Photographer, who was wounded and evacuated during operations on Iwo, 2. Dashiell's archives.

1291 NACPM, RG 127 Box 96 (Iwo) A45-2, 21st Rgt. Journal, 16 March 1945, R-3 Log, Time 1200; NACPM, RG 127 Container 14, Dashiell (Report in the mid 200s).

1292 Joseph Picard, "Iwo Jima Not Pretty as Suribachi Picture: Clark Veteran Returning 50 Years Later," News Tribune (NJ), 26 Feb. 1995.

1293 NACPM, RG 127 Container 14, Dashiell, #263, 1-3.

1294 MCRDSDA, 2nd Blt., 24th Rgt., 4th MarDiv, Battle Reports, Iwo, Narrative, 35.

1295 Interview Graves, 7 May 2017. Leighton Willhite also verifies Graves' testimony. He was a driver in the Sherman tank *Lorraine* attached to the 5th MarDiv. Interview Willhite, 10 May 2017.

1296 *Documents on the Tokyo International Military Tribunal Charter*, 37; Interview Graves, 7 May 2017; NACPM, RG 127 Container 14, Dashiell, #204.

1297 King, 149; McNeill, "Reluctant Warrior," 40; Horie, 105.

1298 Victoria, *Zen at War*, 102; Moore, 75; Gandt, 87.

1299 Prange, Gordon W., Goldstein, Donald M., and Dillon, Katherine V., *God's Samurai: Lead Pilot at Pearl Harbor*, D.C., 2004, 199-204; Kakehashi, xix.

1300 Newcomb, 233.

1301 King, 156-7.

1302 Quote from Newcomb, 234. See also Horie, 107.

1303 Newcomb, 234.

1304 Kakehashi, xviii.

1305 MCHDQV, HQ, 1st Btl., 21st Rgt., 3d MarDiv, FMF, In Field, 6 April 1945, Report Col. Williams, 9-11.

1306 NACPM, RG 127 Box 96 (Iwo) A45-2, 21st Rgt. Journal, 19 March 1945, R-3 Log, Time 0926, CG statement.

1307 Ibid., 20 March 1945, R-3 Log, Sent 2123; MCRDSDA, 2nd Blt., 24th Marines, 4th MarDiv, Op. Journal, 3 March 45, Times 1510 & 1516.

1308 Ibid., 21 March 1945, R-3 Log.

1309 Ibid., 22 March 1945, R-3 Log, Sent 1400.

1310 NACPM, RG 127 Box 96 (Iwo) A45-2, 21st Rgt. Journal, 24 March 1945, R-3 Log, Sent 1645.

1311 NACPM, RG 127 Container 14, Dashiell, #200-1.

1312 See Drea, 147-57, 206.

1313 NACPM, RG 127 Box 96 (Iwo) A45-2, 21st Rgt. Journal, 23 March 1945, R-3 Log, sent 0715 & 27 March 1945, R-3 Log, Sent 1510.

1314 NASLPR, Harry Linn Martin, Testimony of 1st Lt. Norris L. Bowen, Jr., 10 April 1945, 1-2.
1315 Ibid., 2.
1316 Ibid., 1.
1317 Crowl & Isely, 500.
1318 Ross, 335-7; Newcomb, 241; Kakehashi, xvi; Hallas, *Uncommon Valor on Iwo Jima*, 343. To read how the airmen responded to this attack, see Brown & Yelling, 91-100.
1319 Kakehashi, 192-6; Burrell, *Ghosts of Iwo Jima*, 80; Hallas, *Uncommon Valor on Iwo Jima*, 344.
1320 Kakehashi, 194.
1321 Toland, Vol. II, 830; Wheeler, 57. Yet, another story has Kuribayashi and Nakane committing suicide together using pistols. Horie, 155.
1322 McNeill, "Reluctant Warrior," 43; Burleigh, 331-2.
1323 Dower, 232-33; Burrell, *Ghosts of Iwo Jima*, 46; Bradley, *Flyboys*, 5, 293; Davis, "Operation Olympic," 20-1; Miller, "Deathtrap Island," 10; Edgerton, 300; Cook & Cook, 14-5, 263-4, 364; Drea, 231.
1324 Sakai, 309.
1325 Ibid., 308-9.
1326 Frank, 95, 107.
1327 Horie, 67.
1328 Tanaka, 8, 250. Of the 2.3 million military deaths Japan suffered, 1.4 million were due to "starvation, malnutrition and…diseases." See also Harries & Harries, 399, 403.
1329 This quote comes from Elie Wiesel's essay "Why I Write" in his book *From the Kingdom of Memory*.
1330 Butow, 405.
1331 *Documents on the Tokyo International Military Tribunal Charter*, 538; Interview Yellin, 2 June 2017. See newsreel "Why We Fight: The Battle for China (1944)." https://www.youtube.com/watch?v=2QvDk316BKo; https://archive.org/details/gov.archives.arc.36072; Takashi Yoshida, 23, 28, 38-9; Toland, Vol. I, 289-90; F. Tillman Durdin, "All Captives Slain: Civilians Also Killed as Japanese Spread Terror in Nanking," *NY Times*, 18 Dec. 1937.
1332 Patterson, 247; Mosley, 171.
1333 Interview Lee, 4 April 2017; Notes by Woody on manuscript 25 June 2017; NASLPR, John Warner.
1334 MCHDQV, Oral History, Clifton Cates, 52-3. MOH recipient and China Marine Mitchell Paige witnessed the same crimes in Shanghai in 1937 as Cates. Larry Smith, *Beyond Glory*, 10.

1335 From Jon Hoffman's unfinished biography of General Lewis William Walt, Chapter 3, p. 24, First Draft.

1336 Brackman, 180-1, 186.

1337 Lord Russell of Liverpool, 289; Brackman, 180-1.

1338 David M. Kennedy, "The Horror: Should the Japanese atrocities in Nanking be equated with the Nazi Holocaust?," *The Atlantic Monthly*, Vol. 281, No. 4 (April 1998), 110–116.

1339 Lord Russell of Liverpool, 289.

1340 Ibid., 295.

1341 Ienaga, 209-210.

1342 Harries & Harries, 226, 270; Bix, 364, 379.

1343 Modder, 30.

1344 Harries & Harries, 270.

1345 Harries & Harries, 285; Bix, 379.

1346 Toll, *Pacific Crucible*, 37.

1347 Ibid., 46.

1348 Edgerton, 275; Scott, 510; Frank, *Tower of Skulls*, 512; Crowe, 132.

1349 Toll, *Pacific Crucible*, 300.

1350 Edgerton, 314.

1351 NACPM, RG 226, Box 368 (Records Off. US Strategic Services), Offices of Jap Forces, 8 July 1944, 3. When one asks the question why did America not do more to stop Japan's "ethnocide" in China since it knew about it, an answer that can be given is simply, the U.S. did not care. Historian Yuki Tanaka wrote: "It is believed that the racism against Asians prevalent among Westerners at that time was a major contributing factor to their indifference toward Japanese atrocities" (Tanaka, 254).

1352 Butow, 437.

1353 Wallace & Williams, 105.

1354 Wallace & Williams, 111; Barenblatt, 229–30.

1355 Kennedy, *The Rise and Fall of Great Powers*, 350; NACPM, RG 127 Box 14 (3d MarDiv), HQ, FMF, Intel Bulletin #4-44, Capt. Whipple, Disposition Japanese Ground Strength, 1; Bix, 396; Drea, 250.

1356 Harries & Harries, 479; Ienaga, 167.

1357 Joshua A. Fogel (ed.), *The Nanjing Massacre in History and Historiography*, Berkeley, 2000, Mark Eykholt, "Aggression, Victimization, and Chinese Historiography of the Nanjing Massacre," 16.

1358 Butow, 101-2.

1359 Wakabayashi (ed.), *The Nanking Atrocity, 1937-38*, Akira, "The Nanking Atrocity: An Interpretive Overview," 40.

1360 Ibid., 48.

1361 UGSL, Hosch Papers, Tokyo War Crimes Trials, Conventional War Crimes (Atrocities), Part B, Ch. VIII, 1023; Modder, 23.
1362 Wakabayashi (ed.), *The Nanking Atrocity, 1937-38*, Akira, "The Nanking Atrocity: An Interpretive Overview," 49.
1363 Wallace & Williams, 217; Modder, 23-4; Lord Russell of Liverpool, 291; Harries & Harries, 234.
1364 Frank, *Tower of Skulls*, 122; Goldman & Shulatov, 32-3; Bix, 351.
1365 Bix, 351.
1366 Ibid., 337.
1367 Ibid., 338.
1368 Harries & Harries, 320-1.
1369 Carroll, 123; Bradsher, "Thousands March in Anti-Japan Protest in Hong Kong"; *Documents on the Tokyo International Military Tribunal Charter*, 541; UGSL, Hosch Papers, Tokyo War Crimes Trials, Conventional War Crimes (Atrocities), Part B, Ch. VIII, 1023-4.
1370 Hough, 20; Toll, *Pacific Crucible*, 248, 269.
1371 *Hong Kong's War Crimes Trials*, Linton, "War Crimes," 98.
1372 Zeiler, 3.
1373 Carl Richard Mueller (Trans. & ed.), *Georg Büchner Complete Plays and Prose*, NY, 1963, "Danton's Death, Act I, Scene I," 3.
1374 Discussion with Takayuki Matsumoto and Tatsu Kashiwabara, 24 Feb. 1995.
1375 Weiner (ed.), *Race, Ethnicity and Migration in Modern Japan*, Weiner, "Introduction," 2.
1376 Bradley, *Flyboys*, 316; "Japan PM Shinzo Abe Visits Yasukuni WW2 Shrine," *BBC News*, 26 Dec. 2013; Coogan, 439, 511; Burleigh, 561; Yuma Totani, *The Tokyo War Crimes Trial: The Pursuit of Justice in the Wake of World War II* (Cambridge, 2008), 135; Cook & Cook, 4, 151, 405; "Japanese Minister Yoshitaka Shindo Visits Yasukuni Shrine Provoking China's Ire," *South China Morning Post*, 1 Jan. 2014; Keegan, 590; Brackman, 27-8, 185; Potter, 179.
1377 Potter, 179.
1378 Wakabayashi (ed.), *The Nanking Atrocity, 1937-38*, Wakabayashi, "The Messiness of Historical Reality," 13.
1379 Potter, 179.
1380 Hitchens, *god is not Great*, 203. See also *Hong Kong's War Crimes Trials*, Daqun, "Foreword," viii.
1381 Chang, 12; Cook & Cook, 448.
1382 Andrew Glass, "Reagan Visits German War Cemetery, May 5, 1985," *Politico*, 5 May 2018. Historian Richard Frank points out a double standard here. U.S. leaders have conducted visits to Soviet cemeteries where members of the NKVD are buried, and nobody finds this amiss. Likewise,

WWII, Soviet, and later Russian leaders visit Soviet WWII cemeteries, many containing NKVD graves, and there is no outcry. Notes on manuscript by Richard Frank, 2 April 2023.

1383 Wallace & Williams, 243.

1384 Browne, 266-7; Hoyt, xiii, 223. Some evidence indicates that some of Tōjō's ashes did not make it to the family after his cremation but was flown out to the Pacific and scattered amongst the waves. See Mari Yamaguchi, "US Documents Solve Mystery of War Criminal Tojo's Remains," *AP News*, 14 June 2021.

1385 Chang, 12; Cook & Cook, 448.

1386 Cook & Cook, 453; Drea, 50.

1387 Email Dan King to Rigg, 22 Feb. 2018.

1388 Interview Shindo, 9 April 2018.

1389 "Japanese Minister Shindo Visits Yasukuni Shrine Provoking China's Ire," *South China Morning Post*, 1 Jan. 2014.

1390 Tanaka, xvii.

1391 *Hong Kong's War Crimes Trials*, Daqun, "Foreword," viii.

1392 Prange, 724.

1393 Brackman, 35-6.

1394 Dower, 232-3; Bradley, *Flyboys*, 5, 293; Cook & Cook, 172, 184, 324-5, 375; James Martin Davis, "Operation Olympic: An Invasion not Found in History Books," *Omaha World Herald*, Nov. 1987, 20-1; Miller, "Deathtrap Island," 10; Edgerton, 300; Bix, 480, 482; Frank, 188; Frank, Review *Flamethrower*, 8 Aug. 2018; Toland, Vol. II, 934-5; Victoria, *Zen at War*, 138.

1395 Frank, 311; Rhodes, 744; Edgerton, 298; Frank, Review *Flamethrower*, 8 Aug. 2018; Toland, Vol. II, 934, 1025.

1396 Frank, 188, 243, 257, 340, 351-2; Davis, "Operation Olympic," 18; Hane, 353; Cook & Cook, 341-2, 354-64, 367, 459-60; Drea, 247-8, 250; Sledge, 312; Bix, 485; Sieg, "Historians Battle Over Okinawa WW2 Mass Suicides"; James Brooke, "Okinawa Suicides and Japan's Army: Burying the Truth?", *NYT*, 20 June '05; Toland, Vol. II, 897-8; NACPM, RG 127 Box 318 (Saipan-Tinian) HQ Northern Troops Landing Force, Marianas Phase I (Saipan) 1. Civ. Affairs Report 2. Liaison Offs. Report 2. Public Rel. Report, 9 Nov. 1944, HQ VAC, Corps Civ. Affairs Off. to Com. Gen., 13 Aug. 1944, Donald Winder, 3; Harwood, 29; Hough, 259; O'Brien, *The Second Most Powerful Man in the World*, 347-8.

1397 Dennis M. Giangreco, *Hell to Pay: Operation Downfall and the Invasion of Japan, 1945–1947*, Annapolis, 2009.

1398 Ibid., 272.

1399 Cook & Cook, 56, 403, 407-9; Kuhn, Epilog; Patterson, 296; Bix, 508; Toland, Vol. II, 998; Moore, 242.

1400 Bradley, *Flyboys*, 299; Ienaga, 233; Edgerton, 303. Different numbers for Japanese civilians range from 80,000 to 180,000. This study has chosen to use the higher number due to the number of civilians who just disappeared and were unaccounted for after the war. Bradley and Edgerton above indicate that the Soviets lost over 8,000 KIAs, but the Russians have later admitted that their deaths exceeded 12,000 according to historian Richard Frank. Notes on manuscript by Richard Frank, 2 April 2023. Frank's source for this comes from David M. Glantz and Jonathan House, *When Titans Clashed: How the Red Army Stopped Hitler,* Kansas, 1995, Tables A and B, 292-300.

1401 Wallace & Williams, 180; *Materials on the Trial of Former Servicemen of the Japanese army Charged with Manufacturing and Employing Bacteriological Weapons*, 126-31, 272-83; Drea, 251.

1402 Wallace & Williams, 132.

1403 Notes on manuscript by Richard Frank, 2 April 2023.

1404 Frank, 295-6.

1405 Toland, Vol. II, 998-9.

1406 Maslowski, and Millett, 466; Frank, 316-9, 330; Rhodes, 745; Edgerton, 302; Burleigh, 13, 551; Kennedy, *The Rise and Fall of Great Nations*, 356; Toland, Vol. II, 1045, 1052; Scott, 49; Ienaga, 231-2.

1407 Cook & Cook, 403; Bix, 81; Toland, Vol. II, 1054; Ienaga, 232.

1408 Cook & Cook, 202, 257,413.

1409 Ibid., 458.

1410 Brackman, 43-4.

1411 Sakai, 310; Frank, 186-7; Edgerton, 303.

1412 Ienaga, 236.

1413 Toland, Vol. II, 979.

1414 Toland, Vol. II, 1015; Notes on manuscript by Richard Frank, 2 April 2023.

1415 Bradley, *Flyboys*, 298.

1416 Clausewitz, *On War*, 92–3.

1417 Notes on manuscript by Richard Frank, 2 April 2023.

1418 Frank, 163, 359. Werner Gruhl comes to a similar analysis. See Gruhl, 203-4.

1419 Bowie, 273–4, 275.

1420 Ibid., 275.

1421 Notes on manuscript by Richard Frank, 25 Feb. 2023.

1422 Bradley, *Flyboys*, 297.

1423 Ibid.

1424 Frank, 163, 359.

1425 Horie, 114.

1426 Ibid., 47.

1427 Toll, *Pacific Crucible*, 387.

1428 Steinberg, *Island Fighting*, 74; Edgerton, 287; *Japan at War*, 125; Hane, 341. Frank, "Review *Flamethrower*," 25 May 2017; Ross, 11.

1429 Moskin, 316; Steinberg, *Island Fighting*, 166; Frank, 216.

1430 Spector, 314; Hough, 3; Crowl & Isely, 62; Millett, 325-6, 373.

1431 Burrell, *Ghosts of Iwo Jima*, 51. Crowl & Isely, *The U.S. Marines and Amphibious War.*

1432 Crowl & Isely, v, 3; Smith, *Coral and Brass*, 22-3; Krulak, 82-3.

1433 NASLPR, Holland M. Smith, Monthly Chronological Data 1917-1918; Smith, *Coral and Brass*, 32.

1434 Ibid., Monthly Chronological Data, March 1919, p. 1-2.

1435 Kennedy, *Engineers of Victory*, 219, 308; Crowl & Jeter, *The Marines and Amphibious War*; Paterson (ed.), *Major Problems in American Foreign Policy*," John Braeman, "American Military Power and Security," 154; Coram, 50, 73; MCHDQV, Oral History, Victor H. Krulak, 41.

1436 Hough, 4.

1437 Ibid., 3-4.

1438 Hoffman, *Once a Legend*, 134-6; Crowl & Isely, 66.

1439 Coram, 69-71; Richard Goldstein, "Victor H. Krulak, Marine Behind U.S. Landing Craft, Dies at 95," *NYT*, 4 Jan. 2009; Millett, 340. Krulak was the assistant intelligence officer attached to the 4th Marines in China. In 1937, he personally observed the Japanese outside Shanghai at Woosung make amphibious landings with ramped boats like the Higgins boats. His observations and reports helped push General Smith to develop and support Higgins boats. Hoffman, *Once a Legend*, 118; Krulak, 90; MCHDQV, Oral History, Victor H. Krulak, 22, 67.

1440 Email Charles C. Krulak to Rigg, 5 Dec. 2019. Ironically, Krulak got his ideas about how to help Higgins develop the amphibious boat by analyzing how the Japanese utilized their own outside of Shanghai. General Charles C. Krulak said that turning this technology against them, his father helped the Corps use "A Japanese system to defeat...the Japanese." Email Charles C. Krulak to Rigg, 14 Dec. 2019.

1441 Email Charles C. Krulak to Rigg, 14 Dec. 2019; Victor H. Krulak, *Japanese Assault Boats, Shanghai, 1937*, CMP Productions, 2017; Krulak, 90-4; MCHDQV, Oral History, Victor H. Krulak, 23-5, 45, 54-56.

1442 Arthur Herman, *Freedom's Forge: How American Business Produced Victory in World War II*, NY, 2013, 204-6; Smith, *Coral and Brass*, 44-7.

1443 Smith, *Coral and Brass*, 45; Burrell, *Ghosts of Iwo Jima*, 19.

1444 Hough, 5; Crowl & Isely, 202.

1445 Crowl & Isely, 4.

1446 Krulak, *First to Fight*, 36. J. F. C. Fuller, a noted British military historian, "described the amphibious assault as perfected and practiced by the U.S.

Marines as 'in all probability…the most far-reaching tactical innovation of the war.'" Krulak, 87. See Krulak 100-9 and MCHDQV, Oral History, Victor H. Krulak, 49-54 about the amtracs or "alligators."

1447 MCHDQV, Oral History, Erskine, 203-4; Hoffman, *Once a Legend,* 136; MCHDQV, Oral History, Victor H. Krulak, 61; Ross, 39.

1448 Smith, *Coral and Brass,* 140; *Two Score and Ten,* 5.

1449 National Archives, St. Louis Personnel Files, (NASLPR), Graves Erskine; MCHDQV, Oral History, Erskine from 1969-1970, 2, 15, 51, 56, 67.

1450 Hoffman, *Once a Legend,* 306-8.

1451 Hough, 12.

1452 Crowl & Isely, 6.

1453 Lord Russell of Liverpool, 204.

1454 Lord Russell of Liverpool, 38.

1455 Frank, *Tower of Skulls,* 95.

1456 Maslowski, and Millett, 404; Frank, "Review *Flamethrower,*" 25 May 2017.

1457 Maslowski, and Millett, 316.

1458 Ibid., 318.

1459 Hoyt, xii.

1460 Lord Russell of Liverpool, xiii.

1461 Bix, 359–60.

1462 Ibid., 519.

1463 Drea, 250.

1464 Frank, *Tower of Skulls,* 361.

1465 Snow, 102. According to Alan Birch and Martin Cole in their book *Captive Years: The Occupation of Hong Kong 1941-45,* there were indeed some executions of Japanese soldiers in Hong Kong for rape and murder, but it is unclear who prosecuted these sentences. Birch & Cole, 23–4.

1466 Lord Russell of Liverpool, 201.

1467 Mr. James, "The Untold Story of Captain Kudo Shunsaku and the Destroyer Ikazuchi," *Japan Probe,* 19 May 2007.

1468 Neal Robison, "The Japanese Scouting Unknown Soldier Story," *Vanguard Scouting,* 4 February 2021.

1469 Ienaga, 44.

1470 Sabrina Stierwalt, "Why Do We Laugh? We Laugh Even Before We Can Speak. But Why? Science Has Some Answers to the Mystery of Human Laughter, and Some of Them Might Surprise You," *Scientific American,* 9 Feb. 2020.

1471 Ibid.

1472 Kurt Haas & Adelaide Haas, *Understanding Sexuality,* New Paltz, NY, 1993, 564; Harries & Harries, 230, 479; Frank, *Tower of Skulls,* 57; Shu-Fan, 111.

1473 Haas & Haas, 564-5.

1474 Ibid., 565.

1475 Ibid.

1476 Ibid.

1477 Harries & Harries, 260-1.

1478 Ibid., 241.

1479 Ibid., 320-1.

1480 Haas & Haas, 565.

1481 Ibid.

1482 Tanaka, 111.

1483 Harries & Harries, 479.

1484 From 1937 to 1939, Japan did try 420 Japanese soldiers for rape and murder and found them guilty. However, none of the men were executed for
such crimes. Out of the millions of women who must have been raped by
Japanese soldiers, this is a pathetic showing of how Japanese military justice
system worked. Bix, 335.

1485 Shu-Fan, 111.

1486 Mary Bradley, "Experts Reveal Psychology of Killers Who Dismember
Victims," *The Nation*, 9 Feb. 2016.

1487 Raj Persaud, "The Psychology of Corpse Dismemberment—The Motivation
Behind the Most Grotesque of Crimes," *Huffington Post*, 8 August 2012.

1488 Ibid.

1489 Ibid.

1490 Ibid.

1491 Ibid.

1492 Talmud, Tractate of *Shabbat* (the Sabbath), 31a.

1493 Edgerton, 312; Bradley, *Flyboys*, 59.

1494 Ienaga, 46.

1495 Plato, *The Trial and Death of Socrates: Apology*, Cambridge, 1975, 39. See
also Campbell, 65.

1496 Ienaga, 116.

1497 Ienaga, 223; Harries & Harries, 459; Owings (ed.), *The War Years on Guam:
Vol. I*, 6, 15, 18, 45, 151-2, 160, 204. This happened also to some Japanese
POW guards as well in Hong Kong. See Bowie, 205.

1498 Interview Lt. Col. W. K., 6 Jan. 2022.

1499 Ibid.

1500 Bradley & Powers, 236, 238, 320, 344-6; Interview Iwo Jima veteran John
Lauriello, 20 Nov. 2016.

1501 NIDSMDMA, *Senshi-Sosho*, Central Pacific, Op. #2, Peleliu, Angaur, Iwo,
Vol. 13, 391; Crowl & Isely, 483 (loc. 10526); Newcomb, 12, 35; McNeill,
"Reluctant Warrior," 40. Crowl & Isely write that 700 Koreans were on the
island, but NIDSMDMA write 1,600 were garrisoned there.

1502 Lord Russell of Liverpool, 318.
1503 Ibid., 323.
1504 Ibid., 315.
1505 Ibid.
1506 Ibid., 318.
1507 Ienaga, 230.
1508 Ibid., 222.
1509 Yahara, 173, 208.
1510 Ibid., 173, 176–7.
1511 Yahara, *The Battle for Okinawa,* NY, 1985, Commentary by Frank B. Gibney, "Two Views of Battle," xvii.
1512 Horie, xxiv, "Editor's Note," by Robert D. Eldridge and Charles W. Tatum.
1513 Hough, 39, 89.
1514 Interview Graves, 7 May 2017; Email Jarosz to Don Farrell, 11 May 2017; Interview Shayne Jarosz, 12 May 2017; Bingham, 159; Conversation with Heaton, 27 May 2017; Interview Farley, 8 Nov. 2017; IJAA symposium lecture by Iwo veteran Ira Rigger, 17 Feb. 2018;Interview George Bernstein, 22 March 2018.
1515 Ienaga, 184.
1516 Interview Graves, 7 May 2017.
1517 Interview Graves, 7 May 2017; Interview Bernstein, 22 March 2018; Interview Farley, 8 Nov. 2017; IJAA symposium lecture by veteran Ira Rigger, 17 Feb. 2018.
1518 Henri, et al., 109.
1519 Interview Bernstein, 22 March 2018; Interview Bernstein, 23 March 2018.
1520 Historian Jeffrey Ethell interviewed a Japanese Iwo veteran who said some officers had brought their Korean mistresses/comfort women with them to Iwo. Conversation with Heaton, 27 May 2017.
1521 Yahara, 50-1.
1522 Ibid.
1523 See Harries & Harries, 409; Yahara, 50, 83, 91, 93, 117, 144, 151, 162, 164, 172; Ienaga, 191.
1524 Ienaga, 184.
1525 Ibid., 195.
1526 Butow, 506–7.
1527 Steve Rabson, "Case Dismissed: Osaka Court Upholds Novelist Oe Kensaburo for Writing that Japanese Military Ordered 'Group Suicides' in Battle of Okinawa," *The Asia-Pacific Journal,* Vol. 6, Issue 4, 1 April 2008; Ienaga, 185; Mire Koikari, "Chapter 8. Re-visualizing Okinawa: Gender, Race and Cold War US Occupation in The Okinawa Graphic," in Jeremy

E. Taylor (ed.), *Visual Histories of Occupation: A Transcultural Dialogue*, Bloomsbury, 2020, 183-204.

1528 Drea, 262.

1529 Harris, *The End of Faith*, 134.

1530 Scott, 453.

1531 Dante, *Inferno*, XV 137, 78.

1532 Ibid., XV 135, 67–69.

1533 TSHACNCDNM, Vol. 10, 263, Statement Keenan, Chief Counsel, International Military Tribunal Far East, 4 June 1946, Encl. 4.

1534 Ibid., 2.

1535 *Materials on the Trial of Former Servicemen of the Japanese army Charged with Manufacturing and Employing Bacteriological Weapons*, 284.

1536 Horie, xi, "Editor's Note," by Robert D. Eldridge and Charles W. Tatum. See also, Maga, 97-9.

1537 Horie, 167.

1538 Horie, x, xix, xx, "Editor's Note," by Robert D. Eldridge and Charles W. Tatum.

1539 UGSL, Hosch Papers, Tokyo War Crimes Trials, Conventional War Crimes (Atrocities), Part B, Ch. VIII, 1023; Modder, 23.

1540 Horie, 161.

1541 http://ww2-weapons.com/us-navy-in-late-1941/; "Ship Force Levels 1917-present." History.navy.mil; Maslowski, and Millett, 408. WWII Museum web site says there were 458,365 at the end of 1940. http://www.nationalww2museum.org/learn/education/for-students/ww2-history/ww2-by-the-numbers/us-military.html?referrer=https://www.google.com/; Thomas W. Zeiler, *Unconditional Defeat: Japan, America, and the End of World War II*, Wilmington, DE, 2004, 5. Historian Paul Johnson has the number pegged at slightly higher than 16.3 throughout the war writing that there were 11,260,000 soldiers, 4,183,466 sailors, 669,100 Marines and 241,093 coastguardsmen amounting to a total of 16,353,659. Johnson, *A History of the American People*, 780.

1542 See footnote 875.

1543 Dallin, 427; Sebastian Haffner, *The Meaning of Hitler*, Cambridge, 1979, 136; Robert Jay Lifton, *The Nazi Doctors: Medical Killing and the Psychology of Genocide*, NY, 1986, 138; Alan Bullock, *Hitler: A Study in Tyranny*, NY, 1983, 696; Cesarani (ed.), *The Final Solution*, Omer Bartov, "Operation Barbarossa and the Final Solution," 120-1; Ian Kershaw, *The Nazi Dictatorship: Problems and Perspectives of Interpretation*, NY, 1993, 103.

1544 My ancestor, John Linton (8th great-grandfather), a friend of William Penn, left England in 1699 for Pennsylvania after being disinherited by his father, Sir Roger Lynton, for having converted to Quakerism and embraced a religion disloyal to the crown. See Herman LeRoy Collins, *Philadelphia, A*

Story of Progress, NY, 1941; Albert J. Brown, *Clinton County Ohio: Its People, Industries and Institutions*, Indianapolis, IN, 1915, 621.

1545 George M. Marsden, *The Twilight of the American Enlightenment: The 1950s and the Crisis of Liberal Belief*, NY, 2014, xxiii-xxiv; Morris U. Schappes (ed.), *A Documentary History of the Jews in the United States 1654-1875*, NY, 1950, 80.

1546 Comment on manuscript by Colin Heaton, 11 September 2022.

1547 Dan Barker, *Godless: How an Evangelical Preacher Became One of America's Leading Atheists*, Berkeley, 2008, 213.

1548 Christopher Hitchens, *The Portable Atheist*, NY 2007, "Introduction" by Christopher Hitchens, xiii.

1549 Kem Stone, "*The Struggle of Sisyphus: Absurdity and Ethics in the Work of Albert Camus—Moralist Camus – The Plague*," July 2006, http://www.kemstone. com/Nonfiction/Philosophy/Thesis/plague.htm. Kem Stone is a pseud-onym and not the author's real name. For excellent lectures of Camus, see Robert C. Solomon's lectures on him with the Teaching Company entitled "*No Excuses: Existentialism and the Meaning of Life*," Lecture 5, Disc 3, 2000.

1550 Harris, *The End of Faith*, 44.

1551 Numbers 31 (NIV—New International Version, pp. 163-4).

1552 "The slaughter of Midianite women and children is rationalized in pious tradition as a justified punishment for the scheme 'to seduce the sons of Israel to unchastity and then to idolatry,' a scheme that the rabbis attributed to the despised Balaam." Jonathan Kirsch, *Moses: A Life*, NY, 1998, 323. While there is no historical evidence for the Israelites conquering the ancient lands of Canaan, most ultra-religious Jews and strong Christians still believe it happened and thus it is cited here. For a source that discusses the lack of historical evidence for events in the Torah, see H. H. Ben-Sasson (ed.), *A History of the Jewish People*, A. Malamat, "Origins and the Formative Period," Cambridge, 1976, 43, 52-9; Theodor H. Gaster, *Myth, Legend, and Custom in the Old Testament*, NY, 1969, 411; James L. Kugel, *How to Read the Bible: A Guide to Scripture Then and Now*, NY, 2007, 376-85.

1553 Robert Melson, *Revolution and Genocide: On the Origins of the Armenian Genocide and the Holocaust*, University of Chicago, 1996.

1554 Hitler Youth songs referred to Hitler as their "redeemer." Kertzer, 202. In China, people often called Mao their "Savior." Interview with 10th Degree Grand Kung Fu Master Johnny Lee, 13 Feb. 2015.

1555 Jonathan Steinberg, *All or Nothing: The Axis and the Holocaust 1941-1943*, NY, 1991, 244.

1556 Jung Chang and Jon Halliday, *Mao: The Unknown Story*, London, 2006, 3; Ian Kershaw, *The Hitler Myth: Image and Reality in the Third Reich*, Oxford, 1990, 105-20; Kershaw, *The Hitler Myth*, 107. In reference to 70 million, this is a high number put on the genocide by Chang and Halliday. The National Geographic Jan. 2006 edition on genocide numbers places China's extermination under Mao reaching the number of 30 million.

1557 Steinberg, *All or Nothing*, 244.

1558 Hitchens, *god is not Great*, 202–3.

1559 Dawkins, 249.

1560 Wallance, 201.

1561 William B. Breuer, *Sea Wolf: A Biography of John D. Bulkeley, USN*, Novato, CA, 1989, 10-1.

1562 Michael Berenbaum, *The World Must Know: The History of the Holocaust as Told in the United States Holocaust Memorial Museum*, Baltimore, 2007, xxi.

1563 Plato, *The Trial and Death of Socrates: Apology*, Cambridge, 1975, 39; Joseph Campbell, *The Power of Myth with Bill Moyers*, NY, 1991, 65.

1564 Scott, 515.

INDEX

Dachau Concentration Camp (Nazi), 115, 173

Dahmer, Jeffrey, 153, 163

Daigensui, 29

Dallas (Texas, USA), 18

Dante Alighieri (Italian Poet), 20, 22

Danton's Death (German play), 270

Daqun, Judge Liu, 273

Darwin (Australia), 61

Darwin, Evolutionary biologist Charles, 100

Dashiell, Technical Sergeant Dick (USMC), 257

Dawkins, Professor Richard, 337 fn. 34

Day Commemorating the End of the War (Japanese Holiday), 202

DDT, 258

Death Camps (Nazi), 15, 22, 36, 78, 130-131, 135

The Diet (Japanese Legislative Assembly), 24, 58, 204

Doctolero, Lucas, 120-121

Doi, Colonel Teihichi (IJA), 143, 149, 370 fn. 666

Doihara, General Kenji (IJA), 12, 55, 176-182, 271-272, 306

    Nicknamed "Lawrence of Manchuria," 179, 181

Doihara Special Agency, 178

Domei News Agency, 141

Dominican Republic, 283

Domitian (Roman Emperor), 250

Doolittle Raid (April 1942), 170, 187, 200, 265

"Double Tenth" Trial of Singapore, 101

Dowell, Private Cam (USA), 126

Dower, Historian John W., 15-16, 193, 203

Drea, Historian Edward J., 49, 211, 217, 339 fn. 64 & fn. 66, 381 fn. 877

Drugs (See Japan, Drug Empire)

The Dutch, 43, 60, 131, 162

Dutch East Indies (i.e. Indonesia), 59-60, 64, 380 fn. 875

Eastwood, Clint, 11, 159-160, 300

Eden, British Foreign Secretary Anthony, 150

Edgerton, Historian Robert B., 407 fn. 1400

Edson, Brigadier General Mike (USMC), 287

Eguchi, Colonel T. (IJA), 157

Einsatzgruppen (*SS* Killing Squads), 15

Ellis, Major Earl H. (USMC), 53-54

Emerson, Transcendentalist Ralph Waldo, 250

Emperor's Tokyo Division (Imperial Guards—IJA), 143

The Encyclopedia of Genocide (book), 190

England, (See Great Britain)

Epstein, Jeffrey, 163

Ermattungsstrategie (strategy of attrition), 253

Erskine, Lieutenant General Graves (USMC), 179, 223, 225, 258, 286-288

Ethell, Historian Jeffrey, 398-399 fn. 1213, 411 fn. 1520

Europe (European), 34-35, 48, 51, 62, 64, 133, 165, 179

Exodus (the Bible), 106

Fairmont Hotel (San Francisco, California), 114

Farley, Historian James Oelke, 398-399 fn. 1213

Farrell, Proof-Reader Clayton, 416

Farrell, Historian Don, 416

Fascism, 26, 28-29, 40, 44, 46, 48, 54, 59, 272, 289, 308, 312, 341 fn. 100

Fellers, Brigadier General Bonner F. (USA), 202

FDR, see President Franklin Delano Roosevelt

Filipino Soldiers, 103-104, 108, 189-190

First Air Fleet (IJN), 238

First Amendment (Rights under the U.S. Constitution), 314

First Area Army (IJA), 130

First Submarine Force (Truk—IJN), 188

Flags of our Fathers (book), 16, 338 fn. 56

Flamethrower: Iwo Jima Medal of Honor Recipient and U.S. Marine Woody Williams and His Controversial Award, Japan's Holocaust and the Pacific War(-book), 14, 193

Flyboys (book), 338 fn. 56

Flying Tigers (American fighter pilots provided to China to fight the Japanese), 60

Fonte Ridge (Guam), 230-231, 235

Formosa (see Taiwan)

Founding Fathers (United States), 313

France, 207, 283, 285

Frank, Historian Richard, 2, 39, 165, 219-220, 279-281, 339 fn. 66, 341 fn. 94, 354 fn. 308, 363 fn. 522, 380 fn. 875, 391 fn. 1050, 405-406 fn. 1382, 415

Franklin, Bejamin, 314

French Revolution, 24

Freiburg i. Br. (Germany), 270

Fugo Plan, 36

Fuji, Fukuko, 238

Fuji, Major Hajime (IJA), 238

Mt. Fuji (Japan), 45

Fujisawa, Professor Chikao, 45, 47

Fujiwara, Lieutenant Colonel Iwaichi (IJA), 101

Fuller, Historian J.F.C., 408-409 fn. 1446

Fuller, Stuart J., 179

Futsing (China), 187

Gaijin (Japanese for Barbarian), 35, 40, 196, 341 fn. 100

Gallipoli (battle of), 283-284

Garcia, Priscilla, 367 fn. 597

Gaza (Fascist/Hamas Controlled area of Palestine), 312

Geiger, Major General Roy S. (USMC), 229

Geishas (Japanese High-End Prostitutes), 157

Gelernter, Journalist Josh, 197

Gender Equality Law (Japanese, 1999), 197

Geneva Convention, 106, 108, 135, 159, 292, 303

Genghis Khan (Mongolian Warlord), 94, 162

Genroku Akō, 254-255

German government, 314

German Military Delegation to China, 36, 58

German Military, 91-92, 106, 163, 269, 350-352 fn. 272

Germans, 14-15, 30, 32-34, 36, 45, 49, 54, 88, 92-93, 185, 193, 220, 271-272, 274, 283, 302, 318, 373 fn. 723, 382 fn. 891

View of Chinese, 36-37, 88

View of Japanese, 36-37, 88

Germany, 11, 13-15, 22, 26, 33, 35-37, 44, 47, 52, 58, 64, 90, 105, 163, 178, 192-193, 199, 201, 204, 219-220, 270-272, 276, 294, 299, 311, 315

Condemnation of Hiter, 201

Reparations Paid to Victims from WWII, 200, 385 fn. 932

Germany's Supreme Army Command (*OKH*), 58

Ghettos (Nazi), 317

Gibney, Naval Intelligence Officer Frank B. (USN), 217-218, 303-304

Gil, I (Korean in the IJA), 134

Gilbert, Historian Sir Martin, 10, 17

Gittelsohn, Captain and Rabbi Roland E. (USN), 416

Global Combatting Terrorism Network Special Operations Command, 154

Goethe Institute (Freiburg, Germany), 270

Gomi, Soldier Kōsuke (IJA), 68

Gongshan (China), 167

Grand Cross of the German Eagle (Nazi Medal), 178

Graves, Corporal Don (USMC), 257, 304-305, 398 fn. 1213

Gray, Commandant and General Al (USMC), 259

Rampage, 127
Ranau (Indonesia), 107
Rape (by the Japanese), 11, 15, 54, 68-69, 78, 83, 85-86, 88, 93, 99, 113, 119, 125-126, 128-129, 135, 148, 156, 169, 187-189, 196, 295-297, 312, 349-350 fn. 259, 350-352 fn. 272, 355 fn. 324, 367 fn. 597, 369 fn. 648, 371 fn. 677, 373 fn. 723, 410 fn. 1484
 Desecrating of raped women's bodies, 86-87, 119, 297
 Explanation of why Japanese men raped so much, 295-297
The Rape of Asia (Japanese Operation), 93, 146, 206
The Rape of Beijing (Japanese Operation), 276, 317
The Rape of Canton (Japanese Operation), 276, 317
The Rape of Chekiang (Japanese Operation), 188, 200, 265, 276
The Rape of Guam (Japanese Operation), 109-118, 160, 276, 294
 Concentration Camps, 114-115, 117
The Rape of Hong Kong, 146-160, 199, 240-241, 265, 276, 294, 297, 371 fn. 677
The Rape of Korea (Japanese Operation), 51-52, 117
The Rape of Malaya (Japanese Operation), 94-102, 130, 160, 276, 293
The Rape of Manchuria (Japanese Operation), 55, 130, 146-147
The Rape of Manila (Japanese Operation), 95, 101, 119-130, 154-155, 160, 164, 240, 276, 294
 Number of victims, 363 fn. 522
The Rape of Nanking (Japanese Operation), 20-22, 40, 42, 58, 67-93, 100, 127, 140, 150, 160, 193, 197-201, 207, 218, 240, 263-265, 267, 270-271, 276, 294-295, 312, 317, 335 fn. 2, 349 fn. 259, 349-350 fn. 259, 350 fn. 264, 353 fn. 296

The Rape of Nanking (book), 13, 335 fn. 2, 349 fn. 259
The Rape of the Pacific (Japanese Operations), 206
The Rape of the Philippines (Japanese Operation), 95, 103-108, 119-130, 276, 294
The Rape of Shanghai (Japanese Operation), 263, 265, 276, 317
The Rape of Singapore (Japanese Operation), 94-102, 130, 189, 203, 293-294, 357 fn. 377
The Rape of Tientsin, 317
Ramesses II (Egyptian Pharaoh), 250
Ranua (Indonesia), 293
Reagan, President Ronald, 272
Realpolitik, 65
Red Cross Hospital (Hong Kong), 150, 159
Reed, Corporal Jim (USMC), 209, 212-213
Rehe (China—battle of), 178
Renstrom, Gunnery Sergeant Keith A. (USMC), 210-211, 213-214, 225-229, 389 fn. 1010, 394 fn. 1100
Reparations (Japanese), 12, 200, 385 fn. 932
Reynolds, Judge and Major General Russel (USA), 154
Rhode Island (USA), 285
Richie, Alexandra, 109
Rigg, Historian Bryan, 9-12, 18-20, 274
Rigg, Ian, 5
Rigg, Justin, 5
Rigg, Sophia, 5, 20-21
Rigger, Iwo Jima veteran Ira, 398-399 fn. 1213
Riggs, Rev. Charles, 88
Roberts, Historian Sir Andrew, 2, 9, 12
Rommel, Field Marshal Erwin (*Heer*), 61
Rōnin (leaderless *Samurai*), 254
Roosevelt, President Franklin Delano (FDR), 60, 90, 118, 187, 263, 265, 290, 317, 347 fn. 217
Ruff-O'Hearne, Jeanne, 162

ACKNOWLEDGMENTS

A GOOD BOOK IS NEVER written alone. As historian James M. Scott wrote, "Nonfiction books are like historical scavenger hunts," and along the way, there are many who help a historian gather his stories, words, and analysis.[1564] I have so many to thank for their contribution to this work that it would be difficult to name them all, yet several deserve special mention. First, I would like to thank my Yale University professors Paul Kennedy and James Crowley for supporting my study of the Pacific War while I was an undergraduate. Kennedy was generous with his time, conducting a small seminar with me to review the history of the war with Japan. Also, I thank famous author Richard Selzer, who did three independent studies with me at Yale. He was a wonderful mentor and taught me to explore language and find good stories.

While conducting my graduate studies at Cambridge University, I had the honor to study under Jonathan Steinberg. He encouraged me to look into Japanese atrocities during World War II and compare them to what I was learning about Hitler's genocide. His support and guidance during my formative years of learning how to be a scholar are greatly appreciated. He is sorely missed as he passed away in 2021 due to complications from Alzheimer's. He was one of the best teachers I ever had.

Over the past decade and a half, the distinguished Holocaust historian Michael Berenbaum of the University of Judaism honored me by reading all my works and giving invaluable advice and criticism. His support means more to me than he will ever know. Since publication of *Hitler's Jewish Soldiers*, he has been my strongest advocate and supporter. He has been a wonderful *Doktorvater*.

During my research for *Flamethrower*, Richard Frank read my work twice and gave me incredible feedback. He has yet once again done so for this work. Few people get the subject area expert to look at their work once, yet alone twice, and for two works. I am eternally grateful to Frank for his friendship and support. They both mean the world to me.

Since I was a student at Cambridge University, historian and fellow Marine Colin Heaton has consistently shared information with me from his vast collection of oral histories. He has published numerous WWII books and has an incredible knowledge of the personalities from the war. All my books have been enriched by his support and sources.

I am deeply thankful to accomplished Marine Corps historian, Colonel Jon T. Hoffman, who gave me a tough and detailed report on my work in 2017, 2018, and 2022, and helped me reshape this work dramatically. He aided me in finding mistakes and fixing errors. For his careful reading and thorough review, I thank him from the bottom of my heart. He has often read and re-read my work while undergoing cancer treatment. I cannot tell him how much I value his mentorship. He is a dear friend, loyal Marine, and wonderful historical comrade.

Many thanks go to retired Navy Captain Lee Mandel for his support. His work *A Pacifist at Iwo Jima* on Rabbi Roland E. Gittelsohn, the first Marine Corps Jewish Chaplain, is an excellent work on Iwo Jima and the Pacific War. His careful editing and feedback on this current book are greatly appreciated.

Many thanks go to Don Farrell, a historian of the Guam battle. While touring the battlefield of Guam in 2015, he was our tour guide, providing useful insights into the conflict. He has been gracious, helping me find sources and providing excellent proofreading of my manuscript on the Guam section. His book *The Pictorial History of Guam: Liberation 1944* is a good and thorough exploration of that battle.

For his detailed editorial comments and his help with the Japanese and Chinese languages, I am grateful to Clayton Farrell for his support and feedback. He helped me correct several grammatical and conceptional mistakes, and he has helped make this book more accurate.

Many have helped me throughout the years and I cannot thank them enough. I hope this book, in a major way, helps to create a movement to get the Japanese to become honest with their past and acknowledge the pain they caused throughout the world. At the time of the writing of this book, they have been disgraceful in their behavior when it comes to admitting their mistakes during WWII and atoning for their crimes. Let us hope that they start to change their childish ways.